Entrepreneurial Finance
A Practical Approach

Denise M. Lee
KENT STATE UNIVERSITY

CHICAGO
BUSINESS PRESS

This book is dedicated to my husband, Jeffrey, who has often noted, "Sometimes, if you want answers, you have to ask questions."

Cover photo: Gearstd/Shutterstock

Entrepreneurial Finance: A Practical Approach

Copyright © 2020

13-digit ISBN 978-1-948426-12-1

10 9 8 7 6 5 4 3 2 1

Brief Contents

Contents

CHAPTER 11

Cash Harvest, Business Valuation, and Business Exit *309*

CHAPTER 12

Personal Finance and Wealth Management *343*

Preface

The Need for a New Approach to Entrepreneurial Finance

Having taught entrepreneurial finance for five years and having reviewed or used almost every available entrepreneurial finance textbook, I have found most of them have the following shortcomings:

- They ignore the circular nature of entrepreneurship.
- They ignore the fact that most entrepreneurs make decisions for their businesses based on their personal financial realities and goals.
- They do not explain how to do the research to create—or demonstrate how to create—the pro forma financial statements an entrepreneur needs to get his business funded.

Meanwhile, I've found that entrepreneurship students have these things in common:

- They are enthusiastic, creative problem solvers.
- They are nervous around numbers.
- They don't feel they can learn to understand financial statements and the different forms of financial analysis that are essential to sound business decision-making.

The Perspective of a Teacher, Accountant, and Entrepreneur

This is an entrepreneurial finance textbook written by someone who is both a serial entrepreneur and a CPA. It is based on the practices and processes I found worked well in the real world and hence consistently adopted for use in the companies I cofounded and helped manage. This book does not attempt to teach entrepreneurship students everything they need to know about finance. It attempts to teach entrepreneurship students what they need to know about finance in order to succeed as entrepreneurs.

It is important to note that this textbook is based on content I developed over the course of five years while teaching undergraduate entrepreneurial finance classes at a major university. In other words, I've been teaching the majority of the content of this book in the classroom for years. My own entrepreneurial experience helped me decide what material is most important to entrepreneurs and should therefore be included in this book. The teaching process helped me determine how the relevant material can be successfully taught to entrepreneurship students.

Approach

Most people like checklists they can complete that ensure the successful achievement of a goal. Over the years, I've often tried to devise such a checklist for entrepreneurship. What I've found is that such a list is not possible, because entrepreneurship is not linear—like a list is—entrepreneurship is circular. Entrepreneurship is circular because, when starting a new venture, the decisions made in the beginning must very carefully consider the desired ending. This is true because a lot of what can or will ultimately happen with regard to a new venture depends very much upon the decisions made at the new venture's start.

Due to the circular nature of entrepreneurship, I've taken a 360 degree approach to writing this textbook in two different ways. First, in chapter 1 of the book, I alert the student to refer to chapter 11 of the book for guidance before making any major decisions regarding the company he is about to start. Chapter 11 discusses—among other topics—how to position a company for sale. Proper positioning involves activities the entrepreneur should ideally engage in before starting a company and also issues to consider when initially setting up the company. The second way I've taken a 360 degree approach to writing this textbook is that I start the book by talking about the entrepreneur as an individual, before he starts a company. I then focus on how to start, fund, grow, manage, and harvest cash from the business. I end the book by again talking about the entrepreneur as an individual, but this time as an individual who has achieved personal wealth as a result of building a successful company.

Organization

The first part of the book, chapters 1–3, focuses on the education, research, planning, preparation, and decision making an individual should undertake before starting a business. The chapters discuss entrepreneurial failure and what the entrepreneur can do to both minimize the risk of failure for her business and also protect herself as an individual. Protection of the entrepreneur as an individual is important because as long as an entrepreneur owns a business, the personal finances of the entrepreneur and the finances of the business she has created are inextricably linked. This strong financial link is one of the reasons entrepreneurs make decisions for their businesses based on their personal financial realities and goals. Beyond the fact that one discipline focuses on starting a new business and the other focuses on managing an existing business, it is the depth of the relationship between the entrepreneur's personal finances and the finances of the entity she creates that makes entrepreneurial finance fundamentally different from traditional business finance.

Understanding the numbers associated with business isn't a strong point for most entrepreneurs. As a result, at their peril, they tend to avoid learning to read and understand financial statements. The second part of the book, chapters 4–7, addresses this lack of understanding by teaching the basics about financial statements. The chapters also teach basic business jargon and how to perform the critical breakeven analysis that can deter an entrepreneur from starting a business—or pursuing a new line of business—that is doomed to fail. Perhaps most importantly, these chapters explain how to do the research to create—and demonstrate how to create—the pro forma financial statements an entrepreneur needs to get his business funded. In essence, chapters 4–7 were written to answer the number one question I used to get from recently graduated entrepreneurship students before I started teaching the material included in this book: How do I create the financial statements I need to get my business funded?

The third part of the book, chapters 8–10, demonstrates the basic tools needed to manage a business and make informed decisions for that business. The topics addressed include bootstrapping, proper working capital management, and the effective management of what are, for most businesses, two of the largest and riskiest asset categories: accounts receivable and inventory. The chapters also discuss placing appropriate controls over the assets of a business—so that the assets of the business remain the assets of the business—and how to appropriately choose between the many business opportunities and investments that are constantly presented to business owners.

The fourth part of the book, chapters 11 and 12, focuses on how to value a business, how to sell a business (if that result is desired), how to harvest cash from a business (in ways other than selling it), and how to properly manage the personal wealth that often results from successful entrepreneurship. The discussion of personal wealth management effectively closes the loop of the book's discussion of entrepreneurship by bringing us back to once again looking at the entrepreneur as an individual, but this time after he has achieved personal wealth as a result of building a successful company.

It should be noted that this textbook, while it does from time to time address some particulars associated with nonprofit organizations, focuses primarily on for-profit entrepreneurial ventures. Also, to achieve some level of gender neutrality, this book alternates in the use of masculine versus feminine pronouns between chapters throughout the book when referring to an entrepreneur, except when describing a particular Entrepreneur in Action or a person being interviewed in exercises. This is done for purposes of readability only and should not be construed to have any other meaning.

Key Features of This Book

- Chapter Opening Quote—introduces each chapter and reflects the theme of the chapter
- Learning Objectives—help the student and instructor focus on the goals for the chapter
- Entrepreneur in Action segments—illustrate the use of chapter concepts by entrepreneurs in their day-to-day activities
- Key Terms—are highlighted and defined within the chapter, appear as margin notes, are listed at the end of each chapter, and appear again in the glossary; these are the terms the student will learn and use throughout the book
- Figures—consist primarily of the financial statements, schedules, and analyses most often needed and created by an entrepreneur
- Review and Discussion Questions—are designed for use in class or to be assigned as homework in order to make sure the students have grasped the concepts of the chapter
- Exercises—are designed to be assigned as homework to enforce the learning objectives listed at the start of the chapter; these give the student practical experience performing the analyses and creating the financial statements they will need as entrepreneurs
- End of chapter appendices—follow chapters 6 and 9, the chapter 6 appendices illustrating the creation of pro forma financial statements for a service-based business and a smartphone application business, and the chapter 9 appendix including present value and future value tables that may be used for time value of money calculations

Supplements to This Book

Instructor's Manual—every chapter is supported with the following:
- Chapter overview
- Learning objectives
- Detailed chapter outline
- Teaching tips
- Answers to Review and Discussion Questions
- Solutions to Exercises

Test Bank—developed to cover every learning objective and key term for each chapter; presents multiple-choice and true-false questions that are compatible with any learning management system; includes knowledge and application questions, as well as essay questions and answers

PowerPoint Slides—a Microsoft PowerPoint deck of slides for each chapter that provides key chapter topics in outline form along with key figures

Acknowledgments

Thank you to my past Kent State University entrepreneurial finance students for their feedback and their invaluable assistance in helping me refine the concepts and materials included in this textbook.

Thank you as well to the dedicated faculty who reviewed the book and gave me ideas for improving it, including Thomas Allison of Washington State University, Caroline Glackin of Fayetteville State University, David Deeds of the University of St. Thomas, Scott Shane of Case Western Reserve University and Jane Xie of St. Edward's University. I owe special thanks to Talitha Smith of Auburn University for both reviewing the book and also class-testing it for multiple semesters. The guidance she provided from having hundreds of students use early drafts of the manuscript proved immeasurably helpful.

Proper Preparation and the Nascent Entrepreneur

"You hit home runs not by chance, but by preparation."

— Roger Maris, New York Yankee, set a single-season home run record in 1961

Learning Objectives

Understand how entrepreneurial finance is different from traditional business finance.

Know the two major causes of business failure that are, in many cases, avoidable.

Understand what preparation a nascent entrepreneur can undertake before starting a new business that will increase his chances of entrepreneurial success.

Know how a business plan is different from a feasibility analysis and why an entrepreneur should always do a feasibility analysis before starting a business.

Have an appreciation for how an entrepreneur can financially sustain himself during the start-up phase of his business.

Understand why it is a problem for an entrepreneur—or one or more of his business partners—to have a low credit score and what an individual can do to improve a bad credit score.

Understand why it is wise for an entrepreneur to separate himself from his business and what specifically an entrepreneur can do to separate himself from his business.

Know the top legal and financial mistakes entrepreneurs make.

Have an appreciation for the circular nature of entrepreneurship.

Introduction

The personal finances of the nascent entrepreneur and the finances of the start-up venture he creates are inextricably linked. This is true for the following reasons:

- Most new ventures benefit from a significant financial investment from their founders.
- Many founders personally guarantee the debt or contracts of their young start-ups.
- Most new ventures are founded as pass-through entities. A **pass-through entity** is a business whose profits are not taxed at the company level but instead pass through to the business owners' individual tax returns, where they are taxed.

Beyond the fact that one discipline focuses on starting a new business and the other focuses on managing an existing business, it is the depth of the relationship between the entrepreneur's personal finances and the finances of the entity he creates that makes entrepreneurial finance fundamentally different from traditional business finance. **Entrepreneurial finance** is the study of resource acquisition, allocation, and management; financial planning and management; asset and business valuation; cash harvest strategy and contingency planning in the context of a new business venture and the entrepreneur's personal financial goals. In other words, the topic of entrepreneurial finance recognizes that, oftentimes, entrepreneurs make decisions for the businesses they've founded with their personal financial goals—and other personal goals—clearly in mind. Arguably, the relationship between a start-up venture and its founders is most pronounced when the venture is only a concept being contemplated, researched, and considered. Rare is the entrepreneur who doesn't consider his personal financial and professional future when deciding whether or not to actually start a new venture.

The rate of new business failure is notoriously high in all industries. It's interesting to note, however, that the percentage of new businesses that survive the first five years does, in fact, vary by industry. Five-year business survival rates by industry sector, from highest to lowest, are illustrated in figure 1.1.

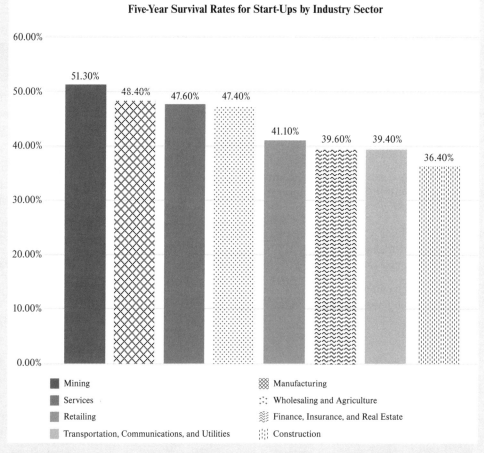

Figure 1.1. Five-year survival rates for start-ups by industry sector. Adapted from: "Are Startup Failure Rates as Bad as They Used to Be?" by Paul Chaney, Small Business Trends, August 7, 2016.

Having noted both the unique relationship between a founder and his start-up, and the high failure rate associated with new ventures, what should a nascent entrepreneur consider when deciding whether or not to pursue starting a company? What can an individual do to increase his chances of entrepreneurial success?

The answers to these questions will, of course, vary dependent upon the nature of the individual entrepreneur and the business concept under consideration, but there are two major causes of business failure that, with some effort on the part of the entrepreneur, are, in many cases, avoidable: poor timing and lack of proper preparation. Whether because of poor timing, lack of proper preparation, or another factor, the mistakes that most severely damage a business tend to be either legal or financial. With the goal of improving the entrepreneur's chances for new venture success, chapter 1 will discuss the optimal timing of the start of an entrepreneurial venture, the preparation an entrepreneur should undertake before starting a new venture, and the top legal and financial mistakes an entrepreneur should avoid making.

Timing

In a March 2015 TED talk, Bill Gross, founder of Idealab, said that after gathering and studying data from hundreds of companies, he had found one factor that seems to affect a start-up company's prospects for success more than any other: timing.[1] Often the timing of the start of an entrepreneurial venture is driven by trends in the market the concept will serve. Other times it is driven by the innovation associated with the concept itself or innovation in the environment in which the concept will exist or function. Still other times it is driven by the entrepreneur himself. It is important to note that, no matter what the reasoning behind it, poor timing is the enemy of the entrepreneur.

Suppose that market research indicates that a certain product or service is currently trending favorably with a market. For example, for the last decade, many individual securities investors have been increasingly favoring investing in exchange traded funds. An **exchange traded fund (ETF)** is a fund that invests in a basket of assets, such as stocks or bonds, and trades on a regulated exchange like the New York Stock Exchange (NYSE). ETFs offer investors an easy way to diversify their investment holdings compared to incurring the expense associated with buying small quantities of a large number of different individual stocks. A long-term upward trend in the popularity of a product—like that exhibited by ETFs—suggests that the time to introduce a new product conforming to the popular trend would be sooner rather than later. As such, the optimal time to introduce a new ETF to the market would likely be sometime in the very near future. This is true because most trends do eventually end, and if an interested entrepreneur waits too long to introduce his product to the market, he may miss the proverbial boat and instead end up boarding a sinking ship of his own making.

Suppose that instead of hopping on a trend, a concept is such that a first-to-market opportunity is available. A first-to-market opportunity generally suggests that the time to introduce a new product to the market is now. This is true because, while certainly no guarantee of success, conventional and anecdotal wisdom indicate that those who reach the market first with a truly innovative new product or service tend to be more profitable and better able to hold onto market share in the long run compared to later (copycat) entrants to the market. Examples like Amazon (which created the first online bookstore) and eBay (which created the first major online auction site) certainly illustrate the attractiveness of a first-to-market opportunity. In certain instances, a first-to-market opportunity can be enticing enough to compel an entrepreneur to start a new venture at a time that is actually personally inconvenient for the entrepreneur. There is nothing really wrong with this as long as the entrepreneur is otherwise well prepared.

pass-through entity
a business whose profits are not taxed at the company level, but instead pass through to the business owners' individual tax returns, where they are taxed

entrepreneurial finance
the study of resource acquisition, allocation, and management; financial planning and management; asset and business valuation; cash harvest strategy; and contingency planning in the context of a new business venture and the entrepreneur's personal financial goals

exchange traded fund (ETF)
a fund that invests in a basket of assets, such as stocks or bonds, and trades on a regulated exchange like the New York Stock Exchange, as many individual stocks do

Generally, the timing is right to start a business when both the customer—and the environment surrounding both the business concept and the customer—are ready for what the entrepreneur has to offer. If either the customer or the environment isn't ready, no matter how well the entrepreneur executes, the likelihood of entrepreneurial failure is high.

Preparation

There is a lot to be said for the entrepreneur being properly prepared before starting a new venture. We've all heard the saying "Success is 90 percent preparation and 10 percent perspiration." Louis Pasteur noted that "Chance favors only the prepared mind." Abraham Lincoln said, "I will prepare and someday my chance will come." Quotes like these have staying power in our culture because they have proven over time to be fundamentally true. Appropriate preparation before you start a new venture, perhaps before you even have an idea for a new venture, will serve you well as an entrepreneur.

So, what should you do? How do you prepare?

Before starting a business, in order to increase his chances for entrepreneurial success, the aspiring entrepreneur should do the following:

- Work in and learn about the industry in which he intends to start the business.
- Establish a large network both within and outside of the industry in which he intends to start the business.
- Complete a full feasibility analysis on the concept under consideration and, if deemed appropriate, also complete a business plan on the concept.
- Personally financially prepare for the pre-revenue and pre-profit phases of the business.
- Learn the basics regarding how an entrepreneur should separate himself from his business.

Feasibility Analysis

business plan
a comprehensive document that focuses on how to build a company, prepared by—and for the benefit of—the entrepreneurs involved, but written with an outside audience of potential investors, lenders, strategic partners or, major talent targets in mind

feasibility analysis
a document that concentrates on assessing the likelihood of economic success of a business, primarily for the benefit of the entrepreneurs contemplating starting that business

The rate of new business failure would likely be significantly lower if every entrepreneur took the time to do a feasibility analysis that includes a breakeven analysis (breakeven analysis will be explained and illustrated in detail in chapter 5). Many successful businesses have been started without a **business plan**—a comprehensive document that focuses on how to build a company, prepared by—and for the benefit of—the entrepreneurs involved, but written with an outside audience of potential investors, lenders, strategic partners, or major talent targets in mind—but no new business should be started without the founding team first completing a full feasibility analysis.

A **feasibility analysis** is a more narrowly focused document than a business plan as it concentrates on assessing the likelihood of economic success of a business, primarily for the benefit of the entrepreneurs contemplating starting that business. A feasibility analysis is performed to answer the following four questions:

1. Are there enough interested customers that a business based on the concept under consideration can actually turn a profit?
2. Is now a good time to introduce this product or service to the market? In other words, has the optimal time to introduce the concept already passed, or has it possibly not yet arrived?
3. Will a business based on the concept under consideration make enough of a profit to actually be worth undertaking considering both the financial and non-financial up-front investment required?

4. Can a cross-functional founding team be quickly and efficiently assembled in order to successfully get the product or service under consideration to market in a timely fashion?

A typical feasibility analysis includes the following major components:

- an executive summary, including the feasibility (i.e., "go" or "no go") decision
- a description of the business concept underlying the proposed business, which should include the following:
  - a detailed description of the proposed product or service
  - a description of the value the product or service will bring to its likely customers
  - a description of the product's or service's likely customers
  - a description of the distribution channels that will most likely be utilized to get the product or service to its customers
- a market (customer) analysis that includes a description of the product's or service's first target customers
- an industry (competitor) analysis that clearly illustrates the product's or service's competitive advantage
- a development plan that describes how the final version of the desired product or service will be realized over time
- a description of the existing or needed management team
- a financial plan that includes the following information:
  - a detailed accounting of the amount of start-up capital required by the business and how and when that start-up capital will be used
  - expected product pricing
  - expected customer demand
  - expected short- and long-term profitability
  - expected working capital needs (**working capital** is the capital required to sustain operations and support business growth after a company's start-up phase)
  - existing and potential sources of capital for the business
  - the expected return on investment
  - a breakeven analysis that supports the proposed business's economic viability

    The financial plan is the element of the feasibility analysis that we'll focus on in this textbook. All of the above components of a financial plan will be fully explained and illustrated in chapters 2–8.
- the expected timeline to launch, including objective milestones whose achievement will clearly indicate progress (or lack thereof)

> **working capital**
> the capital required to sustain operations and support business growth after a company's start-up phase

The Business Plan

While a feasibility analysis primarily proves or disproves a new concept's viability in the marketplace (i.e., if enough people will buy the product or service to make a business based on the concept viable), a business plan is more comprehensive and discusses all the operational and financial aspects of a new business. In other words, a business plan focuses on how to build a company.

The major components of a business plan include all the components of a feasibility analysis, less the "go" or "no go" feasibility decision, with the breadth and depth of each section of the feasibility analysis being fleshed out and expanded by significant additional research. Specifically, a business plan should include the following modified or additional elements:

- the business concept, fleshed out in order to illustrate a comprehensive **business model** (a company's business model indicates how a business concept will make a company—and ultimately the entrepreneur—money)

> **business model**
> how a business concept will make a company—and ultimately the entrepreneur—money

- the expected operational and organizational structures of the business
- a marketing plan (emphasizing the plan for initial market entry)
- a growth plan
- pro forma financial statements for the first three to five years of the business (**pro forma financial statements** are financial statements that attempt to estimate the future financial situation of a company based upon certain identified assumptions)
- a cash harvest strategy, including contingency plans

Pro forma financial statements and cash harvest are elements of a business plan we will focus on later in this textbook. The business model element of a business plan we will take a moment to discuss here.

A business model broadens and extends a business concept by answering the question: How will the company make a profit from the products and services suggested by the business concept? Specifically,

- How will value be created for all of the stakeholders associated with the business?
  - Will customers benefit from the competitive advantage offered by the business and its products and services?
  - Will jobs be created?
  - Will enough cash be generated to allow for payouts of cash to the company's owners?
  - Will lenders and creditors be repaid on a timely basis?
  - Will the company create shared value that benefits both itself and society—or will the company be purely profit-driven?
  The entrepreneur should note that unsatisfied stakeholders usually don't stick around.
- How will competitive advantage be achieved? Significant sales revenue is rarely generated by a company without a clear competitive advantage.
- What are the nature, size, and relative importance of the revenue streams the business model can produce? The entrepreneur needs to identify a clear path for how the business will turn its investment in the products and services it will purchase, build, or develop back into cash to be received by the company in the form of revenue. Multiple revenue streams are preferable to one revenue stream.
- What costs most affect the business's ability to operate on both a short-term and long-term basis? Identifying a business's major costs early on—and understanding when and how those costs will be incurred—helps the entrepreneur plan appropriately regarding how to pay for and minimize such costs.
- Can the efficacy of the business model be sustained over time? In other words, will the planned business model sustain the company long term? If not, is the business model flexible enough to be adapted over time as necessary?

Two examples of business models with which many entrepreneurs are currently finding success are the subscription-based business model and the marketplace business model. Time is a finite resource for every individual and, because of real or perceived time poverty, consumers worldwide are increasingly embracing hassle-free shopping experiences. Evidence of this can be seen in the exponential growth in the number of businesses offering subscription-based products or services. For consumers, the value of the subscription-based business model lies in being able to easily set up the recurring delivery of a product or service, knowing the cost of that product or service will not change without warning and knowing the desired product or service will arrive as scheduled, without the time and trouble of reordering. For start-up businesses, the value of the subscription-based business model lies in the ability of a business to start small and grow in a controlled fashion. For more mature businesses, the value of the subscription-based business model lies in the business being able to fairly accurately predict future revenues due to the subscription-based business model's naturally occurring high rate of repeat sales. Ipsy, Blue Apron, and Dollar Shave Club are examples of some of the top subscription-based product businesses.[2] Netflix and Spotify are examples of some of the top subscription-based service businesses.[3]

A business operating under the marketplace business model is primarily engaged in bringing consumers and the businesses that serve them together in a more convenient fashion than was previously available. A marketplace business facilitates transactions between others, making money by either charging a small fee or taking a small portion of the revenue related to each transaction. Uber has successfully created a marketplace where strangers rent rides from strangers. Airbnb has successfully created a marketplace where strangers rent accommodations from strangers. Amazon has successfully created a marketplace where strangers buy products from strangers. The challenge of the marketplace business model for a start-up business is the need to quickly establish trust and achieve a broad user base. However, once they are established, as long as trust and the broad user base are adequately maintained, a marketplace business generally continues to be successful.

Personal Financial Preparation

Before starting a business, entrepreneur, you should carefully consider three entrepreneurial realities:

1. Most new businesses require a substantial time commitment from the entrepreneur.
2. Most new businesses require a significant financial investment by the entrepreneur.
3. Many start-ups earn no revenue during their first year of operations, and more than half aren't profitable in their first year.[4]

Considering these realities, it's likely you'll increase your chances for entrepreneurial success if you're in a stable life situation—that is, if you're not making major personal life changes during your new venture's start-up period. Your new venture will likely require every spare moment you have to give it. And your new venture will also likely induce certain mental and physical stresses. A wise entrepreneur doesn't voluntarily lump the stresses associated with starting a business on top of personal stresses. A wise entrepreneur adjusts his life and frees up adequate time to pursue a new venture before starting that new venture.

Further, it's likely you'll increase your chances for entrepreneurial success if you're not worried about how you're going to pay your personal bills during your new venture's start-up phase. No potential investor in your company wants to hear that you need money to pay your personal bills or that you need a salary. Saying either of these things sounds unprofessional, and you'll appear to potential investors as having not adequately planned for the start-up phase of your new business.

Generally, you can sustain yourself personally during the start-up phase of your business utilizing one or more of the following resources:

- funds you already have
- income you earn on an ongoing basis from a job or another existing business you may own
- strategic expense minimization
- funds you borrow

Some entrepreneurs have a cache of money they can dip into to survive during the start-up phase of their business. This is usually money they've saved or, perhaps, money they've inherited. Other entrepreneurs, in order to survive, work a job or operate another existing business at the same time they're starting a new business. Still others engage in strategic expense minimization or live off credit cards and other forms of debt until their new business becomes profitable enough that they can start withdrawing cash from the business.

Strategic expense minimization is a process in which many entrepreneurs engage before starting a business with the goal of minimizing expected future outlays of cash. Strategic expense minimization involves making your dollars serve you twice—once for business purposes and once for personal purposes—by investing in assets you can share with your business. Examples include turning the top floor of a building rented by your business into your personal residence, using a business vehicle for personal use instead of having a personal vehicle, and using a business smartphone during off hours as your personal smartphone instead of having a separate personal smartphone.

Strategic expense minimization involves:

- reviewing all of your personal expenses
- determining which are the largest—and thus the most attractive to minimize or eliminate
- determining which expenses can, in fact, be minimized or eliminated—and how
- actually executing the process of minimizing or eliminating the identified expenses

Strategic expense minimization involves truly embracing the entrepreneurial lifestyle at the beginning of a new venture. Strategic expense minimization also often simply makes good financial sense.

Imagine you're an entrepreneur who wants to quit your boring (but well-paying) day job and open a wine bar. How best could you do that?

First, you'd likely consider keeping your day job until the wine bar reaches the minimum level of profitability needed for you to pay your personal bills. Note that your personal bills will likely be significantly lower than your pre–wine bar days if you've engaged in some level of strategic expense minimization.

For example, is it really the best course of action to continue paying the mortgage on your house or the rent on your apartment during the start-up phase of this business? Might it make more sense, for many reasons, to live on the currently unoccupied second floor of the building your business is renting—the building in which you're about to open and operate your wine bar? (I'm guessing your own business would charge you reasonable rent.) And isn't it wise to be physically close to your business when it's in its infancy anyway? And if you have to share a vehicle and a smartphone in order to keep expenses low, wouldn't you prefer to share it with your own business?

As long as you keep diligent records of personal versus business use (as a start, reference Internal Revenue Service tax topic 305—recordkeeping), sharing a car or a smartphone with your business isn't a problem at all.[5, 6, 7] Remember, sharing assets with your business can significantly increase the speed with which you're able to successfully get your new business past the start-up phase and into a state of profitability so that you can quit that day job.

Next, let's consider the issue of taking on debt. For some budding entrepreneurs, taking on personal debt is the only way they can get through the start-up phase of their business.

strategic expense minimization
a process in which many entrepreneurs engage before starting a business with the goal of minimizing expected future outlays of cash

If You Must Rely on Debt

Debt is a useful tool that has historically helped many individuals and businesses achieve goals they otherwise couldn't. But debt is something that should always be thoughtfully considered before it is incurred. Before borrowing to support an entrepreneurial start-up, an entrepreneur should always consider if there are ways to achieve the desired goal without taking on debt. This is important because taking on debt is essentially spending money you haven't yet earned.

Some individuals have no viable alternative to taking on some debt in order to pursue their entrepreneurial goals. If you must take on debt in order to pursue your entrepreneurial goals, be sure to do the following:

- Set a debt limit for yourself such that you can pay back the debt without major hardship should the business fail.
- Develop a budget detailing exactly for what (and only for what) the borrowed dollars will be used.

If you're going rely upon debt, you're obviously going to need to find someone willing to loan you money. Depending on the lender, credit scores can often play an important role in your ability to borrow money.

Your Credit Score

If you're an entrepreneur seeking to borrow money, the personal credit histories of you and your business partners—if, in fact, you have business partners—are going to come under review. One of the first things any lender will look at is your credit score. Your **credit score** is a three-digit number, typically between 300 and 850, which is calculated from your credit report in order to gauge your reliability as a borrower. Your **credit report** is a detailed report of your credit history prepared by a credit bureau.

Lenders and other creditors use your credit score to predict whether you'll pay back your debts on time. Your credit score also helps determine whether you're generally a good risk for a lender (i.e., lenders use it to help determine the interest rate you will pay). Generally, the higher your credit score, the more likely it is you'll be able to get a loan when you need it—and at a reasonable interest rate.

In 1981, the Fair Isaac Corporation (FICO) created a branded version of your credit score called the FICO Score.[8] According to FICO, the FICO Score is the credit score most widely used by U.S. lenders to make loan approval decisions.[9] To compute credit scores, FICO uses information provided by the three major credit reporting agencies—Equifax, Experian, and TransUnion—but FICO itself is not a credit reporting agency. Each of the three major credit reporting agencies also computes a FICO credit score for you based on the FICO formula and the information that has been reported to them about you. This means you may have as many as four different FICO Scores, one computed by each credit reporting agency and one calculated by FICO itself.

It's interesting to note that the credit reporting agencies don't seek out information from creditors or lenders. They build your credit report based solely on the information voluntarily reported to them by creditors. Figure 1.2 (on page 10) shows the factors that determine the average person's credit score.

The percentages in figure 1.2 are based on the relative importance of the five categories for the general population. For individuals falling outside the general population demographic, the relative importance of these categories will be different.

Negative information adversely affects your credit score (i.e., lowers your score). Negative information includes bankruptcy, collection actions, foreclosures, and late

credit score
a three-digit number, typically between 300 and 850, which is calculated from your credit report in order to gauge your reliability as a borrower

credit report
a detailed report of your credit history prepared by a credit bureau

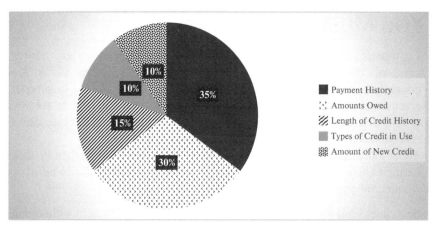

Figure 1.2. The basis for your credit score. Adapted from: Fair Isaac Corporation, "What's in my FICO scores?" 2018.

payments. Fortunately, negative information stays on your credit report for only a certain period of time—usually seven years—so positive behavior such as not taking on too much debt, not opening too many credit card accounts at one time, making on-time debt payments, and overall responsible credit use will improve your credit score over time.

A low credit score generally increases your difficulty of obtaining a loan. It also increases the interest rate you'll be charged on any debt you do obtain. If you plan to take on business partners, you should endeavor to select partners who have good credit. If you currently have bad credit and want to someday start your own business, you should immediately start working to improve your credit score by cleaning up your credit report.

Your Credit Report

It's important to check your credit report regularly. The following factors related to your credit report could negatively affect your credit score:

- The report could include inaccurate information.
- Some of your credit accounts could be missing from the report.
- Information that doesn't belong to you could be included on the report.

If you find inaccurate information, you should immediately file a dispute with the applicable credit reporting agency.

Another important reason to monitor your credit report is the very real threat of identity theft. Identity thieves who have access to too many pieces of your personal information (e.g., your social security number, date of birth, and home address) can take out loans in your name. They can also create other financial disasters you may be completely unaware of—until the Internal Revenue Service or a collection agency comes looking for you.

The Fair Credit Reporting Act requires Equifax, Experian, and TransUnion to provide you with a free copy of your credit report, at your request, once every 12 months. The most efficient way to access these credit reports is by using annual-creditreport.com. Many people make a practice of requesting one free credit report every four months and rotating these requests between the three major credit reporting agencies in order to keep a continuing eye on their credit report. You can also usually get your credit score when checking your credit report for a small fee, typically less than $10. If you want to have more regular access to your credit report and score, and also have a credit reporting agency monitor your credit report, you might want to consider investing in a credit monitoring service offered by one of the three major credit reporting agencies.

The Secured Credit Card

In many instances, the easiest way to build credit (if you don't have any) is to obtain a credit card, use it regularly, and make the required payments on time. So how do you obtain a credit card when you have no credit history? One solution is to get a secured credit card. A **secured credit card** is a real credit card—not a prepaid credit card or debit card—whose application involves opening a certificate of deposit, the amount of which will be the card's credit limit. A **certificate of deposit** (CD) is a promissory note whereby a bank promises to return to the depositor the principal amount deposited with the bank, plus interest, after a stipulated period of time. Certificates of deposit can have terms of less than one year to up to five years or more and usually have a minimum initial deposit of $500.

Your CD is a security deposit for the credit card. You earn interest on your CD, so your deposit will grow over time. The money in the CD account is yours and will remain yours as long as you don't default on your credit card payments. Ideally, at some point before you are ready to start your business, you will be able to trade in your secured credit card for a traditional credit card, thereby regaining access to the funds in the CD account you created when establishing the secured credit card.

secured credit card
a credit card whose application involves opening a certificate of deposit, the amount of which will be the card's credit limit

certificate of deposit
a promissory note whereby a bank promises to return to the depositor the principal amount deposited with the bank, plus interest, after a stipulated period of time

Separation of the Entrepreneur from the Business

Assuming you've successfully completed the many steps suggested thus far in this chapter in order to properly prepare before starting a business, there are some items of general business knowledge you should next learn before starting a business. All involve proper separation of the entrepreneur from his business.

We'll cover legal form of business in chapter 3, but it's good to know in advance of starting a company that an entrepreneur should strive to avoid being the owner of a **sole proprietorship**—a business owned and operated by an individual for profit—or a general partner in a **partnership**—an association of two or more persons who conduct business as co-owners for profit. It's often difficult to legally distinguish the owner of a sole proprietorship or a general partner in a partnership from his business. If it's difficult to distinguish the entrepreneur, as an individual, from his business, this puts both the entrepreneur and the business at risk. In most instances, forming a **corporation**—a legal entity authorized by state law to act as an artificial person in order to conduct business or engage in certain other activities—or a **limited liability company (LLC)**—a hybrid legal business entity authorized by state law featuring some of the characteristics of both partnerships and corporations—will serve the entrepreneur better than operating as sole proprietor or general partner because forming a corporation or an LLC allows the entrepreneur to more clearly separate himself from his business.

Clear separation of the entrepreneur from the business increases the likelihood that a business's financial issues won't become the entrepreneur's personal financial issues. Similarly, clear separation of the entrepreneur from the business increases the likelihood that an entrepreneur's personal financial issues—or the personal financial issues of one or more of the entrepreneur's partners—won't become the business's financial issues. In other words, the financial issues of one party do not necessarily have to become the financial issues of the other party if the entrepreneur properly separates himself from his business.

sole proprietorship
a business owned and operated by an individual for profit

partnership
an association of two or more persons who conduct business as co-owners for profit

corporation
a legal entity authorized by state law to act as an artificial person in order to conduct business or engage in certain other activities

limited liability company (LLC)
a hybrid legal business entity authorized by state law featuring some of the characteristics of both partnerships and corporations

Beyond the choice of legal form of business, an entrepreneur should do the following, as applicable, in order to clearly separate himself from his business:

- Pay the business rent or some reasonable remuneration for any significant business assets the entrepreneur uses for personal purposes (e.g., living on an unused floor of a building rented by the business, as in our earlier wine bar example).
- Make sure the use of any business vehicle is more than 50 percent business use as documented in a daily mileage log that describes the purpose of every mile driven.
- Keep separate bank and debt accounts for personal versus business use.
- Execute a formal operating agreement between the entrepreneur, the partners (if applicable), and the company.
- Always sign business documents as a representative of the company rather than personally.
- Never personally guarantee loans, contracts, or other activities of the business.

If you can't completely separate yourself from the business right at the very beginning of the business, at least be sure to keep meticulous records that clearly indicate business versus personal transactions. You'll need to do this eventually for accounting and tax purposes anyway. It's not an elegant solution, but if the best you can do at the very beginning of your company's operations is make sure all of the documentation related to the business ends up in one clearly designated box or drawer, you'll thank yourself later.

How to Properly Sign a Business Document

At the very earliest stages of any business you start, the need to separate yourself from your business will likely show up immediately with regard to one very important area: your signature. In order to properly separate yourself from your business, when you sign any document related to the business you have formed, you are no longer "Jane Doe." You are "Jane Doe, President, American XL, LLC" or "Jane Doe, Founder, American XL, LLC."

The distinction is important. Signing your name including your company title and your company's name clearly distinguishes you as signing as a representative of the company as opposed to you signing personally. The difference can be critical if problems arise—and, in business, problems often arise.

The Personal Guarantee

personal guarantee
when a third party guarantees the financial obligations of another person or a business

Before you even start your business, you can fall into the trap of failing to separate yourself from the business. A **personal guarantee** occurs when a third party guarantees the financial obligations of another person or a business. Such guarantees can be specific to one obligation or contract, or they can be general in nature. Regarding a personal guarantee, the following are some important items to consider:

- Will you be asked to personally guarantee certain aspects of your business? Probably, yes.
- Should you provide personal guarantees related to your business? No, not if you can avoid it. Why would you tie your personal financial future to a potentially negative financial situation associated with your business if you can avoid doing so?

- Do you have to provide personal guarantees to get what you want?

  No, not necessarily. Sometimes, you can offer other acceptable assurances in lieu of a personal guarantee. Acceptable alternatives to personal guarantees include providing security deposits, funds to be held in escrow, partial payments, and business assets for use as collateral. If someone requests a personal guarantee, ask them why they're requesting it. There are often many ways a vendor's or creditor's concerns can be addressed without resorting to a personal guarantee.

- Can personal guarantees have amount, time, or other limitations?

  Yes, absolutely. If you find yourself in a situation where you absolutely cannot avoid giving a personal guarantee, then at least be sure to limit both the dollar amount and the duration of the guarantee—and also to expressly limit the circumstances or transactions to which the personal guarantee applies.

Entrepreneur in Action 1.1 highlights a situation where someone wanted a personal guarantee. The example demonstrates how asking for a solution that will allay a vendor's or creditor's concerns in lieu of granting a personal guarantee can often work out well for an entrepreneur.

charge-back
when a customer uses a credit card to buy something and then cancels the transaction

Entrepreneur *in Action* 1.1

One Entrepreneur's Response to a Request for a Personal Guarantee

Joe Snyder was at a meeting with his bank about his new company, HowtoStartaBusiness.com. Joe and his web designers had spent months putting together the website, which was designed to instruct first-time entrepreneurs about how to properly set up a new business. It was almost time to launch the website. The last item on the site that needed configuration was the method for processing customer credit card payments for the $29.95 annual fee required to access the site. For that, Joe had been told he needed the cooperation of his bank.

Joe was surprised by the amount of security protocol necessary for a website to securely process credit card payments, but he and his bank had worked their way through all of the necessary paperwork, and Joe was confident he understood what he needed to instruct his web designers to do in order to guarantee all the necessary security measures were properly set up. Joe stood up to leave the meeting when the banker he was dealing with, Martin Mann, explained that there was one more thing he and Joe needed to discuss: how to handle possible credit card charge-backs. Martin explained that a credit card **charge-back** occurs when a customer uses a credit card to buy something and then cancels the transaction. Martin further explained that if Joe's company received the funds from a credit card sale in its bank account and the customer later canceled the sales transaction, there would be a problem if there wasn't enough cash in the company's bank account for the bank to withdraw the amount of the canceled sale. Martin said this type of situation was usually taken care of by the owners of a company guaranteeing they would personally cover any charge-backs exceeding the amount of funds available in the company's bank account.

There was an awkward silence as Joe pondered what was being requested of him. His lawyer had told him to try to avoid personally guaranteeing anything associated with his business. Joe looked at Martin and said he wasn't comfortable giving a personal guarantee and explained why. Martin said he understood, but then he added, "This is how the possibility of charge-backs is usually managed." Joe asked if there wasn't possibly some other way to handle the situation. Martin thought about Joe's request for a moment, left the meeting to consult with his manager, and then returned with a suggestion: If Joe could open a personal savings account at the bank and leave $2,500 on deposit there, his manager would waive the need for the personal guarantee. Martin said that his manager had noted that, after some time had passed and the bank had some historical data regarding Joe's company's average checking account balance and the average rate of charge-backs against the account, the need for Joe to maintain the personal savings account at the bank would likely go away.

Joe asked if the $2,500 would be deemed to be some sort of collateral by the bank. Martin said that it would not. Martin said the $2,500 would instead be characterized as an expression of good faith by Joe to the bank and the personal savings account would not in any way be formally tied to Joe's business. Joe agreed to deposit the $2,500 and happily exited the meeting. He was glad he'd pushed back against the bank's desire for a personal guarantee. He'd much rather deposit $2,500 of his personal funds in his company's bank than have to worry about the potential consequences associated with giving a personal guarantee.

Note that if a business has no assets or no revenues and is seeking a loan from a typical bank, in lieu of or in addition to asking for a personal guarantee, the bank may ask the entrepreneurs involved to pledge specific personal assets as collateral for the loan. As a practical matter, this practice also compromises the goal of keeping the entrepreneur separate from his business and should, therefore, be avoided if at all possible.

The Top 10 Legal and Financial Mistakes Entrepreneurs Make

Not surprisingly, entrepreneurs can err in a variety of ways. In most instances, the mistakes made by entrepreneurs that most severely damage a business are either legal or financial. Below are the top 10 legal and financial mistakes entrepreneurs make:

1. Failing to operate the business in such a way as to avoid litigation.

   As anyone who has ever spent any time in a significant legal battle knows, it's hard to think of a bigger drain of time, energy, and money than suing someone or being sued. It is therefore of paramount importance, when starting and managing a new company, that the entrepreneur make it his mission to avoid ending up in litigation.

2. Failing to keep current with regard to filing tax returns and paying taxes.

   The IRS and the other federal, state, and local entities that have jurisdiction over your business expect to be paid the amounts due to them when those amounts are due. They've heard every excuse imaginable. They aren't interested in yours.

   The IRS and other governmental entities have the power to put liens on your assets, seize your assets, cancel your licenses, suspend your permits, penalize you, fine you, and do a multitude of other unsavory things to both you and your business. The colloquialism "Don't mess with the IRS" has been around for a long time for a reason. Ultimately, the government is going to win, and you are going to lose. In order to avoid time-consuming, complicated, and expensive tax problems, a wise entrepreneur always files the required tax returns on time and always pays the taxes due on time. Period.

3. Failing to put critical agreements, terms of doing business, and other important understandings in writing.

   All your business's major agreements, especially the operating agreement, should be in writing. Even the most honest and well-intentioned human beings can genuinely forget or misremember what has been communicated only verbally. Putting the details of any important agreement into a written document to be signed by all parties concerned gives everyone a chance to reflect upon what's being agreed to and make sure all important issues are fully fleshed out and considered.

   intellectual property
   intangible property created from human intellect, often evidenced by copyrights, trademarks, or patents

   Often, the founders of a company will bring technology, **intellectual property** (intangible property created from human intellect, often evidenced by copyrights, trademarks, or patents), or other assets they have purchased or developed with them to the new company. After the company is formed, who owns these assets? In order to avoid future misunderstandings, the ownership of such assets, and any consideration a founder has received with regard to the contribution of such assets to the start-up, should be fully documented—ideally in an operating agreement.

   Good operating agreements are available online at reasonable prices, or for free, from websites such as ilrg.com (multi-member LLCs) and eforms.com (single-member LLCs). Note that even if a founder is a solo entrepreneur, he should still complete an operating agreement between himself and his company in order to clearly legally separate the person from the business.

Beyond operating agreements and other types of written agreements, it should go without saying that the basic terms of anyone's employment should be put in writing.

4. Allowing oneself to be hurried into signing a written agreement.

Too often, in the rush to make a business grow, entrepreneurs sign whatever is put in front of them, especially if it comes from someone they think they can trust. Keep in mind that whoever drafted a legal document took a lot of time to prepare that document. It makes sense that you should take a lot of time to review the document and make sure it reflects what has been verbally agreed upon before you sign it.

Could taking time to read the document completely involve an awkward silence? Yes. If you find that notion disturbing, request to take the document home for the evening for a thorough review so you can bring it back the next day and sign it after you're fully informed. Doing so could prevent you from agreeing to something that is not in your best interest. Entrepreneur in Action 1.2 (on page 16) presents a situation with an awkward silence. The vignette also shows the benefits of enduring that silence to thoroughly read an important document before signing it.

5. Not planning for disagreements between founders and changes in founders' circumstances.

According to an article on the Bloomberg website, approximately 50 percent of all marriages end in divorce.[10] The "divorce rate" among entrepreneurial business partners is probably much higher. You should anticipate that you and your cofounders will have disputes and, as such, have an agreed-upon procedure for resolving such disputes. You should also have an agreed-upon mechanism so a partner can exit the business, if necessary.

Business partners get sick. They become disabled. They die. Sometimes, they simply lose interest in participating in a business. How circumstances like these and others will be managed should be outlined in a formal operating agreement.

6. Not putting clear payment terms in place for customers.

This is a common mistake for new entrepreneurs. So excited to make those first few sales, the entrepreneur doesn't clearly indicate to the customer when he expects to be paid for what he just sold. It's hard to force payment when a deadline for payment has not been established. Many are the entrepreneurs who never got paid for their first sale because they neglected to establish firm payment terms, including a deadline for payment and specified consequences for late payment.

7. Not adequately identifying, avoiding, reducing, or insuring against the risks that can destroy a business.

A wise entrepreneur is always trying to reduce risk. **Risk management** involves an individual planning for both his business's assets and his personal assets in such a manner as to reduce uncertainty and risk. Common approaches to risk management include:

- risk avoidance
- risk reduction
- risk transfer
- risk assumption

Risk avoidance is characterized by the avoidance of any hazard that exposes a business or an individual to risk. An example of risk avoidance would be instituting a "Cash Only" sales policy at one's business. A business owner does not have to worry about a check bouncing or a credit card charge-back if he

risk management
an individual planning for both his business's assets and his personal assets in such a manner as to reduce uncertainty and risk

risk avoidance
the avoidance of any hazard that exposes a business or an individual to risk

Entrepreneur *in Action* **1.2**

The Crowne Building Company's First Land Purchase Contract

Susan Powell, the founder and chief operating officer of the Wyoming-based Crowne Building Company (Crowne), was about to make the company's first vacant lot purchase. Since Crowne's founding three years ago, it had specialized in building multimillion dollar luxury homes on property already owned by its customers. Business was booming, and Susan had decided it was time to take a risk on a different type of home building: spec home building. Spec home building involves building a residence without a particular buyer in mind and then selling that home on the open market. In order to enter this new area of business, Susan had to first buy a vacant lot, and she had picked out a beauty.

Susan was a little nervous about the transaction because she'd never purchased a vacant lot before. She'd also heard through the grapevine that the land developer from whom she was about to buy the property had a reputation for being dishonest. Susan dismissed such gossip, however, because she felt she was capable of determining for herself who was honest—and who was not. So far, she had a good feeling about the developer. The price negotiations for the property had gone smoothly, and all that was needed to close the deal was Susan's signature on the purchase and financing contract.

Crowne couldn't easily come up with the $250,000 needed to buy the exquisite lot, so Susan had negotiated a 20 percent down payment, with the remainder of the purchase price to be financed by the developer over five years at 4 percent interest. No principal was due to be repaid until the end of year 5, but if Crowne successfully built a house on the property and sold that house within Susan's planned two-year time frame, the developer could be repaid much more quickly than the permitted five years. Susan made sure of this eventuality by requesting that an early repayment option be included in the contract. Susan arrived at the land developer's cattle farm at four in the afternoon, as requested: first, for a tour of the farm; then, to sign the purchase and financing contract.

The tour of the cattle farm was amazing. The property was impressive, and the land developer and his wife were both gracious and friendly. Finally, it was time to retire to the farmhouse kitchen to sign the contract. Susan was treated to hot cocoa and warm cookies, both of which tasted fantastic on the cold November afternoon.

The land developer handed Susan the contract. Susan started to read it. She felt awkward forcing the developer and his wife to sit there while she read the entire contract, but Susan was always thorough in her business dealings. The land developer interrupted Susan after a few minutes and asked her if everything was okay. Susan replied that, yes, everything was fine, so far. The developer noted that the contract reflected what he and Susan had previously agreed upon verbally. Susan said she was sure that it did, but she liked to be thorough and completely read documents before she signed them. The land developer's wife noted that it was almost time for her and her husband to go to church. Susan began to feel uncomfortable, like she was being unreasonable making the developer and his wife sit and wait as she insisted on reading every word of the lengthy contract. Still, Susan stuck to her guns and kept reading. The land developer and his wife started talking to each other about their fund-raising plans for their charitable foundation.

Then, Susan found it. Of course, it must be an accidental error, she thought. The contract said Susan's company would be paying 21 percent interest on the unpaid balance associated with the land purchase, not 4 percent. Susan read on. The early repayment option she had requested was not included in the contract. Susan looked up to see the developer staring at her. There was a challenge in his eyes. The look on his face indicated that the anomalies in the contract were not a mistake. Susan started to speak, faltered, and then said, "I have a feeling I won't be buying this property today, will I?" "Not for 4 percent financing you won't," said the developer, as he snatched the contract out of Susan's hands. As she exited the developer's property, Susan struggled to absorb the depth of his dishonesty and the severity of the financial consequences that would have befallen her young company if she hadn't taken the time to read every word of the contract the developer had prepared for her signature.

does not accept checks or credit cards. Similarly, a business owner does not have to worry about late or unpaid accounts receivable if he does not offer customers the opportunity to make purchases using credit or trade credit. (**Accounts receivable** represent the amounts customers owe a company related to their purchases from that company utilizing the credit or trade credit offered by that company. **Trade credit** is a business-to-business arrangement by which the customer business can purchase items from the supplier business on account—paying no cash at the time of purchase, but instead paying for the items at a later date.)

Risk reduction involves engaging in behaviors and programs specifically designed to reduce risk. An example of a risk reduction behavior would be installing a sprinkler system and a security system at one's business facility.

While by no means guaranteeing that neither will happen, a sprinkler system and a security system do significantly reduce the likelihood that one's business will be destroyed by fire or burglarized.

Risk transfer involves proactively transferring risk to another party. An example of risk transfer would be selling a business's accounts receivable to a factor. A **factor** is a third party who, for a fee that is usually equivalent in amount to 1 percent to 5 percent of the total accounts receivable sold, provides the business owner with immediate cash for the accounts receivable and then goes about collecting the accounts receivable themselves.[11, 12] Another example of risk transfer would be paying for insurance policies that reimburse one for losses associated with one's personal or business assets. The key elements of insurance will be explained in chapter 12.

Risk assumption occurs when one proactively assumes risk because one believes that the loss or cost one is likely to incur by assuming that risk is less than the loss or cost associated with risk avoidance, risk reduction, or risk transfer. For example, many businesses accept checks and credit cards from their customers or offer credit or trade credit to their customers because they believe the cost of the occasional bad check, credit card charge-back, or bad account receivable is more than offset by the increased level of sales they enjoy by assuming the risk of possible customer nonpayment. As a further example, some businesses self-insure their employees' medical coverage because they believe that the amount they will pay out of pocket to settle their employees' medical bills will be less than the cost of the medical insurance premiums they would have to pay in order for an insurance company to settle those medical bills.

8. Expecting too much—or too little—in return for sweat equity.

   Maybe the concept you and your founding team are pursuing was your idea. Maybe you did most of the research to complete the feasibility analysis. Perhaps you've spent long hours fabricating the working prototype for your fledgling product company. Or perhaps you've instead spent long hours working out the operating processes for your fledgling service company. You've been told by your family and friends not to start a business and you've done it anyway. You've been told by naysayers that you're going to fail and you keep going anyway. The mental and physical stresses you've endured are many. Now that you've perfected your product or service, you need funding to grow your fledgling company. It'd be great if you had the money yourself, but you don't. Remember that equity is dear and shouldn't be given away without careful consideration, because once you give away a portion of the ownership of your company, it's unlikely you'll ever get it back. However, remember also that those who can afford to fund your company generally have many promising start-ups from which to choose. A wise entrepreneur thinks far into the future and attempts to determine in advance what he would value highly enough that it would be worth giving up equity to obtain it.

9. Processing payroll internally.

   For those of you who aren't certified public accountants (CPAs) or accountants, you may think doing payroll sounds complicated. You're right. Outsource the payroll function. Outsourcing payroll is actually quite inexpensive and one very wise step to take to help ensure you don't walk into the mine field of trouble described in item 2 of this list.

   You may think because you're a CPA or an accountant, you should do the payroll for your own business. Think again. Of all the things you could be spending your time on, entrepreneur, this is absolutely last on the list. Your time is valuable. Outsource the payroll function.

risk reduction
engaging in behaviors and programs specifically designed to reduce risk

risk transfer
proactively transferring risk to another party

factor
a third party who, for a fee, provides a business owner with immediate cash for accounts receivable and then goes about collecting the accounts receivable themselves

risk assumption
when one proactively assumes risk because one believes that the loss or cost one is likely to incur by assuming that risk is less than the loss or cost associated with risk avoidance, risk reduction, or risk transfer

10. Using vague or ambiguous terms in written agreements.

    Vague terms create confusion. Classic examples of vague terms are the words *many*, *right*, *nice*, and *good*. Depending upon the context in which they're used, your interpretation of the meaning of these words might be entirely different from the interpretation of their meaning by your business partners or others. The whole point of a written agreement is to clarify issues and create understanding, not confusion. Be sure to replace the vague words in any written agreement with specific words that have clear meanings to everyone involved. Ambiguous references, by definition, can have more than one meaning. Classic instances of ambiguity are often caused by the inappropriate use of pronouns. For example, consider the following statement: "Ron Smith is responsible for in-processing all deliveries and will assist Karl Jones with unpacking and stacking all such deliveries. His signature of approval will be required on all packing lists." Whose signature of approval will be required on all packing lists, Ron's or Karl's? Note that rewriting entire sentences, not just trading out a word or two, may be necessary in order to clarify ambiguous references.

The Circular Nature of Entrepreneurship

When starting a new venture, an entrepreneur must be mindful of the circular nature of entrepreneurship. In other words, when starting a new venture, an entrepreneur must be aware that the beginning needs to consider the desired ending.

A lot of what can or will happen with regard to a new venture depends very much upon the decisions made at the new venture's start. Some choices—like those regarding legal form of business—are changeable. Other choices—like some decisions regarding sources of funding—can involve long-term consequences that are not changeable. Legal form of business and sources of funding—topics covered in chapters 2 and 3 of this textbook—are not, however, the only decisions made at a new venture's start that can have a lasting impact on the new venture. Decisions regarding whether or not to pursue patents, in which state a business should legally form, which product or service should be developed first, even the naming of a business can have significant long-term effects on the viability and success of a business. The end shot is that every major decision the entrepreneur makes should clearly support the end game desired by the entrepreneur, whether that end game is selling the company, growing the company, or some other goal—topics covered in chapter 11 of this textbook.

Failure to consider the desired ending at the start of a new venture can create situations that make certain desired endings impossible to attain. A wise entrepreneur carefully considers the impact of every major decision he makes in order to safeguard the flexibility and the overall potential of the entity he starts.

Summary

Before starting a new business, an entrepreneur can increase his chances of entrepreneurial success by:

- choosing the timing of the start of the business carefully—to the extent this is possible
- aiming to be both personally and financially well prepared by:
  - working in and learning about the industry in which he intends to start the business
  - establishing a large network both within and outside of the industry in which he intends to start the business
  - completing a full feasibility analysis on the concept under consideration and, if deemed appropriate, also completing a business plan on the concept

- personally financially preparing for the pre-revenue and pre-profit phases of the business
- learning the basics regarding how an entrepreneur should separate himself from his business
- resolving to avoid making the most common entrepreneurial legal and financial mistakes

In addition, when starting a new venture, an entrepreneur must be mindful of the circular nature of entrepreneurship. In other words, an entrepreneur must be aware that a lot of what can or will happen with regard to a new venture depends very much upon the decisions made at the new venture's start. A wise entrepreneur carefully considers the impact of every major decision he makes in order to safeguard the potential and flexibility of the entity he starts.

Key Terms

accounts receivable	factor	risk avoidance
business model	feasibility analysis	risk management
business plan	intellectual property	risk reduction
certificate of deposit	limited liability company	risk transfer
charge-back	(LLC)	secured credit card
corporation	partnership	sole proprietorship
credit report	pass-through entity	strategic expense
credit score	personal guarantee	minimization
entrepreneurial finance	pro forma financial	trade credit
exchange traded fund	statements	working capital
(ETF)	risk assumption	

Review and Discussion Questions

1. How is entrepreneurial finance different from traditional business finance?
2. What should a nascent entrepreneur do to prepare for starting a new business?
3. What is a business plan and how is it different from a feasibility analysis? Why should an entrepreneur always do a feasibility analysis before starting a business?
4. How can an entrepreneur financially sustain himself during the start-up phase of a new business?
5. Why is it a problem for an entrepreneur—or one or more of his business partners—to have a low credit score? What can an individual do to improve a bad credit score?
6. What can an entrepreneur do to separate himself from his business? Why is it wise for an entrepreneur to separate himself from his business?

Exercises

1. Appropriate preparation before you start a new venture, perhaps before you even have an idea for a new venture, will serve you well as an entrepreneur. Write a two- to three-page paper detailing the following about your favorite entrepreneur: (1) the person's company and the significant products or services it offers, (2) the inspiration for the entrepreneur starting the company (i.e., the problem he wanted to solve), (3) the preparation performed and education completed by the entrepreneur prior to starting the company, (4) the major reasons for the entrepreneur's success, and (5) anything you feel is important about the entrepreneur and his or her company.

2. Before starting a business, an entrepreneur should have established a large network both within and outside of the industry in which he intends to start the business. One of the best ways for an entrepreneur to make, keep in contact with, and keep track of business connections is via LinkedIn (linkedin.com). Review the LinkedIn profiles of a famous entrepreneur, an entrepreneur based in your hometown, and the head of a major corporation. Write two to three paragraphs comparing and contrasting the profiles. Indicate whose profile is the best, in your opinion, and explain why.

3. It is important to check your credit report regularly because (1) the report could include inaccurate information, (2) some of your credit accounts could be missing from the report, and (3) information that doesn't belong to you could be included on your report. Go to annualcreditreport.com and request a free copy of your credit report. Is all of the information in the report correct? Is any important information missing? Is there any information that surprised you? Without disclosing any personal details, write two to three paragraphs describing the process of obtaining the free credit report and any surprises, inaccuracies, or items of interest you may have discovered along the way.

4. One of the top legal and financial mistakes entrepreneurs make is failing to keep current with regard to filing tax returns and paying taxes. That said, how do you keep current with regard to tax law, entrepreneurial finance, and related topics? One great way is to read a magazine that regularly addresses these topics. Search "finance" at entrepreneur.com or inc.com. Read a finance article of your choice. Write two to three paragraphs describing the concepts included in the article and especially highlighting anything you learned as a result of reading the article. Be sure to include the title, date, and web address of the article you read.

5. All your business's major agreements—especially the operating agreement—should be in writing. Read the member-managed operating agreement for your state at ilrg.com. You can read the agreement without paying for it or downloading it. Next, write two to three paragraphs detailing what items included in the agreement are items you likely wouldn't have addressed with potential business partners without such a document prompting you to do so. What items, if any, do you think should be added to the agreement?

Endnotes

1. Ted Conferences, LLC, https://www.ted.com/talks/bill_gross_the_single_biggest_reason_why_startups_succeed, March 2015.

2. Richard Kestenbaum, "Subscription Businesses Are Exploding with Growth," Forbes, August 16, 2017, https://www.forbes.com/sites/richardkestenbaum/2017/08/10/subscription-businesses-are-exploding-with-growth/#377fbb8c6678.

3. Ibid.

4. Ewing Marion Kauffman Foundation (website), Ewing Marion Kauffman Foundation, accessed June 8, 2018, https://www.kauffman.org/.

5. "Topic Number: 305—Recordkeeping," IRS, updated January 3, 2018, https://www.irs.gov/taxtopics/tc305.

6. "Topic Number 510—Business Use of Car," IRS, January 31, 2018, https://www.irs.gov/taxtopics/tc510.

7. "IRS Issues Guidance on Tax Treatment of Cell Phones; Provides Small Business Record-keeping Relief," IRS, September 14, 2011, https://www.irs.gov/newsroom/irs-issues-guidance-on-tax-treatment-of-cell-phones-provides-small-business-recordkeeping-relief.

8. Fair Isaac Corporation, https://www.myfico.com/consumer-division-of-FICO.aspx, 2019.

9. Fair Isaac Corporation, https://www.fico.com/en/products/fico-score, 2019.

10. Ben Steverman, "Boomers Are Making Sure the Divorces Keep Coming," Bloomberg, June 17, 2016, https://www.bloomberg.com/news/articles/2016-06-17/boomers-are-making-sure-the-divorces-keep-coming.

11. J&D Financial Corporation, http://www.jdfinancial.com/factoring-services.php, 2013.

12. Costowl.com, https://www.costowl.com/b2b/cash-advance-accounts-receivable-factoring-cost.html, 2018.

Sources of Funding

"A bank is a place where they lend you an umbrella in fair
weather and ask for it back when it begins to rain."

— **Robert Frost, American poet, four-time Pulitzer Prize winner**

Learning Objectives

Understand the concept of bootstrapping.

Know the common sources of funding available to a U.S. for-profit start-up business.

Have an understanding of the profile of a typical angel investor and the types of companies in which angel investors usually like to invest.

Understand the nature of a typical venture capital investment.

Know the difference between reward-based, lending-based, and equity-based crowdfunding.

Understand the many challenges for investors and companies wishing to participate in equity crowdfunding.

Know the sources of debt financing available to a U.S. for-profit start-up business.

Have an appreciation for the fundamental differences between Regulation D and Regulation A.

Understand how issuing securities under Regulation D or Regulation A compares to issuing securities via an initial public offering.

Understand the sources of funding generally available to U.S. small businesses versus U.S. entrepreneurial ventures.

Introduction

In order to minimize the amount of capital needed to start a business and operate it during its early stages, an entrepreneur should bootstrap her business to the extent reasonably possible. **Bootstrapping** involves borrowing noncash assets, bartering for noncash assets and services, and utilizing strategic negotiation tactics in order to avoid, delay, or minimize the outlay of cash. Bootstrapping involves seeking out what you can "get for free" or purchase "used." At its most basic level, bootstrapping involves embracing the entrepreneurial mindset in order to get a business through its start-up phase until more traditional means of financing the young venture become available. The concept of bootstrapping will be explored in detail in chapter 8.

While it does help minimize the amount of capital a business needs, bootstrapping cannot completely eliminate a business's need for capital. There are two major categories of capital generally available to the typical for-profit business: equity capital and debt capital. **Equity capital** is capital acquired by a business as a result of selling some form of ownership of that business. **Debt capital** is capital acquired by a business with the understanding that the capital will have to be repaid by the business, usually within a defined time period and usually with interest. Other sources of capital for a start-up that involve neither equity nor debt capital include reward-based crowdfunding and grants. **Reward-based crowdfunding** is the accumulation of small amounts of capital from a large number of individuals via a campaign on the internet, such individuals generally expecting nothing in return (other than a news update, a small token gift, or a promised product or service, usually of nominal value). **Grants** are monies provided to an individual or an entity that do not have to be repaid to the provider of the monies (the grantor) as long as the receiver of the monies (the grantee) provides the goods or performs the services for which the grant was approved.

Equity capital, debt capital, reward-based crowdfunding, and grants will all be discussed in detail in this chapter. The regulations that often apply to equity capital and debt capital will also be explored.

bootstrapping
borrowing non-cash assets, bartering for non-cash assets and services, and utilizing strategic negotiation tactics in order to avoid, delay or minimize the outlay of cash

equity capital
capital acquired by a business as a result of selling some form of ownership of that business

debt capital
capital acquired by a business with the understanding that the capital will have to be repaid by the business, within a defined time period, usually with interest

reward-based crowdfunding
the accumulation of small amounts of capital from a large number of individuals via a campaign on the internet, such individuals generally expecting nothing in return (other than a news update, a small token gift, or a promised product or service, usually of nominal value)

grant
an amount of money provided to an individual or an entity that does not have to be repaid to the provider of the money (the grantor) as long as the receiver of the money (the grantee) provides the goods or performs the services for which the grant was approved

Common Sources of Funding

The funding for a start-up venture usually comes from a variety of sources. Below are the most common sources of funding for a typical U.S. for-profit business:

- providers of equity or debt capital, such as:
  - the founders themselves—individuals who generally provide a venture with its very first seed capital either from their personal savings or by taking on personal debt (**seed capital** is the funding required to get a business started and actively pursuing full-scale operations)
  - friends, family, and "fools"—individuals who usually know the founders very well and provide them with secondary seed capital, usually because they believe in either the founders or the business concept they are pursuing
  - **angel investors** (commonly referred to as angels)—individuals, usually successful or retired entrepreneurs or businesspeople, who provide follow-up investment and free mentoring to start-up businesses
  - **venture capital funds**—monies typically used to invest in young, market-driven companies with very large potential upside accumulated by:
    a. private **venture capital firms** (firms typically set up as limited partnerships that gather large sums of money from investors and deploy these monies by investing in the start-ups that survive the venture capital firm's vetting process)
    b. **small business investment companies** (SBICs) (firms similar to venture capital firms that are licensed and regulated by the Small Business Administration)
    c. certain large corporations
  - community development financial institutions (CDFIs)—organizations that aim to expand economic opportunity in low-income communities by

providing access to financing for businesses that support local economic development activity

- providers of equity capital only, such as participants in equity crowdfunding (**equity crowdfunding** is the accumulation of small amounts of capital from a large number of individuals via a campaign on the internet, such individuals receiving an ownership interest in the company in which they invest)
- providers of debt capital only, such as:
  - banks and a variety of other commercial lenders, including lenders who participate in government-supported loan programs
  - participants in lending-based crowdfunding (**lending-based crowdfunding—** also called crowd lending—is the accumulation of small amounts of capital from a large number of individuals via a campaign on the internet, such individuals expecting to be repaid by the company, with interest)
- participants in reward-based crowdfunding

Figure 2.1 is an analysis of the sources of funding for-profit U.S. start-ups have historically used to finance their start-up operations and it indicates that, on average, the founders themselves provide more funding for their start-up businesses than all other sources of funding combined. That said, many start-ups do pursue and successfully obtain at least one outside source of funding. What type of funding—and from what source—depends very much upon the entrepreneur and the nature of her business.

Important items to note when considering which sources of funding are best for your start-up include the following:

- Once you give away or sell any ownership (equity) of your company, it is very unlikely you will ever get it back.
- Investors in start-ups take on a lot of risk and expect a healthy profit on their investment in return. They also expect to eventually be repaid or provided with a means to exit their investment.
- Debt needs to be repaid, and there are limits to the amount of debt any company can obtain and support.

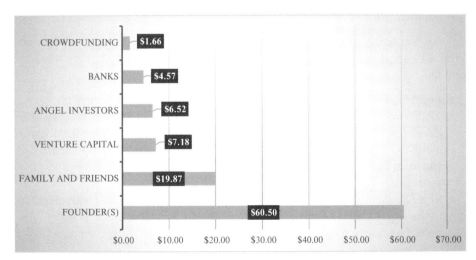

Figure 2.1. Source per $100 of funding for all US Startups Combined, 2013. Source: Adapted from information included at www.entrepreneur.com/article/230011#, 2013.

Note: The amount indicated above for crowdfunding includes no equity crowdfunding as there was no legal mechanism for equity crowdfunding in the United States in 2013.

seed capital
the funding required to get a business started and actively pursuing full-scale operations

angel investor
an individual, usually a successful or retired entrepreneur or business person, who provides follow-up investment and free mentoring to start-up businesses; also referred to as an angel

venture capital fund
monies accumulated by private venture capital firms, small business investment companies (SBICs), and certain large corporations that are typically used to invest in young, market-driven companies with a very large potential upside

venture capital firm
a firm typically set up as a limited partnership that gathers large sums of money from investors and deploys these monies by investing in the start-ups that survive the venture capital firm's vetting process

small business investment companies (SBICs)
firms similar to venture capital firms that are licensed and regulated by the Small Business Administration

equity crowdfunding
the accumulation of small amounts of capital from a large number of individuals via a campaign on the internet, such individuals receiving an ownership interest in the company in which they invest

lending-based crowdfunding
the accumulation of small amounts of capital from a large number of individuals via a campaign on the internet, such individuals expecting to be repaid by the company, with interest; also called crowd lending

Angel Investors

The term "angel investor" originated on Broadway, where it was used to describe the individuals who provided the financing for theatrical productions.[1] Today, angel investors are wealthy individuals—usually making $200,000 or more in income every year or maintaining a net worth of over $1 million, excluding their primary residence—who invest either debt or equity capital—or some combination of both—in start-ups and early-stage companies. In addition to providing funding, because angels are usually successful or retired entrepreneurs or businesspeople, angels also often provide free mentoring to the companies in which they invest. Recent estimates suggest that every two years approximately 300,000 individuals in the United States make an angel investment.[2]

Like all investments in entrepreneurial start-ups, the investments made by angels are considered high risk. As a result, investments in entrepreneurial start-ups normally don't represent more than 10 percent of the total investment portfolio of any given angel.[3]

An angel investor typically looks to invest in a young business with these characteristics:

- Its product, service, or business model has a clear competitive advantage.
- It is pursuing a large or fast-growing market.
- It has a passionate founding team that possesses the skills necessary to successfully deliver the product or service and execute the business model.
- It could potentially return the angel 10 times her investment in five years.[4]

The typical angel investment ranges from $25,000 to $100,000 per company.[5] Recent research by the Kauffman Foundation and Nesta indicates the following about angel investments:

- On any one investment, an angel is more likely than not to lose some or all of her investment.
- Ninety percent of all cash returns are produced by 10 percent of an angel's investments.
- Over a period of approximately four years, the typical U.S. angel investor makes an average 2.5x return on all of her angel investments combined (i.e., an investment of $100,000 would return $250,000).[6] This equates to an approximate 25 percent annual return.

An increasing number of angel investors are organizing themselves into angel groups or angel networks in order to pool their investment capital, share research, and find sources of experienced advice for their portfolio companies:

- *Angel Capital Association* (angelcapitalassociation.org) is a collective of 13,000+ accredited angel investors that make up the largest angel professional development organization in the world. The organization's website includes a link to the website of each angel organization listed so the entrepreneur can learn more about the group, including its investment preferences and processes.
- *Angel Resource Institute* (angelresourceinstitute.org) collaborates with members of the Angel Capital Association to provide educational workshops and published research that supports the development of early-stage ventures.

In addition, websites like Gust.com and Funded.com are designed to provide entrepreneurs with a standardized platform with which to efficiently approach angels for new venture funding. The entrepreneur should note, however, that these and similar platforms do generally charge a fee.

Venture Capital

Private venture capital firms, SBICs, and certain large corporations provide capital sourced from designated venture capital funds to select start-up businesses. Venture capital is typically provided to an early-stage, high-potential, or high-growth start-up company, usually in one of the technology industries. While it can involve a component of debt, a venture capital investment is typically an equity investment that has the following attributes:

- It occurs as the first sophisticated round of investment capital (often referred to as a **Series A** round of investment) to fund a young entity's growth after seed capital has already been provided.
- It is made in the interest of generating returns similar to those desired by angel investors (i.e., 10 times the investment returned in five years).
- It generates a return through an eventual realization event such as the sale of the company or an initial public offering. A **public offering** is an issue of securities offered for sale to the public by a company or other entity. An **initial public offering (IPO)** is a very highly regulated and managed first sale of most or all of the stock of a previously private company—or mostly private company—to the general public.

Because of the high risk that venture capitalists assume by investing in small, early-stage companies, venture capitalists usually ensure that they can exert significant control over the companies, when they deem such control desirable. Venture capitalists deciding to exert control over a young company can oftentimes be quite challenging for the company's founders. This is a reason why some founders reject venture capital as a source of funding.

Venture capital firms are different from **private equity firms**. Private equity firms help manage the mature companies of which they usually buy majority control or full control, often over time. Venture capital firms (and angels) invest in young, typically fast-growing companies and rarely pursue majority control.

Corporations as a source of venture capital are relatively new to the entrepreneurial funding landscape. In the late 1990s, certain large corporations started to recognize the opportunities associated with being invested in the young ventures innovating in their industries. As a result, these corporations—corporations such as Cisco, Intel, and Johnson & Johnson—began to establish multimillion dollar venture capital funds for the purpose of investing in such companies. Currently representing about 25 percent of all venture capital funding, corporate venture capital is widely viewed as a desirable source of funding because of the vast amount of resources and business savvy the corporate entities who created these funds can potentially bring to the table.[7]

Although the U.S. Small Business Administration (SBA) does not itself invest in small businesses, it does license and regulate privately owned and managed investment firms called small business investment companies. SBICs search for and invest in promising U.S. small businesses in need of debt or equity financing. SBICs are similar to venture capital firms in terms of how they operate and in their pursuit of high returns.[8] As of March 31, 2019, the SBA's SBIC program included 304 licensees managing more than $32 billion in assets.[9] SBIC's provided an estimated $7 billion in financing to approximately 1,500 U.S. small businesses during the 12 months ended March 31, 2019.[10] You can learn more about SBICs at sba.gov.

Beyond the benefits associated with having firsthand knowledge of some of the latest innovations about to hit the market, why do private venture capital firms, SBICs, and certain large corporations invest in high-risk start-up businesses? According to the National Bureau of Economic Research, the average annual return a U.S.

Series A
the first sophisticated round of investment capital to fund a young entity's growth after seed capital has already been provided

public offering
an issue of securities offered for sale to the public by a company or other entity

initial public offering (IPO)
a very highly regulated and managed first sale of most or all of the stock of a previously private company—or mostly private company—to the general public

private equity firm
a type of firm that helps manage the mature companies of which it usually buys majority control or full control, often over time

venture capital fund receives on all of its venture capital investments combined is 25 percent—similar to the results achieved by angel investors.[11]

Community Development Financial Institutions

Community development financial institutions aim to expand economic opportunity in low-income communities. They generally do this by providing access to financing for businesses that support local economic development activity, including the creation of local jobs and the creation of—or improvement of access to—affordable housing. CDFI support is usually in the form of a loan or some type of loan support, but it can also sometimes involve an equity investment or a grant. CDFIs come in the form of banks, credit unions, community development loan funds, and community development venture capital funds. There are more than 1,000 nationwide. Financing via a CDFI can make sense when traditional financing from banks or private investors is not an option due to less than perfect credit or because a business generates returns too low to attract angel or venture capital investment. In 2018, CDFI's provided $3.995 billion of financial support to U.S. small and medium-sized businesses in the form of awards, loans, bond guarantees, and tax credit allocations.[12] You can find out if there is a CDFI in your community by visiting cdfifund.gov.

Crowdfunding

As mentioned earlier in this chapter, reward-based crowdfunding is the accumulation of small amounts of capital from a large number of individuals via a campaign on the internet, such individuals generally expecting nothing in return (other than a news update, a small token gift, or a promised product or service, usually of nominal value). The beauty of reward-based crowdfunding is that the entrepreneur receives funding without giving away any ownership or taking on any debt. An additional benefit is that the start-up's "investors" often become its advocates via positive word-of-mouth and promotional social media posts. In some cases, the benefit the "investor" receives is the start-up's product or service, which means that—via its crowdfunding campaign—the start-up is essentially selling its product or service. Such sales can provide **proof of concept**—evidence that a business concept is feasible. Proof of concept makes obtaining follow-up financing via more traditional sources of funding more possible for the start-up.

proof of concept
evidence that a business concept is feasible

As also mentioned earlier in this chapter, lending-based crowdfunding is the accumulation of small amounts of capital from a large number of individuals via a campaign on the internet, such individuals expecting to be repaid by the company, with interest. An advantage of lending-based crowdfunding is that the entrepreneur receives funding without giving away any ownership. In addition, similar to what occurs with reward-based crowdfunding, often the start-up's lenders become its advocates via positive word-of-mouth and promotional social media posts. Although it is an avenue of funding that can often be pursued when traditional avenues of debt financing cannot—lending-based crowdfunding does still, in fact, represent debt financing. As such, additional discussion regarding lending-based crowdfunding is included in the section on "Debt" included later in this chapter.

Additionally mentioned earlier in this chapter, equity crowdfunding is the accumulation of small amounts of capital from a large number of individuals via a campaign on the internet, such individuals obtaining an equity (ownership) position in the company as a result of their investment. Under U.S. federal law, the sale of securities to the public as an investment is regulated by the Securities and Exchange

Commission (SEC). Among other responsibilities, the role of the SEC is to protect individual investors. The SEC, however, generally views accredited investors as savvy enough to take care of themselves when it comes to investing—or wealthy enough to hire someone financially sophisticated to invest their money for them. An **accredited investor** is an individual who makes over $200,000 per year in income or has a net worth greater than $1 million, excluding her primary residence. A general partner, executive officer, or director of a company issuing a **security**—a negotiable financial instrument whereby an investor or lender expects to derive a profit or income—is also considered an accredited investor with regard to that particular company. Angel investors are typically accredited investors.

In 2012, the Jumpstart Our Business Startups (JOBS) Act became law. Title III of that law created a need for the SEC to write rules regarding the registration, disclosure, and compliance requirements related to equity crowdfunding. Specifically, the Act tasked the SEC with creating a structure for equity crowdfunding that exempted it from some of the more burdensome regulations that restrict non-accredited investors from purchasing the non-SEC-registered securities often offered by entrepreneurial start-ups. The typical participant in equity crowdfunding is *not* an accredited investor. The challenge of developing regulations that allowed for equity crowdfunding while still providing protections to its participant investors absorbed much of the SEC's attention for several years.

In October of 2015, the SEC finally promulgated the rules necessitated by Title III of the JOBS Act, thus giving non-accredited investors (individuals who make $200,000 or less per year in income or have a net worth of less than $1 million, excluding their primary residence) the opportunity to invest in start-up companies. In other words, in 2015, within certain guidelines and subject to certain limitations, the SEC created a path for average individuals to become private investors in start-up companies marketing themselves on the internet. The primary motivation for allowing non-accredited investors access to equity crowdfunding was the federal government's desire to open up a new source of capital for entrepreneurs—entrepreneurs being the individuals who created the companies that were responsible for generating approximately two-thirds of U.S. net new jobs from 1995 through 2011—a trend that continues today.[13]

There are limits on the amount non-accredited investors can invest in equity crowdfunding during any 12-month period. If your income is less than $100,000 per year or your net worth is below that amount, you can invest up to the greater of $2,000 or 5 percent of the lesser of your income or net worth.[14] If both your annual income and your net worth exceed $100,000, you can invest up to 10 percent of the lesser of your income or net worth, up to a total limit of $100,000.[15]

Like all investments in start-ups, an investment in equity crowdfunding is considered high risk. There is no guarantee that a new startup will succeed, and if the company fails, the equity shares will become worthless. Further, like most shares sold through **private placements** (the sale of securities directly to a private investor, rather than as part of a public offering), according to **Rule 144 of the Securities Act of 1933** (a rule that, under limited circumstances, provides an exemption from SEC registration requirements and permits for the resale of restricted or control securities, such as those issued in a private placement), the shares of stock purchased via equity crowdfunding cannot be sold (in most instances) for at least one year.[16] Beyond that, there is generally no marketplace for these shares—and in all likelihood there never will be—unless a company is successful enough to decide to register with the SEC and become a public company. Even if a company plans to go public, it still usually takes many years before a company's initial investors can sell their shares. Data from CrunchBase indicates that the average time it takes for a start-up company to go public (considering only those companies who actually choose to pursue this path) is 8.25 years.[17]

accredited investor
an individual who typically makes over $200,000 per year in income or has a net worth greater than $1 million, excluding her primary residence

security
a negotiable financial instrument whereby an investor or lender expects to derive a profit or income

private placement
the sale of securities directly to a private investor, rather than as part of a public offering

Rule 144 of the Securities Act of 1933
a rule that, under limited circumstances, provides an exemption from SEC registration requirements and permits for the resale of restricted or control securities, such as those issued in a private placement

Aside from the above-noted challenges for investors participating in equity crowdfunding, equity crowdfunding also presents the following challenges for the companies who wish to pursue financing using the platform:

seed round
a startup's first significant seed capital received from a source other than the founders or their friends and families

- Equity crowdfunding rules limit start-ups to raising only up to $1 million within a period of 12 months. This can be a problem because the size of the average **seed round**—a seed round is typically a startup's first significant seed capital received from a source other than the founders or their friends and families—is steadily increasing in size in the United States. According to Pitchbook-NVCA Venture Monitor, as of March 31, 2018, the size of the average seed round was $2.2 million.[18] If the average seed round is twice the equity crowdfunding cap, that means many founders will need to pursue additional funding in parallel or in sequence to pursuing crowdfunding. This will, of course, require more money and more time on the part of the start-up and its founders.

- As is true for all crowdfunding campaigns, including reward-based and lending-based crowdfunding, if a company does not raise the full amount of their funding goal, the company does not get to keep any of the money raised—and they lose the money spent on the up-front costs associated with pursuing the crowdfunding campaign.

- Not knowing if their company will even have a successful equity crowdfunding campaign, the founders will need to spend time and money to meet certain requirements of the SEC.

- The founders will need to prepare filings that include a due diligence screening and, in some cases, audited financial statements. (First-time companies and companies wishing to raise less than $500,000 can usually get an exemption from the audit requirement.) How much all of this will cost depends upon what exactly the SEC requires considering the particular instance at hand and how much of the work the founders do themselves versus outsourcing it, but estimates put the range of cost at between $18,000 and $65,000 (or more).[19]

- After a successful equity crowdfunding campaign, periodic updates are required to be filed with the SEC, including ongoing annual reports. Such updates are estimated to cost anywhere between $7,000 and $25,000 per year—dependent upon the nature of the company and its campaign—every year for the remaining life of the company.[20]

- Due to the additional compliance requirements and perceived liability associated with having non-accredited investors, it may be difficult for companies looking to do subsequent rounds of financing to bring in venture capital investment after a successful equity crowdfunding campaign.

capitalization table
a schedule that outlines the entire debt and equity structure of a business, including the order in which lenders and investors will be satisfied in the event of a company's liquidation

A company's **capitalization table** outlines the entire debt and equity structure of the business, as well as the order in which lenders and investors will be satisfied in the event of a company's liquidation. An uncomplicated capitalization table is deemed preferable by potential investors because the more investors and lenders an entrepreneurial venture has, the harder it is to push through major company initiatives.

Because of the costs and time requirements involved, in 2015 the SEC estimated that only 1,900 businesses per year will likely raise capital via equity crowdfunding.[21] Considering the total number of start-ups funded by angels alone was approximately 73,400 in 2014, 1,900 is a very small number indeed.[22] At the time of publishing of this textbook (2019), though complete data is not yet available, all evidence seems to support the supposition that, in the United States, equity crowdfunding is—and will remain—an extremely small source of funding compared to other sources of start-up funding.[23] Given the hurdles and risks associated with equity crowdfunding, many entrepreneurs will likely choose to pursue more traditional avenues of funding, like those offered by Regulation D and Regulation A, which will be discussed later in this chapter.

Debt

Debt is a well-known and often-used means of raising capital. The most attractive aspect of debt is that it does not generally involve giving away ownership of your company or a percentage of its profits. The least attractive aspect of debt is that, unless it converts into an equity investment, it must be repaid, usually with interest.

At the beginning of this chapter, it was noted that the founders themselves, their friends and families, angel investors, venture capital funds, and CDFIs may all be sources of debt capital for a young venture. It is important to note that the promissory notes and other, more sophisticated debt instruments like convertible notes issued by young ventures in exchange for borrowed funds are, in fact, securities, and are therefore, in many instances, subject to federal and state securities laws. **Convertible notes** are securities that document the terms of an investor's loan to a company, but also include an option for the investor to convert the loan into an equity position in the company if desired by the investor at a future time. Convertible notes are a commonly used investment tool of angel investors.

Potential sources of debt capital beyond the founders themselves, their friends and families, angel investors, venture capital funds, and CDFIs include:

- consumer credit
- banks and commercial lenders
- SBA loans
- Capital Access Programs (CAPs)
- lending-based crowdfunding

Most new businesses utilize some type of consumer credit in the form of either personal (founder) credit cards or business credit cards. It should be noted that the reward systems and the costs (annual fees, other fees, and interest rates) associated with credit cards vary widely. Repayment terms also vary. An entrepreneur should take the time to find a personal or business credit card that makes the most sense overall considering all of the costs involved and all of the rewards provided. Also, the entrepreneur will have to make a decision regarding the treatment of any personal credit card use for the benefit of her start-up. An entrepreneur can make the decision to treat the use of her personal credit card for the benefit of her start-up as a loan to be repaid by the start-up at a later date. Alternatively, the entrepreneur can make the decision to treat the use of her personal credit card for the benefit of her start-up as an equity investment in that start-up. Either way, the use of a personal credit card to benefit an entrepreneur's start-up should be clearly documented for later follow-up.

In general, beyond issuing credit cards, banks loan money to businesses in the form of either term loans, equipment (or asset) loans, or lines of credit. Term loans involve borrowing a lump sum of cash that is repaid, with interest, over a predetermined period of time. A downside of term loans is that they can be hard for a start-up business to obtain—especially a start-up business with few or no assets or little or no revenue. Equipment (or asset) loans typically finance a significant portion of a major asset purchase. The repayment term of the loan often mirrors the expected life of the asset, and the asset serves as collateral for the loan. A downside of asset loans is that they usually require that the start-up have the necessary down payment for the asset purchase. This can be a challenge for many young ventures. A business line of credit provides access to funds up to a pre-established credit limit. Interest is paid only on the amounts borrowed, like a credit card, so a line of credit can offer flexibility that term and asset loans cannot. Downsides of business lines of credit include the need

convertible note
a security that documents the terms of an investor's loan to a company, but also includes an option for the investor to convert the loan into an equity position in the company if desired by the investor at a future time; a commonly used tool of angel investors

for the business to have established good credit before applying for the line and, often, the need for the business to pay down the line to $0 at least once each year.

Although small, local banks are sometimes friendlier than large banks, in general, banks are risk-averse and not receptive to lending to start-up companies, especially those that have no assets or no revenues. If a business has no assets or no revenues and is seeking a loan from a typical bank, the bank is likely to ask the entrepreneurs involved to either personally guarantee the loan or pledge specific personal assets as collateral for the loan. As a practical matter, both of these practices compromise the goal of keeping the entrepreneur separate from her business discussed in chapter 1 and should, therefore, be avoided if at all possible.

A 2019 National Federation of Independent Business (NFIB) survey indicated that only about one third of small business owners were able to consistently obtain all of the credit that their businesses needed.[24] Because of the difficulties many entrepreneurs and small business owners encounter when trying to get a loan, they often enlist the help of the SBA. The SBA doesn't make loans to start-ups. It does, however, work to facilitate loans to small businesses via its Guaranteed Loan Program.

When a business applies for an SBA loan, it is actually applying for a commercial loan from one of the SBA's lending partners, structured according to SBA requirements. The SBA then guarantees that the loan will be repaid (up to 85 percent), thus eliminating some of the risk to its lending partner.[25] SBA-guaranteed loans may not be available to a small business if that business has access to other financing at reasonable terms. The requirements to participate in the SBA's Guaranteed Loan Program vary as economic, regulatory, and other conditions vary.[26] You can learn more about the SBA's Guaranteed Loan Program at sba.gov.

A Capital Access Program (CAP) is a loan portfolio insurance program that makes it possible for banks to provide loans to small businesses they might otherwise reject. The insurance aspect of the program works such that, when a loan is made, the lender and borrower each contribute a percentage of the loan—such contribution typically ranging from 2 percent to 7 percent of the total loan amount—into a reserve fund held by the lender.[27] The state then matches the combined lender/borrower contribution. Each participating lender's total CAP reserve fund is then available to cover losses on any loan in the lender's CAP portfolio. CAPs offer banks the flexibility to make loans that may not qualify for an SBA guarantee. CAPs offer entrepreneurs the ability to get a loan more quickly than they often can through the SBA. In order to determine if a CAP exists in your state, check with your state's economic development agency.

Lending-based crowdfunding is a form of crowdfunding that is slowly gaining traction in the United States. Lending-based crowdfunding takes place through internet platforms like LendingClub.com and Prosper.com. The interest rate charged is usually competitive and the crowdfunding approach to lending often facilitates debt financing for entrepreneurs who cannot borrow via other means. Some debt instruments associated with lending-based crowdfunding allow for entering into securities that relate in some way to a company's potential growth. Others are strictly interest-based. Additionally, the debt instruments can be either secured or unsecured.[28] A downside of lending-based crowdfunding is the lack of input from a trained financial advisor like that an entrepreneur would receive when working with a traditional lender. Another downside is lending-based crowdfunding's often rigid repayment terms compared to other forms of debt financing.

Securing debt financing for a start-up is not an easy task for the typical entrepreneur. And beyond just determining a viable path for pursuing debt financing, the entrepreneur must also work to carefully structure any debt financing successfully obtained so that the debt optimally serves the needs of her start-up business. Best practices when structuring debt for a start-up business include:

- negotiating the ability to pay interest only for a period of months or years, ideally until the new venture gets past its start-up phase
- negotiating a fixed, rather than a variable, interest rate
- negotiating a long repayment term with the ability to repay early, if and when desired
- negotiating the ability to renegotiate interest rates, fees, and repayment terms, if and when circumstances change

Grants

Grants are monies provided to an individual or an entity that do not have to be repaid to the provider of the monies (the grantor) as long as the receiver of the monies (the grantee) provides the goods or performs the services for which the grant was approved. In the United States, grants are most often issued by governmental agencies and a wide range of public and private trusts and foundations. According to the Foundation Center, in 2019, U.S. grant-awarding trusts and foundations numbered in excess of 140,000 and disbursed in excess of $250 billion.[29]

The federal government generally does not provide grants related to starting or expanding a business. Federal grants are generally only available to nonprofits and educational institutions related to specific areas of pursuit, such as medicine, education, scientific research, and technology development. Some industry-specific business grants are, however, available through state and local programs, nonprofit organizations, and other groups.[30] Start your search for grant funding by visiting foundationcenter.org or grants.gov.

Sources of Funding for Small Businesses vs. Entrepreneurial Ventures

Before launching into a discussion of what type of entity typically gets what type of funding, it is important to note that there are significant differences between a typical U.S. small business and a more broad-based entrepreneurial venture. A small business tends to come up with ideas that solve local problems. It helps keep money and jobs in the local community. A more broad-based entrepreneurial venture tends to come up with ideas that solve national or world problems. It generates revenues and creates jobs wherever it decides to locate. A small business tends to be more limited in scope and involves innovations that, while important, are not necessarily disruptive. An entrepreneurial venture tends to pursue larger scope, more disruptive ideas that involve a higher degree of risk. A small business owner tends to enjoy operating her business day to day, and while she might desire to grow the business geographically or otherwise, that growth tends to be slow and sure, rather than exponential. The founder of an entrepreneurial venture often enlists others to manage the day-to-day operations of the business while she functions more as a rainmaker and an implementer of sweeping change. Small businesses are the backbone of the U.S. economy. Entrepreneurial ventures propel the U.S. economy forward.

The typical U.S. entrepreneurial venture usually has the opportunity to pursue and obtain funding from any or all of the sources mentioned in this chapter. The funding sources available to the typical U.S. small business are more limited than those available to the typical U.S. entrepreneurial venture. U.S. small businesses generally do not have the market potential to attract angel or venture capital investment, and they also generally do not have the internet appeal to successfully pursue crowdfunding. Grant capital is largely reserved for nonprofit organizations, and most banks are too risk averse to loan money to a start-up venture of any type.

So what sources of start-up funding are available to U.S. small businesses? Usually, a small business begins by utilizing funds from the founders themselves and funds from their friends and families. As the business builds **traction** (evidence—such as sales or another form of positive customer response—that a product or service is being adopted at such a rate that the business model and the business's potential for sustainable growth appear to be validated), dependent upon the type of business, loans sponsored by the SBA, a CDFI, or a CAP often become the next source of funding for the typical U.S. small business. Later, as the business matures, traditional bank financing usually becomes an option.

Regulatory Considerations

Almost every path to securing capital for a young venture, other than perhaps the funding that comes from the entrepreneurs themselves or from their friends and families, involves the issuance of a security. Stocks and bonds are easily identifiable as securities, but the SEC and most states also view an ownership interest in an LLC as a security. Similarly, a limited partnership interest is generally viewed as a security. Additionally, as mentioned previously, dependent upon the circumstances surrounding it, a promissory note or other document detailing debt financing from a nonbank entity can also be viewed as a security.

Prior to 1933, the U.S. securities markets were largely unregulated. The stock market crash of 1929 and the Great Depression it precipitated led to the promulgation of the Securities Act of 1933 and the Securities and Exchange Act of 1934. The Securities Act of 1933 is most relevant to new ventures in that it pertains to the initial offering of securities by a company and the continuing disclosures that must be made once those securities have been issued. The Securities and Exchange Act of 1934 regulates the exchange of securities after they have been issued. Both Acts require that very specific filings be made with the SEC. Such filings can involve the formal registration statements and prospectuses associated with a company offering securities to the public for the first time. Ongoing filings can involve the submission of quarterly financial information and complete annual reports that include audited financial statements.

Beyond the requirements of the 1933 and 1934 federal Acts, state security laws known as "blue sky laws" also exist. Although every state in the United States has securities laws, the laws are not uniform from state to state and sometimes conflict somewhat with federal securities laws. This can sometimes make complying with all of the securities laws applicable to a particular company—or a particular security issued by a company—very challenging. A point that cannot be stressed enough is that, *before an entrepreneur ever thinks of taking either debt or equity capital from an outside investor, the entrepreneur must thoroughly investigate the implications of taking that capital considering the nature of the security to be issued in exchange for the capital and the federal and state securities laws that may affect that security.* Unless the entrepreneur happens to be a CPA or an attorney, this usually means contracting the services of a CPA or an attorney.

Because of the time, money, and effort generally required to comply with securities laws, entrepreneurs often choose to pursue funding via paths that avoid the need to register securities with the SEC. There are two general types of exemption from federal registration: exempt securities and exempt transactions. Exempt securities include, among others, government securities, insurance policies, and **commercial paper**—an unsecured, short-term debt instrument, typically issued in a large denomination ($100,000 or more) by a large bank, a foreign government, or a large corporation with a strong balance sheet, the proceeds of which are typically used to finance accounts receivable or inventory or to meet short-term debt obligations. Exempt transactions include purely **intrastate offerings**—securities whose sale is limited to investors in one state—and certain private placements. The amount of money that

---

traction

evidence—such as sales or another form of positive customer response—that a product or service is being adopted at such a rate that the business model and the business's potential for sustainable growth appear to be validated

commercial paper

an unsecured, short-term debt instrument, typically issued in a large denomination ($100,000 or more) by a large bank, a foreign government, or a large corporation with a strong balance sheet, the proceeds of which are typically used to finance accounts receivable or inventory or to meet short-term debt obligations

intrastate offering

a security whose sale is limited to investors in one state

can be raised with an intrastate offering—and the amount of time permitted to do so—varies by state. As a result, before attempting any intrastate offering, the applicable state's securities laws should be consulted. The exemption related to private placements is best described in an amendment to the Securities Act of 1933 called Regulation D.

Regulation D

Regulation D is a regulation that allows companies to raise capital through the issuance of securities without having to register those securities with the SEC.

Regulation D contains Rules 504 and 506. The only filing requirement associated with each of these rules is to file a Form D with the SEC and certain states (as required by those states). Form D must be filed within 15 days of the first sale of the securities in an offering.[31] The main purpose of Form D is to notify federal and state authorities of the amount and nature of the offering being pursued under Regulation D. It is via Regulation D that many angel investors acquire their equity positions in young companies.

Under *Rule 504* of Regulation D, certain issuers may offer and sell up to $5 million of securities in any 12-month period. Securities offered under Rule 504 may be sold to only accredited investors, and the issuer is not subject to specific disclosure requirements.[32]

Under *Rule 506* of Regulation D, certain issuers may offer and sell an unlimited amount of securities by relying on one of two possible exemptions: Rule 506(b) and 506(c):

> Issuers relying on *Rule 506(b)* may sell to an unlimited number of accredited investors, but to no more than 35 non-accredited investors. Note, however, that the non-accredited investors included in the offering must be financially sophisticated or, in other words, they must have sufficient knowledge and experience in business and financial matters to be able to effectively evaluate the investment under consideration.
>
> Issuers relying on *Rule 506(c)* can, in most instances, advertise their offerings to the general public via the internet, social media, television, radio, etc. Note, however, that only accredited investors are permitted to purchase securities offered under a Rule 506(c) offering that is widely advertised, and the issuer will need to be able to prove that reasonable steps were taken to verify accredited investor status.[33]

While a start-up wanting to raise capital still needs to provide the proper framework and disclosures when pursuing funding via a private placement under Regulation D, overall, the requirements are significantly less than what is prescribed for both a public offering and equity crowdfunding.

Conducting a public offering is a notoriously expensive and time-consuming process usually engaged in by a company well past the start-up phase. In other words, a public offering is generally outside the realm of possibility for the typical start-up company. When looking for major funding, because venture capital investment is relatively rare (less than 9,000 such investments were made in 2018), a start-up is most likely to consider Regulation D or equity crowdfunding.[34] For a start-up seeking investment, the estimated average cost for a Regulation D raise is $15,000 per $1 million of investment versus $100,000 per $1 million of investment for an equity crowdfunding raise.[35] The time between deciding to pursue funding and actually receiving that funding is also less for funding pursued via Regulation D versus funding pursued via equity crowdfunding. Entrepreneur in Action 2.1, (on page 34), illustrates how Regulation D can often be preferable to equity crowdfunding as a means of pursuing funding for a young company.

Regulation D
a regulation that allows companies to raise capital through the sale of securities without having to register those securities with the SEC

Entrepreneur *in Action* **2.1**

The Owners of a Young Company Must Choose an Avenue for Funding Product Development

It was December 2016 and CFO Cory Sanders needed cash for his business, SafeNet, Inc. SafeNet was developing a new app that allowed users to monitor the vital signs of their child under age two via a small chip implanted behind one of the child's ears. Much research in the field of pediatrics had clearly concluded that since children under age two generally can't effectively verbalize how they are feeling, the health issues of small children often aren't recognized until they become acute—meaning the health issues develop to the point of either becoming complicated to address or causing severe pain to the child. The SafeNet application's competitive advantage was that the health-monitoring mechanism it included immediately alerted parents when their child's vital signs suggested the child was mildly ill or in pain so that the parents could take action before the underlying health issue or injury became more complicated to address or more painful to the child.

Developing the app and its accompanying chip was an expensive endeavor. After clearing all of the applicable FDA hurdles, Cory and his partners had developed and field tested a prototype of both with success. Now they were working on a final design that was both commercially viable and able to be mass produced. The final design process was going well except for one thing: the company was quickly running out of cash.

One of Cory's partners, Amy Warren, told Cory she thought SafeNet should pursue equity crowdfunding. She felt the SafeNet product had huge commercial appeal, and it would be easy to raise the $1 million the company needed. Cory was less sure. He had read news articles about the rules recently promulgated by the SEC related to equity crowdfunding, and some of what he had read had made him nervous. As a result, Cory suggested to Amy that he, she, and the other five owners of SafeNet meet the next day to discuss the merits of equity crowdfunding as a means to raise the additional funding their company needed.

Cory came to the meeting prepared. Amy did too. Amy regaled her six business partners with crowdfunding success stories—stories about the successful funding of the *Exploding Kittens* board game, the *Veronica Mars* movie, and the *Wasteland 2* video game. When it was his turn to speak, Cory said that he appreciated the success of all the campaigns Amy had mentioned, but he also said, "Amy, all of the companies you just mentioned participated in reward-based crowdfunding, not equity crowdfunding." Amy responded, "What's the difference?" Cory told Amy and the rest of his business partners, "The difference is actually huge. Individuals who participate in reward-based crowdfunding generally expect nothing in return for their investment other than a news update, a small gift, or sometimes one unit of the product or service their money will help the company develop. Individuals who participate in equity crowdfunding obtain an ownership position in a company as a result of their investment in the company. Our company is currently limited to us seven owners. Do we really want hundreds or thousands more?"

Cory paused to take a breath giving Amy the opportunity to quickly interject, "Well, it might be worth it if we can get the money we need." Cory responded gently, "First, you assume the campaign will be successful and we'll get the money we need. If we have a $1 million funding goal and the campaign falls short of that goal, remember that we get no money at all. Also, it takes money to raise money. The reading I've been doing suggests it will cost tens of thousands of dollars, at minimum, to meet the requirements of the SEC in order to appropriately run and manage an equity crowdfunding campaign. Then every year after the campaign, periodic updates are required to be filed with the SEC. Those updates will also cost money. All in all, I just think it's easier and cheaper to pursue the funding we need using Regulation D."

Amy said, simply, "Why?" Cory continued on, "Seeking funding under Rule 504 of Regulation D would allow us to raise the $1 million of capital we need without having to register with the SEC. The only filing requirement associated with Rule 504 is to file a Form D with the SEC and our state within 15 days of the first sale of the securities in our offering. Regulation D allows us to go after a few accredited investors—angel investors—instead of hundreds or thousands of investors via equity crowdfunding. Plus, the articles I've read suggest that the estimated average cost for a Regulation D raise is significantly less—usually by a factor of five or more—than the average cost of pursuing the same amount of funding via equity crowdfunding. And Regulation D raises also tend to take a lot less time to complete than equity crowdfunding raises."

Amy looked at Cory, then at her other business partners, then back at Cory. "Well," she said, "I'm impressed. You certainly have done your research, Cory, and you've sold me. Regulation D has my vote." The other five owners of SafeNet all nodded in agreement.

Note that the information included in this section regarding Regulation D is general in nature, and any entrepreneur interested in offering securities under Regulation D should investigate the details outlined at sec.gov.

Regulation A and Regulation A+

While Regulation D allows a company to avoid formally registering with the SEC altogether, **Regulation A** is a regulation that allows an exemption from certain registration requirements of the SEC.

Regulation A is usually utilized by young companies that are beyond the start-up phase and seeking funding for growth. Companies utilizing the Regulation A exemption must still file offering statements with the SEC and give potential buyers documentation similar to the prospectus associated with a registered offering; however, companies utilizing the exemption enjoy more limited disclosure requirements than publicly reporting companies.

The original Regulation A exemption related to public offerings of securities that did not exceed $5 million in any one-year period. 2015 updates to Regulation A (creating what is commonly referred to as "**Regulation A+**") allow companies to pursue public offerings under the following two tiers:

1. *Tier 1*: Companies offering securities under Tier 1 can offer up to $20 million in any one-year period. The issuing company must provide an offering circular to the potential investor. That circular must be filed with the SEC and is subject to review and qualification by both the SEC and the securities regulators of the individual states in which the offering is being conducted. Companies are required to issue a report on the final status of the offering, but they are not required to continue to report to the SEC on an ongoing basis.[36]

2. *Tier 2*: Companies offering securities under Tier 2 can offer up to $50 million in any one-year period. As with Tier 1, the issuing company must provide an offering circular and that circular must be filed with SEC, which will review it and may qualify it. What is different for Tier 2 is that the offering circular is not subject to a vetting process by the securities regulators of any individual state. Instead, companies offering securities under Tier 2, in addition to issuing a report on the final status of the offering, become subject to ongoing SEC reporting requirements.[37] Further, the financial statements disclosed in a Tier 2 offering have to be audited by an independent accountant, while those disclosed in a Tier 1 offering do not.[38]

There are no limitations regarding who can invest—or how much they can invest—in an offering under Tier 1 of Regulation A. There are limitations regarding how much certain individuals can invest in an offering under Tier 2. Generally, if the potential investor is not an accredited investor and the securities in question are not going to be listed on a national securities exchange, the investor may invest no more than 10 percent of the greater of her annual income or net worth, excluding primary residence.

Note that the information included above is general in nature, and any entrepreneur interested in offering securities under Regulation A should investigate the details outlined at sec.gov.

Regulation A
a regulation that allows an exemption from certain registration requirements of the SEC

Regulation A+
the name commonly applied to the 2015 updates to Regulation A

Regulation D vs. Regulation A vs. Initial Public Offering

A traditional initial public offering is designed for a large, mature company that has the resources needed to cover the significant accounting and legal expenses associated with "going public." Regulation A gives a smaller company the ability to make a limited-size public offering, including the ability to list Tier 2 offerings on securities exchanges like the Nasdaq Stock Market (commonly referred to as NASDAQ) and the New York Stock Exchange (NYSE). For this reason, a Tier 2 Regulation A offering is sometimes called a "mini-IPO." In other words, Regulation A essentially represents the middle ground between a private placement under Regulation D and a public offering in the form of a full-scale IPO.[39]

In certain ways, however, Regulation A actually has more in common with a traditional IPO than Regulation D. Most important, perhaps, is *the ability of a Regulation A offering to act as a liquidity event for early-stage investors.* The "secondary sales" process associated with Regulation A allows for up to 30 percent of the securities sold during a public offering to originate from a company's current securities holders.[40] Issuing securities under Regulation A, therefore, is often a viable option entrepreneurs can suggest to potential angel and venture capital investors as a means for those investors to exit their investment in a start-up at some time in the future, should they desire to do so.

Summary

The funding for a typical start-up venture often comes from a variety of sources, including the entrepreneurs themselves, their friends and families, angel investors, venture capital funds, various types of crowdfunding, banks and other lenders, and grants. Important items to note when considering which sources of funding are best for your start-up include the following:

- Once you give away or sell any ownership (equity) of your company, it is very unlikely you will ever get it back.
- Investors in start-ups take on a lot of risk and expect a healthy profit on their investment in return. They also expect to eventually be repaid or provided with a means to exit their investment.
- Debt needs to be repaid, and there are limits to the amount of debt any company can obtain and support.

Almost every path to securing capital for a young venture, other than perhaps the funding that comes from the entrepreneurs themselves or from their friends and families, involves the issuance of a security. Because of the time, money, and effort generally required to comply with securities laws, entrepreneurs often choose to pursue funding via paths that avoid the need to register securities with the SEC. There are two general types of exemption from federal registration: exempt securities and exempt transactions. Exempt securities include, among others, government securities, insurance policies, and commercial paper. Exempt transactions include purely intrastate offerings and certain private placements. The amount of money that can be raised with an intrastate offering—and the amount of time permitted to do so—varies by state. The exemption related to private placements is best described in an amendment to the Securities Act of 1933 called Regulation D.

Regulation D is an SEC regulation that allows companies to raise capital through the issuance of securities without having to register those securities with the SEC. It is via Regulation D that many angel investors acquire their equity positions in young companies. Regulation A, in comparison, is an SEC regulation that instead allows an exemption from certain registration requirements of the SEC. Issuing securities under Regulation A is often a viable option entrepreneurs can suggest to potential angel and venture capital investors as a means for those investors to exit their investment in a start-up at some time in the future, should they desire to do so.

Key Terms

accredited investor
angel investor
bootstrapping
capitalization table
commercial paper
convertible note
debt capital
equity capital
equity crowdfunding
grant
initial public offering
  (IPO)

intrastate offering
lending-based
  crowdfunding
private equity firm
private placement
proof of concept
public offering
Regulation A
Regulation A+
Regulation D
reward-based
  crowdfunding

Rule 144 of the Securities
  Act of 1933
security
seed capital
seed round
Series A
small business investment
  companies (SBICs)
traction
venture capital firm
venture capital fund

Review and Discussion Questions

1. What are the common sources of funding for a U.S. for-profit business?
2. What is the profile of a typical angel investor, and in what type of companies do angel investors usually like to invest?
3. Explain the nature of a typical venture capital investment.
4. Aside from the many challenges for the investor participants in equity crowdfunding, equity crowdfunding also presents many challenges for the companies that wish to raise funds using the platform. Describe these challenges.
5. In general, banks are risk-averse and not receptive to lending money to start-up companies. Considering this fact, what alternative sources of debt financing—beyond the founders themselves, their friends and families, angel investors, venture capital funds, and CDFIs—are often available to a start-up? What are some of the main attributes of these alternative sources of debt financing?
6. Many entrepreneurs choose to pursue sources of funding under the auspices of Regulation D or Regulation A. What are the fundamental differences between these two regulations? How does issuing securities under Regulation D or Regulation A compare to issuing securities via an IPO?

Exercises

1. A common source of funding for a start-up venture is friends, family, and "fools." Brainstorm and come up with an idea for a new app. Flesh out the idea into a full business model (see chapter 1) that describes how you would make money with the app. Assume you do not have enough resources available to you to execute the concept on your own and need an investment of $50,000 to develop and launch the app. Interview five of your family members or friends. After explaining the app to them, which of them would be willing to invest in a company created by you to bring the app to market? How much would they be willing to invest, and what would they want in exchange for their investment? If they are not willing to invest, why not? Write a two- to three-page paper describing the app and describing the results of your interviews with your family members or friends regarding investing in your imaginary company.
2. Angel investors are a common source of funding for start-up ventures. Go to angelcapitalassociation.org. Find an angel investor or an angel investor group that is in your state. Explaining that you are an entrepreneurship student seeking to learn about angel investors, contact the angel investor—or a member or

leader of the angel investor group you have chosen—asking them for a short phone interview. During the interview, ask the angel about his or her background and how he or she came to be an angel investor. Ask the angel what he or she specifically looks for when deciding whether or not to invest in a start-up. Last, in light of his or her considerable experience, ask the angel for any advice he or she has for young entrepreneurs. Write two to three paragraphs describing how you came to choose the angel you interviewed and the results of the interview itself.

3. Equity crowdfunding campaigns are a possible source of funding for a start-up venture. Recent successful equity crowdfunding campaigns include those executed by the following companies: Beta Bionics (betabionics.org), Legion M Entertainment (legionm.com/#opening-the-gates-to-hollywood-1), Green Sense Farms (greensensefarms.com), and SwitchPitch (switchpitch.com). Beta Bionics and Legion M used the Wefunder (wefunder.com) funding portal to execute their equity crowdfunding campaigns. Green Sense used StartEngine (startengine.com). SwitchPitch used SeedInvest (seedinvest.com). Either via its company website, the applicable equity crowdfunding portal, or some alternative means, investigate one of the four companies mentioned in the second sentence of this exercise. Write two to three paragraphs explaining the merits of the company and why, if given the opportunity, you would have—or would not have—invested in the company via its equity crowdfunding campaign.

4. Equity crowdfunding is a possible source of funding for a start-up venture. Review a reputable equity crowdfunding website (funding portal) of your choice (examples include Wefunder (wefunder.com), StartEngine (startengine.com), and SeedInvest (seedinvest.com)). Write two to three paragraphs describing the types of opportunities for investment available on the funding portal you have chosen. In what company, if any, would you invest? How much and why? If you cannot find a company in which you would invest, pick any company on the funding portal and then explain what steps would have to be taken by the company/funding portal in order to convince you to invest in that company.

5. Taking on debt is a possible source of funding for a start-up venture. Brainstorm and come up with an idea for a new app. Flesh out the idea into a full business model (see chapter 1) that describes how you would make money with the app. Assume you do not have enough resources available to you to execute the concept on your own and need a loan of $50,000 to develop and launch the app. Explaining that you are an entrepreneurship student seeking to learn about the various sources of funding available to start-up businesses, interview two loan officers—each representing a bank that is local to you. After explaining the app to them, which of them would be willing to make a loan to a company created by you to bring your app to market? How much would each bank be willing to loan, and what restrictions/requirements would be attached to the loan(s), if any? If a bank would be unwilling to make such a loan, why? What suggestions for alternative funding does the bank have? Write a two- to three-page paper describing the app and describing the results of your interviews with the loan officers regarding making a loan to your imaginary company.

Endnotes

1. Prive, Tanya, "Angel Investors: How the Rich Invest," https://www.forbes.com, March 12, 2013.
2. Angel Capital Association, https://www.angelcapitalassociation.org/faqs/#How%20many%20angel%20investors%20are%20there%20in%20the%20U.S.
3. Prive, Tanya, "Angel Investors: How the Rich Invest," https://www.forbes.com, March 12, 2013.

4. Angel Capital Association, http://www.angelcapitalassociation.org/data/Documents/Resources/AngelGroupResearch/Expected%20Returns%20to%20Angel%20Investors.pdf, March 7, 2009.

5. Harroch, Richard, "20 Things All Entrepreneurs Should Know about Angel Investors," https://www.forbes.com, February 5, 2015.

6. Wiltbank, Robert, "Angel Investors Do Make Money, Data Shows 2.5x Returns Overall," https://techcrunch.com, October 13, 2012.

7. Widjaya, Ivan, "Corporate vs. Private VC: What Are the Similarities and Differences?," https://www.fundingnote.com, January 6, 2017.

8. U.S. Small Business Administration, https://www.sba.gov/loans-grants/see-what-sba-offers/what-sba-offers-help-small-businesses-grow, 2017.

9. U.S. Small Business Administration, https://www.sba.gov/sites/default/files/2019-05/SBIC%20Quarterly%20Report%20as%20of%20March%2031%202019_0.pdf, March 2019.

10. Ibid.

11. The National Bureau of Economic Research, https://nber.org/digest/may01/w8066.html, 2017.

12. United States Department of the Treasury, "CDFI Fund's Year in Review 2018, A Year of Investment '18," https://www.cdfifund.gov/Documents/CDFITO2_YIR18_Final508_20190321.pdf#search=year%20in%20review.

13. U.S. Small Business Administration, https://fas.org/sgp/crs/misc/R41523.pdf, December 20, 2018.

14. U.S. Securities and Exchange Commission, https://www.sec.gov/news/pressrelease/2015-249.html, October 30, 2015.

15. Ibid.

16. U.S. Securities and Exchange Commission, https://www.sec.gov/reportspubs/investor-publications/investorpubsrule144htm.html, January 16, 2013.

17. Lake, Rebecca, "Guide to Crowdfunded Investments for Non-Accredited Investors," https://www.investopedia.com, December 18, 2018.

18. PitchBook, https://pitchbook.com/news/reports/1q-2018-pitchbook-nvca-venture-monitor, April 9, 2018.

19. Prive, Tanya, "Why Title III of the JOBS Act May Be a Flop," https://www.forbes.com, November 3, 2015.

20. Ibid.

21. U.S. Securities and Exchange Commission, https://www.sec.gov/rules/final/2015/33-9974.pdf, 2015.

22. Sohl, Jeffrey, "The Angel Investor Market in 2014: A Market Correction in Deal Size," Center for Venture Research, May 14, 2015.

23. Clarence-Smith, Toby, "Has the US Equity Crowdfunding Market Lived up to Expectations?" https://www.toptal.com, January 2018.

24. National Federation of Independent Business, https://www.nfib.com/assets/SBET-Mar-2019.pdf, 2019.

25. U.S. Small Business Administration, https://www.sba.gov/sites/default/files/SDOLoan FactSheet_Oct_2011.pdf, 2011.

26. U.S. Small Business Administration, https://www.sba.gov/loans-grants/see-what-sba-offers/what-sba-offers-help-small-businesses-grow, 2017.

27. United States Department of the Treasury, "SSBCI Program Profile: Capital Access Program," http://www.treasury.gov, May 17, 2011.

28. "What Is Debt-Based Crowdfunding?," https://crowdfund.co, January 13, 2015.

29. Foundation Center, http://foundationcenter.org/gain-knowledge/foundation-data, 2019.

30. U.S. Small Business Administration, https://www.sba.gov/starting-business/finance-your-business/grants, 2017.

31. U.S. Securities and Exchange Commission, https://www.sec.gov/info/smallbus/qasbsec.htm, 2017.

32. U.S. Securities and Exchange Commission, https://www.sec.gov/fast-answers/answers-rule504.html, 2018.

33. U.S. Securities and Exchange Commission, https://www.investor.gov/additional-resources/news-alerts/alerts-bulletins/investor-bulletin-private-placements-under, September 24, 2014.

34. PitchBook, https://pitchbook.com/media/press-releases/us-venture-capital-investment-reached-1309-billion-in-2018-surpassing-dot-com-era, January 10, 2019.

35. Barnett, Chance, "Why Title III of the JOBS Act will Disappoint Entrepreneurs," https://forbes.com, May 13, 2015.

36. U.S. Securities and Exchange Commission, https://www.investor.gov/additional-resources/news-alerts/alerts-bulletins/investor-bulletin-private-placements-under, September 24, 2014.

37. U.S. Securities and Exchange Commission, https://www.sec.gov/oiea/investor-alerts-bulletins/ib_regulationa.html, July 8, 2015.

38. Ibid.

39. U.S. Securities and Exchange Commission, https://www.sec.gov/files/Knyazeva_RegulationA%20.pdf, November 2016.

40. U.S. Securities and Exchange Commission, https://www.sec.gov/oiea/investor-alerts-bulletins/ib_regulationa.html, July 8, 2015.

Legal Forms of Business, Taxation, and Business Owner Compensation

"Nothing is certain except death and taxes."

— **Benjamin Franklin, statesman, diplomat, author, and inventor**

Learning Objectives

Have an understanding of the different legal forms of business organization generally available to a U.S. start-up.

Know the important items to consider when choosing the legal form of business for a start-up.

Understand what the term "unlimited liability" means and which type of business owners have unlimited liability.

Know which legal form of business is generally most conducive to a company successfully obtaining debt or equity financing, and why.

Understand the different ways an owner of a for-profit business might be compensated.

Have an appreciation for the major factors that determine the amount of taxes an individual business owner will pay as a result of owning his business.

Introduction

The legal form of the business chosen by a start-up business's founders has enormous implications for both the start-up and its owners. Certain legal forms of business significantly limit a business owner's personal liability with regard to the business. Other legal forms do not. Certain legal forms of business allow a business owner total control over his business. Other legal forms do not. Certain legal forms of business permit a business owner to write off the initial losses suffered by a start-up on his personal income tax return. Other legal forms do not.

An often-overlooked consideration when choosing legal form of business is the effect that choice has on an entrepreneur's ability to raise funding for the new entity. Historically, investors have shown a clear preference for some legal forms over others. This is because certain legal forms offer flexibility, ease of business expansion, and tax benefits that others do not. Another often-overlooked consideration when choosing legal form of business is the effect that choice has on the options available for business owner compensation. Some legal forms offer options for business owner compensation that others simply do not.

Since the topics of legal form of business, taxation, and business owner compensation are closely related, we will examine the three topics together in this chapter. In addition, we will explore how legal form of business affects a business owner's liability with regard to a business, how it affects his ability to make decisions for and control a business, and also how it affects which sources of funding are generally available to a business.

Legal Forms of Business Organization

A good place to start our conversation about legal form of business is to note that, subject to limitations established by the applicable state in which an enterprise is formed and subject to limitations established by the Internal Revenue Service, the legal form of business organization chosen by an entity's founders is generally not permanent and can be changed. However, changing the legal form of a business—if permitted—does usually involve a lot of work and expense. Hence, taking the time to choose the most favorable legal form of organization at the outset of a business is ideal. Figure 3.1 illustrates the legal forms of organization U.S. businesses have historically most often used to operate their businesses.

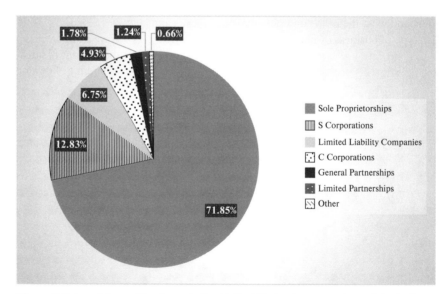

Figure 3.1. Legal form of business in the United States by percentage. Adapted from: Internal Revenue Service, "SOI Tax Stats—Integrated Business Data," 2017.

The legal form of business organization most often utilized in the United States is the sole proprietorship.

Sole Proprietorship

A sole proprietorship is a business owned and operated by an individual for profit. Because they are the only owner of their businesses, sole proprietors have complete decision-making authority and control over their businesses. Unfortunately, sole proprietors also have unlimited liability with regard to their businesses.

What, exactly, does "unlimited liability" mean? Unlimited liability means the owner of the business is:

- personally liable for any debts of the business
- legally liable for any problems the business may have
- responsible for the payment of all legal and tax judgments against the business

In chapter 1 it was noted that it is desirable for the entrepreneur to separate himself from his business in order to minimize the risk to both the business and the entrepreneur. Operating a business as a sole proprietorship does not allow the entrepreneur to separate himself from his business because, legally, the sole proprietor and his business are one and the same. While still required, like any business owner, to obtain any needed licenses or permits to operate the business—and to register to collect, withhold, and remit any applicable sales, payroll, and other taxes—an individual is not required to file any formal paperwork with his applicable state in order to create a sole proprietorship. This is perhaps the reason why the sole proprietorship remains so popular a means for operating a business in the United States. The popularity of the sole proprietorship as a means for operating a business is unfortunate because an individual operating a business as a sole proprietor is leaving himself open to a theoretically unlimited amount of liability, liability that could be largely avoided by instead choosing to operate the business as a corporation or limited liability company.

A sole proprietorship is considered a pass-through entity, which, as we learned in chapter 1, means that the business's profit is not taxed at the company level but instead passes through to the business owner's individual tax return, where it is taxed. Specifically, the typical sole proprietor will file a Schedule C and a Schedule SE with his annual Form 1040 in order to both report the profit related to the sole proprietorship and calculate the income taxes, social security taxes, and Medicare taxes due related to that profit.

Note that, because of their choice to operate their businesses as sole proprietorships, sole proprietors often have difficulty obtaining financing for their businesses for these reasons:

- Sole proprietors can't sell stock—or any form of ownership of the business for that matter—so investors often won't invest.
- Lenders get to choose to whom they want to make a loan and, as a result, business credit is often reserved for larger, more sophisticated businesses that have a formal legal structure in place, such as a corporation or a limited liability company.
- Banks are hesitant to lend to a sole proprietorship because of a perceived lack of credibility when it comes to repayment if the business fails and because, by definition, when the sole proprietor dies, the business dies with him.[1]

Partnership

A partnership is an association of two or more persons who carry on a business as co-owners for a profit. Most partnerships exist in one of three forms:

1. General partnership: In a general partnership, each partner is 100 percent liable for the acts of the partnership, and each partner has unlimited liability with regard to the business. Partners typically create a partnership agreement detailing the specifics of their partnership. Some—but not all—states require that a general partnership file a certificate of partnership or similar document with the state in order to provide notice of the existence of the partnership.

2. Limited partnership: A limited partnership consists of one or more general partners and one or more limited partners. Limited partners generally function as investors who don't play an active role in the business and whose liability is limited to the amount they invest in the partnership. Each general partner has unlimited liability with regard to the business. In order to form a limited partnership, the partners must register the partnership with its applicable state.

3. Limited liability partnership (LLP): The limited liability partnership exists in different forms in different states, but typically resembles a limited liability company as all of the partners have a form of limited liability and may participate in the day-to-day management of the partnership. In some states, the LLP legal form is limited to use only by licensed professionals, such as physicians, lawyers, accountants, and architects. The LLP form of business organization typically shields each partner from personal liability for any costs or losses stemming from the professional malpractice of the other partners. In order to form an LLP, the partners must register the partnership with its applicable state.

Similar to operating a business as a sole proprietor, electing to be a general partner in a partnership does not allow the entrepreneur to separate himself from his business. As previously mentioned, a general partner has unlimited liability with regard to the partnership, but what is perhaps more alarming is the liability to which a general partner exposes himself with respect to the actions and potential actions of the other general partners of the business. A general partner in a partnership can act on behalf of the entire business without the knowledge or permission of the other general partners. As a result, theoretically, a general partner can become personally liable for acts of the partnership of which he wasn't even aware. Consequently, being a general partner in a partnership is, for most individuals, the riskiest—and therefore the least desirable—form of business ownership. There is no doubt that the general partners in a partnership enjoy much more decision-making authority and control over a business than its limited partners. The price the general partners pay for that authority and control, however, is unlimited personal liability with regard to both the business and any business decisions made by the other general partners related to that business. An individual considering being a general partner in a partnership should give serious consideration to reconfiguring his partnership interest such that he can be a limited partner instead of a general partner.

As mentioned earlier, a limited partner is basically an investor who has his liability limited to the amount of his investment in the partnership. It is important to note, however, that a limited partner can inadvertently dissolve his role as a limited partner—and become liable as a general partner—if he begins to take an active role in the management of the company. An individual considering being a limited partner in a partnership should be sure he is comfortable with the role of being an investor in the business as opposed to being a manager of the business.

In most circumstances, a limited partner of a limited partnership can die or otherwise withdraw from his role as partner without causing dissolution of the entire partnership. If, however, a general partner of a limited partnership dies or withdraws from his role as partner, dissolution of the entire partnership is not an impossibility.

Legally, in order for the limited partnership to continue, there must be a continuing general partner—or a new general partner must be elected or brought into the partnership. Electing a new general partner or bringing a new general partner into the partnership is a process about which most partners would prefer there be a previously agreed-upon set of procedures. Such procedures should ideally be thoughtfully detailed in a partnership agreement.

If a general partner of a general partnership dies or otherwise withdraws from his role as partner, under the default regulations of many states, when no written partnership agreement exists, the general partnership automatically dissolves. However, if a partnership agreement exists, then that agreement overrides state default regulations and governs the fate of the general partnership. As with electing or bringing in a new general partner, managing the death or withdrawal of a general partner is a process about which most partners would prefer there be a previously agreed-upon set of procedures. Such procedures should also ideally be thoughtfully detailed in a partnership agreement.

Like a sole proprietorship, a partnership is considered a pass-through entity, which means the net income of the business is included on the partners' individual tax returns, usually in accordance with the partners' respective business ownership percentages. Note however that, if they desire to do so, the partners may execute a partnership agreement that allocates income to the partners based on metrics other than the partners' respective business ownership percentages—metrics such as the amount of new business brought into the firm or the number of billable hours worked for the firm during an applicable period.

Due to their chosen legal form of organization, the partners of a partnership often have difficulty obtaining financing for their businesses. The reasons are many:

- Partnerships cannot sell stock in the business.
- Investors generally don't want the unlimited liability associated with being a general partner.
- Investors generally don't want the limitation on their activity in the business associated with being a limited partner.
- Investors who aren't an appropriately licensed professional often can't legally invest in a limited liability partnership.
- Venture capitalists and angels often won't invest because they don't want pass-through income on their personal income tax returns.
- Lenders get to choose to whom they want to make a loan and, as a result, business credit is often reserved for larger, more sophisticated businesses that have a "more formal" legal structure in place, like a corporation or a limited liability company.

Corporation

A corporation is a legal entity authorized by state law to act as an artificial person in order to conduct business or engage in certain other activities. A corporation can sue or be sued and has the right to hold property. All corporations are initially formed as C corporations. More specifically, a **C corporation** is the formal corporate form of all corporations, by default, unless the corporation meets certain requirements and proactively requests Subchapter S tax status from the Internal Revenue Service, thereby becoming an S corporation. An **S corporation**, more formally known as a Subchapter S corporation, is a private corporation with special tax status granted by Internal Revenue Service such that it is taxed similar to a partnership rather than as a corporation.

The predominant legal form of business in use by entities participating in an initial public offering (IPO) is the C corporation. (There are publicly traded LLCs.

C corporation
the formal corporate form of all corporations, by default, unless the corporation meets certain requirements and proactively requests Subchapter S tax status from the Internal Revenue Service, thereby becoming an S corporation

S corporation
a private corporation with special tax status granted by Internal Revenue Service such that it is taxed similar to a partnership rather than as a corporation; more formally known as a Subchapter S corporation

Examples include Fortress Investment Group, LLC (FIG) and Och-Ziff Capital Management Group, LLC (OZM). However, the state laws governing LLCs often make it impossible (or extremely difficult) for LLCs to do an IPO. Delaware is generally considered the friendliest state for LLCs pursuing IPOs.) Note, however, that most U.S. corporations exist as private corporations, i.e., the corporation's stock is held by relatively few shareholders and is not offered for purchase to the general public.

The major advantages associated with using the C corporation as the legal form of business organization for a start-up follow:

- A corporation is generally considered to offer its owners the highest form of liability protection as owner liability is generally limited to the amount invested in the corporation. A corporation's liability for damages or debts is limited to its assets, and its officers are generally protected from personal claims, unless they act outside of their authority or outside of the law.
- Transfer of ownership is easy because the transfer of stock is easy.
- The shareholders of a C corporation do not personally pay income tax on the profit of the business unless they actually receive consideration in the form of a dividend. A **dividend** is a payment, usually in the form of cash, made by a C corporation to one or more of its shareholders as authorized by the C corporation's board of directors. As discussed in more detail later in this chapter, because they are owners of pass-through entities, sole proprietors and owners of entities taxed as partnerships (this can include partnerships, LLCs, and S corporations) personally pay income tax on the profit of the business whether or not they actually receive a cash payout of this profit. This can discourage some individuals from wanting to be owners of these types of entities.
- In conjunction with the advantages of C corporations listed above, it's usually easier for a C corporation to obtain debt or equity financing compared to businesses organized in alternative legal forms for the following reasons:
  - A corporation can sell stock in the business.
  - Beyond issuing just common stock, a C corporation has the ability to issue convertible notes, preferred stock, and stock options and also to develop and maintain other sophisticated debt, equity, or compensation offerings that other legal forms of business generally cannot. **Common stock** is an equity security representing the fundamental ownership of a company issued by a public or private corporation in order to raise financial capital. **Preferred stock** is a class of ownership of a C corporation that has a higher claim on the assets and earnings of the corporation than the corporation's common stock. **Stock options** are contracts that give the contract's owner the right to buy or sell one or more shares of stock at a specified price for a specified period of time.
  - Due to securities regulations, tax concerns, and their own legal form of business organization, many investors can or will invest only in C corporations.
  - Lenders get to choose to whom they want to make a loan and, as a result, business credit is often reserved for larger, more sophisticated businesses that have a formal legal structure in place, like a corporation or a limited liability company.

The major disadvantages associated with using the C corporation as the legal form of business organization for a start-up follow:

- A C corporation's shareholders cannot write off the initial losses often suffered by a start-up on their personal income tax returns.
- Dividends to the C corporation's common shareholders are not guaranteed and occur at the pleasure of the board of directors.

dividend

a payment, usually in the form of cash, made by a C corporation to one or more of its shareholders as authorized by the C corporation's board of directors

common stock

an equity security representing the fundamental ownership of a company issued by a public or private corporation in order to raise financial capital

preferred stock

a class of ownership of a C corporation that has a higher claim on the assets and earnings of the corporation than the corporation's common stock

stock option

a contract that gives its owner the right to buy or sell one or more shares of stock at a specified price for a specified period of time

- The C corporation's income is taxed once at the business level, then again at the shareholder level (if that income is, in fact, distributed in the form of a dividend).
- Control of the corporation lies with the officers of the company and the board of directors who elect the officers of the company. (Note that, in order to maintain some level of decision-making authority and control over the entity he creates, it is wise for an entrepreneur to be both an officer and a member of the board of directors of the corporation he founds.)
- There is significant ongoing paperwork required to properly maintain a corporation.

As previously mentioned, all corporations are initially formed as C corporations. If, however, it meets certain requirements and requests Subchapter S tax status from the Internal Revenue Service, a C corporation can become an S corporation. Subchapter S tax status stipulates that an S corporation be taxed similar to a partnership rather than as a corporation. As indicated in figure 3.1, the S corporation is the second most often utilized legal form of business in the United States.

S corporations do not themselves pay income tax. Like other pass-through entities taxed as partnerships, their owners (shareholders, in the case of an S corporation) pay the tax on their share of the business's income via their individual tax returns.

The major advantages associated with using the S corporation as the legal form of business organization for a start-up follow:

- A corporation is generally considered to offer its owners the highest form of liability protection as owner liability is generally limited to the amount invested in the corporation. A corporation's liability for damages or debts is limited to its assets, and its officers are generally protected from personal claims, unless they act outside of their authority or outside of the law.
- Transfer of ownership is easy because the transfer of stock is easy.
- As will be discussed in more detail later in this chapter, social security and Medicare taxes do not apply to the pass-through profits remaining after "reasonable" salaries have been paid to the owner-employees of an S corporation or an entity taxed as an S corporation. This fact has, in the past, led many owners to choose the S corporation—or the LLC taxed as an S corporation—as their business's legal and tax form of business. (The manner in which S corporation profits are taxed is likely the reason why the S corporation is the second most utilized legal form of business in the United States.)
  The passage of the Tax Cuts and Jobs Act in December of 2017, and its corresponding reduction of the corporate tax rate to 21 percent, along with the introduction of an up to 20 percent deduction of the qualified business income of certain pass-through businesses, complicated the taxation of business profits. The 2017 Tax Cuts and Jobs Act may in fact, for at least some business owners, make the S corporation—or the LLC taxed as an S corporation—a less attractive legal form of business than in the past.

The major disadvantages associated with using the S corporation as the legal form of business organization for a start-up follow:

- Control of the corporation lies with the officers of the company and the board of directors who elect the officers of the company. (Note that, in order to maintain some level of decision-making authority and control over the entity he creates, it is wise for an entrepreneur to be both an officer and a member of the board of directors of the corporation he founds.)
- There is significant ongoing paperwork required to properly maintain a corporation.

- Only one class of stock—and a maximum of 100 shareholders—is permitted.
- S corporation shareholders must be "natural persons," which means business entities may not be shareholders. Also, nonresident aliens may not be shareholders.
- Venture capitalists generally don't—and angel investors often won't—invest in S corporations because:
  - S corporations are permitted to have only one class of stock and venture capitalists and angels often want preferred stock—not common stock—in return for their investment dollars.[2]
  - The fact that S corporations cannot have more than 100 stockholders is viewed as—and can be—a burdensome limitation.
  - Most venture capital firms are organized as limited partnerships or multi-member LLCs. Neither legal entity qualifies as a "natural person," so a venture capital firm cannot be a shareholder of an S corporation.
  - Some venture capitalists won't invest because S corporations are pass-through entities whose income certain limited partners of venture capital firms are legally prohibited from receiving.[3] Other venture capitalists and angels won't invest because they don't want pass-through income on their personal income tax returns.

Special note: In order to avoid a potentially complicated tax issue (i.e., built-in-gain tax), owners wishing to establish an S corporation should request an effective date for their Subchapter S tax election that matches the state-indicated start date of the underlying C corporation.

Limited Liability Company

A limited liability company (LLC) is a hybrid legal business entity authorized by state law featuring some of the characteristics of both partnerships and corporations. Unless its owners (called members) specifically elect otherwise with the Internal Revenue Service, a multi-member LLC is taxed as a partnership and a single-member LLC is taxed as a sole proprietorship. This means the income and losses of the business "pass through" to LLC members' individual tax returns similar to a sole proprietorship or partnership.

LLCs operate under one of two different management structures. The members of an LLC can choose to be a **member-managed LLC**—an LLC where all of the members participate in managing the business—or they can choose to be a **manager-managed LLC**—an LLC where only certain individuals, who may or may not be members of the LLC, are responsible for managing the business. Member-managed LLCs are most common. The requirements vary by state, but generally an LLC that elects to be manager-managed has to expressly indicate such either in its articles of organization, its operating agreement, or both. The two typical scenarios where LLCs opt to be manager-managed are when:

1. The business's ownership is too large or too complex to allow for effective management of the business by all of its members.
2. Some or all of the members are either not skilled at—or are not interested in—managing the business.

The major advantages associated with using the LLC as the legal form of business organization for a start-up follow:

- The legal form provides limited liability for its owners.
- The legal form is generally easy (easier than a corporation) to create and maintain.

member-managed LLC
an LLC where all of the members participate in managing the business

manager-managed LLC
an LLC where only certain individuals, who may or may not be members of the LLC, are responsible for managing the business

The major disadvantage associated with using the LLC as a legal form of business organization is that venture capitalists and angels generally don't invest in LLCs. The reasons for this follow:

- Some venture capitalists won't invest because LLCs are pass-through entities whose income certain limited partners of venture capital firms are legally prohibited from receiving.[4] Other venture capitalists and angels won't invest because they don't want pass-through income on their personal income tax returns.
- Either type of investor might not invest because the LLC's capital structure limits the company's ability to offer sophisticated securities like the preferred stock and convertible notes that angels and venture capitalists often desire.
- An LLC's inability to offer stock options to its employees is viewed as a disadvantage for the company.

The reader should note that, although it is not typical, an LLC may elect to be taxed as a C or an S corporation. Throughout the rest of this textbook, we will assume our single-member LLCs are taxed as sole proprietorships and our multi-member LLCs are taxed as partnerships unless specifically indicated otherwise, but the question does arise as to why an LLC might elect to be taxed as a C or an S corporation instead of as a sole proprietorship or partnership.

Only LLCs that elect to be taxed as a C or an S corporation can pay their owners salaries. The pass-through profits remaining after the payment of reasonable salaries to the owner-employees of an entity taxed as an S corporation are not subject to social security and Medicare taxes. This fact alone might persuade the owners of an LLC to elect to be taxed as an S corporation.

Why then not just form the company as an S corporation?

Because LLCs have benefits:

- They are easier to form.
- They require less paperwork to maintain long term.
- They aren't limited to 100 or fewer owners.
- They're permitted to have other types of business entities, such as LLCs, partnerships, and corporations, as members (however, some states do place restrictions on the ability of a corporation to be a member of an LLC).

We've addressed the question of why an LLC might elect to be taxed as an S corporation. Why then might an LLC elect to be taxed as a C corporation?

An LLC might consider electing to be taxed as a C corporation if both of the following conditions exist:

1. The LLC owners' personal tax rates are higher than the corporate tax rate.
2. The owners plan to leave the business's earnings in the company anyway, in order to fund its growth.

Note that, as Entrepreneur in Action 3.1 illustrates on the next page, both of the above conditions not only need to exist—they need to be expected to continue to exist—in order for it to make sense for an LLC to elect to be taxed as a C corporation.

Franchise

A **franchise** is a business in which the buyer, who is the franchisee, purchases the right to sell goods or services using the systems, processes, or branding of the seller, who is the franchisor. A franchise itself is not a legal form of business. Franchisees pick a legal form under which to operate their franchise. Selecting a legal form like the LLC or corporation does not, however, protect franchisees (or any business

franchise
a business in which the buyer, who is the franchisee, purchases the right to sell goods or services using the systems, processes, or branding of the seller, who is the franchisor

The CEO of an LLC Reconsiders the Company's Tax Status

James Owens, cofounder, co-owner, and CEO of ScreenPerfect, LLC, a South Dakota–based company, had been spending a lot of time dealing with complaints from his business partners—his fellow cofounders of the business who, while still owners of the business, were not working for the business on a daily basis like he was. His business partners—one a high-income attorney and the other a high-income doctor, both of whom were only able to take advantage of the 20 percent qualified business income deduction passed as part of the 2017 tax bill to a very minimal extent—were complaining that while the marginal federal income tax rate for both of them was 35 percent, the company was making cash distributions that averaged only 28 percent of the profits of the business, an amount too small to cover the taxes the owners had to pay on their share of income of the business. James's business partners were also complaining about James's increased use of the company's business line of credit to fund the cash needs of the business. The increased level of borrowing was resulting in an increased amount of interest expense. James, increasingly frustrated with trying to balance the cash needs of the business with the cash needs of his business partners, decided it was time to seek some advice from ScreenPerfect's outside accountant, Alexis Harrison.

Alexis listened to James explain the cash issues with which he was dealing. ScreenPerfect was a mid-stage technology company that continued to need large amounts of cash to fund the final stage of development of its second smartphone protection product—a cell phone protector that successfully eliminated the problem of cracked or broken smartphone screens. The customer reviews from the initial market testing of the new product were in—and they were remarkably good. Customers loved the product. Now it was up to James to finalize the product's design and step up production to prepare to meet the huge customer demand he expected would occur after introducing the new product to the general public.

Alexis understood how revolutionary ScreenPerfect's new product was—and also the cash crunch James was struggling to resolve. She asked James, "What is your plan for the company? What I mean is, do you plan to keep it long term or sell it?" James responded, "The plan has always been to successfully get this second product to market, ramp up sales, and then sell the company as soon as possible." Alexis thought about this for a moment and then said, "I think I may have a solution for you."

Alexis then suggested to James that he consider transforming ScreenPerfect from an LLC taxed as a partnership to an LLC taxed as a C corporation. She noted that this would eliminate his business partners having to include their share of the company's net income on their personal income tax returns, so their complaints about that issue would disappear. The solution would also allow James to justify eliminating the company's cash distributions to the owners of the business, since their tax liability related to the company's profits would be eliminated. This cash could then be used to do two things: pay the corporate income tax that would now be due (at a tax rate of 21 percent) and help fund the continuing cash needs of the business. Alexis noted that while her proposed solution wouldn't completely eliminate the company's need to borrow from its line of credit, it would reduce that need. Alexis further noted that if the partners intended to keep the company long term and eventually start pulling cash from it, changing the LLC's tax status to C corporation wasn't something she'd recommend, but considering the tax situations of James's partners and the intention of ScreenPerfect's owners to sell the company in the near future, the solution did seem like it might work for them.

James thanked Alexis profusely and smiled. He decided he was definitely going to schedule a meeting with his business partners and present them with Alexis's proposed solution.

owner, for that matter) with regard to any contract they might personally sign or any transaction they might personally guarantee in relation to the franchise or the business. Note that most franchisors do require franchisees to personally guarantee certain aspects of the business operations associated with their franchise agreements.

Nonprofit

nonprofit organization
an entity that is run like a business, but whose main purpose is not to make a profit but instead to support some aspect of the public or private sector; also called a not-for-profit organization

Nonprofit organizations (or not-for-profit organizations) are run like a business, but their main purpose is not to make a profit but instead to support some aspect of the public or private sector. A nonprofit itself is not a legal form of business. Nonprofits must pick a legal form of business under which to operate. Most states advise—and some require—that nonprofit organizations be set up as corporations. Some states, including California, Michigan, Minnesota, Ohio, and Tennessee, allow for nonprofit LLCs.[5] Delaware and Texas allow for the formation of an LLC with a nonprofit purpose.[6] Virginia does not distinguish between for-profit and nonprofit LLCs.[7]

Properly set up nonprofits are largely funded by grants and donations and staffed by both volunteers and employees. Nonprofits can pay their directors and employees—and provide them with employee benefits—within reason. Nonprofits usually do not issue stock, they do not have owners, and they never pay dividends.

Forming a proper nonprofit organization under the regulations of a particular state does not automatically make an entity exempt from federal income taxes. Once the nonprofit has been created by filing the necessary documents with the applicable state, if the organization wants to be exempt from federal income taxes, the founders or officers of the nonprofit must file an application for such exemption with the IRS. Note that, while in many states a federal income tax exemption qualifies the nonprofit as being exempt from state income taxes, property taxes, sales taxes, and other types of taxes, this is not true in all states. State and local laws vary on this issue and should be thoroughly investigated.

Only a state-recognized nonprofit organization that has achieved federal tax-exempt status can successfully compete for most private and public grants, qualify for low-cost postage rates, and be exempt from most taxes. More importantly, a properly set up nonprofit organization allows individuals to deduct the amounts donated to the nonprofit on their individual income tax returns (within IRS limits), while shielding the founders' personal assets from liability.[8]

Types of Business Owner Compensation

An owner of a for-profit business may be compensated in one of the following ways:

- **distribution**—a disbursement, usually in the form of cash, to an owner of a pass-through entity business
- salary
- dividend
- **capital gain**—the profit made by an investor after selling an asset whose value has appreciated beyond the amount invested to acquire or build the asset
- some combination of the above

Legal form of business determines, to some extent, which of these options is available to the business owner.

Once a business becomes profitable enough to allow for it, owners of the following types of entities—all of which are pass-through entities—may pay themselves by taking a distribution from their companies as needed or desired:

- sole proprietorships
- entities taxed as sole proprietorships (i.e., most single-member LLCs)
- partnerships
- entities taxed as partnerships (i.e., most multi-member LLCs)
- S corporations
- entities taxed as an S corporation (i.e., usually LLCs that have elected to be taxed as an S corporation)

It has been noted many times in this chapter that the profits of a pass-through entity are not taxed at the company level, but instead pass through to the business owners' individual tax returns, where they are taxed. It is important to note that a pass-through entity's profits are taxed on the business owners' individual tax returns whether or not the owners receive any of that profit in the form of a distribution. Further, the distributions business owners receive are not themselves taxed. The two

distribution
a disbursement, usually in the form of cash, to an owner of a pass-through entity business

capital gain
the profit made by an investor after selling an asset whose value has appreciated beyond the amount invested to acquire or build the asset

items—the taxation of a business's profits and the distributions to a business's owners—may in fact occur quite independent of each other in terms of timing.

An owner-employee of a C corporation or a company that is taxed as a C corporation may choose to receive compensation from the business via salary. In addition, any shareholder of a C corporation, including its officers and employees, may receive compensation from the business in the form of a dividend. Dividend payments are usually made at the discretion of a C corporation's board of directors from the cache of otherwise uncommitted cash remaining after the corporation has paid all of the income taxes on its net income.

An owner-employee of an S corporation or a company that is taxed as an S corporation is required by the IRS to receive reasonable compensation from the business via salary. Determining reasonable compensation usually involves the entrepreneur investigating what other businesses in the same industry are paying individuals doing the same work he is doing. After he receives reasonable compensation via salary, an owner-employee of an S corporation or a company that is taxed as an S corporation can exercise the option to receive additional compensation from the business in the form of a distribution.

Note that, generally, there is no guarantee that dividends to stockholders or distribution payments to owners will be authorized or paid by a company. For this reason (and for many other reasons), it is wise for an entrepreneur to be both an officer and a member of the board of directors of the corporation he founds or, in the instance of a noncorporate entity, to designate minimum required distribution payments in an operating agreement.

Beyond the possibility of harvesting cash from his company via distributions, dividends, or salary, an entrepreneur can also sell all or part of his ownership interest in his company—after its value appreciates over the amount he has invested to acquire or build that ownership interest—in order to make a profit in the form of a capital gain on the sale. The problem with harvesting cash from a company via capital gain is that—while it is an option available to a business of any legal form—it involves selling all or part of the company. This is something the business owner may not necessarily wish to do.

Once a business owner understands which compensation options are available to him, the factor that most affects his decision regarding how to be compensated is taxes. For the remainder of this chapter, we will take a look at the major taxes that affect most U.S. businesses and their owners and how these taxes can influence the decisions business owners make regarding legal form of business and how to be compensated by their businesses.

Federal, State, and Local Corporate Income Taxes

The Tax Cuts and Jobs Act of 2017 reduced the U.S. federal corporate income tax rate from 35 percent to 21 percent. However, 44 states and the District of Columbia also impose income taxes on C corporations and entities taxed as C corporations. The rules for determining corporate taxable income vary widely from state to state, as do the tax rates that apply. State corporate tax rates range from 3 percent in North Carolina to 12 percent in Iowa.[9] The average state corporate income tax rate in the United States is 6 percent.[10]

Instead of imposing income tax on the profits of C corporations, Nevada, Ohio, Texas, and Washington instead impose a gross receipts tax.[11] Gross receipts taxes are generally believed to result in a higher tax burden than corporate income taxes. South Dakota and Wyoming are the only states that levy neither a corporate income tax nor a gross receipts tax.[12]

Only seven states allow their localities to levy a corporate income tax.[13] Except for New York City, which is responsible for approximately 90 percent of the corporate income tax revenue collected by all U.S. local governments annually, the amount of corporate income tax these localities collect is generally negligible.[14] The corporate income tax calculations of local governments are usually based on the corporate income tax calculations of their applicable state.

It is usually worthwhile for a business owner to investigate the relevant state and local corporate income tax rates that will apply to the profits of his business when considering where to locate or expand that business. You can start your research regarding the state and local corporate income tax rates that may apply to your business by visiting the website of the department of taxation for each state in which you are interested in locating or expanding your business.

Payroll Taxes

A list of the items that fall under the general category of "payroll taxes" for a typical business owner includes:

- withholdings from employee paychecks for individual federal, state, and local income taxes
- withheld and accrued social security and Medicare
- federal and state unemployment
- workers' compensation

A brief discussion of each of these items follows.

Federal Individual Income Taxes

An amount estimated to equal the amount of federal income taxes due from the employee to the Internal Revenue Service is usually withheld by the employer from the employee's paycheck. Federal income tax due related to any applicable income not processed through payroll is expected to be paid to the IRS in the form of quarterly estimated tax payments due in April, June, September, and January.

A table indicating U.S. individual income tax rates follows in figure 3.2.

Note that an individual pays federal income tax at a given tax rate only on those dollars earned within a tax bracket's range. For example, a single person with taxable income of $20,000 will pay federal income tax at a rate of 10 percent on his first

Marginal Tax Rate	Single Taxable Income	Married Filing Jointly or Qualified Widow(er) Taxable Income	Married Filing Separately Taxable Income	Head of Household Taxable Income
10%	$0–$9,525	$0–$19,050	$0–$9,525	$0–$13,600
12%	$9,526–$38,700	$19,051–$77,400	$9,526–$38,700	$13,601–$51,800
22%	$38,701–$82,500	$77,401–$165,000	$38,701–$82,500	$51,801–$82,500
24%	$82,501–$157,500	$165,001–$315,000	$82,501–$157,500	$82,501–$157,500
32%	$157,501–$200,000	$315,001–$400,000	$157,501–$200,000	$157,501–$200,000
35%	$200,001–$500,000	$400,001–$600,000	$200,001–$300,000	$200,001–$500,000
37%	$500,001+	$600,001+	$300,001+	$500,001+

Figure 3.2. 2018 U.S. individual income tax rates. Adapted from: Information included at https://www.taxpolicycenter.org/feature/analysis-tax-cuts-and-jobs-act.

$9,525 of taxable income and at a rate of 12 percent on the remaining $10,475 of taxable income.

State and Local Individual Income Taxes

Amounts estimated to equal the amount of state and local income taxes due from the employee to the applicable taxing agencies are usually withheld by the employer from the employee's paycheck. State and local income taxes due related to any applicable income not processed through payroll are typically expected to be paid to the applicable taxing agencies in the form of quarterly estimated tax payments due in April, June, September, and January.

Note that some state and local tax entities do not levy an income tax on the individual taxpayer. Such states include Alaska, Florida, Nevada, South Dakota, Texas, Washington, and Wyoming.[15] New Hampshire and Tennessee don't tax an individual's earned income, but they do tax interest and dividend income.[16] Be aware that the states that don't tax individual income tend to levy higher property and sales taxes in order to make up for the lack of income tax revenue.

Social Security and Medicare

Federal social insurance taxes are imposed on both employers and employees, consisting of a tax of 12.4 percent on wages up to an annual wage maximum for social security ($128,400 for 2018) and a tax of 2.9 percent on all wages for Medicare.[17] Generally, the employer and employee each pay 50 percent of the total social security and Medicare taxes due related to the individual employee's wages. Note, however, that an additional 0.9 percent Medicare tax—payable 100 percent by the employee—is assessed on employee wages over $200,000 ($250,000 if married and filing jointly, $125,000 if married and filing separately).[18]

For owners of pass-through entities who *are not* the owners of an S corporation or an entity taxed as an S corporation, the owner pays both sides of the social security and Medicare taxes due related to the profit that flows through to his individual tax return, but he gets a small discount via IRS Schedule SE (7.65 percent off the income base upon which these taxes are calculated) and the ability to deduct half of the tax paid on his IRS Form 1040.[19, 20]

For owners of pass-through entities who *are* the owners of an S corporation or an entity taxed as an S corporation, social security and Medicare taxes do not apply to the pass-through profits remaining after "reasonable" salaries have been paid to the owner-employees of an S corporation or an entity taxed as an S corporation.

Social security and Medicare taxes due related to any applicable income not processed through payroll are expected to be paid to the IRS in the form of quarterly estimated tax payments due in April, June, September, and January.

Federal and State Unemployment

Generally, employers are subject to unemployment taxes imposed by both the state governments that have jurisdiction over them and the federal government. The tax is usually a percentage of "taxable" wages, up to an applicable wage cap.

A federal unemployment rate of 6 percent is imposed on the first $7,000 of an employee's wages.[21] This rate can be reduced to as low as 0.6 percent based upon an employer's contributions to applicable state unemployment insurance funds.[22]

State unemployment rates and wage caps vary widely by state.[23] The state unemployment rate paid by any individual company will also often consider the employer's historical experience rating (in very general terms, a rating based on the employer's history of terminating employees for reasons other than employee gross misconduct, i.e., the employer's history of terminating employees via general layoffs).

Note that owner earnings processed through a payroll system are, in most states, subject to unemployment taxes.

Workers' Compensation

Although technically not a tax, when employers think about payroll taxes, they usually include workers' compensation in the mix. Workers' compensation is a form of state-based social insurance paid for by employers that provides wage replacement and medical benefits to employees injured in the course of employment. Workers' compensation benefits employers in that, although there are exceptions, workers' compensation statutes generally make the employer immune from any liability to the employee above the amount provided for in the applicable state's workers' compensation statutes.

All states in the United States, except Texas, require that an employer provide workers' compensation coverage for its employees, although this requirement often doesn't kick in until the business reaches a certain minimum number of employees, as determined by applicable state statute.[24, 25]

The median state workers' compensation rate for 2012 (the latest year for which information is available) was 1.88 percent.[26] A workers' compensation rate may be applied to different wage types and is subject to different wage minimums and wage caps, dependent upon the state in question.[27] Workers' compensation rates also vary dependent upon the type of work being performed by an employee, i.e., the workers' compensation rate for a construction worker will typically be much higher than that for an office clerk because the work performed by a construction worker typically leads to a higher rate of injury and a higher severity of injury than the work performed by an office clerk.

Owners of sole proprietorships, partners in a partnership, and members of most LLCs are not (in most instances) considered employees and, in most states, have the option to elect into or out of workers' compensation coverage.[28] Individuals who are the sole owner of a corporation with no employees may exempt themselves from coverage in many states. Owners who have earnings processed through a payroll system are usually included in a company's workers' compensation coverage, although this is not required in all states.

A Complicating Factor: State and Local Government Tax Incentives for Businesses

In recent years the amount and type of tax incentives offered by state and local governments have increased substantially. Programs vary widely by state and municipality. Tax incentives can focus on revitalizing communities by encouraging businesses to locate or grow their operations there. They can relate to job creation. They can also focus on promoting desired behaviors or encouraging the development or expansion of certain industries. An example of a popular tax incentive is the tax credit for hiring recently discharged U.S. veterans offered by 15 states: Alabama, Alaska, California, Connecticut, Florida, Illinois, Missouri, New Jersey, New Mexico, New York, Oklahoma, Utah, Vermont, West Virginia, and Wisconsin.[29]

It is important to note that, in some instances, an incentive that appears at first glance to be attractive may have conditions or requirements that make it an unsatisfactory option for a particular business. In other instances, finding the time to identify and apply for a particular incentive may be a challenge. Still, it is usually worthwhile for a business owner to investigate the tax incentives available to his business—as well as the relevant state and local income tax rates that will apply to the profits of the business—when considering where to locate or expand the business. You can start your research regarding the tax and other incentives offered to businesses in your area by visiting businessfacilities.com/state-by-state-incentives-guide.

The Tax Consequences of Business Ownership and Business Owner Compensation

Now that we have reviewed some of the basics of U.S. corporate income taxes, individual income taxes, and payroll taxes, let's take a look at how all three of these elements—and the broader U.S. tax code—can affect the legal form of business chosen by an entrepreneur and also how the entrepreneur might choose to be compensated by his business. Our analysis will consider the fact that, the larger the percentage of his company that he owns, the more the business owner feels not only the pain of every tax dollar paid by himself as an individual, but also the pain of every tax dollar paid by his business.

For example, a 100 percent owner-employee of an entity taxed as a C or an S corporation is effectively paying both sides of the social security and Medicare taxes related to any salary he may take. He is also absorbing the full effect of any unemployment or workers' compensation paid related to that salary. A 100 percent owner of a C corporation, likewise, is absorbing the full effect of any corporate income taxes paid by his corporation. An owner who owns less than 100 percent of his company will feel less than 100 percent of the effect of these types of taxes, but obviously, the higher his ownership percentage, the more the taxes paid by his business will be felt by the business owner.

The Tax Consequences of Business Owner Compensation via Salary

As mentioned earlier in this chapter, a salary is required to be paid to an owner-employee of an S corporation or an entity that is taxed as an S corporation. An owner-employee of a C corporation or an entity that is taxed as a C corporation may choose whether or not to pay himself a salary. Note that, even in the instances where they are legally required, these salaries may, in fact, be quite minimal and appropriately reflective of the company's minimal resources and lack of profitability during the start-up phase of a business.

If an entrepreneur pays himself a salary, he will have federal income taxes, state and local income taxes (as applicable), and social security and Medicare taxes withheld from his paycheck, just like any other employee. His company will also pay social security and Medicare taxes based on the amount of his salary. Additionally, his company will most likely pay workers' compensation, federal unemployment, and state unemployment taxes based upon all or part of his salary (dependent upon the state(s) in which the business operates).

The good news is that the entrepreneur's salary—along with all of the workers' compensation, federal unemployment, state unemployment, social security, and Medicare taxes paid by his company related to that salary—is tax deductible by the company. That means the company's net income is reduced when the entrepreneur pays himself a salary. A reduced net income translates to less corporate income taxes to be paid by the entrepreneur's C corporation (or entity taxed as a C corporation) or less income taxes to be paid by the entrepreneur himself (via his individual tax return) on his share of the profits of his S corporation (or entity taxed as an S corporation).

The Tax Consequences of Business Owner Compensation via Dividend

The payment of dividends relates only to an owner of a C corporation or an entity taxed as a C corporation. Note that, in the instance of an owner being paid via dividend, the income is double-taxed. First, the corporation pays corporate income tax on its taxable net income at the U.S. corporate income tax rate of 21 percent. The owner then pays personal income tax on the dividend he receives. (Note that workers' compensation, federal unemployment, state unemployment, social security, and Medicare taxes do not apply to dividend income.)

The amount of federal income tax the owner will pay on the dividend he receives depends upon whether the dividend is classified as an ordinary dividend or a qualified dividend. **Ordinary dividends** are dividends that are not qualified dividends. Ordinary dividends are taxed at the same rate as a taxpayer's ordinary income (see figure 3.2). **Qualified dividends** are dividends that meet the Internal Revenue Service requirements to—in most instances—be taxed at a lower rate than an ordinary dividend. The federal income tax rates on qualified dividends are indicated in figure 3.3.

In order to be taxed at the qualified dividend rate, a dividend:

ordinary dividend
a dividend that is not a qualified dividend

qualified dividend
a dividend that meets the Internal Revenue Service requirements to—in most instances—be taxed at a lower rate than an ordinary dividend

- must be paid by a U.S. corporation, by a corporation incorporated in a U.S. possession, or by a foreign corporation that meets certain requirements
- must not be included in the category of dividends that the IRS specifically identifies in its Publication 17 as "dividends that are not qualified dividends"
- must relate to a stock that meets certain stock holding period requirements (Specifically, you must have held the stock for more than 60 days during the 121-day period that begins 60 days before the ex-dividend date. There is an exception for preferred stock. In the case of preferred stock, you must have held the stock more than 90 days during the 181-day period that begins 90 days before the ex-dividend date if the dividends are due to periods totaling more than 366 days. If the preferred dividends are due to periods totaling less than 367 days, the holding period previously indicated applies.)[30]

(Note: This author believes the stock holding period requirements indicated above make a good case for the need for tax code simplification!)

Qualified Dividend Tax Rate	Single Taxpayers with taxable income of:	Married Filing Jointly with taxable income of:	Married Filing Separately with taxable income of:	Head of Household with taxable income of:
0%	$0–$38,600	$0–$77,200	$0–$38,600	$0–$51,700
15%–18.8%*	$38,601–$425,800	$77,201–$479,000	$38,601–$239,500	$51,701–$452,400
20%–23.8%*	Over $425,800	Over $479,000	Over $239,500	Over $452,400
* 3.8% Net investment income tax enacted in 2013.				

Figure 3.3. 2018 U.S. qualified dividend tax rates. Adapted from: Information included at https://taxfoundation.org.

Most states tax dividends as ordinary income.[31] The tax treatment of dividends by local tax entities varies widely. Some local tax entities tax dividends as ordinary income, while others do not consider dividends to be taxable at all. The states with the highest combined federal, state, and local marginal tax rates on dividends are California (33 percent), Hawaii (31.6 percent), and New York (31.5 percent).[32] To the extent any dividends received are taxable, in order to avoid tax penalties, the entrepreneur must be sure to make appropriate federal, state, and local estimated tax payments, as required.

The Tax Consequences of Business Owner Compensation via Capital Gain

An entrepreneur can "get paid" for the effort expended to start and run a successful business by selling all or part of that business. If an entrepreneur sells all or part of a business he has owned for one year or less, any profit made is considered a short-term capital gain. Short-term capital gains are taxed on the federal level at the same rate as a taxpayer's ordinary income (see figure 3.2). If, however, an entrepreneur sells all or part of a business he has owned for more than one year, any profit made is considered a long-term capital gain. The federal tax rates on long-term capital gains are generally lower than the federal tax rates on ordinary income. The federal tax rates on long-term capital gains (which mirror the federal tax rates on qualified dividends) are indicated in figure 3.4.

It usually takes considerable time to build a business worth selling. It also usually takes considerable time to sell all or part of a business. As a result, it is usually true that an entrepreneur will pay the long-term capital gains tax rate on the capital gain he realizes as a result of selling all or part of his business.

In the instance of an entrepreneur selling a long-term interest in all or part of his business, the business itself generally pays no tax on the transaction, and as we have noted, the tax rate paid by the entrepreneur is relatively low. The combination of these two likelihoods makes selling all or part of the business an attractive option tax-wise for an entrepreneur desiring to harvest cash from his business. The only problem is that many business owners don't want to have to sell all or part of their company in order to harvest cash at a low tax rate.

Note that, as with dividends, workers' compensation, federal unemployment, state unemployment, social security, and Medicare taxes do not apply to capital gains. Most states either tax capital gains as ordinary income or have codified a special tax treatment specifically for capital gains.[33] The tax treatment of capital gains by local tax entities varies widely. Some local tax entities tax capital gains as ordinary income, while others do not consider capital gains to be taxable at all. To the extent any capital gains earned are taxable, in order to avoid tax penalties, the entrepreneur must be sure to make appropriate federal, state, and local estimated tax payments, as required.

Long-Term Capital Gain Tax Rate	Single Taxpayers with taxable income of:	Married Filing Jointly with taxable income of:	Married Filing Separately with taxable income of:	Head of Household with taxable income of:
0%	$0–$38,600	$0–$77,200	$0–$38,600	$0–$51,700
15%–18.8%*	$38,601–$425,800	$77,201–$479,000	$38,601–$239,500	$51,701–$452,400
20%–23.8%*	Over $425,800	Over $479,000	Over $239,500	Over $452,400

* 3.8% Net investment income tax enacted in 2013.

Figure 3.4. 2018 U.S. long-term capital gain tax rates. Adapted from: Information included at https://taxfoundation.org.

The Tax Consequences of Business Owner Compensation via Distribution

Distributions are paid only by pass-through entities. Taking distributions from one's own company is therefore a possibility for a sole proprietor, a partner in a partnership, and members of most LLCs. It is also possible, as mentioned earlier, that after they receive reasonable compensation, an owner-employee of an S corporation or a company that is taxed as an S corporation can exercise the option to receive additional compensation from the business in the form of a distribution. Owners of C corporations—and owners of entities taxed as C corporations—cannot take distributions from their companies.

It was noted earlier in this chapter that the profits of a pass-through entity are not taxed at the company level, but instead pass through to the business owners' individual tax returns, where they are taxed. It was further noted that these businesses' profits are taxed on the business owners' individual tax returns whether or not the owners actually receive the profit in the form of a distribution. For a pass-through entity, while the business's profits are taxed on the business owners' individual tax returns, the distributions business owners receive are not themselves taxed. The two items—the taxation of a business's profits and the distributions to a business's owners—may in fact occur quite independent of each other in terms of timing. If an owner's portion of the business's profits for the year was higher or lower than the distribution he received, he would pay tax based not on the amount of the distribution he received, but on the higher or lower profit number.

Federal income taxes and self-employment (social security and Medicare) taxes apply to the profits of most pass-through entities (but not the pass-through profits remaining after "reasonable" salaries have been paid to the owner-employees of an S corporation or an entity taxed as an S corporation). Most states tax pass-through profits as ordinary income. The tax treatment of pass-through entity profits by local tax entities varies widely. Most local tax entities tax pass-through profits as ordinary income, but some others do not consider pass-through entity profits to be taxable at all. To the extent any pass-through profits are taxable, in order to avoid tax penalties, the entrepreneur must be sure to make appropriate federal, state, and local estimated tax payments, as required.

Unemployment and workers' compensation "taxes" typically do not apply to pass-through entity profits. This means, however, that a sole proprietor, a partner in a partnership, or a member of a typical LLC also doesn't receive the potential benefits associated with these forms of social safety net—unless he happens to be on the payroll of another company that pays for these benefits on his behalf.

Legal Form of Business and Business Owner Compensation—Making the Decision

So what is the optimal legal form of business? And given the choice (and because they set up the company, entrepreneurs generally do have a choice), how ideally should an entrepreneur be compensated—distributions, dividends, salary, capital gain, or some combination thereof? The answer to both of these questions is: it depends.

Overall, the entrepreneur needs to realize that how much tax an individual business owner pays as a result of owning his business depends very much upon:

- the business's legal form of organization
- how the business has elected to be taxed considering its legal form of organization
- the amount and type of "compensation" the business owner receives from the business (distributions, dividends, salary, capital gain, or some combination thereof)
- the business owner's personal tax situation, including among other things his personal tax elections, the amounts and types of income he receives from sources other than the business in question, the amounts and types of his tax deductions, and the state and local municipalities in which he lives and in which he operates his business or businesses

Because the last two items on the above list are individual-specific, it is impossible to point to one type of cash harvest strategy (distributions, dividends, salary, capital gain, or some combination thereof) as always being superior tax-wise to the others for an entrepreneur.

It was mentioned earlier in this chapter that, because of the exemption from social security and Medicare taxes enjoyed by the pass-through profits remaining after "reasonable" salaries have been paid to the owner-employees of an S corporation or an entity taxed as an S corporation, in the past, many owners chose the S corporation—or the LLC taxed as an S corporation—as their business's legal and tax form of business. The passage of the Tax Cuts and Jobs Act in December of 2017, and its corresponding reduction of the corporate tax rate to 21 percent—along with the introduction of an up to 20 percent deduction of the qualified business income (QBI) of certain pass-through businesses (the QBI deduction generally isn't available for income from businesses that provide professional financial services or operate as professional practices)—significantly complicated the taxation of business profits. The result of this is that, in certain instances, choosing to be a C corporation or an entity taxed as a C corporation may be a more appealing option than in the past for certain business owners. In reality, a major tax change like that precipitated by the Tax Cuts and Jobs Act of 2017 will require that most business owners take the time to review their business's legal form of business and business tax elections—and the type of compensation they receive from their business—in order to determine the most effective way to minimize taxes moving forward.

The U.S. tax code is long and complicated. In 2016, the Washington Examiner estimated it to be 74,608 pages long—and that was before the addition of the new tax code required as a result of the Tax Cuts and Jobs Act of 2017.[34] The discussion included in this chapter is designed to teach a future business owner the basics of business and personal taxation, but it is by no means comprehensive. So how can a future business owner determine the most tax-effective form of compensation for himself and his business partners? And considering that the forms of compensation available to a business owner depend, to some extent, upon the business's legal form, how can a future business owner determine the optimal legal form of organization for his business?

Several elements come into play in this decision-making process. First, most start-ups are not profitable—or at least not significantly profitable—in their first year. This otherwise undesirable element of starting a business allows the entrepreneur some time to figure out how best to position his company—and how best to compensate himself—in order to minimize taxes. Second, subject to limitations established by the applicable state in which an enterprise is formed and subject to limitations established by the Internal Revenue Service, the choice of legal form of business is generally not permanent and can be changed. This usually gives the entrepreneur the leeway to correct any mistakes he's made and also to make any needed adjustments as his circumstances—or the circumstances surrounding his business—change. Last, an entrepreneur doesn't necessarily need to be a tax expert, but he does need to consult with one. Before an entrepreneur starts a business, or at least before that business becomes significantly profitable, he should meet with a tax expert to develop a strategy to minimize—dependent on the goal of the entrepreneur—either the amount of his individual tax bill, the amount of his business's tax bill, or the amount of his individual tax bill and his business's tax bill combined.

Summary

Important items to contemplate when considering which legal form of business organization is best for your start-up include:

- how the choice of legal form of business affects an entity's possible sources of funding
- the amount of liability you are willing to expose yourself to as a business owner
- the amount of control you wish to exert over the entity you create
- how the choice of legal form of business affects the options available for business owner compensation
- the amount of taxes you and your business are likely to pay

It is usually easier for a C corporation to engage in equity or debt financing than businesses organized in an alternative legal form. Also, the corporation is generally viewed as top tier in terms of limiting the liability of its owners. Partnerships are generally regarded as the lowest tier in terms of limiting the liability of its owners since, beyond the fact that a general partner has unlimited liability with regard to the partnership, a general partner in a partnership has the ability to bind the partnership without the knowledge or permission of the other general partners. As a result, theoretically, a general partner can become personally liable for acts of the partnership of which he wasn't even aware.

Because a nonprofit entity is a mission-oriented entity that must adhere to strict, self-imposed rules—as well as federal and sometimes state regulations—those who create a nonprofit corporation arguably have the least control over the entity they create. Also, the founders of a corporation can easily lose the ability to affect the direction and operation of the entity they create if they fail to establish themselves both as members of the board of directors and as officers of the corporation. Those who create single-member LLCs (and sole proprietorships, though this legal form is not recommended) arguably have the most control over the entities they create.

Distribution as a form of compensation is available only to owners of pass-through entity businesses. Salary as a form of owner compensation is available only to owner-employees of corporations or entities taxed as a corporation. Dividend as a form of compensation is available only to owners of C corporations. Capital gain as a form of owner compensation is available to any type of business owner, but also involves selling all or part of the applicable business.

All businesses with employees pay payroll taxes, but only businesses that are C corporations or entities taxed as a C corporation pay income taxes. The profits of all other legal and tax forms of business pass through to the individual income tax returns of their owners, where they are taxed. As discussed in detail in this chapter, the personal tax consequences of business ownership vary significantly dependent upon many factors, the most significant of which include the business's legal form of business, how the business has elected to be taxed considering its legal form of business, the amount and type of "compensation" the business owner receives from the business, and the business owner's personal tax situation.

Key Terms

C corporation	franchise	preferred stock
capital gain	manager-managed LLC	qualified dividend
common stock	member-managed LLC	S corporation
distribution	nonprofit organization	stock option
dividend	ordinary dividend	

Review and Discussion Questions

1. Can a company's legal form of organization be changed? Explain your answer.
2. What does "unlimited liability" mean, and what type of business owners have unlimited liability?
3. What legal form is most conducive to a company successfully obtaining debt or equity financing, and why?
4. What are the different ways an owner of a for-profit business might be compensated?
5. What are the major factors that determine the amount of taxes an individual business owner will pay as a result of owning his business?

Exercises

1. Request a 10-minute phone interview with an owner of one of each of the following types of businesses: a local manufacturer, a local boutique retailer, and a local restaurant. Ask each business owner about the legal form of business under which his or her company operates. Why did each business owner pick the legal form of business that they did? Is the business's current legal form the same as its original legal form? If there was a change, why? Are any of the business owners currently considering a change in legal form for their business? If yes, why? Summarize the results of your interviews in a two-page paper.
2. The taxation of individual and corporate income varies widely at the state and local level. Investigate the individual and corporate income taxes levied by your state and local governments. Assume you are an entrepreneur about to start a direct-mail printing company. Does the combined tax burden of your state and local governments appear to be heavy or light in comparison with other areas of the United States? What factors affect the answer to this question, if any? Write two to three paragraphs summarizing the results of your research, supported by appropriate sources.
3. Generally, employers are subject to unemployment taxes imposed by both the state governments that have jurisdiction over them and the federal government. Workers' compensation is a form of state-based social insurance paid for by employers that provides wage replacement and medical benefits to employees injured in the course of employment. Investigate your state's unemployment and workers' compensation regulations. Assume you are an owner-employee of an entity that is an S corporation or an entity taxed as an S corporation. Would your business be required to pay into your state's unemployment or workers' compensation systems on your behalf? If yes, how would the amount of any such contribution be determined? What factors affect the answer to these questions, if any? Write two to three paragraphs summarizing the results of your research, supported by appropriate sources.

4. In recent years the amount and type of tax and other incentives offered to businesses by state and local governments have increased substantially. Assume you are an entrepreneur about to start a company that will manufacture an innovative new type of protective case for smartphones and employ 20 people. Investigate the incentives offered by your state and local governments that might benefit this type of business. What factors might affect your company's ability to take advantage of these incentives, if any? Write two to three paragraphs summarizing the results of your research, supported by appropriate sources.

5. Assume you are an entrepreneur about to start a company that will code smartphone applications. Assume that you are willing and able to set up this company anywhere in the United States. What legal form of business would you choose? In what state would you choose to set up the business? Within that state, in what local municipality or county would you choose to set up the business? What factors most affect your decision regarding legal form of business and where to locate your business? Citing appropriate sources, write a two-page paper supporting your choices considering, among other things, applicable state and local individual and corporate income tax rates, state unemployment rates, workers' compensation rules and rates, and the tax and other incentives offered by the applicable state and local governments.

Endnotes

1. U.S. Small Business Administration, https://www.sba.gov/starting-business/choose-your-business-structure/sole- proprietorship, 2017.
2. Startup Lawyer, https://startuplawyer.com/venture-capital/why-startups-are-corporation-for-venture-capital, July 17, 2008.
3. Feit, Ryan, "Don't Let Venture Capitalists Force You to Convert to a C-Corporation," https://www.inc.com, January 14, 2015.
4. Ibid.
5. Hearst Newspapers, Inc., https://smallbusiness.chron.com/state-allows-formation-notforprofit-llc-65770.html, 2017.
6. Ibid.
7. Ibid.
8. Internal Revenue Service, https://www.irs.gov/pub/irs-pdf/p526.pdf, January 19, 2017.
9. Pomerleau, Kyle, "The United States' Corporate Income Tax Rate Is Now More in Line with Those Levied by Other Major Nations," https://taxfoundation.org, February 12, 2018.
10. Ibid.
11. Scarboro, Morgan, "State Corporate Income Tax Rates and Brackets for 2017," https://taxfoundation.org, February 27, 2017.
12. Ibid.
13. Tax Policy Center, https://www.taxpolicycenter.org/briefing-book/how-do-state-and-local-corporate-income-taxes-work, 2018.
14. Ibid.
15. Loudenback, Tanza, "What Americans Pay in State Income Taxes, Ranked from Highest to Lowest," https://www.businessinsider.com, April 8, 2018.
16. Ibid.
17. Social Security Administration, https://www.ssa.gov/news/press/factsheets/colafacts2018.pdf
18. Ibid.
19. Internal Revenue Service, https://www.irs.gov/pub/irs-pdf/f1040sse.pdf, 2017.
20. Internal Revenue Service, https://www.irs.gov/pub/irs-pdf/f1040.pdf, 2017.
21. Internal Revenue Service, https://taxmap.irs.gov/taxmap/pubs/p15-013.htm, 2019.
22. Ibid.
23. American Payroll Association, https://www.americanpayroll.org/members/stateui/state-ui-2, 2017.
24. United States Department of Labor, https://www.dol.gov/owcp/dfec/regs/compliance/wc.htm, 2017.

25. Hearst Newspapers, Inc., https://smallbusiness.chron.com/workers-comp-compliance-65721. html, 2017.

26. Business and Legal Resources, https://hr.blr.com/HR-news/HR-Administration/Workers-Workmen-Compensation/50-state-study-on-workers-comp-rates-released#, October 11, 2012.

27. United States Department of Labor, https://www.dol.gov/owcp/dfec/regs/compliance/wc.htm, 2017.

28. Ibid.

29. Orion ICS, LLC, https://www.oriontalent.com/hire-military/state-tax-credits-for-hiring-veterans.aspx, 2018.

30. Internal Revenue Service, https://www.irs.gov/publications/p17/ch08.html, 2017.

31. Pomerleau, Kyle, "How High Are Personal Dividends Income Tax Rates in Your State?," https://taxfoundation.org/how-high-are-personal-dividends-income-tax-rates-your-state/, March 11, 2014.

32. Ibid.

33. Tax Foundation, https://taxfoundation.org/how-high-are-capital-gains-tax-rates-your-state/, 2014.

34. Russell, Jason, "Look at How Many Pages Are in the Federal Tax Code," https://www.washingtonexaminer.com, April 15, 2016.

Financial Statements

"I'm a big advocate of financial intelligence."

— **Daymond John, television personality, founder and CEO of FUBU**

Learning Objectives

Be able to read and understand the income statements, balance sheets, and statements of cash flows of a for-profit business.

Understand the difference between audited, reviewed, and compiled financial statements.

Have an understanding of the limitations of financial statements and why an individual should use caution when making decisions based on a company's financial statements.

Introduction

Understanding the numbers associated with business isn't a strong point for most entrepreneurs. As a result, at their peril, they tend to avoid learning to read and understand financial statements. Not understanding the numbers associated with your business is a mistake for several reasons:

- Understanding your company is impossible without understanding the numbers behind it. For-profit businesses exist to make a profit. Profitability is defined by numbers. Nonprofits exist to serve some mission. Nonprofits can't execute their mission without money. Money is defined by numbers.
- You can't succeed in business negotiations if you don't understand basic business jargon. Most business jargon relates to issues associated with profitability. Profitability, as already mentioned, is defined by numbers.

- You can't improve your business's profitability if you don't understand your business's weaknesses. A business's weaknesses are exposed by its numbers.
- If you don't understand the numbers behind your business, you're at the mercy of those who do. Not everyone has your best interest in mind, entrepreneur. You need to be your own advocate. You need to learn to read and understand financial statements.

An owner understanding the financial statements associated with her business is critical to the success of that business. Entrepreneur in Action 4.1 illustrates the type of negative outcome that can result when an owner doesn't understand his own company's financial statements.

Entrepreneur *in Action* 4.1

An Entrepreneur's Embarrassing Moment

Tyler Kelly, the founder and owner of Cadence Caster Manufacturing, Inc., was a smart guy. A smart guy who had never learned to understand financial statements. Understanding financial statements was something Tyler didn't feel he needed to do. He paid his accountant for that sort of thing.

It was the beginning of Cadence's fourth year of operations, and Tyler wanted to obtain a line of credit from a bank to support a desired expansion of the business. Expanding the business meant, among other things, that the business would need to purchase more inventory in order to build and sell more product and it would also need to be able to support the resultant increased level of accounts receivable. On the day of the scheduled meeting with the bank, Tyler's accountant commented to Tyler that he'd be happy to go with him to the meeting. Tyler confidently said, "No. I can sell the bank on my own." A few hours later, Tyler left Cadence's manufacturing facility and headed to the bank for the meeting.

The meeting started out with the usual friendly greetings and handshakes. Then the individual representing the bank, Pete Antonio, invited Tyler to sit down and relax while they talked. Tyler explained his desire to establish a line of credit with Pete's

bank in order to fund the expansion of his business. Pete nodded in understanding. He said he had reviewed Cadence's financial statements—which had been sent over at his request by Cadence's accountant—and he had some questions. Pete asked, "Why is your company's owner's equity so low when your company's net income for the last two years has been so high? Also, what exactly is included in the cost of goods sold, miscellaneous expense, and accounts payable line items on your company's financial statements? Last, what circumstances generated the deferred tax asset on your company's balance sheet?"

Tyler stared at the banker, mute and stunned. An awkward moment passed. Another awkward moment passed. Pete began to look a bit disturbed and then asked, "Are you able to answer these questions for me, Mr. Kelly?" Tyler replied shortly, "No." Pete shook his head in a manner that expressed some irritation on his part and said, "Mr. Kelly, how do you expect me to authorize a line of credit to expand a business you, its owner, do not appear to understand?" Tyler, embarrassed, stood up, apologized for wasting the banker's time, and left the meeting. He realized he had just learned the hard way why it is necessary for a business owner to understand the financial statements of the company he owns.

Financial Statements

Every for-profit business, regardless of its legal form, creates the same basic financial statements. Internal parties (i.e., entrepreneurs and the talent they recruit) use these financial statements to manage and control the business. External parties (i.e., potential investors, lenders, and grantors of funds) use them to evaluate the profit potential, creditworthiness, and financial health of the business.

Financial statements are often historical in nature in that they tell us about the past, but they may be forward looking, as in the instance of pro forma financial statements. **Pro forma financial statements** are financial statements created by an entrepreneur that attempt to estimate the future financial results of a company based upon certain identified assumptions. Pro forma financial statements will be discussed and illustrated in detail in chapters 6 and 7.

There are three basic financial statements:

1. The **income statement** is a summary of the revenue and expenses of a business over a specified period of time.
2. The **statement of financial position** (also called the balance sheet) is a summary of the assets, liabilities, and equity of a business at a specific point in time.
3. The **statement of cash flows** is a summary of the cash receipts and cash expenditures of a business over a specified period of time.

The financial statements of a company whose stock is publicly traded (i.e., traded on a public stock exchange, such as the New York Stock Exchange) are required by the Securities and Exchange Commission to be audited every year by an independent auditor who is a certified public accountant (CPA). **Audited financial statements** have been successfully formally examined by an outside, independent auditor. Examination includes an in-depth investigation of a business's accounting policies and practices, accounting records, and internal financial statements with the goal of providing reasonable assurance that the final financial statements shared with those outside the company fairly present the financial position, performance, continued viability, and risks associated with the company under audit.

The financial statements of privately held companies (i.e., companies whose stock is not traded on a public stock exchange) aren't normally audited unless there's a specific contractual, legal, or regulatory obligation to do so, usually as a result of the company's relationship or potential relationship with an investor, lender, or other interested party. However, in order to ensure the accuracy and professional presentation of her business's financial statements, it's often wise for an entrepreneur to use an independent CPA or outside accountant to review or compile a start-up entity's financial statements.

Reviewed financial statements have been subjected to inquiry and analytical procedures by an outside accountant who expresses limited assurance that the financial statements fairly present the financial position, performance, continued viability, and risks associated with the company under review. A review is a "does it make sense?" analysis that's useful when an organization needs some assurance about the adequacy and fairness of its financial statements—but not the higher level of assurance provided by an audit. **Compiled financial statements** have been prepared by an accountant outside a company based upon the data provided by that company. An accountant who prepares compiled financial statements does so without providing any of the assurances associated with an audit or a review.

Accounting Information Systems

All businesses need some sort of **accounting information system**, a usually software-based system that provides the data that:

- helps the entrepreneur effectively operate the business
- allows for the preparation of period- or year-end financial statements, tax documents (i.e., W-2s and Form 1099s), and tax filings

pro forma financial statements financial statements created by an entrepreneur that attempt to estimate the future financial results of a company based upon certain identified assumptions

income statement a summary of the revenue and expenses of a business over a specified period of time

statement of financial position a summary of the assets, liabilities, and equity of a business at a specific point in time; also called a balance sheet

statement of cash flows a summary of the cash receipts and cash expenditures of a business over a specified period of time

audited financial statements financial statements that have been successfully formally examined by an outside, independent auditor; examination includes an in-depth investigation of a business's accounting policies and practices, accounting records, and internal financial statements, with the goal of providing reasonable assurance that the final financial statements shared with those outside the company fairly present the financial position, performance, continued viability, and risks associated the company under audit

reviewed financial statements financial statements that have been subjected to inquiry and analytical procedures by an outside accountant who expresses limited assurance that the financial statements fairly present the financial position, performance, continued viability, and risks associated with the company under review

compiled financial statements financial statements that have been prepared by an accountant outside a company based on the data provided by that company; an accountant who prepares compiled financial statements does so without providing any of the assurances associated with an audit or a review

accounting information system a usually software-based system that provides the data needed to effectively operate a business and prepare that business's period- or year-end financial statements, tax documents (i.e., W-2s and Form 1099s), and tax filings

For most entrepreneurial start-ups, hiring a full-time accountant as an employee of the organization to manage the accounting information system and prepare period- or year-end financial statements, tax documents, and tax returns is overkill. Someone within the entrepreneurial organization can almost always effectively manage the organization's accounting information system. And, depending upon the level of expertise and interest of the entrepreneur, either the entrepreneur or an outside accountant can usually effectively prepare the organization's financial statements, tax documents, and tax returns.

Using canned accounting and tax software (e.g., QuickBooks, NetSuite) as the basis for an organization's accounting information system is a good option, but someone still has to take on the responsibility of identifying the software that best suits the particular start-up and setting up the system. Even when considering and utilizing only the most popular and user-friendly canned software, this is an arduous task. Using an outside accountant to help select and set up a new venture's accounting information system can save the entrepreneur a lot of time—time generally better utilized managing and growing the young business. An optimally set up accounting information system can save the entrepreneur a tremendous amount of effort with regard to billing customers, paying vendors, and managing the business's working capital. An optimally set up accounting information system can also save the entrepreneur—or the outside accountant—a tremendous amount of legwork with regard to completing the necessary period- or year-end financial statements, tax documents, and tax filings for the business. Most entrepreneurs eventually learn that the money spent to have an outside, appropriately skilled accountant select and optimally set up their new venture's accounting information system is money very well spent. Outside accountants tend to pay for themselves in terms of recognizing and avoiding the accounting and tax problems that can cost an entrepreneur money.

Note that, beyond just annual financial statements, investors, lenders, or others might require monthly or quarterly financial statements for the business. Having a well-functioning accounting information system will make the generation of these financial statements a relatively pain-free process.

The Income Statement

Having a good accounting information system in place will help facilitate the creation of the first of the three basic financial statements: the income statement. Before looking at the income statement itself, defining the key terms typically seen on that statement is wise:

- **Sales** (also called revenue and sales revenue) represents the monies received as a result of a business selling its products and services.
- **Returns and allowances** (also called sales returns and allowances or simply sales allowances or returns) represents refunded sales dollars from one or more of three sources:
  - returns of product
  - allowances given in lieu of returns of product
  - allowances given on the sales price of services, because services generally can't be returned
- **Net sales** (also called net revenue) equals sales minus returns and allowances.
- **Cost of goods sold** (COGS) represents the amount it costs a company to create, build, or purchase the product it sells. Note that the cost of inventory, once a company has sold that inventory, becomes cost of goods sold.
- **Cost of sales** (also called cost of revenue and cost of services) represents the direct costs associated with delivering services to the clients of service-based businesses.

sales
the monies received as a result of a business selling its products and services; also called revenue and sales revenue

returns and allowances
refunded sales dollars; also called sales returns and allowances or simply sales allowances or returns

net sales
sales minus returns and allowances; also called net revenue

cost of goods sold
the amount it costs a company to create, build, or purchase the product it sells; the cost of inventory—once a company has sold that inventory—becomes cost of goods sold; often referred to as COGS

cost of sales
the direct costs associated with delivering services to the clients of service-based businesses; also called cost of revenue and cost of services

- **Gross profit** equals net sales (or sales, if there is no net sales amount) minus cost of goods sold, cost of sales, cost of revenue, or cost of services.
- **Operating expenses** includes all of an enterprise's expenses—except interest and income taxes—that are not included in cost of goods sold, cost of sales, cost of revenue, or cost of services.
- **Depreciation expense** (also called depreciation) represents the wearing out of certain of a business's fixed assets over time, valued in dollars.
- **Operating income** equals gross profit minus operating expenses. Operating income represents the earnings from business operations—before interest and income taxes are considered—and is generally viewed as a key indicator of the relative success or failure of a business model.
- **Interest expense** (also called interest) represents the amount of interest incurred by a business related to its liabilities and debt.
- **Provision for income taxes** (also called income tax expense) represents the amount of income taxes incurred by a C corporation or an entity taxed as a C corporation, related generally to the net income it generates.
- **Net income** (also called profit and net profit) equals operating income minus interest expense for most sole proprietorships, partnerships, LLCs, and S corporations. For a C corporation or an entity taxed as a C corporation, net income equals operating income minus interest expense and minus the provision for income taxes.

Now that we've established the basic vocabulary used in income statements, let's view some sample income statements. Figure 4.1 is an example of an income statement for a product-based company.

gross profit
net sales (or sales, if there is no net sales amount) minus cost of goods sold, cost of sales, cost of revenue, or cost of services

operating expenses
all of an enterprise's expenses—except interest and income taxes—that are not included in cost of goods sold, cost of sales, cost of revenue, or cost of services

depreciation expense
an expense amount that represents the wearing out of certain of a business's fixed assets over time, valued in dollars; also called depreciation

operating income
gross profit minus operating expenses; operating income represents the earnings from business operations—before interest and income taxes are considered—and is generally viewed as a key indicator of the relative success or failure of a business model

interest expense
the amount of interest incurred by a business related to its liabilities and debt; also called interest

provision for income taxes
the amount of income taxes incurred by a C corporation or an entity taxed as a C corporation, related generally to the net income it generates; also called income tax expense

net income
operating income minus interest expense for most sole proprietorships, partnerships, LLCs, and S corporations; for a C corporation or an entity taxed as a C corporation, net income equals operating income minus interest expense and minus the provision for income taxes; also called profit and net profit

The Michael Stanwick Company Income Statement For the Year Ended December 31, 2018		
Gross sales	$445,000	
Less: Returns and allowances	5,000	
Net sales		$440,000
Less: Cost of goods sold		125,000
Gross profit		315,000
Less: Operating expenses:		
Wages expense	126,000	
Equipment rental expense	36,000	
Utilities expense	6,500	
Property tax expense	2,750	
Depreciation expense	3,500	
Insurance expense	3,600	
Total operating expenses		178,350
Operating income		136,650
Less: Interest expense		10,000
Net income		$126,650

FIGURE 4.1. Income statement for a product-based company that isn't a C corporation or an entity taxed as a C corporation.

While there's no hard-and-fast rule regarding the proper order of the expenses listed within operating expenses, general practice is to present the most significant expenses first. An expense's significance within the category of operating expenses is typically determined by considering both the item's dollar amount and the item's importance to the financial statement reader.

Cost of Sales, Cost of Revenue, and Cost of Services

We know the income statement in figure 4.1 is for a product-based company because "cost of goods sold" suggests the sale of a good, an item of product. The income statement for a service-based business generally does not include a line for cost of goods sold because either no goods are sold or the goods that are sold are insignificant in amount and only sold in order to support the company's service business.

While it does not accumulate cost of goods sold, a service-based business (e.g., an accounting, architectural, engineering, or law firm) does accumulate costs associated with delivering services to its clients. Depending upon the industry in which the business operates—and depending upon the purpose of the financial statement itself—a service business may present the direct costs associated with delivering services to its clients on its income statements by means of a line item called cost of sales, cost of revenue, or cost of services. Expenses that comprise this type of line item vary by industry and may include the following:

- hourly wages paid to the workers who deliver the services
- fees paid to independent contractors and professionals on a by-project basis

The Michael Stanwick Company Income Statement For the Year Ended December 31, 2018		
Gross sales	$445,000	
Less: Sales allowances	5,000	
Net sales		$440,000
Less: Cost of sales		125,000
Gross profit		315,000
Less: Operating expenses:		
Wages expense	162,000	
Utilities expense	6,500	
Property tax expense	2,750	
Depreciation expense	3,500	
Insurance expense	3,600	
Total operating expenses		178,350
Operating income		136,650
Less: Interest expense		10,000
Net income		$126,650

FIGURE 4.2. Income statement for a service-based company that isn't a C corporation or an entity taxed as a C corporation and whose industry uses the term "cost of sales."

- transportation costs to deliver the services
- sales commissions
- any expense incurred only when the services are sold or that varies in direct relationship to the amount of the services sold

Examples of expenses generally not considered part of cost of sales, cost of revenue, or cost of services include the following:

- salaries
- rents
- utilities
- any expense that's generally fixed in nature and doesn't vary—or doesn't vary significantly—with the amount of the services sold

Figure 4.2 is another example of an income statement. This one is for a service-based company whose industry typically uses the term "cost of sales."

Figure 4.3 is also an example of an income statement for a service-based company, but it's for a company whose industry typically doesn't use the terms "cost of sales," "cost of revenue," or "cost of services." Note that the income statement doesn't include a line for gross profit.

The income statements we've look at thus far are for entities that are not a C corporation or an entity taxed as a C corporation (i.e., sole proprietorships, partnerships, S corporations, and LLCs not taxed as a C corporation [i.e., most LLCs]). The income statements of entities that are not a C corporation or an entity taxed as a C corporation don't show a provision for income taxes. This is because these businesses are pass-through entities whose income flows through to the business owners' individual tax returns, where it is taxed. The primary difference between the income statement of a C corporation or an entity taxed as a C corporation and every other type of entity is that the income statement of a C corporation or an entity taxed as

The Michael Stanwick Company Income Statement For the Year Ended December 31, 2018		
Gross sales	$445,000	
Less: Sales allowances	5,000	
Net sales		$440,000
Less: Operating expenses:		
Wages expense	257,000	
Marketing expense	30,000	
Utilities expense	6,500	
Property tax expense	2,750	
Depreciation expense	3,500	
Insurance expense	3,600	
Total operating expenses		303,350
Operating income		136,650
Less: Interest expense		10,000
Net income		$126,650

FIGURE 4.3. Income statement for a service-based company that isn't a C corporation or an entity taxed as a C corporation and whose industry doesn't use a term like "cost of sales."

a C corporation typically includes a provision for income taxes (sometimes called income tax expense).

The income statement in figure 4.4 shows an income statement for a C corporation. Note the provision for income taxes included on the statement.

Beyond the provision for income taxes, note that this income statement includes two other lines we haven't seen before:

1. **net income before income taxes**—a subtotal unique to the income statement of a C corporation or entity taxed as a C corporation that usually appears immediately before the line for the provision for income taxes

2. **earnings per share of common stock**—an element sometimes included on the income statement of a C corporation (but not on the income statement of an entity taxed as a C corporation) calculated by dividing net income by the number of the corporation's outstanding shares of common stock

A pass-through entity that has elected to be taxed as a C corporation wouldn't have any shares of common stock; therefore, its income statement wouldn't include earnings per share of common stock. Technically, an S corporation could present earnings per share of common stock on its income statement. However, this is not common practice.

net income before income taxes

a subtotal unique to the income statement of a C corporation or entity taxed as a C corporation that usually appears immediately before the line for the provision for income taxes

earnings per share of common stock

an element sometimes included on the income statement of a C corporation (but not on the income statement of an entity taxed as a C corporation) calculated by dividing net income by the number of the corporation's outstanding shares of common stock

The Stanwick Corporation Income Statement For the Year Ended December 31, 2018		
Gross sales	$445,000	
Less: Returns and allowances	5,000	
Net sales		$440,000
Less: Cost of goods sold		125,000
Gross profit		315,000
Less: Operating expenses:		
Wages expense	126,000	
Equipment rental expense	36,000	
Utilities expense	6,500	
Property tax expense	2,750	
Depreciation expense	3,500	
Insurance expense	3,600	
Total operating expenses		178,350
Operating income		136,650
Less: Interest expense		10,000
Net income before income taxes		126,650
Less: Provision for income taxes		26,650
Net income		$100,000
Earning per share of common stock		$ 1.00

FIGURE 4.4. Income statement for a C corporation.

The Balance Sheet and the Basic Accounting Equation

Next, we'll examine the statement of financial position, more commonly referred to as the balance sheet, the second of the three basic financial statements. As we did with the income statement, before looking at the balance sheet itself, let us first review the definitions of the key terms one would typically see on that statement:

- An **asset** is an item of value owned by a business.
- A **current asset** is an item of value that's either cash or an asset that will likely be converted into cash within the next 12 months.
- The term accounts receivable refers to the amounts customers owe a company related to their purchases from that company utilizing the credit or trade credit offered by that company.
- A **prepaid asset** is typically an expense that's been paid for in advance of the period of its use. A common example is prepaid insurance. Insurance usually needs to be paid for in advance of the period for which coverage is provided. As the coverage period expires or partially expires, the amount of prepaid insurance included on the balance sheet decreases and the amount of insurance expense included on the income statement increases. Prepaid assets are usually current assets.
- **Fixed assets** (also called noncurrent assets, long-term assets, and property, plant, and equipment) is a balance sheet subtotal made up of major assets that will likely not be converted into cash within the next 12 months. Which of the four indicated terms is utilized generally depends on the makeup of the major assets included in the subtotal.
- **Accumulated depreciation** is a contra-asset included on the balance sheet that represents the cumulative wearing out of certain of a business's fixed assets over time, valued in dollars. In other words, accumulated depreciation is an account that accumulates all the depreciation expense included on a company's income statements over time related to an asset or group of assets currently included on a company's balance sheet.
- **Net fixed assets** (also called net noncurrent assets, net long-term assets, and net property, plant, and equipment), for most businesses, equals fixed assets minus accumulated depreciation.
- A **liability** is an amount owed to others. A business's assets are partially financed by its liabilities.
- A **current liability** is an amount owed to others that will need to be paid within the next 12 months.
- **Accounts payable** is a current liability that typically represents amounts owed to the vendors that provide essential products and services to a business so the business can, in turn, provide products and services to its customers. Accounts payable often includes significant amounts owed related to the purchase of inventory.
- **Short-term portion of long-term debt** is a current liability that represents that portion of the principal of one or more major long-term borrowings (e.g., a mortgage payable) that's due to be repaid within the next 12 months. Reference appendix B at the end of chapter 6 for an illustration of the calculation of the short-term portion of long-term debt.
- A **long-term liability** (also called a noncurrent liability) is an amount owed to others that doesn't need to be paid within the next 12 months.
- **Equity** is the amount by which the assets of a business exceed the liabilities of a business. The equity section of a balance sheet will vary in form and format depending upon the legal form of the business.

asset
an item of value owned by a business

current asset
an item of value that's either cash or an asset that will likely be converted into cash within the next 12 months

prepaid asset
typically, an expense that's been paid for in advance of the period of its use

fixed assets
a balance sheet subtotal made up of major assets that will likely not be converted into cash within the next 12 months; also called noncurrent assets, long-term assets, and property, plant, and equipment

accumulated depreciation
a contra-asset included on the balance sheet that represents the cumulative wearing out of certain of a business's fixed assets over time, valued in dollars

net fixed assets
for most businesses, fixed assets minus accumulated depreciation; also called net noncurrent assets, net long-term assets, and net property, plant, and equipment

liability
an amount owed to others

current liability
an amount owed to others that will need to be paid within the next 12 months

accounts payable
a current liability that typically represents amounts owed to the vendors that provide essential products and services to a business so the business can, in turn, provide products and services to its customers

short-term portion of long-term debt
a current liability that represents that portion of the principal of one or more major long-term borrowings that's due to be repaid within the next 12 months

long-term liability
an amount owed to others that doesn't need to be paid within the next 12 months; also called noncurrent liability

equity
the amount by which the assets of a business exceed the liabilities of a business

Now that we've established important terms, let's review some example balance sheets. Figure 4.5 is an example of a balance sheet for a sole proprietorship or a single-member LLC.

Note that on a balance sheet, the amount for total assets must always equal the amount for total liabilities and equity. This fact is represented by the **basic accounting equation**, which can be written in multiple ways, but is most often seen in one of the two following forms:

1. Total assets = Total liabilities + Total equity: This form of the equation emphasizes that the assets of a company can be paid for in one of two ways: debt or equity.
2. Total equity = Total assets – Total liabilities: This form of the equation emphasizes that we can always determine total equity if we know total assets and total liabilities. Knowing this fact is especially handy when attempting to build a balance sheet.

The current assets on a balance sheet are typically presented in the order of most to least "liquid." **Liquidity in relation to the general topic of finance** refers to the ease with which an asset can be converted into cash without significant loss of value. **Liquidity in relation to an asset on a balance sheet** refers to how quickly an asset can be turned into cash. Cash is obviously the most liquid current asset. Accounts receivable are generally viewed as more liquid than inventory because accounts receivable represent cash a business is waiting to collect from its customers.

basic accounting equation
Total assets = Total liabilities + Total equity

liquidity (in relation to the general topic of finance)
the ease with which an asset can be converted into cash without significant loss of value

liquidity (in relation to an asset on a balance sheet)
how quickly an asset can be turned into cash

The Michael Stanwick Company Balance Sheet As of December 31, 2018			
Cash		$ 4,000	
Accounts receivable		75,000	
Inventory		97,500	
Prepaid insurance		2,500	
Total current assets			$179,000
Land		125,000	
Building	$350,000		
Less: Accumulated depreciation	75,000		
		275,000	
Equipment	45,000		
Less: Accumulated depreciation	7,500		
		37,500	
Net fixed assets			437,500
Total assets			$616,500
Accounts payable		$ 55,000	
Notes payable-bank		10,000	
Taxes payable		4,500	
Short-term portion of long-term debt		21,000	
Total current liabilities			$ 90,500
Building mortgage payable		185,000	
Equipment loan payable		35,000	
Total long-term liabilities			220,000
Total liabilities			310,500
Owner's equity			306,000
Total liabilities and owner's equity			$616,500

FIGURE 4.5. Balance sheet for a sole proprietorship or a single-member LLC.

Inventory, on the other hand, represents an asset that first has to be sold and thereby turned into accounts receivable, which in turn represent cash a business is waiting to collect from its customers.

While there's no hard-and-fast rule regarding the proper order of the assets listed within fixed assets, common practice is to present the least significant assets first and build toward the more significant assets—or vice versa. In other words, there's usually some logic behind the chosen order of presentation. An asset's significance within the category of fixed assets is usually determined by considering both the item's dollar amount and the item's importance to the financial statement reader. If the business owns land, that land is often listed as the first fixed asset because land isn't depreciated while most other fixed assets are.

Accounts payable, if they exist, are usually listed as the first current liability. Short-term portion of long-term debt, if it exists, is usually listed as the last current liability. Otherwise, similar to fixed assets, there's no hard-and-fast rule regarding the proper order of the liabilities listed within the current liabilities section of a balance sheet.

We can tell that the balance sheet in figure 4.5 is a balance sheet for a sole proprietorship or a single-member LLC because the term "owner's equity" is used to describe the equity on the balance sheet. "Owner's equity," as opposed to the plural "owners' equity," indicates a solo business owner who's not a shareholder of a corporation. Owner's equity reflects the cumulative amount the owner has invested into the business, plus or minus the amount of the business's net income or net loss for each year, less any distributions that have been paid to the owner.

Figure 4.6 presents another balance sheet. This example is for a multi-member LLC.

Stanwick Enterprises, LLC
Balance Sheet
As of December 31, 2018

Cash		$ 4,000	
Accounts receivable		75,000	
Inventory		97,500	
Prepaid insurance		2,500	
Total current assets			$179,000
Land		125,000	
Building	$350,000		
Equipment	45,000		
Less: Accumulated depreciation	82,500		
		312,500	
Net fixed assets			437,500
Total assets			$616,500
Accounts payable		$55,000	
Notes payable-bank		10,000	
Taxes payable		4,500	
Short-term portion of long-term debt		21,000	
Total current liabilities			$90,500
Building mortgage payable		185,000	
Equipment loan payable		35,000	
Total long-term liabilities			220,000
Total liabilities			310,500
Owners' equity			306,000
Total liabilities and owners' equity			$616,500

FIGURE 4.6. Balance sheet for a multi-member LLC.

Beyond the fact that the title of the financial statement gives us a pretty solid hint, we can tell this balance sheet is for a multi-member LLC because the term "owners' equity" is used to describe the equity on the balance sheet. The plural "owners' equity," as opposed to the singular "owner's equity," indicates multiple business owners who are neither partners in a partnership nor shareholders of a corporation.

Note that the fixed-assets section of the balance sheet in figure 4.6 is presented differently than that of the balance sheet presented in figure 4.5. The balance sheet for the multi-member LLC (figure 4.6) presents accumulated depreciation as one line item that relates to a group of assets. The balance sheet for the sole proprietorship or single-member LLC (figure 4.5) presents a separate line of accumulated depreciation for each applicable fixed asset. Both presentations are frequently used and generally accepted. Figure 4.7 presents side by side only the assets sections of these two balance sheets (i.e., figures 4.5 and 4.6) in order to clearly illustrate the difference.

The Michael Stanwick Company Assets Section of Balance Sheet As of December 31, 2018			Stanwick Enterprises, LLC Assets Section of Balance Sheet As of December 31, 2018		
Cash		$ 4,000	Cash		$ 4,000
Accounts receivable		75,000	Accounts receivable		75,000
Inventory		97,500	Inventory		97,500
Prepaid insurance		2,500	Prepaid insurance		2,500
Total current assets		$179,000	Total current assets		$179,000
Land		125,000	Land		125,000
Building	$350,000		Building	$350,000	
Less: Accumulated depreciation	75,000		Equipment	45,000	
		275,000	Less: Accumulated depreciation	82,500	
Equipment	45,000				312,500
Less: Accumulated depreciation	7,500		Net fixed assets		437,500
		37,500	Total assets		$616,500
Net fixed assets		437,500			
Total assets		$616,500			

FIGURE 4.7. Different presentations of the fixed-assets section of a balance sheet.

As mentioned previously, owners' equity reflects the cumulative amount the owners have invested into the business, plus or minus the amount of the business's net income or net loss for each year, minus any distributions that have been paid to the owners. A balance sheet for a partnership would look just like the balance sheets already presented, except that the equity section would look like that shown in figure 4.8.

Note that although indicating the amount of each partner's equity account on the balance sheet of a partnership is common, it is not mandatory. Note also that the amount of each partner's equity account typically reflects the amount she has invested into the partnership, plus her portion of the partnership's net income or net loss for each year, minus any distributions that have been made to her.

Michael Stanwick and Partners Equity Section of a Balance Sheet for a Partnership As of December 31, 2018		
Partners' equity:		
Michael Stanwick	$168,300	
Rebecca Stanwick	76,500	
Joseph Kelley	61,200	
Total partners' equity		306,000
Total liabilities and partners' equity		$616,500

FIGURE 4.8. Equity section of a balance sheet for a partnership.

Our next example highlights the financials of another kind of entity. Figure 4.9 presents a balance sheet for a corporation.

Beyond the title of the financial statement telling us so, we know the balance sheet in figure 4.9 is for a corporation because the equity section of this balance sheet

The Stanwick Corporation Balance Sheet As of December 31, 2018			
Cash		$ 4,000	
Accounts receivable		75,000	
Inventory		97,500	
Prepaid insurance		2,500	
Total current assets			$179,000
Land		125,000	
Building	$350,000		
Equipment	45,000		
Less: Accumulated depreciation	82,500		
		312,500	
Net fixed assets			437,500
Total assets			$616,500
Accounts payable		$55,000	
Notes payable-bank		10,000	
Taxes payable		4,500	
Short-term portion of long-term debt		21,000	
Total current liabilities			$ 90,500
Building mortgage payable			220,000
Total liabilities			310,500
Preferred stock, $5 par (10,000 shares)	$ 50,000		
Common stock, $0.10 par (100,000 shares)	10,000		
Paid-in capital in excess of par, common	50,000		
Total paid-in capital		110,000	
Retained earnings		196,000	
Total stockholders' equity			306,000
Total liabilities and stockholders' equity			$616,500

FIGURE 4.9. Balance sheet for a corporation.

is quite different from the equity sections of the other balance sheets we've looked at thus far. Here are some terms related specifically to corporate balance sheets:

- Common stock (also called common shares), as first defined in chapter 3, is an equity security representing the fundamental ownership of a company issued by a public or private corporation in order to raise financial capital. The number of common shares outstanding is used to determine the earnings per share and book value per share of a company.

- **Paid-in capital in excess of par** (also called additional paid-in capital) represents the cumulative amount shareholders paid for the common stock of a company beyond its par value. (**Par value** is an arbitrary dollar amount indicated on a stock certificate, usually because a par value is required by state law.) In the balance sheet shown in figure 4.9, shareholders paid $0.60 per share for 100,000 shares of stock. $0.10 of the $0.60 represents the par value of each share ($0.10 x 100,000 shares = the $10,000 common stock value included on the balance sheet). The amount paid in excess of par for each share is the remaining $0.50 of the $0.60 ($0.50 x 100,000 shares = the $50,000 paid-in capital in excess of par value included on the balance sheet).

- **Retained earnings** represents the cumulative earnings of a company not distributed to stockholders via dividends (C corporations) or distributions (S corporations) but instead retained in the corporation for future investment.

- Preferred stock (also called preferred shares), as introduced in chapter 3, is a class of ownership of a C corporation that has a higher claim on the assets and earnings of the corporation than the corporation's common stock. Preferred stock generally has a dividend that must be paid out before dividends can be paid to the common stockholders, and preferred shareholders usually don't have voting rights.

Details regarding the nature of preferred stock are specific to each issuance; however, preferred stock usually has characteristics of both debt (i.e., "guaranteed" dividends, which are similar in nature to interest) and equity (potential capital appreciation). Though preferred stock can be issued only by a C corporation, it is by no means issued by all C corporations and, as a result, is absent from many corporate balance sheets.

We'll discuss both preferred and common stock in more detail in chapter 12.

- **Deferred taxes** is a balance sheet line item unique to C corporations and entities taxed as a C corporation. A deferred tax item usually arises due to differences in the treatment of an asset or expense for accounting versus tax purposes because of differences in accounting and tax rules.

The classic example of this is the difference between the accounting and tax depreciation of an asset. For purposes of accounting, a business might depreciate an asset, such as a piece of equipment, using the straight-line, half-year convention depreciation method (see chapter 6 for an illustration of this method). The IRS, however, might require that the asset be depreciated using a more accelerated depreciation method, such as the modified accelerated cost recovery system (MACRS). If an asset is depreciated more quickly for tax purposes than for accounting purposes, the depreciation expense on the company's income tax return will be more than the depreciation expense on the company's income statement. This will result in taxable income being less than accounting net income. A deferred tax liability is created when taxable income is less than accounting net income, resulting in the need for fewer taxes to be paid than the net income on the income statement would seem to indicate. When the depreciation situation reverses in the future—as it always will for each individual asset—tax depreciation expense will then be less than accounting

---

paid-in capital in excess of par
the cumulative amount shareholders paid for the common stock of a company beyond its par value; also called additional paid-in capital

par value
an arbitrary dollar amount indicated on a stock certificate, usually because a par value is required by state law

retained earnings
the cumulative earnings of a company not distributed to stockholders via dividends (C corporations) or distributions (S corporations) but instead retained in the corporation for future investment

deferred taxes
a balance sheet line item unique to C corporations and entities taxed as a C corporation that usually arises due to differences in the treatment of an asset or expense for accounting versus tax purposes because of differences in accounting and tax rules

depreciation expense. Taxable income will correspondingly be higher than accounting net income, resulting in the need for more taxes to be paid than the net income on the income statement would seem to indicate. As the depreciation situation reverses, the deferred tax liability previously created is eliminated over time.

A deferred tax asset is created when an item or situation comes into existence that will reduce a corporation's future taxable income. An example of this would be when a company has suffered a net loss during the current year that it expects to use as a loss carryforward to reduce a future year's taxable income.

Note that the terms "stockholder" and "shareholder" are generally used interchangeably to refer to an individual or an entity that owns a corporation's stock. Best practices suggest selecting and consistently using one term or the other so as not to create unnecessary confusion.

Also note that, while the presentation isn't specific to a corporate balance sheet and can be used by virtually any legal form of business, the liabilities section of our example corporate balance sheet (figure 4.9) is somewhat different from the liabilities sections of the other balance sheets we have looked at thus far (figures 4.5 and 4.6). Specifically, because the corporate balance sheet (figure 4.9) happens to include only one long-term liability, a "total long-term liabilities" subtotal would be redundant and therefore isn't used. The liabilities section of our example multi-member LLC balance sheet (figure 4.6) and the liabilities section of our example corporate balance sheet (figure 4.9) are presented side by side in figure 4.10 in order to clearly illustrate the difference.

Stanwick Enterprises, LLC Liabilities Section of Balance Sheet As of December 31, 2018		The Stanwick Corporation Liabilities Section of Balance Sheet As of December 31, 2018	
Accounts payable	$55,000	Accounts payable	$55,000
Notes payable-bank	10,000	Notes payable-bank	10,000
Taxes payable	4,500	Taxes payable	4,500
Short-term portion of long-term debt	21,000	Short-term portion of long-term debt	21,000
Total current liabilities	$90,500	Total current liabilities	$90,500
Building mortgage payable	185,000	Building mortgage payable	220,000
Equipment loan payable	35,000		
		Total liabilities	$310,500
Total long-term liabilities	220,000		
Total liabilities	$310,500		

FIGURE 4.10. Different presentations of the liabilities section of a balance sheet.

S Corporations—a Truly Hybrid Legal Form

Nowhere more clearly than on its financial statements does an S corporation illustrate how truly hybrid a legal form of business it is. On its balance sheet, an S corporation looks like a C corporation. This is because, like a C corporation, an S corporation issues shares of common stock. Therefore, the equity section of the balance sheet of an S corporation will include line items for common stock and retained earnings. The equity section may also include a line item for paid-in capital in excess of par. The equity section of the balance sheet for an S corporation will not, however, include a line for preferred stock, as S corporations are precluded from issuing preferred stock because they may have only one class of stock and must issue common stock.

In its accounting practices, an S corporation is like a partnership. This is because details regarding the balances of the individual shareholders' capital accounts must be maintained and reported on various required annual individual and summary tax schedules.

On its income statement, an S corporation most closely resembles a typical LLC. The similarity exists because, beyond other considerations, like the typical LLC, an S corporation doesn't pay corporate income tax.

Understanding Owner's Equity and Retained Earnings

Entrepreneurs often fail to understand how much owner's equity and retained earnings can tell a potential investor, lender, or grantor of funds about both the entrepreneurs behind the company and the company itself. Understanding owner's equity and retained earnings begins with understanding how they are calculated. (Note that, for purposes of this discussion, owners' equity and owner's equity are being treated as being the same thing—which they are, except that the first represents the equity of a company with multiple owners and the second represents the equity of a company with one owner.)

In order to determine this year's ending owner's equity balance, one would do the following:

- Begin with last year's ending owner's equity balance.
- Add any equity investment in the company that has occurred during the current year.
- Add the business's net income or deduct the business's net loss for the current year.
- Deduct any distributions paid to the owner during the current year.

To illustrate the point, let's assume the source of the December 31, 2018 owners' equity balance of $306,000 for Stanwick Enterprises, LLC is as follows:

$300,000	(owners' equity as of December 31, 2017)
+ 0	(equity investment in the company during 2018)
+ 126,650	(the business's 2018 net income according to its income statement)
– <u>120,650</u>	(distributions paid to the business's owners during 2018)
$306,000	(owners' equity as of December 31, 2018)

The above information becomes very significant if the owners of Stanwick Enterprises, LLC are seeking outside equity investment in the company in 2019. If a potential investor with access to the financial statements of the company asked its owners if anyone had provided new equity capital to the company in 2018, and the owners said that no one had, the potential investor would be able to figure out that the owners of the company had taken distributions of $120,650 during 2018. In other words, immediately before seeking outside investment in the company, the owners took $120,650 out of the company in the form of distributions. A wise potential investor would likely wonder why the owners aren't choosing to reinvest in this business but are instead seeking outside sources of funding.

Alternatively, in order to determine this year's ending retained earnings balance for a corporation, one would do the following:

- Begin with last year's ending retained earnings balance.
- Add the business's net income or deduct the business's net loss for the current year.
- Deduct any dividends (C corporation) or distributions (S corporation) paid to shareholders during the current year.

Note that any new equity investment in a corporation would affect the common stock account—and could affect the preferred stock or additional paid-in capital accounts—but would not affect the retained earnings account. As an example, let's assume the source of the December 31, 2018 retained earnings balance of $196,000 for the Stanwick Corporation is as follows:

$207,345	(retained earnings as of December 31, 2017)
+ 100,000	(the business's 2018 net income according to its income statement)
– 111,345	(dividends paid during 2018)
$196,000	(retained earnings as of December 31, 2018)

Again, the above information becomes very significant if the company is seeking additional equity investment. A potential investor would be able to tell by looking at the company's December 31, 2017 and December 31, 2018 balance sheets that the company had received no new equity investment in 2018. The potential investor would also be able to deduce, if she had access to the 2018 statement of cash flows for the company, that $111,345 of dividends had been paid to the shareholders of the company during 2018. Depending upon the financial goals of the potential investor, this might encourage or discourage her investment in the company.

The Statement of Cash Flows

The statement of cash flows is the third of the three basic financial statements. It summarizes the cash receipts and cash expenditures of a business over a specified period of time. As with the income statement and balance sheet, before looking at a statement of cash flows, we'll define the key terms typically seen on that statement. A statement of cash flows generally includes the following three major sections:

1. **cash flows from operating activities**, which typically does the following:
   - considers a business's net income or net loss
   - adds back depreciation expense to net income or net loss because depreciation is a noncash expense
   - identifies all the cash received and paid out by the business as a result of its day-to-day operations during a specified period by identifying the dollar change in noncash current asset and current liability balance sheet line items from the beginning of the period to the end of the period
2. **cash flows from investing activities**, which typically includes summary information regarding the purchase or sale of investments in the financial markets, the purchase or sale of fixed assets, the making or collection of loans, and any insurance settlement proceeds related to fixed assets
3. **cash flows from financing activities**, which typically includes summary information regarding the sale or repurchase of stock, the receipt of debt proceeds or the repayment of debt, and the payment of dividends or distributions

cash flows from operating activities
a section of the statement of cash flows that considers a business's net income or net loss, adds back depreciation expense to net income or net loss because depreciation is a noncash expense, and identifies all the cash received and paid out by the business as a result of its day-to-day operations during a specified period by identifying the dollar change in balance sheet line items from the beginning of the period to the end of the period

cash flows from investing activities
a section of the statement of cash flows that typically includes summary information regarding the purchase or sale of investments in the financial markets, the purchase or sale of fixed assets, the making or collection of loans, and any insurance settlement proceeds related to fixed assets

cash flows from financing activities
a section of the statement of cash flows that typically includes summary information regarding the sale or repurchase of stock, the receipt of debt proceeds or the repayment of debt, and the payment of dividends or distributions

The net increase or decrease in cash included on a statement of cash flows represents the overall change in a company's cash balance during the period in question. As illustrated in figure 4.11, the net increase or decrease in cash for the current year, plus the cash balance on the previous balance sheet, equals the cash balance on the current balance sheet.

As further discussed and illustrated in chapters 6 and 7, while potential investors and lenders sometimes require a formal statement of cash flows like the one illustrated in figure 4.11, entrepreneurs often create a simpler version of the statement, called a pro forma reconciliation of cash, to accompany the pro forma balance sheets and income statements they create. Whether looking at a statement of cash flows or a reconciliation of cash, one should be sure to note the major sources of a company's cash receipts. A potential investor's or lender's view of a company receiving most of its cash as a result of the acquisition of new debt is quite different from a potential investor's or lender's view of a company receiving most of its cash as a result of net income from its successful business operations.

Finally, as will be further discussed and illustrated in chapter 6, it should be noted that—depending upon the nature of the business and the industry in which it operates—the financial statements of a business can look quite different from those illustrated in this chapter. As examples to illustrate this point, the financial statements of a CPA firm and a smartphone application business are illustrated in the appendices to chapter 6.

The Stanwick Corporation		
Statement of Cash Flows		
For the Year Ended December 31, 2018		
Cash flows from operating activities:		
Net income		$ 88,655
Adjustments to reconcile net income to net cash flows from operating activities:		
Depreciation expense	$ 3,500	
Increase in accounts receivable	(12,000)	
Increase in inventory	(18,500)	
Increase in accounts payable	8,500	
Increase in notes payable	1,500	
Increase in taxes payable	6,500	
		(10,500)
Net cash flows from operating activities		78,155
Cash flows from investing activities:		
Purchase of building	(150,000)	
Net cash flows from investing activities		(150,000)
Cash flows from financing activities:		
Proceeds from issuance of preferred stock	50,000	
Proceeds from mortgage payable	45,000	
Repayment of bank loan	(22,155)	
Net cash flows from financing activities		72,845
Net increase in cash		1,000
Cash balance, December 31, 2017		3,000
Cash balance, December 31, 2018		$ 4,000

FIGURE 4.11. Example statement of cash flows.

Financial Statements—a Few Words of Caution

A few words of caution are in order with regard to the practice of reviewing financial statements. Generally, we must keep in mind that:

- Accounting general practices and tax rules vary over time, by type of entity, and by industry.
- The values of the assets included on a balance sheet are generally based on those assets' costs.
- The book value (equity section) indicated by the balance sheet of a business rarely reflects the market value of the business.
- Financial statements are created by people—and people are fallible.

First, when reviewing financial statements, we must remember that accounting general practices and tax rules vary over time, by type of entity, and by industry. As a result, in order to avoid serious errors in decision making, we must be sure we understand the rules that apply to the particular financial statements we're reviewing. For example, most companies depreciate their fixed assets differently for accounting purposes than for tax purposes. For both accounting and tax purposes, within certain limits, a company can establish the useful life of its assets and also choose among multiple possible methods of depreciating those assets. Further complicating the depreciation issue is the fact that, over time, the tax depreciation methods available for use by companies—and sometimes required by the IRS to be used by companies—have changed. Before arriving at conclusions about a company's fixed assets, we would obviously want to understand both the company's fixed-asset useful life assumptions and the depreciation methods the company has historically been using for both accounting and tax purposes.

As another example, the financial statements of a nonprofit entity are different from the financial statements of a for-profit entity. Instead of an income statement, nonprofits prepare a statement of activities that typically lists their revenue and expenses, often grouped by mission versus non-mission activities. A nonprofit's statement of financial position is different from that of a for-profit entity because, given that a nonprofit entity has no owners per se, the statement includes no equity section. A nonprofit's statement of financial position instead includes a net assets section that breaks out restricted- versus nonrestricted-use net assets.

As a third example, the inventory on the balance sheets of companies in certain industries (e.g., typically industries involving perishable or time-restricted goods, such as food and designer clothing) tends to be valued using the intuitive first in, first out (FIFO) method of inventory valuation. The FIFO method of inventory valuation generally expenses inventory to cost of goods sold assuming the first inventory item purchased is the first inventory item sold, the second inventory item purchased is the second inventory item sold, and so on.

The inventory on the balance sheets of companies in many other industries is often valued using the last in, first out (LIFO) method of inventory valuation—a method that expenses inventory to cost of goods sold in the exact opposite way the FIFO method does. The LIFO method of inventory valuation expenses inventory to cost of goods sold assuming the most recent inventory item purchased is the most recent inventory item sold, which generally means the inventory included on the balance sheet of a company using the LIFO method is valued using the cost associated with inventory items purchased long ago. As the costs associated with inventory increase or decrease over time, the method of inventory valuation a company uses can significantly affect both the value of the inventory included on a company's balance sheet and the amount of cost of goods sold included on a company's income statement.

Next, when reviewing financial statements, we must remember that the values of the assets included on a balance sheet are generally based on those assets' costs. This means that the value of an asset indicated on a balance sheet may not reflect anything approaching its actual (i.e., market) value, especially when considering accumulated depreciation and other possible adjustments to an asset's value. For example, the building a business purchased 20 years ago that is still in use today is valued on that company's balance sheet at the amount it cost to purchase the building 20 years ago. If the market value of that building today is much higher than what the building cost, the higher value won't be reflected on today's balance sheet. Reductions in the value of an asset below cost are, however, usually reflected on a balance sheet.

Third, when reviewing financial statements, we must remember that, because the assets on the balance sheet are cost based, the equity on the balance sheet is also effectively cost based. The book value (equity section) indicated by the balance sheet of a business therefore rarely reflects the market value of the business. The value of a business may be much more than the equity section of its balance sheet indicates if the market values of the assets on the balance sheet have significantly appreciated since their purchase. Alternatively, the value of a business may be less than the equity section of its balance sheet indicates if, for instance, a major product recall or a lawsuit calls into question the business's ability to continue to operate long term. However, the most common reason the equity section of a balance sheet doesn't reflect the true value of a business is because a balance sheet generally completely ignores the value of the expected future net income associated with a business.

Last, when reviewing financial statements, we must remember that financial statements are created by people. People sometimes make honest errors when creating financial statements. People also sometimes manipulate financial statements to make their companies look more robust in order to win over potential business partners, investors, or lenders. Don't forget the lessons taught by Kenneth Lay (Enron), Bernie Ebbers (WorldCom), and Bernie Madoff. A wise individual reviews the financial statements prepared by others armed with a solid fundamental knowledge of both the nature and limitations of financial statements—and also armed with a healthy dose of skepticism.

Summary

The ability to read and understand financial statements is a critical skill for all people participating in business, including entrepreneurs. The three traditional financial statements an entrepreneur should be able to read and understand are the income statement, the statement of financial position (balance sheet), and the statement of cash flows. In this chapter, we reviewed the fundamentals associated with income statements, balance sheets, and statements of cash flows of a variety of types of entities in detail. Chapter 6 will illustrate and explain how entrepreneurs can, if they desire, create a simpler version of a statement of cash flows, called a pro forma reconciliation of cash, to accompany the pro forma balance sheets and income statements they create.

Financial statements, while key to understanding the performance and financial position of a company, do have limitations:

- Accounting general practices and tax rules vary over time, by type of entity, and by industry. This can make financial statements challenging to understand and complicate meaningful comparisons of the financial statements of different companies.
- The values of the assets included on a balance sheet are generally based on the costs of those assets. This means that the value of an asset indicated on a balance sheet may not reflect anything approaching its actual (i.e., market)

value, especially when considering accumulated depreciation and other allowances and adjustments.

- The book value (equity section) indicated by the balance sheet of a business usually doesn't reflect the market value of the business for two reasons:
  - The assets on the balance sheet are cost based, so the equity on the balance sheet is also effectively cost based.
  - A balance sheet generally completely ignores the value of the future years of net income associated with a business.
- Financial statements are created by people. People sometimes make honest errors when creating financial statements. Dishonest people sometimes manipulate financial statements to make their companies look more robust than they really are. A wise individual reviews the financial statements prepared by others armed with a solid fundamental knowledge of both the nature and limitations of financial statements—and also armed with a healthy dose of skepticism.

Key Terms

accounting information system

accounts payable

accumulated depreciation

asset

audited financial statements

basic accounting equation

cash flows from financing activities

cash flows from investing activities

cash flows from operating activities

compiled financial statements

cost of goods sold

cost of sales

current asset

current liability

deferred taxes

depreciation expense

earnings per share of common stock

equity

fixed assets

gross profit

income statement

interest expense

liability

liquidity (in relation to an asset on a balance sheet)

liquidity (in relation to the general topic of finance)

long-term liability

net fixed assets

net income

net income before income taxes

net sales

operating expenses

operating income

paid-in capital in excess of par

par value

prepaid asset

pro forma financial statements

provision for income taxes

retained earnings

returns and allowances

reviewed financial statements

sales

short-term portion of long-term debt

statement of cash flows

statement of financial position

Review and Discussion Questions

1. Every for-profit business, regardless of its legal form, creates the same basic financial statements. List and describe the three basic financial statements.

2. It is often either necessary or wise for an entrepreneur to use an independent CPA or outside accountant to audit, compile, or review a start-up's financial statements. Define audited, compiled, and reviewed financial statements and explain the differences between them.

3. Answer the following questions about financial statement line items:
   a. What line items are found only on the income statements of C corporations and entities taxed as a C corporation?
   b. What line items are found only on the balance sheets of C and S corporations?

    c. What line items are found only on the balance sheets of C corporations and entities taxed as a C corporation?

    d. What line items are found only on the balance sheets of C corporations?

4. Explain how an S corporation's accounting practices and financial statements illustrate the hybrid nature of that legal form.

5. How is an ending owner's equity balance determined? How is an ending retained earnings balance determined? What's the primary difference between the two calculations?

6. Why should we use caution when making decisions based on a company's financial statements?

Exercises

1. Construct a complete, properly formatted income statement for the year ended December 31, 2019, for ABC Company, an LLC, using the following information:

Utilities expense	$23,000
Equipment rental expense	$25,500
Interest expense	$4,500
Management salaries expense	$100,000
Gross sales	$905,000
Sales and marketing expense	$15,000
Payroll tax expense	$12,300
Sales returns and allowances	$1,500
Cost of goods sold	$567,000
Rent expense	$24,000
Depreciation expense	$3,000

2. Construct a complete, properly formatted balance sheet as of December 31, 2019, for ABC Company, an LLC owned by one individual, using the following information:

Accumulated depreciation	$11,000
Equipment loan	$18,000
Payroll taxes payable	$2,200
Accounts receivable	$91,000
Equipment	$55,000
Office furniture	$12,500
Cash	$6,000
Accounts payable	$33,000
Inventory	$100,000
Sales taxes payable	$5,400
Management salaries payable	$11,400
Computers	$7,500
Equipment rent payable	$1,900
Short-term portion of equipment loan	$1,800

3. Construct a complete, properly formatted income statement for the year ended December 31, 2019, for XYZ Company, a corporation, using the following information:

Utilities expense	$12,000
Insurance expense	$18,500
Interest expense	$5,200
Management salaries expense	$65,000
Payroll tax expense	$17,500
Sales	$775,000
Marketing expense	$26,500
Provision for income taxes	$13,500
Cost of services	$465,000
Rent expense	$40,000
Depreciation expense	$8,000

4. Construct a complete, properly formatted balance sheet as of December 31, 2019, for XYZ Company, a corporation, using the following information:

Accumulated depreciation	$22,400
Equipment loan payable	$10,000
Payroll taxes payable	$1,300
Accounts receivable	$52,000
Building	$75,700
Cash	$5,400
Accounts payable	$13,200
Equipment	$11,800
Inventory	$86,400
Mortgage payable	$48,000
Management salaries payable	$4,800
Common stock	$50,000
Short-term portion of long-term debt	$8,300

5. Answer the following questions using the incomplete statement of cash flows for the Zany Company provided on page 88.

a. If cash is equal to $57,544 at December 31, 2019, what did cash equal at December 31, 2018?

b. If net cash provided by operating activities is $186,448, what is net income?

c. Why is depreciation expense treated as an add back to net income in order to determine net cash provided by operating activities?

The Zany Company Statement of Cash Flows For the Year Ended December 31, 2019		
Cash flows from operating activities		
Net income		
Adjustments to reconcile net income to net cash provided by operating activities:		
Depreciation expense	$ 48,557	
Increase in accounts receivable	(16,321)	
Increase in inventory	(18,500)	
Increase in accounts payable	6,941	
Increase in sales taxes payable	550	
		21,227
Net cash provided by operating activities		186,448
Cash flows from investing activities:		
Acquisition of new facility	(250,000)	
Proceeds from fire insurance settlement	100,000	
Net cash outflow from investing activities		(150,000)
Cash flows from financing activities:		
Proceeds from new facility mortgage	50,000	
Payment of old facility mortgage	(42,155)	
Net cash inflow from financing activities		7,845
Net increase in cash		$ 44,293

6. Using the information provided, determine the amount of cash Ted Herbick, the owner of Herbick Enterprises, LLC, took in the form of distributions from his company in 2019.

Net income for 2019:	$258,500
Owner's equity as of December 31, 2018:	$352,400
Owner's equity as of December 31, 2019:	$445,000
Equity investment during 2019:	$100,000

7. Using the information provided, determine the amount of dividends that were paid to the shareholders of the Zwicker Corporation in 2019.

Net income for 2019:	$358,000
Retained earnings as of December 31, 2018:	$452,000
Retained earnings as of December 31, 2018:	$450,000
Equity investment during 2019:	$250,000

Traditional Financial Statement Analysis and Breakeven Analysis

"Don't ever let your business get ahead of the financial side
of your business. . . . Know your numbers."

— **Tilman J. Fertitta, owner of the Houston Rockets, Golden Nugget Casinos, and Landry's restaurant chain**

Learning Objectives

Be able to perform vertical, horizontal, ratio, and breakeven analysis on the financial statements of a for-profit business.

Be able to draw conclusions and make decisions from the results of vertical, horizontal, ratio, and breakeven analysis.

Introduction

Historical financial statements tell us about the past activities and financial results of a company. Business owners and managers, as well as individuals outside a company, analyze historical financial statements to determine a business's current and potential operational effectiveness, profitability, and cash flows. Historical financial statements are helpful when comparing a company's current performance to two things:

1. its past performance
2. the performance of other companies operating in the same industry

Pro forma financial statements are financial statements created by an entrepreneur that attempt to estimate the future financial results of a company based upon certain identified assumptions. Pro forma financial statements are an entrepreneur's best attempt to predict the future operational effectiveness, profitability, and cash flows of a business, often with the goal of obtaining funding for the business.

In chapter 4, we focused on learning about financial statements that are historical in nature. The preparation of pro forma financial statements will be fully explained and illustrated in chapters 6 and 7. In this chapter we will focus on financial statement analysis, which can involve the use of historical financial statements, pro forma financial statements, or both.

Financial Statement Analysis

Whether financial statement analysis involves the use of historical financial statements, pro forma financial statements, or both, depends upon the purpose of the analysis being undertaken:

- Are we trying to determine the areas in which our business didn't do well in the past? This analysis would involve the use of historical financial statements.
- Are we trying to determine what we can do to improve our company's performance? This analysis would likely involve the use of both historical and pro forma financial statements.
- Are we trying to determine if we should even start a company? This analysis would involve the use of pro forma financial statements.

There are four basic methods of financial statement analysis:

1. vertical
2. horizontal
3. ratio
4. breakeven

An entrepreneur can't fix his business's problems if he doesn't understand what those problems are. Vertical, horizontal, and ratio analysis are the forms of analysis traditionally used to determine which areas within a company are problematic and therefore require close monitoring or adjustment by the business owner.

Breakeven analysis is the form of analysis most relevant to a business owner contemplating adding a new product or service to his company's offerings or an entrepreneur contemplating starting a new venture. Breakeven analysis helps a business owner determine the minimum number of units that must be sold, the minimum revenue that must be brought in, and the minimum price that must be charged in order to make introducing a new product or service—or starting a new business—worthwhile. Understanding the minimum number of units that must be sold, the minimum revenue that must be brought in, and the minimum price that must be charged is obviously quite useful when trying to operate a business. It's even more useful when trying to determine if one should start a business.

To introduce the topic of breakeven, this chapter will illustrate breakeven analysis for a proposed new product line. Chapter 6 will continue the subject of breakeven by illustrating a breakeven analysis for a proposed new business. For now, let's begin our study of financial statement analysis by taking a look at vertical and horizontal analysis.

Vertical and Horizontal Analysis of an Income Statement

Vertical analysis is the process of using a single line item on a financial statement as a constant and determining how all the other line items relate as a percentage of that constant. A vertical analysis of an income statement is typically used to determine how much of a company's net sales (or sales, if there is no line for net sales) is being consumed by each line of the income statement.

If the constant is net sales, then the formula is:

Percentage of net sales = (Amount of applicable income statement line item ÷ Net sales) x 100

Horizontal analysis is a determination of the percentage increase or decrease in each line item on a financial statement from a base time period to a successive time period.

The formula is:

Percentage change = [(New amount − Old amount) ÷ Old amount] x 100

Note: This equation indicates how a percentage change should always be calculated, not just for purposes of doing horizontal analysis.

The income statement in figure 5.1 illustrates both vertical and horizontal analysis.

vertical analysis
the process of using a single line item on a financial statement as a constant and determining how all the other line items relate as a percentage of that constant

horizontal analysis
a determination of the percentage increase or decrease in each line item on a financial statement from a base time period to a successive time period

The Suzanna Jones Company Income Statement For the Years Ended December 31, 2018, and December 31, 2019				
			Vertical Analysis	Horizontal Analysis
	2018	2019	2019	2018-2019
Gross sales	$ 430,125	$ 452,137	101.11%	5.12%
Less: Returns	4,123	4,952	1.11%	20.11%
Net sales	426,002	447,185	100.00%	4.97%
Less: Cost of goods sold	202,221	213,584	47.76%	5.62%
Gross profit	223,781	233,601	52.24%	4.39%
Less: Operating expenses				
Wages and payroll taxes	78,454	82,665	18.49%	5.37%
Rent	24,000	26,000	5.81%	8.33%
Equipment rental	14,955	15,884	3.55%	6.21%
Marketing	15,000	20,010	4.47%	33.40%
Miscellaneous	18,455	19,456	4.35%	5.42%
Total operating expenses	150,864	164,015	36.68%	8.72%
Operating income	72,917	69,586	15.56%	-4.57%
Less: Interest	8,451	7,266	1.62%	-14.02%
Net income	$ 64,466	$ 62,320	13.94%	-3.33%

Figure 5.1. Vertical and horizontal analysis of an income statement.

With regard to the financial statement and financial analysis in figure 5.1, note that:

comparative financial statements
financial statements that present more than one period or date of financial statement information side by side in such a way that the reader can easily compare the different periods or dates

- The financial statement is comparative. **Comparative financial statements** present more than one period or date of financial statement information side by side in such a way that the reader can easily compare the different periods or dates. Note that the most recent financial statement information—the 2019 information in the example provided—may be presented either to the right or to the left of the older information. Determining which column contains the most recent information is one of the first tasks that should be undertaken when studying a comparative financial statement.
- For the vertical analysis only, because every line item on the 2019 income statement is being compared to net sales, the net sales line equals 100 percent. In other words, the item net sales is 100 percent, and vertical analysis determines how much of that 100 percent each line item on the income statement represents.
- For the vertical analysis only, the percentages add and subtract in the same manner as the income statement lines they are associated with add and subtract.

The significant findings associated with the example vertical analysis are that the company's gross profit percentage is about 52 percent and its profit percentage is about 14 percent. These percentages may or may not be good, depending upon the

Entrepreneur *in Action* 5.1

A New Co-Owner of a Business Makes a Misstep

Miranda Esser was a CPA who had recently become a co-owner and the CFO of Bayex Pharmaceuticals, LLC. Miranda's business partners—the founders of the company—were thrilled to finally have an in-house accountant handling all of the accounting and tax demands of their young, mid-sized pharmaceutical firm. Miranda had been with the company for a little less than three months when the CEO and cofounder of the company, Victor Dennison, called a meeting of the top management of Bayex to review the company's most recent operating results.

At the meeting, Miranda handed out copies of all of the company's historical financial statements—the company had been operating just shy of three years—and settled in to listen to Bayex's top managers' comments on the company's financial results. After several comments were made by a few of the company's various executives, Victor looked at Miranda and asked her, "Why is the profitability of the company down this year when sales are up?" Miranda, surprised by the question, responded, "Um, I'm not sure." Victor, who had a reputation for being no nonsense and abrupt—a person who rarely pulled any punches—frowned and asked, "Isn't it your job to be able to answer a question like that? If not, I'm not sure what we're paying you for." Miranda, surprised and hurt, murmured something about not having had enough time. Victor looked at the others in the room in exasperation and said, "This doesn't exactly inspire one's confidence, does it?" Miranda, embarrassed, stood up and said she'd be back to answer Victor's question in just a few minutes. She then walked briskly to her office and quickly performed a horizontal and verti-

cal analysis of the company's most recent two years of financial statements. The reason for this year's decrease in profitability was now clear to her.

Miranda walked back into the meeting, sat down, and waited for an opportunity to speak. Finally, Victor stopped talking, looked at her, and waited. Miranda said, "The most significant increase in expense this past year relates to salesperson salaries and related salesperson expenses." Victor sighed and said, "Well, I think I know what that's about." Miranda and the other members of top management waited to hear more. Victor continued, "At the beginning of last year, our Director of Sales said adding one more salesperson to each state would 'guarantee' an increased level of sales. I guess he wasn't wrong. Bayex's sales are up. The problem seems to be that we clearly aren't achieving enough of an increase in sales to justify the expense of having an extra salesperson in each state. I think we may need to let all of these salespeople go." Miranda, still smarting from being admonished for not doing proper financial analysis, jumped in quickly and said, "Maybe I could run a state-by-state cost-benefit analysis to determine if any of the extra salespeople we hired are worth keeping?" Victor considered this for a moment, nodded, and said, "Good thinking, Miranda. Let's not be as quick to fire these people as we were to hire them. Please do the necessary analysis and report back to us, by the end of the week if possible, which salespeople we should consider keeping versus letting go." Miranda smiled, feeling a bit vindicated, and responded, "I certainly will do that."

performance of the company in the past and whether the company compares favorably or unfavorably to its competitors.

The horizontal analysis presented in combination with the vertical analysis gives us a more complete picture. We can see that returns are increasing faster than sales. We can also see that operating expenses in total and marketing expense in particular are also increasing faster than sales. Finally, we see the effect of these two negative trends on profitability: both operating income and net income are less this year than last year, even though sales have increased.

Overall, the vertical and horizontal analysis in figure 5.1 suggests that the company has issues that are detrimental to its profitability. Knowing where these problems are gives the entrepreneur the ability to do research within his company, find the ultimate source of the problems, and then eradicate the problems. For example, an increase in product returns would suggest the need to take a look at the product itself. Has its quality decreased? Have there been changes to the product that customers don't like? An increase in product returns would also suggest the need to take a look at the company's sales practices and terms of sale. Have sales practices changed such that customers feel pressured to buy a product they really don't want? Or do the terms of sale perhaps allow customers to return the product too easily? Entrepreneur in Action 5.1 further illustrates how vertical and horizontal analysis of an income statement can help business owners find the source of a business's problems so they can fix those problems.

Vertical and Horizontal Analysis of a Balance Sheet

Next, we'll explore vertical and horizontal analysis of a balance sheet. Vertical analysis of a balance sheet is carried out by using total assets as a constant and dividing every figure on the balance sheet by total assets:

Percentage of total assets = (Amount of applicable balance sheet line item ÷ Total assets) x 100

Horizontal analysis of a balance sheet is performed the same way as horizontal analysis of an income statement. The formula remains unchanged:

Percentage change = [(New amount – Old amount) ÷ Old amount] x 100

Figure 5.2 (on page 94) illustrates both vertical and horizontal analysis of a balance sheet.

With regard to the financial statement and financial analysis in figure 5.2, note that:

- For the vertical analysis only, because every line item on the 2019 balance sheet in figure 5.2 is being compared to total assets, the total assets line equals 100 percent. In other words, the item total assets is 100 percent, and vertical analysis determines how much of that 100 percent each line item on the balance sheet represents.
- For the vertical analysis only, because the basic accounting equation tells us that total assets always equals total liabilities and equity, the total liabilities and equity line also equals 100 percent.
- For the vertical analysis only, the percentages add and subtract in the same manner as the balance sheet lines they are associated with add and subtract.

The significant findings associated with the vertical analysis of the example balance sheet are that a powerful majority of the company's assets are fixed assets and that the company's assets are financed two to one by equity versus debt. The indicated percentages may or may not be good, depending upon the nature of the

			Vertical Analysis	Horizontal Analysis
The Suzanna Jones Company Balance Sheet As of December 31, 2018, and December 31, 2019				
	2018	2019	2019	2018–2019
Cash	$ 4,255	$ 5,662	1.53%	33.07%
Accounts receivable	8,451	7,866	2.12%	-6.92%
Inventory	22,587	23,599	6.36%	4.48%
Prepaid insurance	2,534	2,955	0.80%	16.61%
Total current assets	37,827	40,082	10.80%	5.96%
Land	55,000	55,000	14.83%	0.00%
Buildings	174,300	183,764	49.54%	5.43%
Equipment	166,500	166,500	44.88%	0.00%
Less: Accumulated depreciation	69,650	74,387	20.05%	6.80%
Net fixed assets	326,150	330,877	89.20%	1.45%
Total assets	$ 363,977	$ 370,959	100.00%	1.92%
Accounts payable	$16,485	$41,089	11.08%	149.25%
Wages and payroll taxes payable	8,300	17,859	4.81%	115.17%
Short-term portion of mortgage and bank loan payable	6,700	7,981	2.15%	19.12%
Total current liabilities	31,485	66,929	18.04%	112.57%
Mortgage payable	45,000	40,000	10.78%	-11.11%
Bank loan payable	10,000	15,750	4.25%	57.50%
Total long-term liabilities	55,000	55,750	15.03%	1.36%
Total liabilities	86,485	122,679	33.07%	41.85%
Owner's equity	277,492	248,280	66.93%	-10.53%
Total liabilities and owner's equity	$ 363,977	$ 370,959	100.00%	1.92%

Figure 5.2. Vertical and horizontal analysis of a balance sheet.

company in the past and whether the company compares favorably or unfavorably to its competitors.

As was the case with the income statement, the horizontal analysis presented in combination with the vertical analysis gives us a more complete picture of the strengths and weaknesses of the balance sheet. Percentage-wise, the increases in cash and prepaid insurance are significant, but the dollar amount increases are not significant, so little or no effort would likely be put into determining the source of these changes. Much more pressing is the almost 42 percent increase in total liabilities and the large increases in accounts payable, wages and payroll taxes payable, and bank loan payable that appear to have driven that change. Such a large increase in liabilities without a corresponding increase in either sales or assets is a bit disturbing. What happened to the funds that were borrowed? Were they wasted? Were they stolen? Were they put to good use in some way that just isn't showing up yet on the income statement or the balance sheet? A business owner would certainly want to investigate this particular phenomenon.

Ratio Analysis

A ratio is nothing more than a numerical relationship between two variables, often expressed as a decimal or a fraction. **Ratio analysis** is a form of evaluation that uses a variety of ratios to determine the health of a business, especially as that business compares to other firms in the same industry.

The different types of ratios typically used to perform ratio analysis include:

- liquidity ratios—ratios that indicate how much of a firm's current assets are available to meet short-term creditors' claims
- activity ratios—ratios that indicate how effectively a business is managing its assets
- leverage, or debt, ratios—ratios that indicate the role of debt in financing the activities of a business
- profitability ratios—ratios that help potential investors and creditors determine how much of an investment will be returned each year via the earnings of a business

Our discussion of ratio analysis will focus only on the ratios pertinent to a typical young venture. We'll begin with liquidity ratios.

ratio analysis
a form of evaluation that uses a variety of ratios to determine the health of a business, especially as that business compares to other firms in the same industry

Liquidity Ratios

While not technically a ratio, working capital is probably one of the most common ways to initially evaluate the financial health of a company. Working capital is the capital required to sustain operations and support business growth after a company's start-up phase.

Working capital is calculated by subtracting a company's current liabilities from its current assets, as follows:

Working capital = Current assets – Current liabilities

Positive working capital is an indicator that a company has the ability to pay its obligations in the short run. Negative working capital indicates a company faces short-term challenges with regard to paying its bills. Figure 5.3 (on page 96) presents the same balance sheet information included in figure 5.2. The total current assets and total current liabilities amounts as of December 31, 2019, are highlighted.

Using the highlighted amounts, we can determine working capital as of December 31, 2019, as follows:

Working capital = $40,082 – $66,929
              = ($26,847)

Working capital of ($26,847) suggests that The Suzanna Jones Company will likely soon be challenged to pay its bills.

Like working capital, the **current ratio** is an indicator of a company's ability to pay its obligations in the short run. The current ratio is calculated by dividing a company's current assets by its current liabilities:

Current ratio = Current assets ÷ Current liabilities

A current ratio of less than one indicates a company faces short-term challenges with regard to paying its bills. Continuing to use the balance sheet in figure 5.3, we can calculate the current ratio as of December 31, 2019, as follows:

Current ratio = $40,082 ÷ $66,929
            = 0.599

current ratio
a ratio that indicates a company's ability to pay its obligations in the short run

The Suzanna Jones Company Balance Sheet As of December 31, 2018, and December 31, 2019		
	2018	2019
Cash	$ 4,255	$ 5,662
Accounts receivable	8,451	7,866
Inventory	22,587	23,599
Prepaid insurance	2,534	2,955
Total current assets	37,827	40,082
Land	55,000	55,000
Buildings	174,300	183,764
Equipment	166,500	166,500
Less: Accumulated depreciation	79,650	74,387
Net fixed assets	316,150	330,877
Total assets	$ 353,977	$ 370,959
Accounts payable	$ 16,485	$ 41,089
Wages and payroll taxes payable	8,300	17,859
Short-term portion of mortgage and bank loan payable	6,700	7,981
Total current liabilities	31,485	66,929
Mortgage payable	45,000	40,000
Bank loan payable	10,000	15,750
Total long-term liabilities	55,000	55,750
Total liabilities	86,485	122,679
Owner's equity	267,492	248,280
Total liabilities and owner's equity	$ 353,977	$370,959

Figure 5.3. Location of total current assets and total current liabilities on a balance sheet.

Concurring with the working capital calculation of ($26,847), the current ratio of 0.599 suggests that The Suzanna Jones Company will likely soon be challenged to pay its bills.

Activity Ratios

Activity ratios indicate how effectively a business is managing its assets. Accounts receivable is one of the largest assets on the balance sheet of many companies. Accounts receivable represent the amounts customers owe a company related to their purchases from that company utilizing the credit or trade credit offered by that company. A customer purchase using a credit card issued by a financial institution, a bank credit card branded Mastercard or Visa, for example, doesn't represent a true accounts receivable to a business. This is because purchases utilizing these types of credit cards are more or less immediately converted by a business into cash at the business's local bank. True accounts receivable represent the amounts customers owe a company because that company has approved the customer to purchase from them on credit, up to an established credit limit, subject to the specific credit terms developed by that company.

The **accounts receivable turnover ratio** allows us to determine how fast a company is turning its credit sales into cash. The ratio involves two formulas:

Accounts receivable turnover = Credit sales ÷ Average net accounts receivable

where

Average net accounts receivable = (Beginning net accounts receivable + ending net accounts receivable) ÷ 2

A special note regarding reserve for bad debts: Average net accounts receivable refers to average accounts receivable net of a reserve for bad debts. When a company can determine, based on its history, that a certain percentage of its accounts receivable are typically not collectible—or when a company has identified specific individual accounts receivable that are likely not collectible—the company should establish a **reserve for bad debts**. A reserve for bad debts is an estimate of the amount of the accounts receivable included on the balance sheet that won't be collected, typically included on the balance sheet as a contra-asset account to accounts receivable—similar to the way accumulated depreciation is presented on the balance sheet as a contra-asset to one or more fixed assets—as illustrated here:

Accounts receivable	$8,026
Less: Reserve for bad debts	160
Net accounts receivable	$7,866

If a reserve for bad debts is insignificant, as in the example above, it may not warrant a separate line item on the balance sheet, and the accounts receivable indicated on the balance sheet might, in fact, technically be net accounts receivable. In other cases, as in the case of a start-up, there may be no history with which to estimate a reserve for bad debts, so determination of the item is left to a future time when a reasonable estimate can be made. An insignificant reserve for bad debts like the one in the example above is typically created or increased via a charge to miscellaneous expense. A reduction in the reserve for bad debts would similarly result in a decrease in miscellaneous expense.

If a reserve for bad debts is significant (i.e., significant as a percentage of total accounts receivable), a company may want to more methodically track the amount of accounts receivable written off and expected to be written off. The creation and subsequent adjustment in amount of a significant reserve for bad debts would likely warrant the creation and subsequent adjustment in amount of a bad debt expense account rather than the miscellaneous expense account.

Figure 5.4 (on page 98) shows the balance sheet and income statement presented earlier, but with the amounts for accounts receivable and 2019 net sales highlighted.

Let's use the highlighted amounts and assume 20 percent of 2019 net sales are credit sales:

Credit sales = $447,185 x 0.20
= $89,437

Average net accounts receivable = (8,451 + $7,866) ÷ 2
= $8,158.50

Accounts receivable turnover = $89,437 ÷ $8,158.50
= 10.96

An accounts receivable turnover of 10.96 means that, on average, the company turned its accounts receivable into cash 10.96 times during 2019.

Accounts receivable turnover becomes more meaningful when it's translated into days. The formal name for the average number of days it takes a firm to collect

accounts receivable turnover ratio
a ratio that indicates how fast a company is turning its credit sales into cash

reserve for bad debts
an estimate of the amount of the accounts receivable included on the balance sheet that won't be collected, typically included on a balance sheet as a contra-asset account to accounts receivable

The Suzanna Jones Company Balance Sheet As of December 31, 2018, and December 31, 2019	2018	2019
Cash	$ 4,255	$ 5,662
Accounts receivable	8,451	7,866
Inventory	22,587	23,599
Prepaid insurance	2,534	2,955
Total current assets	37,827	40,082
Land	55,000	55,000
Buildings	174,300	183,764
Equipment	166,500	166,500
Less: Accumulated depreciation	79,650	74,387
Net fixed assets	316,150	330,877
Total assets	$ 353,977	$ 370,959
Accounts payable	$ 16,485	$ 41,089
Wages and payroll taxes payable	8,300	17,859
Short-term portion of mortgage and bank loan payable	6,700	7,981
Total current liabilities	31,485	66,929
Mortgage payable	45,000	40,000
Bank loan payable	10,000	15,750
Total long-term liabilities	55,000	55,750
Total liabilities	86,485	122,679
Owner's equity	267,492	248,280
Total liabilities and owner's equity	$ 353,977	$ 370,959

The Suzanna Jones Company Income Statement For the Years Ended December 31, 2018, and December 31, 2019	2018	2019
Gross sales	$ 430,125	$ 452,137
Less: Returns	4,123	4,952
Net sales	426,002	447,185
Less: Cost of goods sold	202,221	213,584
Gross profit	223,781	233,601
Less: Operating expenses		
Wages and payroll taxes	78,454	82,665
Rent	24,000	26,000
Equipment rental	14,955	15,884
Marketing	15,000	20,010
Miscellaneous	18,455	19,456
Total operating expenses	150,864	164,015
Operating income	72,917	69,586
Less: Interest	8,451	7,266
Net income	$ 64,466	$ 62,320

Figure 5.4. Location of accounts receivable and net sales on financial statements.

average collection period
the average number of days it takes a firm to collect its accounts receivable

its accounts receivable is the **average collection period**. The formula for the average collection period is as follows:

Average collection period = Days per year ÷ Accounts receivable turnover

Extending our example above, we can calculate the following:

Average collection period = 365 ÷ 10.96
= 33.3 days

Is 33.3 days good or bad? The answer to that question depends upon the terms for payment a company has stated to its customers. If the terms for payment are 45 days, then a 33.3-day average collection period is good because it means customers are, on average, paying the company early. However, if the payment terms are 30 days, then a 33.3-day average collection period indicates that some customers are paying late—and that's a situation that should be investigated and corrected.

inventory turnover ratio
a ratio that indicates how many times per year, on average, a company sells—and therefore must replace—all of its inventory

The **inventory turnover ratio** suggests how fast a firm is moving its inventory. It indicates how many times per year, on average, a company sells—and therefore must replace—all of its inventory.

The ratio involves two formulas:

Inventory turnover = Cost of goods sold ÷ Average inventory at cost

where

Average inventory = (Beginning inventory + Ending inventory) ÷ 2

Figure 5.5 shows the same balance sheet and income statement we've been using, but now the dollar amounts for inventory and 2019 cost of goods sold are highlighted.

Using the highlighted amounts, we can determine inventory turnover as follows:

$$\text{Average inventory} = (\$22{,}587 + \$23{,}599) \div 2$$
$$= \$23{,}093$$

$$\text{Inventory turnover} = \$213{,}584 \div \$23{,}093$$
$$= 9.25$$

An inventory turnover of 9.25 means the company sold—and had to replace—its inventory, on average, 9.25 times during 2019.

The Suzanna Jones Company Balance Sheet As of December 31, 2018, and December 31, 2019			The Suzanna Jones Company Income Statement For the Years Ended December 31, 2018, and December 31, 2019		
	2018	2019		2018	2019
Cash	$ 4,255	$ 5,662	Gross sales	$ 430,125	$ 452,137
Accounts receivable	8,451	7,866	Less: Returns	4,123	4,952
Inventory	22,587	23,599	Net sales	426,002	447,185
Prepaid insurance	2,534	2,955	Less: Cost of goods sold	202,221	213,584
Total current assets	37,827	40,082	Gross profit	223,781	233,601
			Less: Operating expenses		
Land	55,000	55,000	Wages and payroll taxes	78,454	82,665
Buildings	174,300	183,764	Rent	24,000	26,000
Equipment	166,500	166,500	Equipment rental	14,955	15,884
Less: Accumulated			Marketing	15,000	20,010
depreciation	79,650	74,387	Miscellaneous	18,455	19,456
Net fixed assets	316,150	330,877	Total operating expenses	150,864	164,015
			Operating income	72,917	69,586
Total assets	$353,977	$370,959	Less: Interest	8,451	7,266
			Net income	$ 64,466	$ 62,320
Accounts payable	$ 16,485	$ 41,089			
Wages and payroll taxes payable	8,300	17,859			
Short-term portion of mortgage and bank loan payable	6,700	7,981			
Total current liabilities	31,485	66,929			
Mortgage payable	45,000	40,000			
Bank loan payable	10,000	15,750			
Total long-term liabilities	55,000	55,750			
Total liabilities	86,485	122,679			
Owner's equity	267,492	248,280			
Total liabilities and owner's equity	$353,977	$370,959			

Figure 5.5. Location of inventory and cost of goods sold on financial statements.

Like accounts receivable turnover, inventory turnover becomes more meaningful when it's translated into days:

365 days per year ÷ Inventory turnover of 9.25 = 39.46

On average, this company sold—and had to replace—its inventory approximately every 39 days in 2019. This is good information to know when negotiating terms with vendors.

Leverage Ratios

debt-to-equity ratio

a ratio that indicates what percentage of a business's assets are financed with debt compared to equity

Leverage, or debt, ratios indicate the role of debt in financing the activities of a business. The **debt-to-equity ratio** indicates what percentage of a business's assets are financed with debt compared to equity. The formula is as follows:

Debt to equity = Total liabilities ÷ Equity

Figure 5.6 presents the same balance sheet we've been using. This time, the amounts for total liabilities and equity as of December 31, 2019, are highlighted.

The Suzanna Jones Company Balance Sheet As of December 31, 2018, and December 31, 2019		
	2018	2019
Cash	$ 4,255	$ 5,662
Accounts receivable	8,451	7,866
Inventory	22,587	23,599
Prepaid insurance	2,534	2,955
Total current assets	37,827	40,082
Land	55,000	55,000
Buildings	174,300	183,764
Equipment	166,500	166,500
Less: Accumulated depreciation	79,650	74,387
Net fixed assets	316,150	330,877
Total assets	$353,977	$370,959
Accounts payable	$16,485	$41,089
Wages and payroll taxes payable	8,300	17,859
Short-term portion of mortgage and bank loan payable	6,700	7,981
Total current liabilities	31,485	66,929
Mortgage payable	45,000	40,000
Bank loan payable	10,000	15,750
Total long-term liabilities	55,000	55,750
Total liabilities	86,485	122,679
Owner's equity	267,492	248,280
Total liabilities and owner's equity	$353,977	$370,959

Figure 5.6. Location of total liabilities and equity on a balance sheet.

Using the highlighted numbers, we can calculate the debt-to-equity ratio as follows:

$$\text{Debt to equity} = \$122{,}679 \div \$248{,}280$$
$$= 0.494$$

A debt-to-equity ratio of 0.494 means the company is financed by roughly $0.49 of debt for every dollar of equity.

The **debt-to-total assets ratio** indicates what percentage of a business's assets are owned by its creditors. The formula is as follows:

debt-to-total assets ratio
a ratio that indicates what percentage of a business's assets are owned by its creditors

$$\text{Debt to total assets} = \text{Total liabilities} \div \text{Total assets}$$

Figure 5.7 shows our same balance sheet for The Suzanna Jones Company. This time, the amounts for total assets and total liabilities as of December 31, 2019, are highlighted.

Using the highlighted amounts, we can calculate the debt-to-total assets ratio as follows:

$$\text{Debt to total assets} = \$122{,}679 \div \$370{,}959$$
$$= 0.331$$

The Suzanna Jones Company Balance Sheet As of December 31, 2018, and December 31, 2019		
	2018	2019
Cash	$ 4,255	$ 5,662
Accounts receivable	8,451	7,866
Inventory	22,587	23,599
Prepaid insurance	2,534	2,955
Total current assets	37,827	40,082
Land	55,000	55,000
Buildings	174,300	183,764
Equipment	166,500	166,500
Less: Accumulated depreciation	79,650	74,387
Net fixed assets	316,150	330,877
Total assets	$ 353,977	$ 370,959
Accounts payable	$16,485	$41,089
Wages and payroll taxes payable	8,300	17,859
Short-term portion of mortgage and bank loan payable	6,700	7,981
Total current liabilities	31,485	66,929
Mortgage payable	45,000	40,000
Bank loan payable	10,000	15,750
Total long-term liabilities	55,000	55,750
Total liabilities	86,485	122,679
Owner's equity	267,492	248,280
Total liabilities and owner's equity	$ 353,977	$ 370,959

Figure 5.7. Location of total assets and total liabilities on a balance sheet.

The Suzanna Jones Company Income Statement For the Years Ended December 31, 2018, and December 31, 2019		
	2018	2019
Gross sales	$ 430,125	$ 452,137
Less: Returns	4,123	4,952
Net sales	426,002	447,185
Less: Cost of goods sold	202,221	213,584
Gross profit	223,781	233,601
Less: Operating expenses		
Wages and payroll taxes	78,454	82,665
Rent	24,000	26,000
Equipment rental	14,955	15,884
Marketing	15,000	20,010
Miscellaneous	18,455	19,456
Total operating expenses	150,864	164,015
Operating income	72,917	69,586
Less: Interest	8,451	7,266
Net income	$ 64,466	$ 62,320

Figure 5.8. Location of operating income and interest expense on an income statement.

A debt-to-total assets ratio of 0.331 means debt finances approximately 33 percent of the company's assets.

times-interest-earned ratio
a ratio that illustrates the relationship between the amount of interest a company must pay its creditors on an annual basis and a company's annual operating income

The **times-interest-earned ratio** illustrates the relationship between the amount of interest a company must pay its creditors on an annual basis and a company's annual operating income. Here's the formula:

Times interest earned = Operating income ÷ Interest

Figure 5.8 shows The Suzanna Jones Company's income statement with the amounts for 2019 operating income and interest highlighted.

Inserting the highlighted amounts into our equation, we get the following:

Times interest earned = $69,586 ÷ $7,266
= 9.58

A times-interest-earned ratio of 9.58 tells lenders that the company earned enough operating income to pay its interest expense not just once, but if needed, the company could actually have paid it 9.58 times. This suggests the company may be able to afford to take on more debt. The ability to make the interest payments on debt is an absolute minimum standard most lenders review annually.

Profitability Ratios

Profitability ratios help potential investors and creditors determine how much of an investment will be returned each year via the earnings of a business. The **gross margin** is the percentage of each dollar of net sales (or sales, if there is no net sales amount) that remains after cost of goods sold has been considered. The formula is as follows:

gross margin
the percentage of each dollar of net sales (or sales, if there is no net sales amount) that remains after cost of goods sold has been considered

Gross margin = Gross profit ÷ Net sales

Figure 5.9 shows our example income statement with the amounts we need to determine gross margin for 2019 highlighted.

The Suzanna Jones Company Income Statement For the Years Ended December 31, 2018, and December 31, 2019		
	2018	2019
Gross sales	$ 430,125	$ 452,137
Less: Returns	4,123	4,952
Net sales	426,002	447,185
Less: Cost of goods sold	202,221	213,584
Gross profit	223,781	233,601
Less: Operating expenses		
Wages and payroll taxes	78,454	82,665
Rent	24,000	26,000
Equipment rental	14,955	15,884
Marketing	15,000	20,010
Miscellaneous	18,455	19,456
Total operating expenses	150,864	164,015
Operating income	72,917	69,586
Less: Interest	8,451	7,266
Net income	$ 64,466	$ 62,320

Figure 5.9. Location of net sales and gross profit on an income statement.

Inserting the highlighted amounts into the equation, we get the following:

Gross margin = $233,601 ÷ $447,185

= 0.522

= 52.2%

A gross margin of 52.2 percent means approximately $0.52 of every $1 of net sales equals gross profit.

The **profit margin** is the percentage of each dollar of net sales (or sales, if there is no net sales amount) that remains after all expenses, including interest and taxes, have been considered. To determine profit margin, use this formula:

Profit margin = Net income ÷ Net sales

profit margin
the percentage of each dollar of net sales (or sales, if there is no net sales amount) that remains after all expenses, including interest and taxes, have been considered

The Suzanna Jones Company Income Statement For the Years Ended December 31, 2018, and December 31, 2019		
	2018	2019
Gross sales	$ 430,125	$ 452,137
Less: Returns	4,123	4,952
Net sales	426,002	447,185
Less: Cost of goods sold	202,221	213,584
Gross profit	223,781	233,601
Less: Operating expenses		
Wages and payroll taxes	78,454	82,665
Rent	24,000	26,000
Equipment rental	14,955	15,884
Marketing	15,000	20,010
Miscellaneous	18,455	19,456
Total operating expenses	150,864	164,015
Operating income	72,917	69,586
Less: Interest	8,451	7,266
Net income	$ 64,466	$ 62,320

Figure 5.10. Location of net sales and net income on an income statement.

Figure 5.10 (on page 103) highlights the data we need to determine the profit margin for 2019 for The Suzanna Jones Company.

Inserting the highlighted numbers into the equation, we get the following:

$$\text{Profit margin} = \$62{,}320 \div 447{,}185$$
$$= 0.139$$
$$= 13.9\%$$

A profit margin of 13.9 percent means approximately $0.14 of every $1 of net sales equals profit.

The **return-on-assets ratio (ROA)** (also referred to as the return-on-investment ratio [ROI]) tells us how much profit a firm is earning on its assets. It's calculated as a percentage of those assets and involves two formulas:

$$\text{Return on assets} = \text{Net income} \div \text{Average total assets}$$

where

$$\text{Average total assets} = (\text{Beginning total assets} + \text{Ending total assets}) \div 2$$

Figure 5.11 presents our example balance sheet and income statement with the information we need to calculate 2019 return on assets highlighted.

return-on-assets ratio

a ratio that indicates how much profit a firm is earning on its assets, calculated as a percentage of those assets; sometimes referred to as ROA ratio, also called return-on-investment (ROI) ratio

The Suzanna Jones Company Balance Sheet As of December 31, 2018, and December 31, 2019	2018	2019
Cash	$ 4,255	$ 5,662
Accounts receivable	8,451	7,866
Inventory	22,587	23,599
Prepaid insurance	2,534	2,955
Total current assets	37,827	40,082
Land	55,000	55,000
Buildings	174,300	183,764
Equipment	166,500	166,500
Less: Accumulated depreciation	79,650	74,387
Net fixed assets	316,150	330,877
Total assets	$ 353,977	$ 370,959
Accounts payable	$ 16,485	$ 41,089
Wages and payroll taxes payable	8,300	17,859
Short-term portion of mortgage and bank loan payable	6,700	7,981
Total current liabilities	31,485	66,929
Mortgage payable	45,000	40,000
Bank loan payable	10,000	15,750
Total long-term liabilities	55,000	55,750
Total liabilities	86,485	122,679
Owner's equity	267,492	248,280
Total liabilities and owner's equity	$ 353,977	$ 370,959

The Suzanna Jones Company Income Statement For the Years Ended December 31, 2018, and December 31, 2019	2018	2019
Gross sales	$ 430,125	$ 452,137
Less: Returns	4,123	4,952
Net sales	426,002	447,185
Less: Cost of goods sold	202,221	213,584
Gross profit	223,781	233,601
Less: Operating expenses		
Wages and payroll taxes	78,454	82,665
Rent	24,000	26,000
Equipment rental	14,955	15,884
Marketing	15,000	20,010
Miscellaneous	18,455	19,456
Total operating expenses	150,864	164,015
Operating income	72,917	69,586
Less: Interest	8,451	7,266
Net income	$ 64,466	$ 62,320

Figure 5.11. Location of total assets and net income on financial statements.

Inserting the highlighted amounts into the equations, we get the following:

Average total assets = ($353,977 + $370,959) ÷ 2

= $362,468

Return on assets = $62,320 ÷ $362,468

= 0.1719

= 17.19%

A return on assets of 17.19 percent means the company, on average, generates about $0.17 of profit for every $1 of assets it holds.

The **return-on-equity ratio (ROE)** indicates how much profit a firm is earning on the amounts invested in the company—and the profits retained in the company— by the company's owners. It's calculated as a percentage of the company's equity using the following formulas:

Return on equity = Net income ÷ Average equity

where

Average equity = (Beginning equity + Ending equity) ÷ 2

return-on-equity ratio
a ratio that indicates how much profit a firm is earning on the amounts invested in the company—and the profits retained in the company—by the company's owners, calculated as a percentage of the company's equity; sometimes referred to as ROE ratio

The Suzanna Jones Company Balance Sheet As of December 31, 2018, and December 31, 2019		
	2018	2019
Cash	$ 4,255	$ 5,662
Accounts receivable	8,451	7,866
Inventory	22,587	23,599
Prepaid insurance	2,534	2,955
Total current assets	37,827	40,082
Land	55,000	55,000
Buildings	174,300	183,764
Equipment	166,500	166,500
Less: Accumulated depreciation	79,650	74,387
Net fixed assets	316,150	330,877
Total assets	$ 353,977	$ 370,959
Accounts payable	$ 16,485	$ 41,089
Wages and payroll taxes payable	8,300	17,859
Short-term portion of mortgage and bank loan payable	6,700	7,981
Total current liabilities	31,485	66,929
Mortgage payable	45,000	40,000
Bank loan payable	10,000	15,750
Total long-term liabilities	55,000	55,750
Total liabilities	86,485	122,679
Owner's equity	267,492	248,280
Total liabilities and owner's equity	$ 353,977	$ 370,959

The Suzanna Jones Company Income Statement For the Years Ended December 31, 2018, and December 31, 2019		
	2018	2019
Gross sales	$ 430,125	$ 452,137
Less: Returns	4,123	4,952
Net sales	426,002	447,185
Less: Cost of goods sold	202,221	213,584
Gross profit	223,781	233,601
Less: Operating expenses		
Wages and payroll taxes	78,454	82,665
Rent	24,000	26,000
Equipment rental	14,955	15,884
Marketing	15,000	20,010
Miscellaneous	18,455	19,456
Total operating expenses	150,864	164,015
Operating income	72,917	69,586
Less: Interest	8,451	7,266
Net income	$ 64,466	$ 62,320

Figure 5.12. Location of equity and net income on financial statements.

Figure 5.12 (on page 105) shows our example balance sheet and income statement with the beginning equity, ending equity, and 2019 net income highlighted.

Inserting the highlighted amounts into our formulas, we get the following:

$$\text{Average equity} = (\$267{,}492 + \$248{,}280) \div 2$$
$$= \$257{,}886$$

$$\text{Return on equity} = \$62{,}320 \div \$257{,}886$$
$$= 0.2417$$
$$= 24.17\%$$

A return on equity of 24.17 percent means the company generates approximately $0.24 of profit on every $1 of equity retained in the company by its owner.

Vertical, Horizontal, and Ratio Analysis—Resources and Best Practices

The purpose of doing vertical, horizontal, and ratio analysis is to compare your company's most recent performance against its past performance and the performance of other companies in your industry. You may be able to compare your company to friendly, privately held competitor companies that will readily share their financial information with you, but this is unlikely. In most cases, you'll have to look elsewhere for financial results against which to compare your company.

Good source publications for industry-specific financial ratios are available online and at libraries. Here are some of the best sources:

- Yahoo Industry Center (free access via the internet—a good place to start)
- IBISWorld
- Bizminer
- *Almanac of Business and Industrial Financial Ratios*
- *Industry Norms & Key Business Ratios* (Dun & Bradstreet)
- Value Line Investment Survey
- S&P Capital IQ
- Mergent Online

Additional sources that are also good:

- annual reports of publicly held companies
- trade journals relevant to your company's industry
- general business and industry publications

Vertical, horizontal, and ratio analysis are tools that allow an owner-manager to identify issues of concern regarding a company's performance so the owner can determine and implement a course of corrective action. Vertical, horizontal, and ratio analysis also form a basis for establishing a company's current and future financial standards and goals.

When performing financial statement analysis, it's important to always use a combination of vertical, horizontal, and ratio analysis in order to obtain a clear and complete picture of an individual firm's performance. It's also important to remember to compare a company's performance with competitor and industry information from more than one source because firm size, the financial information included, and how that information is compiled will vary by source.

Breakeven Analysis

For a business, **breakeven** is the point at which that business's net income equals zero. Chapter 1 noted that the rate of new business failure would likely be significantly lower if every entrepreneur took the time to do a breakeven analysis before starting a business. A breakeven analysis for a proposed new business will be illustrated in chapter 6.

For a product line, breakeven is the point at which that product line's net income equals zero. It was noted earlier in this chapter that breakeven analysis helps a business owner determine the minimum number of units that must be sold, the minimum revenue that must be brought in, and the minimum price that must be charged in order to make introducing a new product or service worthwhile. If a business owner determines that his business can't produce enough product, sell enough product, or charge enough for a product so as not to lose money on that product, the decision of whether or not to introduce the product becomes a pretty simple one. Breakeven analysis involves three formulas:

1. Breakeven sales units = Total fixed costs ÷ Unit contribution

   where

   Unit contribution = Price – Variable cost per unit

2. Breakeven revenue = Total fixed costs ÷ Gross margin

   where

   Gross margin = Gross profit ÷ Net sales

   or

   Gross margin = Unit contribution ÷ Price

3. Breakeven price = Fixed cost per unit + Variable cost per unit

   where

   Fixed cost per unit = Fixed costs ÷ Units

Breakeven sales units equals the number of units that must be sold over an indicated period of time in order to not lose money. **Breakeven revenue** equals the amount of revenue that must be brought in over an indicated period of time in order to not lose money. **Breakeven price** equals the minimum price at which a product or service must be sold—under a given set of cost and sales unit conditions—in order to not lose money.

To illustrate breakeven calculations, let's assume Suzanna Jones, whose company has been featured thus far in this chapter, manufactures and sells eclectic apparel in the state of New York. Let's further assume that Lynn Graham, Jones's friend who lives in Arizona, is considering selling Jones's line of dresses at her upscale boutique. Graham recently read an outstanding book on entrepreneurial finance, so she understands the importance of doing breakeven calculations to assess the financial feasibility of adding a new product line before she actually begins taking the steps to add that product line.

The first thing Graham will need to do is determine the variable and fixed costs associated with adding the new product line, likely by talking with Jones, other individuals who already sell Jones's line of dresses, and anyone else who becomes a relevant source of information as a result of those conversations.

breakeven
the point at which the net income of a business, or a selected segment of a business (e.g., a product line), equals zero

breakeven sales units
the number of units that must be sold over an indicated period of time in order to not lose money

breakeven revenue
the amount of revenue that must be brought in over an indicated period of time in order to not lose money

breakeven price
the minimum price at which a product or service must be sold—under a given set of cost and sales unit conditions—in order to not lose money

variable cost
a cost that changes in total with a change in the volume of production or sales, but is generally fixed on a per-unit basis

fixed cost
a cost that remains the same amount in total over a specified period of time

mixed cost
a cost that includes elements of both variable and fixed costs

A **variable cost** is a cost that changes in total with a change in the volume of production or sales, but is generally fixed on a per-unit basis. For example, if each turtleneck sweater a company produces requires $6.53 of material, $6.53 is a variable cost associated with producing the turtleneck sweater. If a company produces and sells 10 sweaters this month, the variable cost per unit for material is still $6.53, but the total variable cost for material—known from here forward as cost of goods sold (COGS)—is $65.30.

A **fixed cost** is a cost that remains the same amount in total over a specified period of time. For example, a company's monthly rent of $500, as specified by the company's lease, is a fixed cost. A change in the company's level of production or sales doesn't increase or decrease the monthly rent.

A **mixed cost** is a cost that includes elements of both variable and fixed costs. An example of a mixed cost might be a water bill that includes a fixed charge per month for use of the city sewer system and a charge for water based on the actual amount of water used. For purposes of breakeven analysis, a mixed cost is separated into its variable and fixed elements. The variable portion of the cost is grouped with the other variable costs. The fixed portion of the cost is grouped with the other fixed costs.

Note that, for purposes of breakeven analysis, all costs are ultimately categorized as being either fixed or variable. We categorize every cost as being either fixed or variable for purposes of breakeven analysis because—on both a total and per-unit basis—fixed and variable costs act exactly opposite of each other in response to a change in the number of units produced or sold.

Returning to our example, let's assume that Graham negotiates with Jones to buy each dress at a wholesale price of $33 and pay $1 per dress for shipping. Let's further assume that, after talking with her customers, her employees, and Jones, Graham decides that she and her employees will sell each dress at the suggested retail price of $100 and Graham will pay her employees a sales commission equal to 10 percent of suggested retail price. The only other costs that will vary directly with sales will be the cost of the high-end boutique bags and ribbons Graham and her employees use to package customer purchases—the cost of such being $1 per unit of apparel.

Based on the above information, the estimated total variable cost associated with each unit of apparel purchased from Jones will be $45, calculated in figure 5.13.

Next, Graham will want to calculate unit contribution. Unit contribution is the amount of the sales price left over after applicable variable costs have been considered. The formula for unit contribution, therefore, is as follows:

Unit contribution = Price – Variable cost per unit

Knowing her expected sales price per unit is $100, Graham can determine the unit contribution for each item of apparel to be purchased from Jones. See figure 5.14.

After talking with Jones and some individuals who already sell Jones's line of dresses, Graham determines that she will need to rent some special clothing racks and shelving to properly showcase the dresses. These rentals are the only new fixed costs Graham's business will incur directly related to the proposed new product line. However, Graham would like the new product line to also cover $5,000 of her business's overall fixed costs. In other words, Graham is planning to allocate $5,000 of the annual fixed costs of her business to the new product line. The total annual fixed

Cost per unit of apparel	$ 33.00
Sales commission per unit	10.00
Shipping per unit	1.00
Boutique wrap per unit	1.00
Total variable cost per unit	$ 45.00

Figure 5.13. Calculation of total variable cost per unit for a proposed new product line.

Price	$ 100.00
Less: Variable cost per unit	45.00
Unit contribution	$ 55.00

Figure 5.14. Calculation of unit contribution for a proposed new product line.

costs the proposed new product line must then cover amount to $6,800 per year, as calculated in figure 5.15.

Note that a new product line—or any new product or service being evaluated using breakeven analysis—may have direct fixed costs, allocated fixed costs, both direct and allocated fixed costs, or neither type of fixed cost. Allocated fixed costs are generally allocated at the discretion of the business owner.

At this point, Graham has all the information she needs to calculate breakeven sales units:

Breakeven sales units = Total fixed costs ÷ Unit contribution

= $6,800 ÷ $55

= 123.64 = 124 units

Note that when calculating breakeven sales units, one must always round up to the next whole unit. (No one wants to buy 0.64 [64 percent] of a dress.) The above calculation indicates that Graham's shop needs to sell 124 units of the new product line each year in order to not lose money on the proposed new product line.

Because Graham has negotiated the same price for every unit of the new apparel to be purchased—and because she intends to sell every unit of that apparel for the same price—she can perform the following simple calculation to determine breakeven revenue for the proposed new product line:

Breakeven revenue = Price x Breakeven sales units

= $100 x 124

= $12,400

Note that while the technique of multiplying sales price by breakeven sales units to arrive at breakeven revenue works when analyzing an individual product or service, the best practice is to use the formal breakeven revenue formula presented at the beginning of this section when computing breakeven revenue for an entire company, unless that company sells only one product.

The calculation of breakeven revenue for the proposed new product line using the formula presented at the beginning of this section follows:

Breakeven revenue = Total fixed costs ÷ Gross margin

where

Gross margin = Gross profit ÷ Net sales

Observe that whether Graham sells one, 100, or 500 units of the proposed new product line, the gross margin of the new product line is the same, as figure 5.16 (on page 110) illustrates.

Clothing rack rental	$ 600
Shelving rental	1,200
Allocated fixed costs	5,000
Total annual fixed costs	$ 6,800

Figure 5.15. Calculation of total annual fixed costs for a proposed new product line.

Price	$100.00	x 1 unit =	Sales	$ 100.00
Less: Variable cost per unit	45.00	x 1 unit =	Less: Cost of goods sold	45.00
Unit contribution	$ 55.00	x 1 unit =	Gross profit	$ 55.00
Gross margin (Unit contribution ÷ Price) = 55%			Gross margin (Gross profit ÷ Sales) = 55%	

Price	$100.00	x 100 units =	Sales	$10,000.00
Less: Variable cost per unit	45.00	x 100 units =	Less: Cost of goods sold	4,500.00
Unit contribution	$ 55.00	x 100 units =	Gross profit	$ 5,500.00
Gross margin (Unit contribution ÷ Price) = 55%			Gross margin (Gross profit ÷ Sales) = 55%	

Price	$100.00	x 500 units =	Sales	$50,000.00
Less: Variable cost per unit	45.00	x 500 units =	Less: Cost of goods sold	22,500.00
Unit contribution	$ 55.00	x 500 units =	Gross profit	$27,500.00
Gross margin (Unit contribution ÷ Price) = 55%			Gross margin (Gross profit ÷ Sales) = 55%	

Figure 5.16. Calculation of gross margin for a proposed new product line.

Recall that gross margin is the percentage of each dollar of net sales (or sales, if there is no net sales amount) that remains after cost of goods sold has been considered. In figure 5.16, gross margin is calculated using sales rather than net sales. This is not unusual when performing breakeven analysis. Next, observe that the gross profit for one unit of a product, that product's gross profit per unit, is the same as that product's unit contribution. Further observe that unit contribution divided by price yields the same gross margin as gross profit divided by sales. This will always be so. As a result, we now have an alternative formula for gross margin:

Gross margin = Unit contribution ÷ Price

Returning to the calculation of breakeven revenue, referencing the total fixed costs determined in figure 5.15, Graham can determine breakeven revenue as follows:

$$\text{Breakeven revenue} = \text{Total fixed costs} \div \text{Gross margin}$$
$$= \$6,800 \div 0.55$$
$$= \$12,363.64$$

Note that the $12,363.64 breakeven revenue number was determined by rounding the solution of $6,800 divided by 55 percent up to the next whole cent. Further note that the $12,363.64 breakeven revenue number differs from the $12,400 breakeven revenue number calculated previously using sales price and breakeven sales units. This is because the $12,400 breakeven revenue number was calculated after breakeven sales units had been rounded up to whole units.

Finally, in order to know how much she can afford to discount the dresses, should that become necessary, Graham may want to calculate a breakeven price for the proposed new product line. In order to calculate a breakeven price, however, Graham will need to estimate the expected annual sales units of the proposed new product line. Assuming Graham believes she can sell 15 of the new dresses per month, the breakeven price for the proposed new product line would be $82.78, calculated as follows:

Breakeven price = Fixed cost per unit + Variable cost per unit

where

Fixed cost per unit = Fixed costs ÷ Units

First, Graham will need to determine how many dresses per year her business will sell:

15 dresses per month x 12 months in a year = 180 dresses per year

Graham can then use the formulas to determine the fixed cost per unit and the breakeven price:

Fixed cost per unit = $6,800 ÷ 180

$$= \$37.78$$

Breakeven price = $37.78 + $45.00

$$= \$82.78$$

Breakeven price equals the minimum price at which a product or service must be sold—under a given set of cost and sales unit conditions—in order to not lose money. The results of the above calculation therefore suggest that, to avoid losing money on the proposed new product line, Graham should never sell one of the dresses for less than $82.78.

Summary

Historical financial statements tell us about the past activities and financial results of a company. Business owners and managers, as well as individuals outside a company, analyze historical financial statements to determine a business's current and potential operational effectiveness, profitability, and cash flows. Historical financial statements are helpful when comparing a company's current performance to two things:

1. its past performance
2. the performance of other companies operating in the same industry

Pro forma financial statements are financial statements created by an entrepreneur that attempt to estimate the future financial results of a company based upon certain identified assumptions. Pro forma financial statements are an entrepreneur's best attempt to predict the future operational effectiveness, profitability, and cash flows of a business, often with the goal of obtaining funding for the business. Financial statement analysis can involve the use of historical financial statements, pro forma financial statements, or both.

There are four basic methods of financial statement analysis:

1. vertical
2. horizontal
3. ratio
4. breakeven

An entrepreneur uses vertical, horizontal, and ratio analyses to determine which areas within a company are problematic and therefore require close monitoring or adjustment. When performing financial statement analysis, it's important to always use a combination of vertical, horizontal, and ratio analyses in order to obtain a clear and complete picture of an individual firm's performance.

Breakeven analysis is the form of analysis most relevant to a business owner contemplating adding a new product or service to a company's offerings or an entrepreneur contemplating starting a new venture. For a business, breakeven is the point at which that business's net income equals zero. For a product line, breakeven is the point at which that product line's net income equals zero. In order to introduce the topic of breakeven, a breakeven analysis for a proposed new product line was illustrated in this chapter. A breakeven analysis for a proposed new business will be illustrated in chapter 6.

Key Terms

accounts receivable turn-
  over ratio
average collection period
breakeven
breakeven price
breakeven revenue
breakeven sales units
comparative financial
  statements

current ratio
debt-to-equity ratio
debt-to-total assets ratio
fixed cost
gross margin
horizontal analysis
inventory turnover ratio
mixed cost
profit margin

ratio analysis
reserve for bad debts
return-on-assets ratio
return-on-equity ratio
times-interest-earned ratio
variable cost
vertical analysis

Review and Discussion Questions

1. Explain the difference between historical financial statements and pro forma financial statements.
2. What are the four basic methods of financial statement analysis? How do they differ?
3. List and describe the different types of ratios typically used to perform ratio analysis.
4. Define breakeven for a product line, and explain why performing a breakeven analysis on a proposed new product line can be helpful to a business owner.
5. Explain the two categories into which costs are ultimately grouped for purposes of breakeven analysis and why they're categorized in this manner.

Exercises

1. Perform a 2019 vertical analysis and a 2018–2019 horizontal analysis of the income statements for DMZ, LLC provided below. What areas of concern, if any, do these analyses highlight? Explain your answer.

DMZ, LLC Income Statements For the Years Ended December 31, 2018, and December 31, 2019		
	2018	2019
Gross sales	$ 1,045,623	$ 1,125,844
Less: Returns	10,546	10,995
Net sales	1,035,077	1,114,849
Less: Cost of goods sold	425,689	431,258
Gross profit	609,388	683,591
Less: Operating expenses	308,119	313,774
Operating income	301,269	369,817
Less: Interest	12,251	11,602
Net income	$ 289,018	$ 358,215

2. Perform a 2019 vertical analysis and a 2018–2019 horizontal analysis of the balance sheets for DMZ, LLC provided below. What areas of concern, if any, do these analyses highlight? Explain your answer.

DMZ, LLC Balance Sheets As of December 31, 2018, and December 31, 2019		
	2018	2019
Cash	$ 28,421	$ 1,274
Accounts receivable	225,019	333,558
Inventory	319,887	321,006
Prepaid insurance	3,500	3,750
Total current assets	576,827	659,588
Equipment	385,000	385,000
Less: Accumulated depreciation	21,150	63,450
Net fixed assets	363,850	321,550
Total assets	$940,677	$981,138
Accounts payable	$331,822	$401,693
Wages and payroll taxes payable	25,889	26,145
Short-term portion of mortgage payable	21,014	20,085
Total current liabilities	378,725	447,923
Mortgage payable	245,000	224,915
Total liabilities	623,725	672,838
Owner's equity	316,952	308,300
Total liabilities and owner's equity	$940,677	$981,138

3. Perform a full ratio analysis for 2019 using the balance sheets and income statements for DMZ, LLC provided below. Assume 100 percent of net sales are credit sales. What areas of concern, if any, does this analysis highlight? Explain your answer.

DMZ, LLC Balance Sheets As of December 31, 2018, and December 31, 2019			DMZ, LLC Income Statements For the Years Ended December 31, 2018, and December 31, 2019		
	2018	2019		2018	2019
Cash	$ 28,421	$ 1,274	Gross sales	$ 1,045,623	$ 1,125,844
Accounts receivable	225,019	333,558	Less: Returns	10,546	10,995
Inventory	319,887	321,006	Net sales	1,035,077	1,114,849
Prepaid insurance	3,500	3,750	Less: Cost of goods sold	425,689	431,258
Total current assets	576,827	659,588	Gross profit	609,388	683,591
			Less: Operating expenses	308,119	313,774
Equipment	385,000	385,000	Operating income	301,269	369,817
Less: Accumulated			Less: Interest	12,251	11,602
depreciation	21,150	63,450	Net income	$ 289,018	$ 358,215
Net fixed assets	363,850	321,550			
Total assets	$940,677	$981,138			
Accounts payable	$331,822	$401,693			
Wages and payroll taxes payable	25,889	26,145			
Short-term portion of mortgage payable	21,014	20,085			
Total current liabilities	378,725	447,923			
Mortgage payable	245,000	224,915			
Total liabilities	623,725	672,838			
Owner's equity	316,952	308,300			
Total liabilities and owner's equity	$940,677	$981,138			

4. Using the information provided below that relates to a company that produces and sells only one product, calculate unit contribution, breakeven sales units, breakeven price, and breakeven revenue for that product.

Tiny's Manufacturing Company
Selected Financial Information and Income Statement
For the Year Ended December 31, 2019

Price:	$ 2,500	Sales	$ 50,000
Variable cost:	$ 1,125	Less: Cost of goods sold	22,500
Units sold:	20	Gross profit	27,500
		Less: Fixed costs	12,500
		Net income	$ 15,000

5. Using the information provided below for a company that produces and sells three products and allocates fixed costs based on sales revenue, calculate unit contribution, breakeven sales units, breakeven price, and breakeven revenue for each product.

The Imperial Manufacturing Company
Selected Financial Information and Income Statement
For the Year Ended December 31, 2019

	Product A	Product B	Product C		
Price:	$ 750	$ 500	$ 250	Sales	$ 1,000,000
Variable cost:	$ 525	$ 325	$ 125	Less: Cost of goods sold	599,375
Allocated portion of				Gross profit	400,625
fixed costs:	$ 15,469	$ 62,188	$ 47,344	Less: Fixed costs	125,000
Units sold:	165	995	1,515	Net income	$ 275,625

Pro Forma Financial Statements

"Before you can become a millionaire, you must learn to think like one."

— Thomas J. Stanley, business theorist and author of the best-selling book *The Millionaire Next Door*

Learning Objectives

Be able to create a pro forma pre-revenue balance sheet.

Be able to create the first pro forma post-revenue balance sheet and all of the pro forma income statements associated with the first years of a for-profit business.

Be able to create the detail schedules that support these financial statements.

Introduction

Potential investors typically request pro forma financial statements for at least three to five years into the future in order to determine if a business is a good choice for their investment dollars. Before they'll consider lending to a business or guaranteeing a loan to a business, most lenders and the Small Business Administration will typically require the same. As business owners, we use the pro forma financial statements we create for our own purposes. We use them to develop internal budgets for our business, plan for its future, and make sure we have the resources we need to grow the business. Perhaps most important, as entrepreneurs, we use pro forma financial statements to determine if a proposed business is expected to be profitable enough to be worth pursuing.

In chapter 1, we discussed the fact that no new business should be started without the founding team first completing a full feasibility analysis. We then discussed the merits of a proper feasibility analysis, noting that it should include a financial plan that provides the following information:

- a detailed accounting of the amount of start-up capital required by the business and how and when that start-up capital will be used
- expected product pricing
- expected short- and long-term profitability
- expected working capital needs
- existing and potential sources of capital for the business
- expected return on investment
- a breakeven analysis that supports the proposed business's economic viability

Chapter 1 also noted that, while a feasibility analysis proves or disproves a new concept's viability in the marketplace, a business plan is more comprehensive and discusses all the operational and financial aspects of a new business. In addition, a business plan includes all the components of a feasibility analysis (less the "go" or "no go" feasibility decision) but should also include the following expanded or additional sections and subsections:

- the business concept, fleshed out into a comprehensive business model
- the expected operational and organizational structures of the business
- a marketing plan
- a growth plan
- pro forma financial statements for the first three to five years of the business (supported by documented research)
- a cash harvest strategy, including contingency plans

Chapters 6 and 7 will illustrate how to create pro forma financial statements and the detail schedules that support them. Specifically, in chapter 6, we'll see how to create the following elements:

- a schedule of start-up costs, which is a detailed accounting of the amount of start-up capital required by a business, and how and when that start-up capital will be used
- a pro forma pre-revenue balance sheet and a pro forma start-up phase expense statement, including reconciliations of cash and equity
- a list of assumptions—based on documented research—that underlies the creation of the post-start-up phase pro forma financial statements
- depreciation, cost of goods sold, and estimated sales schedules, as applicable
- the first pro forma post-revenue balance sheet, including reconciliations of cash and equity
- all the pro forma income statements associated with the first years of a business

Chapter 7 will illustrate how to create balance sheets for years 2–5 of a new enterprise and pro forma statements of cash flows. A current or potential investor or lender may require them.

Pro Forma Financial Statements

In Latin, *pro forma* means "for form" or "for the sake of form." Pro forma financial statements are financial statements that attempt to estimate the future financial results of a company—in the form of estimated or projected financial statements—based upon certain identified assumptions. Pro forma financial statements indicate the amount of capital needed to start a company, tell us when the entity will become profitable, and inform us regarding the ongoing financial position of the company. Pro forma financial statements also give the entrepreneur fair warning regarding when a business is likely to be in danger of running out of cash.

Pro forma financial statements are created based upon many lists, reconciliations, and detail schedules developed by the entrepreneur. It's important to note that the worth of pro forma financial statements is determined by the quality of the research that underlies the lists, reconciliations, and detail schedules used to create them. Someone serious about investing in or lending to a business will want to thoroughly understand the research that is the basis for the numbers included in the pro forma financial statements. If a potential investor or lender understands and respects the research behind the numbers—and can trace how the research translates into the numbers on the pro forma financial statements—the potential investor or lender will likely buy into the notion that the pro forma financial statements are reasonable estimates of a proposed business's expected future financial results. Without both research and clear documentation of that research, pro forma financial statements are often viewed as pie in the sky wild guesses of the future with nothing to back them up except the passion and optimism of the entrepreneur. Investors don't invest—and lenders don't lend—based on entrepreneurial passion and optimism.

There are three traditional pro forma financial statements:

1. the pro forma income statement
2. the pro forma balance sheet
3. the pro forma statement of cash flows

Beyond pro forma income statements and pro forma balance sheets for a start-up entity (we'll illustrate an alternative to the pro forma statement of cash flows—the reconciliation of cash—later in this chapter), the entrepreneur will also want to develop a schedule that details all the costs that will be incurred pre-revenue (i.e., before the new venture's first sale occurs). This schedule is critical because it indicates how much capital the entrepreneur will need to have raised before endeavoring to start a new venture.

The Schedule of Start-up Costs and Industry Research

A schedule of start-up costs details all the costs that will be incurred before a new venture's first sale occurs. A schedule of start-up costs, like many schedules the entrepreneur will create, begins with a list of words rather than numbers.

As stated in the previous section, the worth of pro forma financial statements is determined by the quality of the research that underlies the lists, reconciliations, and detail schedules used to create them. The schedule of start-up costs is one of these schedules. The entrepreneur develops a schedule of start-up costs as a result of **industry research**—research performed to provide insight regarding the size and complexity of an industry, the number and nature of its participants, and the economic, political, market, and other factors that affect it. This research involves a variety of aspects:

industry research
research performed to provide insight regarding the size and complexity of an industry, the number and nature of its participants, and the economic, political, market, and other factors that affect it

- reading industry trade journals and other trade association publications and reaching out to trade associations for detailed follow-up information, as needed
- attending industry trade shows to assess which companies currently dominate the industry, which companies are up-and-comers, and which individuals are considered industry experts (these likely include future competitors, so caution is warranted)
- talking to industry experts and asking them open-ended questions
- reading future competitors' annual reports and any other relevant competitor information—a business librarian can be helpful with this research
- talking to those who sell or service future competitors' products or services

- talking to those who use future competitors' products or services
- buying and using future competitors' products or services

Using these resources, the entrepreneur gleans information, sorts it, and evaluates it in terms of its relevance to her proposed venture. The entrepreneur then organizes the appropriate information from her research into a list of start-up costs. Ultimately, the entrepreneur will create the schedule of start-up costs based upon the list of start-up costs and her best guesses considering all the industry research she has performed.

To illustrate the process of creating a schedule of start-up costs, let's assume two entrepreneurs have decided to open a high-end apparel store called the Fifth Avenue Apparel Shoppe (the Shoppe) in a major U.S. city. The store's grand opening is planned for October 1, 2020. At the beginning of its start-up phase, the entrepreneurs expect to be able to deposit $150,000 in the new venture's checking account: $25,000 of their own money and $125,000 to be secured from an angel investor in exchange for one-third ownership of the new venture.

Two founders of successful stores similar to the one our entrepreneurs wish to create (Starr Evans, founder of Hautey Boutique, and Michele Quinn, founder of MTQ Apparel) have indicated to the entrepreneurs that they should expect it to take four months to prepare the space they rent for the store's grand opening. As a result of their industry research and conversations with industry experts like Evans and Quinn, the budding entrepreneurs have developed the following preliminary list of start-up costs related to the business:

- rent
- utilities
- business insurance
- store design and decoration
- clothing inventory
- accessories inventory
- checkout counters and furniture
- clothing racks and shelving
- computers and software
- security system

With a preliminary list of start-up costs expressed in words, the next step is to attach a number—a realistic, researched dollar amount—to each item on the list. Each cost item—and the number attached to it—should be supported with at least one meaningful and respected source of information and a time frame, as applicable. After our entrepreneurs have assigned a dollar amount to each item on the preliminary list of start-up costs, they flesh out that list based on their ongoing industry research in order to develop the finalized list of start-up costs shown in figure 6.1.

Using the list of start-up costs and other details provided by their industry experts and ongoing industry research, our entrepreneurs then develop a schedule of start-up costs for the proposed business. Figure 6.2 shows that schedule.

Notice that in addition to scheduling out the amounts on the list of start-up costs over the estimated four-month start-up phase time frame, the schedule in figure 6.2 includes notes regarding when certain items are to be paid. This information will become important as we look at the next step of creating the pro forma financial statements for this business: developing a pro forma pre-revenue balance sheet and a pro forma start-up phase expense statement, including reconciliations.

Notice further that our entrepreneurs expect to have $150,000 to start their business and start-up costs total only $120,250. It appears that seeking out lenders or additional investors (i.e., beyond the one planned angel investor) isn't necessary—at least not at this time.

Fifth Avenue Apparel Shoppe, LLC List of Start-up Costs			
Expense Type	Amount	Time Frame	Source of Information
Rent	$ 5,000	per month	Xcel Realty and Management Company
Utilities	$ 500	per month	Xcel Realty and Management Company
Business insurance	$ 250	per month*	McGoohan Insurance Services, LLC
Store design and decoration	$10,000	during the four months before opening	Starr Evans, founder, Hautey Boutique Michele Quinn, founder, MTQ Apparel Smythe Brothers Store Interiors Consulting
Clothing inventory	$30,000	in the two months before opening	Starr Evans, founder, Hautey Boutique Michele Quinn, founder, MTQ Apparel Natalia Wasaki, Apparel Wholesalers, Inc.
Accessories inventory	$10,000	in the two months before opening	Starr Evans, founder, Hautey Boutique Michele Quinn, founder, MTQ Apparel Natalia Wasaki, Apparel Wholesalers, Inc.
Checkout counters and furniture	$12,000	two months before opening	Starr Evans, founder, Hautey Boutique Michele Quinn, founder, MTQ Apparel Smythe Brothers Store Interiors Consulting
Clothing racks and shelving	$20,000	in the two months before opening	Starr Evans, founder, Hautey Boutique Michele Quinn, founder, MTQ Apparel Smythe Brothers Store Interiors Consulting
Computers and software	$10,000	two months before opening	Starr Evans, founder, Hautey Boutique Michele Quinn, founder, MTQ Apparel Chris Rayburn, Retail Systems, Inc.
Security system	$ 5,000	three months before opening	Starr Evans, founder, Hautey Boutique Michele Quinn, founder, MTQ Apparel Chris Rayburn, Retail Systems, Inc.

*The cost of months 1 and 2 is due during month 1.

Figure 6.1. List of start-up costs for the Fifth Avenue Apparel Shoppe.

Fifth Avenue Apparel Shoppe, LLC Schedule of Start-up Costs					
	June 2020	July 2020	August 2020	September 2020	For the Four Months Ended September 30, 2020
Rent	$ 5,000	$ 5,000	$ 5,000	$ 5,000	$ 20,000
Utilities	500	500	500	500	2,000
Insurance	500	250	250	250	1,250
Store design and decoration	4,000	3,000	2,000	1,000	10,000
Clothing inventory	–	–	10,000	20,000	30,000
Accessories inventory	–	–	5,000	–	10,000
Checkout counters and furniture	–	–	12,000	5,000	12,000
Clothing racks and shelving	–	–	10,000	10,000	20,000
Computers and software	–	–	10,000	–	10,000
Security system	–	5,000	–	–	5,000
Total	$10,000	$13,750	$54,750	$41,750	$120,250

Notes: Rent is paid on the first day of the month to which it applies.
    Utilities are paid in the month after the services are used.
    Insurance is paid in the month previous to the month to which it applies.
    All other costs are paid in the same month as incurred.

Figure 6.2. Schedule of start-up costs for the Fifth Avenue Apparel Shoppe.

The Pro Forma Pre-Revenue Balance Sheet and the Pro Forma Start-up Phase Expense Statement, Including Reconciliations of Cash and Equity

markup
the amount added to the cost of a good to determine its sales price

Before we turn our discussion to creating the first pro forma financial statement—the pro forma pre-revenue balance sheet—it's wise to note that an entrepreneur's approach to creating pro forma financial statements for an entity will vary somewhat depending upon the nature of the entity in question, its associated business model, and the industry in which it operates. Throughout this chapter and chapter 7, we'll work through the creation of pro forma financial statements for a retailer of high-end apparel. Retailers buy and resell products, so their business model is rather simple and largely focuses on units purchased, units sold, and expected **markup**—the amount added to the cost of a good to determine its sales price. The approaches to creating pro forma financial statements for more complicated business models, while generally the same as what this chapter presents, will vary somewhat and, in some cases, require more detailed analysis. Also, the high-end apparel retailer example illustrated throughout this chapter and chapter 7 is an LLC—a pass-through entity. As a result, the reconciliation of equity illustrated throughout this chapter and chapter 7 will be a reconciliation of owners' equity. If our example company were instead a corporation, the reconciliation of equity would be a reconciliation of retained earnings. In order to illustrate pro forma financial statements for alternative types of entities—including an entity that is a corporation—detailed examples of how to create pro forma financial statements for a service-based business and a C corporation smartphone application business are included as appendices at the end of this chapter.

As a founding team faces the challenge of creating a pro forma pre-revenue balance sheet, they may be questioning why this particular financial statement needs to be created in the first place. There are many reasons, but one is probably more important than all the others: every entrepreneur needs to know how much cash is available at the end of the start-up phase of her business, immediately before the business commences operations. In the instance of the Fifth Avenue Apparel Shoppe, our entrepreneurs need to know they have enough cash to maintain adequate change in the cash register and also pay the store's bills and employees until significant cash receipts from product sales occur.

The pro forma pre-revenue balance sheet (pre-revenue balance sheet), the pro-forma start-up phase expense statement (expense statement), and their associated reconciliations of cash and equity (reconciliations) are created more or less simultaneously using the schedule of start-up costs our entrepreneurs have already created.

The schedule of start-up costs includes information about all the costs associated with the start-up phase of a business. Assuming, as is typical for most start-ups, there are no loan payments, dividend payments, or distribution payments expected to be made during the start-up phase of the business, each cost associated with the start-up phase of a business represents one of two things: an asset or an expense. This means each cost included on the schedule of start-up costs ends up in one of two places: either on the pre-revenue balance sheet or on the expense statement.

Using this knowledge, we can formulate the beginnings of a pre-revenue balance sheet, an expense statement, and their associated reconciliations for the Fifth Avenue Apparel Shoppe, as illustrated in figure 6.3.

Figure 6.3 shows that each line item's total from the schedule of start-up costs has been placed on either the pre-revenue balance sheet if it's an asset (i.e., clothing inventory, accessories inventory, checkout counters and furniture, clothing racks and shelving, computers and software, security system) or on the expense statement

Fifth Avenue Apparel Shoppe, LLC Schedule of Start-up Costs For the Four Months Ended September 30, 2020		Fifth Avenue Apparel Shoppe, LLC Pro Forma Pre-Revenue Balance Sheet As of September 30, 2020		Fifth Avenue Apparel Shoppe, LLC Pro Forma Start-up Phase Expense Statement, Including Reconciliations of Cash and Owners' Equity For the Four Months Ended September 30, 2020	
Rent	$ 20,000	Cash		Rent	$ 20,000
Utilities	2,000	Prepaid insurance		Utilities	2,000
Insurance	1,250	Clothing inventory	30,000	Insurance	1,250
Store design and decoration	10,000	Accessories inventory	10,000	Store design and decoration	10,000
Clothing inventory	30,000	Total current assets			
Accessories inventory	10,000				
Checkout counters and		Checkout counters and		Reconciliation of Cash:	
furniture	12,000	furniture	12,000	Beginning cash	$ 150,00
Clothing racks and shelving	20,000	Clothing racks and shelving	20,000	Less: Cash outlays for	
Computers and software	10,000	Computers and software	10,000	assets	
Security system	5,000	Security system	5,000	Less: Cash outlays for	
Total	$120,250	Total fixed assets	47,000	expenses	
				Ending cash	
Notes: Rent is paid on the first day of the month to which it applies.		Total assets		Reconciliation of Owners' Equity:	
Utilities are paid in the month after the services are used.		Total liabilities		Beginning owners' equity	$150,000
Insurance is paid in the month previous to the month to which it applies.		Owners' equity		Less: Start-up phase expenses	
				Ending owners' equity	
All other costs are paid in the same month as incurred.		Total liabilities and owners' equity			

Figure 6.3. Pro forma pre-revenue balance sheet and pro forma start-up phase expense statement, including reconciliations of cash and owners' equity, working copy 1.

if it's an expense (i.e., rent, utilities, insurance, store design and decoration). The individual fixed-asset amounts have then been summed to arrive at a total of $47,000. Note that the term "fixed assets" rather than "net fixed assets" has been used to describe the $47,000 total on the pre-revenue balance sheet because a new venture typically does not begin depreciating its fixed assets until it commences business operations. Last, note that $150,000 has been included on each of the two different reconciliations. The $150,000 represents the expected beginning cash amount, which is also the expected beginning owners' equity amount.

Before moving forward in our effort to create a pre-revenue balance sheet, it's wise to review the nature of a few specific items included on a balance sheet:

- A current asset is an item of value that's either cash or an asset that will likely be converted into cash within the next 12 months.
- A prepaid asset is typically an expense that has been paid for in advance of the period of its use. A common example is prepaid insurance. Insurance usually needs to be paid for in advance of the period to which it relates. As that period expires or partially expires, the amount of prepaid insurance included on the balance sheet decreases, and the amount of insurance expense included on the income statement increases. Prepaid assets are often current assets.
- A current liability is an amount owed to others that will need to be paid within the next 12 months.

The creation of a proper pro forma balance sheet requires that the entrepreneur recognize when prepaid assets and payables will result from the activities of the start-up. When a product or service is paid for in advance of its receipt or use, a pre-paid asset generally results. When a product or service is paid for after its receipt or use, a payable generally results.

In our example, the Shoppe pays for most items in the same month the product or service is received or used, but this is not true in every case. The notes on our schedule of start-up costs indicate that business insurance is paid in the month previous to the month to which it applies and utilities are paid in the month after the services are used. As you may know from experience with your personal car insurance and home utilities, this timing is typical for insurance and utilities expenses. The fact that business insurance is paid in the month previous to the month to which it applies means the balance sheet will have a line item for prepaid insurance. The fact that utilities are paid in the month after the services are used means the balance sheet will have a line item for utilities payable.

We are now ready to take our process of developing pro forma financial statements a few steps further by adding prepaid insurance and utilities payable to our pre-revenue balance sheet and our expense statement. Note that, because we've utilized all the information on the schedule of start-up costs except the notes, we retain only the notes from that schedule on the next iteration of our first pro forma financial statement, which is included in figure 6.4.

Note first that prepaid insurance in the amount of $250 has been added to the pre-revenue balance sheet and the expense statement has been adjusted to reflect the fact that only part of the $1,250 paid for insurance during the start-up phase of

Fifth Avenue Apparel Shoppe, LLC Pro Forma Pre-Revenue Balance Sheet As of September 30, 2020		Fifth Avenue Apparel Shoppe, LLC Pro Forma Start-up Phase Expense Statement, Including Reconciliations of Cash and Owners' Equity For the Four Months Ended September 30, 2020		
Cash		Rent		$20,000
Prepaid insurance	250	Utilities		2,000
Clothing inventory	30,000	Insurance	$1,250	
Accessories inventory	10,000	Less: Prepaid insurance	250	
Total current assets				1,000
		Store design and decoration		10,000
Checkout counters and furniture	12,000	Start-up phase expenses		33,000
Clothing racks and shelving	20,000	Less: Utilities payable		500
Computers and software	10,000	Total cash outlays for expenses		$ 32,500
Security system	5,000			
Total fixed assets	47,000	Reconciliation of Cash:		
		Beginning cash		$150,000
Total assets		Less: Cash outlays for assets		
		Less: Cash outlays for expenses		32,500
Utilities payable	$ 500	Ending cash		
Total liabilities				
		Reconciliation of Owners' Equity:		
Owners' equity		Beginning owners' equity		$150,000
		Less: Start-up phase expenses		33,000
Total liabilities and owners' equity		Ending owners' equity		

Notes: Rent is paid on the first day of the month to which it applies.
 Utilities are paid in the month after the services are used.
 Insurance is paid in the month previous to the month to which it applies.
 All other costs are paid in the same month as incurred.

Figure 6.4. Pro forma pre-revenue balance sheet and pro forma start-up phase expense statement, including reconciliations of cash and owners' equity, working copy 2.

the business relates to the months of June–September 2020. Because our entrepreneurs are generally always paying one month ahead for insurance, the September payment for insurance is really a payment for October (the June payment of $500 related $250 to June and $250 to July). Hence, the September payment for insurance represents prepaid insurance—an asset—rather than insurance expense. Note also that a total for start-up phase expenses has been calculated and this total has been utilized in the reconciliation of owners' equity.

Notice next that utilities payable in the amount of $500 has been added to the pre-revenue balance sheet and the expense statement has been adjusted to reflect the fact that not the entire $2,000 of utilities cost included on the schedule of start-up costs has actually been paid. Since our entrepreneurs are always paying one month behind for utilities, the estimated $500 utility bill that relates to September will be received and paid in October. Notice also that a total for cash outlays for expenses has been calculated and this total has been utilized in the reconciliation of cash.

Learning how to properly reflect prepaids and payables on balance sheets and expense statements like those included in this chapter can be challenging. Keep in mind, however, that once you know how to treat one prepaid asset, you know how to treat them all. The same is true for payables.

Next, we'll complete the reconciliations of cash and owners' equity and calculate the totals and subtotals on our pre-revenue balance sheet. This will get us to the fully completed and final version of the pro forma pre-revenue balance sheet and pro forma start-up phase expense statement, including reconciliations of cash and owners' equity, as shown in figure 6.5. Observe that the notes included in figure 6.4 are appropriately excluded from figure 6.5.

The total for cash outlays for assets of $87,250 was arrived at by totaling all the assets purchased with cash included on the pre-revenue balance sheet (i.e., prepaid insurance, clothing inventory, accessories inventory, checkout counters and furniture,

Fifth Avenue Apparel Shoppe, LLC Pro Forma Pre-Revenue Balance Sheet As of September 30, 2020		Fifth Avenue Apparel Shoppe, LLC Pro Forma Start-up Phase Expense Statement, Including Reconciliations of Cash and Owners' Equity For the Four Months Ended September 30, 2020		
Cash	$ 30,250	Rent		$ 20,000
Prepaid insurance	250	Utilities		2,000
Clothing inventory	30,000	Insurance	$1,250	
Accessories inventory	10,000	Less: Prepaid insurance	250	
Total current assets	70,500			1,000
		Store design and decoration		10,000
Checkout counters and furniture	12,000	Start-up phase expenses		33,000
Clothing racks and shelving	20,000	Less: Utilities payable		500
Computers and software	10,000	Total cash outlays for expenses		$ 32,500
Security system	5,000			
Total fixed assets	47,000	Reconciliation of Cash:		
		Beginning cash		$150,000
Total assets	$117,500	Less: Cash outlays for assets		87,250
		Less: Cash outlays for expenses		32,500
Utilities payable	$ 500	Ending cash		$ 30,250
Total liabilities	500			
		Reconciliation of Owners' Equity:		
Owners' equity	117,000	Beginning owners' equity		$150,000
		Less: Start-up phase expenses		33,000
Total liabilities and owners' equity	$117,500	Ending owners' equity		$117,000

Figure 6.5. Pro forma pre-revenue balance sheet and pro forma start-up phase expense statement, including reconciliations of cash and owners' equity, final version.

clothing racks and shelving, computers and software, security system). Once a total was determined for cash outlays for assets, an amount for September 30, 2020 cash was able to be calculated on the reconciliation of cash. This amount was then replicated on the balance sheet. Next an amount for September 30, 2020 owners' equity was calculated on the reconciliation of owners' equity. This amount was then also replicated on the balance sheet.

The last step was to compute the necessary subtotals and totals on the pre-revenue balance sheet and verify that the dollar amount for total assets equals the dollar amount for total liabilities and equity—as required by the basic accounting equation. Because the basic accounting equation works on this balance sheet, we can be reasonably assured that all the asset and expense items on the pre-revenue balance sheet and expense statement have been treated appropriately.

At this point, we have completed the schedule of start-up costs, the pro forma pre-revenue balance sheet, and the pro forma start-up expense statement, including reconciliations of cash and equity. We have created the foundation upon which the rest of the pro forma financial statements will be based.

The First Pro Forma Income Statement and Market Research

The next statement to complete for the Fifth Avenue Apparel Shoppe is its first pro forma income statement. Oftentimes, the first income statement for a business will provide information on a monthly basis (see the appendices to this chapter for examples). However, because the retail industry tends to view its operations more on a quarterly (i.e., seasonal) basis than monthly, we'll create our first income statement from a quarterly point of view. In addition, like most start-ups, the Fifth Avenue Apparel Shoppe will commence operations midyear. For businesses commencing operations late in the year, this can create the need for a first income statement that actually incorporates more than one year. Because the Fifth Avenue Apparel Shoppe is opening its doors late in the year—on October 1, 2020—it makes sense for the company's first income statement to encapsulate its first five quarters of operations, October 1, 2020–December 31, 2021.

Before creating the first pro forma income statement, a list of assumptions relevant to that income statement and all the pro forma financial statements that will follow it must be developed. This list should define the hours of operation of the business, the nature and extent of the use of employees during those hours of operation, relevant details regarding the business model itself, and information that will help define the future revenues, expenses, assets, liabilities and equity of the company. In order to create this list of assumptions, the entrepreneur will consider the industry research already performed and the schedule of start-up costs already created. Beyond this, the entrepreneur will want to engage in **market research**. Market research involves the identification of one or more specific markets and the determination of their relative sizes and characteristics. The goal of the market research performed by an entrepreneur prior to the start of a business is to identify and understand all the potential customers of the business under consideration. When doing market research, the entrepreneur should do the following:

- Talk to those who sell or service future competitors' product or services.
- Talk to industry experts—some of them may be future competitors, so caution is warranted.
- Perform **primary market research**, which is research conducted by communicating directly with current or potential customers.

The importance of primary market research can't be stressed enough. An entrepreneur needs to remember that the information obtained directly from potential

market research
research performed to identify one or more specific markets and determine their relative sizes and characteristics in order to identify and understand all the potential customers of the business under consideration

primary market research
research conducted by communicating directly with current or potential customers

customers generally trumps the information received from all other sources. An entrepreneur who does not perform proper market research—or who does not heed the needed adjustments or actions suggested by that research—significantly increases the probability that her new venture will fail.

The information that will ultimately end up on the list of assumptions is gleaned by the entrepreneur from the performance of industry and market research. The entrepreneur sorts and evaluates all this information in terms of its relevance to the particular venture under consideration. Ultimately, the entrepreneur will create the list of assumptions based upon the decisions she makes after considering all the information available in light of her vision for the entity she wishes to create. Figure 6.6 (on page 128) is the list of assumptions for the Shoppe developed by our entrepreneurs.

Using the information provided in figure 6.6, we'll first estimate weekly gross payroll. We can determine from the list of assumptions that our entrepreneurs expect to pay two employees to work a 6.5-hour shift Tuesday through Saturday and one employee to work a 6.5-hour shift on Sunday. This represents a total of 11 shifts of 6.5 hours each per week. Employees will be paid at a rate of $10 per hour, so estimated weekly gross payroll can be calculated as follows:

11 shifts per week x 6.5-hour shifts x $10 per hour = $715

Next, we'll calculate depreciation expense for the fixed assets purchased during the Fifth Avenue Apparel Shoppe's start-up phase. The information in the list of assumptions indicates that the Fifth Avenue Apparel Shoppe plans to depreciate its fixed assets using the straight-line, half-year convention depreciation method. This depreciation method is relatively simple and generally a perfectly acceptable way to choose to depreciate assets for purposes of preparing pro forma financial statements.

Salvage value is the amount for which an asset is expected to be sold after a business has fully depreciated the asset and ceased using it. The straight-line depreciation method indicates that one would take the cost of an asset or group of assets (minus any salvage value), divide that asset or group of assets by the expected useful life of the assets or group of assets, and the result would represent annual depreciation expense. The more commonly used straight-line, half-year convention depreciation method determines annual depreciation expense for the middle years of life of an asset or group of assets in exactly this manner, but depreciation expense for the first and last years is calculated differently. The first and last years' depreciation expense would equal half the annual depreciation expense calculated for the middle years, illustrated as follows for the $47,000 of depreciable fixed assets included on the Fifth Avenue Apparel Shoppe's pre-revenue balance sheet:

$47,000 ÷ 5 = $9,400 (years 2–5 annual depreciation expense)

$9,400 ÷ 2 = $4,700 (years 1 and 6 annual depreciation expense)

Figure 6.7 (on page 129) shows the full depreciation schedule for the Fifth Avenue Apparel Shoppe's 2020 fixed-asset acquisitions. Note that when using the half-year convention, we technically depreciate an asset or group of assets over its useful life, plus one year. Note further that, in the above calculations, in keeping with what is stated in our list of assumptions, we assumed a salvage value of $0 for our fixed assets. Assuming a salvage value of $0 is acceptable if our entrepreneurs expect to use the applicable fixed assets until they aren't suitable for anything except the trash bin. Such an expectation is not unusual for new ventures that are often strapped for cash.

Thus far, the creation of the schedules, statements, and reconciliations for the Fifth Avenue Apparel Shoppe has involved the use of spreadsheets that utilize formulas. Creating schedules, statements, and reconciliations that utilize formulas is wise because, within a spreadsheet that is well set up, if one number changes, all the other numbers automatically recalculate to reflect that change. Setting up spreadsheets to

salvage value

the amount for which an asset is expected to be sold after a business has fully depreciated the asset and ceased using it

---

Fifth Avenue Apparel Shoppe, LLC
List of Assumptions

General Operational and Payroll Information

| Store hours: | Tuesday–Saturday 10:00 a.m.–9:00 p.m. |
| | Sunday Noon–8:00 p.m. |

Needed employees:	Three: 1 Tuesday–Saturday 9:30 a.m.–4:00 p.m.
	1 Tuesday–Saturday 3:30 p.m.–10:00 p.m.
	1 Sunday 11:30 a.m.–6:00 p.m.

In order to keep payroll to a minimum and effectively manage the business, one or both of the two founding entrepreneurs will always be present during the store's hours of operation. Employees will be paid $10 per hour. Payroll taxes, unemployment, and workers' compensation combined are expected to equal 13.5% of gross payroll. Employee pay per hour is expected to increase 20% from its year 2021 amount in 2022 and then another 5% in 2024.

Information Regarding Expected Inventory Pricing, Inventory Sales (Cost of Goods Sold), and Inventory Levels

| Target margin for clothing: | 60% until December 31, 2023, 65% beginning January 1, 2024 |
| Target margin for accessories: | 75% until December 31, 2024, 80% beginning January 1, 2025 |

Expected inventory turnover rate for 2020: Four times per year. In other words, for 2020, after business operations commence, it is expected that, on average, the business will sell and replace its inventory at a rate of four times per year, or once per quarter. After 2020, cost of goods sold (COGS) is expected to increase 10% each quarter through the end of 2021. Although COGS will increase, inventory levels are expected to remain at $30,000 (clothing) and $10,000 (accessories) through the end of 2021 due to expertise gained in inventory management. COGS is expected to increase to $45,000 (clothing) and 15,000 (accessories) per quarter for 2022. COGS is expected to increase to $48,500 (clothing) and $16,500 (accessories) per quarter for 2023 and stabilize there.

Information Regarding Expected Fixed-Asset Purchases, Disposals, and Depreciation

- The $47,000 of fixed assets to be purchased during the start-up phase of the business are expected to have a useful life of five years and a salvage value of $0, and will, like all the business's expected fixed assets, be depreciated using the straight-line, half-year convention depreciation method.
- No new fixed assets are expected to be purchased after the start-up phase until 2023, when the business expects to purchase $5,000 of new software with a salvage value of $0. In addition, at the beginning of 2025, the business expects to purchase $12,500 of new, higher-end computers with a salvage value of $1,250.
- By the end of 2025, the $10,000 of computers and software purchased during the start-up phase of the business are expected to be fully depreciated, phased out, and abandoned (i.e., thrown out). These are expected to be the first fixed assets disposed of by the business.

Information Regarding Expected Non-Payroll Expenses

- Store design and decoration expense is expected to terminate in September 2020.
- Cleaning and maintenance expense is expected to cost $250 per month beginning in October 2020 and remain the same amount through the end of 2025.
- Miscellaneous expense is expected to amount to 5% of the prior period's COGS.
- Rent is expected to remain at $5,000 per month through September 30, 2023, then increase 5% to $5,250 on October 1, 2023. Rent is expected to continue to be paid on the first day of the month to which it relates.
- Utilities expense is expected to continue to be paid in the month after the services are used and is expected to remain unchanged at approximately $500 per month until it increases 3% in 2022 and then another 2% in 2024.
- Insurance expense is expected to continue to be paid one month in advance and is expected to remain unchanged at approximately $250 per month until it increases 10% in 2022 and then stabilizes.

Information Regarding Expected Payables

- At December 31, 2021, accounts payable, including payables related to cleaning and maintenance and miscellaneous expenses, is expected to approximate 85% of clothing and accessories inventory.
- At December 31, 2021, payroll payable is expected to equal one-sixth of fourth quarter 2021 payroll expense.
- At December 31, 2021, payroll taxes payable is expected to equal one-sixth of fourth quarter 2021 payroll tax expense.
- At December 31, 2021, sales tax payable is expected to approximate one month's sales multiplied by the sales tax rate of 6% (calculated as one-third of fourth quarter 2021 sales x 0.06).

Other Information

Each of the three owners of the company is expected to begin taking a $10,000-per-month cash distribution starting in April 2021.

Figure 6.6. List of assumptions for the Fifth Avenue Apparel Shoppe.

automatically recalculate in this manner takes time, but it's worth the effort because creating pro forma financial statements involves a lot of estimating—and then re-estimating—as new information is discovered.

Beyond just using formulas, however, it's sometimes wise to establish conspicuous cells for key data that will likely be experimented with or changed often. Such is the case with the cost of goods sold schedule, the next schedule we'll prepare for the Fifth Avenue Apparel Shoppe.

Fifth Avenue Apparel Shoppe, LLC	
Depreciation Schedule	
Total fixed assets:	$47,000
Useful life in years:	5
Depreciation method:	Straight-line, half-year convention
Year	**Depreciation Expense**
2020	$ 4,700
2021	9,400
2022	9,400
2023	9,400
2024	9,400
2025	4,700
Total	$47,000

Figure 6.7. Depreciation schedule for year 2020 fixed-asset acquisitions.

Cost of goods sold represents the cost of all the items sold by a business over an indicated period. For a retail business, it's often easier to estimate the amount of product the business will move (i.e., expected cost of goods sold) than the specific price at which the product will move (i.e., sales). We'll create our cost of goods sold and estimated sales schedules assuming this premise.

The industry and market research conducted by our entrepreneurs suggests that, after business operations commence, the Fifth Avenue Apparel Shoppe's owners should expect an inventory turnover rate of four turns per year for 2020. Because there are four quarters in a year, this translates into one inventory turn per quarter. We learned in chapter 5 that an inventory turn means that, during the indicated period, in theory, a business will sell 100 percent of its inventory and therefore have to replace it. For the Fifth Avenue Apparel Shoppe, this means the business's combined beginning clothing and accessories inventory of $40,000 will equal its cost of goods sold for fourth quarter 2020. (Remember: The inventory we sell—once we have sold it—becomes cost of goods sold.)

The industry and market research conducted by our entrepreneurs further suggests that the Fifth Avenue Apparel Shoppe's owners should expect cost of goods sold to increase 10 percent per quarter in 2021. All the cost of goods sold information combined suggests the cost of goods sold numbers indicated in figure 6.8.

Note that the expected quarterly growth of cost of goods sold of 10 percent is conspicuously set up in a separate cell in figure 6.8. The reason is so we can easily

Fifth Avenue Apparel Shoppe, LLC						
Cost of Goods Sold Schedule						
Expected quarterly growth:	10%					
	Fourth Quarter 2020	First Quarter 2021	Second Quarter 2021	Third Quarter 2021	Fourth Quarter 2021	For the Year Ended December 31, 2021
Clothing	$30,000	$33,000	$36,300	$39,930	$43,923	$153,153
Accessories	10,000	11,000	12,100	13,310	14,641	51,051
Total	$40,000	$44,000	$48,400	$53,240	$58,546	$204,204

Figure 6.8. Cost of goods sold schedule for the first five quarters of operations and for the year ended December 31, 2021.

experiment with our cost of goods sold numbers by changing the 10 percent to a different percentage and then reviewing the results after the spreadsheet automatically recalculates.

In retail sales, one typically takes the cost of an item and then adds a markup to arrive at a sales price. One then estimates how many units of that item one expects to sell over a period of time in order to arrive at the expected total sales dollars related to that item. When estimating sales for a retailer like the Fifth Avenue Apparel Shoppe, instead of estimating sales units and determining a sales price for every item the store might sell, it's usually easier to determine an average expected margin (i.e., markup in percentage terms) by product line and apply that to expected cost of goods sold by product line to arrive at expected sales by product line. Because our entrepreneurs' industry experts have provided them with an average margin to target for both the clothing line and the accessories line, we can use the cost of goods sold numbers from figure 6.8 to estimate sales. Specifically, note the following calculation of the sales amount for clothing for fourth quarter 2020 using the cost of goods sold amount for clothing for fourth quarter 2020.

First, we need the formula:

Sales amount = Cost of item ÷ (1 − Expected average margin for that item)

Next, we fill in the numbers:

Sales amount = $30,000 ÷ (1 − 0.60)
$$= \$30,000 \div 0.40$$
$$= \$75,000$$

Finally, we do the proof:

$75,000 (Sales) x 0.60 (Expected average margin) = $45,000 (Markup)
$30,000 (Cost of item) + $45,000 (Markup) = $75,000 (Sales)

Cost of goods sold for clothing for fourth quarter 2020 of $30,000 translates to a sales amount for clothing for fourth quarter 2020 of $75,000. Sales amounts for clothing for each of the other four quarters and sales amounts for accessories for each of the five quarters would be calculated in the same way. Figure 6.9 shows the resulting estimated sales schedule.

Note that the target margins are conspicuously set up in separate cells so we can easily experiment with expected sales by changing these percentages. We do this for two reasons:

1. The Fifth Avenue Apparel Shoppe's industry experts likely have a much better idea how much product the Fifth Avenue Apparel Shoppe will sell (i.e., cost of goods sold) than exactly how much the Fifth Avenue Apparel Shoppe will sell that product for (i.e., sales).

Fifth Avenue Apparel Shoppe, LLC Estimated Sales Schedule						
Target margin for clothing:	60%					
Target margin for accessories:	75%					
	Fourth Quarter 2020	First Quarter 2021	Second Quarter 2021	Third Quarter 2021	Fourth Quarter 2021	For the Year Ended December 31, 2021
Clothing	$ 75,000	$ 82,500	$ 90,750	$ 99,825	$109,808	$382,883
Accessories	40,000	44,000	48,400	53,240	58,564	204,204
Total	$115,000	$126,500	$139,150	$153,065	$168,372	$587,087

Figure 6.9. Estimated sales schedule for the first five quarters of operations and for the year ended December 31, 2021.

2. The target margins applied to the cost of goods sold numbers are what drive the sales numbers shown in figure 6.9.

When estimating sales for a proposed new entity, remember the following:

- As much as reasonably possible, sales need to be built from the bottom up rather than estimated from the top down.
- An entity's sales often don't begin in the same month, the same quarter, or even the same year the entity commences business operations.
- Sales for most entities start at some sort of reasonable base level, then slowly gain momentum over time.
- Sales can only exist to the extent of a new entity's ability to deliver its products or services to its customers.

How not to estimate sales: "I think I can capture 1 percent of a $2 billion market. That's $20 million of sales per year!" The aforementioned is a top-down approach to estimating sales rather than the bottom-up approach recommended above. Also, no one believes you. A top-down approach to estimating sales does, however, provide a good sanity check for sales numbers built from the bottom up (i.e., sales numbers generated by considering costs and margins on a period-by-period basis). Sales numbers built from the bottom up—like those in figure 6.9—are much more believable than sales estimated using a top-down approach. This is because sales numbers built from the bottom up are based on research and take into account the specifics associated with a particular business venture.

At this point, we've calculated amounts for expected weekly gross payroll, annual depreciation, quarterly cost of goods sold, and quarterly sales. It's now time to start building the first pro forma income statement. We start this process by introducing the numbers we've already calculated into a standard income statement format in a manner such as shown in figure 6.10. Note that, although we've referred to our first pro forma income statement in the singular thus far in this chapter, technically we are preparing an income statement that includes multiple periods of time. Hence, the formal income statement shown at figure 6.10 is appropriately entitled "Pro Forma Income Statements."

Note that quarterly gross payroll equals our previously calculated weekly gross payroll number of $715 x 13 because there are 13 weeks in a calendar quarter. Note also that the annual depreciation expense number of $9,400 for 2021—a number

	Fourth Quarter 2020	First Quarter 2021	Second Quarter 2021	Third Quarter 2021	Fourth Quarter 2021	For the Year Ended December 31, 2021
Sales	$115,000	$126,500	$139,150	$153,065	$168,372	$587,087
Cost of goods sold	40,000	44,000	48,400	53,240	58,564	204,204
Gross profit	75,000	82,500	90,750	99,825	109,808	382,883
Operating expenses:						
Payroll	9,295	9,295	9,295	9,295	9,295	37,180
Depreciation	4,700	2,350	2,350	2,350	2,350	9,400
Total operating expenses						
Net income						

Fifth Avenue Apparel Shoppe, LLC — Pro Forma Income Statements — For the First Five Quarters of Operations and for the Year Ended December 31, 2021

Figure 6.10. Pro forma income statements for the first five quarters of operations and for the year ended December 31, 2021, working copy 1.

included on the depreciation schedule we previously created—is spread out equally over the four quarters of 2021.

We can now start adding the other information we know to these preliminary income statements. We know from the schedule of start-up costs that rent is $5,000 per month, and we know from the list of assumptions that it's expected to remain that amount through September 30, 2023, so $5,000 per month x 3 months = $15,000 rent per quarter.

We also know from the list of assumptions that we can expect payroll taxes, unemployment, and workers' compensation combined to equal 13.5 percent of gross payroll. Accordingly, we'll lump these three items together into a single line item called payroll taxes on our pro forma income statements. We've already calculated quarterly gross payroll and included it on our preliminary income statement, so estimating quarterly payroll taxes is an easy calculation:

$$\text{Quarterly payroll taxes} = \text{Quarterly gross payroll} \times 0.135$$
$$= \$9,295 \times 0.135$$
$$= \$1,255$$

According to the list of assumptions, utilities and insurance expenses are expected to remain unchanged at $500 per month and $250 per month, respectively, until 2022, so we'll utilize the monthly expense amounts to calculate a quarterly expense amount for each of these expenses. Then, we'll include the quarterly expense amounts on our preliminary income statement.

Adding what we know about rent, payroll tax, utility, and insurance expenses, we arrive at the updated preliminary income statements shown in figure 6.11.

In order to complete the pro forma income statements, we must next add lines for cleaning and maintenance expense and miscellaneous expense. Our list of assumptions indicates that cleaning and maintenance expense is expected to be $250 per month ($750 per quarter). Miscellaneous expense is to be calculated as a percentage of the prior month's cost of goods sold—translating to a fourth quarter 2020 expense

	Fourth Quarter 2020	First Quarter 2021	Second Quarter 2021	Third Quarter 2021	Fourth Quarter 2021	For the Year Ended December 31, 2021
Sales	$115,000	$126,500	$139,150	$153,065	$168,372	$587,087
Cost of goods sold	40,000	44,000	48,400	53,240	58,564	204,204
Gross profit	75,000	82,500	90,750	99,825	109,808	382,883
Operating expenses:						
Rent	15,000	15,000	15,000	15,000	15,000	60,000
Payroll	9,295	9,295	9,295	9,295	9,295	37,180
Payroll taxes	1,255	1,255	1,255	1,255	1,255	5,019
Utilities	1,500	1,500	1,500	1,500	1,500	6,000
Insurance	750	750	750	750	750	3,000
Depreciation	4,700	2,350	2,350	2,350	2,350	9,400
Total operating expenses						
Net income						

Fifth Avenue Apparel Shoppe, LLC
Pro Forma Income Statements
For the First Five Quarters of Operations and for the Year Ended December 31, 2021

Figure 6.11. Pro forma income statements for the first five quarters of operations and for the year ended December 31, 2021, working copy 2.

of $0, because there was no third quarter 2020 cost of goods sold, and a first quarter 2021 expense of $2,000 (fourth quarter 2020 cost of goods sold x 5% = $40,000 x 0.05 = $2,000). After these two line items are added to the pro forma income statements, we simply calculate subtotals and totals to arrive at the final version of our first pro forma income statements for the Shoppe, as shown in figure 6.12.

Note that the rightmost column in figure 6.12 represents an annual total provided for informational purposes that does not include the fourth quarter of 2020. The results for fourth quarter 2020 have been boxed so as to hopefully impress this point upon the financial statement reader. Note also that the income statements in figure 6.12 include no line for operating income. This is because the income statements don't include a line item for interest expense. Finally, note that the rightmost column in figure 6.12 totals properly horizontally, but not vertically. This is because the numbers displayed in the spreadsheet used to create figure 6.12 have been rounded.

The following example illustrates the effects of the rounding inherent in spreadsheet calculations:

$382,882.50	rounds to	$382,883
-132,881.30	rounds to	-132,881
$250,001.20		$250,002

The $250,001.20 appears as $250,001 in our spreadsheet because the spreadsheet displays a rounded down number, but $382,883 minus $132,881 equals $250,002. So how do we deal with such a problem? Most preparers of financial statements handle this problem by including a phrase similar to the following at the bottom of each of their affected financial statements: "Due to rounding, some totals may not correspond with the sum of the separate figures."

	Fourth Quarter 2020	First Quarter 2021	Second Quarter 2021	Third Quarter 2021	Fourth Quarter 2021	For the Year Ended December 31, 2021
Sales	$115,000	$126,500	$139,150	$153,065	$168,372	$587,087
Cost of goods sold	40,000	44,000	48,400	53,240	58,564	204,204
Gross profit	75,000	82,500	90,750	99,825	109,808	382,883
Operating expenses:						
Rent	15,000	15,000	15,000	15,000	15,000	60,000
Payroll	9,295	9,295	9,295	9,295	9,295	37,180
Payroll taxes	1,255	1,255	1,255	1,255	1,255	5,019
Utilities	1,500	1,500	1,500	1,500	1,500	6,000
Insurance	750	750	750	750	750	3,000
Depreciation	4,700	2,350	2,350	2,350	2,350	9,400
Cleaning and maintenance	750	750	750	750	750	3,000
Miscellaneous	–	2,000	2,200	2,420	2,662	9,282
Total operating expenses	33,250	32,900	33,100	33,320	33,562	132,881
Net income	$ 41,750	$ 49,600	$ 57,650	$ 66,505	$ 76,246	$250,001

Fifth Avenue Apparel Shoppe, LLC
Pro Forma Income Statements
For the First Five Quarters of Operations and for the Year Ended December 31, 2021

Figure 6.12. Pro forma income statements for the first five quarters of operations and for the year ended December 31, 2021, final version.

The First Pro Forma Post-Revenue Balance Sheet

The first pro forma post-revenue balance sheet is usually set up to be compared with the pro forma pre-revenue balance sheet. This presentation allows the financial statement reader to easily see the progress the entity is expected to make during its initial months or quarters of operations. The entrepreneur will prepare reconciliations of cash and equity in concert with the first post-revenue balance sheet, but note that a pro forma start-up phase expense statement does not need to be prepared in conjunction with the post-revenue reconciliations of cash and equity. This is because the business has moved past its start-up phase into its operational phase and therefore generates income statements.

Figure 6.13 is the first iteration of the Fifth Avenue Apparel Shoppe's post-revenue balance sheet and related reconciliations.

What we see in figure 6.13 is that the post-revenue balance sheet creation process has been initiated by setting up the balance sheet and its associated reconciliations based on items already known. Specifically, the pre-revenue balance sheet has been duplicated, and then a second column has been added for the December 31, 2021 post-revenue balance sheet. Next, the cash amount on the pre-revenue balance sheet ($30,250) has been replicated on the reconciliation of cash, and the owners' equity amount on the pre-revenue balance sheet ($117,000) has been replicated

Fifth Avenue Apparel Shoppe, LLC Pro Forma Balance Sheets As of September 30, 2020, and December 31, 2021			Fifth Avenue Apparel Shoppe, LLC Pro Forma Reconciliations of Cash and Owners' Equity For the Five Quarters Ended December 31, 2021	
	(Pre-Revenue) September 30, 2020	(Post-Revenue) December 31, 2021		
Cash	$ 30,250		Reconciliation of Cash:	
Prepaid insurance	250	250		
Clothing inventory	30,000	30,000	Beginning cash	$ 30,250
Accessories inventory	10,000	10,000		
Total current assets	70,500			
Checkout counters and furniture	12,000	12,000		
Clothing racks and shelving	20,000	20,000		
Computers and software	10,000	10,000		
Security system	5,000	5,000		
Less: Accumulated depreciation	–			
Net fixed assets	47,500			
Total assets	$117,500		Reconciliation of Owners' Equity:	
Utilities payable	$ 500	$ 500	Beginning owners' equity	$117,000
Total liabilities	500		Add: Net income for the five quarters ended December 31, 2021	291,751
			Less: Distributions to owners from April–December 2021	270,000
Owners' equity	117,000			
Total liabilities and owners' equity	$117,500			

Figure 6.13. Pro forma pre-revenue balance sheet and pro forma post-revenue balance sheet, including post-revenue reconciliations of cash and owners' equity, working copy 1.

on the reconciliation of owners' equity. Last, the expected total net income for the first five quarters of operations of $291,751 has been posted to the reconciliation of equity. Note that net income for fourth quarter 2020 must be added to net income for 2021 in order to arrive at total net income for the first five quarters of operations.

Additional balance sheet and reconciliation amounts have been determined using the information included in the list of assumptions (see figure 6.6). For instance, the list of assumptions suggests that distributions related to the first five quarters of the business are expected to equal $270,000 (April–December 2021 represents nine months; 9 months x $10,000 per month x 3 owners = $270,000). $270,000 of distributions have accordingly been included on the reconciliation of owners' equity. The list of assumptions doesn't mention anything about expected new equity investment during fourth quarter 2020 or 2021, so this line item hasn't been included on the reconciliation of equity.

Our list of assumptions indicates there are expected to be no purchases or disposals (i.e., sales or abandonments) of fixed assets until after 2021, so the dollar amounts of the fixed assets will stay the same and have therefore been replicated on the December 31, 2021 balance sheet. Our list of assumptions also indicates that clothing and accessories inventories are expected to stay at the same levels through the end of 2021, so the dollar amounts of these two line items have also been replicated on the December 31, 2021 balance sheet. In addition, our list of assumptions indicates insurance and utilities expenses are expected to remain unchanged at $500 per month and $250 per month, respectively, until 2022. Percentage increases or decreases in expenses—or the lack thereof—are usually mirrored in their related prepaids or payables. As a result, the dollar amounts of the prepaid asset related to insurance expense and the payable related to utilities expense can be reasonably assumed to stay the same and have therefore been replicated on the December 31, 2021 balance sheet. Finally, we know we generally start depreciating our assets once business operations have commenced, so the balance sheet has been adjusted to recognize that fact by changing the term "fixed assets" to "net fixed assets" and adding a line for accumulated depreciation.

Note that, as a result of creating the post-revenue balance sheet next to the pre-revenue balance sheet, we are creating our first comparative balance sheets. When creating comparative balance sheets, there are a few special items to remember:

- Assuming no fixed assets have been sold or abandoned during the current period, accumulated depreciation at the end of the current period is calculated as follows:

    Accumulated depreciation at the beginning of the current period

    + Current period depreciation expense
    _____

    Accumulated depreciation at the end of the current period

    If a fixed asset has been sold or abandoned during the current period, after performing the above calculation, the dollar amount of accumulated depreciation associated with the sold or abandoned fixed asset—and the dollar amount of the fixed asset itself—should be removed from the current period balance sheet. The sold or abandoned fixed asset and its associated accumulated depreciation should not, however, be removed from the prior period's balance sheet.

    In addition to adjusting the current period balance sheet to reflect that a fixed asset has been sold or abandoned, the cost, the salvage value, and any related future depreciation expense related to the sold or abandoned fixed asset should also be removed from the business's forward-looking depreciation schedules, as applicable.

- In the instance of an entity that is not a corporation, owner's equity at the end of the current period is calculated as follows:

> Owner's equity at the beginning of the current period
> + Current period projected net income or – current period projected net loss
> + Expected current period new equity investment
> – Expected current period distributions to the owner
> _____
> Owner's equity at the end of the current period

- In the instance of a corporation, retained earnings at the end of the current period is calculated as follows:

> Retained earnings at the beginning of the current period
> + Current period projected net income or – current period projected net loss
> – Expected current period dividends (C corporation) or distributions (S corporation)
> _____
> Retained earnings at the end of the current period

Fifth Avenue Apparel Shoppe, LLC Pro Forma Balance Sheets As of September 30, 2020, and December 31, 2021			Fifth Avenue Apparel Shoppe, LLC Pro Forma Reconciliations of Cash and Owners' Equity For the Five Quarters Ended December 31, 2021	
	(Pre-Revenue) September 30, 2020	(Post-Revenue) December 31, 2021		
Cash	$ 30,250		Reconciliation of Cash:	
Prepaid insurance	250	250		
Clothing inventory	30,000	30,000	Beginning cash	$ 30,250
Accessories inventory	10,000	10,000		
Total current assets	70,500			
Checkout counters and furniture	12,000	12,000		
Clothing racks and shelving	20,000	20,000		
Computers and software	10,000	10,000		
Security system	5,000	5,000		
Less: Accumulated depreciation	–	14,100		
Net fixed assets	47,000	32,900		
Total assets	$ 117,500		Reconciliation of Owners' Equity:	
Accounts payable	$ –	$ 34,000	Beginning owners' equity:	$117,000
Payroll payable	–	1,552	Add: Net income for the five quarters	
Payroll taxes payable	–	210	ended December 31, 2021	291,751
Utilities payable	500	500	Less: Distributions to owners from	
Sales tax payable	–	3,364	April–December 2021	270,000
Total liabilities	500	39,626	Ending owners' equity	$138,751
Owners' equity	117,000	138,751		
Total liabilities and owners' equity	$ 117,500	$178,377		

Figure 6.14. Pro forma pre-revenue balance sheet and pro forma post-revenue balance sheet, including post-revenue reconciliations of cash and owners' equity, working copy 2.

Note that any new equity investments expected to occur during the current period would be reflected in the common stock, paid-in capital in excess of par, or preferred stock accounts, not the retained earnings account. Reference appendix 6-B at the end of this chapter for an illustration of the treatment of new equity investment for a corporation.

Returning to our example, figure 6.14 is the second iteration of our post-revenue balance sheet and related reconciliations.

In the second iteration, since no fixed assets are expected to be sold or abandoned during the period between the end of the start-up phase of the business and the beginning of 2022, the $14,100 amount for accumulated depreciation was determined as follows:

	Accumulated depreciation at the beginning of the current period	$ 0
+	Current period depreciation expense	14,100
	Accumulated depreciation at the end of the current period	$14,100

Note that the $14,100 depreciation expense number sources from the pro forma income statements for the first five quarters of operations shown at figure 6.12 (depreciation expense for fourth quarter 2020 + depreciation expense for 2021 = $4,700 + $9,400 = $14,100). Next, a total was calculated for net fixed assets.

The list of assumptions in figure 6.6 includes specific information regarding expected payables. The information is shown again in figure 6.15.

Each payable indicated on the balance sheet shown at figure 6.14 is based on a number that has already been calculated elsewhere. Determining the amounts for these items was, therefore, a matter of simple multiplication:

Accounts payable = December 31, 2021 clothing and accessories
                 inventory x 0.85
               = $40,000 x 0.85
               = $34,000

Payroll payable = Fourth quarter 2021 payroll expense x 0.167
              = $9,295 x 0.167
              = $1,552

Payroll taxes payable = Fourth quarter 2021 payroll tax expense x 0.167
                    = $1,255 x 0.167
                    = $210

Sales tax payable = Fourth quarter 2021 sales x 0.333 x 0.06
                = $168,372 x 0.333 x 0.06
                = $3,364

- At December 31, 2021 accounts payable, including payables related to cleaning and maintenance and miscellaneous expenses, is expected to approximate 85% of clothing and accessories inventory.
- At December 31, 2021, payroll payable is expected to equal one-sixth of fourth quarter 2021 payroll expense.
- At December 31, 2021, payroll taxes payable is expected to equal one-sixth of fourth quarter 2021 tax expense.
- At December 31, 2021, sales tax payable is expected to approximate one month's sales multiplied by the sales tax rate of 6 percent (calculated as one-third of fourth quarter 2021 sales x 0.06).

Figure 6.15. Assumptions regarding expected payables (excerpt from figure 6.6).

After these payable amounts were posted to the balance sheet, a total was calculated for total liabilities. Next, the reconciliation of owners' equity was completed by calculating the applicable total and then posting the result on the December 31, 2021 balance sheet. After owners' equity was posted to the balance sheet, a total was calculated for total liabilities and equity.

In order to complete the pro forma comparative balance sheet, all that is needed now is to determine the December 31, 2021 cash balance and then calculate the remaining December 31, 2021 balance sheet subtotals and totals. December 31, 2021 cash will be determined by completing the reconciliation of cash, as shown in figure 6.16, the final version of our pro forma pre-revenue balance sheet, pro forma post-revenue balance sheet, and related reconciliations of cash and owners' equity.

The reconciliation of cash was completed by first adding the net income for the applicable five quarters to beginning cash and then adding back depreciation expense—a noncash expense. Next, adjustments were made for the changes in noncash asset and liability line items. None of the noncash asset line items changed from September 30, 2020 to December 31, 2021, so no adjustments related to these assets were needed on the reconciliation of cash. Note that the change in accumulated

Fifth Avenue Apparel Shoppe, LLC Pro Forma Balance Sheets As of September 30, 2020, and December 31, 2021			Fifth Avenue Apparel Shoppe, LLC Pro Forma Reconciliations of Cash and Owners' Equity For the Five Quarters Ended December 31, 2021	
	(Pre-Revenue) September 30, 2020	(Post-Revenue) December 31, 2021		
Cash	$ 30,250	$105,227	Reconciliation of Cash:	
Prepaid insurance	250	250		
Clothing inventory	30,000	30,000	Beginning cash	$ 30,250
Accessories inventory	10,000	10,000	Add: Net income for the five quarters	
Total current assets	70,500	145,477	ended December 31, 2021	291,751
			Add: Depreciation for the five	14,100
Checkout counters and	12,000	12,000	quarters ended December 31, 2021	
furniture			Adjustments for changes in noncash	
Clothing racks and shelving	20,000	20,000	assets and liabilities:	
Computers and software	10,000	10,000	Increase in accounts payable	34,000
Security system	5,000	5,000	Increase in payroll payable	1,552
Less: Accumulated			Increase in payroll taxes payable	210
depreciation	-	14,100	Increase in sales tax payable	3,364
Net fixed assets	47,000	32,900	Less: Distributions to owners from	
			April–December 2021	270,000
Total assets	$117,500	$178,377	Ending cash	$105,227
Accounts payable	$ -	$ 34,000	Reconciliation of Owners' Equity:	
Payroll payable	-	1,552		
Payroll taxes payable	-	210	Beginning owners' equity	$117,000
Utilities payable	500	500	Add: Net income for the five quarters	
Sales tax payable	-	3,364	ended December 31, 2021	291,751
Total liabilities	500	39,626	Less: Distributions to owners from	
			April–December 2021	270,000
Owners' equity	117,000	138,751	Ending owners' equity	$138,751
Total liabilities and owners' equity	$117,500	$178,377		

Figure 6.16. Pro forma pre-revenue balance sheet and pro forma post-revenue balance sheet, including post-revenue reconciliations of cash and owners' equity, final version.

depreciation has already been accounted for by adding back depreciation expense on the reconciliation. While none of the noncash asset line items changed, four of the five payable line items on the balance sheet did change. In fact, in all four instances, the payable increased. An increase in a payable is caused by delaying paying a bill. Delaying paying a bill is a source of cash, so the increase in each of the four payables was treated as a source of cash or add back to cash on the reconciliation.

Note the proper treatment of the following types of items on a reconciliation of cash:

- An increase in a payable is a source of cash or an add back to cash.
- A decrease in a payable is a use of cash or a deduction from cash.
- An increase in a noncash asset is a use of cash or a deduction from cash.
- A decrease in a noncash asset is a source of cash or an add back to cash.

The reconciliation of cash was finalized by adding a line item for expected distributions to owners during the applicable five quarters, totaling the reconciliation, and replicating the indicated ending cash balance on the post-revenue balance sheet. Once the balance sheet included the cash balance, totals for current assets and total assets were calculated. The last step was to verify the dollar amount for total assets equals the dollar amount for total liabilities and equity. The fact that the two amounts are equal suggests that the post-revenue balance sheet has likely been completed correctly.

Year 2 and Subsequent Year Pro Forma Income Statements

Given that the owners of the Fifth Avenue Apparel Shoppe would probably want to understand more than just the expected short-term profitability of their business, they'll likely want to prepare additional pro forma income statements reaching two, three, or four years further into the future in order to determine the expected long-term profitability of the business. To that end, using the information included in the list of assumptions at figure 6.6, we'll first prepare a cost of goods sold schedule for years 2022–2025 of the business's operations. Figure 6.17 shows that schedule.

To determine 2022 cost of goods sold for clothing, we multiplied the expected quarterly cost of goods sold for clothing for 2022 by a factor of four, as there are four quarters in a year. The other cost of goods sold numbers were calculated similarly by product line. The cost of goods sold schedule in figure 6.17 indicates how much product our entrepreneurs expect to sell. As we did for our first pro forma income

Fifth Avenue Apparel Shoppe, LLC Cost of Goods Sold Schedule				
Assumptions: Cost of good sold = $45,000 (clothing) and $15,000 (accessories) per quarter for 2022. Cost of goods sold = $48,500 (clothing) and $16,500 (accessories) per quarter for 2023 and beyond.				
	2022	2023	2024	2025
Clothing	$180,000	$194,000	$194,000	$194,000
Accessories	60,000	66,000	66,000	66,000
Total	$240,000	$260,000	$260,000	$260,000

Figure 6.17. Cost of goods sold schedule for years 2022–2025.

statement, we can gross up the cost of goods sold numbers to sales numbers by applying the following formula:

Sales amount = Cost of item ÷ (1 − Expected average margin for that item)

Figure 6.18 illustrates the resulting estimated sales schedule.

Fifth Avenue Apparel Shoppe, LLC **Estimated Sales Schedule**				
Target margin for clothing:		60% until December 31, 2023 65% beginning January 1, 2024		
Target margin for accessories:		75% until December 31, 2024 80% beginning January 1, 2025		
	2022	2023	2024	2025
Clothing	$450,000	$485,000	$554,286	$554,286
Accessories	240,000	264,000	264,000	330,000
Total	$690,000	$794,000	$818,286	$884,286

Figure 6.18. Estimated sales schedule for years 2022–2025.

Next, we expand our depreciation schedule from that shown in figure 6.7 to that shown in figure 6.19 by including the fixed-asset acquisitions expected in 2023 and 2025.

Fifth Avenue Apparel Shoppe, LLC **Depreciation Schedule**				
	2020	2023	2025	
Fixed asset acquisitions:	$47,000	$5,000	$12,500	
Less: Salvage value:	-	-	1,250	
Depreciable value:	$47,000	$5,000	$11,250	
Useful life in years:	5	5	5	
Depreciation method:	Straight-line, half-year convention	Straight-line, half-year convention	Straight-line, half-year convention	
Year	Depreciation	Depreciation	Depreciation	Annual Depreciation
2020	$ 4,700	$ -	$ -	$ 4,700
2021	9,400	-	-	9,400
2022	9,400	-	-	9,400
2023	9,400	500	-	9,900
2024	9,400	1,000	-	10,400
2025	4,700	1,000	1,125	6,825
2026	-	1,000	2,250	3,250
2027	-	1,000	2,250	3,250
2028	-	500	2,250	2,750
2029	-	-	2,250	2,250
2030	-	-	1,125	1,125
Total	$47,000	$5,000	$11,250	$63,250

Figure 6.19. Expanded depreciation schedule.

Fifth Avenue Apparel Shoppe, LLC Pro Forma Income Statements For the Years Ended December 31, 2022, 2023, 2024, and 2025				
	2022	2023	2024	2025
Sales	$690,000	$749,000	$818,286	$884,286
Cost of goods sold	240,000	260,000	260,000	260,000
Gross profit	450,000	489,000	558,286	624,284
Operating expenses:				
Rent				
Payroll				
Payroll taxes				
Utilities				
Insurance				
Depreciation	9,400	9,900	10,400	6,825
Cleaning and maintenance				
Miscellaneous				
Total operating expenses				
Net income				

Figure 6.20. Pro forma income statements for the years ended December 31, 2022, 2023, 2024, and 2025, working copy.

Inputting the information we've determined thus far results in the preliminary pro forma income statements presented in figure 6.20. Note that, as when we prepared the first pro forma income statement, although we've referred to the second pro forma income statement we are creating in the singular thus far in this chapter, technically we are preparing an income statement that includes multiple periods of time. Hence, the formal income statement shown at figure 6.20 is appropriately entitled "Pro Forma Income Statements."

We can now complete the pro forma income statements by fleshing out operating expenses for years 2022–2025 utilizing the expense information included on our list of assumptions at figure 6.6. Figure 6.21 includes the relevant information from that list.

After reflecting the data in figure 6.21 in our operating expenses for 2022–2025, the final version of our pro forma income statements for years 2022–2025 looks as shown in figure 6.22 (on page 142).

Those are some pretty fat profits! The profits are fat enough, in fact, that they likely make our entrepreneurs pretty comfortable that this business can support the monthly distributions they deem reflective of their full-time engagement in the business and that also are needed to keep their angel investor happy.

- Employee pay per hour is expected to increase 20% from its year 2021 amount in 2022 and then another 5% in 2024.
- Cleaning and maintenance expense is expected to cost $250 per month beginning in October 2020 and remain the same amount through the end of 2025.
- Miscellaneous expense is expected to amount to 5% of the prior period's COGS.
- Rent will remain at $5,000 per month through September 30, 2023, then increase 5% to $5,250 on October 1, 2023. Rent is expected to continue to be paid on the first day of the month to which it relates.
- Utilities expense is expected to remain unchanged at approximately $500 per month until it increases 3% in 2022 and then another 2% in 2024.
- Insurance expense is expected to continue to be paid one month in advance and is expected to remain unchanged at approximately $250 per month until it increases 10% in 2022 and then stabilizes.

Figure 6.21. Assumptions regarding expected expenses (excerpts from figure 6.6).

Fifth Avenue Apparel Shoppe, LLC Pro Forma Income Statements For the Years Ended December 31, 2022, 2023, 2024, and 2025				
	2022	2023	2024	2025
Sales	$690,000	$749,000	$818,286	$884,286
Cost of goods sold	240,000	260,000	260,000	260,000
Gross profit	450,000	489,000	558,286	624,284
Operating expenses:				
Rent	60,000	60,750	63,000	63,000
Payroll	44,616	44,616	46,847	46,847
Payroll taxes	6,023	6,023	6,324	6,324
Utilities	6,180	6,180	6,304	6,304
Insurance	3,300	3,300	3,300	3,300
Depreciation	9,400	9,900	10,400	6,825
Cleaning and maintenance	3,000	3,000	3,000	3,000
Miscellaneous	10,211	12,000	13,000	13,000
Total operating expenses	142,729	145,769	152,175	148,600
Net income	$307,271	$343,231	$406,111	$475,686

Figure 6.22. Pro forma income statements for the years ended December 31, 2022, 2023, 2024, and 2025, final version.

Pro Forma Financial Statements and Potential Investors and Lenders

Thus far, we've completed the following pro forma financial statements and major schedules for the Fifth Avenue Apparel Shoppe:

- schedule of start-up costs for the four months ended September 30, 2020
- pre-revenue balance sheet for September 30, 2020, including reconciliations of cash and owners' equity
- start-up phase expense statement for the four months ended September 30, 2020
- post-start-up phase list of assumptions
- income statement for the first five quarters of operations and the year ended December 31, 2021
- post-revenue balance sheet for December 31, 2021, including reconciliations of cash and owners' equity
- income statements for the years ended December 31, 2022, 2023, 2024, and 2025

The question next arises as to which of these financial statements and schedules our entrepreneurs would likely want to show to an interested investor or lender. The pro forma financial statements and schedules that should be shared with an interested investor or lender include, at minimum:

- the list of assumptions
- the pre-revenue and post-revenue balance sheets
- the income statements for all periods

The list of assumptions should be shared with potential investors and lenders because it explains the research and logic behind all the numbers on both the pro

	Fifth Avenue Apparel Shoppe, LLC Pro Forma Income Statements For the Three Months Ended December 31, 2020, and for the Years Ended December 31, 2021, 2022, 2023, 2024 and 2025					
	For the Three Months Ended December 31, 2020	2021	2022	2023	2024	2025
Sales	$115,000	$587,087	$690,000	$749,000	$818,286	$884.286
Cost of goods sold	40,000	204,204	240,000	260,000	260,000	260,000
Gross profit	75,000	382,883	450,000	489,000	558,286	624,286
Operating expenses:						
Rent	15,000	60,000	60,000	60,750	63,000	63,000
Payroll	9,295	37,180	44,616	44,616	46,847	46,847
Payroll taxes	1,255	5,019	6,023	6,023	6,324	6,324
Utilities	1,500	6,000	6,180	6,180	6,304	6,304
Insurance	750	3,000	3,300	3,300	3,300	3,300
Depreciation	4,700	9,400	9,400	9,900	10,400	6,825
Cleaning and maintenance	750	3,000	3,000	3,000	3,000	3,000
Miscellaneous	–	9,282	10,210	12,000	13,000	13,000
Total operating expenses	33,250	132,881	142,729	145,769	152,175	148,600
Net income	$ 41,750	$250,001	$307,271	$343,231	$406,111	$475,686

Figure 6.23. Pro forma income statements for the three months ended December 31, 2020, and for the years ended December 31, 2021, 2022, 2023, 2024, and 2025.

forma balance sheets and the pro forma income statements. Figure 6.16 shows the two pro forma balance sheets together in one financial statement. At the discretion of our entrepreneurs, these balance sheets could be shared with interested investors or lenders exactly as presented in figure 6.16—or they could be shared without the reconciliations of cash and equity. Further, at the discretion of our entrepreneurs, the balance sheets could also be shown without the terms "pre-revenue" and "post-revenue" above their respective balance sheet dates. In order to finalize a pro forma financial statements package suitable to be shared with potential investors or lenders, our entrepreneurs would likely want to combine all the pro forma income statements into one financial statement. Figure 6.23 illustrates what such a statement might look like.

Note that the pro forma income statement shown in figure 6.23 includes only annual information for 2021. The pro forma income statement for the first five quarters of operations (see figure 6.12 on page 133)—which provides quarterly information for 2021—could be provided to potential investors or lenders as a supplemental financial statement, if so desired by our entrepreneurs. Also, note that in keeping with the slightly more formal tone of the income statement included in figure 6.23, the term "fourth quarter 2020" has been changed to "for the three months ended December 31, 2020."

Pro Forma Balance Sheets for Year 2 and Subsequent Years and Pro Forma Statements of Cash Flows

At this point, we have yet to do the balance sheets for years 2022, 2023, 2024, and 2025. And have you noticed that while we have done a few cash reconciliations, we have not yet created any formal statements of cash flows?

When you're asked to create pro forma financial statements for your start-up company, don't prepare statements of cash flows, and postpone creating balance sheets for years 2–5. There are multiple reasons for this rather nontraditional approach. The reasons to not prepare statements of cash flows are as follows:

- A reconciliation of cash (like those we've created in this chapter) is usually an acceptable replacement for a statement of cash flows.
- A cash flow issue will identify itself in the form of a negative cash balance on the reconciliation of cash and the pro forma balance sheet. If a cash flow issue is identified, the entrepreneur can adjust the applicable list of assumptions, the reconciliation of cash, the reconciliation of equity (if applicable), and the pro forma financial statements in a way that acknowledges that, in order to resolve the cash flow issue, one or both of the following must occur:
  - The business must obtain additional equity investment—a source of cash on the reconciliation of cash and an addition to the reconciliation of owners' equity, but not an addition to the reconciliation of retained earnings in the event of a corporation. In the event of a corporation, additional equity investment would be reflected as an increase in the appropriate equity account(s) on the balance sheet.
  - The business must obtain new or additional debt financing—a source of cash on the reconciliation of cash, a new liability—or an increase to an existing liability—on the balance sheet, and likely new or increased interest expense on the income statement.
- Creating formal statements of cash flows is time-consuming and challenging work. If we can produce the information we need without constructing these statements, time is freed up to spend on other challenges. The entrepreneur can always create additional pro forma annual, quarterly, or monthly income statements and their related balance sheets, cash reconciliations, and equity reconciliations—as needed—in order to illustrate in detail the consequences associated with an expected major capital expenditure or working capital need.

The reasons to postpone preparing balance sheets for years 2–5 are as follows:

- As this chapter has illustrated, balance sheets are much more time consuming and difficult to create than income statements.
- Pro forma balance sheets tend to get more and more unrealistic as we proceed further and further into the future. This is because pro forma balance sheets are estimates based upon the pro forma income statements, which are themselves estimates.
- Every time the pro forma income statements (or early pro forma balance sheets) are updated with new information, which will happen often, every existing pro forma balance sheet, reconciliation of cash, reconciliation of equity, and statement of cash flows dated on or after that change will also have to be updated. Considering item 1 of this list, that is quite unappealing.
- Investors and lenders spend most of their time looking at income statements and very little time looking at balance sheets. Note that, if an investor or lender really wants to see balance sheets for years 2–5, you can always prepare them if you feel the potential reward is worth the time spent.

Given all this, how does an entrepreneur create pro forma balance sheets for years 2–5 and pro forma statements of cash flows if a current or potential investor or lender insists upon them? The creation of these financial statements for a proposed new enterprise will be discussed and illustrated in detail in chapter 7. Before an entrepreneur performs the extra work to create additional pro forma financial statements, however, she should first perform a breakeven analysis on the proposed new venture using the financial statement information she has already developed.

Breakeven Analysis—Feasibility of a Proposed New Business

As mentioned in previous chapters of this textbook, the rate of new business failure would likely be significantly lower if every entrepreneur took the time to do a breakeven analysis before starting a business. The Fifth Avenue Apparel Shoppe example we've been exploring in this chapter is clearly expected to be a very profitable venture, but it's always good for an entrepreneur to understand the hurdles her new venture must clear in order to not lose money. A breakeven analysis clarifies these hurdles.

In chapter 5, we calculated the breakeven sales units, breakeven price, and breakeven revenue related to a proposed new product. When a business has a limited number of products—and the pricing and variable costs associated with those products are not complex, as was the case with our chapter 5 example—calculating breakeven sales units and breakeven price for each individual product makes sense. When a business sells many different products with many different variable costs at many different prices—as will be the case with the Fifth Avenue Apparel Shoppe—calculating breakeven sales units and breakeven price for each individual product doesn't make sense, at least not at the planning stage of the business. However, calculating breakeven revenue for the business does make sense.

Breakeven revenue is the minimum revenue a business must bring in over an indicated period of time in order to not lose money. It's also the minimum revenue needed to make starting a new venture worthwhile. If we determine we can't bring in enough revenue to cover our costs, then the decision about whether or not to start a new venture becomes pretty simple. The relevant formulas for the calculation of breakeven revenue follow:

Breakeven revenue = Total fixed costs ÷ Gross margin

where

Gross margin = Gross profit ÷ Net sales

Because we have completed pro forma income statements for the Fifth Avenue Apparel Shoppe, we have the information we need to calculate breakeven revenue. Focusing on year 2021 for purposes of our calculations, we first need to determine the gross margin for the proposed business. Reviewing the income statement for 2021 included in figure 6.12, we see that the expected gross profit for 2021 is $382,883 and the expected sales for 2021 are $587,087 (note that, as first discussed in chapter 5, when there is no net sales line on an income statement, we instead use the amount on the sales line to calculate gross margin). Therefore, the Fifth Avenue Apparel Shoppe's gross margin for 2021 equals 65.2 percent, calculated as follows:

Gross margin = Gross profit ÷ Net sales

Therefore,

Gross margin = $382,883 ÷ $587,087
= 0.652
= 65.2%

Next, we need to determine the total fixed costs for the proposed business. Remember that a variable cost is a cost that changes in total with a change in the volume of production or sales, but is generally fixed on a per-unit basis. Recall, too, that a fixed cost is a cost that remains the same amount in total over a specified period of time. Given these facts, figure 6.24 (on page 146) is a summary of the variable and fixed costs included on the Fifth Avenue Apparel Shoppe's income statement for 2021.

Fifth Avenue Apparel Shoppe, LLC Summary of Variable and Fixed Costs For the Year Ended December 31, 2021		
	Variable Costs	Fixed Costs
Cost of goods sold	$204,204	$ –
Rent	–	60,000
Payroll	–	37,180
Payroll taxes	–	5,019
Utilities	–	6,000
Insurance	–	3,000
Depreciation	–	9,400
Cleaning and maintenance	–	3,000
Miscellaneous	9,282	–
Total	$231,486	$123,599

Figure 6.24. Summary of variable and fixed costs for the year ended December 31, 2021.

Having determined values for both total fixed costs and gross margin, we can now calculate breakeven revenue. After rounding up to the next whole dollar, breakeven revenue for year 2021 for the Fifth Avenue Apparel Shoppe is $189,570, calculated as follows:

Breakeven revenue = Total fixed costs ÷ Gross margin

Therefore,

Breakeven revenue = $123,599 ÷ 0.652
= $189,570

This breakeven revenue number makes sense because we can see in the pro forma income statement at figure 6.12 that, at sales of $587,087, the proposed business is, in fact, quite profitable. Breakeven revenue for this company should then be well below $587,087, as the number we have calculated for breakeven revenue, in fact, is. Note that the breakeven revenue we have calculated is based on the company's expected annual fixed costs for 2021 of $123,599. If and when the expected annual fixed costs for 2021 change, breakeven revenue for 2021 will change accordingly.

Breakeven hurdles such as breakeven revenue should be included in the feasibility analysis for a proposed new venture. If the two entrepreneurs looking to start the Fifth Avenue Apparel Shoppe are planning to use their feasibility analysis to entice the desired $125,000 angel investment, demonstrating that the expected revenue of the proposed new venture far exceeds the breakeven revenue of the proposed new venture is an excellent starting point for a conversation with an interested investor.

Pro Forma Financial Statements for Alternative Types of Entities

As mentioned earlier in this chapter, as practical matter, an entrepreneur's approach to creating pro forma financial statements for an entity will vary depending upon the nature of the entity in question, its associated business model, and the industry in which it operates. In this chapter, we've illustrated the creation of pro forma financial statements using the example of a retailer of high-end apparel. Detailed examples of how to create pro forma financial statements for a service-based business and a C corporation smartphone application business are included as appendices to this chapter. Note that these examples also include guidance on the treatment of the following topics not addressed in the apparel retailer example utilized throughout this chapter:

- accounts receivable (appendix 6-A)
- debt (appendices 6-A and 6-B)
- new equity investment for a pass-through entity (appendix 6-A)
- new equity investment for a corporation (appendix 6-B)
- initial net losses (appendix 6-B)
- dividends (appendix 6-B)

The treatment of a fixed-asset disposal will be illustrated in chapter 7.

A Word of Caution Regarding Pro Forma Financial Statements

It's worth noting that there's no such thing as a "correct" pro forma financial statement. All pro forma financial statements are an entrepreneur's best guess of the future based on research and logic. Because all pro forma financial statements are inherently guesses, they're eminently attackable and defendable only with regard to the quality of the research that provides the foundation upon which they were created. If the research that underlies pro forma financial statements is poor, no matter how well the statements follow the form, function, and logic suggested in this chapter, they will have little value.

Summary

In this chapter, we completed the following pro forma financial statements and major schedules for an example business:

- schedule of start-up costs
- pre-revenue balance sheet, including reconciliations of cash and equity
- start-up phase expense statement
- post-start-up phase list of assumptions
- income statement for the period of a business's initial operations
- post-revenue balance sheet, including reconciliations of cash and equity
- income statements for the years subsequent to the period of a business's initial operations

When you're asked to create pro forma financial statements for your start-up company, don't prepare statements of cash flows, and postpone creating balance sheets for years 2–5. There are multiple reasons for this rather nontraditional approach. The reasons to not prepare statements of cash flows are as follows:

- A reconciliation of cash is usually an acceptable replacement for a statement of cash flows.
- A cash flow issue will identify itself in the form of a negative cash balance on the reconciliation of cash and the pro forma balance sheet.
- Creating formal statements of cash flows is time-consuming and challenging work. We can always instead create additional detailed pro forma balance sheets and income statements as their creation becomes warranted.

The reasons to postpone preparing balance sheets for years 2–5 are as follows:

- Balance sheets are much more time consuming and difficult to create than income statements.

- Pro forma balance sheets tend to get more and more unrealistic as we proceed further and further into the future.
- Every time the pro forma income statements (or early pro forma balance sheets) are updated with new information, every existing pro forma balance sheet, reconciliation of cash, reconciliation of equity, and statement of cash flows dated on or after that change will also have to be updated.
- Investors and lenders spend most of their time looking at income statements and very little time looking at balance sheets.

How does an entrepreneur create pro forma balance sheets for years 2–5 and pro forma statements of cash flows if a current or potential investor or lender insists upon them? The creation of these financial statements for a proposed new enterprise will be discussed and illustrated in detail in chapter 7.

Breakeven hurdles should be included in the feasibility analysis for a proposed new venture. When a business sells many different products with many different variable costs at many different prices, calculating breakeven sales units and breakeven price for each individual product doesn't make sense, at least not at the planning stage of the business. However, calculating breakeven revenue for the business does make sense. Breakeven revenue is the minimum revenue a business must bring in over an indicated period of time in order to not lose money. It's also the minimum revenue needed to make starting a new venture worthwhile. A feasibility analysis demonstrating that the expected revenue of a proposed new venture far exceeds the breakeven revenue of that new venture is a significant asset to any entrepreneur desiring to pursue outside funding for the new venture.

There is no such thing as a "correct" pro forma financial statement. All pro forma financial statements are an entrepreneur's best guess of the future based on research and logic. If the research that underlies pro forma financial statements is poor, no matter how well the statements follow the form, function, and logic suggested in this chapter, they will have little value.

Key Terms

industry research	markup	salvage value
market research	primary market research	

Review and Discussion Questions

1. Why does an entrepreneur need to create pro forma financial statements?
2. What are the three traditional pro forma statements for a for-profit business?
3. What detail schedules typically need to be created in conjunction with the creation of pro forma financial statements?
4. Describe what a schedule of start-up costs is and how it is created.
5. When creating comparative balance sheets, there are a few special items to remember. List and describe those items.
6. What is breakeven revenue, and why should every entrepreneur calculate it for any new venture she's considering starting?

Exercises

1. An entrepreneur and an angel investor with $100,000 to invest plan to open a retail store called Affordably Haute on October 1, 2020, following a four-month start-up phase. Using the schedule of start-up costs provided below, complete

the pro forma pre-revenue balance sheet and pro forma start-up phase expense statement, including reconciliations of cash and owners' equity, included below for Affordably Haute Apparel Shoppe, LLC.

Affordably Haute Apparel Shoppe, LLC Schedule of Start-up Costs					
	June 2020	July 2020	August 2020	September 2020	For the Four Months Ended September 30, 2020
Rent	$2,500	$2,500	$2,500	$2,500	$10,000
Utilities	275	275	275	275	1,100
Insurance	500	250	250	250	1,250
Cleaning and maintenance	500	300	300	300	1,200
Store design and decoration	5,000	4,000	3,000	2,000	14,000
Clothing inventory	–	–	12,000	15,500	27,500
Accessories inventory	–	–	3,000	–	8,500
Checkout counters and furniture	–	–	8,500	5,500	8,500
Clothing racks and shelving	–	–	6,000	3,000	9,000
Computers and software	–	–	10,000	–	10,000
Security system	–	5,000	–	–	5,000
Total	$8,575	$12,325	$45,825	$29,325	$96,050

Notes: Rent is paid on the first day of the month to which it applies.
     Utilities are paid in the month after the services are used.
     Insurance is paid in the month previous to the month to which it applies.
     All other costs are paid in the same month as incurred.
     Store design and decoration expense will terminate in September 2020.

Affordably Haute Apparel Shoppe, LLC Pro Forma Pre-Revenue Balance Sheet As of September 30, 2020	Affordably Haute Apparel Shoppe, LLC Pro Forma Start-up Phase Expense Statement, Including Reconciliations of Cash and Owners' Equity For the Four Months Ended September 30, 2020
Cash	Rent
Prepaid insurance	Utilities
Clothing inventory	Insurance
Accessories inventory	Less: Prepaid insurance
Total current assets	
	Cleaning and maintenance
Checkout counters and furniture	Store design and decoration
Clothing racks and shelving	Start-up phase expenses
Computers and software	Less: Utilities payable
Security system	Total cash outlays for expenses
Total fixed assets	
	Reconciliation of Cash:
Total assets	Beginning cash
	Less: Cash outlays for assets
Utilities payable	Less: Cash outlays for expenses
Total liabilities	Ending cash
Owners' equity	Reconciliation of Owners' Equity:
	Beginning owners' equity
Total liabilities and owners' equity	Less: Start-up phase expenses
	Ending owners' equity

2. An entrepreneur with $52,500 plans to open a convenience store called Kevin's Convenience Store on June 1, 2020, following a two-month start-up phase. Using the schedule of start-up costs provided below, create a pro forma pre-revenue balance sheet and a pro forma start-up phase expense statement, including reconciliations of cash and owner's equity, for Kevin's Convenience Store, LLC.

Kevin's Convenience Store, LLC Schedule of Start-up Costs			
	April 2020	May 2020	For the Two Months Ended May 31, 2020
Rent	$ 4,000	$ 2,000	$ 6,000
Utilities	400	400	800
Insurance	600	300	950
Cleaning and maintenance	200	200	400
Food inventory	–	10,000	10,000
Non-food inventory	–	7,500	7,500
Checkout counters and equipment	8,500	–	8,500
Racks and shelving	6,000	–	6,000
Computers and software	5,000	–	5,000
Security system	4,500	–	4,500
Total	$29,200	$20,400	$49,600

Notes: Rent is paid on the first day of the month to which it applies.
Utilities are paid in the month after the services are used.
Insurance is paid in the month previous to the month to which it applies.
All other costs are paid in the same month as incurred.

3. You've decided to open an apparel store called Bargain Basement on July 1, 2020, following a four-month start-up phase. A list of assumptions for Bargain Basement Apparel Shoppe, LLC follows:

Bargain Basement Apparel Shoppe, LLC
List of Assumptions for July 1, 2020–December 31, 2021

General Operational and Payroll Information

Store hours:	Tuesday–Saturday: 10:00 a.m.–9:00 p.m.
	Sunday: Noon–8:00 p.m.

Needed employees: Three:	1 Tuesday–Saturday 9:00 a.m.–4:00 p.m.
	1 Tuesday–Saturday 3:00 p.m.–10:00 p.m.
	1 Sunday 11:00 a.m.–6:00 p.m.

Employees will be paid $11 per hour. Total payroll taxes, unemployment, and workers' compensation (i.e., payroll taxes) are expected to equal 13.5% of gross payroll. In order to keep payroll to a minimum and effectively manage the business, the founder will be present during most of the store's hours of operation.

Information Regarding Expected Inventory Pricing and Inventory Sales (Cost of Goods Sold)

Target margin for clothing:	40%
Target margin for accessories:	35%

Expected inventory turnover rate for 2020: 12 times per year. In other words, for 2020, after business operations commence, it is expected that, on average, the business will sell and replace its inventory at a rate of 12 times per year, or once every month. The company's June 30, 2020 pro forma pre-revenue balance sheet includes $20,000 of clothing inventory and $7,500 of accessories inventory. Beginning the first quarter of 2021, cost of goods sold (COGS) is expected to increase 7.5% each quarter through the end of 2021.

Information Regarding Expected Fixed-Asset Purchases, Disposals, and Depreciation

The business is expected to purchase $29,900 of depreciable fixed assets during the start-up phase of the business (March–June 2020). All these fixed assets are expected to have a useful life of five years and a salvage value of $0, and will be depreciated using the straight-line, half-year convention depreciation method. No additional fixed assets are expected to be purchased—and no fixed assets are expected to be disposed of—until after 2021.

Information Regarding Expected Non-Payroll Expenses

- Rent is expected to be $1,750 per month and will remain the same amount through September 30, 2023.
- Miscellaneous expense is expected to amount to 2% of the prior period's COGS.
- Utilities, insurance, and cleaning and maintenance expenses aren't expected to change from their third quarter 2020 amounts of $1,500, $600, and $1,350, respectively.

Using the information included above, do the following:

a. Calculate expected quarterly gross payroll for each of the first six quarters of Bargain Basement's operations.

b. Calculate expected quarterly cost of goods sold for each of the first six quarters of Bargain Basement's operations.

c. Calculate expected quarterly sales for each of the first six quarters of Bargain Basement's operations.

d. Create a depreciation schedule.

e. Complete the following pro forma income statements:

Bargain Basement Apparel Shoppe, LLC Pro Forma Income Statements For the First Six Quarters of Operations and for the Year Ended December 31, 2021							
	Third Quarter 2020	Fourth Quarter 2020	First Quarter 2021	Second Quarter 2021	Third Quarter 2021	Fourth Quarter 2021	For the Year Ended December 31, 2021
Sales							
Cost of goods sold							
Gross profit							
Operating expenses:							
Rent							
Payroll							
Payroll taxes							
Utilities	1,500						
Insurance	600						
Depreciation							
Cleaning and maintenance	1,350						
Miscellaneous							
Total operating expenses							
Net income							

4. Three avid hunters have decided to open a hunting supply store called Erin's Hunting Supply on July 1, 2020, following a three-month start-up phase. A list of assumptions for Erin's Hunting Supply, LLC follows:

Erin's Hunting Supply, LLC
List of Assumptions for July 1–December 31, 2020

General Operational and Payroll Information

| Store hours: | Monday–Sunday: 9:00 a.m.–9:00 p.m. |

| Needed employees: Eight: | 4 Monday–Sunday 8:00 a.m.–3:00 p.m. |
| | 4 Monday–Sunday 3:00 p.m.–10:00 p.m. |

Employees will be paid $15.00 per hour. Total payroll taxes, unemployment, and workers' compensation (i.e., payroll taxes) are expected to equal 12% of gross payroll.

Information Regarding Expected Inventory Pricing and Inventory Sales (Cost of Goods Sold)

Target margin for hunting equipment:	50%
Target margin for clothing:	40%
Target margin for other inventory:	35%

Expected inventory turnover rate for 2020: 6 times per year. In other words, for 2020, after business operations commence, it is expected that, on average, the business will sell and replace its inventory at a rate of 6 times per year, or 50% every month. The company's June 30, 2020 pro forma pre-revenue balance sheet includes $100,000 of hunting equipment inventory, $70,000 of clothing inventory, and $30,000 of other inventory. Beginning August 2020, cost of goods sold (COGS) is expected to increase 5% each month through the end of 2020.

Information Regarding Expected Fixed-Asset Purchases, Disposals, and Depreciation

The business is expected to purchase $35,700 of depreciable fixed assets during the start-up phase of the business (April–June 2020). All these fixed assets are expected to have a useful life of five years and a salvage value of $0, and will be depreciated using the straight-line, half-year convention depreciation method. No additional fixed assets are expected to be purchased—and no fixed assets are expected to be disposed of—until after 2020.

Information Regarding Expected Non-Payroll Expenses

- Rent is expected to be $6,750 per month and will remain the same amount through March 31, 2023.
- Miscellaneous expense is expected to amount to 5% of the prior period's COGS.
- Utilities, insurance, and cleaning and maintenance expenses aren't expected to change from their June 2020 amounts of $1,450, $1,350, and $300, respectively.

Using the information included above, do the following:
   a. Calculate expected monthly gross payroll for each of the first six months of Erin's Hunting Supply's operations. (Hint: Calculate daily gross payroll and then calculate monthly gross payroll considering the number of days in each applicable month.)
   b. Calculate expected monthly cost of goods sold for each of the first six months of Erin's Hunting Supply's operations.
   c. Calculate expected monthly sales for each of the first six months of Erin's Hunting Supply's operations.
   d. Create a depreciation schedule.
   e. Complete the following pro forma income statements:

	July 2020	August 2020	September 2020	October 2020	November 2020	December 2020	For the Six Months Ended December 31, 2020
Sales							
Cost of goods sold							
Gross profit							
Operating expenses:							
Rent							
Payroll							
Payroll taxes							
Utilities							
Insurance							
Depreciation							
Cleaning and maintenance							
Miscellaneous							
Total operating expenses							
Net income							

Erin's Hunting Supply, LLC
Pro Forma Income Statements
For the First Six Months of Operations and for the Six Months Ended December 31, 2020

5. Using the assumptions provided below, complete the following pro forma comparative balance sheets and related reconciliations of cash and owner's equity for Bargain Basement:

Bargain Basement Apparel Shoppe, LLC
List of Assumptions for July 1, 2020–December 31, 2021

- Although cost of goods sold will increase, inventory levels are expected to remain the same at $20,000 for clothing and $7,500 for accessories through the end of 2021 due to expertise gained in inventory management.

- No fixed assets are expected to be purchased, sold, or abandoned during the time frame of July 1, 2020–December 31, 2021.

- Insurance and utilities expenses are expected to remain at their monthly expense amounts of $200 and $500, respectively. Insurance is expected to continue to be paid one month in advance. Utilities are expected to continue to be paid in the month after the services are used.

- Accounts payable is expected to approximate 90% of clothing and accessories inventory.

- Payroll payable is expected to equal one-third of payroll expense for fourth quarter 2021.

- Payroll taxes payable is expected to equal one-third of payroll tax expense for fourth quarter 2021.

- Sales tax payable is expected to approximate one-third of fourth quarter 2021 sales multiplied by 0.055.

Information for
Fourth Quarter 2021

Sales	$179,775
Payroll	$ 11,011
Payroll taxes	$ 1,486

- The owner will begin taking distributions of $10,000 per month beginning January 2021.

Bargain Basement Apparel Shoppe, LLC Pro Forma Balance Sheets As of June 30, 2020, and December 31, 2021		
	(Pre-Revenue) June 30, 2020	(Post-Revenue) December 31, 2021
Cash	$ 24,300	
Prepaid insurance	200	
Clothing inventory	20,000	
Accessories inventory	7,500	
Total current assets	52,000	
Checkout counters and furniture	7,500	
Clothing racks and shelving	7,400	
Computers and software	10,000	
Security system	5,000	
Less: Accumulated depreciation	–	
Net fixed assets	29,900	
Total assets	$ 81,900	
Accounts payable	$ –	
Payroll payable	–	
Payroll taxes payable	–	
Utilities payable	500	
Sales tax payable	–	
Total liabilities	500	
Owners' equity	81,400	
Total liabilities and owners' equity	$ 81,900	

Bargain Basement Apparel Shoppe, LLC
Pro Forma Reconciliations of Cash and Owners' Equity
For the Six Quarters Ended December 31, 2021

Reconciliation of Cash:

Beginning cash
  Add: Net income for the six quarters
    ended December 31, 2021 209,640
  Add: Depreciation for the six quarters
    ended December 31, 2021 8,970
  Adjustments for changes in noncash
    assets and liabilities:
    Increase in accounts payable
    Increase in payroll payable
    Increase in payroll taxes payable
    Increase in sales tax payable
  Less: Distributions during the six quarters
    ended December 31, 2021
Ending cash

Reconciliation of Owners' Equity:

Beginning owners' equity
  Add: Net income for the six quarters
    ended December 31, 2021
  Less: Distributions during the six quarters
    ended December 31, 2021
Ending owners' equity

6. Using the assumptions provided below, complete the following pro forma comparative balance sheets and related reconciliations of cash and owners' equity for Erin's Hunting Supply:

Erin's Hunting Supply, LLC
List of Assumptions for July 1–December 31, 2020

- Inventory levels are expected to be $110,000 for hunting equipment, $75,000 for clothing, and $32,500 for other items at December 31, 2020.

- No fixed assets are expected to be purchased, sold, or abandoned during the time frame of July 1, 2020–December 31, 2020.

- Rent, insurance, and utilities expenses are expected to remain at their monthly expense amounts of $6,750, $1,350, and $1,450, respectively. Rent and insurance are expected to continue to be paid one month in advance. Utilities are expected to continue to be paid in the month after the services are used.

- Accounts payable is expected to approximate 30% of inventory.

- Payroll payable is expected to equal one-half of payroll expense for December 2020.

- Payroll taxes payable is expected to equal one-half of payroll tax expense for December 2020.

- Sales tax payable is expected to approximate December 2020 sales multiplied by 0.06.

	Information for December 2020
Sales	$231,531
Payroll	$ 26,040
Payroll taxes	$ 3,125

- Each of the three owners of the company is expected to begin taking a $15,000-per-month cash distribution starting in October 2020.

Erin's Hunting Supply, LLC Pro Forma Balance Sheets As of June 30, 2020, and December 31, 2020		
	(Pre-Revenue) June 30, 2020	(Post-Revenue) December 31, 2020
Cash	$ 10,645	
Prepaid rent	6,750	
Prepaid insurance	1,350	
Hunting equipment inventory	100,000	
Clothing inventory	70,000	
Other inventory	30,000	
Total current assets	218,745	
Checkout counters	5,700	
Racks and shelving	9,850	
Computers and software	12,650	
Security system	7,500	
Less: Accumulated depreciation	–	
Net fixed assets	35,700	
Total assets	$254,445	
Accounts payable	$ –	
Payroll payable	–	
Payroll taxes payable	–	
Utilities payable	1,450	
Sales tax payable	–	
Total liabilities	1,450	
Owners' equity	252,995	
Total liabilities and owners' equity	$254,445	

Erin's Hunting Supply, LLC
Pro Forma Reconciliations of Cash and Owners' Equity
For the Six Months Ended December 31, 2020

Reconciliation of Cash:

Beginning cash

Add: Net income for the six months
   ended December 31, 2020 290,340

Add: Depreciation for the six months
   ended December 31, 2020 3,570

Adjustments for changes in noncash
   assets and liabilities:

Increase in inventory

Increase in accounts payable

Increase in payroll payable

Increase in payroll taxes payable

Increase in sales tax payable

Less: Distributions during the six months
   ended December 31, 2020

Ending cash

Reconciliation of Owners' Equity:

Beginning owners' equity

Add: Net income for the six months
   ended December 31, 2020

Less: Distributions during the six months
   ended December 31, 2020

Ending owners' equity

7. Calculate the estimated annual sales for years 2022–2025, create a depreciation schedule, and complete the following pro forma income statements for Affordably Haute Apparel Shoppe, LLC considering the following assumptions:

Affordably Haute Apparel Shoppe, LLC
List of Assumptions for 2022–2025

	2022	2023	2024	2025
Target margin for clothing:	57.5%	60%	60%	62.5%
Target margin for accessories:	47.5%	50%	50%	52.5%

Expected cost of goods sold:	2022	2023	2024	2025
Clothing	$144,487	$158,935	$163,703	$166,977
Accessories	49,702	54,672	56,859	58,565
	$194,189	$213,607	$220,562	$225,542

During the start-up phase of the business in 2020, $32,500 of depreciable fixed assets are expected to be purchased. An additional $15,000 of depreciable fixed assets are expected to be purchased in 2023. No fixed assets are expected to be disposed of until after 2025. All fixed assets are expected to have a useful life of five years and a salvage value of $0, and will be depreciated using the straight-line, half-year convention depreciation method.

Information regarding expected expenses :

- In 2022, payroll is expected to increase 15% from its year 2021 level and then stabilize.
- Payroll taxes are expected to be 13.5% of payroll.
- Insurance expense is expected to increase 5% every year after 2021.
- Miscellaneous expense is expected to amount to 3.5% of the prior period's cost of goods sold.
- Rent, utility, and cleaning and maintenance expenses are expected to remain the same amount from 2021–2025.

Affordably Haute Apparel Shoppe, LLC
Pro Forma Income Statements
For the Years Ended December 31, 2021, 2022, 2023, 2024, and 2025

	2021	2022	2023	2024	2025
Sales	$390,875				
Cost of goods sold	183,784				
Gross profit	207,091				
Operating expenses:					
Rent	30,000				
Payroll	71,136				
Payroll taxes	9,603				
Utilities	3,300				
Insurance	3,000				
Depreciation	6,500				
Cleaning and maintenance	3,600				
Miscellaneous	5,848				
Total operating expenses	132,987				
Net income	$ 74,104				

8. Calculate cost of goods sold and estimated annual sales for years 2021–2025, create a depreciation schedule, and complete the following pro forma income statements for Kevin's Convenience Store, LLC considering the following assumptions:

Kevin's Convenience Store, LLC
List of Assumptions for 2021–2025

	2021	2022	2023	2024	2025
Target margin for food inventory:	45%	46%	47%	48%	49%
Target margin for non-food inventory:	35%	36%	37%	38%	39%

Cost of goods sold for December 2020 is expected to equal $5,000 for food inventory and $3,750 for non-food inventory. Cost of goods sold for 2021 is expected to equal December 2020 cost of goods sold times 12, plus 10%. After 2021, cost of goods sold is expected to increase annually as follows:

2022	2023	2024	2025
7.5%	5%	2.5%	0%

During the start-up phase of the business in 2020, $24,000 of depreciable fixed assets with a salvage value of $0 are expected to be purchased. An additional $10,000 of depreciable fixed assets with a salvage value of $1,000 are expected to be purchased in 2023. No fixed assets are expected to be disposed of until after 2025. All fixed assets are expected to have a useful life of five years and will be depreciated using the straight-line, half-year convention depreciation method.

Information regarding expected expenses:

- In 2022, payroll is expected to increase 5% from its year 2021 level of $22,880 and then stabilize.
- Payroll taxes are expected to be 13% of payroll.
- Insurance expense is expected to be $300 per month in 2021 and increase 3% every year after 2021.
- Miscellaneous expense is expected to amount to $1,225 for 2021. Miscellaneous expense is expected to amount to 2% of the prior period's cost of goods sold for years 2022–2025.
- Rent is expected to be $2,000 per month until it increases 5% in July 2023.
- Utilities are expected to be $400 per month in 2021 and increase 2% every year thereafter.
- Cleaning and maintenance expense is expected to be $500 per month in 2021 and 2022 and increase 5% in 2023.

Kevin's Convenience Store, LLC
Pro Forma Income Statements
For the Years Ended December 31, 2021, 2022, 2023, 2024, and 2025

	2021	2022	2023	2024	2025
Sales					
Cost of goods sold					
Gross profit					
Operating expenses:					
Rent					
Payroll					
Payroll taxes					
Utilities					
Insurance					
Depreciation					
Cleaning and maintenance					
Miscellaneous					
Total operating expenses					
Net income					

9. Like many retail stores, Bargain Basement's only expenses that vary directly with its sales are its cost of goods sold and its miscellaneous expenses. Using this information and the information below, create a schedule summarizing Bargain Basement's variable and fixed costs for 2022 and 2025 and calculate breakeven revenue for Bargain Basement for 2022 and 2025.

Bargain Basement Apparel Shoppe, LLC Pro Forma Income Statements For the Years Ended December 31, 2022, 2023, 2024, and 2025				
	2022	2023	2024	2025
Sales	$702,605	$737,735	$815,970	$856,769
Cost of goods sold	416,527	437,353	459,221	482,182
Gross profit	286,078	300,382	356,749	374,587
Operating expenses:				
Rent	21,000	21,300	22,200	22,200
Payroll	44,044	48,448	48,448	48,448
Payroll taxes	5,946	6,540	6,540	6,540
Utilities	6,180	6,365	6,556	6,753
Insurance	2,640	2,904	3,194	3,514
Depreciation	5,980	5,980	6,980	4,990
Cleaning and maintenance	5,400	5,400	5,400	5,400
Miscellaneous	7,934	8,331	8,747	9,184
Total operating expenses	99,124	105,268	108,065	107,029
Net income	$186,954	$195,114	$248,684	$267,558

10. Like many retail stores, Erin's Hunting Supply's only expenses that vary directly with its sales are its cost of goods sold and its miscellaneous expenses. Using this information and the information below, create a schedule summarizing Erin's Hunting Supply's variable and fixed costs for 2021, 2023, and 2025 and calculate breakeven revenue for Erin's Hunting Supply for 2021, 2023, and 2025.

Erin's Hunting Supply, LLC Pro Forma Income Statements For the Years Ended December 31, 2021, 2022, 2023, 2024, and 2025					
	2021	2022	2023	2024	2025
Sales	$2,591,268	$2,694,918	$2,802,715	$2,858,769	$2,915,945
Cost of goods sold	1,428,403	1,485,539	1,530,106	1,560,708	1,576,315
Gross profit	1,162,865	1,209,379	1,272,610	1,298,062	1,339,630
Operating expenses:					
Rent	81,000	81,000	84,000	84,000	84,000
Payroll	324,576	337,559	347,686	354,640	358,186
Payroll taxes	38,949	40,507	41,772	42,557	42,982
Utilities	17,400	18,096	18,639	19,012	19,202
Insurance	16,200	16,848	17,353	17,701	17,878
Depreciation	7,140	7,140	7,140	7,140	3,570
Cleaning and maintenance	3,600	3,744	3,856	3,933	3,973
Miscellaneous	55,256	71,420	74,277	76,505	78,035
Total operating expenses	544,121	576,314	594,673	605,487	607,826
Net income	$ 618,743	$ 633,065	$ 677,937	$ 692,575	$ 731,804

Example Pro Forma Financial Statements for a Service-Based Business, Including the Treatment of Accounts Receivable, Debt, and New Equity Investment

Two sisters who are certified public accountants (CPAs) have decided to open an accounting firm called Ross and Ross, CPAs on July 1, 2020, following a three-month start-up phase. The sisters have $150,000 they plan to invest in this business, but that amount of cash won't quite cover expected start-up costs. As a result, the sisters have negotiated a $25,000 loan to the business. They expect to receive the proceeds of the loan on May 31, 2020. The interest rate on the loan is 6 percent, and interest is payable on the first day of each month starting on July 1, 2020. The entrepreneurs have negotiated that no principal payment is due related to the loan until June 1, 2022, and that the loan can be paid back early. The bank requires the loan to be paid back in full by June 1, 2025, but the sisters plan to repay the loan in full on July 1, 2021.

Using the details provided above about the $25,000 loan the sisters have negotiated for the business, we can calculate expected monthly interest expense for June 2020–June 2021 for Ross & Ross, CPAs as follows:

Monthly interest expense calculation: ($25,000 x 0.06) ÷ 12 = $125

Figure 6-A.1 shows the schedule of start-up costs the sisters have developed for their business.

Ross and Ross, CPAs Schedule of Start-up Costs			
	April 2020	May 2020	June 2020	For the Three Months Ended June 30, 2020
Rent	$15,000	$ 7,500	$ 7,500	$ 30,000
Utilities	500	500	500	1,500
Insurance	2,000	1,000	1,000	4000
Employee recruitment and training	–	2,500	7,500	10,000
Office design and decoration	2,000	2,000	1,000	5,000
Interest	–	–	125	125
Computers and software	–	30,000	20,000	50,000
Office equipment	–	–	25,000	25,000
Shelving and storage	–	10,000	10,000	20,000
Desks and furniture	–	12,000	–	12,000
Security system	–	2,500	–	2,500
Total	$19,500	$68,000	$72,625	$160,125

Notes: Rent is paid on the first day of the month to which it applies.
    Utilities are paid in the month after the services are used.
    Insurance is paid in the month previous to the month to which it applies.
    Interest is paid on the first day of each month beginning July 2020.
    All other costs are paid in the same month as incurred.
    Office design and decoration expense will terminate in June 2020.

Figure 6-A.1. Schedule of start-up costs for Ross and Ross, CPAs.

Using the problem information, the monthly interest expense information, and the schedule of start-up costs, we can create the pro forma pre-revenue balance sheet and pro forma start-up phase expense statement, including reconciliations of cash and owners' equity, as shown in figure 6-A.2.

The next step in the pro forma financial statement creation process is to create the pro forma income statements for the first six months of the business's operations. Before we can do that, however, we first need to calculate expected monthly gross payroll and expected monthly billings for these same six months. We also need to create a depreciation schedule for 2020 fixed-asset acquisitions based on the assumptions of the sister entrepreneurs. The applicable calculations and depreciation schedule follow the list of assumptions in figure 6-A.3.

Using the information in figure 6-A.3 allows us to create the monthly gross payroll and billings schedule shown in figure 6-A.4 (page 164) and the depreciation schedule shown in figure 6-A.5 (page 164).

Now, using the information included in the list of assumptions and the information we have just calculated, we can create pro forma income statements for Ross and Ross, CPAs for its first six months of operations, as indicated in figure 6-A.6 (page 165).

Next, using the pro forma income statements in figure 6-A.6 and the list of assumptions shown at figure 6-A.3, we can complete the pro forma comparative balance sheets and related reconciliations of cash and owners' equity. Figure 6-A.7 (page 166) illustrates the results.

Ross and Ross, CPAs Pro Forma Pre-Revenue Balance Sheet As of June 30, 2020		Ross and Ross, CPAs Pro Forma Start-up Phase Expense Statement, Including Reconciliations of Cash and Owners' Equity For the Three Months Ended June 30, 2020		
Cash	$ 15,500	Rent	$30,000	
Prepaid rent	7,500	Less: Prepaid rent	7,500	
Prepaid insurance	1,000			$ 22,500
Total current assets	24,000	Utilities		1,500
		Insurance	4,000	
Computers and software	50,000	Less: Prepaid insurance	1,000	
Office equipment	25,000			3,000
Shelving and storage	20,000	Employee recruitment and training		10,000
Desks and furniture	12,000	Office design and decoration		5,000
Security system	2,500	Interest		125
Total fixed assets	109,500	Start-up phase expenses		42,125
		Less: Utilities payable		500
Total assets	$133,500	Less: Interest payable		125
		Total cash outlays for expenses		$ 41,500
Utilities payable	$ 500			
Interest payable	125	Reconciliation of Cash:		
Total current liabilities	625	Beginning cash		$175,000
		Less: Cash outlays for assets		118,000
Loan payable	25,000	Less: Cash outlays for expenses		41,500
		Ending cash		$ 15,500
Total liabilities	25,625			
		Reconciliation of Owners' Equity:		
Owners' equity	107,875	Beginning owners' equity		$150,000
		Less: Start-up phase expenses		42,125
Total liabilities and owners' equity	$133,500	Ending owners' equity		$107,875

Figure 6-A.2. Pro forma pre-revenue balance sheet and pro forma start-up phase expense statement, including reconciliations of cash and owners' equity.

Ross and Ross, CPAs
List of Assumptions

General Operational and Payroll Information

Hours of operation: Monday–Friday 8:00 a.m.–6:00 p.m., Saturday as needed

Needed employees: July 2020: 3
              August 2020: 4
              September 2020: 5
              October–December 2020: 6

The founders will review their employees' work and manage the business. Employees will be paid $35 per hour. Total payroll taxes, unemployment, and workers' compensation (i.e., payroll taxes) are expected to equal 13.5% of gross payroll. Employee benefits are estimated to be 10% of gross payroll. Employees are expected to perform their duties such that they generate 2,000 billable hours per year. Employee hours will be billed at $100 per hour. An employee will not be hired until the founders are comfortable the employee can sell enough business to keep the employee working at 100% of required billable hours.

- A seventh employee is expected to be hired in time to begin work on January 1, 2021.
- An eighth employee is expected to be hired in time to begin work on January 1, 2022.
- A ninth employee is expected to be hired in time to begin work on January 1, 2023.
- A tenth employee is expected to be hired in time to begin work on January 1, 2024.

Employees will receive a 10% raise in January 2023 and a 5% raise in January 2025. New employees will be hired at the rate currently being paid other employees. Beginning in 2023, employees are expected to generate 2,200 billable hours per year. The company expects to be able to increase its employees' billing rate per hour by 15% in January 2023. The company expects to be able to increase its employees' billing rate per hour by another 10% in January 2025.

Information Regarding the 2020 $25,000 loan and New Equity Investment

The business's 2020 $25,000 loan, the proceeds of which are expected to be received by the business on May 31, 2020, is a 6% interest loan with interest payable on the first day of each month starting on July 1, 2020. The entrepreneurs have negotiated that no principal payment is due related to the loan until June 1, 2022, and that the loan can be paid back early. The bank requires that the loan be paid back in full by June 1, 2025, but the entrepreneurs plan to repay the loan in full on July 1, 2021. The entrepreneurs plan to make a new equity investment in the company in the amount of $25,000 in December 2020 in preparation to pay off the $25,000 loan on July 1, 2021.

Information Regarding Expected Fixed-Asset Purchases, Disposals, Depreciation, and Related Debt

Like all the other fixed assets of this business—except the building to be purchased in 2023—the $109,500 of depreciable fixed assets expected to be purchased by the business during its start-up phase in April–June 2020 are expected to have a useful life of five years and a salvage value of $0, and will be depreciated using the straight-line, half-year convention depreciation method. The business expects to purchase $30,000 in new computers and software upgrades in 2024. No fixed assets are expected to be sold or abandoned until the end of 2025, when 50% of the computers and software acquired in May and June of 2020 are expected to be disposed of.

In early January 2023, the business plans to spend $400,000 to buy an office building. The building is valued at $300,000. The land on which the building sits is valued at $100,000. The building is to be financed over 10 years by a $250,000, 6%, fixed principal mortgage. The building will be depreciated using the straight-line, half-year convention depreciation method assuming a useful life of 40 years. The building will be assumed to have a salvage value of $0 since the firm plans to tear down and rebuild the building at the end of its useful life.

Information Regarding Expected Non-Employee-Related Expenses

- Cleaning and maintenance expense for the office is expected to cost $250 per month beginning in July of 2020 and remain the same amount through the end of 2025.
- Miscellaneous expense, which includes ongoing employee recruitment and training expenses, is expected to amount to 1% of the current period's billings.
- Rent will continue to be paid one month in advance, will remain at $7,500 per month through the end of 2022, and will then terminate.
- Property tax expense related to the office building to be purchased in 2023 is expected to amount to $6,000 per year.
- Utilities expense is expected to continue to be paid in the month after the services are used and is expected to increase 20% from its 2020 monthly expense amount of $500 beginning in January 2023, and then stabilize.
- Insurance expense is expected to continue to be paid one month in advance and is expected to increase 10% from its 2020 monthly expense amount of $1,000 beginning in July 2021, and then another 15% in January 2023, after which it will stabilize.

Information Regarding Expected Accounts Receivable and Payables

- At December 31, 2020, accounts receivable is expected to approximate 100% of December 2020 billings.
- At December 31, 2020, accounts payable is expected to approximate 100% of December 2020 employee benefits, cleaning and maintenance, and miscellaneous expense amounts.
- At December 31, 2020, payroll payable is expected to approximate 50% of December 2020 payroll expense.
- At December 31, 2020, payroll taxes payable is expected to approximate 50% of December 2020 payroll tax expense.

Figure 6-A.3. List of assumptions for Ross and Ross, CPAs.

	July 2020	August 2020	September 2020	October 2020	November 2020	December 2020	For the Six Months Ended December 31, 2020

Ross and Ross, CPAs
Gross Payroll and Billings Schedule

	July 2020	August 2020	September 2020	October 2020	November 2020	December 2020	For the Six Months Ended December 31, 2020
Number of Employees (A)	3	4	5	6	6	6	
Number of Billable Hours (B) (2,000 ÷ 12)	166.67	166.67	166.67	166.67	166.67	166.67	1,000
Hourly Pay Rate (C)	$ 35	$ 35	$ 35	$ 35	$ 35	$ 35	
Hourly Billing Rate (D)	$ 100	$ 100	$ 100	$ 100	$ 100	$ 100	
Gross Payroll (A) x (B) x (C)	$17,500	$23,333	$29,167	$ 35,000	$ 35,000	$ 35,000	$175,000
Billings (A) x (B) x (D)	$50,000	$66,667	$83,333	$100,000	$100,000	$100,000	$500,000

Figure 6-A.4. Gross payroll and billings for the first six months of operations and for the six months ended December 31, 2020.

Note that the balance sheets in figure 6-A.7 don't include a reserve for bad debts. This is because such a reserve would be based on an entity's historical experience of bad debts or on its list of identified individual accounts receivable that are likely not collectible, neither of which a proposed start-up would have. Note further the movement of the $25,000 loan payable from a long-term payable to a short-term payable. This is because the sister entrepreneurs plan to pay off the loan in July 2021, which is less than 12 months out from December 31, 2020. Note last the treatment of the December 2020 new equity investment of $25,000 as an addition to both the reconciliation of cash and the reconciliation of owners' equity.

The next step in our process of pro forma financial statement creation is the creation of the pro forma income statements for years 2021, 2022, 2023, 2024, and 2025. The assumptions that support the creation of these income statements are included in figure 6-A.3. Figure 6-A.8 (page 167) shows the partial loan amortization table and interest calculations needed to create the income statements.

Ross and Ross, CPAs
Depreciation Schedule

Total fixed assets:	$109,500
Useful life in years:	5
Depreciation method:	Straight-line, half-year convention

Year	Depreciation Expense
2020	$ 10,950
2021	21,900
2022	21,900
2023	21,900
2024	21,900
2025	10,950
Total	$109,500

Figure 6-A.5. Depreciation schedule for year 2020 fixed-asset acquisitions.

	July 2020	August 2020	September 2020	October 2020	November 2020	December 2020	For the Six Months Ended December 31, 2020
Billings	$50,000	$66,667	$83,333	$100,000	$100,000	$100,000	$500,000
Operating expenses:							
Payroll	17,500	23,333	29,167	35,000	35,000	35,000	175,500
Payroll taxes	2,363	3,150	3,938	4,725	4,725	4,725	23,62640,
Employee benefits	1,750	2,333	2,917	3,500	3,500	3,500	17,500
Rent	7,500	7,500	7,500	7,500	7,500	7,500	45,000
Utilities	500	500	500	500	500	500	3,000
Insurance	1,000	1,000	1,000	1,000	1,000	1,000	6,000
Depreciation	1,825	1,825	1,825	1,825	1,825	1,825	10,950
Cleaning and maintenance	250	250	250	250	250	250	1,500
Miscellaneous	500	667	833	1,000	1,000	1,000	5,000
Total operating expenses	33,188	40,558	47,930	55,300	55,300	55,300	287,576
Operating income	16,812	26,109	35,403	44,700	44,700	44,700	212,424
Interest expense	125	125	125	125	125	125	750
Net income	$16,687	$25,984	$32,278	$44,575	$44,575	$44,575	$211,674

Table title: Ross and Ross, CPAs — Pro Forma Income Statements — For the First Six Months of Operations and for the Six Months Ended December 31, 2020

Figure 6-A.6. Pro forma income statements for the first six months of operations and for the six months ended December 31, 2020.

Lenders typically create loan amortization tables related to the loans they make. Such tables are helpful to both the lender and the borrower in terms of understanding the amount and timing of the payments that need to be made or received related to a loan and also the total amount of interest to be paid or received over the life of the loan. Figure 6-A.8 is an example of a partial loan amortization table for a fixed-principal loan. A fixed-principal loan is just that, a loan for which the amount of principal to be repaid each month is fixed and will remain unchanged for the life of the loan. Because the principal amount to be repaid each month is fixed, but the amount of interest due each month changes as the amount of unpaid principal related to the loan decreases each month, the amount of the payment due related to the loan is generally different each month. The principal amount due each month is usually calculated as the loan amount divided by the number of months the loan will be outstanding. For the Ross and Ross, CPAs fixed-principal loan illustrated in figure 6-A.8, the monthly principal amount was calculated as follows:

$250,000 ÷ 120 months = $2,083.33

Fixed-principal loans are not an uncommon configuration for U.S. bank loans to businesses. An example of a loan amortization table for an alternative type of loan—a fixed-payment loan—is illustrated in appendix 6-B to this chapter. Note that the loan example in appendix 6-B also illustrates how to calculate the short- and long-term portions of a loan using a loan amortization table.

Figures 6-A.9 and 6-A.10 (both on page 168), show the remaining calculations needed to create the pro forma income statements for years 2021, 2022, 2023, 2024, and 2025. The pro forma income statement for the first six months of operations is then added to these income statements to create the financial statement shown in figure 6-A.11 (page 169).

Ross and Ross, CPAs Pro Forma Balance Sheets As of June 30, 2020, and December 31, 2020			Ross and Ross, CPAs Pro Forma Reconciliations of Cash and Owners' Equity For the Six Months Ended December 31, 2020	
	(Pre-Revenue) June 30, 2020	(Post-Revenue) December 31, 2020		
Cash	$ 15,500	$187,737	Reconciliation of Cash:	
Accounts receivable	–	100,000		
Prepaid rent	7,500	7,500	Beginning cash	$15,500
Prepaid insurance	1,000	1,000	Add: Net income for the six months	
Total current assets	24,000	296,237	ended December 31, 2020	211,674
			Add: Depreciation for the six months	
Computers and software	50,000	50,000	ended December 31, 2020	10,950
Office equipment	25,000	25,000	Adjustments for changes in noncash	
Shelving and storage	20,000	20,000	assets and liabilities:	
Desks and furniture	12,000	12,000	Increase in accounts receivable	(100,000)
Security system	2,500	2,500	Increase in accounts payable	4,750
Less: Accumulated depreciation	–	10,950	Increase in payroll payable	17,500
Net fixed assets	109,500	98,550	Increase in payroll taxes payable	2,363
			Increase in short-term portion of	
Total assets	$133,500	$394,787	loan payable	25,000
			Decrease in loan payable	(25,000)
Accounts payable	$ –	$ 4,750	Add: New equity investment	
Payroll payable	–	17,500	during the six months ended	
Payroll taxes payable	–	2,363	December 31, 2020	25,000
Utilities payable	500	500	Ending cash	$187,737
Interest payable	125	125		
Short-term portion of loan payable	–	25,000	Reconciliation of Owners' Equity:	
Total current liabilities	625	50,238		
			Beginning owners' equity	$107,875
Loan payable	25,000	–	Add: Net income for the six months	
			ended December 31, 2020	211,674
Total liabilities	25,625	50,238	Add: Net equity investment during	
			the six months ended	
Owners' equity	107,875	344,549	December 31, 2020	25,000
			Ending owners' equity	$344,549
Total liabilities and owners' equity	$133,500	$394,787		

Figure 6-A.7. Pro forma pre-revenue balance sheet and pro forma post-revenue balance sheet, including post-revenue reconciliations of cash and owners' equity.

Loan Amortization Table—Fixed-Principal Loan

Principal Amount =	$	250,000.00
Interest Rate =		6.00%
Number of Years =		10

Payment	Principal	Interest	Payment	Loan Balance	
January 2023	$ 2,083.33	$ 1,250.00	$ 3,333.33	$ 247,916.67	
February 2023	2,083.33	1,239.58	3,322.92	245,833.33	
March 2023	2,083.33	1,229.17	3,312.50	243,750.00	
April 2023	2,083.33	1,218.75	3,302.08	241,666.67	
May 2023	2,083.33	1,208.33	3,291.67	239,583.33	
June 2023	2,083.33	1,197.92	3,281.25	237,500.00	
July 2023	2,083.33	1,187.50	3,270.83	235,416.67	
August 2023	2,083.33	1,177.08	3,260.42	233,333.33	
September 2023	2,083.33	1,166.67	3,250.00	231,250.00	
October 2023	2,083.33	1,156.25	3,239.58	229,166.67	
November 2023	2,083.33	1,145.83	3,229.17	227,083.33	
December 2023	2,083.33	1,135.42	3,218.75	225,000.00	January–December 2023 interest = $ 14,312.50
January 2024	2,083.33	1,125.00	3,208.33	222,916.67	
February 2024	2,083.33	1,114.58	3,197.92	220,833.33	
March 2024	2,083.33	1,104.17	3,187.50	218,750.00	
April 2024	2,083.33	1,093.75	3,177.08	216,666.67	
May 2024	2,083.33	1,083.33	3,166.67	214,583.33	
June 2024	2,083.33	1,072.92	3,156.25	212,500.00	
July 2024	2,083.33	1,062.50	3,145.83	210,416.67	
August 2024	2,083.33	1,052.08	3,135.42	208,333.33	
September 2024	2,083.33	1,041.67	3,125.00	206,250.00	
October 2024	2,083.33	1,031.25	3,114.58	204,166.67	
November 2024	2,083.33	1,020.83	3,104.17	202,083.33	
December 2024	2,083.33	1,010.42	3,093.75	200,000.00	January–December 2024 interest = $ 12,812.50
January 2025	2,083.33	1,000.00	3,083.33	197,916.67	
February 2025	2,083.33	989.58	3,072.92	195,833.33	
March 2025	2,083.33	979.17	3,062.50	193,750.00	
April 2025	2,083.33	968.75	3,052.08	191,666.67	
May 2025	2,083.33	958.33	3,041.67	189,583.33	
June 2025	2,083.33	947.92	3,031.25	187,500.00	
July 2025	2,083.33	937.50	3,020.83	185,416.67	
August 2025	2,083.33	927.08	3,010.42	183,333.33	
September 2025	2,083.33	916.67	3,000.00	181,250.00	
October 2025	2,083.33	906.25	2,989.58	179,166.67	
November 2025	2,083.33	895.83	2,979.17	177,083.33	
December 2025	2,083.33	885.42	2,968.75	175,000.00	January–December 2025 interest = $ 11,312.50
January 2026	2,083.33	875.00	2,958.33	172,916.67	
February 2026	2,083.33	864.58	2,947.92	170,833.33	
↓	↓	↓	↓	↓	
November 2032	2,083.33	20.83	2,104.17	2,083.33	
December 2032	2,083.33	10.42	2,093.75	(0.00)	
Total	$ 250,000.00	$ 75,625.00			

Figure 6-A.8. Partial loan amortization table and interest calculations related to the 2023 fixed-principal loan.

Ross and Ross, CPAs Gross Payroll and Billings Schedule					
	2021	2022	2023	2024	2025
Number of employees (A)	7	8	9	10	10
Number of billable hours (B)	2,000	2,000	2,200	2,200	2,200
Hourly pay rate (C)	$ 35.00	$ 35.00	$ 38.50	$ 38.50	$ 49.43
Hourly billing rate (D)	$ 100.00	$ 100.00	$ 115.00	$115.00	$ 126.50
Gross payroll (A) x (B) x (C)	$ 490,000	$ 560,000	$ 762,300	$ 847,000	$ 889,460
Billings (A) x (B) x (D)	$1,400,000	$1,600,000	$2,277,000	$2,530,000	$2,783,000

Figure 6-A.9. Gross payroll and billings for years 2021–2025.

Ross and Ross, CPAs Depreciation Schedule				
	2020	2023	2024	
Fixed-asset acquisitions:	$ 109,500	$ 300,000	$ 30,000	
Less: Salvage value:	-	-	-	
Depreciable value:	$ 109,500	$ 300,000	$ 30,000	
Useful life in years:	5	40	5	
Depreciation method:	Straight-line, half-year convention	Straight-line, half-year convention	Straight-line, half-year convention	

Year	Depreciation	Depreciation	Depreciation	Annual Depreciation
2020	$ 10,950	$ -	$ -	$ 10,950
2021	21,900	-	-	21,900
2022	21,900	-	-	21,900
2023	21,900	3,750	-	25,650
2024	21,900	7,500	3,000	32,400
2025	10,950	7,500	6,000	24,450
2026	-	7,500	6,000	13,500
2027	-	7,500	6,000	13,500
2028	-	7,500	6,000	13,500
2029	-	7,500	3,000	10,500
2030	-	7,500	-	7,500
Years 2031–2062*	-	240,000	-	240,000
2063	-	3,750	-	3,750
Total	$109,500	$300,000	$30,000	$439,500

*Depreciation for 2023 acquisitions for Years 2031–2062: $7,500 x 32 years = $240,000

Figure 6-A.10. Expanded depreciation schedule.

	For the Six Months Ended December 31, 2020	2021	2022	2023	2024	2025
Ross and Ross, CPAs Pro Forma Income Statements For the Six Months Ended December 31, 2020, and for the Years Ended December 31, 2021, 2022, 2023, 2024, and 2025						
Billings	$500,000	$1,400,000	$1,600,000	$2,277,000	$2,530,000	$2,783,000
Operating expenses:						
Payroll	175,000	490,000	560,000	762,300	847,000	889,460
Payroll taxes	23,626	66,150	75,600	102,911	114,345	120,077
Employee benefits	17,500	49,000	56,000	76,230	84,700	88,946
Rent	45,000	90,000	90,000	–	–	–
Utilities	3,000	6,000	6,000	7,200	7,200	7,200
Insurance	6,000	12,600	13,200	15,180	15,180	15,180
Depreciation	10,950	21,900	21,900	25,650	32,400	24,450
Property taxes	–	–	–	6,000	6,000	6,000
Cleaning and maintenance	1,500	3,000	3,000	3,000	3,000	3,000
Miscellaneous	5,000	14,000	16,000	22,770	25,300	27,830
Total operating expenses	287,576	752,650	841,700	1,021,241	1,135,125	1,182,143
Operating income	212,424	647,350	758,300	1,255,760	1,394,875	1,600,857
Interest expense	750	750	–	14,313	12,812	11,313
Net income	$211,674	$646,600	$758,300	$1,241,447	$1,382,063	$1,589,544

Figure 6-A.11. Pro forma income statements for the six months ended December 31, 2020, and for the years ended December 31, 2021, 2022, 2023, 2024, and 2025.

Example Pro Forma Financial Statements for a C Corporation Smartphone Application Business, Including the Treatment of Debt, Initial Net Losses, New Equity Investment, and Dividends

Three entrepreneurs have developed a concept for a disruptive smartphone application called ParkItFast. The app allows users to quickly find the closest open parking space considering the user's location. Beyond just indicating the location of the closest open parking space, however, the app also indicates the most efficient route to get to the space, the cost of the space, and the time limitation—if any—associated with the space, and how long the space has been available. After extensive industry and market research, the three entrepreneurs are confident the app can be a commercial success and have decided to pursue its development and distribution. The development of the application is expected to be outsourced.

Experienced smartphone application developers have helped the three entrepreneurs estimate the start-up costs for the proposed new business that will serve as the umbrella under which the app will be developed and distributed. The entrepreneurs have $25,000 they plan to invest in this business, but they know that amount of cash won't cover the expected start-up costs. As a result, the entrepreneurs have realized they will need to finance the majority of the cost of the development and distribution of the app using a combination of $200,000 of outside equity investment and $100,000 of debt. The entrepreneurs have been advised that, for liability reasons—automobiles are involved—and in order to make the company more attractive to outside investors, they should set up the new company as a C corporation. Combining their own $25,000 with the expected $200,000 of outside equity investment suggests that the 1 million shares of $0.01 par value common stock the new C corporation will issue at its founding will be purchased by the entrepreneurs and outside investors at a price of $0.225 per share ($225,000 ÷ 1,000,000 shares = $0.225 per share). Figure 6-B.1 (page 172) shows the schedule of start-up costs the entrepreneurs have developed for their proposed business, which they plan to name ParkItFast, Inc.

Using the problem information and the schedule of start-up costs, we can create the pro forma pre-revenue balance sheet and pro forma start-up phase expense statement, including reconciliations of cash and retained earnings, as shown in figure 6-B.2 (page 173).

Note that, as is the case in most situations for most companies, ParkItFast's application development costs are expensed rather than capitalized as a fixed asset. Note further that figure 6-B.2 includes something we haven't seen before: a reconciliation of retained earnings. Remember from chapter 4 that retained earnings represent the cumulative earnings of a company not distributed to stockholders via dividends (C corporations) or distributions (S corporations) but instead retained in the corporation for future investment. As we see evidenced in figure 6-B.2, the beginning retained earnings balance for a start-up that has not yet commenced with any business activity—including start-up phase activity—will always be $0. The loss generated by start-up activities (i.e., the start-up phase expenses indicated on the pro forma start-up phase expense statement) will be included in the reconciliation of retained earnings as a reduction of retained earnings. Note that it is not uncommon, as is the case with ParkItFast, Inc., that a C corporation in its beginning stages have a negative retained earnings balance. A negative retained earnings balance is

ParkItFast, Inc. Schedule of Start-up Costs				
	January 2020	February 2020	March 2020	For the Three Months Ended March 31, 2020
Rent	$ 1,000	$ 500	$ 500	$ 2,000
Insurance	300	150	150	600
Application development costs	8,500	8,500	8,000	25,000
Application hosting	–	100	100	200
Computers	7,500	–	–	7,500
Software	4,500	–	–	4,500
Total	$21,800	$9,250	$8,750	$39,800

Notes: Rent is paid in the month previous to the month to which it applies.
Insurance is paid in the month previous to the month to which it applies.
Application hosting is paid in the month after the services are used.
All other costs are paid in the same month as incurred.

Figure 6-B.1. Schedule of start-up costs for ParkItFast, Inc.

acceptable as long as stockholders' equity remains positive in total. The common stock and paid-in capital in excess of par amounts included on the balance sheet are calculated as follows:

1,000,000 shares issued x $0.01 par value per share = $10,000 common stock

$225,000 total equity investment – $10,000 common stock = $215,000 paid-in capital in excess of par

The next step in the pro forma financial statement creation process is to create the pro forma income statements for the first nine months of the business's operations. Before we can do that, however, we first need to calculate the expected revenue for these same nine months. We also need to create a depreciation schedule based on the assumptions of the entrepreneurs. The applicable revenue calculations and depreciation schedule follow the list of assumptions in figure 6-B.3 (page 174).

Using the information included in figure 6-B.3 allows us to create the monthly revenue schedule shown in figure 6-B.4 (page 175), the depreciation schedule shown in figure 6-B.5 (page 176), and the loan amortization table and the related calculations shown in figure 6-B.6 (page 177).

As mentioned in appendix 6-A, lenders typically create loan amortization tables related to the loans they make. Such tables are helpful to both the lender and the borrower in terms of understanding the amount and timing of the payments that need to be made or received related to a loan and also the total amount of interest to be paid or received over the life of the loan. Figure 6-B.6 is an example of a loan amortization table for a fixed-payment loan. A fixed-payment loan is just that, a loan for which the monthly payment is a fixed amount for the life of the loan. Fixed-payment loans are not an uncommon configuration for standard U.S. home mortgage and car loans.

Note that whether for a fixed-payment loan like that presented in figure 6-B.6 or for a fixed-principal loan like that illustrated in appendix 6-A of this chapter, the short-term portion of a loan equals the sum of the loan principal payments due to be paid in the next 12 months. The amount of the applicable principal payments is usually determined by consulting the loan's amortization table. The long-term portion of a loan equals the total principal amount of the loan still due to be repaid less the short-term portion of the loan.

ParkItFast, Inc. Pro Forma Pre-Revenue Balance Sheet As of March 31, 2020		ParkItFast, Inc. Pro Forma Start-up Phase Expense Statement, Including Reconciliations of Cash and Retained Earnings For the Three Months Ended March 31, 2020	
Cash	$185,300	Rent	$2,000
Prepaid rent	500	Less: Prepaid rent	500
Prepaid insurance	150		$ 1,500
Total current assets	185,950	Insurance	600
		Less: Prepaid insurance	150
Computers	7,500		450
Software	4,500	Application development costs	25,000
Total fixed assets	12,000	Application hosting	200
		Start-up phase expenses	27,150
Total assets	$197,950	Less: Application hosting payable	100
		Total cash outlays for expenses	$ 27,050
Application hosting payable	$100		
Total liabilities	100	Reconciliation of Cash:	
		Beginning cash	$225,000
Common stock, $0.01 par,		Less: Cash outlays for assets	12,650
1,000,000 shares	10,000	Less: Cash outlays for expenses	27,050
Paid-in capital in excess of par	215,000	Ending cash	$ 185,300
Retained earnings	(27,150)		
Total stockholders' equity	197,850	Reconciliation of Retained Earnings:	
		Beginning retained earnings	$ –
Total liabilities and stockholders' equity	$197,950	Less: Start-up phase expenses	27,150
		Ending retained earnings	$ (27,150)

Figure 6-B.2. Pro forma pre-revenue balance sheet and pro forma start-up phase expense statement, including reconciliations of cash and retained earnings.

Now, using the information included in the list of assumptions and the information we have just calculated, we can create pro forma income statements for ParkIt Fast for its first nine months of operations, as indicated in figure 6-B.7 (page 178).

Note that the interest expense numbers in figure 6-B.7 source from the loan amortization schedule included in figure 6-B.6. Note also that, although there is a small amount of net income in November and December 2020, the provision for income taxes for those months is $0 because, overall for 2020, the business has incurred a net loss. Next, using the pro forma income statements in figure 6-B.7 and the list of assumptions in figure 6-B.3 (page 174), we can complete the pro forma comparative balance sheets and related reconciliations of cash and retained earnings. Figure 6-B.8 (page 179) illustrates the results.

Note that the post-revenue balance sheet reflects the expected December 2020 new equity investment of $50,000 in exchange for 50,000 shares of common stock. The $50,000 of new equity investment drives the increases in the balances of common stock and paid-in capital in excess of par on the balance sheet, calculated as follows:

50,000 additional shares x $0.01 par value = $500 increase common stock

$50,000 new equity investment – $500 increase in common stock = $49,500 increase in paid-in capital in excess of par

The $50,000 of new equity investment is also included in the reconciliation of cash.

ParkItFast, Inc.
List of Assumptions

General Operational and Payroll Information

The three founding entrepreneurs are expected to be on the Board of Directors and to be the officers of the company (i.e., CEO, CFO and COO). Any outside investor providing $100,000 or more in equity funding will be offered the opportunity to be on the Board of Directors. The officers of the company are expected to be compensated as follows:

> December 31, 2020: $1,000 each
> January–June 2021: $0 each
> July 2021–December 2021: $2,500 per month each
> 2022 and beyond: $60,000 per year each

Total payroll taxes, unemployment, and workers' compensation (i.e., payroll taxes) are expected to equal 15% of gross payroll.

Information Regarding Expected Fixed-Asset Purchases, Disposals, Depreciation, and Related Debt

All the fixed assets of this business—except the servers to be purchased in September 2020—are expected to have a useful life of three years and a salvage value of $0, and will be depreciated using the straight-line, half-year convention depreciation method. The business expects to purchase $9,000 of new computers and $6,000 of new software in 2023. No fixed assets are expected to be sold or abandoned until the end of 2023, when the computers and software acquired in 2020 are expected to be disposed of. The $100,000 of servers to be purchased in September 2020 are expected to have a useful life of five years, a salvage value of $10,000, and will be depreciated using the straight-line, half-year convention depreciation method. The $100,000 server purchase will be financed with a $100,000 loan, the proceeds of which are expected to be received by the business on August 31, 2020. The loan is a 5-year, 6% interest, fixed payment loan with interest payable on the last day of each month starting on September 30, 2020.

Information Regarding Expected Revenues

Users paying to use the application will have an advertisement-free experience for $0.99 per month. 200 paying users are expected in April 2020, the month of the application's launch. The number of new paying users is expected to increase 25% month over month throughout 2020. The number of new paying users in 2021 is expected to equal the number of new paying users for December 2020 x 12 months x a growth factor of 4. The number of new paying users in 2022 is expected to be double that of 2021. New paying users are expected to plateau at 150,000 per year in 2023. The number of paying users retained in any period is expected to equal 95% of the prior period's paying users.

Users not paying to use the application will experience advertising within the application. 800 nonpaying users are expected in April 2020, the month of the application's launch. The number of new nonpaying users is expected to increase 50% month over month throughout 2020. The number of new nonpaying users in 2021 is expected to equal the number of new nonpaying users for December 2020 x 12 months x a growth factor of 4. The number of new nonpaying users in 2022 is expected to be double that of 2021. New nonpaying users are expected to plateau at 2,000,000 per year in 2023. The number of nonpaying users retained in any period is expected to equal 95% of the prior period's nonpaying users.

Revenues derived from nonpaying users will be advertisement driven. At any time, the number of active nonpaying users is expected to be 50% of all nonpaying users. Hours spent using the application per month per active user is estimated at five. The number of advertisements displayed per hour per user is expected to be six. The click rate on advertisements and revenue per click are expected to be the industry norms of 5% and $0.50, respectively.

Information Regarding Expected Non-Payroll Expenses

- Cost of goods sold representing the fees to be charged by the most popular app stores is expected to equal 30% of revenue from paying users.
- Marketing expense is expected to be as follows: April 2020: $50,000; May 2020: $40,000; June 2020: $30,000; July 2020: $20,000; August 2020 and every month beyond August 2020: $10,000.
- Application maintenance expense is expected to equal $2,000 per month for the months of April 2020–December 2021, $2,200 per month for years 2022 and 2023, and $2,500 per month for years 2024 and 2025. A $50,000 application upgrade—to be financed by $50,000 of new equity investment in December 2020—is to take place in early 2021. In exchange for the expected $50,000 of new equity investment in December 2020, the investor will receive 50,000 shares of ParkItFast, Inc. common stock. Like the application development costs incurred during the start-up phase of the business, all application upgrades and maintenance will be outsourced and expensed.
- During April–September 2020, hosting expense is expected be equal to 2% of monthly revenue, plus a $100 monthly base fee. Hosting expense is expected to terminate in September 2020 as the business's new servers are expected to take over hosting responsibility for the application on October 1, 2020.
- Rent (which includes utilities) will continue to be paid one month in advance to the business incubator in which ParkItFast's founders plan to start the business, will remain at $500 per month through the end of 2022, and is then expected to increase to $3,000 per month in January 2023 when ParkItFast is expected to be successful enough to be required to leave the business incubator.
- Insurance expense will continue to be paid one month in advance, will remain at $150 per month through the end of 2020, will increase to 1% of revenue in 2021, and will then stabilize at $10,000 per year in 2022. Prepaid insurance at December 31, 2020, is expected to approximate $250.
- Miscellaneous expense is expected to equal 5% of monthly revenue in 2020 and $1,000 per month every month thereafter.
- The corporate income tax is expected to be 21%.

Information Regarding Expected Payables

- At December 31, 2020, payroll payable is expected to be $0 as the officers of the company will be paid on the last day of the month.
- At December 31, 2020, payroll taxes payable is expected to be insignificant as the company will remit payroll taxes, as applicable, on the last day of the month. Any payroll taxes not paid on the last day of the month are expected to be minimal in amount and have been considered in the determination of accounts payable.
- At December 31, 2020, accounts payable is expected to equal 50% of the current month's miscellaneous expense, plus 25% of the current month's marketing expense, plus $200 of estimated payroll taxes payable.

Figure 6-B.3. List of assumptions for ParkItFast, Inc.

ParkItFast, Inc.
Revenue Schedule

	April 2020	May 2020	June 2020	July 2020	August 2020	September 2020	October 2020	November 2020	December 2020	For the Nine Months Ended December 31, 2020
Number of paying users—new	200	250	313	391	488	610	763	954	1,192	
Number of paying users—retained	—	190	418	694	1,030	1,443	1,950	2,578	3,355	
Number of paying users	200	440	731	1,085	1,519	2,053	2,713	3,531	4,547	
Monthly subscription price	$0.90	$ 0.99	$ 0.99	$ 0.99	$ 0.99	$ 0.99	$ 0.99	$ 0.99	$ 0.99	
Revenue from paying users	$ 198	$ 436	$ 723	$1,074	$ 1,503	$ 2,033	$ 2,686	$ 3,496	$ 4,501	$16,650
Number of nonpaying users—new	800	1,200	1,800	2,700	4,050	6,075	9,113	13,669	20,503	
Number of nonpaying users—retained	—	190	1,321	5,664	9,431	15,035	23,395	35,894	54,603	
Number of nonpaying users	200	1,390	3,121	5,664	9,431	15,035	23,395	35,894	54,603	
Active user rate	50%	50%	50%	50%	50%	50%	50%	50%	50%	
Number of active, nonpaying users (A)	100	695	1,560	2,832	4,716	7,517	11,698	17,947	27,301	
Hours spent per month per user (B)	5	5	5	5	5	5	5	5	5	
Number of advertisements displayed per hour per user (C)	6	6	6	6	6	6	6	6	6	
Number of advertisements displayed per month (A) x (B) x (C) = (D)	3,000	20,850	46,808	84,967	141,469	225,520	350,932	538,416	819,043	
Click rate on advertisements (E)	5%	5%	5%	5%	5%	5%	5%	5%	5%	
Revenue per click (F)	$0.50	$ 0.50	$ 0.50	$ 0.50	$ 0.50	$ 0.50	$ 0.50	$ 0.50	$ 0.50	
Revenue from nonpaying users (D) x (E) x (F)	$ 75	$ 521	$1,170	$2,124	$ 3,537	$ 5,638	$ 8,773	$13,460	$20,476	$55,775
Total revenue	$ 273	$ 957	$1,893	$3,198	$ 5,040	$ 7,671	$11,460	$16,460	$16,956	$72,425

Figure 6-B.4. Revenue schedule for the first nine months of operations and for the nine months ended December 31, 2020.

ParkItFast, Inc. Depreciation Schedule				
	2020	2020	2023	
Fixed-asset acquisitions:	$ 12,000	$100,000	$ 15,000	
Less: Salvage value:	–	10,000	–	
Depreciable value:	$ 12,000	$ 90,000	$ 15,000	
Useful life in years:	3	5	3	
Depreciation method:	Straight-line, half-year convention	Straight-line, half-year convention	Straight-line, half-year convention	
Year	Depreciation	Depreciation	Depreciation	Annual Depreciation
2020	$ 2,000	$ 9,000	$ –	$ 11,000
2021	4,000	18,000	–	22,000
2022	4,000	18,000	–	22,000
2023	2,000	18,000	2,500	22,500
2024	–	18,000	5,000	23,000
2025	–	9,000	5,000	14,000
2026	–	–	2,500	2,500
Total	$12,000	$90,000	$15,000	$117,000

Figure 6-B.5. Depreciation schedule.

The ParkItFast, Inc. example we've been utilizing throughout this appendix includes no expected dividend payments to stockholders. This is not unusual for a young company. Assume for a moment, however, for purposes of illustration, that instead of providing $50,000 of new equity investment to the company in December 2020, the stockholders are expecting to receive a dividend of $0.025 per share in that month. If this were the case, note that the $25,000 dividend (1,000,000 shares x $0.025 dividend per share = $25,000) would be included on ParkItFast's reconciliations of cash and retained earnings as illustrated in figure 6-B.9 (page 180).

Returning to the post-revenue balance sheet at figure 6-B.8, notice that the balance sheet reflects both the short- and long-term portions of the August 31, 2020 $100,000 loan. The short-term portion of the loan equals the sum of the loan principal payments due to be paid in the next 12 months, as calculated in figure 6-B.6. The long-term portion of the loan equals the total principal amount of the loan still due to be repaid, less the short-term portion of the loan, calculated as follows:

Loan balance due to be repaid at the end of December 2020	$94,224
– Short-term portion of the loan	18,037
Long-term portion of the loan	$76,187

The next step in our process of pro forma financial statement creation is the creation of the pro forma income statements for years 2021, 2022, 2023, 2024, and 2025. The assumptions and depreciation schedule that support the creation of these income statements are included in figures 6-B.3 and 6-B.5, respectively. The revenue schedule that supports the creation of these income statements is shown at figure 6-B.10 (page 180).

Loan Amortization Table—Fixed-Payment Loan

				Principal Amount =	$ 100,000.00
				Interest Rate =	6.00%
				Number of Years =	5

Payment	Principal	Interest	Payment	Loan Balance	
September 2020	$ 1,433.28	$ 500.00	$ 1,933.28	$ 98,566.72	
October 2020	1,440.45	492.83	1,933.28	97,126.27	
November 2020	1,447.65	485.63	1,933.28	95,678.62	
December 2020	1,454.89	478.39	1,933.28	94,223.74	
January 2021	1,462.16	471.12	1,933.28	92,761.58	
February 2021	1,469.47	463.81	1,933.28	91,292.10	
March 2021	1,476.82	456.46	1,933.28	89,815.29	
April 2021	1,484.20	449.08	1,933.28	88,331.08	
May 2021	1,491.62	441.66	1,933.28	86,839.46	
June 2021	1,499.08	434.20	1,933.28	85,340.37	
July 2021	1,506.58	426.70	1,933.28	83,833.80	
August 2021	1,514.11	419.17	1,933.28	82,319.69	
September 2021	1,521.68	411.60	1,933.28	80,798.00	
October 2021	1,529.29	403.99	1,933.28	79,268.71	
November 2021	1,536.94	396.34	1,933.28	77,731.78	
December 2021	1,544.62	388.66	1,933.28	76,187.16	January–December 2021 interest payments = $ 5,162.78
					January–December 2021 principal payments = $18,036.58
January 2022	1,552.34	380.94	1,933.28	74,634.81	
February 2022	1,560.11	373.17	1,933.28	73,074.71	
March 2022	1,567.91	365.37	1,933.28	71,506.80	
April 2022	1,575.75	357.53	1,933.28	69,931.05	
May 2022	1,583.62	349.66	1,933.28	68,347.43	
June 2022	1,591.54	341.74	1,933.28	66,755.89	
July 2022	1,599.50	333.78	1,933.28	65,156.39	
August 2022	1,607.50	325.78	1,933.28	63,548.89	
September 2022	1,615.54	317.74	1,933.28	61,933.35	
October 2022	1,623.61	309.67	1,933.28	60,309.74	
November 2022	1,631.73	301.55	1,933.28	58,678.01	
December 2022	1,639.89	293.39	1,933.28	57,038.12	January–December 2022 interest payments = $ 4,050.32
					January–December 2022 principal payments = $19,149.04
January 2023	1,648.09	285.19	1,933.28	55,390.03	
February 2023	1,656.33	276.95	1,933.28	53,733.70	
March 2023	1,664.61	268.67	1,933.28	52,069.09	
April 2023	1,672.93	260.35	1,933.28	50,396.15	
May 2023	1,681.30	251.98	1,933.28	48,714.85	
June 2023	1,689.71	243.57	1,933.28	47,025.15	
July 2023	1,698.15	235.13	1,933.28	45,326.99	
August 2023	1,706.65	226.63	1,933.28	43,620.35	
September 2023	1,715.18	218.10	1,933.28	41,905.17	
October 2023	1,723.75	209.53	1,933.28	40,181.42	
November 2023	1,732.37	200.91	1,933.28	38,449.04	
December 2023	1,741.03	192.25	1,933.28	36,708.01	January–December 2023 interest payments = $ 2,869.25
					January–December 2023 principal payments = $20,330.11
January 2024	1,749.74	183.54	1,933.28	34,958.27	
February 2024	1,758.49	174.79	1,933.28	33,199.78	
March 2024	1,767.28	166.00	1,933.28	31,432.50	
April 2024	1,776.12	157.16	1,933.28	29,656.38	
May 2024	1,785.00	148.28	1,933.28	27,871.38	
June 2024	1,793.92	139.36	1,933.28	26,077.46	
July 2024	1,802.89	130.39	1,933.28	24,274.57	
August 2024	1,811.91	121.37	1,933.28	22,462.66	
September 2024	1,820.97	112.31	1,933.28	20,641.69	
October 2024	1,830.07	103.21	1,933.28	18,811.62	
November 2024	1,839.22	94.06	1,933.28	16,972.40	
December 2024	1,848.42	84.86	1,933.28	15,123.98	January–December 2024 interest payments = $ 1,615.33
					January–December 2024 principal payments = $21,584.03
January 2025	1,857.66	75.62	1,933.28	13,266.32	
February 2025	1,866.95	66.33	1,933.28	11,399.37	
March 2025	1,876.28	57.00	1,933.28	9,523.09	
April 2025	1,885.66	47.62	1,933.28	7,637.42	
May 2025	1,895.09	38.19	1,933.28	5,742.33	
June 2025	1,904.57	28.71	1,933.28	3,837.76	
July 2025	1,914.09	19.19	1,933.28	1,923.67	January–August 2025 interest payments = $ 342.27
August 2025	1,923.67	9.62	1,933.29	0.00	January–August 2025 principal payments = $15,123.98
Total	$ 100,000.00	$ 15,996.81			

Figure 6-B.6. Loan amortization table and interest and principal calculations related to the August 2020 fixed-payment loan.

ParkItFast, Inc.
Pro Forma Income Statements
For the First Nine Months of Operations and for the Nine Months Ended December 31, 2020

	April 2020	May 2020	June 2020	July 2020	August 2020	September 2020	October 2020	November 2020	December 2020	For the Nine Months Ended December 31, 2020
Revenue from paying users	$ 198	$ 436	$ 723	$ 1,074	$ 1,503	$ 2,033	$ 2,686	$ 3,496	$ 4,501	$ 16,650
Revenue from nonpaying users	75	521	1,170	2,124	3,537	5,638	8,773	13,460	20,476	55,775
Total revenue	273	957	1,893	3,198	5,040	7,671	11,460	16,956	24,977	72,425
Cost of goods sold–paying users	59	131	217	322	451	610	806	1,049	1,350	4,995
Gross profit	214	826	1,676	2,876	4,589	7,061	10,654	15,908	23,627	67,430
Operating expenses:										
Marketing	50,000	40,000	30,000	20,000	10,000	10,000	10,000	10,000	10,000	190,000
Application upgrades and maintenance	2,000	2,000	2,000	2,000	2,000	2,000	2,000	2,000	2,000	18,000
Hosting	105	119	138	164	201	253	–	–	–	981
Payroll	–	–	–	–	–	–	–	–	3,000	3,000
Payroll taxes	–	–	–	–	–	–	–	–	450	450
Rent	500	500	500	500	500	500	500	500	500	4,500
Insurance	150	150	150	150	150	150	150	150	150	1,350
Depreciation	1,222	1,222	1,222	1,222	1,222	1,222	1,222	1,222	1,222	11,000
Miscellaneous	14	48	95	160	252	384	573	848	1,249	3,621
Total operating expenses	53,991	44,039	34,105	24,196	14,325	14,509	14,445	14,720	18,571	232,902
Operating income	(53,778)	(43,213)	(32,428)	(21,320)	(9,736)	(7,448)	(3,792)	1,188	5,056	(165,472)
Interest expense	–	–	–	–	–	500	493	486	478	1,957
Net income (net loss) before income taxes	(53,778)	(43,213)	(32,428)	(21,320)	(9,736)	(7,948)	(4,284)	702	4,578	(167,428)
Provision for income taxes	–	–	–	–	–	–	–	–	–	–
Net income (net loss)	$(53,778)	$(43,213)	$(32,428)	$(21,320)	$(9,736)	$(7,948)	$(4,284)	$ 702	$ 4,578	$(167,428)

Figure 6-B.7. Pro forma income statements for the first nine months of operations and for the nine months ended December 31, 2020.

ParkItFast, Inc. Pro Forma Balance Sheets As of March 31, 2020, and December 31, 2020		
	(Pre-Revenue) March 30, 2020	(Post-Revenue) December 31, 2020
Cash	$ 185,300	$ 76,220
Prepaid rent	500	500
Prepaid insurance	150	250
Total current assets	185,950	76,970
Computers	7,500	7,500
Software	4,500	4,500
Servers	-	100,000
Accumulated depreciation	-	(11,000)
Net fixed assets	12,000	101,000
Total assets	$ 197,950	$ 177,970
Accounts payable	$ -	$ 3,325
Application hosting payable	100	-
Short-term portion of loan payable	-	18,037
Total current liabilities	100	21,361
Loan payable	-	76,187
Total liabilities	100	97,548
Common stock, $0.01 par, 1,000,000 shares at March 31, 2020, 1,050,000 shares at December 31, 2020	10,000	10,500
Paid-in capital in excess of par	215,000	264,500
Retained earnings	(27,150)	(194,578)
Total shareholders' equity	197,850	80,422
Total liabilities and shareholders' equity	$ 197,950	$ 177,970

ParkItFast, Inc. Pro Forma Reconciliations of Cash and Retained Earnings For the Nine Months Ended December 31, 2020	
Reconciliation of Cash:	
Beginning cash	$ 185,300
Add: Net loss for the nine months ended December 31, 2020	(167,428)
Add: Depreciation for the nine months ended December 31, 2020	11,000
Adjustments for changes in noncash assets and liabilities:	
Increase in prepaid insurance	(100)
Increase in servers	(100,000)
Increase in accounts payable	3,325
Increase in application hosting payable	(100)
Increase in short-term portion of loan payable	18,037
Increase in loan payable	76,187
Add: New equity investment during the nine months ended December 31, 2020	50,000
Ending cash	$ 76,220
Reconciliation of Retained Earnings:	
Beginning retained earnings	$ (27,150)
Add: Net loss for the nine months ended December 31, 2020	(167,428)
Ending retained earnings	$ (194,578)

Figure 6-B.8. Pro forma pre-revenue balance sheet and pro forma post-revenue balance sheet, including post-revenue reconciliations of cash and retained earnings.

ParkItFast, Inc.
Pro Forma Reconciliations of Cash and Retained Earnings
For the Nine Months Ended December 31, 2020

Reconciliation of Cash:

Beginning cash	$ 185,300
Add: Net loss for the nine months ended December 31, 2020	(167,428)
Add: Depreciation for the nine months ended December 31, 2020	11,000
Adjustments for changes in noncash assets and liabilities:	
Increase in prepaid insurance	(100)
Increase in servers	(100,000)
Increase in accounts payable	3,325
Increase in application hosting payable	(100)
Increase in short-term portion of loan payable	18,037
Increase in loan payable	76,187
Less: Dividends paid to stockholders during the nine months ended December 31, 2020	25,000
Ending cash	$ 1,220

Reconciliation of Retained Earnings:

Beginning retained earnings	$ (27,150)
Add: Net loss for the nine months ended December 31, 2020	(167,428)
Less: Dividends paid to stockholders during the nine months ended December 31, 2020	25,000
Ending retained earnings	$ (219,578)

Figure 6-B.9. Reconciliations of cash and retained earnings reflecting a $25,000 dividend.

ParkItFast, Inc.
Revenue Schedule

	2020	2021	2022	2023	2024
Number of paying users–new	57,216	114,432	150,000	150,000	150,000
Number of paying users–retained	4,320	58,459	164,246	298,534	426,107
Number of paying users	61,536	172,891	314,246	448,534	576,107
Monthly subscription price	$ 0.99	$ 0.99	$ 0.99	$ 0.99	$ 0.99
Revenue from paying users	$ 60,920	$ 171,162	$ 311,104	$ 444,049	$ 570,346
Number of non-paying users–new	984,144	1,968,288	2,000,000	2,000,000	2,000,000
Number of non-paying users–retained	51,873	984,216	2,804,879	4,564,635	6,236,403
Number of non-paying users	1,036,017	2,952,504	4,804,879	6,564,635	8,236,403
Active user rate	50%	50%	50%	50%	50%
Number of active, non-paying users (A)	518,008	1,476,252	2,402,439	3,282,317	4,118,201
Hours spent per month per user (B)	5	5	5	5	5
Number of advertisements displayed per hour per user (C)	6	6	6	6	6
Number of advertisements displayed per month (A) x (B) x (C) = (D)	15,540,250	44,287,558	72,073,180	98,469,521	123,546,045
Click rate on advertisements (E)	5%	5%	5%	5%	5%
Revenue per click (F)	$ 0.50	$ 0.50	$ 0.50	$ 0.50	$ 0.50
Revenue from non-paying users (D) x (E) x (F)	$ 388,506	$ 1,107,189	$ 1,801,829	$ 2,461,738	$ 3,088,651
Total revenue	$ 449,426	$ 1,278,351	$ 2,112,933	$ 2,905,787	$ 3,658,997

Figure 6-B.10. Revenue schedule for years 2021–2025.

The pro forma income statements for the first nine months of operations and years 2021, 2022, 2023, 2024, and 2025 are shown at figure 6-B.11. Note that for years 2021–2025, the provision for income taxes is calculated by multiplying net income before income taxes by the corporate tax rate of 21%. For purposes of pro forma financial statement creation, this type of basic provision for income taxes calculation is perfectly acceptable because the typical entrepreneur does not have enough tax knowledge–and is not expected to have enough tax knowledge–to calculate more sophisticated provision for income taxes numbers and their related deferred tax asset and deferred tax liability amounts.

ParkItFast, Inc. Pro Forma Income Statements For the Nine Months Ended December 31, 2020, and for the Years Ended Ended December 31, 2021, 2022, 2023, 2024 and 2025						
	For the Nine Months Ended December 31, 2020	2021	2022	2023	2024	2025
Revenue–paying users	$ 16,650	$ 60,920	$ 171,162	$ 311,104	$ 444,049	$ 570,346
Revenue–nonpaying users	55,775	388,506	1,107,189	1,801,829	2,461,738	3,088,651
Total revenue	72,425	449,426	1,278,351	2,112,933	2,905,787	3,658,997
Cost of goods sold–paying users	4,995	18,276	51,349	93,331	133,215	171,104
Gross profit	67,430	431,150	1,227,002	2,019,602	2,772,572	3,487,893
Operating expenses:						
Marketing	190,000	120,000	120,000	120,000	120,000	120,000
Application upgrades and maintenance	18,000	74,000	26,400	26,400	30,000	30,000
Hosting	981	–	–	–	–	–
Payroll	3,000	45,000	180,000	180,000	180,000	180,000
Payroll taxes	450	6,750	27,000	27,000	27,000	27,000
Rent	4,500	6,000	6,000	36,000	36,000	36,000
Insurance	1,350	4,494	10,000	10,000	10,000	10,000
Depreciation	11,000	22,000	22,000	22,500	23,000	14,000
Miscellaneous	3,621	12,000	12,000	12,000	12,000	12,000
Total operating expenses	232,902	290,244	403,400	433,900	438,000	429,000
Operating income	(165,472)	140,906	823,602	1,585,702	2,334,572	3,058,893
Interest expense	1,957	5,163	4,050	2,869	1,615	342
Net income (net loss) before income taxes	(167,428)	135,743	819,552	1,582,833	2,332,957	3,058,551
Provision for income taxes	–	28,506	172,106	332,395	489,921	642,296
Net income (net loss)	$ (167,428)	$ 107,237	$ 647,446	$ 1,250,438	$ 1,843,036	$ 2,416,255

Figure 6-B.11. Pro forma income statements for the nine months ended December 31, 2020, and the years ended December 31, 2021, 2022, 2023, 2024, and 2025.

Pro Forma Balance Sheets for Year 2 and Subsequent Years and Pro Forma Statements of Cash Flows

"You must always be able to predict what's next and then have the flexibility to evolve."

— **Marc Benioff, American billionaire entrepreneur, founder of Salesforce**

Learning Objectives

Be able to create the pro forma balance sheets for years 2–5 of a new business using the percentage of sales method.

Be able to create the pro forma statements of cash flows for a new business using the pro forma reconciliations of cash already created for the venture.

Introduction

Whether an entrepreneur is preparing a feasibility analysis, a business plan, or both, pro forma financial statements that clearly illustrate the expected future profitability and continued viability of a proposed new business are vital. An entrepreneur will find it nearly impossible to bring on talented business partners, interest investors or lenders, or otherwise significantly move the business forward without them.

Chapter 6 illustrated the creation of the following items for an example company, the Fifth Avenue Apparel Shoppe:

- a schedule of start-up costs
- a pro forma pre-revenue balance sheet, including reconciliations of cash and equity
- a pro forma start-up phase expense statement
- a comprehensive list of assumptions

- cost of goods sold, estimated sales, and depreciation schedules
- a pro forma post-revenue balance sheet, including reconciliations of cash and equity
- all the pro forma income statements associated with the first years of the business

Chapter 7 illustrates how to create pro forma balance sheets for years 2–5 of a new enterprise and pro forma statements of cash flows, should a current or potential investor or lender require them. In order to illustrate the creation of a complete and comprehensive set of pro forma financial statements for a proposed new enterprise, we'll continue to work with the Fifth Avenue Apparel Shoppe example from chapter 6.

The Percentage of Sales Method

percentage of sales method
a technique used to develop a pro forma balance sheet based on the fact that the assets and liabilities of a company typically vary with its sales

The further we move into the future, the harder it is to include on our list of assumptions expectations about the future of our business that we can feel confident about, especially the dollar amount of certain future balance sheet line items. The percentage of sales method can help us overcome this problem. The **percentage of sales method** is a technique used to develop a pro forma balance sheet based on the fact that the assets and liabilities of a company typically vary with its sales. The method allows us to incorporate into our balance sheets those assumptions and expectations related to the future of our company about which we are confident, while also providing a logical framework for estimating balance sheet amounts about which we are less confident.

The theory behind the method is that any increase or decrease in a company's sales will cause a subsequent, related buildup or reduction in both the assets and the liabilities of the company. The relevant formula follows:

Percentage increase or decrease in sales = [(Current year sales – Previous year sales) ÷ Previous year sales] x 100

The seven-step process follows:

1. Calculate or determine the expected percentage increase or decrease in sales from the previous year to the current year (i.e., the current year being the year for which we are trying to develop a balance sheet).
2. Increase or decrease every line item amount—but not the subtotal or total amounts—on the previous year balance sheet by the percentage increase or decrease calculated in step 1 in order to generate a preliminary pro forma balance sheet for the current year.
3. Adjust the preliminary balance sheet generated in step 2 for items known or expected.
4. Calculate subtotals and totals. When we do this, we'll usually note that the amount for total assets isn't the same as the amount for total liabilities and equity. This is because the expected percentage increase or decrease in sales is being used to determine the amounts for cash and equity.
5. Create a reconciliation of cash and a reconciliation of equity.

6. Adjust the cash and equity line items on the preliminary current year balance sheet to reflect the balances indicated by the applicable reconciliations, then recalculate the necessary subtotals and totals on the balance sheet.

7. Verify that the amount for total assets is the same as the amount for total liabilities and equity. If the two amounts are equal, we have likely completed our pro forma balance sheet correctly.

Creating a Pro Forma Balance Sheet Using the Percentage of Sales Method

Returning to the Fifth Avenue Apparel Shoppe example first presented in chapter 6, figure 7.1 shows the pro forma comparative balance sheets and the post-revenue reconciliations of cash and equity prepared in chapter 6.

Figure 7.2 (on page 186) and Figure 7.3 (on page 187) show the company's pro forma income statements and list of assumptions, respectively.

Fifth Avenue Apparel Shoppe, LLC Pro Forma Balance Sheets As of September 30, 2020, and December 31, 2021			Fifth Avenue Apparel Shoppe, LLC Pro Forma Reconciliations of Cash and Owners' Equity For the Five Quarters Ended December 31, 2021	
	(Pre-Revenue) September 30, 2020	(Post-Revenue) December 31, 2021		
Cash	$ 30,250	$105,227	Reconciliation of Cash:	
Prepaid insurance	250	250		
Clothing inventory	30,000	30,000	Beginning cash	$ 30,250
Accessories inventory	10,000	10,000	Add: Net income for the five	
Total current assets	70,500	145,477	quarters ended December 31, 2021	291,751
			Add: Depreciation for the five	
Checkout counters and			quarters ended December 31, 2021	14,100
furniture	12,000	12,000	Adjustments for changes in	
Clothing racks and shelving	20,000	20,000	noncash assets and liabilities:	
Computers and software	10,000	10,000	Increase in accounts payable	34,000
Security system	5,000	5,000	Increase in payroll payable	1,552
Less: Accumulated			Increase in payroll taxes payable	210
depreciation	–	14,100	Increase in sales tax payable	3,364
Net fixed assets	47,000	32,900	Less: Distributions to owners from	
			April–December 2021	270,000
Total assets	$117,500	$178,377	Ending cash	$105,227
Accounts payable	$ –	$ 34,000		
Payroll payable	–	1,552	Reconciliation of Owners' Equity:	
Payroll taxes payable	–	210		
Utilities payable	500	500	Beginning owners' equity	$117,000
Sales tax payable	–	3,364	Add: Net income for the five	
Total liabilities	500	39,626	quarters ended December 31, 2021	291,751
			Less: Distributions to owners from	
Owners' equity	117,000	138,751	April–December 2021	270,00
			Ending owners' equity	$138,751
Total liabilities and owners' equity	$117,500	$178,377		

Figure 7.1. Pro forma pre- and post-revenue balance sheets and post-revenue reconciliations of cash and owners' equity for the Fifth Avenue Apparel Shoppe.

	For the Three Months Ended December 31, 2020	2021	2022	2023	2024	2025
	Fifth Avenue Apparel Shoppe, LLC Pro Forma Income Statements For the Three Months Ended December 31, 2020, and for the Years Ended December 31, 2021, 2022, 2023, 2024, and 2025					
Sales	$115,000	$587,087	$690,000	$749,000	$818,286	$884,286
Cost of goods sold	40,000	204,204	240,000	260,000	260,000	260,000
Gross profit	75,000	382,883	450,000	489,000	558,286	624,286
Operating expenses:						
Rent	15,000	60,000	60,000	60,750	63,000	63,000
Payroll	9,295	37,180	44,616	44,616	46,847	46,847
Payroll taxes	1,255	5,019	6,023	6,023	6,324	6,324
Utilities	1,500	6,000	6,180	6,180	6,304	6,304
Insurance	750	3,000	3,300	3,300	3,300	3,300
Depreciation	4,700	9,400	9,400	9,900	10,400	6,825
Cleaning and maintenance	750	3,000	3,000	3,000	3,000	3,000
Miscellaneous	-	9,282	10,210	12,000	13,000	13,000
Total operating expenses	33,250	132,881	142,729	145,769	152,175	148,600
Net income	$ 41,750	$250,001	$307,271	$343,231	$406,111	$475,686

Figure 7.2. Pro forma income statements for the Fifth Avenue Apparel Shoppe.

Because, as evidenced by figure 7.1, a balance sheet already exists for the Fifth Avenue Apparel Shoppe as of December 31, 2021, the next balance sheet we need to create for the proposed business is for December 31, 2022. Using the information included in the company's income statement in Figure 7.2, we'll execute step 1 of the percentage of sales method of balance sheet creation by determining the percentage increase or decrease in sales from 2021 to 2022:

Percentage increase or decrease in sales = [(Current year sales – Previous year sales) ÷ Previous year sales] x 100

= [($690,000 – $587,087) ÷ $587,087] x 100

= 0.1753 x 100

= 17.53%

Step 2 of the percentage of sales method indicates that we should increase every line item on the previous year's balance sheet by the expected percentage increase in sales in order to generate a preliminary pro forma balance sheet for the current year. Doing so results in the preliminary 2022 balance sheet included in figure 7.4 (on page 188).

Next, step 3 of the percentage of sales method indicates that we should adjust the preliminary balance sheet (figure 7.4) for what we know or expect. What we know or expect for 2022 can be gleaned from the balance sheet for 2021, the income statement for year 2022, and the list of assumptions for the Fifth Avenue Apparel Shoppe. Specifically, what we know or expect for 2022 is as follows:

- Employee pay per hour is expected to increase 20 percent in 2022.
- No new fixed assets are expected to be purchased or disposed of in 2022.
- Utilities expense is expected to increase 3 percent in 2022
- Insurance expense is expected to increase 10 percent in 2022.
- Distributions for 2022 are expected to total $360,000.
- Depreciation expense for 2022 is expected to be $9,400, according to the pro forma income statement for that year.
- Net income for 2022 is expected to equal $307,271, according to the pro forma income statement for that year.

Fifth Avenue Apparel Shoppe, LLC
List of Assumptions

General Operational and Payroll Information

| Storehours: | Tuesday–Saturday 10:00 a.m.–9:00 p.m. |
| | Sunday Noon–8:00 p.m. |

Needed employees: Three:	1 Tuesday–Saturday 9:30 a.m.–4:00 p.m.
	1 Tuesday–Saturday 3:30 p.m.–10:00 p.m.
	1 Sunday 11:30 a.m.–6:00 p.m.

In order to keep payroll to a minimum and effectively manage the business, one or both of the two founding entrepreneurs will always be present during the store's hours of operation. Employees will be paid $10 per hour. Payroll taxes, unemployment, and workers' compensation combined are expected to equal 13.5% of gross payroll. Employee pay per hour is expected to increase 20% from its year 2021 amount in 2022 and then another 5% in 2024.

Information Regarding Expected Inventory Pricing, Inventory Sales (Cost of Goods Sold), and Inventory Levels

| Target margin for clothing: | 60% until December 31, 2023, 65% beginning January 1, 2024 |
| Target margin for accessories: | 75% until December 31, 2024, 80% beginning January 1, 2025 |

Expected inventory turnover rate for 2020: Four times per year. In other words, for 2020, after business operations commence, it is expected that, on average, the business will sell and replace its inventory at a rate of four times per year, or once per quarter. After 2020, cost of goods sold (COGS) is expected to increase 10% each quarter through the end of 2021. Although COGS will increase, inventory levels are expected to remain at $30,000 (clothing) and $10,000 (accessories) through the end of 2021 due to expertise gained in inventory management. COGS is expected to increase to $45,000 (clothing) and 15,000 (accessories) per quarter for 2022. COGS is expected to increase to $48,500 (clothing) and $16,500 (accessories) per quarter for 2023 and stabilize there.

Information Regarding Expected Fixed-Asset Purchases, Disposals, and Depreciation

- The $47,000 of fixed assets to be purchased during the start-up phase of the business are expected to have a useful life of five years, a salvage value of $0, and will, like all the business's expected fixed assets, be depreciated using the straight-line, half-year convention depreciation method.
- No new fixed assets are expected to be purchased after the start-up phase until 2023, when the business expects to purchase $5,000 of new software with a salvage value of $0. In addition, at the beginning of 2025, the business expects to purchase $12,500 of new, higher-end computers with a salvage value of $1,250.
- By the end of 2025, the $10,000 of computers and software purchased during the start-up phase of the business are expected to be fully depreciated, phased out, and abandoned (i.e., thrown out). These are expected to be the first fixed assets disposed of by the business.

Information Regarding Expected Non-Payroll Expenses

- Store design and decoration expense is expected to terminate in September 2020.
- Cleaning and maintenance expense is expected to cost $250 per month beginning in October 2020 and remain the same amount through the end of 2025.
- Miscellaneous expense is expected to amount to 5% of the prior period's COGS.
- Rent is expected to remain at $5,000 per month through September 30, 2023, then increase 5% to $5,250 on October 1, 2023. Rent is expected to continue to be paid on the first day of the month to which it relates.
- Utilities expense is expected to continue to be paid in the month after the services are used and is expected to remain unchanged at approximately $500 per month until it increases 3% in 2022 and then another 2% in 2024.
- Insurance expense is expected to continue to be paid one month in advance and is expected to remain unchanged at approximately $250 per month until it increases 10% in 2022 and then stabilizes.

Information Regarding Expected Payables

- At December 31, 2021, accounts payable, including payables related to cleaning and maintenance and miscellaneous expenses, is expected to approximate 85% of clothing and accessories inventory.
- At December 31, 2021, payroll payable is expected to equal one-sixth of fourth quarter 2021 payroll expense.
- At December 31, 2021, payroll taxes payable is expected to equal one-sixth of fourth quarter 2021 payroll tax expense.
- At December 31, 2021, sales tax payable is expected to approximate one month's sales multiplied by the sales tax rate of 6% (calculated as one-third of fourth quarter 2021 sales x 0.06).

Other Information

Each of the three owners of the company is expected to begin taking a $10,000-per-month cash distribution starting in April 2021.

Figure 7.3. List of assumptions for the Fifth Avenue Apparel Shoppe.

		Fifth Avenue Apparel Shoppe, LLC Pro Forma Balance Sheets As of December 31, 2021, and December 31, 2022		
	2021	Expected Percentage Increase in Sales	2022
Cash	$105,227	17.53%	$123,673
Prepaid insurance	250	17.53%	294
Clothing inventory	30,000	17.53%	35,259
Accessories inventory	10,000	17.53%	11,753
Total current assets	145,477		
Checkout counters and furniture	12,000	17.53%	14,104
Clothing racks and shelving	20,000	17.53%	23,506
Computers and software	10,000	17.53%	11,753
Security system	5,000	17.53%	5,877
Less: Accumulated depreciation	14,100	17.53%	16,572
Net fixed assets	32,900		
Total assets	$178,377		
Accounts payable	$ 34,000	17.53%	$ 39,960
Payroll payable	1,552	17.53%	1,824
Payroll taxes payable	210	17.53%	247
Utilities payable	500	17.53%	588
Sales tax payable	3,364	17.53%	3,954
Total liabilities	39,626		
Owners' equity	138,751	17.53%	163,074
Total liabilities and owners' equity	$178,377		

Figure 7.4. Pro forma balance sheets for December 31, 2021, and December 31, 2022, working copy 1.

Adjusting the preliminary 2022 balance sheet in figure 7.4 for what we know or expect results in the preliminary 2022 balance sheet included in figure 7.5.

It was noted in chapter 6 that percentage increases or decreases in expenses—or the lack thereof—are usually mirrored in their related prepaids or payables. Insurance expense is expected to increase 10 percent in 2022, so on the preliminary balance sheet in figure 7.5, the prepaid insurance line item has been increased 10 percent. No fixed-asset purchases or disposals are planned for 2022, so the amounts of the December 31, 2022 fixed-asset line items have been adjusted to equal the amounts of the December 31, 2021 fixed-asset line items. Because no fixed-asset disposals are planned for 2022, December 31, 2021 accumulated depreciation plus 2022 depreciation expense should equal December 31, 2022 accumulated depreciation, so the preliminary balance sheet has been adjusted to reflect that. Employee pay per hour is expected to increase 20 percent in 2022, so both payroll payable and payroll taxes payable have been increased 20 percent. Last, utilities expense is expected to increase 3 percent in 2022, so the utilities payable line item has been increased 3 percent.

Step 4 of the percentage of sales method indicates we should calculate the subtotals and totals on our balance sheet. Figure 7.6 (on page 190) shows our preliminary 2022 balance sheet after doing so.

Fifth Avenue Apparel Shoppe, LLC Pro Forma Balance Sheets As of December 31, 2021, and December 31, 2022			
	2021	Expected Percentage Increase in Sales	2022
Cash	$105,227	17.53%	$123,673
Prepaid insurance	250		275
Clothing inventory	30,000	17.53%	35,259
Accessories inventory	10,000	17.53%	11,753
Total current assets	145,477		
Checkout counters and furniture	12,000		12,000
Clothing racks and shelving	20,000		20,000
Computers and software	10,000		10,000
Security system	5,000		5,000
Less: Accumulated depreciation	14,100		23,500
Net fixed assets	32,900		
Total assets	$178,377		
Accounts payable	$ 34,000	17.53%	$ 39,960
Payroll payable	1,552		1,862
Payroll taxes payable	210		252
Utilities payable	500		515
Sales tax payable	3,364	17.53%	3,954
Total liabilities	39,626		
Owners' equity	138,751	17.53%	163,074
Total liabilities and owners' equity	$178,377		

Figure 7.5. Pro forma balance sheets for December 31, 2021, and December 31, 2022, working copy 2.

Note that, in figure 7.6, the amount for total assets isn't the same as the amount for total liabilities and equity. This is because the expected percentage increase in sales is currently being used to determine the amounts for cash and owners' equity. In order to correct this, as indicated by step 5 of the percentage of sales method, we must create reconciliations of cash and owners' equity, as shown in figure 7.7 (on page 191).

The reconciliations in figure 7.7 were created the same way as demonstrated in chapter 6. The only meaningful difference is that, because we're moving the business forward in time and the business is therefore becoming more mature, we're including more assets and liabilities on the business's balance sheet. As a result, there are more adjustments for changes in noncash assets and liabilities on the reconciliation of cash.

Step 6 of the percentage of sales method indicates we should next adjust the cash and equity line items on our preliminary balance sheet to reflect the balances indicated by their respective reconciliations. After that, we'll recalculate the necessary subtotals and totals on the balance sheet. Figure 7.8 (on page 192) shows our finalized pro forma comparative balance sheets for 2021 and 2022.

Fifth Avenue Apparel Shoppe, LLC Pro Forma Balance Sheets As of December 31, 2021, and December 31, 2022			
	2021	Expected Percentage Increase in Sales	2022
Cash	$105,227	17.53%	$123,673
Prepaid insurance	250		275
Clothing inventory	30,000	17.53%	35,259
Accessories inventory	10,000	17.53%	11,753
Total current assets	145,477		170,960
Checkout counters and furniture	12,000		12,000
Clothing racks and shelving	20,000		20,000
Computers and software	10,000		10,000
Security system	5,000		5,000
Less: Accumulated depreciation	14,100		23,500
Net fixed assets	32,900		23,500
Total assets	$178,377		$194,460
Accounts payable	$ 34,000	17.53%	$ 39,960
Payroll payable	1,552		1,862
Payroll taxes payable	210		252
Utilities payable	500		515
Sales tax payable	3,364	17.53%	3,954
Total liabilities	39,626		46,543
Owners' equity	138,751	17.53%	163,074
Total liabilities and owners' equity	$178,377		$209,617

Figure 7.6. Pro forma balance sheets for December 31, 2021, and December 31, 2022, working copy 3.

Note that, as is required by step 7 of the percentage of sales method—and by the basic accounting equation—in figure 7.8 the amount for total assets now equals the amount for total liabilities and equity. Note further that, ultimately, only four balance sheet line items ended up changing by the 17.53 percent increase in sales expected from year 2021 to year 2022, specifically:

1. clothing inventory
2. accessories inventory
3. accounts payable
4. sales tax payable

Every other number on the December 31, 2022 balance sheet was determined via alternative means. This result is not unusual.

Fifth Avenue Apparel Shoppe, LLC Pro Forma Reconciliations of Cash and Owners' Equity For the Year Ended December 31, 2022	
Reconciliation of Cash:	
Beginning cash	$ 105,227
Add: Net income for the year ended December 31, 2022	307,271
Add: Depreciation for the year ended December 31, 2022	9,400
Adjustments for changes in noncash assets and liabilities:	
Increase in prepaid insurance	(25)
Increase in clothing inventory	(5,259)
Increase in accessories inventory	(1,753)
Increase in accounts payable	5,960
Increase in payroll payable	310
Increase in payroll taxes payable	42
Increase in utilities payable	15
Increase in sales tax payable	590
Less: Distributions to owners during the year ended December 31, 2022	360,000
Ending cash	$ 61,778
Reconciliation of Owners' Equity:	
Beginning owners' equity	$138,751
Add: Net income for the year ended December 31, 2022	307,271
Less: Distributions to owners during the year ended December 31, 2022	360,000
Ending owners' equity	$ 86,022

Figure 7.7. Pro forma reconciliations of cash and owners' equity for the year ended December 31, 2022.

To recap, with regard to the percentage of sales method, remember the following:

- After all is said and done, we only use our applicable percentage increase or decrease in sales to estimate pro forma balance sheet line items we don't know or can't estimate through other means.
- If we expect an expense to increase or decrease a certain percentage in the coming year, it's reasonable to expect any related payable or prepaid to increase or decrease by that same percentage by the end of the year.
- Subtotals and totals should subtotal and total (i.e., they should not be determined using the percentage increase or decrease in sales).
- Cash and equity should be determined by creating the appropriate reconciliations (i.e., they should not be determined using the percentage increase or decrease in sales).

Now that we've learned how to create a pro forma balance sheet using the percentage of sales method, let's turn our attention to the statement of cash flows.

Fifth Avenue Apparel Shoppe, LLC Pro Forma Balance Sheets As of December 31, 2021, and December 31, 2022		
	2021	2022
Cash	$105,227	$ 61,778
Prepaid insurance	250	275
Clothing inventory	30,000	35,259
Accessories inventory	10,000	11,753
Total current assets	145,477	109,065
Checkout counters and furniture	12,000	12,000
Clothing racks and shelving	20,000	20,000
Computers and software	10,000	10,000
Security system	5,000	5,000
Less: Accumulated depreciation	14,100	23,500
Net fixed assets	32,900	23,500
Total assets	$178,377	$132,565
Accounts payable	$ 34,000	$ 39,960
Payroll payable	1,552	1,862
Payroll taxes payable	210	252
Utilities payable	500	515
Sales tax payable	3,364	3,954
Total liabilities	39,626	46,543
Owners' equity	138,751	86,022
Total liabilities and owners' equity	$178,377	$132,565

Figure 7.8. Pro forma balance sheets for December 31, 2021, and December 31, 2022, final version.

The Statement of Cash Flows

As first discussed in chapter 4, a statement of cash flows is a summary of the cash receipts and cash expenditures of a business over a specified period of time. A statement of cash flows generally includes the following three major sections:

1. cash flows from operating activities, which typically does the following:
   - considers a business's net income or net loss
   - adds back depreciation expense to net income or net loss because depreciation is a noncash expense
   - shows all the cash received by the business and all the cash paid out by the business as a result of its day-to-day operations during a specified period by identifying the dollar change in noncash current asset and current liability balance sheet line items from the beginning of the period to the end of the period
2. cash flows from investing activities, which typically includes summary information regarding the purchase or sale of investments in the financial markets, the purchase or sale of fixed assets, the making or collection of loans, and any insurance settlement proceeds related to fixed assets
3. cash flows from financing activities, which typically includes summary information regarding the sale or repurchase of stock, the receipt of debt proceeds or the repayment of debt, and the payment of dividends or distributions

The Stanwick Corporation Statement of Cash Flows For the Year Ended December 31, 2018		
Cash flows from operating activities:		
Net income		$ 88,655
Adjustments to reconcile net income to net cash flows from operating activities:		
Depreciation expense	$ 3,500	
Increase in accounts receivable	(12,000)	
Increase in inventory	(18,500)	
Increase in accounts payable	8,500	
Increase in notes payable	1,500	
Increase in taxes payable	6,500	
		(10,500)
Net cash flows from operating activities		78,155
Cash flows from investing activities:		
Purchase of building	(150,000)	
Net cash flows from investing activities		(150,000)
Cash flows from financing activities:		
Proceeds from issuance of preferred stock	50,000	
Proceeds from mortgage payable	45,000	
Repayment of bank loan	(22,155)	
Net cash flows from financing activities		72,845
Net increase in cash		1,000
Cash balance, December 31, 2017		3,000
Cash balance, December 31, 2018		$ 4,000

Figure 7.9. An example statement of cash flows.

Figure 7.9 is the example statement of cash flows from chapter 4. A statement of cash flows like the one in figure 7.9 provides detailed information about three areas of interest related to a business over a specified period of time:

1. the business's sources of cash
2. the business's uses of cash
3. the business's beginning and ending balances of cash

Essentially, the reconciliation of cash we learned to create in chapter 6 already provides us with this information. It's also quite close in look and function to a formal statement of cash flows. The next section of this chapter illustrates how to transform a pro forma reconciliation of cash into a pro forma statement of cash flows when an interested party has requested one.

Creating a Pro Forma Statement of Cash Flows from a Pro Forma Reconciliation of Cash

For the most part, transforming a pro forma reconciliation of cash into a pro forma statement of cash flows involves reorganizing the information on the reconciliation of cash into the format required by a statement of cash flows and then adding subtotals and totals. Figure 7.10 (on page 194) illustrates the transformation of the pro

Fifth Avenue Apparel Shoppe, LLC Pro Forma Reconciliation of Cash For the Five Quarters Ended December 31, 2021	
Beginning cash	$ 30,250
Add: Net income for the five quarters ended December 31, 2021	291,751
Add: Depreciation for the five quarters ended December 31, 2021	14,100
Adjustments for changes in noncash assets and liabilities:	
Increase in accounts payable	34,000
Increase in payroll payable	1,552
Increase in payroll taxes payable	210
Increase in sales tax payable	3,364
Less: Distributions to owners from April–December 2021	270,000
Ending cash	$105,227

Fifth Avenue Apparel Shoppe, LLC Pro Forma Statement of Cash Flows For the Five Quarters Ended December 31, 2021		
Cash flows from operating activities:		
Net income		$ 291,751
Adjustments to reconcile net income to net cash flows from operating activities:		
Depreciation	$ 14,100	
Increase in accounts payable	34,000	
Increase in payroll payable	1,552	
Increase in payroll taxes payable	210	
Increase in sales tax payable	3,364	
		53,226
Net cash flows from operating activities		344,977
Cash flows from financing activities:		
Distributions to owners from April–December 2021	(270,000)	
Net cash flows from financing activities		(270,000)
Net increase in cash		74,977
Cash balance, September 30, 2020		30,250
Cash balance, December 31, 2021		$ 105,227

Figure 7.10. Transformation of a pro forma reconciliation of cash into a pro forma statement of cash flows.

forma reconciliation of cash for the five quarters ended December 31, 2021, into a pro forma statement of cash flows for the same period for the Fifth Avenue Apparel Shoppe.

The pro forma statement of cash flows presented in figure 7.10 follows the standard format of most statements of cash flows. Net income—or net loss—is usually the first line item included on the statement. Depreciation expense is generally the first line item of the reconciliation of net income to net cash flows from operating activities. Depreciation expense is typically followed by the increases or decreases in the noncash current asset and current liability accounts. The net cash flows from operating activities subtotal is usually followed by the cash flows from investing activities and cash flows from financing activities sections of the financial statement. Increases or decreases in noncurrent assets and liabilities are typically reflected in these sections. The statement of cash flows typically ends with a reconciliation of the cash balance on the current balance sheet to the cash balance on the balance sheet that immediately precedes it.

Note that not every increase or decrease in the noncash asset and liability accounts on a reconciliation of cash is always reflected on its associated statement of cash flows. In the event of an increase or decrease in an asset or liability account that doesn't involve cash (e.g., when a fully depreciated fixed asset with no salvage value is disposed of in exchange for $0 or when an amount on a balance sheet is reclassified from long term to short term or vice versa), the statement of cash flows wouldn't reflect that particular increase or decrease in account. Note further that the statement of cash flows in figure 7.10 doesn't include a section for cash flows from investing activities. This is because no investing activities are expected to occur during the period covered by the financial statement. This is not unusual.

| Fifth Avenue Apparel Shoppe, LLC |
| Pro Forma Reconciliation of Cash |
| For the Year Ended December 31, 2022 |

Beginning cash	$105,227
Add: Net income for the year ended December 31, 2022	307,271
Add: Depreciation for the year ended December 31, 2022	9,400
Adjustments for changes in noncash assets and liabilities:	
Increase in prepaid insurance	(25)
Increase in clothing inventory	(5,259)
Increase in accessories inventory	(1,753)
Increase in accounts payable	5,960
Increase in payroll payable	310
Increase in payroll taxes payable	42
Increase in utilities payable	15
Increase in sales tax payable	590
Less: Distributions to owners during the year ended December 31, 2022	360,000
Ending cash	$ 61,778

| Fifth Avenue Apparel Shoppe, LLC |
| Pro Forma Statement of Cash Flows |
| For the Year Ended December 31, 2022 |

Cash flows from operating activities:		
Net income		$ 307,271
Adjustments to reconcile net income to net cash flows from operating activities:		
Depreciation	$ 9,400	
Increase in prepaid insurance	(25)	
Increase in clothing inventory	(5,259)	
Increase in accessories inventory	(1,753)	
Increase in accounts payable	5,960	
Increase in payroll payable	310	
Increase in payroll taxes payable	42	
Increase in utilities payable	15	
Increase in sales tax payable	590	
		9,280
Net cash flows from operating activities		316,551
Cash flows from financing activities:		
Distributions to owners during the year ended December 31, 2022	(360,000)	
Net cash flows from financing activities		(360,000)
Net increase in cash		(43,449)
Cash balance, December 31, 2021		105,227
Cash balance, December 31, 2022		$ 61,778

Figure 7.11. Transformation of the 2022 pro forma reconciliation of cash into the 2022 pro forma statement of cash flows.

We created the December 31, 2022 pro forma balance sheet and its related reconciliation of cash for the Fifth Avenue Apparel Shoppe earlier in this chapter. The balance sheet for December 31, 2021, the income statement for 2022, and the list of assumptions for the company were all developed in chapter 6. This means we have all the information needed to transform the Fifth Avenue Apparel Shoppe's 2022 reconciliation of cash into its 2022 statement of cash flows. Figure 7.11 illustrates the transformation.

Note that this statement of cash flows has a net decrease in cash rather than a net increase in cash. This is also not unusual, especially for a start-up entity.

Creating Pro Forma Balance Sheets and Pro Forma Statements of Cash Flows for Years 3, 4, and 5

In order to create pro forma balance sheets for the Fifth Avenue Apparel Shoppe for December 31, 2023, 2024, and 2025, the percentage of sales method of balance sheet creation will need to be repeated three more times. In order to create pro forma statements of cash flows for the years ended December 31, 2023, 2024, and 2025, the process of transforming a reconciliation of cash into a statement of cash flows will also need to be repeated three more times. The creation of all six of these financial statements will be illustrated in this section.

As previously mentioned in chapter 6, during the course of their creation—and after their creation, as new information becomes available—pro forma financial statements are frequently changed and updated. Note that a change to any line item of any pro forma financial statement will necessitate an update to every existing balance sheet, reconciliation of cash, reconciliation of equity, and statement of cash flows dated on or after that change. This is one reason why it's usually wise to postpone creating pro forma balance sheets for years 2–5 and pro forma statements of cash flows until a potential investor or lender specifically requests them. In this chapter, we're operating under the assumption that some investor or lender does, in fact, require them. So, we'll proceed with completing the full complement of year 2023, 2024, and 2025 pro forma financial statements for the Fifth Avenue Apparel Shoppe. The pro forma income statements for these years were already created in chapter 6, so the rest of this chapter will concern itself only with the creation of the needed balance sheets and statements of cash flows.

Referencing the applicable annual income statements in figure 7.2, we have the information we need to calculate the percentage increase in sales for years 2023, 2024, and 2025:

Percentage increase or decrease in sales = [(Current year sales − Previous year sales) ÷ Previous year sales] x 100

Percentage increase in sales for 2023 = [($749,000 − $690,000) ÷ $690,000] x 100 = 0.0855 x 100 = 8.55%

Percentage increase in sales for 2024 = [($818,286 − $749,000) ÷ $749,000] x 100 = 0.0925 x 100 = 9.25%

Percentage increase in sales for 2025 = [($884,286 − $818,286) ÷ $818,286] x 100 = 0.0807 x 100 = 8.07%

What we know or expect will affect the 2023 balance sheet can be gleaned from the balance sheet for 2022, the income statement for year 2023, and the list of assumptions for the Fifth Avenue Apparel Shoppe. Specifically, what we know or expect for 2023 is as follows:

- Employee pay per hour is expected to increase 20 percent in 2022 and another 5 percent in 2024 (i.e., payroll, payroll taxes, and their related payables aren't expected to change in 2023).
- $5,000 of new software with a useful life of five years and a salvage value of $0 is expected to be purchased in 2023. The new software will be depreciated using the straight-line, half-year convention method of depreciation. No fixed-asset disposals are expected in 2023.
- Utilities expense is expected to increase 3 percent in 2022 and another 2 percent in 2024 (i.e., the expense and its related payable aren't expected to change in 2023).
- Insurance expense is expected to increase 10 percent in 2022 and then stabilize (i.e., the expense and its related prepaid aren't expected to change in 2023).
- Distributions for 2023 are expected to be $360,000.
- Depreciation expense for 2023 is expected to be $9,900, according to the pro forma income statement for that year.
- Net income for 2023 is expected to be $343,231, according to the pro forma income statement for that year.

Utilizing this information, the previously calculated percentage increase in sales for 2023 of 8.55 percent, and the percentage of sales method of balance sheet

Fifth Avenue Apparel Shoppe, LLC Pro Forma Balance Sheets as of December 31, 2022, and December 31, 2023			Fifth Avenue Apparel Shoppe, LLC Pro Forma Reconciliations of Cash and Owners' Equity for the Year Ended December 31, 2023	
	2022	2023		
Cash	$ 61,778	$ 49,644	Reconciliation of Cash:	
Prepaid insurance	275	275		
Clothing inventory	35,259	38,274	Beginning cash	$ 61,778
Accessories inventory	11,753	12,758	Add: Net income for the year ended	
Total current assets	109,065	100,951	December 31, 2023	343,231
			Add: Depreciation for the year ended	
Checkout counters and furniture	12,000	12,000	December 31, 2023	9,900
Clothing racks and shelving	20,000	20,000	Adjustments for changes in noncash assets	
Computers and software	10,000	15,000	and liabilities:	
Security system	5,000	5,000	Increase in clothing inventory	(3,015)
Less: Accumulated depreciation	23,500	33,400	Increase in accessories inventory	(1,005)
Net fixed assets	23,500	18,600	Increase in computers and software	(5,000)
			Increase in accounts payable	3,417
Total assets	$132,565	$119,551	Increase in sales tax payable	338
			Less: Distributions to owners during the	
Accounts payable	$ 39,960	$ 43,377	year ended December 31, 2023	360,000
Payroll payable	1,862	1,862	Ending cash	$ 49,644
Payroll taxes payable	252	252		
Utilities payable	515	515		
Sales tax payable	3,954	4,292	Reconciliation of Owners' Equity:	
Total liabilities	46,543	50,298		
			Beginning owners' equity	$ 86,022
Owners' equity	86,022	69,253	Add: Net income for the year ended	
			December 31, 2023	343,231
Total liabilities and owners'			Less: Distributions to owners during the	
equity	$132,565	$119,551	year ended December 31, 2023	360,000
			Ending owners' equity	$ 69,253

Figure 7.12. Pro forma balance sheets for December 31, 2022, and December 31, 2023, and related reconciliations.

creation, we can develop the Fifth Avenue Apparel Shoppe's pro forma balance sheet and related reconciliations for 2023. Figure 7.12 has the results. Note that, ultimately, only four balance sheet line items ended up changing by the 8.55 percent increase in sales expected from year 2022 to year 2023 (i.e., clothing inventory, accessories inventory, accounts payable, sales tax payable). Every other number on the December 31, 2023 balance sheet was determined via alternative means.

At this point in the chapter, among other financial statements and schedules, we've created the balance sheets for 2022 and 2023 and the reconciliation of cash for 2023 for the Fifth Avenue Apparel Shoppe. Utilizing this information, the company's income statement for 2023, and the list of assumptions supporting the creation of its pro forma financial statements, we have all the information needed to transform the Fifth Avenue Apparel Shoppe's 2023 reconciliation of cash into its 2023 statement of cash flows. Figure 7.13 (on page 198) shows the transformation.

Note in figure 7.13 the addition of a new section to the company's statement of cash flows: cash flows from investing activities. The increase in computers and software noted on the reconciliation of cash is related to the purchase of a fixed asset—a noncurrent asset. Increases or decreases in noncurrent assets and liabilities are typically reflected in the cash from investing activities or cash from financing activities sections of a statement of cash flows. The purchase of a fixed asset is considered an investing activity of the business, so this fixed-asset acquisition requires creating the cash flows from investing activities section on the statement of cash flows.

Fifth Avenue Apparel Shoppe, LLC Pro Forma Reconciliation of Cash For the Year Ended December 31, 2023	
Beginning cash	$61,778
Add: Net income for the year ended December 31, 2023	343,231
Add: Depreciation for the year ended December 31, 2023	9,900
Adjustments for changes in noncash assets and liabilities:	
Increase in clothing inventory	(3,015)
Increase in accessories inventory	(1,005)
Increase in computers and software	(5,000)
Increase in accounts payable	3,417
Increase in sales tax payable	338
Less: Distributions to owners during the year ended December 31, 2023	360,000
Ending cash	$49,644

Fifth Avenue Apparel Shoppe, LLC Pro Forma Statement of Cash Flows For the Year Ended December 31, 2023		
Cash flows from operating activities:		
Net income		$ 343,231
Adjustments to reconcile net income to net cash flows from operating activities:		
Depreciation	$ 9,900	
Increase in clothing inventory	(3,015)	
Increase in accessories inventory	(1,005)	
Increase in accounts payable	3,417	
Increase in sales tax payable	338	
		9,635
Net cash flows from operating activities		352,866
Cash flows from investing activities:		
Purchase of new software	(5,000)	
Net cash flows from investing activities		(5,000)
Cash flows from financing activities:		
Distributions to owners during the year ended December 31, 2023	(360,000)	
Net cash flows from financing activities		(360,000)
Net decrease in cash		(12,134)
Cash balance, December 31, 2022		61,778
Cash balance, December 31, 2023		$ 49,644

Figure 7.13. Transformation of the 2023 pro forma reconciliation of cash into the 2023 pro forma statement of cash flows.

Moving on to year 2024, what we know or expect will affect the 2024 balance sheet is included on the 2023 balance sheet, the 2024 income statement, and the list of assumptions for the Fifth Avenue Apparel Shoppe. We know or expect the following:

- Employee pay per hour is expected to increase 5 percent in 2024.
- No fixed-asset purchases or disposals are expected in 2024.
- Utilities expense is expected to increase 2 percent in 2024.
- Insurance expense is expected to increase 10 percent in 2022 and then stabilize (i.e., the expense and its related prepaid aren't expected to change in 2024).
- Distributions for 2024 are expected to be $360,000.
- Depreciation expense for 2024 is expected to be $10,400, according to the pro forma income statement for that year.
- Net income for 2024 is expected to be $406,111, according to the pro forma income statement for that year.

Utilizing this information, the previously calculated percentage increase in sales for 2024 of 9.25 percent, and the percentage of sales method of balance sheet creation, we can now develop the Fifth Avenue Apparel Shoppe's pro forma balance sheet and related reconciliations for 2024. Figure 7.14 shows the balance sheet and its reconciliations.

Fifth Avenue Apparel Shoppe, LLC Pro Forma Balance Sheets As of December 31, 2023, and December 31, 2024			Fifth Avenue Apparel Shoppe, LLC Pro Forma Reconciliations of Cash and Owners' Equity For the Year Ended December 31, 2024	
	2023	2024		
Cash	$ 49,644	$105,960	Reconciliation of Cash:	
Prepaid insurance	275	275		
Clothing inventory	38,274	41,814	Beginning cash	$ 49,644
Accessories inventory	12,758	13,938	Add: Net income for the year ended	
Total current assets	100,951	161,987	December 31, 2024	406,111
			Add: Depreciation for the year ended	
Checkout counters and furniture	12,000	12,000	December 31, 2024	10,400
Clothing racks and shelving	20,000	20,000	Adjustments for changes in noncash assets	
Computers and software	15,000	15,000	and liabilities:	
Security system	5,000	5,000	Increase in clothing inventory	(3,540)
Less: Accumulated depreciation	33,400	43,800	Increase in accessories inventory	(1,180)
Net fixed assets	18,600	8,200	Increase in accounts payable	4,012
			Increase in payroll payable	93
Total assets	$119,551	$170,187	Increase in payroll taxes payable	13
			Increase in utilities payable	10
Accounts payable	$ 43,377	47,389	Increase in sales tax payable	397
Payroll payable	1,862	1,955	Less: Distributions to owners during the	
Payroll taxes payable	252	265	year ended December 31, 2024	360,000
Utilities payable	515	525	Ending cash	$105,960
Sales tax payable	4,292	4,689		
Total liabilities	50,298	54,823		
			Reconciliation of Owners' Equity:	
Owners' equity	69,253	115,364		
			Beginning owners' equity	$ 69,253
Total liabilities and owners' equity	$119,551	$170,187	Add: Net income for the year ended December 31, 2024	406,111
			Less: Distributions to owners during the year ended December 31, 2024	360,000
			Ending owners' equity	$115,364

Figure 7.14. Pro forma balance sheets for December 31, 2023, and December 31, 2024, and related reconciliations.

At this point in the chapter, among other financial statements and schedules, we've created the balance sheets for 2023 and 2024 and the reconciliation of cash for 2024 for the Fifth Avenue Apparel Shoppe. Utilizing this information, the company's income statement for 2024, and the list of assumptions supporting the creation of its pro forma financial statements, we have all the information needed to transform the Fifth Avenue Apparel Shoppe's 2024 reconciliation of cash into its 2024 statement of cash flows. Figure 7.15 (on page 200) illustrates the transformation.

Moving on to our last year of interest, 2025, what we know or expect will affect the 2025 balance sheet can be gleaned from what is included on the 2024 balance sheet, the 2025 income statement, and the list of assumptions for the Fifth Avenue Apparel Shoppe. Specifically, we know or expect the following:

- Employee pay per hour is expected to increase 20 percent in 2022 and another 5 percent in 2024 (i.e., payroll, payroll taxes, and their related payables aren't expected to change in 2025).
- A purchase of $12,500 of new, higher-end computers with a useful life of five years and a salvage value of $1,250 is expected at the beginning of 2025. The new computers will be depreciated using the straight-line, half-year convention method of depreciation. By the end of 2025, the $10,000 of computers and software purchased during the start-up phase of the business—which have

Fifth Avenue Apparel Shoppe, LLC Pro Forma Reconciliation of Cash For the Year Ended December 31, 2024	
Beginning cash	$ 49,644
Add: Net income for the year ended December 31, 2024	406,111
Add: Depreciation for the year ended December 31, 2024	10,400
Adjustments for changes in noncash assets and liabilities:	
Increase in clothing inventory	(3,540)
Increase in accessories inventory	(1,180)
Increase in accounts payable	4,012
Increase in payroll payable	93
Increase in payroll taxes payable	13
Increase in utilities payable	10
Increase in sales tax payable	397
Less: Distributions to owners during the year ended December 31, 2024	360,000
Ending cash	$ 105,960

Fifth Avenue Apparel Shoppe, LLC Pro Forma Statement of Cash Flows For the Year Ended December 31, 2024		
Cash flows from operating activities:		
Net income		$406,111
Adjustments to reconcile net income to net cash flows from operating activities:		
Depreciation	$ 10,400	
Increase in clothing inventory	(3,540)	
Increase in accessories inventory	(1,180)	
Increase in accounts payable	4,012	
Increase in payroll payable	93	
Increase in payroll taxes payable	13	
Increase in utilities payable	10	
Increase in sales tax payable	397	
		10,205
Net cash flows from operating activities		416,316
Cash flows from financing activities:		
Distributions to owners during the year ended December 31, 2024	(360,000)	
Net cash flows from financing activities		(360,000)
Net increase in cash		56,316
Cash balance, December 31, 2023		49,644
Cash balance, December 31, 2024		$ 105,960

Figure 7.15. Transformation of the 2024 pro forma reconciliation of cash into the 2024 pro forma statement of cash flows.

an expected salvage value of $0—are expected to be completely depreciated, phased out, and abandoned (i.e., thrown out).

■ Utilities expense is expected to increase 3 percent in 2022 and another 2 percent in 2024 (i.e., the expense and its related payable aren't expected to change in 2025).

■ Insurance expense is expected to increase 10 percent in 2022 and then stabilize (i.e., the expense and its related prepaid aren't expected to change in 2025).

■ Distributions for 2025 are expected to be $360,000.

■ Depreciation expense for 2025 is expected to be $6,825, according to the pro forma income statement for that year.

■ Net income for 2025 is expected to be $475,686, according to the pro forma income statement for that year.

Utilizing this information, the previously calculated percentage increase in sales for 2025 of 8.07 percent, and the percentage of sales method of balance sheet creation, we can now develop the company's 2025 pro forma balance sheet and related reconciliations, as shown in figure 7.16.

The calculations in figure 7.17 (on page 202) clarify how the December 31, 2025 balances for computers and software and accumulated depreciation were determined considering the purchases and disposals expected to occur during 2025.

Note that the typical expectation regarding the disposal of a fixed asset when creating pro forma financial statements is that the fixed asset will be assigned a

Fifth Avenue Apparel Shoppe, LLC Pro Forma Balance Sheets As of December 31, 2024, and December 31, 2025			Fifth Avenue Apparel Shoppe, LLC Pro Forma Reconciliations of Cash and Owners' Equity For the Year Ended December 31, 2025		
	2024	2025			
Cash	$105,960	$215,675	Reconciliation of Cash:		
Prepaid insurance	275	275			
Clothing inventory	41,814	45,188	Beginning cash		$ 105,960
Accessories inventory	13,938	15,063	Add: Net income for the year		
Total current assets	161,987	276,201	ended December 31, 2025		475,686
			Add: Depreciation for the year		
Checkout counters and			ended December 31, 2025		6,825
furniture	12,000	12,000	Adjustments for changes in		
Clothing racks and shelving	20,000	20,000	noncash assets and liabilities:		
Computers and software	15,000	17,500	Increase in clothing inventory		(3,374)
Security system	5,000	5,000	Increase in accessories inventory		(1,125)
Less: Accumulated			Increase in computers and		
depreciation	43,800	40,625	software	$ (2,500)	
Net fixed assets	8,200	13,875	Adjust for disposals during the		
			year ended December 31,		
Total assets	$170,187	$290,076	2025	(10,000)	
			Purchases of computers during		
Accounts payable	$ 47,389	$ 51,213	the year ended December 31,		
Payroll payable	1,955	1,955	2025		(12,500)
Payroll taxes payable	265	265	Increase in accounts payable		3,824
Utilities payable	525	525	Increase in sales tax payable		378
Sales tax payable	4,689	5,067	Less: Distributions to owners		
Total liabilities	54,823	59,026	during the year ended December		
			31, 2025		360,000
			Ending cash		$ 215,675
Owners' equity	115,364	231,050			
Total liabilities and			Reconciliation of Owners' Equity:		
owners' equity	$170,187	$290,076			
			Beginning owners' equity		$ 115,364
			Add: Net income for the year		
			ended December 31, 2025		475,686
			Less: Distributions to owners		
			during the year ended December		
			31, 2025		360,000
			Ending owners' equity		$ 231,050

Figure 7.16. Pro forma balance sheets for December 31, 2024, and December 31, 2025, and related reconciliations.

salvage value of $0 and then abandoned sometime after it is fully depreciated—or that the fixed asset will be sold for its designated salvage value sometime after it is fully depreciated with regard to the amount of its cost minus its salvage value. The list of assumptions indicates that the $10,000 of computers and software to be purchased during the start-up phase of the Fifth Avenue Apparel Shoppe are expected to have a salvage value of $0 and be completely depreciated at the time of their abandonment at the end of 2025. As a result, as indicated in figure 7.17 (on page 202), we can determine that the accumulated depreciation related to the $10,000 of computers and software expected to be abandoned at the end of 2025 should equal $10,000. If the computers and software did in fact have a salvage value—the salvage value being the amount the computers and software are ultimately expected to be sold for—the amount of the salvage value and the amount of the accumulated depreciation related to the computers and software would be determined by referring to the depreciation

Calculation of December 31, 2025 Computers and Software:		Calculation of December 31, 2025 Accumulated Depreciation:	
Balance at December 31, 2024	$15,000	Balance at December 31, 2024	$43,800
Add: Purchases during 2025	12,500	Add: Depreciation expense for 2025	6,825
Less: Disposals during 2025	10,000	Less: Accumulated Depreciated related	
Balance at December 31, 2025	$17,500	to computers disposed of during 2025	10,000
		Balance at December 31, 2025	$40,625

Figure 7.17. Calculation of the December 31, 2025 balances for computers and software and accumulated depreciation.

schedule that includes the applicable fixed assets. Note that reconciliation of cash covering the time period during which the computers and software are ultimately expected to be sold would include a line item entitled something like "proceeds from the sale of computers and software" for the amount of the sales proceeds–the amount of the salvage value–such line located below the adjustments for changes in noncash assets and liabilities section of the reconciliation. The proceeds from the sale would be included in the cash flows from investing activities section of the company's statement of cash flows, if in fact a statement of cash flows was prepared.

At this point in the chapter, among other financial statements and schedules, we've created the balance sheets for 2024 and 2025 and the reconciliation of cash for 2025 for the Fifth Avenue Apparel Shoppe. Utilizing this information, the company's income statement for 2025, and the list of assumptions supporting the creation of its pro forma financial statements, we have all the information needed to transform the Fifth Avenue Apparel Shoppe's 2025 reconciliation of cash into its 2025 statement of cash flows. Figure 7.18 shows the transformation.

Our list of assumptions indicates that the computers and software expected to be purchased in 2020 (recall our list of start-up costs included in figure 6.1 in chapter 6) will be assigned no salvage value and are expected to be abandoned–rather than sold–in 2025. As mentioned earlier in this chapter, in the event of an increase or decrease in an asset or liability account that doesn't involve cash (e.g., when a fully depreciated fixed asset with no salvage value is disposed of in exchange for $0), the increase or decrease in that asset or liability account isn't reflected on the statement of cash flows. Interestingly, because of this, the reconciliation of cash in figure 7.18 arguably provides a clearer picture than the statement of cash flows regarding all the changes expected to occur with respect to the business's computers and software during 2025.

Making Adjustments to Plans Based on a New Venture's Completed Pro Forma Financial Statements

One of the many purposes of pro forma financial statements is to provide the entrepreneurs who create them with information about the expected future financial results of a proposed new venture. Once the creation of pro forma financial statements is complete, it is in the entrepreneurs' best interest to review the statements carefully in order to determine what adjustments, if any, may be needed with regard to the entrepreneurs' plans for the proposed new business. Our Fifth Avenue Apparel Shoppe example illustrates this important point.

The net income numbers on the company's pro forma income statements and the cash and the equity numbers on the pro forma balance sheets are sure to impress any potential investor or lender, especially considering the high cash distribution

Fifth Avenue Apparel Shoppe, LLC Pro Forma Reconciliation of Cash For the Year Ended December 31, 2025		
Beginning cash		$ 105,960
Add: Net income for the year ended December 31, 2025		475,686
Add: Depreciation for the year ended December 31, 2025		6,825
Adjustments for changes in noncash assets and liabilities:		
Increase in clothing inventory		(3,374)
Increase in accessories inventory		(1,125)
Increase in computers and software	$(2,500)	
Adjust for disposals during the year ended December 31, 2025	(10,000)	
Purchases of computers during the year ended December 31, 2025		(12,500)
Increase in accounts payable		3,824
Increase in sales tax payable		378
Less: Distributions to owners during the year ended December 31, 2025		360,000
Ending cash		$ 215,675

Fifth Avenue Apparel Shoppe, LLC Pro Forma Statement of Cash Flows For the Year Ended December 31, 2025		
Cash flows from operating activities:		
Net income		$ 475,686
Adjustments to reconcile net income to net cash flows from operating activities:		
Depreciation	$ 6,825	
Increase in clothing inventory	(3,374)	
Increase in accessories inventory	(1,125)	
Increase in accounts payable	3,824	
Increase in sales tax payable	378	
		6,529
Net cash flows from operating activities		482,215
Cash flows from investing activities:		
Acquisition of computers	(12,500)	
Net cash flows from investing activities		(12,500)
Cash flows from financing activities:		
Distributions to owners during the year ended December 31, 2025	(360,000)	
Net cash flows from financing activities		(360,000)
Net increase in cash		109,715
Cash balance, December 31, 2024		105,960
Cash balance, December 31, 2025		$ 215,675

Figure 7.18. Transformation of the 2025 pro forma reconciliation of cash into the 2025 pro forma statement of cash flows.

numbers indicated on the pro forma reconciliations of cash and statements of cash flows. Ideally, this information, especially the cash distribution numbers, should start our entrepreneurs thinking about when and how to create an exit for their expected angel investor. It's unlikely our entrepreneurs will be happy long term with the arrangement of paying out $120,000 in cash distributions annually to their angel investor. One of the most important revelations the preparation and review of the pro forma financial statements for the Fifth Avenue Apparel Shoppe may provide our entrepreneurs is that they are likely offering their angel investor too high a percentage ownership of the proposed new venture. A $120,000 recurring annual cash distribution—an annual cash distribution with no indicated end date, no less—in exchange for a one-time investment of $125,000 suggests there should be an adjustment to the terms our two entrepreneurs ultimately offer their angel investor.

Summary

In the instance an entrepreneur needs to create pro forma balance sheets for years 2–5 for a proposed new venture because a current or potential investor or lender specifically requests them, the percentage of sales method is a good way to develop such balance sheets. The percentage of sales method is a mechanism for developing pro forma balance sheets based on the fact that the assets and liabilities of a company typically vary with its sales. The method allows us to incorporate into our balance sheets those assumptions and expectations related to the future of our company about which we are confident, while also providing a logical framework for estimating balance sheet amounts about which we are less confident.

The reconciliation of cash we learned to create in chapter 6 is actually quite close in look and function to a formal statement of cash flows. In the instance an entrepreneur needs to create pro forma statements of cash flows for a proposed new venture because a current or potential investor or lender specifically requests them, transforming pro forma reconciliations of cash into pro forma statements of cash flows is actually a fairly straightforward process. The transformation generally involves reorganizing the information on the reconciliation of cash into the format required by a statement of cash flows and then adding subtotals and totals.

One of the many purposes of pro forma financial statements is to provide the entrepreneurs who create them with information about the expected future financial results of a proposed new business. Once the creation of pro forma financial statements is complete, it is in the entrepreneurs' best interest to review the statements carefully in order to determine what adjustments, if any, may be needed with regard to the entrepreneurs' plans for the proposed new venture.

Key Term

percentage of sales method

Review and Discussion Questions

1. What is the percentage of sales method of balance sheet creation, and what theory is behind the method?
2. Describe the seven-step process associated with the percentage of sales method of balance sheet creation.
3. What is a statement of cash flows, and what are its major sections? Briefly describe each section.
4. What are the similarities and differences between a reconciliation of cash and a statement of cash flows?
5. Once the creation of pro forma financial statements is complete, why is it in an entrepreneur's best interest to review the statements carefully? Provide an example to support your answer.

Exercises

1. Complete the following pro forma comparative balance sheet and reconciliations of cash and equity for the Unique Gifts Shop using the percentage of sales method and the following list of assumptions:

List of Assumptions Relevant to Unique Gifts Shop's 2021 Balance Sheet

Expected sales for 2020: $700,000
Expected sales for 2021: $735,000
Expected net income for 2021: $115,200

- A $10,000 purchase of computers and software with a salvage value of $0 will occur in 2021. No other fixed assets are expected to be purchased in 2021. No fixed assets are expected to be sold or abandoned in 2021.

- Depreciation expense for 2021 is expected to be $9,400.

- The owners expect to take $100,000 in distributions in 2021.

Unique Gifts Shop, LLC Pro Forma Balance Sheets As of December 31, 2020, and December 31, 2021			Unique Gifts Shop, LLC Pro Forma Reconciliations of Cash and Owners' Equity For the Year Ended December 31, 2021
	2020	2021	
Cash	$ 14,885		Reconciliation of Cash:
Prepaid insurance	1,350		
Inventory	187,112		Beginning cash
Total current assets	203,347		Add: Net income for the year ended December 31, 2021
			Add: Depreciation for the year ended December 31, 2021
Checkout counters and furniture	22,500		
Shelving	7,500		Adjustments for changes in noncash assets and liabilities:
Computers and software	12,500		Increase in prepaid insurance
Less: Accumulated depreciation	9,500		Increase in inventory
Net fixed assets	33,000		Increase in computers and software
			Increase in accounts payable
Total assets	$236,347		Increase in payroll payable
			Increase in payroll taxes payable
Accounts payable	$ 25,800		Increase in utilities payable
Payroll payable	4,800		Increase in sales tax payable
Payroll taxes payable	720		Less: Distributions to owners during the year ended December 31, 2021
Utilities payable	485		
Sales tax payable	9,000		Ending cash
Total liabilities	40,805		
			Reconciliation of Owners' Equity:
Owners' equity	195,542		
			Beginning owners' equity
Total liabilities and owners' equity	$236,347		Add: Net income for the year ended December 31, 2021
			Less: Distributions to owners during the year ended December 31, 2021
			Ending owners' equity

2. Complete the following pro forma comparative balance sheet and reconciliations of cash and equity for Affordably Haute Apparel Shoppe using the percentage of sales method and the list of assumptions provided.

List of Assumptions Relevant to Affordably Haute's 2022 Balance Sheet

Expected sales for 2021: $390,875
Expected sales for 2022: $434,640
Expected net income for 2022: $94,618

- All fixed assets are expected to have a useful life of five years and a salvage value of $0, and will be depreciated using the straight-line, half-year convention method of depreciation. During the start-up phase of the business in 2020, $32,500 of fixed assets were purchased. No fixed-asset purchases or disposals are expected to take place in 2021 or 2022.

- Payroll expense is expected to increase 15 percent in 2022.

- Payroll taxes are expected to remain 13.5 percent of payroll.

- Insurance expense is expected to increase 5 percent in 2022.

- Utilities expense is expected to remain the same for 2022 as it was for 2021.

Affordably Haute Apparel Shoppe, LLC
Pro Forma Balance Sheets
As of December 31, 2021, and December 31, 2022

	2021	2022
Cash	$ 134,701	
Prepaid insurance	250	
Clothing inventory	27,500	
Accessories inventory	8,500	
Total current assets	170,951	
Checkout counters and furniture	8,500	
Clothing racks and shelving	9,000	
Computers and software	10,000	
Security system	5,000	
Less: Accumulated depreciation	9,750	
Net fixed assets	22,750	
Total assets	$ 193,701	
Accounts payable	$ 27,000	
Payroll payable	8,892	
Payroll taxes payable	1,200	
Utilities payable	275	
Sales tax payable	2,429	
Total liabilities	39,796	
Owners' equity	153,905	
Total liabilities and owners' equity	$ 193,701	

Affordably Haute Apparel Shoppe, LLC
Pro Forma Reconciliations of Cash and Owners' Equity
For the Year Ended December 31, 2022

Reconciliation of Cash:

Beginning cash
  Add: Net income for the year
    ended December 31, 2022
  Add: Depreciation for the year
    ended December 31, 2022
  Adjustments for changes in
    noncash assets and liabilities:

Ending cash

Reconciliation of Owners' Equity:

Beginning owners' equity
  Add: Net income for the year
    ended December 31, 2022
Ending owners' equity

---

3. Complete the following computers and software and accumulated depreciation calculations and pro forma comparative balance sheet and reconciliations of cash and equity for Campbell & Associates, an architectural firm, using the percentage of sales method and the list of assumptions provided.

List of Assumptions Relevant to the Campbell & Associates 2021 Balance Sheet

Expected sales for 2020: $1,300,000
Expected sales for 2021: $1,397,500
Expected net income for 2021: $131,800

- In 2021, a $30,000 purchase of computers and software is expected and $5,000 of fully depreciated computers and software with a salvage value of $0 are expected to be abandoned (i.e., thrown out). A $50,000 building addition is also planned for 2021. No other fixed-asset purchases or disposals are expected to occur in 2021.
- Depreciation expense for 2021 is expected to be $12,500.
- The firm expects to reduce its accounts payable to $2,500 by the end of 2021.
- Payroll, payroll tax, and utilities expenses are expected to remain the same for 2021 as they were for 2020.
- Of the $100,000 remaining due on the mortgage payable on December 31, 2021, $54,000 is due to be paid in 2022.
- In order to finance the business's 2021 fixed-asset purchases and pay down of debt, the owners plan to invest $50,000 in the business at the beginning of 2021.

Calculation of December 31, 2021 Computers and Software:	Calculation of December 31, 2021 Accumulated Depreciation:
Balance at December 31, 2020	Balance at December 31, 2020
Add: Purchases during 2021	Add: Depreciation expense for 2021
Less: Disposals during 2021	Less: Accumulated depreciation related
Balance at December 31, 2021	to computers disposed of during 2021
	Balance at December 31, 2021

Campbell and Associates Pro Forma Balance Sheets As of December 31, 2020, and December 31, 2021			Campbell and Associates Pro Forma Reconciliations of Cash and Owners' Equity For the Year Ended December 31, 2021
	2020	2021	
Cash	$ 1,623		Reconciliation of Cash:
Prepaid insurance	1,350		
Accounts receivable	57,919		
Total current assets	60,892		
Land	100,000		
Building	250,000		
Computers and software	22,500		
Office furniture	7,500		
Less: Accumulated depreciation	45,000		
Net fixed assets	335,000		
Total assets	$ 395,892		
Accounts payable	$ 28,800		
Payroll payable	25,700		
Payroll taxes payable	3,855		Reconciliation of Owners' Equity:
Utilities payable	1,400		
Short-term portion of mortgage payable	60,000		
Total current liabilities	119,755		
Mortgage payable	100,000		
Total liabilities	219,755		
Owners' equity	176,137		
Total liabilities and owners' equity	$ 395,892		

4. Complete the following computers and software and accumulated depreciation calculations and answer the following questions for Campbell & Associates assuming the same problem information as for exercise 3, except that the $5,000 of computers and software expected to be abandoned in 2021 are now expected to have a salvage value of $500, be fully depreciated with regard to the amount of cost minus salvage value in 2021, and be sold for $500 at the end of 2021.

   a. If the computers and software are sold for their salvage value in 2021, what additional line item would need to be included in the 2021 reconciliation of cash?
   b. Where specifically would this additional line item appear on the 2021 reconciliation of cash?
   c. Where would the proceeds from the sale of the computers and software be included on the company's statement of cash flows, if in fact a statement of cash flows was prepared?

Calculation of December 31, 2021 Computers and Software:	Calculation of December 31, 2021 Accumulated Depreciation:
Balance at December 31, 2020	Balance at December 31, 2020
Add: Purchases during 2021	Add: Depreciation expense for 2021
Less: Disposals during 2021	Less: Accumulated depreciation related
Balance at December 31, 2021	to computers disposed of during 2021
	Balance at December 31, 2021

5. Complete the following statement of cash flows for July 1–December 31, 2020, for Ross and Ross, CPAs. Note that the increase in short-term portion of loan payable of $25,000 and the decrease in loan payable of $25,000 included on the pro forma reconciliation of cash represent the reclassification of a $25,000 bank loan from long term at June 30, 2020, to short term at December 31, 2020.

Ross and Ross, CPAs Pro Forma Reconciliation of Cash For the Six Months Ended December 31, 2020		Ross and Ross, CPAs Pro Forma Statement of Cash Flows For the Six Months Ended December 31, 2020
Beginning cash	$ 15,500	Cash flows from operating activities:
Add: Net income for the six months		Net income
ended December 31, 2020	211,674	
Add: Depreciation for the six months		Adjustments to reconcile net income
ended December 31, 2020	10,950	to net cash flows from operating
Adjustments for changes in noncash		activities:
assets and liabilities:		Depreciation
Increase in accounts receivable	(100,000)	Increase in accounts receivable
Increase in accounts payable	4,750	Increase in accounts payable
Increase in payroll payable	17,500	Increase in payroll payable
Increase in payroll taxes payable	2,363	Increase in payroll taxes payable
Increase in short-term portion of loan		
payable	25,000	Net cash flows from operating
Decrease in loan payable	(25,000)	activities
Add: New equity investment during the		
six months ended December 31, 2020	25,000	Cash flows from financing activities:
Ending cash	$ 187,737	New equity investment during the six
		months ended December 31, 2020
		Net cash flows from financing
		activities
		Net increase in cash
		Cash balance, July 30, 2020
		Cash balance, December 31, 2020

6. Complete the statement of cash flows for the year ended December 31, 2022, for Bargain Basement.

Bargain Basement Apparel Shoppe, LLC Pro Forma Reconciliation of Cash For the Year Ended December 31, 2022	
Beginning cash	$ 155,121
Add: Net income for the year ended December 31, 2022	186,954
Add: Depreciation for the year ended December 31, 2022	5,980
Adjustments for changes in noncash assets and liabilities:	
Increase in prepaid insurance	(20)
Increase in clothing inventory	(1,710)
Increase in accessories inventory	(641)
Increase in accounts payable	2,116
Increase in payroll payable	314
Increase in payroll taxes payable	42
Increase in utilities payable	15
Increase in sales tax payable	282
Less: Distributions to owners during the year ended December 31, 2022	120,000
Ending cash	$ 228,453

Bargain Basement Apparel Shoppe, LLC Pro Forma Statement of Cash Flows For the Year Ended December 31, 2022
Cash flows from operating activities:
Net income

Adjustments to reconcile net income
  to net cash flows from operating
  activities:

Working Capital Management, Bootstrapping, and Controls over Assets

"It's not how much money you make, but how much money you keep."

— **Robert Kiyosaki, author and founder of Rich Dad Company**

Learning Objectives

Have knowledge of the practices and techniques associated with proper working capital management and bootstrapping.

Have an understanding of the concepts and practices associated with placing proper controls over a business's assets.

Introduction

In the normal course of its operations, a business accumulates many short- and long-term liabilities that must be paid. But, for a variety of reasons, the cash generated by a business's operations—that is, the cash needed to pay these liabilities—often comes in sporadically. Even businesses that are profitable and growing are not immune to this problem. In addition to sporadic cash flow, entrepreneurs often don't have access to the full amount of start-up capital they wish to have before starting a new business. Sometimes, even if they do have access to the full amount of start-up capital they desire, entrepreneurs choose not to utilize certain outside sources of funding because they want to maintain a higher level of ownership—and therefore more control—over the venture they're starting.

Proper working capital management and bootstrapping can help an entrepreneur overcome both cash flow issues and the issues associated with a business being underfunded. This chapter introduces and illustrates the concepts and techniques associated with proper working capital management and bootstrapping.

Assuming the entrepreneur has a good business concept, has created a solid business model, and has mastered and applied the techniques of proper working capital management and bootstrapping, the entrepreneur's business will likely begin at some point to accumulate assets. Assets that are attractive to others. Assets that others may consider ripe for the taking. An entrepreneur who doesn't take the time to properly secure the assets of her business is likely to lose those assets. This chapter also discusses the concepts and practices associated with placing proper controls over a business's assets.

Working Capital Management

As first noted in chapter 5, positive working capital represents the amount by which the current assets of a business exceed the current liabilities of a business. Conversely, negative working capital is the amount by which the current liabilities of a business exceed the current assets of a business. A position of positive working capital is obviously the situation in which an entrepreneur would prefer to function.

working capital management
the art of controlling current assets and current liabilities in such a way that a firm will maintain adequate cash and inventory levels, maximize the return on its assets, and minimize the size of the payments needed to settle its liabilities

Working capital management is the art of controlling current assets and current liabilities in such a way that a firm will maintain adequate cash and inventory levels, maximize the return on its assets, and minimize the size of the payments needed to settle its liabilities. Working capital management typically focuses on the effective and efficient management of cash, marketable securities, accounts receivable, inventory, accounts payable, accrued liabilities, and short-term debt. This chapter will address best practices to manage all these asset and liability categories except marketable securities. The management of marketable securities will be discussed in chapter 12.

Cash Management

The three goals of cash management are to:

1. Sustain an adequate level of cash (i.e., never run out of cash).
2. Achieve and maintain positive cash flow.
3. Obtain the highest return reasonably possible on idle cash.

We'll address the first two topics, sustaining an adequate level of cash and achieving and maintaining positive cash flow, in this chapter. We'll discuss the third topic, how to obtain the highest return reasonably possible on idle cash, in chapter 12.

Start-up Phase

Sustaining an adequate level of cash is critical for any business, but never running out of cash is particularly critical for a start-up because a start-up likely doesn't have the ability to borrow to cover a cash shortfall. Start-ups also usually go through a period of zero revenue: the start-up phase of the business. During a young venture's start-up phase, the entity is preparing to commence—but has not yet commenced—business operations, so a lot of cash is flowing out of the business, but no cash is flowing into the business because the entity has no sales.

How can an entrepreneur ensure that her start-up won't run out of cash? Because no one can predict the future with 100 percent accuracy, there are no guarantees. However, the pro forma financial statements created by the entrepreneur give pretty good guidance regarding the amount of cash needed to cover the entity's start-up phase, when cash will start to flow into the business, and when the business will, in fact, become cash flow positive. To the extent the entrepreneur has created pro forma balance sheets, reconciliations of cash, or statements of cash flows, the pro forma financial statements also provide information regarding an entity's expected cash balances at different points in time. In other words, the pro forma financial statements she has created can help the entrepreneur identify how much cash the entity needs—and when—so she can pursue the funding necessary to provide reasonable assurance that the entity will not run out of cash.

Proper assessment of an entity's cash needs is especially critical for a **high-growth start-up**, which is a business designed to be **scalable**—a business designed to perform well under continually increasing operational demands. High-growth start-ups often burn through cash for years before becoming cash flow positive because capturing market share is usually the most critical element to the future success of the company. Companies that require a large user base or a large customer base to succeed, companies such as Amazon, Facebook, and Twitter, are often unprofitable and cash flow negative for years before first becoming profitable and then finally becoming cash flow positive. This makes securing access to both short- and long-term sources of capital for the business a critical requirement for the entrepreneur who founds a high-growth start-up.

high-growth start-up
a business designed to be scalable

scalable
designed to perform well under continually increasing operational demands

Turning the Corner to Positive Cash Flow

In terms of order of occurrence, profitability usually occurs before a business becomes cash flow positive. This is because a business—especially a growing business—can be profitable but still experience negative cash flow. A growing business is often investing in its future by spending cash on items such as improved technology and other fixed assets that it can't immediately expense. Also, a business may be investing in inventory whose return of cash consistently lags behind its sale. For example, if a manufacturer of office furniture decides to expand its operations by increasing the amount of furniture it produces and sells, the manufacturer must use its cash to purchase additional **raw materials inventory**—the fundamental materials or components a company uses to produce its final product—items such as wood, steel, nails, and glue. Next, the company must manufacture **finished goods inventory**—inventory items that have been translated into a final product ready to be sold by the business—from that raw materials inventory. Then the manufacturer must sell that finished goods inventory, most likely to a retailer or wholesaler on trade credit. Selling the inventory on trade credit means an account receivable, not cash, is generated from the sale. At this point, the company is more profitable because it has sold more product, but its cash flow is actually worse than before the company's expansion because the company has paid out cash for an increased level of raw materials inventory but has not yet received any cash from the sales made possible by the investment in that inventory. However, as the office furniture manufacturer's growth plateaus, assuming the company is profitable, the company's cash flow will likely improve overall or, at minimum, return to the same condition it was pre-expansion.

raw materials inventory
the fundamental materials or components a company uses to produce its final product

finished goods inventory
inventory items that have been translated into a final product ready to be sold by the business

It's worth noting that many business owners and stakeholders use cash flow rather than net income as the gauge of an entity's relative success and as a tool to make decisions. This is because a business can be profitable and still go out of business because it runs out of cash. Example 8.1 (on page 214) illustrates how a profitable business can have such poor cash flow that it threatens the continued viability of the business.

Example 8.1

The Madison Capital Products Company (MCPC), a profitable company operating well beyond breakeven, manufactures medical capital equipment. A typical item the company manufactures requires an investment of $35,000 of parts inventory and sells for $60,000. As the other costs associated with building, selling, and delivering a typical item of equipment amount to about $5,000, MCPC makes a gross profit per unit of approximately $20,000 on each item of capital equipment it manufactures and sells ($60,000 sales revenue – $40,000 cost of goods sold = $20,000 gross profit). Still, MCPC continually struggles with cash flow. The situation has gotten so bad that MCPC's chief financial officer recently called a meeting to warn MCPC's owners that the business is likely to run out of cash in 60 days or less. After the meeting, in an attempt to determine the cause of MCPC's ongoing cash flow issue, Clara, one of MCPC's owners, decided to schedule out the timing of the major cash flows of the business (i.e., the company's payments for parts inventory and its collection of related accounts receivable). Figure 8.1 shows the result of her work.

As a result of her work, Clara discovered a major source—if not *the* source—of MCPC's cash flow problem. Every time MCPC receives an order from a customer, the cash inflow of $60,000 generated by that sale is preceded by 45 days by a cash outflow of $35,000 required to pay for the parts inventory needed to manufacture the product. Clara observed that, interestingly, the more customer orders MCPC receives, the worse its overall cash flow problem becomes.

MCPC currently orders most of the parts required to manufacture a piece of equipment only after receiving an order from a customer for that equipment. MCPC's owners have analyzed the wisdom of purchasing and holding parts in inventory prior to receiving a customer order, but being a young company, they're not certain how long they'll continue to use the parts they currently use. MCPC also manufactures a lot of custom capital equipment, and that makes it difficult to determine which parts to hold—versus not hold—in inventory. Beyond these issues, purchasing and holding parts in inventory would require a significant investment of cash on the part of MCPC—cash MCPC doesn't currently have because the owners knowingly chose to start the business in an underfunded position in order to avoid taking outside funding

The Madison Capital Products Company Analysis of the Major Cash Flows Associated with the Manufacture and Sale of One Unit of Product		
	Number of Days	Cash Inflows and (Outflows)
Production time after receipt of customer order:		
Average number of days to order and receive parts inventory	5	
Average number of days until required to pay for parts inventory	30	
MCPC pays its parts vendors on day 35 (30 days after receipt of parts inventory)	–	$ (35,000)
Average number of additional production days until the product is ready to ship	5	
Total production time after receipt of customer order	40	
Post-production time until customer payment:		
Average number of days the product is in shipment	5	
Average number of days to train and invoice the customer	5	
Average number of days until the customer is required to pay for the product	30	
Total post-production time until customer payment	40	
Customer pays MCPC on day 80 (30 days after invoiced for the product)	–	$ 60,000
Total time from order receipt to customer payment	80	

(cash flow arrow spanning: 45 days)

Figure 8.1. Analysis of the major cash flows associated with the manufacture and sale of one unit of product.

(i.e., in order to maintain full ownership and control of the company). MCPC isn't in a position to manufacture product at a faster pace, and the company has already minimized shipment and customer training days to the smallest number possible. So, what steps can MCPC take to correct its cash flow problem?

MCPC is a classic example of a profitable company with a cash flow challenge. Even though it's a young company, MCPC can likely manage its cash flow challenge by obtaining a line of credit from a bank. Profitable companies with cash flow challenges like the one MCPC has are exactly the type of companies for which banks have developed a wide variety of commercial line of credit options.

Note that in order to increase the likelihood that MCPC will not only be offered a line of credit, but also be offered a line of credit with reasonable terms, it may be in MCPC's best interests to do the following:

- Illustrate for the bank the source of the cash flow problem. Banks are more likely to loan funds to support the delivery of sold product than to support other types of projects and expenses.
- Offer to collateralize the line of credit with the inventory purchases the line of credit will fund.

Beyond seeking a bank line of credit, MCPC can take additional steps to correct its cash flow problem. We'll address those steps later in the chapter in the section on bootstrapping.

Everyday Operations

For a business past the start-up phase that has achieved positive cash flow, albeit perhaps on an irregular basis, good cash management, at its most basic level, generally involves performing the following best practices on a consistent basis:

- depositing cash and checks as soon as possible
- invoicing and collecting from customers on a timely basis
- paying bills when they're due, but not before they're due
- making strategic decisions regarding how much cash needs to be kept on hand versus how much cash is not currently needed and is therefore available to be invested in order to achieve a return

It should go without saying that most of the cash and checks received by a business throughout a normal day of its operations should be deposited in the bank that same day. This generally isn't an issue with regard to online sales. The online purchases made by a business's customers using a bank credit card—a credit card branded Mastercard or Visa, for example—are essentially cash sales in that they are more or less automatically converted into cash that is then deposited by the applicable banks into the business's designated checking account either on the day of the sale or on the day following the sale. Unfortunately, with regard to brick and mortar sales, the reality is that many businesses, especially start-up and small businesses, sometimes allow cash and checks to languish for days without being deposited in the company's checking account. Beyond the obvious fact that such a practice can create or exaggerate a cash flow problem, it also creates an opportunity for the applicable cash and checks to be stolen.

Cash sales normally do not present challenges with regard to invoicing and collecting from customers on a timely basis. Noncash sales require more effort. With noncash sales, consistently invoicing customers on a timely basis requires the owner of a product-based business to put a system in place that effectively connects the reduction of inventory related to the sale of a product to the invoicing of the customer who purchased the product. A service-based business requires a system that connects the current or future payment of an employee related to a service the employee provided to the invoicing of the customer who purchased the service. If such invoicing can be made to happen on an automatic basis with the assistance of appropriate software, all the better. Consistent and timely invoicing is the first step to receiving timely cash payments related to noncash sales to customers. We'll discuss the timely collection of invoices related to noncash sales—accounts receivable—in the next section.

In order to not forget to pay their bills, many individuals pay their bills upon receipt. While this is in many ways an admirable personal financial practice, the habit usually doesn't translate well to an entrepreneurial endeavor. Paying bills when they're due, not before they're due, is a proper working capital management practice to which many debt-phobic entrepreneurs may have to adjust. As Entrepreneur in Action 8.1 illustrates, entrepreneurs sometimes inadvertently create completely avoidable cash flow problems for their businesses as a result of their poor working capital management practices.

The last item on our best practices list—making a decision regarding how much cash needs to be kept on hand versus invested—involves determining the amount of cash needed both at the business's physical location and in the business's checking account. This determination is largely the result of the entrepreneur considering the nature of the start-up itself and what's suggested by anecdotal evidence about the business's operations, if such evidence exists. At the very beginning of a venture, until the entrepreneur can have some business operations history upon which to reflect, it's usually wise to keep excess cash—that is, cash currently unneeded—largely uninvested in order to have it available for use as needed. A more mature business than a start-up would, however, likely invest any excess cash in a marketable security of some type in order to keep that cash contributing positively to the bottom line of the company.

Entrepreneur *in Action* 8.1

An Entrepreneur's Self-Created Cash Flow Problem

Stephanie Haag, an entrepreneur who had recently started her first business, had an ongoing cash flow problem. Like her competition, Stephanie offered trade credit to her customers, but she was considering eliminating trade credit because waiting 30 days to be paid by her customers left her in a continual cash crunch. Stephanie had decided to talk to her friend, Elizabeth Howell, a more seasoned entrepreneur, about the problem.

In the café where they met, Elizabeth listened as Stephanie explained her situation. Elizabeth then explained to Stephanie that a growing business experiencing cash flow problems is not unusual and suggested that Stephanie talk to her bank about setting up a business line of credit.

Stephanie balked at the suggestion. She told Elizabeth that she had been taught to always avoid debt and didn't want her business indebted to a bank. Elizabeth, who had known Stephanie for a very long time, smiled and gently asked if she could look at Stephanie's internal accounting records. Stephanie, whose business was located around the corner from the café, agreed.

After looking at the accounting records less than 10 minutes, Elizabeth announced that she had two suggestions for Stephanie that might make it possible for her to avoid having to obtain a line of credit from a bank and also to avoid having to withdraw trade credit from her customers. Elizabeth noted that first, however, she needed to confirm two items of information with Stephanie. Intrigued, Stephanie agreed.

Elizabeth looked at Stephanie, again smiled, and asked her point blank, "Stephanie, I know how much you dislike debt and owing people money. Are you paying your business's bills as soon as you receive them?" Stephanie proudly replied, "Yes, absolutely." Elizabeth's face broke into a full-fledged grin as she next said, "Well, stop doing that and you'll eliminate the biggest part of your cash flow problem. If you have 30 days to pay a bill, take the 30 days."

Stephanie contemplated this, looked at Elizabeth, and quietly said, "Okay. I can do that."

Elizabeth then asked, "How many days does it take you to invoice your customers after you deliver product to them?" Stephanie responded, "I'm not sure. It varies." Elizabeth then said, "Based on what I saw when I looked at your accounting records, it looks like it usually takes you about 10 days. You realize, of course, that your customer can't pay you until you invoice them."

Stephanie thought a moment, laughed quietly to herself, and then said, "So, I've basically been creating most of this cash flow problem myself?" Elizabeth replied, "Yes, but now you know how to fix it!"

Accounts Receivable Management

Accounts receivable represent the amounts customers owe a company related to their purchases from that company utilizing the credit offered by that company. As discussed in chapter 5, a customer purchase made using a credit card issued by a financial institution, such as a bank credit card branded Mastercard or Visa, doesn't represent a true account receivable to a business. That's because purchases utilizing these types of credit are usually more or less immediately converted into cash at the business's local bank. A true account receivable represents the amount a customer owes a company because that company has approved the customer to purchase from the company on credit, up to an established credit limit, subject to the specific credit terms developed by the company.

One example of this would be a manufacturer approving a retailer who routinely sells its products to purchase those products using trade credit. Terms might be such that the manufacturer authorizes the retailer a credit limit of $10,000 and 30 days to pay. The manufacturer who allows the retailer to pay for product in 30 days would hold an account receivable from the retailer. The retailer would, in turn, carry an account payable to the manufacturer on its balance sheet.

The reason businesses offer customers the ability to pay later (i.e., the reason businesses carry accounts receivable on their balance sheets) is to increase sales. Individuals and businesses tend to buy more products and services when they don't have to immediately pay for those products and services. However, a business must manage its accounts receivable properly in order to maximize the overall profitability of the business. An enterprise must carefully compare the costs of carrying accounts receivable with the benefits received.

The following are common options associated with offering credit to customers:

- A business issues its own credit card (e.g., Macy's offers its customers a Macy's credit card).
- A business offers its customers trade credit, potentially featuring a variety of time frames and other terms associated with repayment.
- A business offers credit to its customers via its own credit card or via trade credit and then more or less immediately factors (i.e., sells) these accounts receivable to another firm at a discount in order to turn the accounts receivable into cash quickly.

If an entrepreneur chooses to offer credit, she must establish a credit policy, which means she must determine three things:

1. to whom she will grant credit
2. the terms of the credit granted
3. how she'll monitor credit and deal with delinquent accounts

Credit terms are the rules a business establishes regarding the required payments associated with the use of credit by a customer. Credit terms vary by industry, but U.S. credit terms commonly do the following:

- Indicate that no interest charge will apply to amounts paid in full within a stated number of days for payment, usually 30 days, after an applicable purchase.
- State the interest rate or late fee that will apply to amounts owed that remain unpaid after the stated number of days for payment.
- State a minimum portion of the total amount owed that must be repaid each month.
- Indicate a maximum amount of credit the customer will be permitted.

In order to speed up collections of accounts receivable, cash discounts are often offered to business customers. The offer of a cash discount is often inherent in the terms stated for credit repayment. One example is 2/10 net 30, which means that, if the customer pays the invoice on or before the tenth day after the invoice date, a 2 percent discount is permitted to be taken with regard to the total amount of the invoice. Otherwise, 100 percent of the invoice amount is due to be paid on the thirtieth day after the invoice date. We'll discuss the costs and benefits associated with offering or taking advantage of cash discounts in the "Accounts Payable Management" section of this chapter. This is appropriate because, as discussed earlier, your company's accounts receivable represent other individuals' or companies' accounts payable.

To properly manage its accounts receivable, a business must perform ongoing analysis and monitoring of its accounts receivable. Determining and evaluating the average accounts receivable collection period and creating and evaluating an aging of accounts receivable are two effective ways to analyze and monitor accounts receivable.

We first learned about average collection period in chapter 5. As a review, average collection period is determined by first calculating accounts receivable turnover and then using accounts receivable turnover to calculate average collection period, as illustrated in example 8.2.

Example 8.2

MRH, LLC's most recent 12 months of sales amount to $4,265,000. Ninety percent of these sales are credit sales. The net accounts receivable amounts on MRH's balance sheet at the beginning and end of the applicable 12-month period are $400,000 and $500,000, respectively. MRH offers 30-day payment terms to its customers approved for trade credit. Determine MRH's average collection period.

The formula for calculating accounts receivable turnover is as follows:

$$\text{Accounts receivable turnover} = \text{Credit sales} \div \text{Average net accounts receivable}$$

where

$$\text{Average net accounts receivable} = (\text{Beginning accounts receivable} + \text{Ending accounts receivable}) \div 2$$

That means the calculation of MRH's average net accounts receivable is as follows:

$$\text{Average net accounts receivable} = (\$400,000 + \$500,000) \div 2$$
$$= \$450,000$$

And the accounts receivable turnover is this:

$$\text{Accounts receivable turnover} = (\$4,265,000 \times 0.9) \div \$450,000$$
$$= 8.53$$

Average collection period is the number of days in a year divided by accounts receivable turnover:

$$\text{Average collection period} = 365 \text{ days} \div 8.53$$
$$= 42.79$$
$$= 43 \text{ days}$$

If the average collection period is less than the number of days indicated by a company's stated credit terms, then the accounts receivable are likely generally in good shape. In addition, the company may want to consider offering credit to more of its customers—or more credit to its existing credit customers—as a way to increase sales. If the average collection period exceeds what's indicated by a company's credit terms, as is the case in example 8.2, the company must work to speed up its collections of accounts receivable. A good first step in the effort to speed up the collection of accounts receivable is to create an **aging of accounts receivable**, a schedule that categorizes unpaid customer invoices based on the number of days they have been outstanding. Business owners and managers use an aging of accounts receivable to determine the effectiveness of a business's accounts receivable collection practices.

aging of accounts receivable
a schedule that categorizes unpaid customer invoices based on the number of days they have been outstanding

In order to create an aging of accounts receivable, an entrepreneur should perform the following three steps:

1. Determine the various accounts receivable that exist at a selected point in time.
2. Determine the various lengths of time those accounts have been outstanding.
3. Categorize all the amounts due into selected time frames of interest.

Figure 8.2 is an example of an aging of accounts receivable.

An aging of accounts receivable like that in figure 8.2 provides the business owner with the information to do the following:

- Identify delinquent customers.
- Deny additional credit to identified delinquent customers until they bring their accounts current.
- Pressure delinquent customers for payment.
- Turn the accounts of customers not responding to pressure for payment over to a collection agency, if needed.
- Write off an account receivable when no reasonable hope of customer payment exists.

The aging shown in figure 8.2 indicates that, while six other companies are also past due on their accounts, we have a very clear understanding of which customer should get the first phone call. Considering the amount the Honorable Company owes the Michael Stanwick Company, the Honorable Company may—all by themselves—be creating a major cash flow problem for the Michael Stanwick Company.

With regard to writing off an account receivable, we also learned in chapter 5 that when a company can determine, based on its history, that a certain percentage

	The Michael Stanwick Company Aging of Accounts Receivable As of April 30, 2020			
	Days Outstanding			
Customer	0–30	31–60	61–90	90+
Blough, Inc.	$ 6,398	$ –	$ –	$ –
Franklin Co.	101,110	10,555	–	–
Grimm, LLC	4,800	5,047	–	–
Honorable Co.	–	–	–	110,500
J. Akers Co.	–	–	3,352	–
Jewell, Inc.	5,755	3,466	–	–
Moor, LLC	14,500	–	–	–
Sissman Co.	5,982	–	–	–
Thompson Co.	–	–	486	–
Wiggins Co.	7,200	10,343	–	–
Totals	$ 145,745	$ 29,411	$ 3,838	$ 110,500

Figure 8.2. Example aging of accounts receivable.

of its accounts receivable are typically not collectible—or when a company has identified specific individual accounts receivable that are likely not collectible—the company should establish a reserve for bad debts. A reserve for bad debts is an estimate of the amount of the accounts receivable included on a balance sheet that won't be collected and is presented as a contra-asset account to accounts receivable on the balance sheet. An example is illustrated below for the April 30, 2020 accounts receivable of the Michael Stanwick Company:

Accounts receivable	$289,494
Less: Reserve for bad debts	3,838
Net accounts receivable	$285,656

In this instance, while the Honorable Company is the Michael Stanwick Company's most significant late payer, because the company thinks the $110,500 amount due is collectible, the $110,500 isn't included in the reserve for bad debts. However, the Michael Stanwick Company does deem the amounts owed by the Thompson Company and the J. Akers Company—the two accounts on the aging that are in the 61–90 days outstanding range—as uncollectible. As a result, these two accounts make up the $3,838 reserve for bad debts indicated above.

An insignificant reserve for bad debts like the one above is typically created or increased via a charge to miscellaneous expense. A reduction in the reserve for bad debts would similarly result in a decrease of miscellaneous expense. In order to more methodically keep track of the amount of accounts receivable written off and expected to be written off, the creation or adjustment in amount of a significant reserve for bad debts (i.e., significant as a percentage of total accounts receivable) would likely warrant the creation or adjustment of a bad debt expense account rather than miscellaneous expense. When a bad account receivable is written off, both accounts receivable and the reserve for bad debts are decreased by the amount of the uncollectible accounts receivable.

Note that, in the case of a start-up, there may be no history with which to estimate a reserve for bad debts. As a result, the item is left to be determined when information exists such that a reasonable estimate can be made. If no reserve for bad debts exists, a young company would likely choose to write off an uncollectible account receivable by directly decreasing accounts receivable by the amount of the bad debt and then charging the amount written off, depending upon whether or not the amount written off is significant, to either miscellaneous expense or bad debt expense.

Inventory Management

For many businesses, inventory represents the company's largest current asset. Considering this, it's wise to note that there are many different types of inventory that might be included on a company's balance sheet. The following are the most commonly used inventory categorizations:

- Raw materials inventory, as mentioned previously, is comprised of the fundamental materials or components a company uses to produce its final product. At some point, raw materials inventory usually ends up being included in work-in-process inventory. Note that a raw material to one company may be a final product to another company. For example, stainless steel is a raw material to an appliance manufacturer, but it's the final product of a steel manufacturer.

- **Work-in-process inventory** consists of inventory items that are in the process of being assembled, modified, or otherwise translated into finished goods inventory.
- Finished goods inventory, as mentioned previously, is comprised of inventory items that have been translated into a final product ready to be sold by the business. Virtually all finished goods inventory has, at some point, been work-in-process inventory
- **Maintenance, repair, and operating (MRO) inventory** consists of items that are kept on hand not to be sold, but instead to help the firm maintain consistent operations. These inventory items are generally not fabricated, assembled, or otherwise manufactured by the firm itself. An example of an MRO inventory item would be a replacement part kept on hand to keep key manufacturing equipment continually operating.

The two primary goals of inventory management are to:

1. Keep inventory at a minimum level to maximize available cash.
2. Keep enough inventory on hand to always satisfy production or customer demand.

These goals compete. As discussed in the "Cash Management" section of this chapter, maintaining an adequate level of cash and positive cash flow are critical to the short- and long-term success of a company. That said, maintaining an adequate level of inventory is also critical to a company's short- and long-term success.

Running out of a particular item of inventory is commonly called a **stockout**. When a customer enters the retail outlet of her choice, be it a traditional brick-and-mortar store or an online store, she expects to find what she's shopping for in stock and readily available for purchase. When she finds this isn't the case, if she can find the desired item at an alternative retail outlet, she'll likely purchase the item there. At this point, the original retail outlet sought out by the customer has lost a sale. But this may not be the end of the negative effect of the stockout. When a customer uses an alternative retailer, there's always a risk she'll decide she prefers that retailer to the one she's been using. She may therefore permanently switch to making all her purchases from the alternative retailer. In other words, the original retailer, the retailer that experienced the stockout, doesn't lose just one sale. The retailer loses the customer entirely.

A stockout can go beyond hurting only the retailer, however. Let's assume again that a customer enters the retail outlet of her choice and doesn't find what she's looking for due to a stockout. If the customer is unwilling to investigate whether the product is available at an alternative retailer, or if, after investigating, she can't find the product at an alternative retailer, the customer may purchase a substitute product. In this case, the retailer doesn't lose a sale, the producer of the out-of-stock product loses a sale. But, again, this may not be the end of the negative effect of the stockout. When a customer uses a substitute product, there's always a risk she'll decide she prefers the substitute product to the original product. As a result, she may permanently switch to purchasing the substitute product. In other words, the producer of the original good, the producer of the good for which the retailer experienced the stockout, doesn't lose just one sale. That producer loses the customer entirely.

Keeping enough inventory on hand to always satisfy production or customer demand is obviously important, but that doesn't mean an entrepreneur shouldn't still make an effort to effectively manage—and, to the extent reasonably possible, minimize—the costs associated with purchasing and holding inventory. In order to minimize total inventory costs while meeting production demand or maintaining customer satisfaction, two points of information must generally be determined for every inventory item held in significant quantity by a company: economic order quantity and reorder point. Let's explore both.

work-in-process inventory
inventory items that are in the process of being assembled, modified, or otherwise translated into finished goods inventory

maintenance, repair, and operating inventory
items that are kept on hand not to be sold, but instead to help the firm maintain consistent operations; often referred to as MRO inventory

stockout
running out of a particular item of inventory

Economic Order Quantity

Economic order quantity (EOQ) refers to the optimal quantity a business should purchase every time it places an order for an inventory item. EOQ attempts to balance ordering costs against storage costs. Ordering costs usually, most significantly, are the costs associated with the utilization of an employee's time. Storage costs are usually, most significantly, the costs associated with maintaining warehouse or other facility storage space, the costs associated with the utilization of an employee's time, and the costs associated with the special assets and equipment (e.g., shelving, forklifts) needed to manage inventory. EOQ provides the order size that, at a given purchase price for an inventory item, will minimize the overall costs associated with purchasing and holding that item.

The EOQ formula is as follows:

$$EOQ = \sqrt{\frac{2DK}{CP}}$$

where

D = the annual demand for an inventory item

K = the cost to order the item

C = the average cost to hold one dollar of inventory for one year (average holding cost), calculated by dividing average annual inventory holding costs by average total inventory value

P = the unit purchase price of the item

EOQ is best illustrated via example. Let's consider one.

Example 8.3

The San Francisco Manufacturing Company has a warehouse that incurs, on average, total annual costs of $110,000. The total amount of inventory the company has on hand at any time, virtually all of which is stored in the warehouse, averages $1 million. The purchase price per unit of the inventory item the company wishes to evaluate, item QX1, is $40. The company's owners estimate that placing an order costs the company $16.50 and the annual demand for inventory item QX1 is 3,800 units. What is the EOQ for inventory item QX1?

To calculate the EOQ for inventory item QX1, we must first calculate average holding cost—the cost to hold one dollar of inventory for one year:

$$Average\ holding\ cost = Average\ annual\ inventory\ holding\ cost \div Average\ total\ inventory$$
$$= \$110,000 \div \$1,000,000$$
$$= \$0.11$$

Now we have all the information we need to calculate the EOQ:

$$EOQ = \sqrt{\frac{2DK}{CP}}$$
$$= \sqrt{\frac{(2)(3,800)(\$16.50)}{(\$0.11)(\$40.00)}}$$
$$= \sqrt{28,500}$$
$$= 168.82$$
$$= 169$$

The EOQ of 169 calculated in example 8.3 suggests that an order size of 169 will minimize the San Francisco Manufacturing Company's overall costs associated with purchasing and holding inventory item QX1. Note that when calculating an EOQ, it's generally wise to round to whole units. This is because businesses usually don't order partial units of inventory items.

The EOQ model inherently assumes that an order, once placed, is received instantaneously. As a practical matter, we know this is hardly ever the case. As a result, beyond knowing how much to order (i.e., the EOQ), we must also determine when to order (i.e., the reorder point).

Reorder Point

Reorder point (ROP) is the optimal quantity of an item that should be remaining in inventory when a business places an order for more of that item. The formula is as follows:

$$ROP = LD + SS$$

where:

> L = lead time, the time (in days) that lapses between order placement and order receipt
>
> D = average daily demand, the quantity of an inventory item that is used or sold daily
>
> SS = safety stock, the quantity of stock kept on hand to cover variability in demand

reorder point
the optimal quantity of an item that should be remaining in inventory when a business places an order for more of that item

Continuing with example 8.3, assuming it takes three days from the time the company places an order for item QX1 until it receives the order, the lead time for inventory item QX1 is three days. If the San Francisco Manufacturing Company uses 3,800 units of inventory item QX1 per year and operates 350 days per year, the average daily demand for inventory item QX1 is 11 units (3,800 units ÷ 350 operating days per year = 10.86 = 11 units). Note that, as when calculating an EOQ, when calculating an ROP, it's generally wise to round to whole units. However, because the goal is to not run out of inventory, in the instance of calculating an ROP, we generally always want to round up to the next whole unit.

Safety stock is the number of units of an item of inventory a company expects will be remaining in inventory when a new order for that item arrives. The purpose of safety stock is to cover daily variations in production or customer demand, and the number can be rather subjective. If the most the San Francisco Manufacturing Company has ever used or sold of inventory item QX1 in one day is 15 units, the company might set its safety stock for that item at 12 units, calculated as follows:

safety stock
the number of units of an item of inventory a company expects will be remaining in inventory when a new order for that item arrives

$$\text{Safety stock per day} = \text{Maximum daily demand} - \text{Average daily demand}$$
$$= 15 \text{ units} - 11 \text{ units}$$
$$= 4 \text{ units}$$

Safety stock = 4 units per day x 3 days of lead time = 12 units

The ROP, then, would be calculated as follows:

$$ROP = LD + SS$$
$$= (3)(11) + 12$$
$$= 45$$

With regard to example 8.3, an ROP of 45 means that when the unit level of inventory item QX1 hits 45, we should order the previously calculated EOQ of 169 units. Note that vendor discounts, especially quantity and cumulative purchase discounts, sometimes have the power to persuade an entrepreneur to temporarily ignore the EOQs and ROPs that have been meticulously established for certain critical inventory items. For more information on vendor discounts, reference the "Accounts Payable Management" section of this chapter.

Current Liabilities Management

Current liabilities management focuses on minimizing the amount of the cash payments needed to appropriately settle accounts payable, accrued liabilities, and short-term debt obligations on a timely basis. As entrepreneurs, our primary concern with current liabilities is to make sure we pay these obligations when they're due, as the consequences associated with not doing so can sometimes be significant.

Accounts Payable Management

Accounts payable are amounts a business owes to its vendors. Usually, the amounts are for recurring purchases. For many businesses, the largest portion of accounts payable typically relates to purchases of inventory.

The usual goal of accounts payable management is to pay out as little cash as possible in order to properly settle these obligations. The primary way this is accomplished is by gathering information about or requesting vendor discounts and then systematically taking advantage of the discounts. The secondary way this is accomplished is by making sure amounts due are paid on time in order to avoid interest charges and late fees.

Vendors often offer several types of discounts. The most common are trade, cash, quantity, and cumulative purchase discounts. A vendor can offer these discounts individually or in combination, or a vendor may not offer them at all. Let's take a closer look at each type of discount.

Trade Discount

trade discount
an amount deducted from the list price of an item when specific services are performed by a trade customer

trade customer
a recurring customer approved to purchase product on trade credit

A **trade discount** is an amount deducted from the list price of an item when specific services are performed by a **trade customer**, a recurring customer approved to purchase product on trade credit. Examples of specific services include functioning as a retailer of product, picking up inventory (instead of having it delivered), displaying point-of-sale promotional pieces, and providing local advertising.

Trade discounts may be expressed as a single amount, such as 25 percent, or in a series of amounts, such as 25/20/10. Using 25/20/10 as our example of a trade discount expressed in a series of amounts, 25 percent might be the normal discount from retail price to wholesale price, 20 percent might be the allowance for no delivery service, and 10 percent might be the allowance for the customer displaying point-of-sale promotional pieces. Often, the overall effect of a series of trade discounts is expressed in one of two forms:

net cost rate
the actual percentage of list price paid after taking advantage of a series of trade discounts

single equivalent discount
the total trade discount received, expressed in one percentage

1. **net cost rate**—the actual percentage of list price paid after taking advantage of a series of trade discounts
2. **single equivalent discount**—the total trade discount received, expressed in one percentage

We'll explore trade discounts further with example 8.4.

Example 8.4

If the San Francisco Manufacturing Company plans to take advantage of all aspects of an offered 25/20/10 trade discount, what price will the company pay for an item with a list price of $500? What net cost rate will the company pay? What single equivalent discount rate will the company receive? Let's find out.

In order to determine what price the company will pay for an item with a list price of $500, we'll first need to calculate the price after the initial 25 percent trade discount:

$$\text{Discounted price} = \text{List price} - \text{Discount}$$
$$= \$500 - (\$500 \times 0.25)$$
$$= \$500 - \$125$$
$$= \$375$$

Next, we'll adjust this price for the 20 percent follow-up discount:

$$= \$375 - (\$375 \times 0.20)$$
$$= \$375 - \$75$$
$$= \$300$$

Now we can determine the final purchase price of the product considering the third and final discount of 10 percent:

$$= \$300 - (\$300 \times 0.10)$$
$$= \$300 - \$30$$
$$= \$270$$

Next, let's determine the net cost rate:

$$\text{Net cost rate} = \text{Price paid} \div \text{List price}$$
$$= \$270 \div \$500$$
$$= 0.54$$
$$= 54\%$$

Finally, let's determine the single equivalent discount for our example:

$$\text{Single equivalent discount} = 1 - \text{Net cost rate}$$
$$= 1 - 0.54$$
$$= 0.46$$
$$= 46\%$$

Assuming it has more than one associated discount percentage, a single equivalent discount is not equal to the sum of its associated discount percentages. Rather, the discounts are taken in succession, as demonstrated in example 8.4. Note that, in example 8.4, the single equivalent discount is 46 percent while the sum of its associated discount percentages is 55 percent (25% + 20% + 10% = 55%).

Cash Discount

A **cash discount** is a discount offered to a credit customer to entice the customer to pay their bill early, rather than waiting until the last permitted day to pay. The seller views a cash discount as a sales discount. The customer views it as a purchase discount. The terms of a cash discount play an important role in determining how an invoice will ultimately be paid.

cash discount
a discount offered to a credit customer to entice the customer to pay her bill early

Cash discounts normally appear on an invoice stated in terms such as 2/10, net 30. These terms mean the customer will get a 2 percent discount on the amount of the invoice if payment is made on or before the tenth day after the invoice date. Otherwise, 100 percent of the invoice amount is due on the thirtieth day after the invoice date. If the invoice is paid after 30 days, the credit agreement between the seller and the purchaser normally stipulates that a monthly interest charge or a late fee may be added to the unpaid balance. Example 8.5 illustrates an instance of a cash discount.

Example 8.5

A $25,000 invoice dated May 1 indicates terms of 2/10, net 30. What are the options associated with paying this invoice on a timely basis?

There are essentially two options associated with paying this invoice on a timely basis:

1. Option 1: Settle the $25,000 invoice with a payment of $24,500 on or before May 11, determined as follows:

   May 1 + 10 days = May 11

   $25,000 x 0.02 = $500 discount

   $25,000 invoice amount – $500 discount = $24,500

2. Option 2: Settle the $25,000 invoice with a payment of $25,000 on or slightly before May 31, determined as follows:

   May 1 + 30 days = May 31

   There is no discount associated with this option.

Continuing with example 8.5, note that a customer choosing option 2 will pay the equivalent of 36.7 percent annual interest as a result of delaying payment. The logic supporting this statement is that if one doesn't take advantage of the cash discount, holding on to $24,500 for a period of 20 days will cost $500, or 2.04 percent, calculated as follows:

$$\$500 \div \$24,500 = 0.0204$$
$$= 2.04\%$$

The 2.04 percent, however, is an annual rate. The customer isn't paying $500 to hold on to $24,500 for a whole year. The customer is paying $500 to hold on to $24,500 for 20 days, which results in the following calculation:

$$.0204 \times (360 \div 20) = 0.3672$$
$$= 36.72\%$$

In essence, holding on to $24,500 for 20 days will effectively cost 36.72 percent interest. (Note: Interest rate calculations often use 360 days instead of 365 days to represent one year.)

Considering the interest rates involved, there are two significant lessons to learn here:

1. It's often worthwhile to borrow money to take advantage of cash discounts.
2. An entrepreneur should think twice before offering cash discounts to customers.

```
┌─────────────────────────────────────────────┐
│                                             │
│   Quantity Discount Available for Inventory Item QX1   │
│                                             │
│     Quantity Ordered          Price per Item    │
│        0–199                    $40.00          │
│        200–399                  $36.00          │
│        400+                     $34.00          │
│                                             │
└─────────────────────────────────────────────┘
```

Figure 8.3. Example of quantity discount pricing.

Quantity Discount

A **quantity discount** is a discount based on the number of units ordered by a customer. Figure 8.3 illustrates quantity discount pricing.

> **quantity discount**
> a discount based on the number of units ordered by a customer

Vendors offer quantity discounts to secure the loyalty of valued customers, improve cash flow as a result of moving more inventory, and improve the efficiency of operations by increasing the average number of units per customer order. Quantity discounts are often designed to encourage customers to order quantities in excess of their calculated EOQs. Whether or not a business owner should order in excess of a calculated EOQ to take advantage of a quantity discount depends very much upon the business's expected demand for the applicable inventory item and the other anticipated demands on the business's short-term cash flow.

Cumulative Purchase Discount

A **cumulative purchase discount (cumulative purchase rebate)** is a discount or rebate—above and beyond any applicable trade, cash, or quantity discount—available after a designated purchase threshold has been met by a customer. A typical cumulative purchase discount relates to the total purchases of a particular item over the course of an entire year. These discounts or rebates can be significant and are often buried in the fine print of credit agreements or similar paperwork, only to be emphasized by a vendor when that vendor has a need to move product before year end. For example, a paragraph within a credit agreement might state, "If you buy 12,501 units or more of product A over the course of the calendar year, you are entitled to a 1 percent rebate on your total calendar-year purchases of that item."

> **cumulative purchase discount**
> a discount or rebate—above and beyond any applicable trade, cash, or quantity discount—available after a designated purchase threshold has been met by a customer; also referred to as a cumulative purchase rebate

Note that if a unit of product A costs $85, the cumulative purchase rebate amounts to a minimum of $10,625.85, calculated as follows:

12,501 units x $85 x 0.01 = $10,625.85

The opportunity for such a large discount or rebate might persuade an entrepreneur to purchase additional units of product A before December 31 in order to take advantage of the discount or rebate. As with a quantity discount, whether or not taking advantage of a cumulative purchase discount is a wise choice for a business would depend very much upon the business's expected demand for product A and the other anticipated demands on the business's short-term cash flow.

Accrued Liabilities Management

Accrued liabilities are those obligations of a firm that accumulate over time during the normal course of operations. These liabilities typically include payroll, payroll taxes, certain employee-related benefits, property taxes, and sales taxes. Accrued liabilities are usually current liabilities.

> **accrued liabilities**
> obligations of a firm that accumulate over time during the normal course of operations and typically include items such as payroll, payroll taxes, certain employee-related benefits, property taxes, and sales taxes

The area of accrued liabilities tends to be where entrepreneurs get themselves into the most trouble. Because many accrued liabilities involve a relationship between an entrepreneur's business and a government entity, when accrued liabilities aren't paid on time, the penalties can be severe.

For many entrepreneurs, the best way to avoid a problem with accrued liabilities is to deliberately and systematically (i.e., as the taxes are withheld, accrued, or collected) funnel the funds needed to pay accrued liabilities into a bank account separate from the business's regular checking account. This is especially true for the amounts associated with withheld and accrued payroll taxes and collected sales taxes. The practice of funneling the funds needed to pay accrued liabilities into a bank account separate from the business's regular checking account helps the entrepreneur avoid the problem of not having the funds needed to pay the applicable tax amounts when they are due. Not having the funds needed to pay payroll and sales tax amounts when they are due—because the entrepreneur has inadvertently spent the funds on something else—is a common reason why entrepreneurs sometimes find themselves in trouble with federal, state, and local government entities.

Management of Short-Term Debt

Short-term debt generally consists of business obligations other than accrued liabilities and accounts payable that need to be paid within the next 12 months. Short-term debt may include the following:

- short-term portion of long-term debt
- bank lines of credit
- short-term loans
- notes payable, which are often incident specific (e.g., such as when an entrepreneur makes a short-term loan to her business)

Short-term portion of long-term debt is the amount of principal due to be paid in the next 12 months related to a business's long-term loans, typically loans related to major fixed-asset purchases. As illustrated in appendix 6-B at the end of chapter 6, the short-term portion of long-term debt can be determined by looking at the loan amortization tables associated with a company's loans. Making larger-than-required or faster-than-required loan payments are both effective ways not only to pay off the principal amount owed on a loan earlier than scheduled, but also to reduce the overall amount of interest paid on a loan. Note that not all lenders allow early repayment of a loan. An entrepreneur should therefore be sure that the option to repay the loan early, whether via a lump sum payment or via larger or faster loan payments than are required, is a clause included in—or added to—any loan document her company signs.

A bank line of credit is a means for borrowing extended by a bank that operates similar to a credit card. With a bank line of credit, a company obtains a credit limit, but the company isn't obligated to make payments unless it actually borrows money. A line of credit is normally obtained from a company's primary bank and must usually be repaid in full at least once a year. A business utilizes a line of credit when the business's cash outflows exceed its cash inflows due to variability (seasonal or otherwise) in the business's operations. To that end, a line of credit is usually established by a company as a cushion to be tapped into in the event of a cash shortage or the threat of a cash shortage. In order to obtain the best interest rate possible on a line of credit, the terms of a line of credit should be negotiated and put into writing well before the line of credit is actually needed.

short-term loan
a loan that often fills the gap when a line of credit is temporarily unable to meet all of a company's short-term cash needs

A **short-term loan** is a loan that often fills the gap when a line of credit is temporarily unable to meet all of a company's short-term cash needs. Alternatively, sometimes a short-term loan is the default position into which a company is forced when the company can't meet its requirement to repay 100 percent of its line of credit balance to its lender once a year. When the need for a short-term loan arises, especially when a venture is young, although getting a short-term loan from a bank is sometimes possible, it's usually best to turn to the venture's founders and angels for assistance. For a start-up venture, a **note payable** is typically a short-term loan to the company from a stakeholder—often a founder or an angel investor. This option is ideal because a venture can usually negotiate significantly better and more flexible interest and repayment terms with a founder or angel than with an outside lender.

Notes payable should be clearly documented in writing and made fully transparent to all parties concerned. Those to whom the note is payable, even if this is a founder of the business, should be paid interest at least annually based on the outstanding amount of the note and its stated interest rate. A properly documented note payable that pays interest to the applicable lender provides clarity to those both within and outside of the business that the cash infusion being made is not an equity investment but rather an amount that is expected to be repaid.

note payable
for a start-up venture, typically a short-term loan to the company from a stakeholder—often a founder or an angel investor

Bootstrapping as a Source of Cash

As first defined in chapter 2, bootstrapping involves borrowing noncash assets, bartering for noncash assets and services, and utilizing strategic negotiation tactics in order to avoid, delay, or minimize the outlay of cash. At its most basic level, bootstrapping involves embracing the entrepreneurial mindset in order to get the business through its start-up phase until more traditional means of financing the young venture become available.

There are many effective bootstrapping practices. A few examples follow:

- choosing to commence business operations via a kiosk, mobile cart, or vehicle rather than from a permanent physical location
- choosing to commence business operations from your home
- choosing to commence business operations in a free or low-cost business incubator
- asking a landlord for rent-free months during an entity's start-up period
- asking a landlord for reduced rent
- convincing a retailer to display or sell your product in a prominent area of her store free of charge to your company by arguing that your product will drive increased foot traffic to her store
- convincing a business owner to allow you to offer your services in an appropriate area of her space free of charge to your company by arguing that your service complements her business and will thus drive new customers to her business or increase her current customers' level of satisfaction with her business
- utilizing independent contractors—instead of hiring employees—to the extent reasonably possible, for as long as possible (because employees are often the largest expense of a business)
- borrowing or buying used office furniture, vehicles, or equipment instead of purchasing new
- trading services with other entrepreneurial ventures (e.g., preparing a marketing plan and marketing materials for free for a young accounting firm in exchange for free accounting services)

As these examples illustrate, bootstrapping involves seeking out what you can get for free, get for a reduced price, or purchase used. Bootstrapping also involves thoroughly assessing a situation and the plethora of benefits or outcomes that can be gleaned from the situation before committing a company's resources to that situation. In its most concrete terms, bootstrapping involves, to the fullest extent possible, getting your business the resources it needs in legal and ethical ways that don't involve spending cash or that minimize the amount of cash that must be spent until more traditional means of financing the venture become available.

Unfortunately, working capital management is a specific area of bootstrapping often overlooked by entrepreneurs. Strategically requesting customer deposits and effectively managing accounts receivable, inventory, and accounts payable can be well worth the effort put forth and can significantly improve a venture's overall cash flow and profitability. Ultimately, bootstrapping working capital can make it possible to start or maintain a business that an entrepreneur didn't think she had the resources to start or maintain at all.

As discussed earlier in this chapter, a business can be profitable and growing and still experience cash flow problems. To illustrate a few ways most businesses can successfully bootstrap working capital, we'll return to and continue to work with example 8.1 from the "Cash Management" section of this chapter.

Figure 8.1, presented earlier in this chapter, illustrates the current cash flow problem of MCPC, a manufacturer of medical capital equipment. Specifically, every time MCPC receives an order from a customer, the cash inflow of $60,000 generated by that sale is preceded by 45 days by a cash outflow of $35,000 required to pay for the parts inventory needed to manufacture the product. Fortunately, there are ways to resolve a cash flow challenge of this type that eliminate—or minimize—the need to utilize a bank line of credit.

Bootstrapping working capital involves always asking for better terms than those offered by any vendor, creditor, or lender in order to maximize your business's cash flow and overall financial performance. Note that this does not mean paying for items later than what is indicated by agreed-upon payment terms.

Let's assume that, in order to improve their business's cash flow, MCPC's owners successfully negotiate 90-day payment terms instead of 30-day payment terms with their parts vendors. Reaching such an agreement with vendors isn't necessarily easy, but it also happens every day. Figure 8.4 illustrates the effects of this change in payment terms on MCPC's cash flow.

In this example, the owners of MCPC have worked themselves out of a situation where they were temporarily cash flow negative as a result of every customer

The Madison Capital Products Company Analysis of the Major Cash Flows Associated with the Manufacture and Sale of One Unit of Product		
	Number of Days	Cash Inflows and (Outflows)
Production time after receipt of customer order:		
Average number of days to order and receive parts inventory	5	
Average number of production days until the product is ready to ship	35	
Total production time after receipt of customer order	40	
Post-production time until customer payment:		
Average number of days the product is in shipment	5	
Average number of days to train and invoice the customer	5	
Average number of days until the customer is required to pay for the product	30	
Total post-production time until customer payment	40	
Customer pays MCPC on day 80 (30 days after invoiced for the product)	–	$ 60,000
Total time from order receipt to customer payment	80	15 days
MCPC pays its parts vendors on day 95 (90 days after receipt of parts inventory)	–	$ (35,000)

Figure 8.4. Analysis of the major cash flows associated with the manufacture and sale of one unit of product—90-day vendor payment terms.

order and into a situation where they are never cash flow negative as a result of a customer order. This is obviously a big improvement. Observe that MCPC really doesn't even necessarily need vendor payment terms of 90 days. Terms closer to 80 days would work if MCPC's owners are confident their customers will consistently pay in 30 days.

Beyond asking vendors, creditors, and lenders for better terms, bootstrapping working capital may also involve asking customers for better terms, including pre-payments or deposits. Let's assume that MCPC can't get its parts vendors to agree to 90-day payment terms, but the company does successfully get its parts vendors to agree to less aggressive—but still extended—payment terms of 45 days. Next, let's assume that MCPC successfully negotiates with its customers that they'll pay a down payment of 50 percent on their equipment orders with MCPC. Basically, MCPC is utilizing some of its customers' cash to help finance the manufacture of the product of which these customers will ultimately take delivery. Figure 8.5 illustrates the effects of these changes in its customer and vendor payment terms on MCPC's cash flow.

This cash flow situation isn't a perfect scenario. However, if MCPC does have to borrow to have cash to fund its operations, having to borrow $5,000 for 30 days per customer order is much better than having to borrow $35,000 for 45 days per customer order (reference figure 8.1).

As this example illustrates, asking vendors and customers for better terms can have a huge impact on a company's cash flows and, therefore, ultimately on its profit-ability. Note that customer deposits or prepayments are categorized as current liabili-ties on a company's balance sheet if the applicable products or services are expected to be delivered to the customer within the next 12 months. Customer deposits or prepayments are categorized as noncurrent liabilities on a company's balance sheet

The Madison Capital Products Company Analysis of the Major Cash Flows Associated with the Manufacture and Sale of One Unit of Product		
	Number of Days	Cash Inflows and (Outflows)
Customer pays MCPC a 50% deposit with their order	–	$ 30,000
Production time after receipt of customer order:		
Average number of days to order and receive parts inventory	5	
Average number of production days until the product is ready to ship	35	50
Total production time after receipt of customer order	40	days
Post-production time until final customer payment:		
Average number of days the product is in shipment	5	
Average number of days to train and invoice the customer	5	
MCPC pays its parts vendors on day 50 (45 days after receipt of parts inventory)	–	$ (35,000)
Average number of days until the customer makes its final payment for the product	30	
Total post-production time until final customer payment	40	30 days
Customer pays MCPC the remaining 50% due on day 80 (30 days after invoiced)	–	$ 30,000
Total time from order receipt to final customer payment	80	

Figure 8.5. Analysis of the major cash flows associated with the manufacture and sale of one unit of product—50 percent customer deposit and 45-day vendor payment terms.

if the applicable products or services are expected to be delivered to the customer more than 12 months into the future.

Effective Controls over Business Assets

The steps an entrepreneur needs to take to protect her business's assets depend very much upon the nature of her business, the types of assets it holds, and how many and which individuals have access to these assets. An owner of a high-cash business, especially in the first few months or years of that business, needs to be on-site during the business's hours of operation, period. The owner needs to constantly monitor and minimize the amount of cash in the cash register to minimize the temptation for employees and others to steal. A software-assisted customer checkout process that's tied to the business's inventory system will help maintain some control over cash, but in the end, there are always ways to work outside of these systems, especially if employees collude in order to do so.

Not depositing cash on the same day it's received is an invitation for theft. Most employees know where their employers store the cash that's not in the cash register. As a result, sometimes, employees are unable to resist the urge to steal. Other times, employees share this information with their family members or friends who, in turn, use the information to steal from the business.

An owner, especially in the first few months or years of a business, should open all the business's postal mail herself. This practice becomes even more critical if the business receives cash or checks in the mail. An owner should also perform a weekly cursory review of all the emails received at the business's main contact email address. Often, the way an owner learns that something is amiss with her business is via information in the postal mail or in an email that's inconsistent with either the owner's knowledge or with the information provided by the business's internal accounting and data processing systems. If an owner is delegating the mail opening and review process to others, she's forfeiting the opportunity to find such inconsistencies.

Until an organization is of the size to warrant a full-time accountant or chief financial officer (CFO), all checks issued by the business should be signed by an owner. After an organization has a full-time accountant or CFO, all checks of a significant amount—to be determined by the owner(s)—should require two signatures, one of which is an owner's signature. Even after employing a full-time accountant or CFO, an owner should still routinely review the business's daily cash balances and monthly bank statements for irregularities. Accountants and CFOs stealing from the businesses that employ them is, unfortunately, not a rare occurrence.

An owner should perform surprise physical inventory counts in order to identify the nature and amount of any lost, damaged, or stolen inventory. Surprise physical inventory counts don't give those who are guilty the opportunity to effectively cover their tracks like scheduled physical inventory counts can.

It should go without saying that an owner should password protect every computer and generously use physical locks to safeguard easily transportable assets. Security cameras may be in order, especially in areas where cash is transferred from customers to the business, but security cameras are rendered ineffective if persons other than the owner(s) know about their existence and placement or how to delete the data collected by the cameras.

All in all, owners who don't take basic precautions to protect their assets can expect to lose those assets. Utilizing the practices above in combination with performing background checks on key employees (see Entrepreneur in Action 8.2) can give an entrepreneur some level of comfort that her assets are reasonably well protected.

Entrepreneur *in Action* 8.2

The Background Check of an Employee Largely Pays Off

Amy and her husband, Max, are the founders and co-owners of a quickly growing investment management company called SmartInvest. SmartInvest's customers are wealthy individuals who don't have time to research and manage their own stock and bond portfolios, so they pay SmartInvest to do this work for them.

Recently, Amy has been working a lot of hours trying to keep up with the company's growing number of clients. Max has suggested that Amy hire an assistant to help her, but Amy, who doesn't enjoy the process of interviewing and hiring employees, has been unwilling to do so. After one particularly long and difficult Monday, however, Amy reluctantly agreed to start looking for an assistant.

Amy utilized a popular employment-related platform to announce the available position and within a few days had identified 11 promising candidates she wished to interview. She diligently dug in and had interviewed 10 of the recruits by the following Thursday. Unfortunately, Amy didn't feel that any of the candidates she had interviewed quite fit the bill. She was working up the energy to conduct the eleventh interview when she received a phone call from her mother requesting that Amy take her to her doctor's appointment that afternoon. Max encouraged Amy to take a much needed afternoon off and spend some time with her mother, so Amy did.

Max decided he would take some of the burden off Amy by interviewing the eleventh candidate himself. Max liked the candidate, Donna Ryder, immediately upon meeting her and hired her on the spot at the end of the interview.

When Amy arrived home, Max proudly announced that he had filled the job opening for her assistant. Amy wasn't at all pleased and told him, "I would very much have preferred to hire my own assistant, thank you." Max got the message, apologized for not fully thinking before acting, and then asked Amy to give Donna a chance. Amy reluctantly agreed.

From the start, Amy was not impressed with Donna. Sure, she was friendly and accommodating—perhaps a little too friendly and accommodating—but Amy wasn't sure Donna possessed the skills required to perform the needed work. All this quickly became moot, however, when Max landed a major new client and asked Amy if she would mind if he borrowed Donna for a few weeks because he was swamped with work. Amy agreed.

A few weeks later, Donna stopped Amy on the front steps of SmartInvest and asked when she would get the opportunity to work with Amy and her clients. Donna said she was eagerly anticipating the work. Amy's stomach clenched as she realized she didn't trust Donna. Amy smiled at Donna and gently said that she'd like to do a routine background check on Donna before allowing Donna access to her clients' information. Donna said, "Of course!" Later that afternoon, Donna formally agreed to the background check by signing the required paperwork. Amy sent the paperwork to the background check company and returned to her stack of work. Donna continued working with Max.

Ten days later, Amy pulled an envelope from the background check company out of her company's post office box at the local post office. Amy opened the envelope and stared in dismay at the information the background check company had uncovered. Donna Ryder was only one of Donna's names. She had four aliases. She also had multiple convictions for identity theft and bank fraud. Last, Amy's jaw dropped as she read that Donna also had a conviction for armed robbery. A stranger in the post office walked up to Amy, touched her on the shoulder, and asked if she was okay. Amy looked at her and said, "No, but I will be soon."

From her car in the post office parking lot, Amy called Max and read him the results of Donna's background check. Max was silent for a moment. Then, in a panicked voice, he asked, "What should we do?" Amy told Max to do nothing right now, let Donna leave at the end of the day as usual, then stop her in the parking lot and fire her. At the end of the day, Max did exactly as Amy had suggested.

When Amy arrived back at the office, she and Max went through Donna's desk and found that all the work Max had given Donna to do since her hiring had been stuffed, uncompleted, in her bottom desk drawer. Max meekly asked Amy if she had given Donna access to any of their clients' personal or financial information. Amy responded that thankfully, she had not. She then looked quickly at Max, who immediately confirmed that he hadn't either. Max said, "There is one problem though." Amy looked at Max, raised her eyebrows, and waited. Max then said, "I did give her access to *our* personal and financial information." Amy stared at Max in horror.

Summary

Even businesses that are profitable and growing can struggle with cash flow issues. Often, proper working capital management and bootstrapping can help an entrepreneur overcome both cash flow issues and the issues associated with a business being underfunded.

Working capital management is the art of controlling current assets and current liabilities in such a way that a firm will maintain adequate cash and inventory levels, maximize the return on its assets, and minimize the size of the payments needed to settle its liabilities. Working capital management typically focuses on the effective and efficient management of cash, marketable securities, accounts receivable, inventory, accounts payable, accrued liabilities, and short-term debt.

Bootstrapping involves borrowing noncash assets, bartering for noncash assets and services, and utilizing strategic negotiation tactics in order to avoid, delay, or minimize the outlay of cash. Unfortunately, effective working capital management is a specific area of bootstrapping often overlooked by entrepreneurs. Strategically requesting customer deposits and effectively managing accounts receivable, inventory, and accounts payable can be well worth the effort put forth and can significantly improve a venture's overall cash flow and profitability. Ultimately, bootstrapping working capital can make it possible to start or maintain a business an entrepreneur didn't think she had the resources to start or maintain at all.

Assuming the entrepreneur has a good business concept, has created a solid business model, and has mastered and applied the techniques of proper working capital management and bootstrapping, the entrepreneur's business will likely begin at some point to accumulate assets. An entrepreneur who doesn't take the time to properly secure the assets of her business is likely to lose those assets. The last section of this chapter discussed effective controls over assets.

Key Terms

accrued liabilities

aging of accounts receivable

cash discount

cumulative purchase discount

economic order quantity

finished goods inventory

high-growth start-up

maintenance, repair, and operating inventory

net cost rate

note payable

quantity discount

raw materials inventory

reorder point

safety stock

scalable

short-term loan

single equivalent discount

stockout

trade customer

trade discount

working capital management

work-in-process inventory

Review and Discussion Questions

1. Define and explain the concept of working capital management.

2. Define and explain the concept of cash management.

3. Explain the potential consequences of an inventory stockout for both the retailer and the producer of a good.

4. Define bootstrapping, list five examples of effective bootstrapping practices included in the chapter, and devise a bootstrapping practice of your own, explaining how the practice could help a business avoid, delay, or minimize the outlay of cash.

5. What does it mean to bootstrap working capital? What positive effects can bootstrapping working capital bring about?

6. What steps can a business owner take to safeguard her business's cash and other assets?

Exercises

1. The Sweetie Candy Company's calendar year 2020 sales amounted to $5,665,000. Of these sales, 95 percent were credit sales. The net accounts receivable amounts on the Sweetie Candy Company's balance sheets as of December 31, 2019, and December 31, 2020, were $428,675 and $468,841, respectively. The Sweetie Candy Company offers 30-day payment terms to its customers for whom it has approved trade credit. Determine and evaluate the Sweetie Candy Company's average collection period for 2020.

2. Burton and Associates, LLC's income statement for the year ended December 31, 2021, included $2,875,069 of sales, all of which were credit sales. Its comparative balance sheets for December 31, 2020, and December 31, 2021, included $341,067 and $362,213 of accounts receivable, respectively, the aging of which is included below:

Burton and Associates, LLC Aging of Accounts Receivable As of December 31, 2020					Burton and Associates, LLC Aging of Accounts Receivable As of December 31, 2021				
	Days Outstanding					Days Outstanding			
Customer	0–30	31–60	61–90	90+	Customer	0–30	31–60	61–90	90+
Crawley, Inc.	$ 22,538	$ –	$ –	$ –	Crawley, Inc.	$ –	$ 26,114	$ –	$ –
Franklin Co.	98,115	9,221	–	–	Franklin Co.	101,260	–	–	–
Gilmore and Co.	13,104	–	–	–	Gilmore and Co.	–	10,266	–	–
Integrity Co.	–	–	33,335	85,250	Integrity Co.	–	109,566	–	–
J. Jenkins, Inc.	8,966	–	3,133	–	J. Jenkins, Inc.	–	–	–	21,000
Jones, LLC	7,023	166	–	–	Jones, LLC	–	–	–	20,118
M. Pekala, LLC	6,788	–	–	–	M. Pekala, LLC	6,994	6,541	–	–
Stettler, Inc.	26,951	–	–	–	Stettler, Inc.	22,009	–	–	–
Taylor Co.	1,046	–	–	–	Taylor Co.	9,102	–	–	–
XYZ, Inc.	16,402	9,029	–	–	XYZ, Inc.	15,021	14,222	–	–
Totals	$ 200,933	$ 18,416	$ 36,468	$ 85,250	Totals	$ 154,386	$ 166,709	$ –	$ 41,118

Burton and Associates, LLC's comparative balance sheets include no reserve for bad debts at December 31, 2020, or December 31, 2021. Assuming the company's payment terms are 30 days, do the following:

a. Calculate accounts receivable turnover for 2021.

b. Calculate the average collection period for 2021.

c. Comment on the status of the company's accounts receivable at December 31, 2021. Do collections seem to be improving? Explain your answer.

3. Bob King is the owner of King's Carpeting, LLC, a company that manufactures carpet. Bob estimates that the annual demand for carpet trim X15, the inventory item Bob is currently analyzing, is 58,500 yards. Bob further estimates that it costs his company $5.85 to place an order. King's Carpeting has a warehouse for which the average cost to hold one dollar of inventory for one year equals $0.05. The price per yard for carpet trim X15 is $10. It takes five days to receive an order of carpet trim X15 from King's Carpeting's supplier once an order is placed, and the highest quantity of carpet trim X15 King's Carpeting has ever used in one day is 175 yards. Assuming King's Carpeting operates 350 days per year, what are King's Carpeting's EOQ and ROP for carpet trim X15?

4. The Sweetie Candy Company produces and sells, on average, 3.6 million units per year of its signature product: a three-ounce dark chocolate pretzel and toffee candy bar. One ounce of sugar goes into the production of each of these

candy bars. The Sweetie Candy Company operates 365 days per year and typically uses 225,000 pounds of sugar per year to produce its dark chocolate pretzel and toffee candy bars. It takes one day to receive an order of sugar from the company's discount sugar supplier once an order is placed, and the company estimates that it costs $20 to place an order for sugar. The company has a warehouse that incurs, on average, total annual costs of $6,000. The total amount of inventory the company has on hand at any time, virtually all of which is stored in the warehouse, averages $100,000. The highest quantity of sugar the company has ever used in one day is 679 pounds. The company orders sugar by the pound at a cost of $0.52 per pound. What are the Sweetie Candy Company's EOQ and ROP for sugar?

5. If you plan to take advantage of all aspects of an offered 25/15/5 trade discount, what price will you pay for an item with a list price of $1,000? What net cost rate will you be paying? What single equivalent discount rate are you receiving?

6. You have to pay a $35,000 invoice with stated terms of 1/10, net 30.
   a. What do the terms 1/10, net 30 mean?
   b. What options are available associated with paying this invoice on a timely basis?
   c. What effective interest rate are you paying if you elect to pay $35,000 on the thirtieth day after the invoice date?

7. You have to pay a $15,000 invoice with stated terms of 1/15, net 30.
   a. What do the terms 1/15, net 30 mean?
   b. What options are available associated with paying this invoice on a timely basis?
   c. What effective interest rate are you paying if you elect to pay $15,000 on the thirtieth day after the invoice date?

Time Value of Money

"Compound interest is the eighth wonder of the world. He who understands it, earns it. He who does not, pays it."

— **Albert Einstein, theoretical physicist and developer of the theory of relativity**

Learning Objectives

Understand the difference between simple interest and compound interest.

Understand the difference between a stated rate of interest and an effective rate of interest.

Have an appreciation for the concept of time value of money.

Be able to calculate the present value and future value of a lump sum, a stream of unequal payments, and an ordinary annuity.

Introduction

Businesses must invest in people, technology, fixed assets, or other businesses in order to continue to grow and generate increasing amounts of revenue and, ideally, increasing amounts of profit. Decisions regarding whether or not to invest in people, technology, and fixed assets are referred to as capital budgeting decisions. Decisions regarding whether or not to buy a business involve determinations of business value.

Individuals must invest in people, financial assets, or **capital assets**—assets that have an expected useful life in excess of one year—in order to become financially secure and lead happy, successful lives. Decisions regarding whether or not to invest in certain people, financial assets, or capital assets are referred to as personal wealth management decisions.

Chapters 10, 11, and 12 will discuss capital budgeting, business valuation, and personal wealth management. Before we can talk about these topics, however, we must first understand the concept of time value of money because it's integral to all three topics.

Time Value of Money

capital asset
an asset that has an expected useful life in excess of one year

time value of money
the loss of purchasing power that occurs as a result of the interest considerations associated with the passage of time

One of the most fundamental concepts in all of finance is **time value of money**, the loss of purchasing power that occurs as a result of the interest considerations associated with the passage of time. Put more simply, the basic principle underlying time value of money is that a dollar in your possession today is worth more than a dollar you'll receive in the future because a dollar in your possession today can be invested and turned into more than a dollar. In other words, time affects the value of money. As with many financial concepts, the concept of time value of money is best illustrated with an example.

Example 9.1

Today, Bryce Easterday, the owner of Easterday Construction, Inc., is in a good mood. He recently learned that the group of investors building the new casino in his home state of Missouri has accepted his company's bid to do the bulk of the construction work. But there's one catch: The investors don't want to pay the bid price of $13,250,000 in the manner Easterday Construction's bid has outlined. The investors want to stretch out the payments over a longer period of time. Figure 9.1 details the schedule outlined in the bid and the alternative payment plan suggested by the casino investors.

Easterday Construction, Inc. Missouri Casino Project			
Payment Plan Outlined by Easterday Construction:		Alternative Payment Plan Suggested by the Casino Investors:	
Down payment—due on day 1 of the project	$ 1,250,000	Down payment—due on day 1 of the project	$ 750,000
Payment 1—due at the end of Year 1 of the project	5,000,000	Payment 1—due at the end of Year 1 of the project	1,750,000
Payment 2—due at the end of Year 2 of the project	4,000,000	Payment 2—due at the end of Year 2 of the project	2,500,000
Payment 3—due at the end of Year 3 of the project	3,000,000	Payment 3—due at the end of Year 3 of the project	3,500,000
		Payment 4—due at the end of Year 4	–
	$ 13,250,000	Payment 5—due at the end of Year 5	4,750,000
		Bonus—to be paid at the end of Year 5	662,500
			$ 13,912,500

Figure 9.1. Payment plans related to the construction of a proposed casino.

The investors know stretching out the payments over a longer period of time will likely create a financial hardship for Easterday Construction, so they have included a hefty 5 percent bonus in their suggested alternative payment plan to help ease the pain. The bonus certainly makes the alternative payment plan look very attractive, but Bryce is unsure. Should Easterday Construction accept the alternative payment plan offered by the casino investors? Note that Easterday Construction can borrow money via its bank line of credit at an interest rate of 6 percent.

Time value of money calculations like those we'll learn about in this chapter are a relatively straightforward way to objectively answer the question of whether or not Bryce should accept the alternative payment plan suggested by the casino investors. We'll return to this example and perform the necessary calculations to answer the question at hand after we've reviewed some of the basics regarding simple interest, compound interest, and time value of money.

Simple Interest

Interest is the price (i.e., rent) charged for money that's borrowed or loaned. It's the premium paid by the user of funds to the supplier of funds expressed as a percentage of the amount of the funds in question. **Simple interest** is the amount of interest earned or charged on a stated principal amount when there's no compounding of interest. The stated principal amount is the base amount that is loaned, borrowed, saved, or invested. Compounding of interest, commonly called **compound interest**, involves earning or charging interest on both a stated principal amount and the interest that has been previously earned or charged. The next section of this chapter addresses compound interest. The simple interest formula follows:

$I = prt$

where:

I = Interest
p = Principal
r = Rate
t = Time

Let's look at two examples that illustrate the concept of simple interest.

interest
the price (i.e., rent) charged for money that's borrowed or loaned

simple interest
the amount of interest earned or charged on a stated principal amount when there's no compounding of interest

compound interest
the amount of interest earned or charged on both the stated principal amount and the interest that has been previously earned or charged

Example 9.2

What is the interest due on $1,000 borrowed for one year at 3.5 percent?

$I = (\$1,000)(0.035)(1)$
$= \$35$

Example 9.3

What is the interest due on $1,000 borrowed for six months at 3.5 percent?
Six months represents one half of a year, resulting in the following calculation:

$I = (\$1,000)(0.035)(0.5)$
$= \$17.50$

The total amount due related to a loan or investment—the loan or investment's maturity amount—is equal to the principal borrowed or invested, plus interest. The formula for maturity amount follows:

$$M = p + I$$

where

> M = Maturity amount (i.e., total amount due)
> p = Principal
> I = Interest

Example 9.4 illustrates the calculation of maturity amount.

Example 9.4

What is the maturity amount of $1,000 borrowed for four years at a simple interest rate of 3.5 percent?

$$I = prt$$
$$= (\$1,000)(0.035)(4)$$
$$= \$140$$

$$M = p + I$$
$$= \$1,000 + \$140$$
$$= \$1,140$$

Compound Interest

As noted earlier, compound interest is different from simple interest in that compound interest involves earning or charging interest on both a stated principal amount *and* the interest that has been previously earned or charged. It's interesting to note that, as illustrated in example 9.5, the simple interest formula can actually be used to calculate compound interest.

Example 9.5

What is the value at the end of year 3 (what is the maturity value) of a three-year, $15,000 certificate of deposit (CD) earning 5 percent per year, assuming compound interest?

$$I = prt$$

Year 1 = ($15,000)(0.05)(1)
           = $750.00

Year 2 = (15,000 + $750)(0.05)(1)
           = $787.50

Year 3 = (15,000 + $750 + $787.50)(0.05)(1)
           = $826.88

Total interest earned = $750.00 + $787.50 + $826.88
                              = $2,364.38

$$M = p + I$$

CD maturity value = $15,000 + $2,364.38

= $17,364.38

For purposes of comparison, in example 9.6, let's recompute example 9.5 assuming simple interest.

Example 9.6

What is the value at the end of year 3 of a three-year, $15,000 CD earning 5 percent per year, assuming simple interest?

$I = prt$

Year 1 interest = ($15,000)(0.05)(1)

= $750

Year 2 interest = (15,000)(0.05)(1)

= $750

Year 3 interest = (15,000)(0.05)(1)

= $750

Total interest earned = $750 + $750 + $750

= $2,250

$M = p + I$

CD maturity value = $15,000 + $2,250

= $17,250

Now, let's compare the total interest amounts:

The compound interest earned over three years:	$2,364.38
The simple interest earned over three years:	$2,250.00
The amount by which compound interest exceeds simple interest:	$ 114.38

In our example, when the CD's interest is calculated assuming compound interest rather than simple interest, $114.38 more interest is earned over the CD's three-year term.

A **stated rate of interest** is the rate of interest that's listed or quoted, normally on an annual basis, that disregards compounding. Assuming the same stated rate of interest is being utilized for both calculations, except in the instance of interest being compounded annually for one year or less, compound interest will result in more interest being earned or charged than simple interest. Note that in the real world, in this textbook, and unless specifically indicated otherwise, interest is typically calculated as compound interest rather than as simple interest.

stated rate of interest
the rate of interest that's listed or quoted, normally on an annual basis, that disregards compounding

Compound Interest and Future Value

Future value (FV) is the value at some future point in time of an amount loaned, borrowed, saved, or invested today. The formula follows:

$FV = PV(1 + i)^n$

where

FV = Future value
PV = Present value

future value
the value at some future point in time of an amount loaned, borrowed, saved, or invested today

i = Interest rate per period

n = Number of compounding periods per year multiplied by the number of years

Present value (PV) is the value in today's dollars of some amount to be received or paid in the future. We can bypass the multiple individual steps involved in computing compound interest using the simple interest formula by instead using the future value formula, as illustrated in the example 9.7.

Example 9.7

Referring back to example 9.5, if one wanted to determine the value at the end of year 3 of a three-year, $15,000 CD earning 5 percent per year assuming compound interest, one could more expeditiously calculate that value as follows:

$$FV = PV(1+i)^n$$
$$= \$15,000(1.05)^3$$
$$= \$15,000(1.157625)$$
$$= \$17,364.38$$

Examples 9.5 and 9.6 illustrate that a 5 percent interest rate can result in different interest and maturity amounts depending upon whether the 5 percent is calculated as simple interest or compound interest. This concept can be confusing for many people. That's why banks and certain other financial institutions are often required to provide clarification to consumers regarding the actual rate of interest they'll pay on money borrowed—or the actual rate of interest they'll earn on money invested or deposited—by disclosing an effective annual interest rate.

Effective Annual Interest Rate

As previously discussed, a stated rate of interest is the rate of interest that is listed or quoted, normally on an annual basis, that disregards compounding. As also discussed, assuming the stated rate of interest is being utilized for both calculations, except in the instance of interest being compounded annually for one year or less, compound interest will result in more interest being earned or charged than simple interest. The **effective annual interest rate** is the actual interest rate paid by the borrower or earned by the investor after interest compounding is taken into consideration. Let's look at the formula for the effective annual interest rate:

$$\text{Effective annual interest rate} = \left(\left(1 + \frac{i}{n} \right)^n - 1 \right) \times 100$$

where

i = Stated rate of interest

n = Number of compounding periods per year

Let's look at an example using this equation.

Example 9.8

A bank quotes a 5 percent annual loan rate. The bank wants monthly loan payments and compounds interest monthly. What's the effective annual interest rate associated with this loan?

$$\text{Effective annual interest rate} = \left(\left(1 + \frac{i}{n}\right)^n - 1\right) \times 100$$

$$= \left(\left(1 + \frac{0.05}{12}\right)^{12} - 1\right) \times 100$$

$$= ((1.0041667)^{12} - 1) \times 100$$

$$= (1.0512 - 1) \times 100$$

$$= 5.12\%$$

In the calculation, n equals 12 because we want to determine an effective annual interest rate, interest is being compounded monthly, and there are 12 months in one year. The calculation indicates that 5 percent compounded monthly equals an effective annual interest rate of 5.12 percent. In other words, if a borrower agrees to a loan with 5 percent interest compounded monthly, the actual annual interest rate the borrower will pay is 5.12 percent.

Note that the effective rate associated with compounding a stated rate of interest more often than annually always exceeds the stated rate.

Future Value of a Lump Sum

As mentioned earlier, future value (FV) is the value at some future point in time of an amount loaned, borrowed, saved, or invested today. The formula for future value of a lump sum follows:

$$FV = PV(FVF) = PV(1 + i)^n$$

where

FV = Future value
PV = Present value
FVF = Future value factor = $(1 + i)^n$
i = Interest rate per period
n = Number of compounding periods per year multiplied by the number of years

Note that this formula presents two possible methods to compute future value:

1. Utilizing the first portion of the formula [$FV = PV(FVF)$], we can compute future value by looking up the future value factor (FVF) in the present value and future value tables (included in appendix 9-A at the end of this chapter) and then multiplying that factor by the applicable present value (PV).
2. Utilizing the second, full computation formula [$FV = PV(1 + i)^n$], we can compute future value by calculating the future value factor [$(1+i)^n$] using a calculator and then multiplying that factor by the applicable present value (PV).

Example 9.9 illustrates both methods.

Example 9.9

You deposit $12,250 in the bank and leave it there for 20 years earning 3 percent interest, compounded annually. What's the value of this investment after 20 years?

$$FV = PV(FVF) = PV(1 + i)^n$$

$$= \$12,250(1.8061)$$

$$= \$22,124.73$$

or

$$= \$12,250(1+0.03)^{20}$$
$$= \$12,250(1.80611)$$
$$= \$22,124.85$$

The first solution was determined by first looking up the future value factor (*FVF*), 1.8061, in the future value of a lump sum table (in appendix 9-A) considering an interest rate (*i*) of 3 percent and the number of periods (*n*) of 20. Next, this *FVF* was multiplied by the present value (*PV*) of \$12,250 to arrive at \$22,124.73.

The second solution was determined by computing the *FVF* of 1.80611 with a calculator ($1.03^{20} \approx 1.80611$). Next, this *FVF* was multiplied by the present value (*PV*) of \$12,250 to arrive at \$22,124.85.

The present value and future value tables included in appendix 9-A at the end of this chapter include factors for the four different time value of money formulas we'll ultimately discuss in this chapter:

1. future value of a lump sum
2. present value of a lump sum
3. future value of an ordinary annuity
4. present value of an ordinary annuity

Using the factors in the present value and future value tables can help avoid the math errors associated with calculating factors using a calculator, but because the factors in the tables are rounded to four decimal places, using the factors from the tables also generally results in a slightly different solution than the solution determined performing all calculations with a calculator. As a practical matter, a solution arrived at by determining the factor using either the tables or a calculator is an acceptable solution.

Throughout the remainder of this chapter, the solution to an example problem that's presented first—or, in the event of the presentation of only one solution, a solution to an example problem with a factor that includes four decimal spaces—will be a solution determined using a factor from the present value and future value tables. The solution to an example problem that's presented second—or, in the event of the presentation of only one solution, a solution to an example problem with a factor that includes five decimal spaces—will be a solution determined by calculating an applicable factor with a calculator instead of looking up that factor in the tables. In chapters 10–12, factors will usually be rounded to four decimal places, whether determined using the present value and future value tables or determined using a calculator.

We can also use a financial calculator or Microsoft Excel to calculate future value. Every model of financial calculator is somewhat different, so consult a particular calculator's instructions regarding how to calculate future value using that specific calculator. To calculate the solution to example 9.9 using Microsoft Excel, within an Excel spreadsheet, select the cell where the future value should appear, select the FV function (click on the Insert Function tab located under the Formulas tab to locate—or search for—the function), and then click on "OK." A data input box will appear. Enter the following information:

- Rate: .03
- Nper (number of periods): 20
- Pv: -12,250

Next, click on "OK." At this point, a solution of \$22,124.86 should appear in the designated cell. Note that this solution is slightly different from the solutions generated previously using the present value and future value tables and a calculator. This is because the factors in the tables are rounded to four decimal places and the factor determined using a calculator was rounded to five decimal places. Excel calculates and uses factors with an unlimited number of decimal places.

Let's look at another example of the calculation of future value.

Example 9.10

If a vehicle costs $25,000 today, how much will the same vehicle cost in five years if inflation averages 2 percent per year?

$$FV = PV(FVF) = PV(1+i)^n$$
$$= \$25,000(1.1041)$$
$$= \$27,602.50$$

or

$$= \$25,000(1+0.02)^5$$
$$= \$25,000(1.10408)$$
$$= \$27,602$$

In both examples 9.9 and 9.10, the interest was compounded annually. Note that if a stated rate of interest is not indicated as being compounded something other than annually, it should be assumed for purposes of the examples and problems associated with this textbook that the stated rate of interest is compounded annually. In real life, however, a wise entrepreneur would verify this and not assume it. An example of the calculation of the future value of a lump sum where interest is not compounded annually follows.

Example 9.11

What's the future value of $100,000 deposited today if money grows at 4 percent compounded quarterly for four years?

$$FV = PV(FVF) = PV(1+i)^n$$
$$= \$100,000(1.1726)$$
$$= \$117,260$$

or

$$= \$100,000\left(1+\frac{0.04}{4}\right)^{(4\times4)}$$
$$= \$100,000(1.01)^{16}$$
$$= \$100,000(1.17258)$$
$$= \$117,258$$

Because we're compounding interest in some way other than annually, we must take care to make sure the i and the n we use are correct. In example 9.11, the interest rate per period (i) equals 1 percent—or 4 percent ÷ 4—because the compounding indicated in the problem is quarterly, or once every quarter of a year. In other words, because there are four quarters in one year, we divide the stated rate of interest by four to arrive at the i of 1 percent. Correspondingly, because interest is compounded quarterly, the number of periods (n) associated with the $100,000 in question should be stated in quarters, not years. Four quarters in a year multiplied by the four years the $100,000 will be on deposit results in the n of 16 used to solve the example problem.

Present Value of a Lump Sum

As mentioned earlier, present value (PV) is the value in today's dollars of some amount to be received or paid in the future. The formula for the present value of a lump sum follows:

$$PV = FV(PVF) = FV\left(\frac{1}{(1+i)^n}\right)$$

where

FV = Future value
PV = Present value
PVF = Present value factor = $\left(\frac{1}{(1+i)^n}\right)$
i = Interest rate per period
n = Number of compounding periods per year multiplied by the number of years

Let's consider an example of this calculation.

Example 9.12

You need $25,000 in five years to buy a vehicle. If you can earn 7 percent per annum on your money, how much do you need to invest today to have $25,000 in five years?

First, "per annum" means annually. With that in mind, we can find the solution using either the present value of a lump sum table in appendix 9-A at the end of this chapter or the full computation formula. Both methods are illustrated below:

$$PV = FV(PVF) = FV\left(\frac{1}{(1+i)^n}\right)$$
$$= \$25,000(0.7130)$$
$$= \$17,825$$

or

$$= \$25,000\left(\frac{1}{(1+0.07)^5}\right)$$
$$= \$25,000(0.71299)$$
$$= \$17,824.75$$

Examples 9.13, 9.14, and 9.15, which follow, are calculations of the present value of a lump sum where interest is not compounded annually.

Example 9.13

How much do you have to deposit in an account today to achieve a value of $1 million in five years if the annual interest rate earned is 12 percent compounded semiannually?

$$PV = FV(PVF) = FV\left(\frac{1}{(1+i)^n}\right)$$

$$= \$1,000,000(0.5584)$$

$$= \$558,400$$

or

$$= \$1,000,000\left(\frac{1}{\left(\left(1+\dfrac{0.12}{2}\right)^{(5\times2)}\right)}\right)$$

$$= \$1,000,000\left(\frac{1}{(1+0.06)^{10}}\right)$$

$$= \$1,000,000(0.55839)$$

$$= \$558,390$$

Note that we use an *i* of 6 percent because our stated interest rate of 12 percent is compounded semiannually, or twice per year (12% ÷ 2 semiannual periods in a year = 6%). We use an *n* of 10 because there are 10 semiannual periods in 5 years (5 years x 2 semiannual periods in a year = 10 semiannual periods).

Example 9.14

How much do you have to deposit in an account today to achieve a value of $1 million in five years if the annual interest rate earned is 12 percent compounded monthly?

$$PV = FV(PVF) = FV\left(\frac{1}{(1+i)^n}\right)$$

$$= \$1,000,000(0.5504)$$

$$= \$550,400$$

or

$$= \$1,000,000\left(\frac{1}{(1+0.01)^{60}}\right)$$

$$= \$1,000,000(0.55045)$$

$$= \$550,450$$

Note that we use an *i* of 1 percent because our stated interest rate of 12 percent is compounded monthly, or 12 times per year (12% ÷ 12 months in a year = 1%). We use an *n* of 60 because there are 60 months in a five-year period (5 years x 12 months in a year = 60 months).

Observe that, as illustrated in examples 9.13 and 9.14, more frequent compounding results in smaller amounts when we calculate present values. When we calculate future values, the opposite is true: more frequent compounding results in larger amounts.

Example 9.15

What's the present value of $100,000 assuming an interest rate of 9 percent compounded quarterly for five years?

$$PV = FV(PVF) = FV\left(\frac{1}{(1+i)^n}\right)$$

$$= \$100,000\left(\frac{1}{\left(\left(1+\dfrac{0.09}{4}\right)^{(5\times4)}\right)}\right)$$

$$= \$100,000\left(\frac{1}{(1+0.0225)^{20}}\right)$$

$$= \$100,000(0.64082)$$

$$= \$64,082$$

We use an i of 2.25 percent because our stated interest rate of 9 percent is compounded quarterly (9% ÷ 4 quarters in a year = 2.25%). We use an n of 20 because there are 20 quarters in a five-year period (5 years x 4 quarters in a year = 20 quarters).

non-integer interest rates
interest rates that are not whole numbers

Note that the present value and future value tables in appendix 9-A don't include **non-integer** interest rates—interest rates that are not whole numbers—interest rates like the 2.25 percent rate calculated in example 9.15. As a result, we cannot use the present value and future value tables to determine a present value factor for example 9.15 and must use a calculator in order to arrive at a solution for the problem.

As with future value, we can also use a financial calculator or Microsoft Excel to calculate present value. Every model of financial calculator is somewhat different, so consult a particular calculator's instructions regarding how to calculate present value using that specific calculator. To calculate the solution using Microsoft Excel, select the cell where the present value should appear, select the PV function (click on the Insert Function tab located under the Formulas tab to locate—or search for—the function), and then click on "OK." A data input box will appear. Enter the following information:

- Rate: .0225
- Nper: 20
- Fv: –100,000

Next, click on "OK." The solution of $64,081.65 should appear in the designated cell.

Present Value of a Stream of Unequal Payments

In certain instances, we may want to determine the present value of a contract or other stream of potential payments. In many instances, the amount of the individual payments will vary from one period to the next. As it happens, this is exactly the case in example 9.1 (page 238), where Easterday Construction is considering the merits of accepting a series of payments different from what the company outlined in its bid to the casino investors. Figure 9.1 (page 238) details both the timing of the payments related to the $13,250,000 price as outlined by Easterday Construction in its bid and the timing of the payments related to the $13,912,500 alternative payment plan the

Easterday Construction, Inc. Missouri Casino Project									
Present Value of the Payment Plan Outlined by Easterday Construction						Present Value of the Alternative Payment Plan Suggested by the Casino Investors			
Interest Rate: 6%						Interest Rate: 6%			
Year	Future Value		PVF		Present Value	Year	Future Value		PVF		Present Value
0	$ 1,250,000	x	1.0000	=	$ 1,250,000	0	$ 750,000	x	1.0000	=	$ 750,000
1	5,000,000	x	0.9434	=	4,717,000	1	1,750,000	x	0.9434	=	1,650,950
2	4,000,000	x	0.8900	=	3,560,000	2	2,500,000	x	0.8900	=	2,225,000
3	3,000,000	x	0.8396	=	2,518,800	3	3,500,000	x	0.8396	=	2,938,600
Totals	$ 13,250,000				$ 12,045,800	4	–	x	0.7921	=	–
						5	5,412,500	x	0.7473	=	4,044,761
						Totals	$ 13,912,500				$ 11,609,311

Figure 9.2. Calculation of the present values of two streams of unequal payments.

casino investors have suggested. Figure 9.2 shows the calculation of the total present value associated with each stream of payments.

When we have a stream of unequal payments like those indicated in figure 9.1, we have to build a table, calculate the present value of each payment, then sum those individual present values to arrive at a total present value. Figure 9.2 illustrates this process. Note that all the calculations assume an interest rate of 6 percent because Easterday Construction can borrow money at that rate—and if Easterday Construction accepts the casino investors' proposed alternative payment plan, the company may very well have to borrow money in order to remain cash flow positive.

Except for the down payment, Easterday Construction will receive the payments at the end of the year. Easterday Construction will receive the down payment when the contract is signed, on day 1 of the project, indicated as year 0 in Figure 9.2. A payment received on day 1—or a payment received "today"—has a PVF of 1.0000. This is because a dollar received today is worth a dollar—no more, no less.

Observe that all the PVFs in figure 9.2 appropriately relate to the corresponding year a payment is scheduled to be made. With regard to year 1, the PVF is for an i of 6 percent and an n of 1. For year 2, the PVF is for an i of 6 percent and an n of 2, and so on. For year 4, the year no payment is to be made according to the payment plan suggested by the casino investors, the PVF is for an i of 6 percent and an n of 4. There simply is no payment to which to apply the PVF. Last, observe that, because they are both made at the end of year 5, the two payments of $4,750,000 and $662,500 in figure 9.1 have been combined into one payment of $5,412,500 for purposes of the calculation in figure 9.2.

Example 9.1 asks if Easterday Construction should accept the alternative payment plan. At an interest rate of 6 percent, the value of the payment plan Easterday Construction outlined in its bid for the casino is $12,045,800. Compare this with the value of the payment plan proposed by the casino investors of $11,609,311. Even considering the 5 percent bonus the casino investors are offering at the end of year 5, the alternative payment plan is worth significantly less to Easterday Construction than the payment plan it outlined in its bid. Based purely on the numbers, Easterday Construction shouldn't accept the alternative payment plan.

Time value of money can significantly affect the value of a series of payments made over a period of only months instead of years. Entrepreneur in Action 9.1 (on page 250), illustrates this fact.

As with future value and present value, we can often use a financial calculator or Microsoft Excel to calculate the present value of a stream of unequal payments. If using a financial calculator, consult its instruction manual as needed. To calculate the present value for the alternative payment plan suggested by the casino investors

Entrepreneur *in Action* 9.1

A Business Owner Learns the Practical Worth of Time Value of Money

Connie McCain's company, McCain Builders, LLC, was a profitable company, but not as profitable as she wished it to be. McCain Builders constructed large, luxury homes for its wealthy clients. The typical home built by McCain Builders billed out at about $3M and was constructed over a period of approximately 16 months. After reviewing the company's income statement for one par-ticularly disappointing month, Connie called a meeting with her CFO, Bill Bennett, to discuss the company's continued lagging profitability. Bill came to the meeting prepared. He handed out to Connie and her general manager, John Horowitz, a schedule for discussion. The schedule included the following information:

Average total billing for a McCain home: $3M
Average time to construct a McCain home: 16 months
Applicable interest rate: 10%, compounded monthly

Current Customer Payment Terms					
Down payment	10%	$300,000 x 1.00000	=	$300,000
End of Month 4	15%	$450,000 x 0.96735	=	$435,308
End of Month 8	20%	$600,000 x 0.93577	=	$561,462
End of Month 12	25%	$750,000 x 0.90521	=	$678,908
End of Month 16	30%	$900,000 x 0.87566	=	$788,094
		$3,000,000		$2,763,772

Suggested New Customer Payment Terms					
Down payment	20%	$600,000 x 1.00000	=	$600,000
End of Month 4	25%	$750,000 x 0.96735	=	$725,513
End of Month 8	25%	$750,000 x 0.93577	=	$701,828
End of Month 12	20%	$600,000 x 0.90521	=	$543,126
End of Month 16	10%	$300,000 x 0.87566	=	$262,698
		3,000,000		$2,833,165

Average increase in value received per home if the new customer payment terms are adopted: $69,393

While Connie and John reviewed the schedule, Bill noted, "Our company's current customer payment terms reflect the fact that a lot of the materials cost of a high-end home—the cost of items like cabinets, countertops and flooring—is incurred in the last few months of the home's construction. Our current payment terms also mirror the payment terms preferred by our custom-ers' banks. What our current customer payment terms—and the banks—ignore, however, is that a lot of the cost associated with building a high-end home isn't materials cost, it's management labor cost. If we could sell my suggested new customer payment terms to our customers and their banks based on that premise, each home we build would ultimately be more profitable for us because if we receive our cash faster from our customers, we can then more quickly reinvest that cash into new, profitable projects. Right now we're not borrowing money to support our projects, but we're also not doing as many projects as we could be doing because we're allowing our customers to pay us too slowly. The 10 percent rate I used in the schedule I gave you is McCain Build-ing's approximate current monthly profit margin—what I believe is the opportunity cost of the company having to wait to receive cash from its customers."

Connie looked at Bill and said, "So what you're telling me is that by adopting the customer payment terms you suggest, we can improve the overall profitability of the company because we can be involved in more projects at one time?" Bill responded, "Ultimately, yes. Profit will be improved because we will have the cash to be involved in a higher number of profit-generating projects over the course of a year. In other words, this change in customer payment terms would help fund McCain's growth and hence an increase in its profitability." Connie smiled. Bill had just presented the solution she had been seeking. She looked at John. John gave her a nod. Connie then said determinedly to both Bill and John, "Let's get ready to sell these new payment terms to our next round of customers."

using Microsoft Excel, input the future value data for years 1–5 included in figure 9.2 in a spreadsheet in a row (i.e., horizontally) or in a column (i.e., vertically, as indicated in figure 9.2), making sure to include year 4 with $0 as its future value amount and to exclude year 0 and its $750,000 future value amount. Next, select the cell where the present value should appear, select the NPV function (click on the Insert Function tab located under the Formulas tab to locate—or search for—the function), and then click on "OK." A data input box will appear. Enter .06 in the "Rate" Field. Next, click on the "Value 1" data input field, then use the cursor to select the relevant future value data in order to register the applicable data as the values of interest for purposes of the NPV calculation. Next, click on "OK."

At this point, a result of $10,859,136.85 should appear in the designated cell. Next, add the year 0 future value amount (i.e., $750,000) to the result provided by

Microsoft Excel in order to arrive at the correct solution of $11,609,136.85. (Note that in the event there is no year 0 future value amount, only year 1 and subsequent year future value amounts, this step would be unnecessary.) The solution provided by Microsoft Excel differs slightly from the solution indicated in figure 9.2 due to the rounding inherent in the present value and future value tables.

Future Value of a Stream of Unequal Payments

In certain instances, we may want to determine the future value of an investment or other stream of potential payments that we're considering. In many instances, the amount of the individual payments will vary from one period to the next. Let's explore an example of how to calculate the future value of a stream of unequal payments.

Example 9.16

Carin Heller, a successful entrepreneur wishing to retire at age 65, plans to contribute the following amounts to her simplified employee pension individual retirement account (SEP IRA) at the beginning of each year for the next seven years, the payment for year 1 being made today:

Year 1	$35,000
Year 2	$40,000
Year 3	$42,500
Year 4	$45,000
Year 5	$50,000
Year 6	$52,500
Year 7	$55,000

If Carin is confident she can average a 7 percent annual return on her investments, what will the value of her SEP IRA be at the end of year 7?

When we have a stream of unequal payments for which we wish to determine a future value, we have to build a table, calculate the future value for each year, and then sum those individual future values in order to arrive at a total future value. See figure 9.3 for such a table for our example.

	Carin Heller's SEP IRA Calculation of Expected Future Value					
			Interest Rate: 7%			
Year	Present Value		FVF			Future Value
1	$ 35,000	x	1.6058	=		$ 56,202
2	40,000	x	1.5007	=		60,029
3	42,500	x	1.4026	=		59,608
4	45,000	x	1.3108	=		58,986
5	50,000	x	1.2250	=		61,252
6	52,500	x	1.1449	=		60,107
7	55,000	x	1.0700	=		58,850
Totals	$ 320,000					$ 415,035

Figure 9.3. Calculation of the future value of a stream of unequal payments.

Note that the calculation of the individual future values in figure 9.3 is less intuitive than the calculation of the individual present values presented in figure 9.2. For example, the contribution made at the beginning of year 1 will have the entire seven years to grow, hence the FVF of 1.6058 (i = 7 percent, n = 7). The contribution made at the beginning of year 7, however, will have only one year to grow before the end of year 7, hence the FVF of 1.0700 (i = 7 percent, n = 1). Using the example of a middle-year payment, the contribution made at the beginning of year 4 will have four years to grow until the end of year 7 (i.e., years 4, 5, 6, and 7), hence the FVF of 1.3108 (i = 7 percent, n = 4). Note also that if the payments in example 9.16 were made at the end of the year instead of at the beginning of the year, the n for year 1 would be 6 rather than 7, the n for year 2 would be 5 rather than 6, and so on, because effectively, each payment would have one year less time to grow.

While the present value of a stream of unequal payments can be calculated in Microsoft Excel using the NPV function, no function exists in the program to directly calculate the future value of a stream of unequal payments. When using a financial calculator or Microsoft Excel, the future value of a stream of unequal payments must be calculated as illustrated in figure 9.3 by determining the future value of each payment and then adding the individual future values to determine a total future value.

Annuities

So far in this chapter, with regard to time value of money, we've discussed individual lump sums and streams of unequal payments where we have to treat each payment like an individual lump sum in order to calculate the present value or future value of all the payments. We haven't discussed series of equal payments. We'll do that now.

annuity
a series of equal payments

annuity due
an annuity where the payments are made or received at the beginning of each time period

ordinary annuity
an annuity where the payments are made or received at the end of each time period

A series of equal payments is called an **annuity**. An **annuity due** is an annuity where the payments are made or received at the beginning of each time period, such as a payment made on the first day of every month. Because annuities due aren't relevant to the calculations and analyses performed by most start-up ventures, we won't devote any discussion to annuities due in this textbook beyond providing the aforementioned definition. An **ordinary annuity** is an annuity where the payments are made or received at the end of each time period, such as a payment made on the last day of every month. Because ordinary annuities are relevant to the calculations and analyses performed by most start-up entities, we'll discuss and illustrate them in the next two sections.

Future Value of an Ordinary Annuity

The future value of an ordinary annuity is the future value of a series of equal payments where each payment is made at the end of a period in the series. The formula for the future value of an ordinary annuity is as follows:

$$FVOA = A(FVAF) = A\left[\frac{(1+i)^n - 1}{i}\right]$$

where

$FVOA$ = Future value of an ordinary annuity
A = Annuity
$FVAF$ = Future value of annuity factor = $\left[\dfrac{(1+i)^n - 1}{i}\right]$

i = Interest rate per period

n = Number of compounding periods per year multiplied by the number of years

---

Example 9.17

What's the future value of $3,000 invested at the end of each year for 20 years if money earns 3 percent per year?

$$FVOA = A(FVAF) = A\left[\frac{(1+i)^n - 1}{i}\right]$$

$$= \$3,000(26.8704)$$

$$= \$80,611.20$$

or

$$= \$3,000\left[\frac{(1+0.03)^{20} - 1}{0.03}\right]$$

$$= \$3,000\left[\frac{0.80611}{0.03}\right]$$

$$= \$3,000(26.87033)$$

$$= \$80,610.99$$

Note that it's often easier to look up the appropriate factor (26.8704 in the case of example 9.17) in the present value and future value tables than to perform the complicated calculations included in the second solution to example 9.17

Next, let's see an example of the calculation of the future value of an ordinary annuity when interest is not compounded annually.

Example 9.18

What's the future value of $10,000 invested at the end of each quarter for 10 years if money earns 16 percent compounded quarterly?

$$FVOA = A(FVAF) = A\left[\frac{(1+i)^n - 1}{i}\right]$$

$$= \$10,000(95.0255)$$

$$= \$950,255$$

or

$$= \$10,000\left[\frac{\left(1+\dfrac{0.16}{4}\right)^{(10\times4)} - 1}{\left(\dfrac{0.16}{4}\right)}\right]$$

$$= \$10,000\left[\frac{(1+0.04)^{40} - 1}{0.04}\right]$$

$$= \$10,000\left[\frac{3.80102}{0.04}\right]$$

$$= \$10,000(95.02550)$$

$$= \$950,255$$

In this example, the interest rate per period (i) equals 4 percent because the rate of compounding indicated in the problem is quarterly (16% ÷ 4 quarters per year = 4%). Accordingly, the number of periods (n) should be stated in quarters, not years. In this case, n is 40 (4 quarters in a year x 10 years = 40).

Present Value of an Ordinary Annuity

The present value of an ordinary annuity is the present value of a series of equal payments where each payment is made at the end of a period in the series. The formula for the present value of an ordinary annuity is as follows:

$$PVOA = A(PVAF) = A\left[\frac{(1+i)^n - 1}{i(1+i)^n}\right]$$

where

$PVOA$ = Present value of an ordinary annuity

A = Annuity

$PVAF$ = Present value of an annuity factor = $\left[\dfrac{(1+i)^n - 1}{i(1+i)^n}\right]$

i = Interest rate per period

n = Number of compounding periods per year multiplied by the number of years

Example 9.19

What's the present value of a retirement account if you expect to receive $35,000 per year at the end of each year for 25 years and money earns 5 percent compounded annually?

$$PVOA = A(PVAF) = A\left[\frac{(1+i)^n - 1}{i(1+i)^n}\right]$$
$$= \$35,000(14.0939)$$
$$= \$493,286.50$$

or

$$= \$35,000\left[\frac{(1+0.05)^{25} - 1}{0.05(1+0.05)^{25}}\right]$$
$$= \$35,000\left[\frac{2.38635}{0.16932}\right]$$
$$= \$35,000(14.09373)$$
$$= \$493,280.55$$

Next, let's look at examples of the calculation of the present value of an ordinary annuity when interest is not compounded annually.

Example 9.20

What's the present value of $1,500 received at the end of each month for five years if money earns 12 percent compounded monthly?

$$PVOA = A(PVAF) = A \left[\frac{(1+i)^n - 1}{i(1+i)^n} \right]$$

$$= \$1,500(44.9550)$$

$$= \$67,432.50$$

or

$$= \$1,500 \left[\frac{\left(1 + \dfrac{0.12}{12}\right)^{(5 \times 12)} - 1}{\dfrac{0.12}{12}\left(1 + \dfrac{0.12}{12}\right)^{(5 \times 12)}} \right]$$

$$= \$1,500 \left[\frac{(1.01)^{60} - 1}{0.01(1.01)^{60}} \right]$$

$$= \$1,500 \left[\frac{0.81670}{0.01817} \right]$$

$$= \$1,500(44.94772)$$

$$= \$67,421.58$$

In this example, the interest rate per period (i) is 1 percent because the rate of compounding indicated in the problem is monthly and there are 12 months in a year (12% ÷ 12 months = 1%). Accordingly, the number of periods (n) should be stated in months, not years (12 months in a year x 5 years = 60).

Example 9.21

What's the present value of $2,500 received at the end of each month for five years if money earns 10 percent compounded quarterly?

$$PVOA = A(PVAF) = A \left[\frac{(1+i)^n - 1}{i(1+i)^n} \right]$$

$$= \$2,500 \left[\frac{\left(1 + \dfrac{0.10}{4}\right)^{(5 \times 4)} - 1}{\dfrac{0.10}{4}\left(1 + \dfrac{0.10}{4}\right)^{(5 \times 4)}} \right]$$

$$= \$2,500 \left[\frac{(1.025)^{20} - 1}{0.025(1.025)^{20}} \right]$$

$$= \$2,500 \left[\frac{0.63862}{0.04097} \right]$$

$$= \$2,500(15.58750)$$

$$= \$38,968.75$$

We use an i of 2.5 percent because our stated interest rate of 10 percent is compounded quarterly and 10 percent divided by four quarters equals 2.5 percent. We use an n of 20 because there are 20 quarters in a five-year period (5 years x 4 quarters in a year = 20 quarters). Note that, because the present value and future value tables in appendix 9-A at the end of this chapter don't include non-integer interest rates, we must calculate the present value of an annuity factor using a calculator in this instance in order to arrive at a solution for the problem.

Combining Lump Sums and Annuities

As a practical matter, determining the value of a series of payments often involves determining the present values or the future values of both lump sums and annuities. A classic example of an instance when one would need to determine the future value of both lump sums and annuities is when an individual wants to determine the expected future value of a contribution-oriented retirement plan like a 401(k) or an IRA. Example 9.22 illustrates just such a scenario.

Example 9.22

Carol Nightingale opens a SEP IRA in January 2020 and contributes $350 at the end of each month in 2020. She expects to increase the monthly payments she makes to the account by $100 each year until she reaches the maximum monthly contribution she thinks she'll be able to afford: $750. Her SEP IRA is invested in dividend-paying exchange traded funds that average a 7 percent return compounded monthly. She's currently 25 and plans to retire at 70. What's the expected value of Carol's account when she's 70?

To keep all the relevant information organized, Carol would likely construct a table that incorporates both lump sum and annuity calculations, a table like the one in figure 9.4.

The account value of $2,594,589.92 in figure 9.4 was determined by performing the following four steps:

1. The future value of an ordinary annuity was calculated for each of the first four individual years (i.e., 2020, 2021, 2022, and 2023) in order to determine an end of year value for each of these years. Using year 2020 as an example, the end of year value of $4,337.40 associated with the 12 monthly contributions of $350 made in 2020 was determined by multiplying the future value of an

Carol Nightingale's SEP IRA Calculation of Expected Future Value							
Retirement age:		70					
Current age:		25					
Expected growth rate:		7%					
Compounding rate:		Monthly					
Year of Contribution	Years to Retirement at the Beginning of the Year	Monthly Contrbution	FVOA Factor	End of Year Value	FVF	Future Value	Total Contributions
2020	45	$ 350.00	12.39258	$ 4,337.40	21.56419	$ 93,532.58	$ 4,200.00
2021	44	450.00	12.39258	5,576.66	20.11041	112,148.94	5,400.00
2022	43	550.00	12.39258	6,815.92	18.75465	127,830.18	6,600.00
2023	42	650.00	12.39258	8,055.18	17.49028	140,887.30	7,800.00
2024-2064	41	750.00	2826.92122			2,120,190.92	369,000.00
			Total retirement account value			$ 2,594,589.92	$ 393,000.00

Figure 9.4. Combining lump sums and annuities—calculation of the expected future value of a retirement account.

ordinary annuity factor of 12.39258 (the FVOA factor for an *n* of 12 assuming an interest rate of 7 percent compounded monthly [7% ÷ 12 ≈ 0.58333%]) by the $350 monthly payment.

2. The future value of a lump sum was calculated for each of the four end of year values determined in step 1 because each end of year value amount remains in the retirement account and continues to grow for many years. Continuing to use year 2020 as an example, the $93,532.58 amount—the expected future value of the 12 monthly contributions of $350 made in 2020—was determined by multiplying the future value factor of 21.56419 (the FV Factor for *n* = 528 [44 years left until retirement x 12 months per year] and *i* ≈ 0.58333%) by the end of year value of $4,337.40.

3. For the years that follow 2023, the future value of an ordinary annuity was calculated for the 492 (41 years x 12 months in a year) monthly contributions of $750 expected to be made to the account from January 2024 until December 2064. Specifically, the $2,120,190.92 future value amount was determined by multiplying a FVOA factor of 2826.92122 (the FV factor for *n* = 492 and *i* ≈ 0.58333%) by the $750 monthly contribution.

4. All the amounts in the "Future Value" column were totaled.

Note that in example 9.22 a contribution of only $4,200 to Carol's SEP IRA in 2020 is expected to grow to an approximate value of $93,533 by the end of year 2064. Note further that total contributions of only $393,000 to Carol's SEP IRA are expected to grow to an approximate value of $2,594,590 by the end of year 2064. Behold the power of time value of money!

Summary

Time value of money is the loss of purchasing power that occurs as a result of the interest considerations associated with the passage of time. Time value of money is important because capital budgeting, business valuation, and personal wealth management decisions all involve the concept of time value of money.

Simple interest is the amount of interest earned or charged on a stated principal amount when there's no compounding of interest. Compound interest is the amount of interest earned or charged on both the stated principal amount and the interest that has been previously earned or charged. The simple interest formula can be used to calculate compound interest. Alternatively, we can bypass the multiple individual steps involved in computing compound interest using the simple interest formula and instead use the future value formula.

The future value of a lump sum is the value at some future point in time of an amount loaned, borrowed, saved, or invested today. The present value of a lump sum is the value in today's dollars of some amount to be received or paid in the future. Future value of a lump sum and present value of a lump sum may be calculated using their formulas in two ways:

1. looking up the applicable factor in the present value or future value tables and then multiplying that factor by the appropriate lump sum amount
2. calculating the applicable factor using a calculator and then multiplying that factor by the appropriate lump sum amount

Future value of a lump sum and present value of a lump sum may also be determined using either a financial calculator or Microsoft Excel. More frequent compounding results in larger amounts when calculating future values and smaller amounts when calculating present values.

When we want to determine the total present value of a stream of unequal payments, we must calculate the present value of each payment, then sum those individual present values. Similarly, when we want to determine the total future value of a stream of unequal payments, we must calculate the future value of each payment, then sum those individual future values. While the present value of a stream of unequal payments can be calculated in Microsoft Excel using the NPV function, the software doesn't have a function to directly calculate the future value of a stream of unequal payments.

A series of equal payments is called an annuity. With an ordinary annuity, the payments are made or received at the end of each time period, such as a payment made on the last day of every month. As with future value of a lump sum and present value of a lump sum, we can use the tables, the formulas, a financial calculator, or Microsoft Excel to calculate both the present and future values of ordinary annuities.

In real life, determining the value of a series of payments often involves determining the present values or the future values of both lump sums and annuities. A classic example of an instance where one would need to determine the future value of both lump sums and annuities is when someone wants to determine the expected future value of a contribution-oriented retirement plan like an IRA or a 401(k).

Key Terms

annuity	effective annual interest	ordinary annuity
annuity due	rate	present value
capital asset	future value	simple interest
compound interest	interest	stated rate of interest
	non-integer interest rates	time value of money

Review and Discussion Questions

1. Define time value of money. Why is it important?
2. Explain the difference between simple interest and compound interest.
3. Define and explain effective annual interest rate.
4. What's the difference between the present value of a lump sum and the future value of a lump sum? What are the different ways these two items can be calculated?
5. What's an annuity? What are ordinary annuities? What are the two types of ordinary annuities, and how are they different?

Exercises

1. A local bank has offered you a loan with an 8 percent interest rate compounded quarterly. What's the effective annual interest rate you'll pay on this loan?
2. A local bank has offered you a loan with an 8 percent interest rate compounded daily. What's the effective annual interest rate you'll pay on this loan?
3. A credit card company has offered you a credit card with a 12 percent interest rate compounded monthly. What's the effective annual interest rate you'll pay on this credit card?
4. A credit card company has offered you a credit card with a 12 percent interest rate compounded semiannually. What's the effective annual interest rate you'll pay on this credit card?

5. You deposit $8,000 in an account that grows annually at an 8 percent guaranteed rate. Assuming you don't touch the money and the account continually grows at the stated rate, how much will you have in your account at the end of eight years?

6. Compute question 5 with an 8 percent interest rate compounded semiannually.

7. Compute question 5 with interest compounded monthly.

8. Mr. Z needs to make an $8,000 balloon payment on the loan on his house eight years from now. He can earn 8 percent annually on his money. How much money does Mr. Z need to deposit today in order to have the $8,000 he needs in eight years?

9. Compute question 8 assuming Mr. Z can earn 8 percent compounded quarterly.

10. Compute question 8 with the interest compounded monthly.

11. You have decided to retire. Your deferred compensation package at work stipulates the following payments: $8,000 (year 1), $16,000 (year 2), $24,000 (year 3), $32,000 (year 4), $40,000 (year 5), $48,000 (year 6), $56,000 (year 7), $64,000 (year 8), and $72,000 (year 9). How much is this package worth in today's dollars if you can make 9 percent per year on your money?

12. Would the above package be worth more or less to you if the payments were reversed (i.e., you receive $72,000 in year 1, $64,000 in year 2, etc.)? Why? Prove your answer.

13. At the beginning of each year, you deposit the following into a mutual fund that earns 9 percent per year: $8,000 (year 1), $16,000 (year 2), $24,000 (year 3), $32,000 (year 4), $40,000 (year 5), $48,000 (year 6), $56,000 (year 7), $64,000 (year 8), and $72,000 (year 9). How much will the mutual fund account be worth at the end of nine years?

14. Calculate question 13 assuming the payment stream is reversed (i.e., year 1 deposit is $72,000, year 2 deposit is $64,000, etc.).

15. What is the future value of $6,500 invested at the end of each year for eight years if money earns 6 percent per annum?

16. What is the future value of $19,500 invested at the end of each quarter for eight years if money earns 12 percent compounded quarterly?

17. What is the future value of $500 invested at the end of each quarter for 40 years if money earns 9 percent compounded quarterly?

18. What is the present value of a retirement account if you receive $50,000 per year at the end of each year for 35 years and money earns 5 percent compounded annually?

19. What is the present value of $3,000 received at the end of each month for three years if money earns 12 percent compounded monthly?

20. What is the present value of $4,500 received at the end of each quarter for 18 years if money can earn 8 percent compounded quarterly?

Future Value of a Lump Sum Table (FVF)

$$FV = PV(FVF) = PV(1 + i)^n$$

Interest rate

	Number of periods														
	1	2	3	4	5	6	7	8	9	10	11	12	13	14	15
1%	1.0100	1.0201	1.0303	1.0406	1.0510	1.0615	1.0721	1.0829	1.0937	1.1046	1.1157	1.1268	1.1381	1.1495	1.1610
2%	1.0200	1.0404	1.0612	1.0824	1.1041	1.1262	1.1487	1.1717	1.1951	1.2190	1.2434	1.2682	1.2936	1.3195	1.3459
3%	1.0300	1.0609	1.0927	1.1255	1.1593	1.1941	1.2299	1.2668	1.3048	1.3439	1.3842	1.4258	1.4685	1.5126	1.5580
4%	1.0400	1.0816	1.1249	1.1699	1.2167	1.2653	1.3159	1.3686	1.4233	1.4802	1.5395	1.6010	1.6651	1.7317	1.8009
5%	1.0500	1.1025	1.1576	1.2155	1.2763	1.3401	1.4071	1.4775	1.5513	1.6289	1.7103	1.7959	1.8856	1.9799	2.0789
6%	1.0600	1.1236	1.1910	1.2625	1.3382	1.4185	1.5036	1.5938	1.6895	1.7908	1.8983	2.0122	2.1329	2.2609	2.3966
7%	1.0700	1.1449	1.2250	1.3108	1.4026	1.5007	1.6058	1.7182	1.8385	1.9672	2.1049	2.2522	2.4098	2.5785	2.7590
8%	1.0800	1.1664	1.2597	1.3605	1.4693	1.5869	1.7138	1.8509	1.9990	2.1589	2.3316	2.5182	2.7196	2.9372	3.1722
9%	1.0900	1.1881	1.2950	1.4116	1.5386	1.6771	1.8280	1.9926	2.1719	2.3674	2.5804	2.8127	3.0658	3.3417	3.6425
10%	1.1000	1.2100	1.3310	1.4641	1.6105	1.7716	1.9487	2.1436	2.3579	2.5937	2.8531	3.1384	3.4523	3.7975	4.1772
11%	1.1100	1.2321	1.3676	1.5181	1.6851	1.8704	2.0762	2.3045	2.5580	2.8394	3.1518	3.4985	3.8833	4.3104	4.7846
12%	1.1200	1.2544	1.4049	1.5735	1.7623	1.9738	2.2107	2.4760	2.7731	3.1058	3.4785	3.8960	4.3635	4.8871	5.4736
13%	1.1300	1.2769	1.4429	1.6305	1.8424	2.0820	2.3526	2.6584	3.0040	3.3946	3.8359	4.3345	4.8980	5.5348	6.2543
14%	1.1400	1.2996	1.4815	1.6890	1.9254	2.1950	2.5023	2.8526	3.2519	3.7072	4.2262	4.8179	5.4924	6.2613	7.1379
15%	1.1500	1.3225	1.5209	1.7490	2.0114	2.3131	2.6600	3.0590	3.5179	4.0456	4.6524	5.3503	6.1528	7.0757	8.1371
16%	1.1600	1.3456	1.5609	1.8106	2.1003	2.4364	2.8262	3.2784	3.8030	4.4114	5.1173	5.9360	6.8858	7.9875	9.2655
17%	1.1700	1.3689	1.6016	1.8739	2.1924	2.5652	3.0012	3.5115	4.1084	4.8068	5.6240	6.5801	7.6987	9.0075	10.5387
18%	1.1800	1.3924	1.6430	1.9388	2.2878	2.6996	3.1855	3.7589	4.4355	5.2338	6.1759	7.2876	8.5994	10.1472	11.9737
19%	1.1900	1.4161	1.6852	2.0053	2.3864	2.8398	3.3793	4.0214	4.7854	5.6947	6.7767	8.0642	9.5964	11.4198	13.5895
20%	1.2000	1.4400	1.7280	2.0736	2.4883	2.9860	3.5832	4.2998	5.1598	6.1917	7.4301	8.9161	10.6993	12.8392	15.4070

Future Value of a Lump Sum Table (FVF)
$FV = PV(FVF) = PV(1 + i)^n$ (Continued)

Number of periods

Interest rate	16	17	18	19	20	21	22	23	24	25	26	27	28	29	30
1%	1.1726	1.1843	1.1961	1.2081	1.2202	1.2324	1.2447	1.2572	1.2697	1.2824	1.2953	1.3082	1.3213	1.3345	1.3478
2%	1.3728	1.4002	1.4282	1.4568	1.4859	1.5157	1.5460	1.5769	1.6084	1.6406	1.6734	1.7069	1.7410	1.7758	1.8114
3%	1.6047	1.6528	1.7024	1.7535	1.8061	1.8603	1.9161	1.9736	2.0328	2.0938	2.1566	2.2213	2.2879	2.3566	2.4273
4%	1.8730	1.9479	2.0258	2.1068	2.1911	2.2788	2.3699	2.4647	2.5633	2.6658	2.7725	2.8834	2.9987	3.1187	3.2434
5%	2.1829	2.2920	2.4066	2.5270	2.6533	2.7860	2.9253	3.0715	3.2251	3.3864	3.5557	3.7335	3.9201	4.1161	4.3219
6%	2.5404	2.6928	2.8543	3.0256	3.2071	3.3996	3.6035	3.8197	4.0489	4.2919	4.5494	4.8223	5.1117	5.4184	5.7435
7%	2.9522	3.1588	3.3799	3.6165	3.8697	4.1406	4.4304	4.7405	5.0724	5.4274	5.8074	6.2139	6.6488	7.1143	7.6123
8%	3.4259	3.7000	3.9960	4.3157	4.6610	5.0338	5.4365	5.8715	6.3412	6.8485	7.3964	7.9881	8.6271	9.3173	10.0627
9%	3.9703	4.3276	4.7171	5.1417	5.6044	6.1088	6.6586	7.2579	7.9111	8.6231	9.3992	10.2451	11.1671	12.1722	13.2677
10%	4.5950	5.0545	5.5599	6.1159	6.7275	7.4002	8.1403	8.9543	9.8497	10.8347	11.9182	13.1100	14.4210	15.8631	17.4494
11%	5.3109	5.8951	6.5436	7.2633	8.0623	8.9492	9.9336	11.0263	12.2392	13.5855	15.0799	16.7386	18.5799	20.6237	22.8923
12%	6.1304	6.8660	7.6900	8.6128	9.6463	10.8038	12.1003	13.5523	15.1786	17.0001	19.0401	21.3249	23.8839	26.7499	29.9599
13%	7.0673	7.9861	9.0243	10.1974	11.5231	13.0211	14.7138	16.6266	18.7881	21.2305	23.9905	27.1093	30.6335	34.6158	39.1159
14%	8.1372	9.2765	10.5752	12.0557	13.7435	15.6676	17.8610	20.3616	23.2122	26.4619	30.1666	34.3899	39.2045	44.6931	50.9502
15%	9.3576	10.7613	12.3755	14.2318	16.3665	18.8215	21.6447	24.8915	28.6252	32.9190	37.8568	43.5353	50.0656	57.5755	66.2118
16%	10.7480	12.4677	14.4625	16.7765	19.4608	22.5745	26.1864	30.3762	35.2364	40.8742	47.4141	55.0004	63.8004	74.0085	85.8499
17%	12.3303	14.4265	16.8790	19.7484	23.1056	27.0336	31.6293	37.0062	43.2973	50.6578	59.2697	69.3455	81.1342	94.9271	111.0647
18%	14.1290	16.6722	19.6733	23.2144	27.3930	32.3238	38.1421	45.0076	53.1090	62.6686	73.9490	87.2598	102.9666	121.5005	143.3706
19%	16.1715	19.2441	22.9005	27.2516	32.4294	38.5910	45.9233	54.6487	65.0320	77.3881	92.0918	109.5893	130.4112	155.1893	184.6753
20%	18.4884	22.1861	26.6233	31.9480	38.3376	46.0051	55.2061	66.2474	79.4968	95.3962	114.4755	137.3706	164.8447	197.8136	237.3763

(continued on next page)

Future Value of a Lump Sum Table (FVF)
$$FV = PV(FVF) = PV(1 + i)^n \text{ (Continued)}$$

Interest rates

Number of periods

	31	32	33	34	35	36	37	38	39	40	41	42	43	44	45
1%	1.3613	1.3749	1.3887	1.4026	1.4166	1.4308	1.4451	1.4595	1.4741	1.4889	1.5038	1.5188	1.5340	1.5493	1.5648
2%	1.8476	1.8845	1.9222	1.9607	1.9999	2.0399	2.0807	2.1223	2.1647	2.2080	2.2522	2.2972	2.3432	2.3901	2.4379
3%	2.5001	2.5751	2.6523	2.7319	2.8139	2.8983	2.9852	3.0748	3.1670	3.2620	3.3599	3.4607	3.5645	3.6715	3.7816
4%	3.3731	3.5081	3.6484	3.7943	3.9461	4.1039	4.2681	4.4388	4.6164	4.8010	4.9931	5.1928	5.4005	5.6165	5.8412
5%	4.5380	4.7649	5.0032	5.2533	5.5160	5.7918	6.0814	6.3855	6.7048	7.0400	7.3920	7.7616	8.1497	8.5572	8.9850
6%	6.0881	6.4534	6.8406	7.2510	7.6861	8.1473	8.6361	9.1543	9.7035	10.2857	10.9029	11.5570	12.2505	12.9855	13.7646
7%	8.1451	8.7153	9.3253	9.9781	10.6766	11.4239	12.2236	13.0793	13.9948	14.9745	16.0227	17.1443	18.3444	19.6285	21.0025
8%	10.8677	11.7371	12.6760	13.6901	14.7853	15.9682	17.2456	18.6253	20.1153	21.7245	23.4625	25.3395	27.3666	29.5560	31.9204
9%	14.4618	15.7633	17.1820	18.7284	20.4140	22.2512	24.2538	26.4367	28.8160	31.4094	34.2363	37.3175	40.6761	44.3370	48.3273
10%	19.1943	21.1138	23.2252	25.5477	28.1024	30.9127	34.0039	37.4043	41.1448	45.2593	49.7852	54.7637	60.2401	66.2641	72.8905
11%	25.4104	28.2056	31.3082	34.7521	38.5749	42.8181	47.5281	52.7562	58.5593	65.0009	72.1510	80.0876	88.8972	98.6759	109.5302
12%	33.5551	37.5817	42.0915	47.1425	52.7996	59.1356	66.2318	74.1797	83.0812	93.0510	104.2171	116.7231	130.7299	146.4175	163.9876
13%	44.2010	49.9471	56.4402	63.7774	72.0685	81.4374	92.0243	103.9874	117.5058	132.7816	150.0432	169.5488	191.5901	216.4968	244.6414
14%	58.0832	66.2148	75.4849	86.0528	98.1002	111.8342	127.4910	145.3397	165.6873	188.8835	215.3272	245.4730	279.8392	319.0167	363.6791
15%	76.1435	87.5651	100.6998	115.8048	133.1755	153.1519	176.1246	202.5433	232.9248	267.8635	308.0431	354.2495	407.3870	468.4950	538.7693
16%	99.5859	115.5196	134.0027	155.4432	180.3141	209.1643	242.6306	281.4515	326.4838	378.7212	439.3165	509.6072	591.1443	685.7274	795.4438
17%	129.9456	152.0364	177.8826	208.1226	243.5035	284.8991	333.3319	389.9983	456.2980	533.8687	624.6264	730.8129	855.0511	1000.4098	1170.4794
18%	169.1774	199.6293	235.5625	277.9638	327.9973	387.0368	456.7034	538.9100	635.9139	750.3783	885.4464	1044.8268	1232.8956	1454.8168	1716.6839
19%	219.7636	261.5187	311.2073	370.3366	440.7006	524.4337	624.0761	742.6506	883.7542	1051.6675	1251.4843	1489.2664	1772.2270	2108.9501	2509.6506
20%	284.8516	341.8219	410.1863	492.2235	590.6682	708.8019	850.5622	1020.6747	1224.8096	1469.7716	1763.7259	2116.4711	2539.7653	3047.7183	3657.2620

Future Value of a Lump Sum Table (FVF)

$FV = PV(FVF) = PV(1 + i)^n$ (Continued)

Number of periods

Interest rate	46	47	48	49	50	51	52	53	54	55	56	57	58	59	60
1%	1.5805	1.5963	1.6122	1.6283	1.6446	1.6611	1.6777	1.6945	1.7114	1.7285	1.7458	1.7633	1.7809	1.7987	1.8167
2%	2.4866	2.5363	2.5871	2.6388	2.6916	2.7454	2.8003	2.8563	2.9135	2.9717	3.0312	3.0918	3.1536	3.2167	3.2810
3%	3.8950	4.0119	4.1323	4.2562	4.3839	4.5154	4.6509	4.7904	4.9341	5.0821	5.2346	5.3917	5.5534	5.7200	5.8916
4%	6.0748	6.3178	6.5705	6.8333	7.1067	7.3910	7.6866	7.9941	8.3138	8.6464	8.9922	9.3519	9.7260	10.1150	10.5196
5%	9.4343	9.9060	10.4013	10.9213	11.4674	12.0408	12.6428	13.2749	13.9387	14.6356	15.3674	16.1358	16.9426	17.7897	18.6792
6%	14.5905	15.4659	16.3939	17.3775	18.4202	19.5254	20.6969	21.9387	23.2550	24.6503	26.1293	27.6971	29.3589	31.1205	32.9877
7%	22.4726	24.0457	25.7289	27.5299	29.4570	31.5190	33.7253	36.0861	38.6122	41.3150	44.2071	47.3015	50.6127	54.1555	57.9464
8%	34.4741	37.2320	40.2106	43.4274	46.9016	50.6537	54.7060	59.0825	63.8091	68.9139	74.4270	80.3811	86.8116	93.7565	101.2571
9%	52.6767	57.4176	62.5852	68.2179	74.3575	81.0497	88.3442	96.2951	104.9617	114.4083	124.7050	135.9285	148.1620	161.4966	176.0313
10%	80.1795	88.1975	97.0172	106.7190	117.3909	129.1299	142.0429	156.2472	171.8719	189.0591	207.9651	228.7616	251.6377	276.8015	304.4816
11%	121.5786	134.9522	149.7970	166.2746	184.5648	204.8670	227.4023	252.4166	280.1824	311.0025	345.2127	383.1861	425.3366	472.1236	524.0572
12%	183.6661	205.7061	230.3908	258.0377	289.0022	323.6825	362.5243	406.0273	454.7505	509.3206	570.4391	638.8918	715.5588	801.4258	897.5969
13%	276.4448	312.3826	352.9923	398.8813	450.7359	509.3316	575.5447	650.3655	734.9130	830.4517	938.4104	1060.4038	1198.2563	1354.0296	1530.0535
14%	414.5941	472.6373	538.8065	614.2395	700.2330	798.2656	910.0228	1037.4260	1182.6656	1348.2388	1536.9922	1752.1712	1997.4751	2277.1216	2595.9187
15%	619.5847	712.5224	819.4007	942.3108	1083.6574	1246.2061	1433.1370	1648.1075	1895.3236	2179.6222	2506.5655	2882.5503	3314.9329	3812.1728	4383.9987
16%	922.7148	1070.3492	1241.6051	1440.2619	1670.7038	1938.0164	2248.0990	2607.7949	3025.0421	3509.0488	4070.4966	4721.7761	5477.2602	6353.6219	7370.2014
17%	1369.4609	1602.2693	1874.6550	2193.3464	2566.2153	3002.4719	3512.8921	4110.0838	4808.7980	5626.2937	6582.7636	7701.8334	9011.1451	10543.0397	12335.3565
18%	2025.6870	2390.3106	2820.5665	3328.2685	3927.3569	4634.2811	5468.4517	6452.7730	7614.2721	8984.8411	10602.1125	12510.4928	14762.3815	17419.6101	20555.1400
19%	2986.4842	3553.9162	4229.1603	5032.7008	5988.9139	7126.8075	8480.9010	10092.2722	12009.8039	14291.6666	17007.0833	20238.4291	24083.7306	28659.6394	34104.9709
20%	4388.7144	5266.4573	6319.7487	7583.6985	9100.4382	10920.5258	13104.6309	15725.5571	18870.6685	22644.8023	27173.7627	32608.5153	39130.2183	46956.2620	56347.5144

Present Value of a Lump Sum Table (PVF)

$$PV = FV(PVF) = FV\left(\frac{1}{(1+i)^n}\right)$$

Number of periods

Interest rate	1	2	3	4	5	6	7	8	9	10	11	12	13	14	15
1%	0.9901	0.9803	0.9706	0.9610	0.9515	0.9420	0.9327	0.9235	0.9143	0.9053	0.8963	0.8874	0.8787	0.8700	0.8613
2%	0.9804	0.9612	0.9423	0.9238	0.9057	0.8880	0.8706	0.8535	0.8368	0.8203	0.8043	0.7885	0.7730	0.7579	0.7430
3%	0.9709	0.9426	0.9151	0.8885	0.8626	0.8375	0.8131	0.7894	0.7664	0.7441	0.7224	0.7014	0.6810	0.6611	0.6419
4%	0.9615	0.9246	0.8890	0.8548	0.8219	0.7903	0.7599	0.7307	0.7026	0.6756	0.6496	0.6246	0.6006	0.5775	0.5553
5%	0.9524	0.9070	0.8638	0.8227	0.7835	0.7462	0.7107	0.6768	0.6446	0.6139	0.5847	0.5568	0.5303	0.5051	0.4810
6%	0.9434	0.8900	0.8396	0.7921	0.7473	0.7050	0.6651	0.6274	0.5919	0.5584	0.5268	0.4970	0.4688	0.4423	0.4173
7%	0.9346	0.8734	0.8163	0.7629	0.7130	0.6663	0.6227	0.5820	0.5439	0.5083	0.4751	0.4440	0.4150	0.3878	0.3624
8%	0.9259	0.8573	0.7938	0.7350	0.6806	0.6302	0.5835	0.5403	0.5002	0.4632	0.4289	0.3971	0.3677	0.3405	0.3152
9%	0.9174	0.8417	0.7722	0.7084	0.6499	0.5963	0.5470	0.5019	0.4604	0.4224	0.3875	0.3555	0.3262	0.2992	0.2745
10%	0.9091	0.8264	0.7513	0.6830	0.6209	0.5645	0.5132	0.4665	0.4241	0.3855	0.3505	0.3186	0.2897	0.2633	0.2394
11%	0.9009	0.8116	0.7312	0.6587	0.5935	0.5346	0.4817	0.4339	0.3909	0.3522	0.3173	0.2858	0.2575	0.2320	0.2090
12%	0.8929	0.7972	0.7118	0.6355	0.5674	0.5066	0.4523	0.4039	0.3606	0.3220	0.2875	0.2567	0.2292	0.2046	0.1827
13%	0.8850	0.7831	0.6931	0.6133	0.5428	0.4803	0.4251	0.3762	0.3329	0.2946	0.2607	0.2307	0.2042	0.1807	0.1599
14%	0.8772	0.7695	0.6750	0.5921	0.5194	0.4556	0.3996	0.3506	0.3075	0.2697	0.2366	0.2076	0.1821	0.1597	0.1401
15%	0.8696	0.7561	0.6575	0.5718	0.4972	0.4323	0.3759	0.3269	0.2843	0.2472	0.2149	0.1869	0.1625	0.1413	0.1229
16%	0.8621	0.7432	0.6407	0.5523	0.4761	0.4104	0.3538	0.3050	0.2630	0.2267	0.1954	0.1685	0.1452	0.1252	0.1079
17%	0.8547	0.7305	0.6244	0.5337	0.4561	0.3898	0.3332	0.2848	0.2434	0.2080	0.1778	0.1520	0.1299	0.1110	0.0949
18%	0.8475	0.7182	0.6086	0.5158	0.4371	0.3704	0.3139	0.2660	0.2255	0.1911	0.1619	0.1372	0.1163	0.0985	0.0835
19%	0.8403	0.7062	0.5934	0.4987	0.4190	0.3521	0.2959	0.2487	0.2090	0.1756	0.1476	0.1240	0.1042	0.0876	0.0736
20%	0.8333	0.6944	0.5787	0.4823	0.4019	0.3349	0.2791	0.2326	0.1938	0.1615	0.1346	0.1122	0.0935	0.0779	0.0649

Present Value of a Lump Sum Table (PVF)

$$PV = FV(PVF) = FV\left(\frac{1}{(1+i)^n}\right)$$ (Continued)

Number of periods

Interest rate	16	17	18	19	20	21	22	23	24	25	26	27	28	29	30
1%	0.8528	0.8444	0.8360	0.8277	0.8195	0.8114	0.8034	0.7954	0.7876	0.7798	0.7720	0.7644	0.7568	0.7493	0.7419
2%	0.7284	0.7142	0.7002	0.6864	0.6730	0.6598	0.6468	0.6342	0.6217	0.6095	0.5976	0.5859	0.5744	0.5631	0.5521
3%	0.6232	0.6050	0.5874	0.5703	0.5537	0.5375	0.5219	0.5067	0.4919	0.4776	0.4637	0.4502	0.4371	0.4243	0.4120
4%	0.5339	0.5134	0.4936	0.4746	0.4564	0.4388	0.4220	0.4057	0.3901	0.3751	0.3607	0.3468	0.3335	0.3207	0.3083
5%	0.4581	0.4363	0.4155	0.3957	0.3769	0.3589	0.3418	0.3256	0.3101	0.2953	0.2812	0.2678	0.2551	0.2429	0.2314
6%	0.3936	0.3714	0.3503	0.3305	0.3118	0.2942	0.2775	0.2618	0.2470	0.2330	0.2198	0.2074	0.1956	0.1846	0.1741
7%	0.3387	0.3166	0.2959	0.2765	0.2584	0.2415	0.2257	0.2109	0.1971	0.1842	0.1722	0.1609	0.1504	0.1406	0.1314
8%	0.2919	0.2703	0.2502	0.2317	0.2145	0.1987	0.1839	0.1703	0.1577	0.1460	0.1352	0.1252	0.1159	0.1073	0.0994
9%	0.2519	0.2311	0.2120	0.1945	0.1784	0.1637	0.1502	0.1378	0.1264	0.1160	0.1064	0.0976	0.0895	0.0822	0.0754
10%	0.2176	0.1978	0.1799	0.1635	0.1486	0.1351	0.1228	0.1117	0.1015	0.0923	0.0839	0.0763	0.0693	0.0630	0.0573
11%	0.1883	0.1696	0.1528	0.1377	0.1240	0.1117	0.1007	0.0907	0.0817	0.0736	0.0663	0.0597	0.0538	0.0485	0.0437
12%	0.1631	0.1456	0.1300	0.1161	0.1037	0.0926	0.0826	0.0738	0.0659	0.0588	0.0525	0.0469	0.0419	0.0374	0.0334
13%	0.1415	0.1252	0.1108	0.0981	0.0868	0.0768	0.0680	0.0601	0.0532	0.0471	0.0417	0.0369	0.0326	0.0289	0.0256
14%	0.1229	0.1078	0.0946	0.0829	0.0728	0.0638	0.0560	0.0491	0.0431	0.0378	0.0331	0.0291	0.0255	0.0224	0.0196
15%	0.1069	0.0929	0.0808	0.0703	0.0611	0.0531	0.0462	0.0402	0.0349	0.0304	0.0264	0.0230	0.0200	0.0174	0.0151
16%	0.0930	0.0802	0.0691	0.0596	0.0514	0.0443	0.0382	0.0329	0.0284	0.0245	0.0211	0.0182	0.0157	0.0135	0.0116
17%	0.0811	0.0693	0.0592	0.0506	0.0433	0.0370	0.0316	0.0270	0.0231	0.0197	0.0169	0.0144	0.0123	0.0105	0.0090
18%	0.0708	0.0600	0.0508	0.0431	0.0365	0.0309	0.0262	0.0222	0.0188	0.0160	0.0135	0.0115	0.0097	0.0082	0.0070
19%	0.0618	0.0520	0.0437	0.0367	0.0308	0.0259	0.0218	0.0183	0.0154	0.0129	0.0109	0.0091	0.0077	0.0064	0.0054
20%	0.0541	0.0451	0.0376	0.0313	0.0261	0.0217	0.0181	0.0151	0.0126	0.0105	0.0087	0.0073	0.0061	0.0051	0.0042

(continued on next page)

Present Value of a Lump Sum Table (PVF)

$$PV = FV(PVF) = FV\left(\frac{1}{(1+i)^n}\right) \quad \text{(Continued)}$$

Number of periods

Interest rate	31	32	33	34	35	36	37	38	39	40	41	42	43	44	45
1%	0.7346	0.7273	0.7201	0.7130	0.7059	0.6989	0.6920	0.6852	0.6784	0.6717	0.6650	0.6584	0.6519	0.6454	0.6391
2%	0.5412	0.5306	0.5202	0.5100	0.5000	0.4902	0.4806	0.4712	0.4619	0.4529	0.4440	0.4353	0.4268	0.4184	0.4102
3%	0.4000	0.3883	0.3770	0.3660	0.3554	0.3450	0.3350	0.3252	0.3158	0.3066	0.2976	0.2890	0.2805	0.2724	0.2644
4%	0.2965	0.2851	0.2741	0.2636	0.2534	0.2437	0.2343	0.2253	0.2166	0.2083	0.2003	0.1926	0.1852	0.1780	0.1712
5%	0.2204	0.2099	0.1999	0.1904	0.1813	0.1727	0.1644	0.1566	0.1491	0.1420	0.1353	0.1288	0.1227	0.1169	0.1113
6%	0.1643	0.1550	0.1462	0.1379	0.1301	0.1227	0.1158	0.1092	0.1031	0.0972	0.0917	0.0865	0.0816	0.0770	0.0727
7%	0.1228	0.1147	0.1072	0.1002	0.0937	0.0875	0.0818	0.0765	0.0715	0.0668	0.0624	0.0583	0.0545	0.0509	0.0476
8%	0.0920	0.0852	0.0789	0.0730	0.0676	0.0626	0.0580	0.0537	0.0497	0.0460	0.0426	0.0395	0.0365	0.0338	0.0313
9%	0.0691	0.0634	0.0582	0.0534	0.0490	0.0449	0.0412	0.0378	0.0347	0.0318	0.0292	0.0268	0.0246	0.0226	0.0207
10%	0.0521	0.0474	0.0431	0.0391	0.0356	0.0323	0.0294	0.0267	0.0243	0.0221	0.0201	0.0183	0.0166	0.0151	0.0137
11%	0.0394	0.0355	0.0319	0.0288	0.0259	0.0234	0.0210	0.0190	0.0171	0.0154	0.0139	0.0125	0.0112	0.0101	0.0091
12%	0.0298	0.0266	0.0238	0.0212	0.0189	0.0169	0.0151	0.0135	0.0120	0.0107	0.0096	0.0086	0.0076	0.0068	0.0061
13%	0.0226	0.0200	0.0177	0.0157	0.0139	0.0123	0.0109	0.0096	0.0085	0.0075	0.0067	0.0059	0.0052	0.0046	0.0041
14%	0.0172	0.0151	0.0132	0.0116	0.0102	0.0089	0.0078	0.0069	0.0060	0.0053	0.0046	0.0041	0.0036	0.0031	0.0027
15%	0.0131	0.0114	0.0099	0.0086	0.0075	0.0065	0.0057	0.0049	0.0043	0.0037	0.0032	0.0028	0.0025	0.0021	0.0019
16%	0.0100	0.0087	0.0075	0.0064	0.0055	0.0048	0.0041	0.0036	0.0031	0.0026	0.0023	0.0020	0.0017	0.0015	0.0013
17%	0.0077	0.0066	0.0056	0.0048	0.0041	0.0035	0.0030	0.0026	0.0022	0.0019	0.0016	0.0014	0.0012	0.0010	0.0009
18%	0.0059	0.0050	0.0042	0.0036	0.0030	0.0026	0.0022	0.0019	0.0016	0.0013	0.0011	0.0010	0.0008	0.0007	0.0006
19%	0.0046	0.0038	0.0032	0.0027	0.0023	0.0019	0.0016	0.0013	0.0011	0.0010	0.0008	0.0007	0.0006	0.0005	0.0004
20%	0.0035	0.0029	0.0024	0.0020	0.0017	0.0014	0.0012	0.0010	0.0008	0.0007	0.0006	0.0005	0.0004	0.0003	0.0003

Present Value of a Lump Sum Table (PVF)

$$PV = FV(PVF) = FV\left(\frac{1}{(1+i)^n}\right) \quad \text{(Continued)}$$

Number of periods

Interest rate per period	46	47	48	49	50	51	52	53	54	55	56	57	58	59	60
1%	0.6327	0.6265	0.6203	0.6141	0.6080	0.6020	0.5961	0.5902	0.5843	0.5785	0.5728	0.5671	0.5615	0.5560	0.5504
2%	0.4022	0.3943	0.3865	0.3790	0.3715	0.3642	0.3571	0.3501	0.3432	0.3365	0.3299	0.3234	0.3171	0.3109	0.3048
3%	0.2567	0.2493	0.2420	0.2350	0.2281	0.2215	0.2150	0.2088	0.2027	0.1968	0.1910	0.1855	0.1801	0.1748	0.1697
4%	0.1646	0.1583	0.1522	0.1463	0.1407	0.1353	0.1301	0.1251	0.1203	0.1157	0.1112	0.1069	0.1028	0.0989	0.0951
5%	0.1060	0.1009	0.0961	0.0916	0.0872	0.0831	0.0791	0.0753	0.0717	0.0683	0.0651	0.0620	0.0590	0.0562	0.0535
6%	0.0685	0.0647	0.0610	0.0575	0.0543	0.0512	0.0483	0.0456	0.0430	0.0406	0.0383	0.0361	0.0341	0.0321	0.0303
7%	0.0445	0.0416	0.0389	0.0363	0.0339	0.0317	0.0297	0.0277	0.0259	0.0242	0.0226	0.0211	0.0198	0.0185	0.0173
8%	0.0290	0.0269	0.0249	0.0230	0.0213	0.0197	0.0183	0.0169	0.0157	0.0145	0.0134	0.0124	0.0115	0.0107	0.0099
9%	0.0190	0.0174	0.0160	0.0147	0.0134	0.0123	0.0113	0.0104	0.0095	0.0087	0.0080	0.0074	0.0067	0.0062	0.0057
10%	0.0125	0.0113	0.0103	0.0094	0.0085	0.0077	0.0070	0.0064	0.0058	0.0053	0.0048	0.0044	0.0040	0.0036	0.0033
11%	0.0082	0.0074	0.0067	0.0060	0.0054	0.0049	0.0044	0.0040	0.0036	0.0032	0.0029	0.0026	0.0024	0.0021	0.0019
12%	0.0054	0.0049	0.0043	0.0039	0.0035	0.0031	0.0028	0.0025	0.0022	0.0020	0.0018	0.0016	0.0014	0.0012	0.0011
13%	0.0036	0.0032	0.0028	0.0025	0.0022	0.0020	0.0017	0.0015	0.0014	0.0012	0.0011	0.0009	0.0008	0.0007	0.0007
14%	0.0024	0.0021	0.0019	0.0016	0.0014	0.0013	0.0011	0.0010	0.0008	0.0007	0.0007	0.0006	0.0005	0.0004	0.0004
15%	0.0016	0.0014	0.0012	0.0011	0.0009	0.0008	0.0007	0.0006	0.0005	0.0005	0.0004	0.0003	0.0003	0.0003	0.0002
16%	0.0011	0.0009	0.0008	0.0007	0.0006	0.0005	0.0004	0.0004	0.0003	0.0003	0.0002	0.0002	0.0002	0.0002	0.0001
17%	0.0007	0.0006	0.0005	0.0005	0.0004	0.0003	0.0003	0.0002	0.0002	0.0002	0.0002	0.0001	0.0001	0.0001	0.0001
18%	0.0005	0.0004	0.0004	0.0003	0.0003	0.0002	0.0002	0.0001	0.0001	0.0001	0.0001	0.0001	0.0001	0.0001	0.0000
19%	0.0003	0.0003	0.0002	0.0002	0.0002	0.0001	0.0001	0.0001	0.0001	0.0001	0.0001	0.0000	0.0000	0.0000	0.0000
20%	0.0002	0.0002	0.0002	0.0001	0.0001	0.0001	0.0001	0.0001	0.0001	0.0000	0.0000	0.0000	0.0000	0.0000	0.0000

Future Value of Ordinary Annuity Table (FVAF)

$$FVOA = A(FVAF) = A\left[\frac{(1+i)^n - 1}{i}\right]$$

Number of periods

Interest rate	1	2	3	4	5	6	7	8	9	10	11	12	13	14	15
1%	1.0000	2.0100	3.0301	4.0604	5.1010	6.1520	7.2135	8.2857	9.3685	10.4622	11.5668	12.6825	13.8093	14.9474	16.0969
2%	1.0000	2.0200	3.0604	4.1216	5.2040	6.3081	7.4343	8.5830	9.7546	10.9497	12.1687	13.4121	14.6803	15.9739	17.2934
3%	1.0000	2.0300	3.0909	4.1836	5.3091	6.4684	7.6625	8.8923	10.1591	11.4639	12.8078	14.1920	15.6178	17.0863	18.5989
4%	1.0000	2.0400	3.1216	4.2465	5.4163	6.6330	7.8983	9.2142	10.5828	12.0061	13.4864	15.0258	16.6268	18.2919	20.0236
5%	1.0000	2.0500	3.1525	4.3101	5.5256	6.8019	8.1420	9.5491	11.0266	12.5779	14.2068	15.9171	17.7130	19.5986	21.5786
6%	1.0000	2.0600	3.1836	4.3746	5.6371	6.9753	8.3938	9.8975	11.4913	13.1808	14.9716	16.8699	18.8821	21.0151	23.2760
7%	1.0000	2.0700	3.2149	4.4399	5.7507	7.1533	8.6540	10.2598	11.9780	13.8164	15.7836	17.8885	20.1406	22.5505	25.1290
8%	1.0000	2.0800	3.2464	4.5061	5.8666	7.3359	8.9228	10.6366	12.4876	14.4866	16.6455	18.9771	21.4953	24.2149	27.1521
9%	1.0000	2.0900	3.2781	4.5731	5.9847	7.5233	9.2004	11.0285	13.0210	15.1929	17.5603	20.1407	22.9534	26.0192	29.3609
10%	1.0000	2.1000	3.3100	4.6410	6.1051	7.7156	9.4872	11.4359	13.5795	15.9374	18.5312	21.3843	24.5227	27.9750	31.7725
11%	1.0000	2.1100	3.3421	4.7097	6.2278	7.9129	9.7833	11.8594	14.1640	16.7220	19.5614	22.7132	26.2116	30.0949	34.4054
12%	1.0000	2.1200	3.3744	4.7793	6.3528	8.1152	10.0890	12.2997	14.7757	17.5487	20.6546	24.1331	28.0291	32.3926	37.2797
13%	1.0000	2.1300	3.4069	4.8498	6.4803	8.3227	10.4047	12.7573	15.4157	18.4197	21.8143	25.6502	29.9847	34.8827	40.4175
14%	1.0000	2.1400	3.4396	4.9211	6.6101	8.5355	10.7305	13.2328	16.0853	19.3373	23.0445	27.2707	32.0887	37.5811	43.8424
15%	1.0000	2.1500	3.4725	4.9934	6.7424	8.7537	11.0668	13.7268	16.7858	20.3037	24.3493	29.0017	34.3519	40.5047	47.5804
16%	1.0000	2.1600	3.5056	5.0665	6.8771	8.9775	11.4139	14.2401	17.5185	21.3215	25.7329	30.8502	36.7862	43.6720	51.6595
17%	1.0000	2.1700	3.5389	5.1405	7.0144	9.2068	11.7720	14.7733	18.2847	22.3931	27.1999	32.8239	39.4040	47.1027	56.1101
18%	1.0000	2.1800	3.5724	5.2154	7.1542	9.4420	12.1415	15.3270	19.0859	23.5213	28.7551	34.9311	42.2187	50.8180	60.9653
19%	1.0000	2.1900	3.6061	5.2913	7.2966	9.6830	12.5227	15.9020	19.9234	24.7089	30.4035	37.1802	45.2445	54.8409	66.2607
20%	1.0000	2.2000	3.6400	5.3680	7.4416	9.9299	12.9159	16.4991	20.7989	25.9587	32.1504	39.5805	48.4966	59.1959	72.0351

Future Value of Ordinary Annuity Table (FVAF)

$$FVOA = A(FVAF) = A\left[\frac{(1+i)^n - 1}{i}\right] \quad (Continued)$$

Interest rates

	Number of periods														
	16	17	18	19	20	21	22	23	24	25	26	27	28	29	30
1%	17.2579	18.4304	19.6147	20.8109	22.0190	23.2392	24.4716	25.7163	26.9735	28.2432	29.5256	30.8209	32.1291	33.4504	34.7849
2%	18.6393	20.0121	21.4123	22.8406	24.2974	25.7833	27.2990	28.8450	30.4219	32.0303	33.6709	35.3443	37.0512	38.7922	40.5681
3%	20.1569	21.7616	23.4144	25.1169	26.8704	28.6765	30.5368	32.4529	34.4265	36.4593	38.5530	40.7096	42.9309	45.2189	47.5754
4%	21.8245	23.6975	25.6454	27.6712	29.7781	31.9692	34.2480	36.6179	39.0826	41.6459	44.3117	47.0842	49.9676	52.9663	56.0849
5%	23.6575	25.8404	28.1324	30.5390	33.0660	35.7193	38.5052	41.4305	44.5020	47.7271	51.1135	54.6691	58.4026	62.3227	66.4388
6%	25.6725	28.2129	30.9057	33.7600	36.7856	39.9927	43.3923	46.9958	50.8156	54.8645	59.1564	63.7058	68.5281	73.6398	79.0582
7%	27.8881	30.8402	33.9990	37.3790	40.9955	44.8652	49.0057	53.4361	58.1767	63.2490	68.6765	74.4838	80.6977	87.3465	94.4608
8%	30.3243	33.7502	37.4502	41.4463	45.7620	50.4229	55.4568	60.8933	66.7648	73.1059	79.9544	87.3508	95.3388	103.9659	113.2832
9%	33.0034	36.9737	41.3013	46.0185	51.1601	56.7645	62.8733	69.5319	76.7898	84.7009	93.3240	102.7231	112.9682	124.1354	136.3075
10%	35.9497	40.5447	45.5992	51.1591	57.2750	64.0025	71.4027	79.5430	88.4973	98.3471	109.1818	121.0999	134.2099	148.6309	164.4940
11%	39.1899	44.5008	50.3959	56.9395	64.2028	72.2651	81.2143	91.1479	102.1742	114.4133	127.9988	143.0786	159.8173	178.3972	199.0209
12%	42.7533	48.8837	55.7497	63.4397	72.0524	81.6987	92.5026	104.6029	118.1552	133.3339	150.3339	169.3740	190.6989	214.5828	241.3327
13%	46.6717	53.7391	61.7251	70.7494	80.9468	92.4699	105.4910	120.2048	136.8315	155.6196	176.8501	200.8406	227.9499	258.5834	293.1992
14%	50.9804	59.1176	68.3941	78.9692	91.0249	104.7684	120.4360	138.2970	158.6586	181.8708	208.3327	238.4993	272.8892	312.0937	356.7868
15%	55.7175	65.0751	75.8364	88.2118	102.4436	118.8101	137.6316	159.2764	184.1678	212.7930	245.7120	283.5688	327.1041	377.1697	434.7451
16%	60.9250	71.6730	84.1407	98.6032	115.3797	134.8405	157.4150	183.6014	213.9776	249.2140	290.0883	337.5024	392.5028	456.3032	530.3117
17%	66.6488	78.9792	93.4056	110.2846	130.0329	153.1385	180.1721	211.8013	248.8076	292.1049	342.7627	402.0323	471.3778	552.5121	647.4391
18%	72.9390	87.0680	103.7403	123.4135	146.6280	174.0210	206.3448	244.4868	289.4945	342.6035	405.2721	479.2211	566.4809	669.4475	790.9480
19%	79.8502	96.0218	115.2659	138.1664	165.4180	197.8474	236.4385	282.3618	337.0105	402.0425	479.4306	571.5224	681.1116	811.5228	966.7122
20%	87.4421	105.9306	128.1167	154.7400	186.6880	225.0256	271.0307	326.2369	392.4842	471.9811	567.3773	681.8528	819.2233	984.0680	1,181.8816

(continued on next page)

Future Value of Ordinary Annuity Table (FVAF)

$$FVOA = A(FVAF) = A\left[\frac{(1+i)^n - 1}{i}\right] \quad \text{(Continued)}$$

Number of periods

Interest rate period	31	32	33	34	35	36	37	38	39	40	41	42	43	44	45
1%	36.1327	37.4941	38.8690	40.2577	41.6603	43.0769	44.5076	45.9527	47.4123	48.8864	50.3752	51.8790	53.3978	54.9318	56.4811
2%	42.3794	44.2270	46.1116	48.0338	49.9945	51.9944	54.0343	56.1149	58.2372	60.4020	62.6100	64.8622	67.1595	69.5027	71.8927
3%	50.0027	52.5028	55.0778	57.7302	60.4621	63.2759	66.1742	69.1594	72.2342	75.4013	78.6633	82.0232	85.4839	89.0484	92.7199
4%	59.3283	62.7015	66.2095	69.8579	73.6522	77.5983	81.7022	85.9703	90.4091	95.0255	99.8265	104.8196	110.0124	115.4129	121.0294
5%	70.7608	75.2988	80.0638	85.0670	90.3203	95.8363	101.6281	107.7095	114.0950	120.7998	127.8398	135.2318	142.9933	151.1430	159.7002
6%	84.8017	90.8898	97.3432	104.1838	111.4348	119.1209	127.2681	135.9042	145.0585	154.7620	165.0477	175.9505	187.5076	199.7580	212.7435
7%	102.0730	110.2182	118.9334	128.2588	138.2369	148.9135	160.3374	172.5610	185.6403	199.6351	214.6096	230.6322	247.7765	266.1209	285.7493
8%	123.3459	134.2135	145.9506	158.6267	172.3168	187.1021	203.0703	220.3159	238.9412	259.0565	280.7810	304.2435	329.5830	356.9496	386.5056
9%	149.5752	164.0370	179.8003	196.9823	215.7108	236.1247	258.3759	282.6298	309.0665	337.8824	369.2919	403.5281	440.8457	481.5218	525.8587
10%	181.9434	201.1378	222.2515	245.4767	271.0244	299.1268	330.0395	364.0434	401.4478	442.5926	487.8518	537.6370	592.4007	652.6408	718.9048
11%	221.9132	247.3236	275.5292	306.8374	341.5896	380.1644	422.9825	470.5106	523.2667	581.8261	646.8269	718.9779	799.0655	887.9627	986.6386
12%	271.2926	304.8477	342.4294	384.5210	431.6635	484.4631	543.5987	609.8305	684.0102	767.0914	860.1424	964.3595	1,081.0826	1,211.8125	1,358.2300
13%	332.3151	376.5161	426.4632	482.9034	546.6808	618.7493	700.1867	792.2110	896.1984	1,013.7042	1,146.4858	1,296.5289	1,466.0777	1,657.6678	1,874.1646
14%	407.7370	465.8202	532.0350	607.5199	693.5727	791.6729	903.5071	1,030.9981	1,176.3378	1,342.0251	1,530.9086	1,746.2358	1,991.7088	2,271.5481	2,590.5648
15%	500.9569	577.1005	664.6655	765.3654	881.1702	1,014.3457	1,167.4975	1,343.6222	1,546.1655	1,779.0903	2,046.9539	2,354.9969	2,709.2465	3,116.6334	3,585.1285
16%	616.1616	715.7475	831.2671	965.2698	1,120.7130	1,301.0270	1,510.1914	1,752.8220	2,034.2735	2,360.7572	2,739.4784	3,178.7949	3,688.4021	4,279.5465	4,965.2739
17%	758.5038	888.4494	1,040.4858	1,218.3684	1,426.4910	1,669.9945	1,954.8936	2,288.2255	2,678.2238	3,134.5218	3,668.3906	4,293.0169	5,023.8298	5,878.8809	6,879.2907
18%	934.3186	1,103.4960	1,303.1253	1,538.6878	1,816.6516	2,144.6489	2,531.6857	2,988.3891	3,527.2992	4,163.2130	4,913.5914	5,799.0378	6,843.8646	8,076.7603	9,531.5771
19%	1,151.3875	1,371.1511	1,632.6698	1,943.8771	2,314.2137	2,754.9143	3,279.3481	3,903.4242	4,646.0748	5,529.8290	6,581.4965	7,832.9808	9,322.2472	11,094.4741	13,203.4242
20%	1,419.2579	1,704.1095	2,045.9314	2,456.1176	2,948.3411	3,539.0094	4,247.8112	5,098.3735	6,119.0482	7,343.8578	8,813.6294	10,577.3553	12,693.8263	15,233.5916	18,281.3099

Future Value of Ordinary Annuity Table (FVAF)

$$FVOA = A(FVAF) = A\left[\frac{(1+i)^n - 1}{i}\right] \quad \text{(Continued)}$$

Number of periods

	46	47	48	49	50	51	52	53	54	55	56	57	58	59	60
1%	58.0459	59.6263	61.2226	62.8348	64.4632	66.1078	67.7689	69.4466	71.1410	72.8525	74.5810	76.3268	78.0901	79.8710	81.6697
2%	74.3306	76.8172	79.3535	81.9406	84.5794	87.2710	90.0164	92.8167	95.6731	98.5865	101.5583	104.5894	107.6812	110.8348	114.0515
3%	96.5015	100.3965	104.4084	108.5406	112.7969	117.1808	121.6962	126.3471	131.1375	136.0716	141.1538	146.3884	151.7800	157.3334	163.0534
4%	126.8706	132.9454	139.2632	145.8337	152.6671	159.7738	167.1647	174.8513	182.8454	191.1592	199.8055	208.7978	218.1497	227.8757	237.9907
5%	168.6852	178.1194	188.0254	198.4267	209.3480	220.8154	232.8562	245.4990	258.7739	272.7126	287.3482	302.7157	318.8514	335.7940	353.5837
6%	226.5081	241.0986	256.5645	272.9584	290.3359	308.7561	328.2814	348.9783	370.9170	394.1720	418.8223	444.9517	472.6488	502.0077	533.1282
7%	306.7518	329.2244	353.2701	378.9990	406.5289	435.9860	467.5050	501.2303	537.3164	575.9286	617.2436	661.4506	708.7522	759.3648	813.5204
8%	418.4261	452.9002	490.1322	530.3427	573.7702	620.6718	671.3255	726.0316	785.1141	848.9232	917.8371	992.2640	1,072.6451	1,159.4568	1,253.2133
9%	574.1860	626.8628	684.2804	746.8656	815.0836	889.4411	970.4908	1,058.8349	1,155.1301	1,260.0918	1,374.5001	1,499.2051	1,635.1335	1,783.2955	1,944.7921
10%	791.7953	871.9749	960.1723	1,057.1896	1,163.9085	1,281.2994	1,410.4293	1,552.4723	1,708.7195	1,880.5914	2,069.6506	2,277.6156	2,506.3772	2,758.0149	3,034.8164
11%	1,096.1688	1,217.7474	1,352.6996	1,502.4965	1,668.7712	1,853.3360	2,058.2029	2,285.6053	2,538.0218	2,818.2042	3,129.2067	3,474.4194	3,857.6056	4,282.9422	4,755.0658
12%	1,522.2176	1,705.8838	1,911.5898	2,141.9806	2,400.0182	2,689.0204	3,012.7029	3,375.2272	3,781.2545	4,236.0050	4,745.3257	5,315.7647	5,954.6565	6,670.2153	7,471.6411
13%	2,118.8060	2,395.2508	2,707.6334	3,060.6258	3,459.5071	3,910.2430	4,419.5746	4,995.1193	5,645.4849	6,380.3979	7,210.8496	8,149.2601	9,209.6639	10,407.9202	11,761.9498
14%	2,954.2439	3,368.8380	3,841.4753	4,380.2819	4,994.5213	5,694.7543	6,493.0199	7,403.0427	8,440.4687	9,623.1343	10,971.3731	12,508.3654	14,260.5365	16,258.0117	18,535.1333
15%	4,123.8977	4,743.4824	5,456.0047	6,275.4055	7,217.7163	8,301.3737	9,547.5798	10,980.7167	12,628.8243	14,524.1479	16,703.7701	19,210.3356	22,092.8859	25,407.8188	29,219.9916
16%	5,760.7177	6,683.4326	7,753.7818	8,995.3869	10,435.6488	12,106.3526	14,044.3690	16,292.4680	18,900.2629	21,925.3050	25,434.3538	29,504.8504	34,226.6264	39,703.8867	46,057.5085
17%	8,049.7701	9,419.2310	11,021.5002	12,896.1553	15,089.5017	17,655.7170	20,658.1888	24,171.0809	28,281.1647	33,089.9627	38,716.2564	45,299.0199	53,000.8533	62,011.9984	72,555.0381
18%	11,248.2610	13,273.9480	15,664.2586	18,484.8251	21,813.0937	25,740.4505	30,374.7316	35,843.1833	42,295.9563	49,910.2284	58,895.0696	69,497.1821	82,007.6749	96,770.0563	114,189.6665
19%	15,713.0748	18,699.5590	22,253.4753	26,482.6356	31,515.3363	37,504.2502	44,631.0578	53,111.9588	63,204.2309	75,214.0348	89,505.7014	106,512.7847	126,751.2137	150,834.9444	179,494.5838
20%	21,938.5719	26,327.2863	31,593.7436	37,913.4923	45,497.1908	54,597.6289	65,518.1547	78,622.7856	94,348.3427	113,219.0113	135,863.8135	163,037.5763	195,646.0915	234,776.3098	281,732.5718

Present Value of Ordinary Annuity Table (PVAF)

$$PVOA = A(PVAF) = A\left[\frac{(1+i)^n - 1}{i(1+i)^n}\right]$$

Interest rate / *Number of periods*

	1	2	3	4	5	6	7	8	9	10	11	12	13	14	15
1%	0.9901	1.9704	2.9410	3.9020	4.8534	5.7955	6.7282	7.6517	8.5660	9.4713	10.3676	11.2551	12.1337	13.0037	13.8651
2%	0.9804	1.9416	2.8839	3.8077	4.7135	5.6014	6.4720	7.3255	8.1622	8.9826	9.7868	10.5753	11.3484	12.1062	12.8493
3%	0.9709	1.9135	2.8286	3.7171	4.5797	5.4172	6.2303	7.0197	7.7861	8.5302	9.2526	9.9540	10.6350	11.2961	11.9379
4%	0.9615	1.8861	2.7751	3.6299	4.4518	5.2421	6.0021	6.7327	7.4353	8.1109	8.7605	9.3851	9.9856	10.5631	11.1184
5%	0.9524	1.8594	2.7232	3.5460	4.3295	5.0757	5.7864	6.4632	7.1078	7.7217	8.3064	8.8633	9.3936	9.8986	10.3797
6%	0.9434	1.8334	2.6730	3.4651	4.2124	4.9173	5.5824	6.2098	6.8017	7.3601	7.8869	8.3838	8.8527	9.2950	9.7122
7%	0.9346	1.8080	2.6243	3.3872	4.1002	4.7665	5.3893	5.9713	6.5152	7.0236	7.4987	7.9427	8.3577	8.7455	9.1079
8%	0.9259	1.7833	2.5771	3.3121	3.9927	4.6229	5.2064	5.7466	6.2469	6.7101	7.1390	7.5361	7.9038	8.2442	8.5595
9%	0.9174	1.7591	2.5313	3.2397	3.8897	4.4859	5.0330	5.5348	5.9952	6.4177	6.8052	7.1607	7.4869	7.7862	8.0607
10%	0.9091	1.7355	2.4869	3.1699	3.7908	4.3553	4.8684	5.3349	5.7590	6.1446	6.4951	6.8137	7.1034	7.3667	7.6061
11%	0.9009	1.7125	2.4437	3.1024	3.6959	4.2305	4.7122	5.1461	5.5370	5.8892	6.2065	6.4924	6.7499	6.9819	7.1909
12%	0.8929	1.6901	2.4018	3.0373	3.6048	4.1114	4.5638	4.9676	5.3282	5.6502	5.9377	6.1944	6.4235	6.6282	6.8109
13%	0.8850	1.6681	2.3612	2.9745	3.5172	3.9975	4.4226	4.7988	5.1317	5.4262	5.6869	5.9176	6.1218	6.3025	6.4624
14%	0.8772	1.6467	2.3216	2.9137	3.4331	3.8887	4.2883	4.6389	4.9464	5.2161	5.4527	5.6603	5.8424	6.0021	6.1422
15%	0.8696	1.6257	2.2832	2.8550	3.3522	3.7845	4.1604	4.4873	4.7716	5.0188	5.2337	5.4206	5.5831	5.7245	5.8474
16%	0.8621	1.6052	2.2459	2.7982	3.2743	3.6847	4.0386	4.3436	4.6065	4.8332	5.0286	5.1971	5.3423	5.4675	5.5755
17%	0.8547	1.5852	2.2096	2.7432	3.1993	3.5892	3.9224	4.2072	4.4506	4.6586	4.8364	4.9884	5.1183	5.2293	5.3242
18%	0.8475	1.5656	2.1743	2.6901	3.1272	3.4976	3.8115	4.0776	4.3030	4.4941	4.6560	4.7932	4.9095	5.0081	5.0916
19%	0.8403	1.5465	2.1399	2.6386	3.0576	3.4098	3.7057	3.9544	4.1633	4.3389	4.4865	4.6105	4.7147	4.8023	4.8759
20%	0.8333	1.5278	2.1065	2.5887	2.9906	3.3255	3.6046	3.8372	4.0310	4.1925	4.3271	4.4392	4.5327	4.6106	4.6755

Present Value of Ordinary Annuity Table (PVAF)

$$PVOA = A(PVAF) = A\left[\frac{(1+i)^n - 1}{i(1+i)^n}\right] \quad \text{(Continued)}$$

Number of periods

Interest rates	16	17	18	19	20	21	22	23	24	25	26	27	28	29	30
1%	14.7179	15.5623	16.3983	17.2260	18.0456	18.8570	19.6604	20.4558	21.2434	22.0232	22.7952	23.5596	24.3164	25.0658	25.8077
2%	13.5777	14.2919	14.9920	15.6785	16.3514	17.0112	17.6580	18.2922	18.9139	19.5235	20.1210	20.7069	21.2813	21.8444	22.3965
3%	12.5611	13.1661	13.7535	14.3238	14.8775	15.4150	15.9369	16.4436	16.9355	17.4131	17.8768	18.3270	18.7641	19.1885	19.6004
4%	11.6523	12.1657	12.6593	13.1339	13.5903	14.0292	14.4511	14.8568	15.2470	15.6221	15.9828	16.3296	16.6631	16.9837	17.2920
5%	10.8378	11.2741	11.6896	12.0853	12.4622	12.8212	13.1630	13.4886	13.7986	14.0939	14.3752	14.6430	14.8981	15.1411	15.3725
6%	10.1059	10.4773	10.8276	11.1581	11.4699	11.7641	12.0416	12.3034	12.5504	12.7834	13.0032	13.2105	13.4062	13.5907	13.7648
7%	9.4466	9.7632	10.0591	10.3356	10.5940	10.8355	11.0612	11.2722	11.4693	11.6536	11.8258	11.9867	12.1371	12.2777	12.4090
8%	8.8514	9.1216	9.3719	9.6036	9.8181	10.0168	10.2007	10.3711	10.5288	10.6748	10.8100	10.9352	11.0511	11.1584	11.2578
9%	8.3126	8.5436	8.7556	8.9501	9.1285	9.2922	9.4424	9.5802	9.7066	9.8226	9.9290	10.0266	10.1161	10.1983	10.2737
10%	7.8237	8.0216	8.2014	8.3649	8.5136	8.6487	8.7715	8.8832	8.9847	9.0770	9.1609	9.2372	9.3066	9.3696	9.4269
11%	7.3792	7.5488	7.7016	7.8393	7.9633	8.0751	8.1757	8.2664	8.3481	8.4217	8.4881	8.5478	8.6016	8.6501	8.6938
12%	6.9740	7.1196	7.2497	7.3658	7.4694	7.5620	7.6446	7.7184	7.7843	7.8431	7.8957	7.9426	7.9844	8.0218	8.0552
13%	6.6039	6.7291	6.8399	6.9380	7.0248	7.1016	7.1695	7.2297	7.2829	7.3300	7.3717	7.4086	7.4412	7.4701	7.4957
14%	6.2651	6.3729	6.4674	6.5504	6.6231	6.6870	6.7429	6.7921	6.8351	6.8729	6.9061	6.9352	6.9607	6.9830	7.0027
15%	5.9542	6.0472	6.1280	6.1982	6.2593	6.3125	6.3587	6.3988	6.4338	6.4641	6.4906	6.5135	6.5335	6.5509	6.5660
16%	5.6685	5.7487	5.8178	5.8775	5.9288	5.9731	6.0113	6.0442	6.0726	6.0971	6.1182	6.1364	6.1520	6.1656	6.1772
17%	5.4053	5.4746	5.5339	5.5845	5.6278	5.6648	5.6964	5.7234	5.7465	5.7662	5.7831	5.7975	5.8099	5.8204	5.8294
18%	5.1624	5.2223	5.2732	5.3162	5.3527	5.3837	5.4099	5.4321	5.4509	5.4669	5.4804	5.4919	5.5016	5.5098	5.5168
19%	4.9377	4.9897	5.0333	5.0700	5.1009	5.1268	5.1486	5.1668	5.1822	5.1951	5.2060	5.2151	5.2228	5.2292	5.2347
20%	4.7296	4.7746	4.8122	4.8435	4.8696	4.8913	4.9094	4.9245	4.9371	4.9476	4.9563	4.9636	4.9697	4.9747	4.9789

(continued on next page)

Present Value of Ordinary Annuity Table (PVAF)

$$PVOA = A(PVAF) = A\left[\frac{(1+i)^n - 1}{i(1+i)^n}\right] \quad \text{(Continued)}$$

Number of periods

Interest rate	31	32	33	34	35	36	37	38	39	40	41	42	43	44	45
1%	26.5423	27.2696	27.9897	28.7027	29.4086	30.1075	30.7995	31.4847	32.1630	32.8347	33.4997	34.1581	34.8100	35.4555	36.0945
2%	22.9377	23.4683	23.9886	24.4986	24.9986	25.4888	25.9695	26.4406	26.9026	27.3555	27.7995	28.2348	28.6616	29.0800	29.4902
3%	20.0004	20.3888	20.7658	21.1318	21.4872	21.8323	22.1672	22.4925	22.8082	23.1148	23.4124	23.7014	23.9819	24.2543	24.5187
4%	17.5885	17.8736	18.1476	18.4112	18.6646	18.9083	19.1426	19.3679	19.5845	19.7928	19.9931	20.1856	20.3708	20.5488	20.7200
5%	15.5928	15.8027	16.0025	16.1929	16.3742	16.5469	16.7113	16.8679	17.0170	17.1591	17.2944	17.4232	17.5459	17.6628	17.7741
6%	13.9291	14.0840	14.2302	14.3681	14.4982	14.6210	14.7368	14.8460	14.9491	15.0463	15.1380	15.2245	15.3062	15.3832	15.4558
7%	12.5318	12.6466	12.7538	12.8540	12.9477	13.0352	13.1170	13.1935	13.2649	13.3317	13.3941	13.4524	13.5070	13.5579	13.6055
8%	11.3498	11.4350	11.5139	11.5869	11.6546	11.7172	11.7752	11.8289	11.8786	11.9246	11.9672	12.0067	12.0432	12.0771	12.1084
9%	10.3428	10.4062	10.4644	10.5178	10.5668	10.6118	10.6530	10.6908	10.7255	10.7574	10.7866	10.8134	10.8380	10.8605	10.8812
10%	9.4790	9.5264	9.5694	9.6086	9.6442	9.6765	9.7059	9.7327	9.7570	9.7791	9.7991	9.8174	9.8340	9.8491	9.8628
11%	8.7331	8.7686	8.8005	8.8293	8.8552	8.8786	8.8996	8.9186	8.9357	8.9511	8.9649	8.9774	8.9886	8.9988	9.0079
12%	8.0850	8.1116	8.1354	8.1566	8.1755	8.1924	8.2075	8.2210	8.2330	8.2438	8.2534	8.2619	8.2696	8.2764	8.2825
13%	7.5183	7.5383	7.5560	7.5717	7.5856	7.5979	7.6087	7.6183	7.6268	7.6344	7.6410	7.6469	7.6522	7.6568	7.6609
14%	7.0199	7.0350	7.0482	7.0599	7.0700	7.0790	7.0868	7.0937	7.0997	7.1050	7.1097	7.1138	7.1173	7.1205	7.1232
15%	6.5791	6.5905	6.6005	6.6091	6.6166	6.6231	6.6288	6.6338	6.6380	6.6418	6.6450	6.6478	6.6503	6.6524	6.6543
16%	6.1872	6.1959	6.2034	6.2098	6.2153	6.2201	6.2242	6.2278	6.2309	6.2335	6.2358	6.2377	6.2394	6.2409	6.2421
17%	5.8371	5.8437	5.8493	5.8541	5.8582	5.8617	5.8647	5.8673	5.8695	5.8713	5.8729	5.8743	5.8755	5.8765	5.8773
18%	5.5227	5.5277	5.5320	5.5356	5.5386	5.5412	5.5434	5.5452	5.5468	5.5482	5.5493	5.5502	5.5510	5.5517	5.5523
19%	5.2392	5.2430	5.2462	5.2489	5.2512	5.2531	5.2547	5.2561	5.2572	5.2582	5.2590	5.2596	5.2602	5.2607	5.2611
20%	4.9824	4.9854	4.9878	4.9898	4.9915	4.9929	4.9941	4.9951	4.9959	4.9966	4.9972	4.9976	4.9980	4.9984	4.9986

Present Value of Ordinary Annuity Table (PVAF)

$$PVOA = A(PVAF) = A\left[\frac{(1+i)^n - 1}{i(1+i)^n}\right] \quad \text{(Continued)}$$

Number of periods

Interest	46	47	48	49	50	51	52	53	54	55	56	57	58	59	60
1%	36.7272	37.3537	37.9740	38.5881	39.1961	39.7981	40.3942	40.9844	41.5687	42.1472	42.7200	43.2871	43.8486	44.4046	44.9550
2%	29.8923	30.2866	30.6731	31.0521	31.4236	31.7878	32.1449	32.4950	32.8383	33.1748	33.5047	33.8281	34.1452	34.4561	34.7609
3%	24.7754	25.0247	25.2667	25.5017	25.7298	25.9512	26.1662	26.3750	26.5777	26.7744	26.9655	27.1509	27.3310	27.5058	27.6756
4%	20.8847	21.0429	21.1951	21.3415	21.4822	21.6175	21.7476	21.8727	21.9930	22.1086	22.2198	22.3267	22.4296	22.5284	22.6235
5%	17.8801	17.9810	18.0772	18.1687	18.2559	18.3390	18.4181	18.4934	18.5651	18.6335	18.6985	18.7605	18.8195	18.8758	18.9293
6%	15.5244	15.5890	15.6500	15.7076	15.7619	15.8131	15.8614	15.9070	15.9500	15.9905	16.0288	16.0649	16.0990	16.1311	16.1614
7%	13.6500	13.6916	13.7305	13.7668	13.8007	13.8325	13.8621	13.8898	13.9157	13.9399	13.9626	13.9837	14.0035	14.0219	14.0392
8%	12.1374	12.1643	12.1891	12.2122	12.2335	12.2532	12.2715	12.2884	12.3041	12.3186	12.3321	12.3445	12.3560	12.3667	12.3766
9%	10.9002	10.9176	10.9336	10.9482	10.9617	10.9740	10.9853	10.9957	11.0053	11.0140	11.0220	11.0294	11.0361	11.0423	11.0480
10%	9.8753	9.8866	9.8969	9.9063	9.9148	9.9226	9.9296	9.9360	9.9418	9.9471	9.9519	9.9563	9.9603	9.9639	9.9672
11%	9.0161	9.0235	9.0302	9.0362	9.0417	9.0465	9.0509	9.0549	9.0585	9.0617	9.0646	9.0672	9.0695	9.0717	9.0736
12%	8.2880	8.2928	8.2972	8.3010	8.3045	8.3076	8.3103	8.3128	8.3150	8.3170	8.3187	8.3203	8.3217	8.3229	8.3240
13%	7.6645	7.6677	7.6705	7.6730	7.6752	7.6772	7.6789	7.6805	7.6818	7.6830	7.6841	7.6851	7.6859	7.6866	7.6873
14%	7.1256	7.1277	7.1296	7.1312	7.1327	7.1339	7.1350	7.1360	7.1368	7.1376	7.1382	7.1388	7.1393	7.1397	7.1401
15%	6.6559	6.6573	6.6585	6.6596	6.6605	6.6613	6.6620	6.6626	6.6631	6.6636	6.6640	6.6644	6.6647	6.6649	6.6651
16%	6.2432	6.2442	6.2450	6.2457	6.2463	6.2468	6.2472	6.2476	6.2479	6.2482	6.2485	6.2487	6.2489	6.2490	6.2492
17%	5.8781	5.8787	5.8792	5.8797	5.8801	5.8804	5.8807	5.8809	5.8811	5.8813	5.8815	5.8816	5.8817	5.8818	5.8819
18%	5.5528	5.5532	5.5536	5.5539	5.5541	5.5544	5.5545	5.5547	5.5548	5.5549	5.5550	5.5551	5.5552	5.5552	5.5553
19%	5.2614	5.2617	5.2619	5.2621	5.2623	5.2624	5.2625	5.2626	5.2627	5.2628	5.2628	5.2629	5.2629	5.2630	5.2630
20%	4.9989	4.9991	4.9992	4.9993	4.9995	4.9995	4.9996	4.9997	4.9997	4.9998	4.9998	4.9998	4.9999	4.9999	4.9999

Capital Budgeting

"When you make a decision, you need facts."

— Ken Jennings, holder of the record for the longest winning streak on the American game show *Jeopardy!*

Learning Objectives

Have an understanding of the concept of capital budgeting.

Be able to calculate payback and internal rate of return and perform net present value and lowest total cost analysis.

Be able to draw conclusions and make decisions from the results of payback and internal rate of return calculations and net present value and lowest total cost analysis.

Introduction

As business owners, we often invest in assets we expect will result in profitable returns to the business for the long term. As part of this process, we must constantly make decisions for our company about if, when, and how to expand business operations via the acquisition of new equipment, the expansion or improvement of physical facilities, the addition of new lines of products or services, or other means. Most methods of expanding business operations involve the investment of a significant amount of capital—capital that could be devoted to alternative, less-risky pursuits, such as paying off debt or investing in U.S. government securities. **Capital budgeting** is the process we use to justify the acquisition of capital assets (assets that have an expected useful life in excess of one year) or the investment in projects that support the expansion of business operations. This chapter introduces the concepts and calculations associated with capital budgeting.

Taxes, Interest, and Time

capital budgeting
a process used to justify the acquisition of capital assets or the investment in projects that support the expansion of business operations

In chapter 3, we learned that once a business owner understands which compensation options are available to her, the factor that most affects her decision regarding how to be compensated is taxes. We also learned that the larger the percentage of her company that she owns, the more the business owner feels not only the pain of every tax dollar paid by herself as an individual, but also the pain of every tax dollar paid by her business.

In chapter 9, we learned the difference between simple interest and compound interest. We further learned that, assuming the same stated rate of interest is being used for both calculations, except in the instance of interest being compounded annually for one year or less, compound interest will result in more interest being earned or charged than simple interest.

In chapter 9, we also learned about time value of money, the loss of purchasing power that occurs as a result of the interest considerations associated with the passage of time. Put more simply, a dollar in your possession today is worth more than a dollar you'll receive in the future because a dollar in your possession today can be invested and turned into more than a dollar. In other words, time affects the value of money.

Taxes, interest, and time generally work together to determine the value of the opportunities available to us. When evaluating opportunities—entrepreneurial and otherwise—we need to consider the dollar value of the cash flows expected to be generated by the opportunities. We also need to consider the timing, the taxation, and the interest rates associated with these cash flows.

In this chapter, we'll learn about the methods used to make capital budgeting decisions (i.e., the methods used to choose between major business investment alternatives). In chapter 11, we'll learn how to place a value on a business. In chapter 12, we'll review various approaches to determining the value of investment securities, such as stocks and bonds. All of these methods and approaches involve determining the amount of expected cash flows, establishing the timing of the cash flows, evaluating how the cash flows will be taxed, and ascertaining the interest rates associated with the cash flows.

Capital Budgeting

Situations that might require capital budgeting analysis include changes in government regulations, the need or desire to pursue a change in business strategy, and the need or desire to develop or introduce new products or services. Let's consider some examples.

A few years ago, the California Air Resources Board required an equipment upgrade to certain trucks frequently purchased as part of small delivery or work truck fleets because the applicable truck models were found to be significant contributors to California's air quality problems. The businesses that owned such trucks had a decision to make: Either buy an expensive equipment upgrade for the affected trucks or stop using the affected trucks in California, which, for many companies, meant ceasing to do business in California. The owners and managers of these businesses needed to determine if the benefit of continuing to do business in California exceeded the cost of purchasing the equipment upgrade.

As another example, due to the changing costs of communication, labor, and transportation worldwide, many companies are revisiting their twentieth century decisions regarding where certain types of work get done. For example, U.S. manufacturers of off-road vehicles, construction and farm equipment, autos, auto parts, and electronics are increasingly choosing to manufacture their products in the United States. On the other hand, many U.S. businesses are now routinely exporting their computer coding projects to countries such as India. These types of changes in business strategy require determining the lowest-cost avenue for accomplishing a needed task. Further, as the business environment continues to change, ongoing cost analysis is required in order for a business owner to continue to make informed decisions regarding which path forward is the best choice.

As a final example, companies must develop or introduce new products and services in order to stay competitive. Developing or introducing a new product or service can only be justified if the benefits from the new product or service are expected to exceed all of the costs of the new product or service. If a company has multiple possible new products or services it can choose to develop or introduce but has the resources to pursue only one new product or service, the question of whether to introduce becomes further complicated by the question of which to introduce. Fortunately, multiple methods of capital budgeting analysis exist that can provide business owners with the information they need to make these decisions.

Determination of Capital Budgeting Analysis Data

At its most fundamental level, capital budgeting involves either determining if the benefits of pursuing an opportunity exceed the costs of doing so or determining the lowest-cost avenue of accomplishing some needed task. When making a capital budgeting decision, the business owner must determine four types of costs:

1. Start-up costs—the costs that will be incurred before a new asset or project can begin to provide its intended benefit. For example, in the instance of the purchase of a significant new piece of equipment, start-up costs would include the cost of the equipment itself, the cost of its installation, the cost of any needed changes to the company's facilities to accommodate the equipment, and the cost of any needed employee recruitment or training.

2. Operational costs—the costs that will be incurred on an ongoing basis to support a new asset or project. In the instance of the purchase of a significant new piece of equipment, operational costs would include ongoing increased expenditures for items such as maintenance, utilities, and insurance. Operational costs would also include the costs of additional payroll, payroll taxes, and other employee-related expenses.

3. Working capital costs—the costs associated with the increased demands on a business's working capital necessitated by a new asset or project. Working capital costs would include the costs associated with the need to invest in increased

levels of inventory and accounts receivable in order to accommodate an increased level of sales.

4. Tax costs—the additional taxes that may need to be paid as a result of an investment decision. Tax costs would include income taxes on increased net income, real estate taxes on new or improved facilities, and personal property taxes on inventories and equipment, as applicable.

Benefits that must be determined when making a capital budgeting decision include:

- the amount of any increase in net income
- the amount of any decrease in income taxes to be paid due to tax benefits, which are the income-tax-reducing effects of items like the depreciation of fixed assets (which decreases net income and therefore decreases the amount of income taxes that must be paid) and investment tax credits (which directly reduce the amount of income taxes that must be paid)
- the amount of any increase in cash flow (which generally either increases the amount of cash that can be invested in order to earn a return or decreases the amount of debt an entity must carry—and therefore the amount of interest expense an entity must pay)
- the amount of any increase in productivity (and its related reduction in certain costs, such as payroll, payroll tax, and other employee-related expenses)
- the salvage value associated with any fixed-asset purchase

Note that a benefit must take into account the income taxes that must be paid on it before it can be considered a true benefit. Determining the costs and benefits associated with a capital budgeting decision is best illustrated via example.

Example 10.1

QRS, LLC is considering purchasing a piece of equipment that would increase the production capacity of the company such that the company would be able to manufacture a much greater quantity of one of its products, Q14. The purchase price of the equipment is $100,000.

To date, QRS has been unable to meet customer demand for product Q14, and the company's management is confident QRS can sell every extra unit of product Q14 the company can produce. Management believes the new equipment will allow QRS to produce and sell enough additional product to increase its annual gross profit by $27,500.

The company would need to borrow—at 8 percent for three years—$36,000 of the $100,000 needed to purchase the equipment. According to Internal Revenue Service (IRS) regulations, the 10-year asset life piece of equipment would be depreciated for tax purposes using the modified accelerated cost recovery system (MACRS) depreciation method (see the MACRS half-year convention depreciation rate table included in figure 10.1). QRS's management thinks, with proper maintenance, the new equipment would be operational for at least 15 years. The salvage value of the equipment (i.e., the amount for which QRS expects to be able to sell the equipment at the end of year 15) is $10,000. Increased utilities and insurance costs associated with the purchase of this equipment would amount to $1,000 per year. Increased maintenance costs would amount to $1,500 per year.

QRS is an entity taxed as a C corporation. The U.S. corporate income tax rate is 21 percent. Should QRS purchase this piece of equipment?

According to the IRS, a piece of equipment like that described in example 10.1 would likely be required to be depreciated for tax purposes using the MACRS method of depreciation (see the MACRS half-year convention depreciation rates

MACRS Depreciation Rates for 3-, 5-, 7-, 10-, 15-, and 20-Year Property Half-Year Convention						
Year	3-Year	5-Year	7-Year	10-Year	15-Year	20-Year
1	33.33%	20.00%	14.29%	10.00%	5.00%	3.750%
2	44.45%	32.00%	24.49%	18.00%	9.50%	7.219%
3	14.81%	19.20%	17.49%	14.40%	8.55%	6.677%
4	7.41%	11.52%	12.49%	11.52%	7.70%	6.177%
5	–	11.52%	8.93%	9.22%	6.93%	5.713%
6	–	5.76%	8.92%	7.37%	6.23%	5.285%
7	–	–	8.93%	6.55%	5.90%	4.888%
8	–	–	4.46%	6.55%	5.90%	4.522%
9	–	–	–	6.56%	5.91%	4.462%
10	–	–	–	6.55%	5.90%	4.461%
11	–	–	–	3.28%	5.91%	4.462%
12	–	–	–	–	5.90%	4.461%
13	–	–	–	–	5.91%	4.462%
14	–	–	–	–	5.90%	4.461%
15	–	–	–	–	5.91%	4.462%
16	–	–	–	–	2.95%	4.461%
17	–	–	–	–	–	4.462%
18	–	–	–	–	–	4.461%
19	–	–	–	–	–	4.462%
20	–	–	–	–	–	4.461%
21	–	–	–	–	–	2.231%

Figure 10.1. MACRS half-year convention depreciation rates for 3-, 5-, 7-, 10-, 15-, and 20-year property. Adapted from: Internal Revenue Service publication 946, "How to Depreciate Property," https://IRS.gov, 2018.

included in figure 10.1). Note that while a company may use one method of depreciation for general accounting and financial statement preparation purposes (e.g., the straight-line, half-year convention depreciation method we've been using thus far in this textbook), typically, a company uses an alternative method (i.e., a method dictated by IRS rules) to determine depreciation expense for tax purposes. Such differences in the method of depreciation for tax and general accounting purposes are often a source of deferred tax liabilities on C corporation balance sheets (see chapter 4 for a discussion of deferred tax assets and liabilities).

A special note regarding the **Section 179 deduction**: *Subject to a variety of limitations, Section 179 of the U.S. tax code allows businesses to immediately expense up to 100% of the cost of a fixed-asset purchase for tax purposes when that fixed-asset purchase meets certain criteria. Since not all fixed-asset purchases meet the criteria to be expensed under Section 179, and since for a variety of reasons not all businesses elect to utilize the Section 179 deduction, we will assume for purposes of the examples and problems included in this chapter—and throughout the rest of this textbook—that the businesses in question are not taking advantage of the Section 179 deduction with regard to their fixed-asset acquisitions.*

In order to begin our analysis of the proposed equipment purchase in example 10.1, using the depreciation rates in figure 10.1, we'd likely develop a depreciation schedule for the equipment like the one shown in figure 10.2 (on page 284).

As a reminder, salvage value is the amount for which we expect to be able to sell a fixed asset after it's fully depreciated and we're done using it. Note that, as previously illustrated in chapter 6, in order to calculate depreciation expense for a depreciable fixed asset with a salvage value above $0, we must first subtract the salvage value of the fixed asset from the cost of the fixed asset to arrive at the depreciable value of the fixed asset. Then, we depreciate the fixed asset normally.

Section 179 deduction
subject to a variety of limitations, Section 179 of the U.S. tax code allows businesses to immediately expense up to 100% of the cost of a fixed-asset purchase for tax purposes when that fixed-asset purchase meets certain criteria

QRS, LLC Depreciation Schedule		
Equipment cost:		$100,000
Less: Salvage value:		10,000
Depreciable value:		$ 90,000
Useful life in years:		10
Depreciation method:		MACRS, half-year convention

Year	MACRS Depreciation Rate	Depreciation
1	10.00%	$ 9,000
2	18.00%	16,200
3	14.40%	12,960
4	11.52%	10,368
5	9.22%	8,298
6	7.37%	6,633
7	6.55%	5,895
8	6.55%	5,895
9	6.56%	5,904
10	6.55%	5,895
11	3.28%	2,952
Totals	100.00%	$ 90,000

Figure 10.2. Depreciation schedule for QRS's proposed $100,000 equipment purchase.

In the instance of the straight-year, half-year convention depreciation method we've been using, this would involve determining a depreciable value for the asset and then dividing that depreciable value by the number of years of the asset's expected useful life in order to arrive at the depreciation expense number for the middle years of the asset's expected life. Next, we'd divide that depreciation expense number by two to arrive at the depreciation expense number for the first and last years of the asset's expected life. In the specific instance of the $100,000 piece of equipment under consideration in our example, we'd determine a depreciable value for the asset of $90,000 ($100,000 asset cost – $10,000 salvage value) and then divide that depreciable value by the asset's expected useful life of 10 years in order to determine a depreciation expense of $9,000 for years 2–10 of the asset's life. Next, we'd divide the $9,000 by two to arrive at the depreciation expense number for years 1 and 11 of the asset's expected life: $4,500.

In the instance of MACRS depreciation, as indicated in figure 10.2, we'd simply multiply the depreciable value ($90,000) by the IRS-established MACRS percentage applicable to a particular year (e.g., 10 percent for year 1) in order to arrive at the depreciation expense for that particular year ($9,000 for year 1).

Expected Annual After-Tax Benefit

Depreciation isn't the only expense associated with the equipment purchase proposed in example 10.1. QRS will incur increased utilities and insurance costs amounting to $1,000 per year and increased maintenance costs amounting to $1,500 per year. In addition, if the increase in gross profit associated with the purchase of this equipment exceeds the increase in depreciation, utilities, insurance, and maintenance expenses associated with the purchase of the equipment, the company's net income will increase. If the net income increases, the company's overall income tax expense will increase.

In order to determine the interest expense associated with the debt QRS would incur to purchase the equipment, QRS would likely obtain a loan amortization schedule from its lender. Note, however, that for purposes of evaluating the $100,000 proposed equipment purchase, the interest expense associated with this loan would not be treated as a cash flow associated with the project. The reason is because the interest expense relates to the company's decision regarding how to finance the purchase of equipment, rather than the merits of the purchase of the equipment itself.

, So, how do we best determine the net effect of all the costs and benefits associated with this proposed equipment purchase? We calculate the expected annual after-tax benefit (EAATB) associated with each year of owning and operating the equipment, as shown in figure 10.3.

In figure 10.3, note that, for each year, we're working our way from an expected annual increase in gross profit to an expected increase in net income before income

QRS, LLC Expected Annual After-Tax Benefits (EAATBs) of a Proposed $100,000 Equipment Purchase					
	Year 1	Year 2	Year 3	Year 4	Year 5
Expected annual increase in gross profit	$27,500	$27,500	$27,500	$27,500	$27,500
Less: New depreciation expense	9,000	16,200	12,960	10,368	8,298
Less: Increased utilities and insurance expense	1,000	1,000	1,000	1,000	1,000
Less: Increased maintenance expense	1,500	1,500	1,500	1,500	1,500
Expected increase in net income before income taxes (NIBIT)	16,000	8,800	12,040	14,632	16,702
Less: Increase in income tax expense (NIBIT x 21%)	3,360	1,848	2,528	3,073	3,507
Expected increase in net income	12,640	6,952	9,512	11,559	13,195
Add: New depreciation expense	9,000	16,200	12,960	10,368	8,298
Expected annual after-tax benefit (EAATB) (increase in cash flow)	$21,640	$23,152	$22,472	$21,927	$21,493
	Year 6	Year 7	Year 8	Year 9	Year 10
Expected annual increase in gross profit	$27,500	$27,500	$27,500	$27,500	$27,500
Less: New depreciation expense	6,633	5,895	5,895	5,904	5,895
Less: Increased utilities and insurance expense	1,000	1,000	1,000	1,000	1,000
Less: Increased maintenance expense	1,500	1,500	1,500	1,500	1,500
Expected increase in net income before income taxes (NIBIT)	18,367	19,105	19,105	19,096	19,105
Less: Increase in income tax expense (NIBIT x 21%)	3,857	4,012	4,012	4,010	4,012
Expected increase in net income	14,510	15,093	15,093	15,086	15,093
Add: New depreciation expense	6,633	5,895	5,895	5,904	5,895
Expected annual after-tax benefit (EAATB) (increase in cash flow)	$21,143	$20,988	$20,988	$20,990	$20,988
	Year 11	Year 12	Year 13	Year 14	Year 15
Expected annual increase in gross profit	$27,500	$27,500	$27,500	$27,500	$27,500
Less: New depreciation expense	2,952	–	–	–	–
Less: Increased utilities and insurance expense	1,000	1,000	1,000	1,000	1,000
Less: Increased maintenance expense	1,500	1,500	1,500	1,500	1,500
Expected increase in net income before income taxes (NIBIT)	22,048	25,000	25,000	25,000	25,000
Less: Increase in income tax expense (NIBIT x 21%)	4,630	5,250	5,250	5,250	5,250
Expected increase in net income	17,418	19,750	19,750	19,750	19,750
Add: New depreciation expense	2,952	–	–	–	–
Add: Proceeds from sale of equipment at the end of year 15	–	–	–	–	10,000
Expected annual after-tax benefit (EAATB) (increase in cash flow)	$20,370	$19,750	$19,750	$19,750	$29,750

Figure 10.3. EAATBs of QRS's proposed $100,000 equipment purchase.

taxes by subtracting the expected increase in expenses associated with the proposed equipment purchase. We then subtract the increase in income tax expense associated with the expected increase in net income before income taxes to arrive at the expected increase in net income related to the proposed equipment purchase. Last, we add back the noncash expense of depreciation (and in year 15, the anticipated cash proceeds from the sale of the equipment) to the expected increase in net income to arrive at an expected annual after-tax benefit—the increase in cash flow for the company. As mentioned in chapter 8, many business owners and stakeholders use cash flow rather than net income as the gauge of an entity's relative success and as a tool to make decisions. This is because cash flow is a measure of whether a company has enough capital to sustain itself. A business can be profitable and still go out of business because it runs out of cash. Example 8.1 in chapter 8 highlights the critical importance of cash flow by illustrating how a profitable business can have such poor cash flow that it threatens the continued viability of the business.

Now that we've calculated it, how do we use the expected annual after-tax benefit (i.e., the expected increase in cash flow) to determine whether QRS should purchase the $100,000 piece of equipment? The three methods of analysis typically used to make sound capital budgeting decisions are:

1. payback
2. net present value or lowest total cost
3. internal rate of return

Let's explore each of these methods.

Payback Method

payback method

a capital budgeting method that calculates the number of years it will take a business to get back the money it invests in a proposed project or asset purchase

The **payback method** is a capital budgeting method that calculates the number of years it will take a business to get back the money it invests in a proposed project or asset purchase. The formula is

$$Payback = \frac{C}{AEAATB}$$

where

C = Cost of the project

$AEAATB$ = Average expected annual after-tax benefit of the project or asset

We'll use example 10.1 to illustrate the payback method. First, we'll calculate the AEAATB associated with the proposed $100,000 equipment purchase using the expected annual after-tax benefit amounts in figure 10.3. Figure 10.4 shows the calculation of the AEAATB.

Next, utilizing the AEAATB of $21,677 calculated in figure 10.4 and our known $100,000 cost of the proposed equipment purchase, we can calculate payback as follows:

$$Payback = \frac{C}{AEAATB}$$
$$= \frac{\$100,000}{\$21,677}$$
$$= 4.61 \text{ years}$$

Is 4.61 years good or bad?

QRS, LLC Calculation of the Average Expected Annual After-Tax Benefit (AEAATB) of a Proposed $100,000 Equipment Purchase	
Expected annual after-tax benefit (EAATB) for year 1	$ 21,640
Expected annual after-tax benefit (EAATB) for year 2	23,152
Expected annual after-tax benefit (EAATB) for year 3	22,472
Expected annual after-tax benefit (EAATB) for year 4	21,927
Expected annual after-tax benefit (EAATB) for year 5	21,493
Expected annual after-tax benefit (EAATB) for year 6	21,143
Expected annual after-tax benefit (EAATB) for year 7	20,988
Expected annual after-tax benefit (EAATB) for year 8	20,988
Expected annual after-tax benefit (EAATB) for year 9	20,990
Expected annual after-tax benefit (EAATB) for year 10	20,988
Expected annual after-tax benefit (EAATB) for year 11	20,370
Expected annual after-tax benefit (EAATB) for year 12	19,750
Expected annual after-tax benefit (EAATB) for year 13	19,750
Expected annual after-tax benefit (EAATB) for year 14	19,750
Expected annual after-tax benefit (EAATB) for year 15	29,750
Total	$ 325,150 ÷ 15 years = $21,677

Figure 10.4. Calculation of the AEAATB of QRS's proposed $100,000 equipment purchase.

The payback method, which is widely used, has disadvantages:

- It doesn't consider the time value of money.
- It favors investments with a quick return over those with the largest overall return (because it doesn't consider the value of the cash flows that occur beyond the payback period).
- It doesn't always provide a clear answer regarding whether one should invest in a particular opportunity.

For purposes of illustration, consider the expected annual after-tax benefit numbers in figure 10.5 (on page 288), which are associated with an alternative option. In the alternative, instead of performing an estimated $1,500 of annual maintenance on the equipment itself, the company would purchase a $5,000 annual service contract each year for 20 years. This purchase would "guarantee" that the equipment would operate satisfactorily for 20 years instead of 15 years (which means QRS would sell the equipment for its salvage value of $10,000 at the end of year 20 instead of at the end of year 15).

Using this information, we can calculate the AEAATB associated with the $5,000 annual service contract option. Figure 10.6 (on page 289) shows the calculation.

Utilizing the AEAATB of $18,430 and our known cost of the proposed equipment purchase of $100,000, we can calculate payback:

$$Payback = \frac{C}{AEAATB}$$
$$= \frac{\$100,000}{\$18,430}$$
$$= 5.43 \text{ years}$$

Waiting 5.43 years to be "paid back" is obviously less desirable than waiting 4.61 years. So, should QRS purchase the equipment? If the answer to that question is yes, which option should the company choose? Currently, QRS has two options:

1. Option 1: Purchase the $100,000 piece of equipment without the $5,000 annual service contract and perform an estimated $1,500 of annual maintenance on the equipment itself.
2. Option 2: Purchase the $100,000 piece of equipment and pay for the $5,000 annual service contract instead of performing the estimated $1,500 of annual maintenance on the equipment itself.

QRS, LLC Expected Annual After-Tax Benefits (EAATBs) of a Proposed $100,000 Equipment Purchase with a $5,000 Annual Service Contract	Year 1	Year 2	Year 3	Year 4	Year 5
Expected annual increase in gross profit	$27,500	$27,500	$27,500	$27,500	$27,500
Less: New depreciation expense	9,000	16,200	12,960	10,368	8,298
Less: Increased utilities and insurance expense	1,000	1,000	1,000	1,000	1,000
Less: Increased maintenance expense	5,000	5,000	5,000	5,000	5,000
Expected increase in net income before income taxes (NIBIT)	12,500	5,300	8,540	11,132	13,202
Less: Increase in income tax expense (NIBIT x 21%)	2,625	1,113	1,793	2,338	2,772
Expected increase in net income	9,875	4,187	6,747	8,794	10,430
Add: New depreciation expense	9,000	16,200	12,960	10,368	8,298
Expected annual after-tax benefit (EAATB) (increase in cash flow)	$18,875	$20,387	$19,707	$19,162	$18,728

	Year 6	Year 7	Year 8	Year 9	Year 10
Expected annual increase in gross profit	$27,500	$27,500	$27,500	$27,500	$27,500
Less: New depreciation expense	6,633	5,895	5,895	5,904	5,895
Less: Increased utilities and insurance expense	1,000	1,000	1,000	1,000	1,000
Less: Increased maintenance expense	5,000	5,000	5,000	5,000	5,000
Expected increase in net income before income taxes (NIBIT)	14,867	15,605	15,605	15,596	15,605
Less: Increase in income tax expense (NIBIT x 21%)	3,122	3,277	3,277	3,275	3,277
Expected increase in net income	11,745	12,328	12,328	12,321	12,328
Add: New depreciation expense	6,633	5,895	5,895	5,904	5,895
Expected annual after-tax benefit (EAATB) (increase in cash flow)	$18,378	$18,223	$18,223	$18,225	$18,223

	Year 11	Year 12	Year 13	Year 14	Year 15
Expected annual increase in gross profit	$27,500	$27,500	$27,500	$27,500	$27,500
Less: New depreciation expense	2,952	-	-	-	-
Less: Increased utilities and insurance expense	1,000	1,000	1,000	1,000	1,000
Less: Increased maintenance expense	5,000	5,000	5,000	5,000	5,000
Expected increase in net income before income taxes (NIBIT)	18,548	21,500	21,500	21,500	21,500
Less: Increase in income tax expense (NIBIT x 21%)	3,895	4,515	4,515	4,515	4,515
Expected increase in net income	14,653	16,985	16,985	16,985	16,985
Add: New depreciation expense	2,952	-	-	-	-
Expected annual after-tax benefit (EAATB) (increase in cash flow)	$17,605	$16,985	$16,985	$16,985	$16,985

	Year 16	Year 17	Year 18	Year 19	Year 20
Expected annual increase in gross profit	$27,500	$27,500	$27,500	$27,500	$27,500
Less: New depreciation expense	-	-	-	-	-
Less: Increased utilities and insurance expense	1,000	1,000	1,000	1,000	1,000
Less: Increased maintenance expense	5,000	5,000	5,000	5,000	5,000
Expected increase in net income before income taxes (NIBIT)	21,500	21,500	21,500	21,500	21,500
Less: Increase in income tax expense (NIBIT x 21%)	4,515	4,515	4,515	4,515	4,515
Expected increase in net income	16,985	16,985	16,985	16,985	16,985
Add: New depreciation expense	-	-	-	-	-
Add: Proceeds from sale of equipment at the end of year 20	-	-	-	-	10,000
Expected annual after-tax benefit (EAATB) (increase in cash flow)	$16,985	$16,985	$16,985	$16,985	$26,985

Figure 10.5. EAATBs associated with the $5,000 annual service contract option.

QRS, LLC
Calculation of the Average Expected Annual After-Tax Benefit (AEAATB) of a Proposed $100,000 Equipment Purchase with a $5,000 Annual Service Contract

Expected annual after-tax benefit (EAATB) for year 1	$ 18,875
Expected annual after-tax benefit (EAATB) for year 2	20,387
Expected annual after-tax benefit (EAATB) for year 3	19,707
Expected annual after-tax benefit (EAATB) for year 4	19,162
Expected annual after-tax benefit (EAATB) for year 5	18,728
Expected annual after-tax benefit (EAATB) for year 6	18,378
Expected annual after-tax benefit (EAATB) for year 7	18,223
Expected annual after-tax benefit (EAATB) for year 8	18,223
Expected annual after-tax benefit (EAATB) for year 9	18,225
Expected annual after-tax benefit (EAATB) for year 10	18,223
Expected annual after-tax benefit (EAATB) for year 11	17,605
Expected annual after-tax benefit (EAATB) for year 12	16,985
Expected annual after-tax benefit (EAATB) for year 13	16,985
Expected annual after-tax benefit (EAATB) for year 14	16,985
Expected annual after-tax benefit (EAATB) for year 15	16,985
Expected annual after-tax benefit (EAATB) for year 16	16,985
Expected annual after-tax benefit (EAATB) for year 17	16,985
Expected annual after-tax benefit (EAATB) for year 18	16,985
Expected annual after-tax benefit (EAATB) for year 19	16,985
Expected annual after-tax benefit (EAATB) for year 20	26,985
Total	$368,600 ÷ 20 years = $18,430

Figure 10.6. Calculation of the AEAATB associated with the $5,000 annual service contract option.

Option 1 allows QRS to recoup its $100,000 investment in 4.61 years, which is faster than the 5.43 years it will take if QRS chooses option 2. However, note that the total expected after-tax benefit for *all* the years associated with this proposed investment is higher for option 2 ($368,600, see figure 10.6) than for option 1 ($325,150, see figure 10.4 on page 287). So, which option should QRS choose? Unfortunately, the payback method doesn't provide a clear answer. (Note, however, that a payback period that exceeds the expected functional life of the investment under consideration *does* clearly suggest that one shouldn't invest in the opportunity.)

Net Present Value

The **net present value (NPV) method** is a capital budgeting method that considers the time value of money by discounting the future cash flows associated with a proposed project or asset purchase back to the present. The **lowest total cost (LTC) method** is a capital budgeting method similar to the NPV method commonly used by business owners who must replace fixed assets on a regular basis. The NPV method will be discussed in this section. The LTC method will be discussed in a separate section at the end of the chapter.

The NPV method applies the present value of a lump sum calculation to all the cash flows under consideration (and, if applicable and desired, the present value of an ordinary annuity calculation to any consecutive cash flows that happen to be equal in amount). The calculations are made using an interest rate (discount rate) that matches our perceived cost of capital related to a proposed investment.

If calculations are made using a discount rate that matches our perceived cost of capital related to a proposed investment, what might our perceived cost of capital related to that investment be? The answer depends on the circumstances surrounding both the opportunities at hand and the specific company in question.

net present value (NPV) method
a capital budgeting method that considers the time value of money by discounting the future cash flows associated with a proposed project or asset purchase back to the present

lowest total cost (LTC) method
a capital budgeting method similar to the net present value method commonly used by business owners who must replace fixed assets on a regular basis

Returning to our example company, let's consider a few cost of capital scenarios:

- QRS can invest its idle cash in a mutual fund and receive a return on that investment of 4 percent per year. As a result, the opportunity cost associated with investing in the $100,000 piece of equipment could be viewed as 4 percent. Four percent could then be the discount rate QRS decides to use to assess the project.
- QRS can borrow money at 8 percent. Eight percent could then be the discount rate QRS decides to use to assess the project.
- The owners of QRS have previously determined that they want the business to earn a minimum rate of return of 15 percent on every new project in which the firm invests. Fifteen percent could then be the discount rate QRS decides to use to assess the project.

Note that our perceived cost of capital is just that, the cost of capital we perceive based on the opportunities at hand and the specific circumstances surrounding our own company.

Making a Decision Using NPV

When making a decision using NPV, keep the following in mind:

- If the NPV is positive, make the investment.
- If the NPV is negative, don't make the investment.

Making a capital budgeting decision using the NPV method versus the payback method has two primary advantages:

						QRS, LLC				
				Net Present Values (NPVs) of a Proposed $100,000 Equipment Purchase						
				Option 1: $1,500 of Annual Maintenance Expense						
Cash Flow Item	Time Period	Cash Flow Amount	Type of Factor	Factor at 4%	Present Value at 4%	Factor at 8%	Present Value at 8%	Factor at 15%	Present Value at 15%
Equipment Purchase	Today	$(100,000)	PV	1.0000	$(100,000)	1.0000	$(100,000)	1.0000	$(100,000)
EAATB	Year 1	21,640	PV	0.9615	20,807	0.9259	20,036	0.8696	18,818
EAATB	Year 2	23,152	PV	0.9246	21,406	0.8573	19,848	0.7561	17,505
EAATB	Year 3	22,472	PV	0.8890	19,977	0.7938	17,838	0.6575	14,775
EAATB	Year 4	21,927	PV	0.8548	18,743	0.7350	16,117	0.5718	12,538
EAATB	Year 5	21,493	PV	0.8219	17,665	0.6806	14,628	0.4972	10,686
EAATB	Year 6	21,143	PV	0.7903	16,709	0.6302	13,324	0.4323	9,140
EAATB	Year 7	20,988	PV	0.7599	15,949	0.5835	12,246	0.3759	7,889
EAATB	Year 8	20,988	PV	0.7307	15,336	0.5403	11,340	0.3269	6,861
EAATB	Year 9	20,990	PV	0.7026	14,747	0.5002	10,499	0.2843	5,967
EAATB	Year 10	20,988	PV	0.6756	14,179	0.4632	9,722	0.2472	5,188
EAATB	Year 11	20,370	PV	0.6496	13,232	0.4289	8,737	0.2149	4,377
EAATB	Year 12	19,750	PV	0.6246	12,336	0.3971	7,843	0.1869	3,691
EAATB	Year 13	19,750	PV	0.6006	11,862	0.3677	7,262	0.1625	3,209
EAATB	Year 14	19,750	PV	0.5775	11,406	0.3405	6,725	0.1413	2,791
EAATB	Year 15	29,750	PV	0.5553	16,520	0.3152	9,377	0.1229	3,656
			Net Present Values (NPVs)		$ 140,875		$ 85,542		$ 27,094

Figure 10.7. NPVs of QRS's proposed $100,000 equipment purchase—option 1.

1. The future cash flows that will be paid and received are discounted back to the present so a decision can be made on the investment—or a choice can be made between investments—based on objective criteria (i.e., the value of the investment(s) in today's dollars).
2. The interest rates (discount rates) used are determined by, and based on, the expectations of—and the circumstances surrounding—the specific company making the decision.

To illustrate the calculation of NPV, we'll continue with our previous example of the $100,000 equipment purchase under consideration by QRS. Recall that QRS has two options: QRS performing an estimated $1,500 of annual maintenance on the equipment itself or QRS purchasing a $5,000 annual service contract for 20 years. Figures 10.7 and 10.8 show the calculations of the NPVs for the two options.

The source of the cash flow amounts in figures 10.7 and 10.8 are the EAATB amounts in figures 10.3 and 10.5, respectively. The three discount rates (i.e., 4, 8, and 15 percent) are from the three cost of capital scenarios included in the previous section. The factors associated with the different discount rates source from the present value and future value tables in appendix 9-A at the end of chapter 9. The individual present value amounts are calculated by multiplying the cash flow amount for a particular year by its applicable factor. The NPV amount for each discount rate is the sum of the individual present value amounts above it.

QRS, LLC Net Present Values (NPVs) of a Proposed $100,000 Equipment Purchase Option 2: $5,000 Annual Service Contract										
Cash Flow Item	Time Period	Cash Flow Amount	Type of Factor	Factor at 4%	Present Value at 4%	Factor at 8%	Present Value at 8%	Factor at 15%	Present Value at 15%
Equipment Purchase	Today	$(100,000)	PV	1.0000	$(100,000)	1.0000	$(100,000)	1.0000	$(100,000)
EAATB	Year 1	18,875	PV	0.9615	18,148	0.9259	17,476	0.8696	16,414
EAATB	Year 2	20,387	PV	0.9246	18,850	0.8573	17,478	0.7561	15,415
EAATB	Year 3	19,707	PV	0.8890	17,519	0.7938	15,643	0.6575	12,957
EAATB	Year 4	19,162	PV	0.8548	16,380	0.7350	14,084	0.5718	10,957
EAATB	Year 5	18,728	PV	0.8219	15,392	0.6806	12,746	0.4972	9,311
EAATB	Year 6	18,378	PV	0.7903	14,524	0.6302	11,582	0.4323	7,945
EAATB	Year 7	18,223	PV	0.7599	13,848	0.5835	10,633	0.3759	6,850
EAATB	Year 8	18,223	PV	0.7307	13,316	0.5403	9,846	0.3269	5,957
EAATB	Year 9	18,225	PV	0.7026	12,805	0.5002	9,116	0.2843	5,181
EAATB	Year 10	18,223	PV	0.6756	12,311	0.4632	8,441	0.2472	4,505
EAATB	Year 11	17,605	PV	0.6496	11,436	0.4289	7,551	0.2149	3,783
EAATB	Year 12	16,985	PV	0.6246	10,609	0.3971	6,745	0.1869	3,174
EAATB	Year 13	16,985	PV	0.6006	10,201	0.3677	6,245	0.1625	2,760
EAATB	Year 14	16,985	PV	0.5775	9,809	0.3405	5,783	0.1413	2,400
EAATB	Year 15	16,985	PV	0.5553	9,432	0.3152	5,354	0.1229	2,087
EAATB	Year 16	16,985	PV	0.5339	9,068	0.2919	4,958	0.1069	1,816
EAATB	Year 17	16,985	PV	0.5134	8,720	0.2703	4,591	0.0929	1,578
EAATB	Year 18	16,985	PV	0.4936	8,384	0.2502	4,250	0.0808	1,372
EAATB	Year 19	16,985	PV	0.4746	8,061	0.2317	3,935	0.0703	1,194
EAATB	Year 20	26,985	PV	0.4564	12,316	0.2145	5,788	0.0611	1,649
			Net Present Values (NPVs)		$ 151,129		$ 2,245		$ 17,306

Figure 10.8. NPVs of QRS's proposed $100,000 equipment purchase—option 2.

The NPV calculated at each rate for both options is positive, so QRS should definitely move forward with the purchase of the $100,000 piece of equipment. If the NPV were positive in some instances and negative in others, QRS would have to decide what discount rate is the most meaningful before deciding whether to purchase the equipment.

The NPV for option 2 is higher than the NPV for option 1 at the 4 percent discount rate. However, the NPV for option 1 is higher than the NPV for option 2 at the 8 percent and 15 percent discount rates. (This is because as the discount rate increases, the EAATBs associated with the additional years of service the $5,000 annual service contract provides QRS—years 16-20—become increasingly less valuable to QRS.) QRS will have to decide what discount rate is the most meaningful to the business in order to decide whether to purchase the $5,000 annual service contract along with the equipment.

Note that the cash flow amounts in figures 10.7 (page 290) and 10.8 (page 291) represent streams of unequal payments. That being the case, we can, if we desire, use a financial calculator or Microsoft Excel to calculate the NPV. Every model of financial calculator is somewhat different, so consult a calculator's instructions regarding how to calculate NPV. Using Microsoft Excel, if, for example, one wanted to calculate the NPV of the cash flows in figure 10.8 using a 4 percent discount rate, one would perform the following steps:

1. Input the cash flow amounts for years 1-20 in a row (horizontally) or in a column (vertically, as indicated in figure 10.8), making sure to exclude the $100,000 equipment purchase amount that occurs "today."
2. Select the cell where the present value should appear, then select the "NPV" function (click on the Insert Function tab located under the Formulas tab to locate—or search for—the function).
3. Click "OK." A data input box will appear.
4. Input ".04" as the rate.
5. Click the "Value 1" data input field and then use the cursor to select the relevant cash flow data in order to register the applicable data as the values of interest for purposes of the NPV calculation.
6. Click "OK."

At this point, $251,128.16 should appear in the cell where the user initiated the calculation. Next, one would subtract the value associated with the equipment purchase (i.e., $100,000) from the result provided by Excel in order to arrive at a final result of $151,128.16. Note that this solution differs slightly from the solution indicated in figure 10.8 due to rounding both in the figure and in the present value and future value tables from which the present value factors were sourced.

Internal Rate of Return

internal rate of return (IRR)
the actual rate of return of an investment

The **internal rate of return (IRR)** is the actual rate of return of an investment. Its calculation considers the time value of money.

The IRR is the interest rate that matches the present value of the cost of our investment directly to the present value of the future benefits to be received. The IRR, then, is the interest rate that, when used as the discount rate to determine the NPV of a proposed investment, results in an NPV of zero.

Returning to option 2 of our ongoing example, note that, as illustrated in figure 10.9, while the NPV using a discount rate of 15 percent is positive, applying a discount rate of 20 percent to the estimated cash flows results in a negative NPV. This suggests that the IRR associated with option 2 is somewhere between 15 and 20 percent.

		Cash			Present		Present
		Flow	Type of	Factor	Value	Factor	Value
Cash Flow Item	Time Period	Amount	Factor	at 15%	at 15%	at 20%	at 20%
			QRS, LLC				
		Net Present Values (NPVs) of a Proposed $100,000 Equipment Purchase					
		Option 2: $5,000 Annual Service Contract					
Equipment Purchase	Today	$(100,000)	PV	1.0000	$(100,000)	1.0000	$(100,000)
EAATB	Year 1	18,875	PV	0.8696	16,414	0.8333	15,729
EAATB	Year 2	20,387	PV	0.7561	15,415	0.6944	14,157
EAATB	Year 3	19,707	PV	0.6575	12,957	0.5787	11,404
EAATB	Year 4	19,162	PV	0.5718	10,957	0.4823	9,242
EAATB	Year 5	18,728	PV	0.4972	9,311	0.4019	7,527
EAATB	Year 6	18,378	PV	0.4323	7,945	0.3349	6,155
EAATB	Year 7	18,223	PV	0.3759	6,850	0.2791	5,086
EAATB	Year 8	18,223	PV	0.3269	5,957	0.2326	4,239
EAATB	Year 9	18,225	PV	0.2843	5,181	0.1938	3,532
EAATB	Year 10	18,223	PV	0.2472	4,505	0.1615	2,943
EAATB	Year 11	17,605	PV	0.2149	3,783	0.1346	2,370
EAATB	Year 12	16,985	PV	0.1869	3,174	0.1122	1,906
EAATB	Year 13	16,985	PV	0.1625	2,760	0.0935	1,588
EAATB	Year 14	16,985	PV	0.1413	2,400	0.0779	1,323
EAATB	Year 15	16,985	PV	0.1229	2,087	0.0649	1,102
EAATB	Year 16	16,985	PV	0.1069	1,816	0.0541	919
EAATB	Year 17	16,985	PV	0.0929	1,578	0.0451	766
EAATB	Year 18	16,985	PV	0.0808	1,372	0.0376	639
EAATB	Year 19	16,985	PV	0.0703	1,194	0.0313	532
EAATB	Year 20	26,985	PV	0.0611	1,649	0.0261	704
			Net Present Values (NPVs)		$ 17,306		$ (8,139)

Figure 10.9. NPVs of QRS's proposed $100,000 equipment purchase—option 2—using 15 and 20 percent discount rates.

While formulas and other methods exist to calculate IRR, we can calculate IRR most efficiently using a financial calculator or Microsoft Excel. Remember, every model of financial calculator is somewhat different, so one should consult a calculator's instructions regarding how to calculate IRR. To calculate the IRR for the cash flows included in figure 10.9 using Excel, follow these steps:

1. Input all the cash flow data in the spreadsheet, including the $100,000 equipment purchase, in a row (horizontally) or in a column (vertically, as indicated in figure 10.9).
2. Select the cell where the IRR should appear, then select the "IRR" function (click on the Insert Function tab located under the Formulas tab to locate—or search for—the function).
3. Click "OK." A data input box will appear.
4. Use the cursor to select the relevant cash flow data in order to register the applicable data as the values of interest for purposes of the IRR calculation.
5. Click "OK."

The solution of 18 percent should appear in the cell. By adjusting the number of decimal places displayed, the Excel user would arrive at the more specific IRR of 18.15 percent, which is the IRR that results in a zero NPV for option 2 of QRS's proposed $100,000 equipment purchase, as illustrated in figure 10.10 (on page 294).

| | | Cash | | | Present | Factor | Present | | Present |
Cash Flow Item	Time Period	Flow Amount	Type of Factor	Factor at 15%	Value at 15%	at 18.15%	Value at 18.15%	Factor at 20%	Value at 20%
					QRS, LLC				
				Net Present Values (NPVs) of a Proposed $100,000 Equipment Purchase					
				Option 2: $5,000 Annual Service Contract					
Equipment Purchase	Today	$(100,000)	PV	1.0000	$(100,000)	1.0000	$(100,000)	1.0000	$(100,000)
EAATB	Year 1	18,875	PV	0.8696	16,414	0.8464	15,975	0.8333	15,729
EAATB	Year 2	20,387	PV	0.7561	15,415	0.7164	14,604	0.6944	14,157
EAATB	Year 3	19,707	PV	0.6575	12,957	0.6063	11,949	0.5787	11,404
EAATB	Year 4	19,162	PV	0.5718	10,957	0.5132	9,833	0.4823	9,242
EAATB	Year 5	18,728	PV	0.4972	9,312	0.4343	8,134	0.4019	7,527
EAATB	Year 6	18,378	PV	0.4323	7,945	0.3676	6,756	0.3349	6,155
EAATB	Year 7	18,223	PV	0.3759	6,850	0.3111	5,670	0.2791	5,086
EAATB	Year 8	18,223	PV	0.3269	5,957	0.2633	4,799	0.2326	4,239
EAATB	Year 9	18,225	PV	0.2843	5,181	0.2229	4,062	0.1938	3,532
EAATB	Year 10	18,223	PV	0.2472	4,505	0.1887	3,438	0.1615	2,943
EAATB	Year 11	17,605	PV	0.2149	3,783	0.1597	2,811	0.1346	2,370
EAATB	Year 12	16,985	PV	0.1869	3,174	0.1351	2,295	0.1122	1,906
EAATB	Year 13	16,985	PV	0.1625	2,760	0.1144	1,943	0.0935	1,588
EAATB	Year 14	16,985	PV	0.1413	2,400	0.0968	1,644	0.0779	1,323
EAATB	Year 15	16,985	PV	0.1229	2,087	0.0819	1,392	0.0649	1,102
EAATB	Year 16	16,985	PV	0.1069	1,816	0.0694	1,178	0.0541	919
EAATB	Year 17	16,985	PV	0.0929	1,578	0.0587	997	0.0451	766
EAATB	Year 18	16,985	PV	0.0808	1,372	0.0497	844	0.0376	639
EAATB	Year 19	16,985	PV	0.0703	1,194	0.0420	714	0.0313	532
EAATB	Year 20	26,985	PV	0.0611	1,649	0.0356	960	0.0261	704
				Net Present Values (NPVs)	$ 17,306		$ 0		$ (8,139)

Figure 10.10. NPVs of QRS's proposed $100,000 equipment purchase—option 2—using 15 percent, the IRR, and 20 percent as discount rates.

As expected, when using the IRR as the discount rate to calculate the NPV of the cash flows associated with option 2, the NPV for the proposed project is exactly zero. Note that the factors for the 18.15 percent discount rate included in figure 10.10 were calculated using the following present value factor (PVF) formula:

$$PVF = \left(\frac{1}{(1+i)^n} \right)$$

This formula is part of the overall present value of a lump sum formula first presented in chapter 9:

$$PV = FV(PVF)$$

$$= FV\left(\frac{1}{(1+i)^n} \right)$$

where:

FV = Future value
PV = Present value
i = Interest rate per period
n = Number of compounding periods per year multiplied by the number of years

The calculation of IRR can be useful when evaluating investment options in that, if we've determined a minimum rate of return we wish all our investments to generate, the IRR provides the real rate of return associated with an investment that we can compare to that threshold. For example, if QRS's minimum required rate of return on an investment is 15 percent, the company would be willing to invest in either of the two options presented thus far regarding the purchase of the $100,000 piece of equipment because the NPV of both options using a discount rate of 15 percent is positive. If, however, QRS's minimum required rate of return on an investment is 20 percent, option 2 wouldn't be an acceptable investment because option 2's IRR of 18.15 percent is less than 20 percent. Using Microsoft Excel to calculate the IRR for option 1, we can determine the IRR associated with that option to be 20.46 percent. If QRS's minimum required rate of return on an investment is 20 percent, option 1 would meet the threshold of being an acceptable investment for the company. Note that a negative IRR is a strong indicator that we should not invest in an opportunity under consideration.

Income Tax Rate for an Entity Not Taxed as a C Corporation

Entities that aren't a C corporation or an entity taxed as a C corporation do not, themselves, pay income taxes. The owners of such entities report their share of the business's net income on their individual income tax returns, where the income is taxed. In the event a business suffers a net loss, the owners report their share of the business's net loss on their individual income tax returns, where the loss usually serves to reduce the overall amount of income tax the owners pay. As part of this process, a business's owners can deduct the tax depreciation related to their share of the business's fixed assets on their personal income tax returns. For these reasons, and many others, the activities of a business entity greatly affect the amount of income taxes its owners will pay.

As a result of this, the owners of an entity that does not itself pay income taxes still often consider income taxes when making capital budgeting decisions. This is because, even if the business entity itself won't suffer any income tax costs or receive any income tax benefits associated with a business decision, the owners of the entity will. In practice, owners often use the average personal income tax rate of all the entity's owners—or some other agreed-upon income tax rate benchmark—in order to consider the income tax effects of a proposed major capital investment.

Treatment of an Expected Decrease in Net Income Before Income Taxes

Note that, in the event of an expected decrease in net income before income taxes for any particular year when calculating the EAATB associated with an investment under evaluation, a decrease in income tax expense for that year will result. To illustrate, let's assume that, with regard to option 1 of QRS's proposed $100,000 equipment purchase, the expected annual increase in gross profit generated by the equipment purchase is $15,500 instead of $27,500 for years 1, 2, and 3 of the project. The EAATBs for these years would be calculated as shown in figure 10.11 (on page 296).

QRS, LLC Expected Annual After-Tax Benefits (EAATBs) of a Proposed $100,000 Equipment Purchase			
	Year 1	Year 2	Year 3
Expected annual increase in gross profit	$15,500	$15,500	$15,500
Less: New depreciation expense	9,000	16,200	12,960
Less: Increased utilities and insurance expense	1,000	1,000	1,000
Less: Increased maintenance expense	1,500	1,500	1,500
Expected increase (decrease) in net income before income taxes (NIBIT)	4,000	(3,200)	40
Less: Increase (decrease) in income tax expense (NIBIT x 21%)	840	(672)	8
Expected increase (decrease) in net income	3,160	(2,528)	32
Add: New depreciation expense	9,000	16,200	12,960
Expected annual after-tax benefit (EAATB) (increase in cash flow)	$12,160	$13,672	$12,992

Figure 10.11. The treatment of an expected decrease in net income before income taxes.

Focusing on year 2, notice that the proposed equipment purchase will result in an expected decrease in net income before income taxes of $3,200. Because the net income before income taxes of the company as a whole will decrease by $3,200 in year 2 due to the equipment purchase, the company will pay $672 less in income taxes in year 2 ($3,200 x 0.21 = $672). Income tax is an expense. If the company pays $672 less income taxes, the company's net income will decrease in year 2 by $2,528 rather than by $3,200.

Notice last that, for year 2, the add back of the new depreciation expense associated with the proposed equipment purchase results in a positive expected cash flow even though the equipment purchase will have a negative effect on net income. This result is not uncommon.

Calculating NPV Using Present Value of an Ordinary Annuity

The calculations in figures 10.7 (page 290) and 10.8 (page 291) may seem like a lot of work, but remember, you'll likely have determined one appropriate discount rate that you'll consistently use for capital budgeting purposes, rather than continually experiment with multiple discount rates as we've done in many of the schedules thus far in this chapter. Alternatively, you might choose to calculate the IRR for a project rather than its NPV.

A shortcut to calculating NPV does exist, but it can't be utilized in every instance. If there are multiple consecutive years with the same EAATB, one present value of an ordinary annuity (PVOA) calculation can replace multiple present value of a lump sum calculations. Note the transformation of figure 10.7 (page 290) into figure 10.12 by replacing three present value calculations with one PVOA calculation. Similarly, note the transformation of figure 10.8 (page 291) into figure 10.13 by replacing eight present value calculations with one PVOA calculation.

Note that the solutions arrived at in figures 10.12 and 10.13 differ slightly from the solutions indicated in figures 10.7 and 10.8. This difference is due to rounding both in the figures and in the present value and future value tables from which the present value factors were sourced. The PVOAs utilized in figure 10.12 were calculated as shown in figure 10.14 (page 298).

					QRS, LLC					
				Net Present Values (NPVs) of a Proposed $100,000 Equipment Purchase						
				Option 1: $1,500 of Annual Maintenance Expense						
Cash Flow Item	Time Period	Cash Flow Amount	Type of Factor	Factor at 4%	Present Value at 4%	Factor at 8%	Present Value at 8%	Factor at 15%	Present Value at 15%
---	---	---	---	---	---	---	---	---	---
Equipment Purchase	Today	$(100,000)	PV	1.0000	$(100,000)	1.0000	$(100,000)	1.0000	$(100,000)
EAATB	Year 1	21,640	PV	0.9615	20,807	0.9259	20,036	0.8696	18,818
EAATB	Year 2	23,152	PV	0.9246	21,406	0.8573	19,848	0.7561	17,505
EAATB	Year 3	22,472	PV	0.8890	19,977	0.7938	17,838	0.6575	14,775
EAATB	Year 4	21,927	PV	0.8548	18,743	0.7350	16,117	0.5718	12,538
EAATB	Year 5	21,493	PV	0.8219	17,665	0.6806	14,628	0.4972	10,686
EAATB	Year 6	21,143	PV	0.7903	16,709	0.6302	13,324	0.4323	9,140
EAATB	Year 7	20,988	PV	0.7599	15,949	0.5835	12,246	0.3759	7,889
EAATB	Year 8	20,988	PV	0.7307	15,336	0.5403	11,340	0.3269	6,861
EAATB	Year 9	20,990	PV	0.7026	14,747	0.5002	10,499	0.2843	5,967
EAATB	Year 10	20,988	PV	0.6756	14,179	0.4632	9,722	0.2472	5,188
EAATB	Year 11	20,370	PV	0.6496	13,232	0.4289	8,737	0.2149	4,377
EAATB	Years 12-14	19,750	PVOA	1.8026	35,602	1.1052	21,828	0.4908	9,693
EAATB	Year 15	29,750	PV	0.5553	16,520	0.3152	9,377	0.1229	3,656
			Net Present Values (NPVs)		$ 140,874		$ 85,541		$ 27,095

Figure 10.12. NPVs of QRS's proposed $100,000 equipment purchase—option 1—using PVOA.

					QRS, LLC					
				Net Present Values (NPVs) of a Proposed $100,000 Equipment Purchase						
				Option 2: $5,000 Annual Service Contract						
Cash Flow Item	Time Period	Cash Flow Amount	Type of Factor	Factor at 4%	Present Value at 4%	Factor at 8%	Present Value at 8%	Factor at 15%	Present Value at 15%
---	---	---	---	---	---	---	---	---	---
Equipment Purchase	Today	$(100,000)	PV	1.0000	$(100,000)	1.0000	$(100,000)	1.0000	$(100,000)
EAATB	Year 1	18,875	PV	0.9615	18,148	0.9259	17,476	0.8696	16,414
EAATB	Year 2	20,387	PV	0.9246	18,850	0.8573	17,478	0.7561	15,415
EAATB	Year 3	19,707	PV	0.8890	17,519	0.7938	15,643	0.6575	12,957
EAATB	Year 4	19,162	PV	0.8548	16,380	0.7350	14,084	0.5718	10,957
EAATB	Year 5	18,728	PV	0.8219	15,392	0.6806	12,746	0.4972	9,311
EAATB	Year 6	18,378	PV	0.7903	14,524	0.6302	11,582	0.4323	7,945
EAATB	Year 7	18,223	PV	0.7599	13,848	0.5835	10,633	0.3759	6,850
EAATB	Year 8	18,223	PV	0.7307	13,316	0.5403	9,846	0.3269	5,957
EAATB	Year 9	18,225	PV	0.7026	12,805	0.5002	9,116	0.2843	5,181
EAATB	Year 10	18,223	PV	0.6756	12,311	0.4632	8,441	0.2472	4,505
EAATB	Year 11	17,605	PV	0.6496	11,436	0.4289	7,551	0.2149	3,783
EAATB	Years 12-19	16,985	PVOA	4.3734	74,283	2.4646	41,862	0.9645	16,382
EAATB	Year 20	26,985	PV	0.4564	12,316	0.2145	5,788	0.0611	1,649
			Net Present Values (NPVs)		$ 151,128		$ 82,246		$ 17,306

Figure 10.13. NPVs of QRS's proposed $100,000 equipment purchase—option 2—using PVOA.

Calculation of PVOA Factors for Years 12–14			
	4%	8%	15%
PVOA Factor for Year 14	10.5631	8.2442	5.7245
− PVOA Factor for Year 11	8.7605	7.1390	5.2337
PVOA Factor for Years 12-14	1.8026	1.1052	0.4908

Figure 10.14. Calculation of PVOA factors for years 12–14.

Calculation of PVOA Factors for Years 12–19			
	4%	8%	15%
PVOA Factor for Year 19	13.1339	9.6036	6.1982
− PVOA Factor for Year 11	8.7605	7.1390	5.2337
PVOA Factor for Years 12-19	4.3734	2.4646	0.9645

Figure 10.15. Calculation of PVOA factors for years 12–19.

The PVOAs utilized in figure 10.13 were calculated as shown in figure 10.15.

As illustrated in figures 10.14 and 10.15, when calculating a PVOA factor for a series of consecutive equal EAATBs that doesn't include all the years of the investment under consideration, one must determine two things:

1. the PVOA related to the year of the last consecutive equal EAATB
2. the PVOA related to the year before the first consecutive equal EAATB

One must then subtract the second PVOA from the first PVOA in order to arrive at the correct PVOA for the applicable series of consecutive equal EAATBs.

Specifically, referring to figure 10.10 (page 294), years 12-19 all have an EAATB of $16,985, so it makes sense that we might want to calculate the PVOA factor for years 12-19 for each discount rate rather than looking up and utilizing eight different PV factors for each discount rate. Focusing on the PVOA factor for the 4 percent discount rate calculated in figure 10.15, the 4.3734 factor was determined by subtracting the PVOA related to year 11 (the PVOA related to the year before the first consecutive equal EAATB) from the PVOA for year 19 (the PVOA related to the year of the last consecutive equal EAATB).

Lowest Total Cost

As mentioned earlier in the chapter, the lowest total cost (LTC) method is a capital budgeting method similar to the NPV method commonly used by business owners who must replace fixed assets on a regular basis. LTC emphasizes minimizing total cost because the benefit stream (other than the salvage value, if there is any) doesn't change with the fixed asset chosen.

The LTC method is like the NPV method in that LTC utilizes time value of money concepts to discount future costs and benefits back to the present. The major difference between the methods is that there is no chance of a positive NPV when using LTC. The goal is to determine the least expensive purchase option, which is the option with the smallest negative NPV. Example 10.2 presents an LTC problem.

Example 10.2

Thomas Distributing, LLC is a medium-sized freight delivery business owned by Tommie Thomas, a solo entrepreneur. Tommie is faced with the need to replace one of his trucks. He's trying to decide between the three options his local commercial truck dealer has presented, which figure 10.16 details.

It's difficult to tell by looking at figure 10.16 which is the best truck option for Thomas Distributing. Truck A costs the most up front, but it has the lowest engine overhaul cost and it consistently has the lowest annual gas, insurance, and maintenance costs. Truck A also has a $5,000 salvage value. Trucks B and C cost less up

Thomas Distributing, LLC Truck Purchase Options	Truck A	Truck B	Truck C
Truck purchase price	$100,000	$85,000	$79,500
Annual gas, insurance, and maintenance, years 1–4	$ 5,000	$ 6,000	$ 7,000
Engine overhaul, end of year 4	$ 4,500	$ 5,500	$ 6,000
Annual gas, insurance, and maintenance, years 5–8	$ 5,500	$ 6,250	$ 7,150
Salvage value at the end of year 8	$ 5,000	–	–

Figure 10.16. Truck purchase options.

Thomas Distributing, LLC Depreciation Schedule		Truck A	Truck B	Truck C
Truck cost:		$100,000	$85,000	$79,500
Less: Salvage value:		5,000	-	-
Depreciable value:		$ 95,000	$85,000	$79,500
Useful life in years:		7	7	7
Depreciation method:		MACRS, half-year convention	MACRS, half-year convention	MACRS, half-year convention

Year	MACRS Depreciation Rate	Depreciation	Depreciation	Depreciation
1	14.29%	$ 13,576	$12,147	$11,361
2	24.49%	23,266	20,817	19,470
3	17.49%	16,616	14,867	13,905
4	12.49%	11,866	10,617	9,930
5	8.93%	8,484	7,591	7,099
6	8.92%	8,474	7,582	7,091
7	8.93%	8,484	7,591	7,099
8	4.46%	4,237	3,791	3,546
Totals	100.00%	$ 95,000	$85,000	$79,500

Figure 10.17. Depreciation schedule for the truck purchase options.

Thomas Distributing, LLC
Expected Annual After-Tax Benefits (EAATBs) of the Truck Purchase Options

Truck A	Year 1	Year 2	Year 3	Year 4	Year 5	Year 6	Year 7	Year 8
Depreciation expense	$(13,576)	$(23,266)	$(16,616)	$(11,866)	$ (8,484)	$ (8,474)	$ (8,484)	$ (4,237)
Gas, insurance, and maintenance expense, years 1–4	(5,000)	(5,000)	(5,000)	(5,000)	-	-	-	-
Engine overhaul, end of year 4	-	-	-	(4,500)	-	-	-	-
Gas, insurance, and maintenance expense, years 5–8	-	-	-	-	(5,500)	(5,500)	(5,500)	(5,500)
Expected decrease in net income before income taxes (NIBIT)	(18,576)	(28,266)	(21,616)	(21,366)	(13,984)	(13,974)	(13,984)	(9,737)
Less: Decrease in income tax expense (NIBIT x 24%)	(4,458)	(6,784)	(5,188)	(5,128)	(3,356)	(3,354)	(3,356)	(2,337)
Expected decrease in net income	(14,118)	(21,482)	(16,428)	(16,238)	(10,628)	(10,620)	(10,628)	(7,400)
Add: New depreciation expense	13,576	23,266	16,616	11,866	8,484	8,474	8,484	4,237
Add: Proceeds from sale of truck at the end of year 8	-	-	-	-	-	-	-	5,000
Expected annual after-tax benefit (EAATB)	$ (542)	$ 1,784	$ 188	$ (4,372)	$ (2,144)	$ (2,146)	$ (2,144)	$ 1,837

Truck B	Year 1	Year 2	Year 3	Year 4	Year 5	Year 6	Year 7	Year 8
Depreciation expense	$(12,147)	$(20,817)	$(14,867)	$(10,617)	$ (7,591)	$ (7,582)	$ (7,591)	$ (3,791)
Gas, insurance, and maintenance expense, years 1–4	(6,000)	(6,000)	(6,000)	(6,000)	-	-	-	-
Engine overhaul, end of year 4	-	-	-	(5,500)	-	-	-	-
Gas, insurance, and maintenance expense, years 5–8	-	-	-	-	(6,250)	(6,250)	(6,250)	(6,250)
Expected decrease in net income before income taxes (NIBIT)	(18,147)	(26,817)	(20,867)	(22,117)	(13,841)	(13,832)	(13,841)	(10,041)
Less: Decrease in income tax expense (NIBIT x 24%)	(4,355)	(6,436)	(5,008)	(5,308)	(3,322)	(3,320)	(3,322)	(2,410)
Expected decrease in net income	(13,792)	(20,381)	(15,859)	(16,809)	(10,519)	(10,512)	(10,519)	(7,631)
Add: New depreciation expense	12,147	20,817	14,867	10,617	7,591	7,582	7,591	3,791
Add: Proceeds from sale of truck at the end of year 8	-	-	-	-	-	-	-	-
Expected annual after-tax benefit (EAATB)	$ (1,645)	$ 436	$ (992)	$ (6,192)	$ (2,928)	$ (2,930)	$ (2,928)	$ (3,840)

Truck C	Year 1	Year 2	Year 3	Year 4	Year 5	Year 6	Year 7	Year 8
Depreciation expense	$(11,361)	$(19,470)	$(13,905)	$(9,930)	$ (7,099)	$ (7,091)	$ (7,099)	$ (3,546)
Gas, insurance, and maintenance expense, years 1–4	(7,000)	(7,000)	(7,000)	(7,000)	-	-	-	-
Engine overhaul, end of year 4	-	-	-	(6,000)	-	-	-	-
Gas, insurance, and maintenance expense, years 5–8	-	-	-	-	(7,150)	(7,150)	(7,150)	(7,150)
Expected decrease in net income before income taxes (NIBIT)	(18,361)	(26,470)	(20,905)	(22,930)	(14,249)	(14,241)	(14,249)	(10,696)
Less: Decrease in income tax expense (NIBIT x 24%)	(4,407)	(6,353)	(5,017)	(5,503)	(3,420)	(3,418)	(3,420)	(2,567)
Expected decrease in net income	(13,954)	(20,117)	(15,888)	(17,427)	(10,829)	(10,823)	(10,829)	(8,129)
Add: New depreciation expense	11,361	19,470	13,905	9,930	7,099	7,091	7,099	3,546
Add: Proceeds from sale of truck at the end of year 8	-	-	-	-	-	-	-	-
Expected annual after-tax benefit (EAATB)	$ (2,593)	$ (647)	$ (1,983)	$ (7,497)	$ (3,730)	$ (3,732)	$ (3,730)	$ (4,583)

Figure 10.18. EAATBs of the truck purchase options.

				Truck A		Truck B		Truck C	
Cash Flow Item	Time Period	Type of Factor	Factor at 6%	Cash Flow Amount	Present Value	Cash Flow Amount	Present Value	Cash Flow Amount	Present Value
Truck Purchase	Today	PV	1.0000	$(100,000)	$(100,000)	$(85,000)	$(85,000)	$(79,500)	$(79,500)
EAATB	Year 1	PV	0.9434	(542)	(511)	(1,645)	(1,552)	(2,593)	(2,447)
EAATB	Year 2	PV	0.8900	1,784	1,588	436	388	(647)	(576)
EAATB	Year 3	PV	0.8396	188	158	(992)	(833)	(1,983)	(1,665)
EAATB	Year 4	PV	0.7921	(4,372)	(3,463)	(6,192)	(4,905)	(7,497)	(5,938)
EAATB	Year 5	PV	0.7473	(2,144)	(1,602)	(2,928)	(2,188)	(3,730)	(2,788)
EAATB	Year 6	PV	0.7050	(2,146)	(1,513)	(2,930)	(2,066)	(3,732)	(2,631)
EAATB	Year 7	PV	0.6651	(2,144)	(1,426)	(2,928)	(1,948)	(3,730)	(2,481)
EAATB	Year 8	PV	0.6274	1,837	1,152	(3,840)	(2,409)	(4,583)	(2,875)
			Net Present Values (NPVs)		$(105,618)		$(100,512)		$(100,901)

The table is titled: Thomas Distributing, LLC — Net Present Values (NPVs) of the Truck Purchase Options

Figure 10.19. NPVs of the truck purchase options.

front, but they have higher engine overhaul costs and annual gas, insurance, and maintenance costs—and they are expected to have no salvage value. This is a classic example of an instance where the LTC method of capital budgeting can provide some direction regarding which option is the best choice.

Though he doesn't need to borrow money to finance the truck purchase, Tommie can borrow money at 6 percent, so he has decided that 6 percent is a reasonable discount rate to use to decide between the three options. Tommie's personal income tax rate is 24 percent, so that's the tax rate he typically uses to evaluate potential major purchases and projects for his company.

The first step we'll need to take in order to perform an LTC analysis for example 10.2 is to create a depreciation schedule that addresses each of the truck options—a schedule like that included at figure 10.17 (page 299).

Next we'll need to calculate the EAATB associated with each truck for each year. Note that since we are doing LTC analysis, many of the EAATBs we calculate won't actually be a benefit at all—they'll be negative numbers. Figure 10.18 illustrates the calculation of the EAATB for each truck for each year.

Last, we'll use the EAATBs we've calculated to determine a NPV for each truck option using a discount rate of 6 percent. Figure 10.19 shows the calculation of the NPVs for the three truck options.

Figure 10.19 indicates that despite having higher engine overhaul costs and higher annual gas, insurance, and maintenance costs than truck A—and despite having a higher purchase price than truck C—truck B has the smallest negative NPV. This means truck B has the lowest total cost considering the time value of money and income taxes. As a result, based solely on the numbers, truck B appears to be the optimal truck purchase option for Thomas Distributing.

The LTC method can often point a business owner toward the unobvious correct choice. Entrepreneur in Action 10.1 (page 302) illustrates such an instance.

Entrepreneur *in Action* **10.1**

An Entrepreneur Learns the Value of Lowest Total Cost Analysis

Sharon Paulson, founder and owner of Impact Marketing, Inc., was trying to make a decision. She had been outsourcing the printing of her clients' high-end marketing materials for years, but this outsourcing was becoming increasingly expensive. Expensive enough in fact that she had decided that, instead of continuing to outsource the printing, the company should instead buy a high-end printer and print client materials in-house. Sharon had requested and received quotes detailing the purchase price and estimated annual operating costs for three different high-end printers she felt would suit her business's needs. Sharon had taken the time to summarize the details of the quotes as follows:

	Option A	Option B	Option C
Purchase price	$100,000	$ 90,000	$ 80,000
Annual operating cost—Year 1	$ 5,000	$ 10,000	$ 4,750
Annual operating cost—Year 2	$ 5,000	$ 9,500	$ 6,000
Annual operating cost—Year 3	$ 5,000	$ 9,000	$ 7,250
Annual operating cost—Year 4	$ 7,500	$ 6,500	$ 13,000
Annual operating cost—Year 5	$ 7,500	$ 5,000	$ 14,000
Annual operating cost—Year 6	$ 7,500	$ 5,000	$ 15,000
Total annual operating costs	$ 37,500	$ 45,000	$ 60,000
Estimated total cost	$137,500	$135,000	$140,000

Always wishing to minimize her business's costs and maximize its profits, Sharon felt that because it boasted the lowest estimated total cost, Option B was clearly the best choice. Sharon was about to get online and place the order for the Option B printer when her assistant, Marta, a business school graduate and recent new hire, looked over Sharon's shoulder and asked her what she was working on. Sharon explained the reason for her decision to buy a new printer for the business and showed Marta the schedule summarizing the different printer option costs. Marta studied the schedule, was quiet for a moment, and then gently asked, "Is this the only information you're going to use to make your decision?" Sharon said, "Yes. Why do you ask?" Marta then went on to explain that Sharon was ignoring income tax and time value of money considerations if she was making her decision based solely on the numbers included on her summary. Next, Marta sat down, quickly generated a tax depreciation schedule for each of the three options, determined the estimated annual after-tax benefit for each year for each of the options, and determined each option's net present value considering Impact Marketing's 6 percent borrowing rate. Marta then showed Sharon the spreadsheet she had just created. It indicated net present values of $(105,951), $(103,791), and $(102,998), respectively, for printer options A, B, and C. Marta then explained to Sharon that, in fact, Option C was the least expensive purchase option for Impact Marketing because it had the lowest negative net present value. Marta further noted that the analysis she had performed had a name, "It's called Lowest Total Cost."

Sharon was quiet for a moment. She was a bit surprised by the results of Marta's analysis, but then quickly decided she was also quite pleased. Sharon realized happily what a valuable new resource she had in Marta. Always up for learning something new, Sharon said appreciatively to Marta, "Option C it is, then! Thank you, Marta, for taking the time to show me the value of Lowest Total Cost analysis."

Summary

Capital budgeting is the process we use to justify the acquisition of capital assets (assets that have an expected useful life in excess of one year) or the investment in projects that support the expansion of business operations.

The three methods of analysis typically used to make sound capital budgeting decisions are:

1. payback
2. net present value (NPV) or lowest total cost (LTC)
3. internal rate of return (IRR)

The payback method provides useful information regarding how quickly an opportunity will return to us our initial investment in that opportunity. However, payback isn't an optimal method for analyzing a capital budgeting decision because it doesn't consider the time value of money, it favors investments with a quick return over those with the largest overall return, and it doesn't always give a clear answer regarding whether to invest in a particular opportunity. Note, however, that a payback period that exceeds the expected functional life of the investment under consideration does clearly suggest that we shouldn't invest in the opportunity.

When making a decision using NPV, if the NPV is positive, make the investment. If the NPV is negative, don't make the investment. Making a capital budgeting decision using the NPV method versus the payback method has two primary advantages:

1. The future cash flows that will be paid and received are discounted back to the present so a decision can be made on the investment—or a choice can be made between investments—based on objective criteria (i.e., the value of the investment(s) in today's dollars).
2. The interest rates (discount rates) used are determined by, and based on, the expectations of—and the circumstances surrounding—the specific company making the decision.

LTC is a capital budgeting method similar to NPV and is commonly used by business owners who must replace fixed assets on a regular basis. LTC emphasizes minimizing total cost because the benefit stream (other than the salvage value, if there is any) doesn't change with the fixed asset chosen. The LTC method is like the NPV method in that LTC utilizes time value of money concepts to discount future costs and benefits back to the present. The major difference between the methods is that there is no chance of a positive NPV when using LTC. The goal is to determine the least expensive purchase option, which is the option with the smallest negative NPV.

IRR is the actual rate of return of an investment, considers the time value of money in its calculation, and is the interest rate that, when used as the discount rate to determine the NPV of a proposed investment, results in an NPV of zero. The calculation of IRR can be useful when evaluating investment options in that, if we've determined a minimum rate of return we wish all our investments to generate, the IRR provides the real rate of return associated with an investment that we can compare to that threshold. Note that a negative IRR is a strong indicator that we shouldn't invest in the opportunity under consideration.

Key Terms

capital budgeting	lowest total cost (LTC)	payback method
internal rate of return	method	Section 179 deduction
(IRR)	net present value (NPV)	
	method	

Review and Discussion Questions

1. List and define the costs and benefits relevant to capital budgeting analysis.
2. Why is cash flow considered a more appropriate tool for decision making than net income?
3. What three methods of analysis are typically used to make sound capital budgeting decisions? How do we use the results of these three methods of analysis to choose between investment options?
4. NPV calculations are made using a discount rate that matches our perceived cost of capital. Define perceived cost of capital, and provide some examples of perceived cost of capital included in the chapter.
5. When determining NPV or LTC, sometimes, calculating one present value of an ordinary annuity (PVOA) can be utilized as a shortcut to calculating multiple present value of a lump sum. When is this possible, and how is the PVOA factor calculated?

Exercises

1. You're considering purchasing a new limousine for your transportation services business, Miami Luxury Transportation, LLC. You believe the limousine will increase your business's gross profit by $36,000 each year for the next seven years.

   The cost of the limousine will be $85,000. For tax purposes, this five-year asset life vehicle will be depreciated using the MACRS half-year convention depreciation method (see the MACRS half-year convention depreciation rate table included at figure 10.1). You believe you can sell the limousine for $5,000 at the end of year 7.

   Your company is an LLC that's taxed like a partnership, but because the personal income tax situations of you and your business partners are heavily impacted by what happens with the business, you and your business partners have agreed to use an income tax rate of 24 percent when making capital budgeting decisions. As a result of the limousine purchase, your business will experience the following increases in annual expenses: insurance, $1,500; vehicle maintenance, $1,750; and gas expense, $4,800. Because your business can borrow money at 9 percent, you think 9 percent is a reasonable discount rate to use to evaluate this investment decision.

   a. Develop a tax depreciation schedule for this proposed limousine purchase.
   b. Calculate the EAATBs for years 1–7 associated with this proposed limousine purchase.
   c. Determine the payback period associated with this proposed limousine purchase. Based on the results of your calculations, should you purchase the limousine?
   d. Calculate the NPV associated with this proposed limousine purchase. Based on the results of your calculations, should you purchase the limousine?
   e. Use Microsoft Excel to calculate the IRR associated with this proposed limousine purchase.

2. You want to buy a new piece of equipment for your business, Paul Wyland Construction Services, Inc. You believe you can use the equipment in your business to increase your gross profit by $15,000 each year for the next 10 years.

   The equipment costs $150,000, your business has $150,000 of available cash, and your business can currently earn 7 percent on its money. You believe you can sell the equipment at the end of year 10 for $20,000. For tax purposes, this seven-year asset life piece of equipment will be depreciated using the MACRS half-year convention depreciation method (see the MACRS half-year convention depreciation rate table included at figure 10.1).

Insurance for the new equipment would cost $250 per quarter. The utilities and maintenance expenses to support the new equipment would amount to $3,000 per year. Your company's income tax rate is approximately 21 percent.

a. Develop a tax depreciation schedule for this proposed equipment purchase.

b. Calculate the EAATBs for years 1–10 associated with this proposed equipment purchase.

c. Determine the payback period associated with this proposed equipment purchase. Based on the results of your calculations, should you purchase the piece of equipment?

d. Calculate the NPV associated with this proposed equipment purchase. Based on the results of your calculations, should you buy this piece of equipment?

e. Use Microsoft Excel to calculate the IRR associated with this proposed equipment purchase.

3. You're the sole owner of a retail store called Wendy's Wine and Exotic Cheeses. You want to purchase additional coolers so you can stock additional inventory. You believe the coolers will allow you to stock enough additional product to increase your business's gross profit by $12,000 each year for the next 10 years.

The coolers will cost $55,000. For tax purposes, the seven-year asset life coolers will be depreciated using the MACRS half-year convention depreciation method (see the MACRS half-year convention depreciation rate table included at figure 10.1). The coolers are deemed to have a salvage value of $5,000 at the end of year 10.

Your company is an LLC that's taxed like a sole proprietorship, but because your personal income tax situation is heavily impacted by what happens with your business, you use your personal income tax rate of 22 percent when making capital budgeting decisions. As a result of the asset purchase, you'll experience the following increases in annual expenses: personal property taxes, $55; insurance, $1,200; and utilities, $2,400. Because your business can borrow money at 8 percent, you feel 8 percent is a reasonable discount rate to use to evaluate this investment decision.

a. Develop a tax depreciation schedule for this proposed asset purchase.

b. Calculate the EAATBs for years 1–10 associated with this proposed asset purchase.

c. Determine the payback period associated with this proposed asset purchase. Based on the results of your calculations, should you purchase the coolers?

d. Calculate the NPV associated with this proposed asset purchase. Based on the results of your calculations, should you purchase the coolers?

e. Use Microsoft Excel to calculate the IRR associated with this proposed asset purchase.

4. Yu Yan Hsieh owns two restaurants, the Detroit Avenue Diner and the Clifton Avenue Diner, under the umbrella of her company Hsieh Enterprises, LLC. Yu Yan knows she needs to replace her restaurants' kitchen equipment. The grills and ovens have broken down repeatedly, and Yu Yan worries the refrigerators aren't keeping food cold enough. Yu Yan has received quotes from many kitchen equipment dealers and has narrowed the options down to three, the information for which follows:

Hsieh Enterprises, LLC Kitchen Equipment Purchase Options			
	Option A	Option B	Option C
Equipment purchase price	$250,000	$235,000	$215,000
Annual insurance and utilities expense	$ 1,000	$ 1,200	$ 1,450
Annual service contract, years 1–5	$ 1,500	$ 2,400	$ 2,750
Equipment overhaul, end of year 5	$ 5,000	$ 7,500	$ 10,000
Annual service contract, years 6–20	$ 2,500	$ 3,600	$ 3,750
Salvage value at the end of year 20	$ 25,000	$ 23,500	$ 21,500

Yu Yan has been saving money to replace her restaurants' kitchen equipment for years. That said, she doesn't want to spend one dime more than absolutely necessary, so she's currently favoring option C. Yu Yan has determined the EAATBs for each year for each option as shown in the schedule below.

Hsieh Enterprises, LLC Expected Annual After-Tax Benefits (EAATBs) of the Kitchen Equipment Purchase Options			
	Option A	Option B	Option C
Expected annual after-tax benefit for year 1	$ 5,817	$ 4,518	$ 3,444
Expected annual after-tax benefit for year 2	$ 11,325	$ 9,695	$ 8,181
Expected annual after-tax benefit for year 3	$ 7,545	$ 6,142	$ 4,930
Expected annual after-tax benefit for year 4	$ 4,845	$ 3,604	$ 2,608
Expected annual after-tax benefit for year 5	$ (878)	$ (3,903)	$ (6,645)
Expected annual after-tax benefit for year 6	$ 2,157	$ 880	$ 190
Expected annual after-tax benefit for year 7	$ 2,162	$ 885	$ 195
Expected annual after-tax benefit for year 8	$ (252)	$ (1,384)	$ (1,881)
Expected annual after-tax benefit for year 9	$ (2,660)	$ (3,648)	$ (3,952)
Expected annual after-tax benefit for year 10	$ (2,660)	$ (3,648)	$ (3,952)
Expected annual after-tax benefit for year 11	$ (2,660)	$ (3,648)	$ (3,952)
Expected annual after-tax benefit for year 12	$ (2,660)	$ (3,648)	$ (3,952)
Expected annual after-tax benefit for year 13	$ (2,660)	$ (3,648)	$ (3,952)
Expected annual after-tax benefit for year 14	$ (2,660)	$ (3,648)	$ (3,952)
Expected annual after-tax benefit for year 15	$ (2,660)	$ (3,648)	$ (3,952)
Expected annual after-tax benefit for year 16	$ (2,660)	$ (3,648)	$ (3,952)
Expected annual after-tax benefit for year 17	$ (2,660)	$ (3,648)	$ (3,952)
Expected annual after-tax benefit for year 18	$ (2,660)	$ (3,648)	$ (3,952)
Expected annual after-tax benefit for year 19	$ (2,660)	$ (3,648)	$ (3,952)
Expected annual after-tax benefit for year 20	$ 22,340	$19,852	$ 17,548

Assuming Yu Yan considers 6 percent a good discount rate for evaluating the three options and is an adherent to the concept of time value of money, which option should Yu Yan choose? Use the LTC method and PVOA, as applicable, to determine your answer.

5. ParkItFast, Inc. is a technology company that has developed a smartphone application that helps drivers find the empty parking space nearest them quickly. ParkItFast has been leasing big data appliances to support its application, but because the leasing company now only sells the machines outright, ParkItFast's lease—which is coming to an end—isn't renewable. ParkItFast has determined the most cost-effective way to move forward isn't to lease big data appliances anyway. Owning the machines is more cost effective in the long run. But which machines? ParkItFast's management team is trying to decide

between the two options presented by the company's big data appliance dealer of choice:

ParkItFast, Inc. Big Data Appliance Purchase Options	Option A	Option B
Purchase price per machine	$675,000	$240,000
Annual insurance and maintenance expense per machine, year 1	$ 5,000	$ 350
Annual insurance and maintenance expense per machine, years 2–8	$ 15,000	$ 500
Salvage value per machine at the end of year 8	$ 15,000	–

ParkItFast has a choice between buying one mega machine (option A) or three big machines (option B). Both options will satisfy all of ParkItFast's needs. Buying one mega machine is cheaper in terms of purchase price, but if ParkItFast has only one machine, that machine simply can't fail. As a result, the amount of maintenance that will be required on the mega machine is much higher. The amount of electricity required to run the machines is negligible.

ParkItFast pays corporate income tax at a rate of 21 percent. Using the LTC method, the depreciation schedule included below, and a discount rate of 7 percent, which option should ParkItFast choose?

ParkItFast, Inc. Depreciation Schedule	Option A	Option B
Machine cost:	$675,000	$240,000
Number of machines:	x 1	x 3
	$675,000	$720,000
Less: Salvage value:	15,000	–
Depreciable value:	$660,000	$720,000
Useful life in years:	7	7
Depreciation method:	MACRS, half-year convention	MACRS, half-year convention

Year	MACRS Depreciation Rate	Depreciation	Depreciation
1	14.29%	$ 94,314	$102,888
2	24.49%	161,634	176,328
3	17.49%	115,434	125,928
4	12.49%	82,434	89,928
5	8.93%	58,938	64,296
6	8.92%	58,872	64,224
7	8.93%	58,938	64,296
8	4.46%	29,436	32,112
Totals	100.00%	$660,000	$720,000

Cash Harvest, Business Valuation, and Business Exit

"Show me the money."

— Cuba Gooding Jr., American actor, playing Rod Tidwell in the movie *Jerry McGuire*

Learning Objectives

Have knowledge of the cash harvest options available to entrepreneurs.

- Have an understanding of how to position a company for sale, sell a business, and dissolve a business.

Be able to identify and describe the various approaches for determining the value of a business.

Be able to prepare a business valuation using the discounted cash flow method.

Introduction

Cash harvest is a result desired by virtually every entrepreneur and investor. Cash harvest can begin to take place once a company has matured enough to have the cash available to pay out salaries, dividends, or distributions to its owners and investors, as applicable. Cash harvest can also occur when an entrepreneur or a company's investors fully or partially exit the business—and through other means. In this chapter, we'll look at the common means business owners and investors utilize to harvest cash from their companies—means beyond salaries, dividends, or distributions. We'll also look at some of the required planning and typical consequences associated with these means. In addition, we'll look at the various reasons—beyond or in addition to the harvest of cash—that entrepreneurs and investors sometimes exit a business.

A desire to exit a business usually creates the need to determine a value for the business in question. Determining the value of a business might also be necessary for a variety of other reasons, including to properly insure the business, to support a loan to the business, or to complete a proper **buy-sell agreement**, which is a contract between the business's owners that indicates the terms that will surround the purchase of an exiting owner's interest in the business. Multiple approaches for determining the value of a business exist and will be discussed in this chapter. The most commonly used method to value a business—the **discounted cash flow method of business valuation**, a methodology that places a value on a business by determining, at a specified discount rate, the sum of the present values of all of the business's expected future cash flows—will be illustrated in detail in this chapter.

Non-Business-Exit Cash Harvest Options

buy-sell agreement
a contract between a business's owners that indicates the terms that will surround the purchase of an exiting owner's interest in the business

discounted cash flow method of business valuation
a methodology that places a value on a business by determining, at a specified discount rate, the sum of the present values of all of the business's expected future cash flows

leveraged recapitalization
a financial strategy whereby a company takes on substantial debt that is then used to make significant dividend or distribution payments to the company's owners

business succession planning
a process that formally considers the question of who will take over the management of a business in the event the business owner is unwilling or unable to continue managing the business because of a planned retirement or an unplanned event, such as an accident, severe illness, or death

Cash harvest options can be generally categorized into two types: those that don't involve an owner or investor exiting the business and those that do. Some of the cash harvest options that don't involve an owner exiting the business were discussed in chapter 3. They include the following:

- a C corporation paying dividends to its shareholders
- pass-through entities, such as S corporations and limited liability companies (LLCs), paying distributions to their owners
- owner-employees of corporations and entities taxed like a corporation paying themselves a salary

A business's legal form determines which of these options may or may not be available to a business's owners and investors. This is one of the reasons the choice of legal form of business needs to be carefully considered.

Beyond the three options listed above, another cash harvest option often available to the owner of a mature company well beyond the start-up phase—an option that doesn't involve the owner exiting the business and that's less restricted by the business's legal form—is **leveraged recapitalization**. In a leveraged recapitalization designed to benefit a company's owners, the company takes on substantial debt that is then used to make significant dividend or distribution payments to the company's owners. The debt is paid back over time by the company via its ongoing profitable and cash flow positive operations. Leveraged recapitalization is especially desirable in the instance of a C corporation, which can deduct the interest expense incurred for income tax purposes and therefore reduce the corporation's income tax bill. One of the reasons a leveraged recapitalization is attractive to many business owners is because an owner can maintain full ownership of his company while still putting a significant amount of cash in his pocket.

Business Succession Planning

In the instance of an owner choosing to stay with his company rather than exit it, the issue of business succession planning must be addressed. **Business succession planning** formally considers the question of who will take over the management of a business in the event the business owner is unwilling or unable to continue managing the business because of a planned retirement or an unplanned event, such as an accident, severe illness, or death.

Many start-up and small businesses are family-owned. As a result, business succession planning for these types of entities will often begin with discussions with the business owner's spouse and other interested family members. For a family-owned business, the business succession planning process should include consideration of the following major topics:

- a determination of whether there's any desire on the part of one or more family members to manage the business after the incapacitation or exit of the business's current owner-manager
- assuming such a desire exists, a determination of whether the needed knowledge base and skill sets are possessed by the interested family member(s)
- an honest evaluation of whether the company would, perhaps, be better served by outsourcing the management of the company to a non-family member

Whether for a family-owned business or a non-family-owned business, good succession planning involves identifying a planned successor whom the current owner-manager will groom to take his place. Ideally, a good succession plan is in writing and transparent to all of a business's stakeholders so that, when the time comes to institute the plan, the process can move forward with those most affected by the plan both aware of and in agreement with the plan. Effective succession planning results in the transfer of the management of a company to a new leader without distressing surprises and unpleasant disagreements.

Business-Exit Cash Harvest Options

Capital gain is a cash harvest option that was first discussed in chapter 3. A capital gain is the profit made by an investor after selling an asset whose value has appreciated beyond the amount invested to acquire or build that asset. With regard to an entire business, a capital gain results when an owner or investor sells all or part of the company he owns for more than the amount of his associated investment in that company. A capital gain, therefore, involves an owner or investor fully or partially exiting a business. Figure 11.1 outlines the top 10 ways an owner or investor might fully or partially exit a company.

The term liquidate refers to the **liquidation** of a business—concluding the affairs of a business by selling all of its assets, paying all of its liabilities, and distributing any remaining cash to the business's owners. The term dissolve refers to the **dissolution** of a business—legally terminating the existence of a business.

liquidation
concluding the affairs of a business by selling all of its assets, paying all of its liabilities, and distributing any remaining cash to the business's owners

dissolution
legally terminating the existence of a business

Top 10 Business-Exit Scenarios
1. Liquidate and dissolve an unsuccessful company.
2. Liquidate and dissolve a fixed-time or short-term company.
3. Liquidate and dissolve a successful company in order to pursue a different opportunity.
4. Gift or sell all or part of a company to the next generation of the family or other family members.
5. Sell all or part of a company to the company's employees.
6. Sell all or part of a company to a private equity firm.
7. Sell all or part of a company to the general public in the form of a public offering.
8. Sell all of a company to another individual or company (i.e., a competitor, distributor, or supplier).
9. Sell part of a company to an investor, often at the beginning stages of the company.
10. Sell one's ownership interest in a company to one's current business partners.

Figure 11.1. Top 10 business-exit scenarios.

No explanation is needed to understand why an entrepreneur might choose to liquidate and dissolve an unsuccessful company, but successful companies are also sometimes liquidated and dissolved. There are two common instances in which a successful company might be liquidated and dissolved:

1. when a company is a fixed-time or short-term company and the opportunity the company was created to pursue has passed or expired
2. when the owner of a company desires to focus on an alternative opportunity he thinks has more potential, is more lucrative, or is in some other way more attractive than continuing to operate his existing company

Fixed-time or short-term companies are usually companies started to address a temporary problem (e.g., how to implement a new government regulation) or to pursue a short-term trend (e.g., a fashion trend). An entrepreneur who founds a fixed-time or short-term company understands that the company will be operating—hopefully, at a profit—for a fixed or short time and will be liquidated and dissolved when the opportunity has passed or expired.

It may sound counterintuitive to liquidate and dissolve a successful company in order to pursue a different opportunity, but it happens every day. For example, many entrepreneurs aren't skilled at managing—or don't wish to manage—more than one company at a time, so they liquidate and dissolve one company in order to pursue another company with greater potential. Other entrepreneurs don't necessarily wish to be entrepreneurs their entire business career and might choose to accept a job that pays them better than their business does. Still others might wish to retire from their business but find themselves unsuccessful at selling the business.

As an entrepreneur approaches retirement age, gifting a company to the next generation of family or other family members is not unusual, especially if the business is considered by the entrepreneur to be a family business. The transfer of a business to family members as a gift was made more possible in December 2017 when Congress increased the **lifetime basic exclusion for gifts** for an individual from $5.49 million to $11.18 million. The lifetime basic exclusion for gifts is indexed for inflation, so it increases every year after 2018. In 2019, it increased to $11.4 million. The lifetime basic exclusion for gifts represents the amount of assets an individual can exclude when calculating the gift and estate taxes that may be due during the individual's lifetime or at the individual's death. This exclusion is over and above that allowed by an individual's **annual exclusion for gifts**. An individual's annual exclusion for gifts represents the amount of assets an individual can exclude when calculating the gift and estate taxes that may be due related to an individual tax year. Like the lifetime basic exclusion for gifts, the annual exclusion for gifts is also indexed for inflation, but it can increase only in $1,000 increments.[1] The exclusion amount for 2019 remains the same as it was in 2018: $15,000. All of this means that in 2019, using the lifetime basic exclusion for gifts, over an individual's lifetime, $11.4 million of value could be transferred to others tax free. Further, the annual exclusion for gifts allows for the tax-free transfer of an additional $15,000 of wealth each year.

Rather than gift a business to family members, entrepreneurs sometimes choose to sell the business to family members. This is often accomplished by the entrepreneur financing the sale of the company by accepting a promissory note in full or partial payment for the company with the expectation that the promissory note will be repaid out of the future profits of the company. Note that a third option, an entrepreneur selling part of the business to family during his lifetime and then gifting his remaining ownership interest in the business at his death, is also not an unusual arrangement. One of the benefits of this arrangement is that it allows the entrepreneur to maintain some control over the company—and therefore some control over what may be a major source of his post-retirement income—until his death.

lifetime basic exclusion for gifts
the amount of assets an individual can exclude when calculating the gift and estate taxes that may be due during the individual's lifetime or at the individual's death—over and above that allowed by an individual's annual exclusion for gifts

annual exclusion for gifts
the amount of assets an individual can exclude when calculating the gift and estate taxes that may be due related to an individual tax year

Alternatively, an entrepreneur might want to investigate the possibility of structuring a deal to sell all or part of his company to his employees via an **employee stock ownership plan (ESOP)**. An ESOP is an employee benefit plan designed to invest primarily in the stock of the sponsoring employer. Many successful U.S. companies, such as Publix Super Markets, the Davey Tree Expert Company, and Graybar Electrical Supply, are wholly or partially owned by their employees.[2] ESOPs can create a path not only for the owners of successful, closely held companies to exit their companies, but also for those owners to provide a substantial benefit to their employees should they decide to do so. Additionally, there are significant tax advantages associated with ESOPs that make such plans attractive both to a company's owners and to its employees.[3]

Another possibility for the entrepreneur is selling all or part of his company to a private equity firm, which is a firm that invests in other companies it often helps manage. Private equity firms are typically legally organized as privately held limited partnerships, and their investors tend to be large institutions or wealthy individuals. Private equity firms typically buy majority or full control of a mature company, often over time, and often utilizing debt structured in the form of a **leveraged buyout (LBO)**. In an LBO, the debt used to purchase a company is collateralized fully or partially by the assets or cash flows of the company being purchased. The strategy of most private equity firms is to somehow restructure the companies they purchase—or take advantage of the synergies that exist between the different companies the private equity firm owns—in order to improve the companies and then sell them for a price higher than what the private equity firm paid for them.

As first discussed in chapter 2, a public offering is an issue of securities offered for sale to the public by a company or other entity. An initial public offering (IPO) is a very highly regulated and managed first sale of most or all of the stock of a previously private company—or mostly private company—to the general public. A traditional IPO is designed for a large, mature company that has the resources needed to cover the significant accounting and legal expenses associated with going public. While it does happen from time to time, selling all of the ownership of a company to the general public during an IPO is fairly unusual.[4] Most of the time, only part of the ownership is sold. For example, after Facebook went public in 2012, cofounder Mark Zuckerberg still owned approximately 18 percent of the company.[5] A founder selling all of his ownership of a company is usually frowned upon due to concerns regarding the negative effect of founder brain drain—the exodus from the company of the individual(s) who started the company and therefore have the most comprehensive knowledge about the company. Also, a founder wanting to sell 100 percent of his ownership is likely to be viewed by some potential stock purchasers as signaling that the founder feels the company's value is currently at its peak.

An alternative to a full-scale IPO is a public offering under Regulation A. Regulation A gives a smaller company the ability to make a limited-size public offering, including the ability to list Tier 2 offerings on securities exchanges like the Nasdaq Stock Market (commonly referred to as NASDAQ) and the New York Stock Exchange (NYSE). For this reason, a Tier 2 Regulation A offering is sometimes called a "mini-IPO." Whether via a full-scale IPO or a smaller public offering under Regulation A, public offerings represent a viable option for entrepreneurs and investors to partially (and sometimes fully) exit a business.

An entrepreneur might also decide to sell all of his company to an outside individual or company, likely a competitor, distributor, or supplier. Other options include selling part of the company to an investor, often at the beginning stages of the company, or selling his ownership interest in a company to his business partners. We'll discuss how to successfully sell all or part of a company to these three categories of buyers in the remaining sections of this chapter.

employee stock ownership plan (ESOP)
an employee benefit plan designed to invest primarily in the stock of the sponsoring employer

leveraged buyout (LBO)
a financial strategy whereby the debt used to purchase a company is collateralized fully or partially by the assets or cash flows of the company being purchased

Exiting: Positioning a Company for Sale and Selling a Business

For reasons that will become apparent later, the discussion regarding selling part of a company to an investor or selling a portion of a company to one's business partners pairs naturally with the discussion of business valuation included at the end of this chapter. As a result, we'll focus in this section of the chapter on selling an entire company to an outside individual or company.

Attempting to sell a business to an outside individual or company is usually a significant undertaking made even more complicated by the fact that no two businesses—and therefore no two business sales—are exactly alike. It could be that you execute the sale of your company utilizing only the help of a good attorney. This approach is perfectly acceptable when the transaction is fairly uncomplicated. More often, however, you'll execute the sale of your company with the help of one of the following entities:

business broker

a professional who typically sells small companies to individuals

merger and acquisition (M&A) advisor

a professional who usually assists in the sale of businesses larger than those represented by a business broker but smaller than those represented by an investment banking firm

investment banking firm

a firm that usually assists in the sale of companies that are very large, very complex, or both

- a **business broker**—a professional who typically sells small companies (i.e., generally, companies valued at $2 million or less) to individuals[6]
- a **merger and acquisition (M&A) advisor**—a professional who usually assists in the sale of businesses larger than those represented by a business broker but smaller than those represented by an investment banking firm
- an **investment banking firm**—a firm that usually assists in the sale of companies that are very large, very complex, or both (i.e., generally, companies valued from $100 million to over $1 billion)[7, 8]

Whomever you choose to represent you, as the business's owner, you'll undoubtedly have to focus on two major areas: positioning your company for sale and then actually selling the business. While these two areas definitely overlap, they are different in that the first focuses more on research and planning and the second focuses more on the logistics and exertions associated with completing specific tasks.

Proper positioning of a company can make all the difference in terms of whether a company sells, how quickly it sells, and for how much it sells. In order to properly position a company for sale, you should perform the following eight actions:

1. Do the proper research before starting a company.
2. Consider building a business designed to attract specific buyers.
3. Clarify what's being sold.
4. Properly prepare the business for sale.
5. Consider what professional help may be needed to sell the business.
6. Determine what the business is worth.
7. Think ahead to the post-sale transition.
8. Put the company on the market at the right time and for the right reasons.

Attempting to sell a business should only occur after properly positioning the business for sale. In order to sell a business, you should perform the following two additional important steps:

1. Keep the business in top shape during the business sale process.
2. Execute the business sale process.

Each of these 10 areas of activity will vary in depth, breadth, and level of complexity depending on the nature of the business being sold. Still, some generalities are associated with each area of activity that this chapter will address.

Do the Proper Research before Starting a Company

Before you even start your company, you should talk to the entrepreneurs in your industry who were both successful and unsuccessful at selling their businesses and ask questions like the following:

- How quickly and why did the successful entrepreneurs' companies get bought?
- What obstacles had to be overcome to close these deals?
- Why didn't the unsuccessful entrepreneurs' companies get bought?
- What attributes made the companies attractive—or unattractive—to potential purchasers?

Knowing in advance the expectations of potential purchasers enables the entrepreneur to identify and avoid potential deal breakers when building his company. Entrepreneur in Action 11.1 illustrates the kind of insight performing good research before starting a company can provide.

Asking entrepreneurs who have already walked the path you want to walk an open-ended question like "What don't I know that I need to know?" can provide you with general or industry-specific understanding you may not gain otherwise. You have no idea what the response to this kind of question might be or how critical the information you receive might be to your future company's success. In other words,

Entrepreneur *in Action* **11.1**

The Insight Provided by an Open-Ended Question

Kristin Jacobs had been selling medical capital equipment for 10 years. She knew the industry inside and out. She had in-depth knowledge of the products she sold and of her competitors' products. She understood all of the products' benefits. She also understood all of their failings.

Kristin had, over the years, been mentally building a product that could solve some of a typical surgeon's everyday problems and also save money for the hospitals for whom the surgeons work. Kristin was ready to start her own business—one that would design, develop, and manufacture the medical capital equipment product she had in her mind's eye. She was exhilarated by the possibilities before her.

Kristin had been discussing starting her business with a friend who had sold his business several years prior. She had asked him a lot of questions about how to start, build, and sell a business—because selling the business was her ultimate goal. Kristin's friend had given her a lot of great advice, but he had also noted that she really needed to talk to someone in her own industry, the medical industry, an industry with which he was unfamiliar. He had given her the name of the perfect person to talk to: his friend, Willis Fox, an entrepreneur who had recently sold his company, Medivent, to one of the largest players in the medical industry.

Kristin met with Willis and liked him immediately. At Kristin's request, Willis gave her a lot of medical industry-specific advice. Just as Kristin was about to close the meeting, she realized she had one more question for Willis. She asked, "Willis, what don't I know that I need to know in order to build a medical capital equip-

ment company that I can sell five or 10 years from now? In other words, why are some companies unable to get themselves purchased by a larger company? What are the mistakes they make?"

Willis smiled and complimented Kristin for asking such a great question. He then said, "I have three letters for you: F, D, and A." Kristin, a bit confused, looked at Willis and then told him that she already knew the product she wanted to manufacture fell under the auspices of the Food and Drug Administration (FDA) and she was fully prepared to do all the safety testing the FDA required. Willis said that not doing the required safety testing wasn't the reason many medical industry companies couldn't get themselves bought. Rather, the reason they couldn't get themselves bought was because they didn't properly document the safety testing they had done. The documentation required is very specific, almost impossible to reproduce after the fact, and critically important in the eyes of the FDA. Willis concluded, "No documentation, no company sale. Large companies simply will not buy an FDA problem."

Kristin let out a long sigh. Willis said he hoped he hadn't scared her away from pursuing her dream company. Kristin said he had not. He had, in fact, just provided her with critical information of which she had been completely unaware. She then smiled brightly at Willis and thanked him profusely for the insight. Kristin now knew what she needed to do in order to build a medical capital equipment company she could likely someday successfully sell.

the question "What don't I know that I need to know?" will provide you with answers to the questions you didn't even think to ask.

Of course, there are other points to consider before starting your company:

- the importance of intellectual property
- the most common reason large companies buy other companies
- the structure of a typical business purchase in your industry

While it isn't 100 percent necessary, buying intellectual property is attractive to big companies, so having intellectual property—any intellectual property—will likely be helpful if you want to sell your company someday. Remember that sometimes in business, appearance really is everything, and the words "intellectual property" look good in a press release.

Also remember that the managers of large companies, especially the managers of large, publicly held companies, are under continual pressure from their boards of directors and shareholders to reliably introduce new products and services to the market. If large companies aren't successfully developing new products and services internally, they're forced to buy other companies to get access to new products and services. The need to introduce new products and services is one of the most common reasons large companies purchase other companies. If your company has successfully developed quality products or services, especially products or services with a clear competitive advantage, one of the companies they purchase might be yours.

Finally, take a moment to note the structure of a typical acquisition deal in your industry. In many industries, the large companies don't typically buy an entire business entity. Instead, they buy only the assets of other businesses and leave the founders of these businesses with a shell of a company that includes only its liabilities. Large companies often do this to avoid inadvertently buying any unsavory liabilities or potential litigation originating from a company's past. Being aware of the structure of a typical acquisition deal in your industry may affect how you choose to legally organize your business at start-up and the decisions you make for your business as it grows.

Consider Building a Business Designed to Attract Specific Buyers

If you want to sell a business, you first have to build a company that's sellable. In order to do that, you need to understand a potential buyer's intentions and problems. As mentioned earlier, the managers of corporate entities are accountable to both the boards of directors and the shareholders of the companies for which they work. These managers need to demonstrate that the future of the company is sound by continually introducing to the market new products or services or meaningful improvements to existing products and services. In other words, to maintain adequate competitive advantage, these managers need to shepherd the creation of intellectual property. If a large entity isn't successfully innovating and creating intellectual property, that large entity generally buys intellectual property. These large entities are the leaders in their industries—leaders with strong balance sheets; leaders with the means to pay for innovation if they're not creating it.

In order to create a business that's sellable, think forward in time five years and try to identify what the strongest companies in the industry will be fighting over or needing. Then, create a company that, if acquired, will help the acquirer win that fight or meet that need. Ask yourself who would likely buy your business and what tempting product or service or market position you can create that will entice an acquirer to pay a premium price for your business.

Focus on building a company that's an attractive and uncomplicated purchase. Attractive companies have a good reputation and a clear competitive advantage, offer reliable products and services, have multiple growing revenue streams that include identified repeat customers, and, ideally, are profitable. These types of businesses bring high sales prices.

In addition, look for good strategic fit with a buyer. If you think about a good potential acquirer, what attributes does that potential acquirer have? Do you have a vision for how your company and its culture could be successfully integrated into a certain potential acquirer's environment? Can you identify deal breakers that will force your suppliers, distributors, customers, or employees to flee if certain acquirers purchase your business? Don't be afraid to exclude certain unappealing companies from your list of potential acquirers, especially if you believe your personal future will likely be tied to the future of your company's acquirer due to a post-sale consulting agreement; a stock, stock option, or a promissory note arrangement; or any other formal arrangement, financial or otherwise.

Clarify What's Being Sold

Before putting your business on the market, take an inventory of all of the business's assets. This list should include intangibles, such as intellectual property, strategic position in the market place, social media following, company reputation, and similar items. Next, decide what exactly you want to sell. For example, a certain item of intellectual property owned by your company might not be of much value to a potential buyer, but it might be highly valuable to you. As such, you might want to exclude such an item from the sale. As another example, certain items you utilize and keep at the business might be your personal property and not for sale with the business. A potential buyer might feel misled if it is revealed late in the business sale process that the beautiful office furniture, artwork, and antique grandfather clock in your office aren't part of the sale of the business.

You also need to decide if you're willing to sell your business in the form of an asset-only sale. In this case, you sell the assets of the company to the buyer, but not the company itself. An asset-only purchase is often preferable for a buyer, so taking an asset-only purchase off the table as an option could make your business appear less attractive. The downside of an asset-only purchase for you, the seller, is that after the business sale transaction has been completed, you'll still need to settle all of the company's liabilities and other obligations and then dissolve the company.

Properly Prepare the Business for Sale

Proper preparation will make your business more attractive and therefore more likely to sell. Proper preparation will also make it more likely your business will sell at a high price.

Be aware that buyers are interested in profits, not revenue. In order to get the best price for your business, beyond sharing your financial statements, you'll want to be able to produce two or three years of tax returns that are accurate, tie into your business's financial statements, and demonstrate your business's profitability. This can be a problem for some businesses, particularly family-owned businesses, because the owners of family-owned businesses sometimes run everything through the business—including country club fees, expensive meals, car expenses, and vacations disguised as business travel—in order to keep income taxes low. The classic battle between keeping income taxes low and making a business look attractive comes into play here. Loading a business down with tax write-offs makes the business appear less profitable and gives a buyer a good excuse to place a lower value on the business.

Don't wait until the month before you want to put the business up for sale to start correcting any past accounting and tax gray areas that may plague your business. Correcting the excessive write-off of expenses and any accounting or tax mistakes your business might have made will involve creating new financial statements, filing amended tax returns, and likely paying some taxes. This process takes time—and you'll want to have it 100 percent completed before placing your business on the market.

due diligence

the process of a company willingly subjecting itself to a form of investigation by a potential buyer of the business or a potential new partner in the business

A promising potential buyer might be scared off if your business's systems are antiquated; if its books are a mess; if it has lingering, pending, or threatened litigation; or if it has unmotivated or troublesome employees. Untidy facilities, sloppy websites, and poor customer service can also be turnoffs. Take the time to look at your business through the eyes of an outsider and clean up your business's act before attempting to sell the business. Remember that the **due diligence** process—the process of a company willingly subjecting itself to a form of investigation by a potential buyer of the business or a potential new partner in the business—can be exhaustively thorough. Expect everything to be poked, prodded, uncovered, and examined.

Before putting your business on the market, you'll need to identify and resolve potential deal breakers you didn't manage to avoid or foresee. Issues in the areas of company ownership and intellectual property are especially sensitive. For example, a founding member of the company may have left early on without completing paperwork formalizing the member's exit. This can create questions about who the actual owners of the company are, which can create a legal mess that many potential buyers will choose to walk away from. As another example, an independent contractor may have been paid to write key software for the company without being required to assign the proprietary rights to the software to the company in writing. This can create questions about who owns critical intellectual property rights, which can, again, scuttle a deal.

Can your business thrive without you or a key customer? Use the time you're preparing your business for sale to make yourself expendable. This involves building strong teams that have the ability to get things done without you micromanaging them. This also involves documenting your company's policies, procedures, and key operational processes in a way that makes operating the business easy for a new owner. In other words, if your business isn't able to do so already, you should morph it into a business that's able to operate profitably and successfully without you.

Note that a potential buyer will be justifiably concerned if a business is too dependent on one or two major customers. Customers take their business elsewhere every day for reasons that have nothing to do with the quality of the company from which they have been historically making their purchases. A common benchmark that indicates satisfactory revenue diversification is that no single customer represents more than 5 percent of a business's total sales.

Remember that buyers are interested in the future, not the past. Can your business's current upward trend in sales and profitability be expected to continue? Why? Is there growth in your company's future? In what areas specifically, and why? Buyers, understandably, are worried that they'll mistakenly buy a declining or dying business. A smart seller provides the proper evidence to allay those fears. Such evidence can include research on industry trends, interviews with or surveys of current and potential customers, and the demonstration and explanation of the new products and services in a company's pipeline. If you convince a buyer that your business's good times will continue after the buyer purchases the business, you'll have done a lot to increase the likelihood that your company will sell.

Consider What Professional Help May Be Needed to Sell the Business

Selling a business is generally a large and complex transaction—one that often brings significant emotional impact. You've built your business, likely through sweat, blood, and sacrifice. It's your "baby," your pride and joy, and now you're looking to sell it. In addition to providing the necessary expertise to guide you through the business sale process, hiring professional help can aid you in maintaining the emotional distance and objectivity needed to successfully sell your business.

One type of professional help that's almost always required is the guidance provided by a good attorney. When seeking such guidance, it's important to remember that not all attorneys are experienced in handling the sale of a business. Interview several attorneys before hiring one, and make sure the attorney you hire has been involved in the sale of multiple companies—ideally, both large and small, in a variety of industries. Examples of documents your attorney should review or prepare in conjunction with you include the document that summarizes the nature of your business for prospective buyers and the purchase-sale agreement between you, your business, and your business's acquirer.

If your business holds significant assets whose market value can change significantly over time (e.g., real estate, art, precious metals, gems, or coins), the services of a commercial realtor or a professional appraiser may be in order. You may know—or think you know—the value of your business's assets, but what if you're wrong? Also, although you may consider yourself an expert, your opinion regarding value may not hold much weight with a potential buyer. Last, and perhaps most important, you likely don't want to be in the position of having to consider the appraisals of your business's assets presented by a potential buyer without first having seen appraisals of your business's assets prepared by the individuals and firms you choose to represent you and your company's best interests.

A professional business valuation expert can help you determine what your business is worth. You will learn how to prepare a discounted cash flow business valuation later in this chapter, but a valuation prepared by a professional will hold much more weight with a potential buyer than one prepared by you. So, what should you do? Take the time to prepare a discounted cash flow business valuation for your business. If you like the results, you may want to pay to have a more comprehensive business valuation prepared by an expert in order to support the sales price you have determined for your business. If you don't like the results of the discounted cash flow business valuation you've prepared, which may be the case if your business is very young or if its profits and cash flows are low, at least you'll be prepared when confronted with a potential acquirer's valuation of your business. In other words, you'll know in advance that a low valuation number is likely to be presented by a potential buyer, and ideally, you will have already put together an argument regarding why traditional business valuation methods may undervalue your business. Your argument would likely include the fact that traditional business valuation can often ignore subjective business attributes such as a well-recognized brand, an impressive market position, documented and protected intellectual property, a premium business location, anticipated explosive sales growth due to forces outside the business, and other desirable attributes and competitive advantages of the business.

Something many entrepreneurs don't fully appreciate is that when it comes to the business sale process, knowing the proper procedures and etiquette is important. If you're in the process of attempting to sell a business for the first time, realize that you likely don't know the proper procedures and etiquette and that you should proceed cautiously with awareness of this fact. Entrepreneurs who have built successful businesses are usually in the habit of taking the bull by the horns in almost any situation. This type of assertiveness usually works out well for the entrepreneur. However, this type of assertiveness likely won't work out well in the business sale process. Further, unless you already know the potential purchasers of your business well, selling your business typically requires the sophistication and connections of a business broker, a mergers and acquisitions (M&A) advisor, or an investment banking firm. It is through these professionals that you and your company get introduced to potential buyers. It is through these professionals that most deals get done.

A business broker's clients are typically small companies (i.e., generally, companies valued at $2 million or less) that will likely be sold to an individual.[9] Examples of the types of companies sold by business brokers include franchised businesses, single location restaurants, boutique retail stores, and service businesses, such as auto repair shops and hair and nail salons. Ideally, the business broker you choose should

Certified Business Intermediary
a broker certified by the International Business Brokers Association as being both educated and experienced in the art of business brokerage

be a **Certified Business Intermediary**—a broker certified by the International Business Brokers Association as being both educated and experienced in the art of business brokerage—with a successful track record of selling businesses similar to yours.

An M&A advisor's clients are typically larger than those of a business broker and smaller than those of an investment banking firm. Like most business brokers, most M&A advisors are generally perfectly qualified to manage the sale of a business, except that the larger a transaction is, the more structurally complex it tends to be. Be aware that, for transactions that are structurally complex, the relevant state and federal regulatory bodies may require the professionals managing the sale of your business to hold certain licenses, including securities licenses. Many M&A advisors don't hold these types of licenses, which can create the need for an entrepreneur to work with an investment banking firm instead of an M&A advisor.

Typically, an investment bank's clients are very large, very complex, or both. Investment banks typically work with companies valued from $100 million to over $1 billion, but in order to gain expertise in a new industry, small regional investment banks have been known to work with companies valued at less than $20 million.[10, 11] Investment banking firms provide professional services that generally require that they be licensed under securities laws, although these firms are usually also staffed by individuals who hold other professional licenses and certifications. The wide array of skill sets, licenses, and certifications, as well as the vast and diverse business experience of the professionals who work at an investment bank, allows an investment bank to handle the most complex of business sale transactions.

Business brokers usually charge a fee for their services up to or equal to 10 percent of the sales price of a business.[12] For sales under $10 million, M&A advisors and investment banking firms often charge a fee equal to a negotiated, sometimes tiered percentage equal to 3 to 10 percent of the sales price of a business.[13] For sales greater than $10 million, M&A advisors and investment banking firms often charge a fee equal to 5 percent of a minimum sales price, with a tiered, decreasing percentage of sales price scale applying to the portion of the sales price above the minimum sales price.[14, 15] Such a tiered fee system might look something like the following:

- 5 percent of a business's sales price for a minimum sales price of $10 million
- + 4 percent of the next additional $1 million of sales price
- + 3 percent of the second additional $1 million of sales price
- + 2 percent of the third additional $1 million of sales price
- + 1 percent of each additional $1 million of sales price thereafter

Note that the example fee structure above doesn't provide much of an incentive for an M&A advisor or investment bank to work to sell a business at its highest possible price, a point of fact of which a business owner needs to be very much aware. Note also that the example fee structure above represents ballpark estimates at best, as specific data regarding the fees actually charged by most business brokers, M&A advisors, and investment banks is both hard to come by and varies widely.

retainer
a usually nonrefundable deposit against which invoices for work performed and other fees and expenses may be charged

In connection with their fee structure, some business brokers, M&A advisors, and investment banks—and most attorneys—will request a **retainer**, a usually nonrefundable deposit against which invoices for work performed and other fees and expenses may be charged. Likely, the fees and retainer requested by any business broker, M&A advisor, or investment bank will be based on the perceived amount of work required to sell the business and the expected sales price of the business. Ultimately—and remember this important point—all retainers and fees are negotiable and should be debated and haggled until all parties involved arrive at an arrangement with which they are comfortable.

Determine What the Business Is Worth

In terms of the normal sequence of the activities involved in preparing a business for sale, after you've determined what professional help you need to sell the business, you or the professionals you've hired will likely next address the question of what your business is worth. Many different, commonly used "professional" business valuation methods exist. These methods may be used independently but are more often used in combination. Business valuation represents a major topic in and of itself. We'll cover it in detail at the end of this chapter, separate from the current discussion about properly positioning a business for sale and selling a business.

Think Ahead to the Post-Sale Transition

Are you willing to stay on with the business for a while after you've sold it? Sometimes, you can seal a deal by agreeing to stay on as a consultant to the business's new owner for a period of 6–12 months after your business sells. If you're willing to stay on with the business for a specified period of time after selling it, this usually reduces the perceived risk on the part of the buyer and thus increases the perceived value of your company. A founder's willingness to stay on post-sale generally suggests to a potential buyer that all is well, nothing untoward has been hidden, and the founder is so confident of the business's future success he's willing to stay around for a while to personally witness it.

Beyond reducing perceived risk, having the business's founder stay on after the business is sold makes for a smoother transition for the business's new owner. The founder can introduce the new owner to key suppliers, distributors, and customers and nurture the development of these important new relationships. The founder's presence post-sale can also make the business's employees feel they haven't been taken for granted or abandoned. The founder can focus on keeping morale high while the employees work to accept the new owner and perhaps find an improved role for themselves in a company undergoing significant change. Additionally, the founder's presence can make getting answers to key operational questions easy for the new owner. The new owner doesn't need to consult a manual or try to determine which employee might know the answer to a question. The new owner can simply let the founder direct him in learning his new role as owner.

Note that staying on with a business after you've sold it generally needs to be done well—or not done at all. Before agreeing to stay on post-sale, determine that staying on is something you're truly invested in doing because staying on post-sale requires energy, commitment, and significant attention to detail. That said, there's nothing wrong with insisting on being well paid for your time spent consulting post-sale. The consulting fee associated with a founder staying on post-sale is usually negotiated at the same time as the business's sale price and is generally documented via a consulting agreement that's an addendum to the business's overall purchase-sale agreement.

Put the Company on the Market at the Right Time and for the Right Reasons

Selling a business is very much, in some respects, like selling a house. When selling a house, the owner doesn't tell potential buyers his reasons for selling are because he feels the neighborhood is declining, the neighbors are loud and annoying, and the house doesn't get enough sunlight. Rather, the owner says that he wants to move closer to work or family.

So, what are the right reasons for wanting to sell a business? When selling your business, you likely don't want to admit to potential buyers that you want to sell your business because of your own limitations—limitations such as not having the patience, the "know-how," the money, or the energy to build the new product, new service, new operating process, or new functional team your business needs. You'd likely prefer to tell potential buyers your reason for selling is to pursue a different opportunity or to pursue a change in lifestyle, such as spending more time with your kids. There's nothing wrong with this as long you're telling the truth about your business and not trying to disguise the realities associated with it. That said, it's important to have a plan for your life after you exit the business that you can talk about while trying to sell the business. You don't want to look like you're trying to run away from your company.

So, when is the right time to sell a business? The right time to sell your business is when it's strong, not weak. When your business is at a peak of its strength, not in decline. When you don't *need* anyone to buy your company, although it would be nice. The stresses associated with trying to sell a business are significant. Trying to pull off a successful sale when circumstances are less than optimal (e.g., when you've just lost a major customer or when your business is in the middle of a product recall) only makes the sales process harder and more vulnerable to derailment by any new issues that may develop.

Some elements associated with the right time to sell a business may be outside of your control. For example, are the overall market conditions right? In the years following the 2007–2008 financial market crash and recession, business activity in the United States largely stagnated. Many companies were looking for growth, but they were too afraid to pursue acquisitions for multiple reasons. First, their balance sheets were already suffering as a result of the financial crash and recession. Also, banks were hesitant to loan money. In addition, acquisitions are, by definition, risky, and most companies weren't in a position to potentially experience more pain. Trying to sell a business in these overall market conditions was challenging indeed.

Before attempting to sell, look beyond just general market conditions, however. Ascertain the current conditions in your specific industry. While general market conditions might be good, industry-specific conditions may be bad. The reverse can also be true. Almost every general economic crisis boasts at least a few winners. One of the U.S. government's responses to the 2007–2008 financial crisis was the Cash for Clunkers program. While General Motors was facing a cash crunch and bankruptcy, Ford, a company that was better capitalized and therefore had more cash, began ramping up production to meet the government-incentivized increased demand for cars and trucks. As a result of the same financial crisis, in 2007 and 2008, financially strapped Americans became much more price sensitive. The year 2008 was horrible for most U.S. stocks, but Walmart, a company that caters to price-sensitive consumers, saw its stock rise. Along the same lines, McDonald's had an even more remarkable performance in the wake of the 2007–2008 crisis. In 2008, McDonald's sales growth surpassed that of the two previous years and the fast-food giant opened nearly 600 new stores.[16] As a result, McDonald's was one of the best-performing stocks of the financial crisis.[17]

In general, if market conditions aren't good, wait until market conditions improve before attempting to sell your business. However, before delaying, take time to look specifically at the industry players that affect you the most. The businesses supporting Ford, Walmart, and McDonald's generally did okay throughout the 2007–2008 crisis. While other businesses were stagnating or declining, Ford, Walmart, and McDonald's were in growth mode, which meant they were also in acquisition mode.

Beyond the conditions specific to your company, are there strategic reasons you should pursue selling your business now? Rapidly changing technology, upcoming large cash expenditures, increasing globalization, and other business trends can sometimes prove too much for some entrepreneurs. Keep your eyes trained three or four years down the road, and if you don't believe you can keep up, sell before the failure to adapt catches up with you.

Some people find it hard to leave their business. They don't feel ready or think that if they wait, a better offer will come along. Selling a home improvement business in 2006 showed a pretty good return. The housing market was booming, and there was plenty of work and money to go around. Fast-forward a couple of years, and many roofing, siding, home financing, and other housing-related companies had lost a big chunk of their value. Owners who had turned down a good offer for their company in 2006 couldn't scare up half the price in 2008. Remember that timing really is everything, and if you wait too long, the market, the industry, or the "perfect" buyer might pass you by.

Keep the Business in Top Shape during the Business Sale Process

During the time leading up to putting your company on the market, you have ideally spent considerable time preparing your company for sale. When you're actively in the process of selling your business, remembering that you must be careful not to let things slide is important. Contracting sales volume, declining productivity, the loss of employee talent, and a sudden schism with a key supplier or distributor are the kinds of developments that make potential buyers nervous. Making the extra effort to keep things in tip-top shape both operationally and aesthetically can really pay off. Like a house that's up for sale, your business needs to show well every time a potential buyer comes through.

So, whether or not you have any interest left in running the business—and this can be a real issue for entrepreneurs who have mentally and emotionally moved on—you need to make sure that you're keeping your business's records and required payments up to date, its inventory current, and its premises pristinely maintained during the business sale process. Business acquirers want to buy thriving businesses, not neglected ones.

Execute the Business Sale Process

Thus far, this chapter has mostly been about how to prepare a business for sale. Next, we'll discuss how to execute the business sale process—how to actually sell a business. In order to sell your business, you should perform the following six steps:

1. Prepare the selling memo or management presentation document.
2. Make in-person presentations to interested buyers.
3. Compile and deliver the due diligence documents requested by potential buyers who are actively pursuing buying the company.
4. Negotiate and structure the deal.
5. Execute the formal sale of the company at the close.
6. Transition the business post-sale, including, in some instances, effecting the dissolution of the company.

A **selling memo** is a comprehensive description of your business that's likely the first thing business brokers, M&A advisors, and investment banking firms will distribute to the individuals and companies they think will have an interest in buying your company. A selling memo can be anything from a one-page **term sheet** for a small, uncomplicated business—a term sheet is a usually bulleted list of the significant conditions and circumstances associated with a proposed business arrangement—to a flashy yet professional and sophisticated document, likely called a **management presentation** instead of a selling memo, designed to pique a potential buyer's interest in a larger, more complex business. A selling memo usually includes information about a business's major competitors, competitive advantages, key employees, historical financial results, and opportunities for growth. Depending on the sales approach of the applicable business broker, M&A advisor, or investment banking firm, the selling memo or management presentation may or may not include the asking price for the business.

selling memo
a comprehensive description of a business that business brokers, merger and acquisition advisors, and investment banking firms distribute to the individuals and companies they think will have an interest in buying the business

term sheet
a usually bulleted list of the significant conditions and circumstances associated with a proposed business arrangement

management presentation
a flashy yet professional and sophisticated document designed to pique a potential buyer's interest in a large, complex business

In-person presentations to interested potential acquirers can take the form of anything from a fairly informal interview-style meeting with one person at a lunch to a very formal presentation to a company's board of directors. Before an interview or presentation, fully research the individuals to whom you'll be speaking, the companies they represent, and their potential motivations for being interested in your business. Treat every meeting, even the seemingly informal ones, as you would an important job interview, court appearance, or first date. Remember that your body language and attitude, not just the words you speak, matter tremendously. Honesty and polite forthrightness are good qualities to bring to the table, both when meeting with potential acquirers in person and when performing due diligence.

Due diligence regarding the potential sale of a company involves a company willingly subjecting itself to a form of investigation by a potential buyer of the business. Depending on the size and complexity of the business to be acquired, due diligence can be incredibly detail-oriented, thorough, and time consuming. An owner should be prepared to dig up practically any document or analysis ever created by his company. He should also be prepared to create new reports requested by a potential buyer that analyze his company's past activities in new and different ways. In addition, an owner should be prepared to spend a lot of time investigating potential solutions to concerns identified by a potential buyer and forecasting his company's future in both highly specific and very general ways.

As during the in-person presentation process, honesty really is the best policy during the due diligence process. Ideally, you've cleaned up your company's act before getting to due diligence, so no dirty laundry needs airing. If, however, issues remain that need to be addressed, it is best to disclose them as accurately as possible as early as possible.

Note that during due diligence, whether the answers are verbal or written, you should always be careful to qualify your answers as necessary. When asked to do estimates or forecasts, use terms like "approximately" and "best guess." When asked to verify specific facts, use language like "to the best of my knowledge" and "at this time." Honesty is one thing. Giving the impression you can be certain about future events or have access to every known fact is misguided and misleading and can get you into all sorts of trouble.

Deal Negotiation and Deal Structuring

As unfair as it may seem, you'll likely have to go through extensive due diligence before a potential buyer will give you any hint of what they might be willing to offer to pay for your company. Before you get to the point of considering an offer, however, you'll need to have given sufficient thought to a number of other important considerations, namely, your employees, the other stakeholders associated with your business, your business partners, your investors, the forms of payment for your company you find acceptable, and taxes. Also, you'll need to have considered what will likely happen post-close and have identified the important points that, if successfully negotiated, will make the post-close transition more palatable for all.

Have you thought about what the buyer might need to offer your employees to avoid losing key talent? You don't want the business to lose key talent the minute the deal closes, especially if you're going to help manage the post-sale transition. Encourage a potential buyer to offer raises, bonuses, and other extras to keep key employees happy.

Are your lenders, suppliers, distributors, and customers aware that your company is up for sale? Should they be aware? You don't want any unpleasant surprises, such as a lender's unwillingness to let you repay a loan early or a supplier, distributor, or customer refusing to do business with the new owner. It's good practice to know and have considered the terms associated with the repayment of any of the business's debt before attempting to negotiate a deal. It's also wise to give a potential purchaser both a heads-up and a potential solution if you expect certain suppliers, distributors, or customers will abandon the business post-sale.

Have you and your business partners and investors established the parameters for an acceptable versus unacceptable offer? You don't want to find yourself in a situation where certain of the business's owners and investors want to accept an offer from a buyer that the others do not. Before the first offer from a buyer is ever presented, it's wise to get all of the business's owners and investors to agree what is—and what is not—an acceptable offer.

Is stock or an interest-bearing promissory note an acceptable form of payment from a buyer, or do you want a cash-only deal? Note that, often, the stock transferred in exchange for a business is restricted by the buyer from being immediately sold. Sometimes, it can't be sold for years. Beyond that, the acceptance of any company's stock as payment for your business requires that you do due diligence on that company in order to determine your level of comfort with the prospects of that company. What do you think will happen to the market value of the stock you accept in payment for your company? Does a market for the stock even exist?

How much capital gain will the sale generate, and will the sale generate sufficient cash to pay the tax on that capital gain? A large capital gain means a large tax bill that can't be paid for with stock or a promissory note. An expected large tax bill requires that a certain minimum amount of cash be part of any deal struck. Perhaps the deal can be structured so as to lower the expected tax bill of the business's owners and investors. A consultation with a CPA or tax attorney may be necessary to find out.

Be prepared for the fact that the first offer you receive from a potential purchaser will likely be a low ball in terms of money, might attempt to push all of the risk for anything bad that could ever happen to the business onto you, and may demand that you sign an overreaching **non-compete agreement**—an agreement that limits an individual's ability to compete with a business after the individual has been an employee of or sold the business. Your job—and the job of your business broker, M&A advisor, or investment banking firm—is to haggle the low-ball offer into a higher offer, work out a distribution of risk between you and the buyer that's equitable and reasonable, and professionally negotiate the unreasonable non-compete agreement into a reasonable one.

non-compete agreement
an agreement that limits an individual's ability to compete with a business after the individual has been an employee of the business or sold the business

Remember that it's not unusual for buyers to ask you to sign a non-compete agreement. After all, you've built a successful business once already. The last thing the buyer wants you to do is build another one and become a new competitor to the company they just purchased. There are, however, limits to what are considered reasonable terms of a non-compete agreement. Generally, a non-compete agreement is deemed unreasonable if it's for too long a period, covers too large a geographic area, stifles competition to the point of ensuring or maintaining a long-term monopoly, or deprives a person of the ability to make a living. Note that the applicability and importance of each of these factors varies widely depending upon the industries and states in which a business operates.

Do not depend upon your business broker, M&A advisor, investment banking firm, or attorney to negotiate your business's sale for you. Some of these professionals are adept negotiators. Many are not and will look to you to take over the negotiations the minute things get dicey. Beyond this, deal negotiation does require making many decisions that are most appropriately made by the business owner, such as the scope of a non-compete agreement. Be prepared to lead the deal negotiation and make the decisions that need to be made while, of course, listening to the counsel of the professionals you are paying to assist you.

The importance of negotiating a good deal can't be overstated. Entrepreneur in Action 11.2 (on page 326) is an example that illustrates just how important negotiating a good deal can be.

Miguel's $20 Million Deal

Pamela was on the phone with Miguel, her longtime friend from college. Miguel had called with exciting news: He had just sold his first company for $20 million! Pamela expressed congratulations to her entrepreneurial friend with enthusiasm. She was eager to someday herself make the same type of phone call Miguel was making today.

Pamela pressed Miguel for details regarding the deal he had struck. He described the acquiring company and then commented how comfortable he was making the sale of his company to the acquiring company because it was such a solid company. Pamela paused. Then she said, "Miguel, are you accepting this company's stock in payment for your company?" Miguel replied that he was. Pamela paused again, and then asked, "How much cash are you

getting, Miguel?" Miguel told Pamela that the deal was for 100 percent stock and that he had negotiated that he had to hold the stock for only three years before he was permitted to sell it. Pamela pushed forward, "No cash at all? But Miguel, that simply won't do. How will you pay the taxes you'll owe on the deal if you receive no cash and can't sell the stock for three years?" There was silence on the other end of the phone.

Finally, Miguel said in a subdued tone, "I guess I have to go back and renegotiate this deal." Pamela quietly said, "Yes, you do."

After a momentary pause, Miguel took a deep breath and then slowly said to Pamela with the sound of gratitude in his voice, "Thank goodness I called you before signing the papers on this deal. I'll call a meeting this afternoon to start renegotiating the terms."

The Close

By the time you get to a deal's close date, the negotiations—and what may have been a tense relationship between you and your business's acquirer—are over. Your business's acquirer is fully invested in purchasing the business—and you are ready to sell it. In many instances, you and your business's acquirer are about to become a team.

Many business owners are nervous about the business sale close, but most closes are incident-free because, at this point, the buyer has usually invested a lot of time, energy, and money in the effort to buy your business. Backing out at the last minute would be incredibly counterproductive, and it would make the members of the buyer's acquisition team appear incompetent.

At deal close, the buyers and sellers sign paperwork (be sure to keep the pen!). Afterward, the participants typically shake hands, slap backs, take pictures, and approve press releases. The close is a day to be looked forward to and relished. You've worked hard, entrepreneur. Enjoy your day!

The Post-Sale Transition

With the deal done and the paperwork signed, it's time to transition the company. What the post-sale transition looks like depends very much upon the terms of sale of your business. Did you sell your business in its entirety as a legal business entity? Did you sell the business with no requirement to do work for or consult with the new owner? If the answer to both questions is yes, then your post-sale transition is probably limited to you telling your employees about the sale (many business sales are negotiated in confidence or relative confidence), wishing them well with the new owner, packing up your office, and leaving. In reality, the post-sale transition for most business owners is not this simple.

If you sold your business in its entirety as a legal business entity and are bound by a consulting agreement or similar arrangement that requires you to stay on with the company for some period of time post-sale, you're more than likely expected to help integrate the culture of the acquired company into the culture of the acquiring company to whatever degree the acquiring company sees fit. You're probably also expected to handle any employee morale issues and take steps to nip in the bud any potential loss of talent. You're expected to introduce your suppliers, distributors, customers, and other significant business contacts to the buyer and make sure these nascent relationships don't flounder. You're also expected to be an advocate for the new owner, know that you're no longer in charge, and graciously accept that you're no longer in charge.

Some founders have a difficult time accepting the changes they watch being made by a new owner to the business they built. Keep in mind that your business's acquirer most likely bought your business with a plan in mind that involved significant change for the business. Being aware of this and accepting it ahead of time will make the post-sale transition easier for all involved.

Business Dissolution

If you didn't sell your business in its entirety as a legal business entity but sold only the assets of your company, you now have a shell of a company that you need to legally shut down. Some buyers will contractually obligate you to shut down your company within a certain time frame, so it's best not to delay beginning this process so you can deal with any issues that may arise. Alternatively, you may be legally shutting down your business because it has failed, was a short-term business whose time has passed, or simply because you wish to move on and pursue a different, more lucrative opportunity. Whatever the reason, the business dissolution process generally entails the same set of activities and requirements.

As you pay off all the remaining liabilities of your company, it's wise to formally notify your suppliers, your distributors, and all the others with whom you've done business within the last 12 months of your company's impending closure. This is wise and, in some states, required. The process of formal notification forces you to review both old and current accounts payable files, which helps flush out certain accounts you may have forgotten about (e.g., accounts related to long unvisited storage facilities, the trash dumpsters hidden in the back of the building, and certain types of services that automatically renew). The process of formal notification helps you address everything you need to address in order to successfully shut down your company in an "incident free" manner.

Shutting down the business also requires formally closing its government-related accounts. Not completing this important step will result in a series of undesirable notices, penalties, and fees at a later date. Such accounts include accounts for workers' compensation, unemployment, payroll taxes, sales taxes, even post office boxes, and the like. The last tax return of any type filed should be marked "final."

The requirements for formal business dissolution vary by state and by legal form of business. A business legally organized or registered with a particular state (e.g., most LLCs, corporations, and certain partnerships) will likely need to file dissolution paperwork with that state. Some states also require that the business post a public notice of business closure (or impending business closure), usually in an appropriate newspaper or on an appropriate website. Also, before granting a company formal dissolution, many states require notification from their state's tax department that all necessary final tax returns have been filed and all taxes have been paid.

The very last item that should be terminated is the business's checking account. At this point, the circle of life for your business is complete. One of the very first acts associated with the business was setting up the business's checking account, taking money out of your pocket, and depositing that money into the account. One of the very last acts associated with the business is withdrawing the last few dollars left in the account, putting that money into your pocket, and closing the account.

Business Valuation

The reasons to perform a business valuation vary. An entrepreneur may want to determine the value of his business as part of the preparation to sell all or part of it. Perhaps a business valuation is required due to the death of an owner. Alternatively, a business valuation may become necessary because of insurance requirements, because one of the owners wants to exit the business, or because of the tax planning or tax reporting needs of either the business or one of its owners. We have touched upon the concept of business valuation several times in this chapter. Now, we'll address the concept in detail.

Any discussion of business valuation should first include a few remarks about the way in which entrepreneurs often improperly place a value on their business. Specifically, an entrepreneur shouldn't value his business based on the equity number on the company's balance sheet. The equity number on a company's balance sheet is an accounting number that does not reflect a company's true value. Nor should an entrepreneur value his business based on how much time and money the entrepreneur has invested in the business. While how much time and money an entrepreneur has invested in his business is usually quite significant to the entrepreneur, it does not reflect a company's true value. The equity number on a company's balance sheet and the time and money an entrepreneur has invested in the business are both reflective of a business's past. Proper business valuation looks to the future and is ideally based—at least in part—on the expected future cash flows of the business.

Facetiously, but truthfully, a business is worth the price it can command in the marketplace. Determining what that price might be, however, can be a bit tricky. As a result, when valuing a business, an entrepreneur should determine what attributes of his company are most important to potential buyers and then try to assess what potential buyers might be willing to pay for these attributes. Considering the nature and amounts of the assets and liabilities of the business obviously matters. Taking current general economic and industry conditions and trends into consideration is also important. Last, as mentioned earlier in the chapter, an entrepreneur may want to consider paying for a comprehensive professional business valuation. Because it's unwise to use only one approach to business valuation, a comprehensive professional business valuation typically supplements the results of an earnings-based business valuation with the results of an asset-based business valuation and a market-based business valuation.

An **earnings-based business valuation** is predicated on the idea that a business's true value lies in its ability to produce net income and positive cash flow in the future. The discounted cash flow method of business valuation illustrated in the next section of this chapter is the most common method of earnings-based business valuation.

An **asset-based business valuation** is a straightforward business valuation approach by which the value of a business is determined as a result of considering the total value of the company's tangible and intangible assets. The challenge of an asset-based valuation is that it can oversimplify the business valuation process because the approach ignores the value of the company's future earning potential. That's why asset-based valuation, although a common approach for business liquidations and the sale of defunct businesses, isn't as common for thriving companies. Still, if a business holds significant assets (e.g., real estate, intellectual property, or high-cost-per-unit inventory), an asset-based valuation may indeed provide a higher valuation for a company than other valuation approaches.

A **market-based business valuation** attempts to establish the value of a business by comparing the business to be put on the market to similar businesses that have recently been sold. The successful use of this approach depends upon having enough information regarding a sufficient number of recently sold businesses that

earnings-based business valuation
a business valuation approach predicated on the idea that a business's true value lies in its ability to produce net income and positive cash flow in the future

asset-based business valuation
a business valuation approach by which the value of a business is determined as a result of considering the total value of the company's tangible and intangible assets

market-based business valuation
a business valuation approach that attempts to establish the value of a business by comparing the business to be put on the market to similar businesses that have recently been sold

compare reasonably well to the business under consideration. This can be a real problem depending upon the size of the business to be put on the market, the nature of its competitive advantage, and the industry in which it operates. Simply put, getting sales price information on privately held companies is often very difficult. Sales price information is generally much more readily available regarding publicly held companies, but these companies usually don't compare well with the small or medium-sized businesses being put on the market by typical business owners.

Now that we've looked at the three most common approaches to business valuation, let's focus on the most commonly used business valuation method—an earnings-based method—the discounted cash flow method.

The Discounted Cash Flow Method of Business Valuation

Studies of ancient Babylonian mathematics suggest that the Babylonians used techniques similar to the discounted cash flow method when calculating the interest due related to loans.[18] Following the stock market crash of 1929, discounted cash flow analysis was formalized and gained popularity as a valuation method for stocks when investors suddenly became interested in "real value."[19] In many investors' and lenders' opinion, the value number generated by the discounted cash flow method is a "reality check" that can help avoid the pitfalls associated with the overoptimism and tunnel vision that can occur when considering a loan or investment.[20]

The discounted cash flow method isn't just the most common method of earnings-based business valuation. It's the most commonly used method to value a business, period. When accountants, bankers, investors, and others talk about using the discounted cash flow method to determine the value of a business, they're talking about determining, at a specified discount rate, the sum of the present values of all of the business's expected future cash flows. Example 11.1 illustrates the discounted cash flow method of business valuation in detail.

Example 11.1

The Cleveland Machining Corporation commenced operations in 2012. Since then, its founders have grown the business substantially and are considering selling the company to a competitor. The company is in a good position to be put on the market due its history of profitability and positive cash flow. Another attribute that will make the company attractive to potential purchasers is that, due to the major facility renovation and round of equipment replacement completed in 2019, no significant capital expenditures are expected for the business for next 15 years. As part of preparing their company for potential sale, the owners of the Cleveland Machining Corporation have forecasted the company's expected net income and cash flows for the next 15 years by preparing detailed pro forma financial statements. Using the discounted cash flow method of business valuation and the cash flows from operations found on the company's pro forma statements of cash flows as summarized in figure 11.2 (on page 330), what is the value of the Cleveland Machining Corporation using a 15 percent discount rate? What is the value using a 20 percent discount rate? A 25 percent discount rate?

In order to determine the value of the Cleveland Machining Corporation using the discounted cash flow method of business valuation, we must first determine the present values of the expected cash flows provided. Figure 11.3 (page 331) shows the present value calculations at discount rates of 15, 20, and 25 percent. Note that

Cleveland Machining Corporation Expected Cash Flows	
Year	Amount
2020	$425,000
2021	$446,250
2022	$468,563
2023	$491,991
2024	$516,590
2025	$542,420
2026	$569,541
2027	$598,018
2028	$627,919
2029	$659,314
2030	$692,280
2031	$726,894
2032	$763,239
2033	$801,401
2034	$841,471

Figure 11.2. Expected cash flows of the Cleveland Machining Corporation for years 2020–2034.

the factors for the 25 percent discount rate were calculated using the following present value factor (PVF) formula:

$$PVF = \left(\frac{1}{(1+i)^n} \right)$$

This formula is part of the overall present value of a lump sum formula first presented in chapter 9:

$$PV = FV(PVF)$$
$$= FV \left(\frac{1}{(1+i)^n} \right)$$

where:

FV = Future value
PV = Present value
i = Interest rate per period
n = Number of compounding periods per year multiplied by the number of years

While we haven't completed all the calculations necessary to determine the estimated value of this business, it's worth noting here how much the sums of the present values in figure 11.3 differ depending upon the discount rate used. The sum of the present values determined using the 15 percent discount rate ($3,164,117) is more than 60 percent larger than the sum of the present values determined using the 25 percent discount rate ($1,969,599). The sum of the present values of a business's forecasted cash flows is a major component in the determination of the value of a business (see figure 11.4 on page 333). It's not, therefore, hard to imagine, considering the two very disparate numbers of $3,164,117 and $1,969,599, that much research is generally done—and much effort is generally expended—to justify the discount rate used to determine the present values of a business's cash flows.

	**Cleveland Machining Corporation** **Sums of the Present Values of the Expected Cash Flows for Years 2020–2034**
Year	Expected Cash Flow Amount	Type of Factor	Factor at 15%	Present Value at 15%	Factor at 20%	Present Value at 20%	Factor at 25%	Present Value at 25%
2020	$ 425,000	PV	0.8696	$ 369,580	0.8333	$ 354,153	0.8000	$ 340,000
2021	446,250	PV	0.7561	337,410	0.6944	309,876	0.6400	285,600
2022	468,563	PV	0.6575	308,080	0.5787	271,157	0.5120	239,904
2023	491,991	PV	0.5718	281,320	0.4823	237,287	0.4096	201,519
2024	516,590	PV	0.4972	256,849	0.4019	207,618	0.3277	169,287
2025	542,420	PV	0.4323	234,488	0.3349	181,656	0.2621	142,168
2026	569,541	PV	0.3759	214,090	0.2791	158,959	0.2097	119,433
2027	598,018	PV	0.3269	195,492	0.2326	139,099	0.1678	100,347
2028	627,919	PV	0.2843	178,517	0.1938	121,691	0.1342	84,267
2029	659,314	PV	0.2472	162,983	0.1615	106,479	0.1074	70,810
2030	692,280	PV	0.2149	148,771	0.1346	93,181	0.0859	59,467
2031	726,894	PV	0.1869	135,857	0.1122	81,558	0.0687	49,938
2032	763,239	PV	0.1625	124,026	0.0935	71,363	0.0550	41,978
2033	801,401	PV	0.1413	113,238	0.0779	62,429	0.0440	35,262
2034	841,471	PV	0.1229	103,417	0.0649	54,611	0.0352	29,620
				$3,164,117		$ 2,451,116		$ 1,969,599

Figure 11.3. Sums of the present values of the expected cash flows of the Cleveland Machining Corporation for years 2020–2034 using discount rates of 15, 20, and 25 percent.

Terminal Value

When determining the value of a business using the discounted cash flow method, after estimating the cash flows a business will produce over a forecast period and determining the sum of the present values associated with those cash flows, the next step is to come up with a reasonable idea of the value of the company's expected cash flows after the forecast period. If we didn't include the value of post-forecast period cash flows when determining the value of a business, we'd essentially be assuming that the company stopped operating at the end of the forecast period. For example, the forecast period for the Cleveland Machining Corporation (see figure 11.3) is years 2020–2034. If we don't determine a value for the cash flows expected to occur after year 2034, we're effectively assuming the Cleveland Machining Corporation terminates its operations at the end of 2034 when valuing the business.

Forecasting cash flows gets more difficult as we move forward in time. Forecasting cash flows for 10, 15, or 20 years into the future is challenging enough. Imagine trying to forecast the expected cash flows for the entire life of a company. To make the task of business valuation a bit easier, instead of determining the expected cash flows for the entire life of a company, we can instead calculate a **terminal value** that represents the value of all of a company's expected cash flows after a specified forecast period.

terminal value
the value of all of a company's expected cash flows after a specified forecast period

Calculating terminal value involves making some assumptions about a business's long-term cash flows and the growth rate of those cash flows. There are several ways to estimate the terminal value for a company. One long-used and widely accepted method is the **Gordon growth model**.[21] It utilizes the following formula:

$$\text{Terminal value} = \frac{\text{Final projected year cash flow} \times (1 + \text{Long-term cash flow growth rate})}{\text{Discount rate} - \text{Long-term cash flow growth rate}}$$

Gordon growth model
a model for determining the terminal value of a business that assumes a company exists forever and grows at a constant rate forever

This formula eliminates the practical problem of estimating a business's cash flows beyond a reasonable and manageable forecast period. Keep in mind, however, that this formula is based on the major assumption that the cash flow associated with the last year specifically forecasted (year 2034 in our example) will stabilize and then continue to grow at the same rate forever. In other words, the Gordon growth model assumes a company exists forever and grows at a constant rate forever.

No company exists forever, and no company grows at a constant rate forever, but the Gordon growth model works because it takes into account that the further out in time we are from the present, although our cash flow estimates will likely become less and less reliable, the cash flows also become less and less significant to the company considering the time value of money. Note the present value factors indicated below for a 20 percent discount rate for 25, 50, and 100 years into the future. The present value factors have been extended to eight decimal places for purposes of illustration:

Year 25   0.01048260
Year 50   0.00010988
Year 100 0.00000001

Next, consider the present value of a $1 million cash flow in years 25, 50, and 100 of a company's future given these present value factors:

Year 25 $1,000,000 x 0.01048260 = $10,482.60
Year 50 $1,000,000 x 0.00010988 = $109.88
Year 100 $1,000,000 x 0.00000001 = $0.01

A potential buyer reviewing a business valuation that includes a terminal value calculation has a legitimate point that the company he's considering purchasing likely won't exist in 100 years or grow at a constant rate. However, when you consider the present values associated with cash flows earned 50 or 100 years into the future, this objection is easy to overcome.

For purposes of illustrating the calculation of terminal value, let's assume that after 2034, the Cleveland Machining Corporation's cash flows are expected to grow in perpetuity by 4 percent per year. At first glance, a 4 percent growth rate may seem low, but viewed another way, 4 percent growth represents double the 2 percent estimated long-term growth rate for the U.S. economy.

Let's also assume that a fairly conservative discount rate for the machining industry, which is a historically stable and predictable industry, is 25 percent. Using the selected discount rate of 25 percent, and considering our determined long-term cash flow growth rate of 4 percent and our year 2034 expected cash flow number (final projected year cash flow) of $841,471, we arrive at a terminal value of $4,167,285. The calculation is as follows:

$$\text{Terminal value} = \frac{\$841,471 \times (1+0.04)}{0.25-0.04} = \$4,167,285$$

Next, we calculate the present value of the terminal value considering the selected discount rate of 25 percent. Note that it's common practice to use the present value factor for the last forecasted year as the present value factor when calculating the present value of the terminal value. For our example, this means we'll use a present value factor of 0.0352—the present value factor for the year 2034 expected cash flow at a discount rate of 25 percent (refer to figure 11.3)—to calculate the present value of the terminal value of $146,688 ($4,167,285 x 0.0352 = $146,688). We then add the $146,688 present value of the terminal value to the sum of the present values of the expected cash flows for years 2020-2034 using a 25 percent discount rate ($1,969,599) to arrive at the estimated **equity value** of the Cleveland Machining Corporation—the value of the equity of the company—of $2,116,287 (assuming a 25 percent discount rate). See figure 11.4.

Let's say the owners of the Cleveland Machining Corporation don't agree with the $2,116,287 valuation number. They feel the equity of their company is worth more. Specifically, they feel a more aggressive discount rate of 20 percent is justified

equity value
the value of the equity of a company

	Cleveland Machining Corporation Discounted Cash Flow Business Valuation 25% Discount Rate			
Year	Expected Cash Flow Amount	Type of Factor	Factor Amount at 25%	Present Value at 25%
2020	$ 425,000	PV	0.8000	$ 340,000
2021	446,250	PV	0.6400	285,600
2022	468,563	PV	0.5120	239,904
2023	491,991	PV	0.4096	201,519
2024	516,590	PV	0.3277	169,287
2025	542,420	PV	0.2621	142,168
2026	569,541	PV	0.2097	119,433
2027	598,018	PV	0.1678	100,347
2028	627,919	PV	0.1342	84,267
2029	659,314	PV	0.1074	70,810
2030	692,280	PV	0.0859	59,467
2031	726,894	PV	0.0687	49,938
2032	763,239	PV	0.0550	41,978
2033	801,401	PV	0.0440	35,262
2034	841,471	PV	0.0352	29,620
		Sum of the present values of the expected cash flows		$ 1,969,599
		Present value of the terminal value		146,688
		Estimated equity value of the business		$ 2,116,287

Figure 11.4. Equity value of the Cleveland Machining Corporation using the discounted cash flow method and a discount rate of 25 percent.

considering the nature of their business and the stability of the industry in which it operates. Further, they have found evidence that other companies in the industry have been valued using a 20 percent discount rate.

Considering this information, let's recalculate the equity value of the Cleveland Machining Corporation using our previously determined long-term cash flow growth rate of 4 percent, the year 2034 expected cash flow number of $841,471 as the final projected year cash flow, and the more aggressive discount rate of 20 percent. The terminal value using a discount rate of 20 percent is $5,469,562, calculated as follows:

$$\text{Terminal value} = \frac{\$841,471 \times (1 + 0.04)}{0.20 - 0.04} = \$5,469,562$$

Next, we calculate the present value of the terminal value considering the more aggressive discount rate of 20 percent. For our example, this means we'll use a present value factor of 0.0649—the present value factor for the year 2034 expected cash flow at a discount rate of 20 percent (refer to figure 11.3 on page 331)—to calculate the present value of the terminal value of $354,975 ($5,469,562 x 0.0649 = $354,975). We then add the $354,975 present value of the terminal value to the sum of the present values of the expected cash flows for years 2020–2034 using a 20 percent discount rate ($2,451,116) to arrive at the estimated equity value of the business of $2,806,091 (assuming a 20 percent discount rate). See figure 11.5 (page 334).

The calculations in figures 11.4 and 11.5 are estimates of the equity value—the value of the equity—of the Cleveland Machining Corporation. The need to determine equity value arises whenever a portion of a company's ownership is about to be transferred or sold. Equity value is used determine the value of each owner's portion of the business. In order to illustrate, let's continue with our current example,

	Cleveland Machining Corporation Discounted Cash Flow Business Valuation 20% Discount Rate			
Year	Expected Cash Flow Amount	Type of Factor	Factor Amount at 20%	Present Value at 20%
2020	$ 425,000	PV	0.8333	$ 354,153
2021	446,250	PV	0.6944	309,876
2022	468,563	PV	0.5787	271,157
2023	491,991	PV	0.4823	237,287
2024	516,590	PV	0.4019	207,618
2025	542,420	PV	0.3349	181,656
2026	569,541	PV	0.2791	158,959
2027	598,018	PV	0.2326	139,099
2028	627,919	PV	0.1938	121,691
2029	659,314	PV	0.1615	106,479
2030	692,280	PV	0.1346	93,181
2031	726,894	PV	0.1122	81,558
2032	763,239	PV	0.0935	71,363
2033	801,401	PV	0.0779	62,429
2034	841,471	PV	0.0649	54,611

Sum of the present values of the expected cash flows	$ 2,451,116
Present value of the terminal value	354,975
Estimated equity value of the business	$ 2,806,091

Figure 11.5. Equity value of the Cleveland Machining Corporation using the discounted cash flow method and a discount rate of 20 percent.

assuming the 20 percent discount rate and assuming that the Cleveland Machining Corporation has 10,000 shares of common stock outstanding. In this instance, the value of each share of the company's common stock could be argued to be $280.61, calculated as follows:

Value of the equity of the business	$2,806,091
Divided by: Number of common shares	÷ 10,000
Value of one share of stock of the business	$280.61

If instead of wanting to sell their entire business, the owners of the Cleveland Machining Corporation wish to sell only part of the business to a private equity firm or other investor, either the value of the equity of the business or the value of the business's stock could be used as the basis for determining the price for part of the company. For example, if the owners of the Cleveland Machining Corporation wish to sell only 25 percent of the business, the value of 25 percent of the business could be viewed as either $2,806,091 x 0.25 = $701,523 or 10,000 shares x 0.25 x $280.61 = $701,525.

Note that if the company weren't a corporation, the value of any owner's portion of the business would be determined by simply multiplying that owner's ownership percentage by the value of the equity of the business. For example, if the Cleveland Machining Corporation were an LLC instead of a corporation, the value enjoyed by a 51 percent owner would be $2,806,091 x 0.51 = $1,431,106. If the 51 percent owner desired to sell his entire ownership interest to his business partners, his 51 percent of the business could be viewed as being worth $1,431,106. If the 51 percent owner wished to sell only a portion of his ownership interest—let's say 20 percent—to an outside investor, this 20 percent could be viewed as being worth $2,806,091 x 0.20 = $561,218.

Part of the beauty of the discounted cash flow method of business valuation is that it works for companies both young and mature because it's based on the estimated future cash flows of the business. Before bringing in an investor, even in the very early stages of a business, an entrepreneur should estimate the future cash flows of the business and perform a discounted cash flow business valuation for the business in order to help the entrepreneur place a value on the business and accordingly assign an appropriate business ownership percentage to any cash infusion proposed by an investor.

The estimated value of the Cleveland Machining Corporation as a firm—the company's **enterprise value**—would be the estimated equity value of the company, plus any debt on the company's balance sheet, minus the cash on the company's balance sheet. Note that for purposes of calculating enterprise value, debt includes liabilities that typically involve the payment of interest (e.g., mortgages, equipment loans, notes payable, and bank lines of credit). Debt does not include the normally interest-free liabilities associated with the everyday operations of a company (e.g., accounts payable, payroll payable, and taxes payable).

> **enterprise value**
> an estimate of the value of a business, calculated as the estimated equity value of a company, plus any debt on the company's balance sheet, minus the cash on the company's balance sheet

Most business brokers, M&A advisors, and investment banking firms consider enterprise value to be the best estimate of the value of a business to be put on the market for sale. In order to illustrate the concept of enterprise value, let's assume that the Cleveland Machining Corporation has $300,000 of debt and $50,000 of cash on its balance sheet. In this instance, the value of the Cleveland Machining Corporation could be argued to be $3,056,091, calculated as follows:

Value of the equity of the business	$2,806,091
Plus: The business's debt	+ 300,000
Less: The business's cash	– 50,000
Value of the business	$3,056,091

Since the founders of the Cleveland Machining Corporation are considering selling their entire company to a competitor, and since they consider 20 percent a reasonable discount rate, it is likely they will consider $3,056,091 a good starting point for determining an asking price for their company, should they decide to put it on the market.

Discount Rate and Cash Flow Determination for Purposes of Business Valuation

As we have seen in this chapter and in chapters 9 and 10, the discount rate (interest rate) used significantly affects the value of expected cash flows. As a result, as mentioned previously, much research is generally done—and much effort is generally expended—to justify the discount rate used. Because of the high stakes involved, it's unlikely that any discount rate will ever be more heavily scrutinized than that which is used to determine the value of a business.

In general, the discount rates used for business valuation are usually higher than the discount rates used for capital budgeting because of the higher level of uncertainty associated with the relevant forecasted cash flows, because of the increased level of risk perceived by an outsider of a business, and also because of the very real risks associated with business ownership transfer. Discount rates also vary extensively depending upon the real and perceived risks associated with both a specific company and the industry in which it operates. In general, the typical discount rates for large multinational corporations with revenues greater than $1 billion (e.g., McDonald's and Alphabet) range between 10 and 15 percent, the typical discount rates for middle-market companies with revenues between $50 million and $500 million range between 20 and 25 percent, and the typical discount rates for early-stage and start-up companies can be 30 percent or more.[22]

When valuing a business using the discounted cash flow method, most agree that **free cash flow** is the best measure of cash flow to use. Free cash flow is the cash flow generated by a business that's available for distribution to the providers of capital to the business. Using its most straightforward definition, we get the following equation:

Free cash flow = Cash flows from operations – Capital expenditures

Capital expenditures represent the monies paid out by a company to acquire, upgrade, or maintain the major assets (e.g., land, buildings, or equipment) needed by the business to sustain or improve its operations. Cash flows from operations represent the amount of cash a company generates from its business operations. Cash flows from operations can usually be found on a company's statement of cash flows. In the instance of a young company that hasn't yet reached the level of sophistication to create a statement of cash flows, cash flows from operations can be determined by reviewing the company's reconciliation of cash for the following items and then performing the operation indicated:

Net income

+ Depreciation expense

+ Amortization expense

+/– Changes in the noncash working capital accounts on a company's balance sheet
_____

= Cash flows from operations

free cash flow
the cash flow generated by a business that's available for distribution to the providers of capital to the business

Amortization expense is a noncash expense similar to depreciation expense, except that where depreciation expense represents the systematic writing off of a depreciable *tangible* fixed asset's cost over time, amortization expense represents the systematic writing off of an *intangible* asset's cost over time (e.g., costs like those associated with patenting a product).

amortization expense
a noncash expense that represents the systematic writing off of an intangible asset's cost over time

Just as the discount rate used in a business valuation will be heavily scrutinized, the assumptions underlying the determination of the projected net income numbers for the business (i.e., the starting point for the determination of the cash flows for the business) will be heavily scrutinized. That's why it's in the entrepreneur's best interest to make sure that the assumptions underlying any pro forma financial statements he creates are both well researched and reasonable.

If an entrepreneur doesn't expect his business to own major fixed assets or incur any major future capital expenditures, using projected net income (rather than projected cash flow) to perform a business valuation is not unreasonable for a company in pre-start-up phase planning mode or early start-up phase. This is because, in the absence of major fixed assets and anticipated major future capital expenditures, projected net income often approximates projected cash flow. The key to successfully using projected net income to approximate projected cash flow is to clearly indicate to any potential investor or purchaser that this is what is occurring, and then justify the premise.

Ultimately, the entrepreneur needs to remember that the projected net income numbers for the business, the related expected future cash flow numbers for the business, and the discount rate chosen are all infinitely attackable. The adequacy of the assumptions, amounts, and rate(s) used to perform a discounted cash flow business valuation can be expected to be challenged by any individual or company interested in purchasing a business.

Using Business Valuation to Determine Asking Price

The commonly acknowledged advantages of the discounted cash flow method of valuation are that it focuses on the long term instead of the short term, is based on the cash flows of a business, and looks to the future instead of the past. The cash flows utilized are based on the anticipated future earnings of a business. If everyone agrees that the assumptions underlying the anticipated future earnings of the business are reasonable, then the discounted cash flow method offers a value number that's arguably more a function of objective calculations than what can be viewed as the more subjective and somewhat historically based appraisals of value offered by asset- and market-based methods of business valuation.

That said, the discounted cash flow method of business valuation has some commonly acknowledged disadvantages:

- It doesn't work well without a high degree of confidence (or agreement) about the anticipated future cash flows of a business.
- The valuation number it generates is highly dependent upon both the discount rate used and the anticipated long-term growth rate assumed when determining terminal value.

These weaknesses suggest that, as mentioned earlier in this section, although earnings-based approaches are the most popular business valuation methods, for most businesses, some combination of asset-based, market-based, and earnings-based approaches to business valuation is often the best way to determine the asking price for a business.

Beyond simply relying on the results of some combination of formal business valuation approaches, however, an entrepreneur should also apply a gut check to any business valuation number under consideration. As a practical matter, many entrepreneurs consider the information in the professional business valuations presented to them and then determine a recommended asking price for their business considering this information and also based on their instincts. There's nothing wrong with doing this as long as the business owner can effectively verbalize the justification for doing so. Not every attribute of a business can always be boiled down to a number to be included in a professional business valuation. Also, every entrepreneur needs to remember that asking price is simply the starting point for price negotiations. It is uncommon for a buyer—no matter how enamored the buyer may be with a business—to agree to pay asking price for a business. As a result, leaving some wiggle room for negotiation when determining a company's asking price is always a wise choice.

Summary

In this chapter, we looked at the common means—beyond salaries, dividends, or distributions—that business owners and investors utilize to harvest cash from their companies. We also looked at some of the required planning and typical consequences associated with these means.

Cash harvest options can be generally categorized into two types: those that don't involve an owner or investor exiting the business and those that do. Cash harvest options that don't involve an owner or investor exiting the business include the following:

- a C corporation paying dividends to its shareholders
- pass-through entities, such as S corporations and LLCs, paying distributions to their owners

- owner-employees of corporations and entities taxed like a corporation paying themselves a salary
- leveraged recapitalization

Capital gain is a cash harvest option that results when an owner or investor sells all or part of the company he owns for more than the amount of his associated investment in that company. A capital gain, therefore, involves an owner or investor fully or partially exiting the business. Following are the top 10 ways an owner or investor might fully or partially exit his company:

Top 10 Business-Exit Scenarios
1. Liquidate and dissolve an unsuccessful company.
2. Liquidate and dissolve a fixed-time or short-term company.
3. Liquidate and dissolve a successful company in order to pursue a different opportunity.
4. Gift or sell all or part of a company to the next generation of the family or other family members.
5. Sell all or part of a company to the company's employees.
6. Sell all or part of a company to a private equity firm.
7. Sell all or part of a company to the general public in the form of a public offering.
8. Sell all of a company to another individual or company (i.e., a competitor, distributor, or supplier).
9. Sell part of a company to an investor, often at the beginning stages of the company.
10. Sell one's ownership interest in a company to one's current business partners.

A desire to exit a business usually creates the need to determine a value for the business in question. Determining the value of a business might also be necessary for a variety of other reasons, including to properly insure the business, to support a loan to the business, or to complete a proper buy-sell agreement. Multiple approaches for determining the value of a business exist, including asset-based, market-based, and earnings-based approaches. The most commonly used method to value a business—the discounted cash flow method of business valuation—is an earnings-based methodology that places a value on a business by determining, at a specified discount rate, the sum of the present values of all of the business's expected future cash flows. The discounted cash flow method of business valuation was illustrated in detail in this chapter.

In this chapter, we also looked at how to position a company for sale and how to sell a company. In many cases, the amount of time and effort required to properly position a company for sale far exceeds the amount of time and effort required to actually sell it. Proper positioning of a company can make all the difference in terms of whether a company sells, how quickly it sells, and for how much it sells.

Key Terms

amortization expense
annual exclusion for gifts
asset-based business
    valuation
business broker
business succession
    planning
buy-sell agreement
Certified Business
    Intermediary
discounted cash flow
    method of business
    valuation

dissolution
due diligence
earnings-based business
    valuation
employee stock owner-
    ship plan (ESOP)
enterprise value
equity value
free cash flow
Gordon growth model
investment banking firm
leveraged buyout (LBO)
leveraged recapitalization

lifetime basic exclusion
    for gifts
liquidation
management presentation
market-based business
    valuation
merger and acquisition
    (M&A) advisor
non-compete agreement
retainer
selling memo
term sheet
terminal value

Review and Discussion Questions

1. Cash harvest options can be generally categorized into two types: those that don't involve an owner or investor exiting the business and those that do. What cash harvest options don't involve an owner or investor exiting the business?

2. What is business succession planning? When does business succession planning need to be undertaken? What is the result of good business succession planning?

3. Capital gain is a cash harvest option that results when an owner or investor sells all or part of the company he owns for more than the amount of his associated investment in that company. A capital gain, therefore, involves an owner or investor fully or partially exiting the business. What are the top 10 ways an owner or investor might fully or partially exit a company?

4. A comprehensive professional business valuation typically supplements the results of an earnings-based business valuation with the results of an asset-based business valuation and a market-based business valuation. Describe and explain asset-based, market-based, and earnings-based approaches to business valuation.

5. What are the basic steps of the business sale process?

6. What is involved in a typical business dissolution?

7. Define and explain terminal value.

8. Define and explain equity value and enterprise value.

Exercises

1. In April 2012, Facebook purchased Instagram for approximately $715 million. Research the details of this transaction. Write two to three paragraphs that answer the following questions:
   - Why was there such a big difference between the amount Facebook offered for Instagram and the amount Facebook ultimately paid for Instagram?
   - By how much did the amount Facebook ultimately paid for Instagram exceed the valuation financial pundits had placed on Instagram?
   - Looking back at the deal and considering the popularity of Instagram today, do you think Facebook overpaid for Instagram? Why or why not?

2. Go to nceo.org/articles/employee-ownership-100 to find a list of America's largest employee-owned companies. Pick one of the companies, research that company, and write a one-page paper detailing and describing the company, its successes and failures, when the company became employee owned, and how becoming employee owned changed—or didn't change—the company.

3. Go to businessinsider.com/the-biggest-private-equity-deals-in-history-2011-4 to find a list of the 15 largest private equity deals in history. Pick five of the companies on the list that were still in business at the time the article was written and research how those companies are faring today. Does being purchased—or substantially purchased—by a private equity firm appear to have had a positive, negative, or negligible effect on the five companies you chose? Write a two-page paper that references the research you've done and supports the conclusions you've drawn.

4. Your industry typically values a business using a 25 percent discount rate. You've forecasted that your company, Brady Technologies, LLC, will enjoy expected cash flows for the next five years as follows:

Brady Technologies, LLC Expected Cash Flows	
Year	Amount
2020	$350,000
2021	$375,000
2022	$425,000
2023	$475,000
2024	$500,000

Note the following present value factors for a 25 percent discount rate: 0.8000 ($n = 1$), 0.6400 ($n = 2$), 0.5120 ($n = 3$), 0.4096 ($n = 4$), 0.3277 ($n = 5$). Calculate the equity value of your business using the discounted cash flow method, using a 25 percent discount rate, and assuming that the expected cash flow of the last forecasted year will stabilize and continue to grow in perpetuity by 2 percent per year. Next, answer the following questions:

a. If an investor approaches you and wants to invest $180,000 in Brady Technologies, LLC, what percentage ownership of the company might this investment represent? Justify your answer.

b. If you wish to sell your 60 percent ownership interest in Brady Technologies, LLC to your business partners, what would likely be the numerical basis for your asking price?

c. If your company has $250,000 of debt and $25,000 of cash on its balance sheet, what is the enterprise value of your business?

5. Your industry typically values a business using a 20 percent discount rate. You've forecasted that your company, Hi-Fidelity Innovations, LLC, will enjoy expected cash flows for the next 10 years as shown below:

Hi-Fidelity Innovations, LLC Expected Cash Flows	
Year	Amount
2020	$300,000
2021	$315,000
2022	$330,750
2023	$347,288
2024	$364,652
2025	$382,884
2026	$402,029
2027	$422,130
2028	$443,237
2029	$465,398

Calculate the equity value of your business using the discounted cash flow method, using a 20 percent discount rate, and assuming that the expected cash flow of the last forecasted year will stabilize and continue to grow in perpetuity by 2.5 percent per year. By how much would the results differ if we used a 12 percent discount rate instead of 20 percent?

6. Your industry typically values a business using a 25 percent discount rate. You've forecasted that your company, Benson Manufacturing, Inc., will enjoy expected cash flows for the next 15 years as indicated below:

Benson Manufacturing, Inc. Expected Cash Flows	
Year	Amount
2020	$ 600,000
2021	$ 645,000
2022	$ 693,375
2023	$ 745,378
2024	$ 801,281
2025	$ 861,378
2026	$ 925,981
2027	$ 995,429
2028	$ 1,070,087
2029	$ 1,150,343
2030	$ 1,236,619
2031	$ 1,329,365
2032	$ 1,429,068
2033	$ 1,536,248
2034	$ 1,651,466

Note the following present value factors for a 25 percent discount rate: 0.8000 ($n = 1$), 0.6400 ($n = 2$), 0.5120 ($n = 3$), 0.4096 ($n = 4$), 0.3277 ($n = 5$), 0.2621 ($n = 6$), 0.2097 ($n = 2$), 0.1678 ($n = 8$), 0.1342 ($n = 9$), 0.1074 ($n = 10$), 0.0859 ($n = 11$), 0.0687 ($n = 12$), 0.0550 ($n = 13$), 0.0440 ($n = 14$), 0.0352 ($n = 15$). Calculate the equity value of your business using the discounted cash flow method, using a 25 percent discount rate, and assuming that the expected cash flow of the last forecasted year will stabilize and continue to grow in perpetuity by 2 percent per year. Next, answer the following questions:

a. Assuming Benson Manufacturing, Inc. has 100,000 shares of common stock outstanding, what is the value of each share of this stock based on the equity value of the business you just calculated?

b. If your company has $175,000 of debt and $35,000 of cash on its balance sheet, what is the enterprise value of this business?

Endnotes

1. Julie Garber, "The Annual Gift Tax Exclusion," The Balance, https://www.thebalance.com/annual-exclusion-from-gift-taxes-3505637, December 10, 2018.

2. Will Kenton, "Employee Stock Ownership Plan—EOP," Investopedia, https://www.investopedia.com/terms/e/esop.asp, April 23, 2018.

3. "How an Employee Stock Ownership Plan (ESOP) Works," National Center for Employee Ownership, http://www.nceo.org/articles/esop-employee-stock-ownership-plan, January 30, 2018.

4. Amy Fontinelle, "Keeping Control of Your Business after the IPO," Investopedia, https://www.investopedia.com/articles/personal-finance/102715/keeping-control-your-business-after-ipo.asp, October 14, 2018.

5. Susan Ward, "IPO (Initial Public Offering) Definition," The Balance, https://www.the balancesmb.com/ipo-initial-public-offering-definition-2948116, April 22, 2018.

6. Carl Christensen, "Investment Banker vs. M&A Advisor vs. Business Broker," Investment Bank, https://investmentbank.com/investment-banker-vs-ma-advisor-vs-business-broker/, January 30, 2019.

7. Ibid.

8. Brian DeChesare, "Boutique Investment Banks vs. Middle-Market vs. Bulge-Bracket Banks: Got Rankings?," Mergers and Inquisitions, https://www.mergersandinquisitions.com/boutique-middle-market-bulge-bracket/, February 12, 2019.

9. Carl Christensen, "Investment Banker vs. M&A Advisor vs. Business Broker," Investment Bank, https://investmentbank.com/investment-banker-vs-ma-advisor-vs-business-broker/, January 30, 2019.

10. Ibid.

11. Brian DeChesare, "Boutique Investment Banks vs. Middle-Market vs. Bulge-Bracket Banks: Got Rankings?," Mergers and Inquisitions, https://www.mergersandinquisitions.com/boutique-middle-market-bulge-bracket/, February 12, 2019.

12. Darren Dahl, "What You Should Know about Working with Business Brokers," Inc., https://www.inc.com/guides/201106/what-you-should-know-about-working-with-business-brokers.html, June 16, 2011.

13. Nate Nead, "M&A Advisor Fees: Retainers, Successes, and Ancillary Expenses," Investment Bank, https://investmentbank.com/fees/, January 30, 2019.

14. Divestopedia Team, "A Summary of M&A Fees for Sell-Side Transactions," Divestopedia, https://www.divestopedia.com/2/8036/sale-process/investment-bankers/a-summary-of-ma-fees-for-sell-side-transactions, September 7, 2016.

15. Wesley Legg, "Understanding M&A Advisor Fees," Founders Advisors, http://www.foundersib.com/2016/02/25/understanding-ma-advisor-fees/, February 25, 2016.

16. Lawrence Delevingne, "The 25 Who Won the Recession," Business Insider, https://www.businessinsider.com/recession-winners-2009-8, September 1, 2009.

17. Ibid.

18. R. H. Parker, "Discounted Cash Flow in Historical Perspective." *Journal of Accounting Research* 6, no. 1 (Spring 1968): 58–71.

19. "Summary of the DCF Method," Valuebasedmanagement.net, https://www.valuebasedmanagement.net/methods_dcf.html, January 6, 2016.

20. Edward Stephen, "Discounted Cash Flow Valuation: Advantages and Pitfalls," Deal Room, https://www.firmex.com/thedealroom/discounted-cash-flow-valuation-advantages-pitfalls/, September 23, 2016.

21. Jean Folger, "DCF Analysis: Coming Up with a Fair Value," Investopedia, https://www.investopedia.com/university/dcf/dcf4.asp, January 30, 2019.

22. "Discount Rate," Divestopedia, https://www.divestopedia.com/definition/5039/discount-rate, 2019.

Personal Finance and Wealth Management

"Before you invest, investigate. . . . Before you retire, save.
  Before you die, give."

— William A. Ward, frequently quoted American author

Learning Objectives

Understand the concepts of risk management and asset management.

Understand how to maintain financial liquidity and continued personal financial security utilizing the most common U.S. investment vehicles.

Have knowledge of the options and strategies associated with retirement planning, college planning, and estate planning.

Introduction

As long as an entrepreneur owns a business, the personal finances of the entrepreneur and the finances of the business she has created continue to be linked. The strongest financial connections between the entrepreneur and her business usually relate to business owner compensation and the taxation of the profits of the business. This is especially true for young businesses and small businesses.

Whether an entrepreneur decides to dissolve her business, sell all or part of it, or keep the business long term, the personal wealth of the entrepreneur is often quite significantly enhanced by her business. A business generating a profit brings up the happy question of what to do with the resulting excess cash. Excess cash offers the entrepreneur the opportunity to grow her business—either organically or by investing in other businesses. Excess cash also offers the entrepreneur the opportunity to continue to innovate and create—either within or outside of her current business—the innovation process made easier due to the increased level of resources at the entrepreneur's disposal. Additionally, excess cash can provide an exit to investors or be distributed to the business's owners.

As an entrepreneur's personal wealth increases, she needs to increasingly focus on the following three tasks:

1. the protection of assets
2. the maintenance of adequate **financial liquidity**—the preservation of a certain minimum level of cash coupled with the ability to quickly and easily get access to more cash
3. the investment of excess cash in a manner that maximizes the probability of continued financial security

Protecting assets, maintaining adequate financial liquidity, and investing excess cash for continued financial security are all topics this chapter will address.

Risk Management

financial liquidity
the preservation of a certain minimum level of cash coupled with the ability to quickly and easily get access to more cash

A wise entrepreneur is always trying to reduce risk. We noted in chapter 1 that risk management involves an entrepreneur planning for both her business's assets and her personal assets in such a way as to reduce uncertainty and risk, usually by utilizing one of the following approaches:

- risk avoidance
- risk reduction
- risk transfer
- risk assumption

Risk avoidance is characterized by the avoidance of any hazard that exposes a business or an individual to risk (e.g., instituting a cash-only sales policy at one's business). Risk reduction involves engaging in behaviors and programs specifically designed to reduce risk (e.g., installing a sprinkler system and a security system at one's business facility). Risk transfer involves proactively transferring risk to another party, often by paying for insurance policies that reimburse one for losses associated with one's personal or business assets. Risk assumption occurs when one proactively assumes risk because one believes that the loss or cost one is likely to incur by assuming that risk is less than the loss or cost associated with risk avoidance, risk reduction, or risk transfer (e.g., a business deciding to accept checks from customers knowing that, occasionally, a customer will write a bad check).

insurance
an arrangement evidenced in writing by which one party provides a guarantee of compensation for a specified loss incurred by another party in return for the payment of a premium

The topics of risk avoidance, risk reduction, and risk assumption have been addressed in earlier chapters. This chapter will address risk transfer—specifically, risk transfer achieved as a result of paying for insurance policies. **Insurance** is an arrangement evidenced in writing by which one party provides a guarantee of compensation for a specified loss incurred by another party in return for the payment of a premium. Generally, any losses covered must be accidental in nature and beyond the control of the insured. The potential losses to be covered must also not be so large in amount as to be potentially catastrophic to the insurance company.

The types of insurance typically sought out by individuals include health insurance, auto insurance, renter's or homeowner's insurance, and life insurance. Note that most renter's and homeowner's insurance policies don't cover losses due to flooding.[1] If a renter's or homeowner's insurance policy doesn't cover losses due to flooding, the renter or homeowner should consider purchasing flood insurance from the U.S. National Flood Insurance Program in addition to purchasing standard renter's or homeowner's insurance.[2]

Life insurance transfers some of the financial risk associated with death from the insured to an insurance company. There are two basic types of life insurance:

1. **term life insurance**—a life insurance policy for which one pays a yearly premium based primarily on the mortality rate of one's age group
2. permanent or **whole life insurance**—a life insurance policy that allocates part of the premium paid into building a cash value that can be used upon retirement or borrowed against in case of an emergency

Other types of insurance exist that individuals may purchase to cover unexpected life events.

Disability insurance is purchased to replace the income lost when an individual is temporarily unable to work due to an injury, illness, or pregnancy. To the extent such assistance is not paid for by health insurance, Medicare, or Medicaid, **long-term care insurance** pays for the assistance one needs long term in order to perform daily living functions like eating, bathing, dressing, and walking. **Liability insurance** is purchased to transfer to an insurance company the cost associated with damage to the property or person of others that might result from one's actions or the actions of one's business. Most Americans are significantly underinsured with regard to disability, long-term care, and liability risk.

An often relatively inexpensive way to better protect one's assets or the assets of one's business is umbrella insurance. **Umbrella insurance** refers to liability insurance that's in excess of an individual's other specified policies and also potentially primary insurance for losses not covered by an individual's other insurance policies. When an individual has an umbrella insurance policy and a large loss is incurred, the insured's applicable primary insurance policies first pay up to their designated limits, then the umbrella policy pays any additional amount up to the designated limit of the umbrella policy. Because it is secondary insurance, personal umbrella insurance is usually relatively inexpensive.

With regard to business insurance specifically, a business owner typically pays for multiple types of insurance to cover the following areas:

- commercial property
- business autos
- general business liability
- product liability
- professional liability
- business interruption

Commercial property insurance protects a business's physical assets from theft, fire, vandalism, and the effects of many types of natural disasters. Note that a personal homeowner's insurance policy doesn't cover a home-based business in the same way a commercial property insurance policy covers a business operating out of a commercial facility. An entrepreneur operating a business out of her home should specifically ask for insurance to cover her home-based business's inventory, equipment, and other assets in the event of theft, fire, or other unfortunate event.

Business auto insurance protects the cars, trucks, vans, or other vehicles a business uses, and it also protects the business from liability for most forms of damage or mayhem these vehicles might create. Similar to the way an individual's personal homeowner's insurance policy doesn't provide complete coverage for a home-based business, an individual's personal auto insurance policy doesn't cover

term life insurance
a life insurance policy for which one pays a yearly premium based primarily on the mortality rate of one's age group

whole life insurance
a life insurance policy that allocates part of the premium paid into building a cash value that can be used upon retirement or borrowed against in case of an emergency

disability insurance
insurance purchased to replace the income lost when an individual is temporarily unable to work due to an injury, illness, or pregnancy

long-term care insurance
insurance that pays for the assistance one needs long term in order to perform daily living functions like eating, bathing, dressing, and walking, to the extent such assistance is not paid for by health insurance, Medicare, or Medicaid

liability insurance
insurance purchased to transfer to an insurance company the cost associated with damage to the property or person of others that might result from one's actions or the actions of one's business

umbrella insurance
liability insurance that's in excess of an individual's other specified policies and also potentially primary insurance for losses not covered by an individual's other insurance policies

commercial property insurance
insurance that protects a business's physical assets from theft, fire, vandalism, and the effects of many types of natural disasters

business auto insurance
insurance that protects the cars, trucks, vans, or other vehicles used in a business and also protects the business from liability for most forms of damage or mayhem these vehicles might create

incidents related to the business use of a vehicle in the same way a business auto insurance policy does. A personal auto policy may not have high enough coverage levels to adequately protect a business and may not provide any coverage if the vehicle involved in an incident is determined to be used primarily for business. An entrepreneur whose business owns vehicles, who uses her personal vehicle for business, or who has employees who use their personal vehicles while performing duties for her business should specifically ask her insurer for a business auto insurance policy that adequately protects the business with regard to all three situations.

Business liability insurance, sometimes called general liability insurance, protects you and your business from most claims of bodily injury, personal injury, or property damage that arise as a result of your business's operations. Although an entrepreneur should always specifically verify it, **product liability insurance**—insurance that provides coverage for bodily injury and property damage that result from the use of a product manufactured, assembled, or sold by a business—is usually a part of business liability insurance. Note that there's a significant difference between product liability insurance that is term and product liability insurance that follows and covers a product forever. Depending on the nature of a business and the risks associated with any products it produces or sells, the entrepreneur should consider paying the upcharge for the latter type of product liability insurance.

Professional liability insurance, also known as errors and omissions (E&O) insurance, covers a business against negligence claims due to harm that results from professional mistakes or failure to perform. Among other types of businesses that hold such insurance, accounting firms, architectural firms, and medical practices typically carry professional liability insurance.

Catastrophic events happen to businesses and individuals alike. **Business interruption insurance** compensates a business for the profits lost as a result of a catastrophic event. Business interruption insurance may also cover the reasonable expenses associated with operating the business in a temporary location, retraining employees, and otherwise getting a business back up and running.[3] Business interruption insurance can be the difference between a business surviving—or not surviving—after a fire, natural disaster, or other devastation.

business liability insurance
insurance that protects a business and its owners from most claims of bodily injury, personal injury, or property damage that arise as a result of the business's operations; also sometimes called general liability insurance

product liability insurance
insurance that provides coverage for bodily injury and property damage that result from the use of a product manufactured, assembled, or sold by a business

professional liability insurance
insurance that covers a business against negligence claims due to harm that results from professional mistakes or failure to perform; also known as errors and omissions (E&O) insurance

business interruption insurance
insurance that compensates a business for the profits lost as a result of a catastrophic event

Asset Management and Investment Vehicles

Now that we've talked about how to protect what we have, let's talk about how to maximize its potential. In order to achieve financial success in life and enjoy continued financial security, one must do the following:

- Begin to accumulate capital.
- Determine the level of financial liquidity one wishes to maintain.
- Consider one's tolerance for risk.
- Preserve capital by investing in vehicles that provide an after-tax return greater than the inflation rate.
- Actively manage the diversification and allocation of financial assets among the different asset classes and investment vehicles in order to reduce overall investment risk.
- Consider the eventual future distribution of capital via retirement income, college funding, and estate transfer.

Investment vehicles are the specific financial instruments we use to maintain financial liquidity and enjoy continued financial security by generating income and providing for capital growth. Many different investment vehicles exist within each of five main asset classes:

1. cash and cash equivalents
2. bonds and similar debt instruments, including fixed-income exchange traded funds and mutual funds
3. equities, including individual shares of stock and many exchange traded funds and mutual funds
4. real estate
5. commodities, precious metals, and collectables

Some investment vehicles are quite complex, represent exotic combinations of other investment vehicles, and are designed for only the most sophisticated investors. The purpose of the following five sections of this chapter is to familiarize you with only the most common U.S. investment vehicles.

Cash and Cash Equivalents

Cash equivalents are investment securities designed for short-term investing. They're generally high-credit quality, low-risk, highly liquid investments that provide a lower yield than longer-term, higher-risk, less-liquid investments.

As first mentioned in chapter 4, in relation to the general topic of finance, liquidity refers to the ease with which an asset can be converted into cash without significant loss of value. The most liquid asset in existence is cash itself. To maintain adequate financial liquidity, it's desirable to always have a certain amount of cash on hand in order to take advantage of unexpected opportunities and also to pay for unexpected expenses. Beyond simply having cash on hand, however, in order to both maintain adequate financial liquidity and maximize the return on one's assets, investing in a certain amount of cash equivalents is also desirable. Because cash equivalents can be quickly and easily converted into cash without significant loss of value, cash equivalents are generally considered second only to cash in terms of liquidity. However, because they generally offer some type of yield, cash equivalents can also help maximize the overall return on one's assets.

Yield refers to the annual earnings produced by an investment, calculated as a percentage of the value of that investment. These earnings are usually in the form of interest or dividends. Yield is different from an investment's total return in that yield generally doesn't consider an asset's appreciation or depreciation in market value. An investment's yield often, but not always, reflects the risk associated with the underlying investment. In other words, a high yield is often an indicator of high risk, just as a low yield is often an indicator of low risk.

Common cash equivalent investments with a low-risk, low-yield profile include U.S. Treasury bills (often called T-bills), bank certificates of deposit (CDs), banker's acceptances, commercial paper, and money market funds. T-bills are short-term debt instruments issued by the U.S. Department of the Treasury. T-bills mature in one year or less, typically in three or six months, and are considered risk-free investments because they are backed by the full faith and credit of the federal government. In other words, they're backed by the U.S. government's ability to tax.

CDs are promissory notes whereby a bank promises to return to the depositor the principal amount deposited with the bank, plus interest, after a stipulated period. CDs can have terms of less than one year to up to five years or more and usually have a minimum initial deposit of $500.

A **banker's acceptance** is a short-term debt instrument issued by a company that is guaranteed by that company's bank. Banker's acceptances are widely used to provide some level of protection to a seller involved in a high-dollar-value international goods transaction with a purchaser the seller does not know. Essentially

cash equivalents
investment securities designed for short-term investing, generally high-credit quality, low-risk, highly liquid investments that provide a lower yield than longer-term, higher-risk, less-liquid investments

yield
the annual earnings—usually in the form of interest or dividends—produced by an investment, calculated as a percentage of the value of that investment

banker's acceptance
a short-term debt instrument issued by a company that is guaranteed by that company's bank, widely used to provide some level of protection to a seller involved in a high-dollar-value international goods transaction with a purchaser the seller does not know

the purchaser issues a time draft to the seller of the goods, the payment of which is guaranteed by the bank's prior acceptance of it. The bank's acceptance of the time draft is typically indicated by a bank stamp on the face of the time draft that includes authorized bank signatures. The time draft is like a post-dated check guaranteeing payment of a specified amount of funds to the owner of the time draft at a specified date. When the time draft matures, the purchaser's bank simultaneously pays the amount due and charges the purchaser's account for the same amount. The owner of the time draft can sell it for a discounted price to a buyer who's willing to wait until the maturity date of the time draft for her money.

Commercial paper is an unsecured, short-term debt instrument, typically issued in a large denomination ($100,000 or more) by a large bank, a foreign government, or a large corporation with a strong balance sheet, the proceeds of which are typically used to finance accounts receivable or inventory or to meet short-term debt obligations. Commercial paper is typically non-interest-bearing debt issued at a discount from face value, such discount considering applicable current market interest rates.[4] Generally, the higher the current market interest rates, the larger the discount from face value that must be effected in order to render the commercial paper attractive to potential buyers. Usually, commercial paper isn't backed by any form of collateral, so only entities with a very high **credit rating**—an assessment of the creditworthiness of an entity or financial obligation, ideally provided by an objective third party—can easily find buyers without having to offer a substantial discount at the time of the debt issue. As first discussed in chapter 3, because of the time, money, and effort required to comply with securities laws, entities often choose to pursue funding paths that avoid the need to register securities with the Securities and Exchange Commission (SEC). A major benefit of commercial paper is that it doesn't need to be registered with the SEC as long as it matures in 270 days or less.[5] This often makes issuing commercial paper a cost-effective way for large banks, foreign governments, and large corporations to obtain needed short-term financing.

A **money market fund** invests in short-term debt securities such as U.S. Treasury bills, high-quality commercial paper, and banker's acceptances. Money market funds are a type of **mutual fund**, which is an investment vehicle set up by a mutual fund company, a company that collects funds from investors and uses the funds to purchase large blocks of bonds, stocks, and other types of investment securities. Money market funds are regulated by the SEC and generally aim to provide a higher return on excess cash than a bank offers. While most money market funds are carefully managed to deliver on their reputation as a safe investment, excess cash placed in a money market fund isn't as safe as excess cash placed in a financial institution insured by the Federal Deposit Insurance Corporation (FDIC), an independent federal agency that protects the monies on deposit in U.S. banks and savings associations.[6]

When cash isn't invested short term in T-bills, banker's acceptances, commercial paper, or a money market fund, it's usually deposited and held at a bank or similar financial institution, where it's protected by the FDIC. FDIC insurance covers the following types of deposit accounts:

- checking accounts
- savings accounts
- money market deposit accounts—deposit accounts that generally allow for limited check writing privileges and typically pay a higher interest rate than a savings account and a lower interest rate than a CD
- CDs

FDIC insurance is backed by the full faith and credit of the U.S. government. Since the FDIC's establishment in 1933, not a single depositor has lost even a penny of FDIC-insured funds.[7] The current insurance amount is $250,000 per depositor per insured bank for each of 14 account ownership categories, including trust accounts,

credit rating
an assessment of the creditworthiness of an entity or financial obligation, ideally provided by an objective third party

money market fund
a type of mutual fund that invests in short-term debt securities such as U.S Treasury bills, high-quality commercial paper, and banker's acceptances and generally aims to provide a higher return on excess cash than what is offered by a bank

mutual funds
investment vehicles set up by mutual fund companies, companies that collect funds from investors then use the funds to purchase large blocks of bonds, stocks, and other types of investment securities

employee benefit accounts, and certain retirement accounts.[8] Note that FDIC insurance covers only the funds on deposit in checking and savings accounts, money market deposit accounts, and CDs. It doesn't cover funds invested in the other financial products some banks offer.

Bonds

Bonds are contractual agreements between a borrower and a lender of financial capital. Several types of bond are available. These are the most common:

- U.S. Treasury
- other U.S. government (also called agency bonds)
- investment-grade
- mortgage-backed (also called mortgage-backed securities)
- high-yield (also called junk bonds)
- foreign
- municipal

U.S. Treasury bonds are securities issued by the federal government in order to finance its budget deficit. Because they're backed by the full faith and credit of the U.S. government, these bonds are generally considered risk free. However, because they're considered risk free, their yields are low compared to most other bonds. The interest on U.S. Treasury bonds is usually not taxed at the state or local level.

Other U.S. government bonds, called **agency bonds**, are bonds issued by government-sponsored enterprises (GSEs), usually federally chartered, privately owned corporations, such as the Federal National Mortgage Association (Fannie Mae) and the Federal Home Loan Mortgage Corporation (Freddie Mac), and U.S. federal agencies, such as the Government National Mortgage Association (Ginnie Mae) and the Small Business Administration (SBA). GSE bond yields are usually higher than U.S. Treasury bond yields because, unlike U.S. Treasury bonds, GSE bonds aren't full-faith-and-credit obligations of the U.S. government. Nonetheless, their credit risk is still considered minimal. Although they are full-faith-and-credit obligations of the U.S. government, the yields on federal agency bonds—bonds issued by U.S. federal agencies—are also usually higher than U.S. Treasury bond yields—although only slightly—because federal agency bonds are generally perceived as slightly less liquid than U.S. Treasury bonds. The interest on many, but not all, U.S. agency bonds is exempt from taxation at the state and local levels.

Investment-grade corporate bonds are issued by financially sound entities—typically large corporations—with a credit rating of at least Baa3 from Moody's Investor Service or BBB- from Standard & Poor's. Because the risk associated with these bonds is higher than the risk associated with U.S. Treasury and agency bonds, the yields of investment-grade corporate bonds are typically higher than those offered by U.S. Treasury and agency bonds. The risk of default associated with investment-grade bonds is, however, low enough that banks and similar financial institutions are permitted by banking regulations to invest in them. Detailed information about the methodology behind the credit ratings issued by Moody's Investor Service and Standard & Poor's can be found at moodys.com and standardandpoors.com.

Mortgage-backed bonds, often called mortgage-backed securities, are bonds backed by home mortgages. Mortgage-backed securities are created when mortgages are pooled together by a sponsor who packages them for sale to the public in the form of a negotiable security—typically a bond—that is sold in the financial markets. Although private financial institutions can issue mortgage-backed securities, the principal issuers of these types of securities are Fannie Mae, Freddie Mac, and Ginnie Mae. Because the risk associated with them is higher than U.S. Treasury, agency,

agency bonds
bonds issued by government-sponsored enterprises and U.S. federal agencies

investment-grade corporate bonds
bonds issued by financially sound entities—typically large corporations—with a credit rating of at least Baa3 from Moody's Investor Service or BBB- from Standard & Poor's

mortgage-backed bonds
bonds backed by home mortgages, such bonds created when mortgages are pooled together by a sponsor who packages them for sale to the public in the form of a negotiable security that is sold in the financial markets; also called mortgage-backed securities

and investment-grade corporate bonds, mortgage-backed securities typically offer a higher yield than U.S. Treasury, agency, and investment-grade corporate bonds.

High-yield bonds, often called junk bonds, are issued by less financially sound entities than those that issue investment-grade bonds. Junk bonds are issued by entities with a credit rating below Baa3 from Moody's Investor Service or BBB- from Standard & Poor's. The risk of default is distinctly higher with a junk bond than with an investment-grade bond, hence, junk bond yields are generally higher than the yields offered by investment-grade bonds. As noted above, detailed information about the methodology behind the credit ratings issued by Moody's Investor Service and Standard & Poor's is available at moodys.com and standardandpoors.com.

Foreign bonds are bonds issued or sold in the U.S. market by a non-U.S. entity, such bonds often denominated in U.S. dollars. Many U.S. investors find U.S. dollar-denominated foreign bonds attractive because U.S. dollar-denominated foreign bonds allow investors to add foreign investment to their investment portfolios without adding exchange rate exposure. Non-U.S. dollar-denominated foreign bonds exist, but they are less popular with the typical U.S. investor because, even though non-U.S. dollar-denominated foreign bonds typically have higher yields than U.S. dollar-denominated foreign bonds and domestic bonds, their higher yield is due to the added element of currency risk. Specifically, if the U.S. dollar strengthens against the applicable foreign currency, the value of the non-U.S. dollar-denominated foreign bond is diminished. If the U.S. dollar weakens against the applicable foreign currency, the value of the non-U.S. dollar-denominated foreign bond is enhanced.

Municipal bonds are issued by a government or a government agency other than the federal government or one of its GSEs or agencies. Municipal bonds may be either investment-grade or high-yield. The interest related to municipal bonds is, for most taxpayers, exempt from federal taxation. The interest on municipal bonds is also often exempt from state and local income taxation, especially in the instance where a bondholder resides in the same state in which the bond was issued. Municipal bonds typically have a higher yield than U.S. Treasury and other U.S. government bonds, which are lower risk, but a lower yield than corporate bonds, whose interest is taxable. For most taxpayers, a municipal bond's lower, tax-free yield equates to a higher before-tax yield. A municipal bond's before-tax yield is what should be considered when comparing municipal bonds with taxable investment alternatives. Example 12.1 illustrates the calculation of the before-tax yield for a municipal bond.

Example 12.1

The municipality of Lakeville, Iowa, is issuing 5 percent interest rate, 30-year, tax-free municipal bonds. Sandra Owens, an Iowa resident who pays out 30 percent of her income annually for federal, state, and local income taxes, is considering purchasing some of these bonds. When comparing this investment with other potential investments that aren't tax free, what yield should Sandra use?

$$\text{Before-tax yield} = \frac{\text{Tax-free yield}}{1 - \text{Tax rate}}$$

$$= \frac{0.05}{1 - 0.30}$$

$$= 7.14\%$$

The calculation indicates that our Iowa taxpayer should use the before-tax yield of 7.14 percent when comparing these municipal bonds with taxable investment alternatives.

---

high-yield bonds
bonds issued by less financially sound entities than those who issue investment-grade bonds and whose risk of default is distinctly higher than an investment-grade bond; also called junk bonds

foreign bonds
bonds issued or sold in the U.S. market by a non-U.S. entity, such bonds often denominated in U.S. dollars

municipal bonds
bonds issued by a government or a government agency other than the federal government or one of its GSEs or agencies

Before moving into a discussion of bond valuation, let's review some of the basic terminology associated with bonds:

- The **par value of a bond** (also called the face value or the principal value), usually in the denomination of $1,000 or a multiple of $1,000, is the amount paid to a bondholder at a bond's maturity. This amount never changes after a bond is issued.
- The **coupon rate of a bond** (also called the quoted rate or the stated rate) is the rate of interest the bond issuer agrees to pay to the bondholder. This also never changes after a bond is issued.

The par value of a bond, its coupon rate, and the prevailing market interest rate on the issue date of the bond combine to determine the amount of the proceeds the bond issuer receives (the amount the bond purchaser pays) on the issue date of the bond, as example 12.2 illustrates.

par value of a bond
the amount paid to a bondholder at a bond's maturity, usually in the denomination of $1,000 or a multiple of $1,000; also called the face value or the principal value

coupon rate of a bond
the rate of interest the bond issuer agrees to pay to the bondholder; also called the quoted rate or the stated rate

---

Example 12.2

An investor is interested in purchasing a $10,000, five-year, 6 percent interest rate bond to be issued today. The bond pays interest semiannually, and the applicable current market interest rate is 8 percent. What should the investor pay for this bond?

A bond, like most investments, involves a series of future cash flows. To determine the value today of these future cash flows, we must perform present value calculations. Before performing present value calculations, however, we must first determine the recurring cash flow amount associated with the interest component of the bond:

$10,000 \times 0.06 = 600 of annual interest

$600 \div 2 = 300 of semiannual interest

Because this bond's interest is paid semiannually, the bondholder would receive two payments of interest per year, each in the amount of $300. A payment of $300 at the end of each semiannual period for 10 semiannual periods in a row (5 years x 2 semiannual periods in a year = 10 semiannual periods) is an ordinary annuity. As a result, we use the present value of an ordinary annuity formula (in conjunction with the present value of an ordinary annuity table, if so desired) to calculate the present value of the bond interest payments:

$$PVOA = A(PVAF) = A\left[\frac{(1+i)^n - 1}{i(1+i)^n}\right]$$

$$= $300(8.1109)$$

$$= $2,433.27$$

The present value of an ordinary annuity factor for an n of 10 and an i of 4 percent (8% ÷ 2 semiannual periods per year = 4%) is 8.1109. Note that in our calculations, we used the bond coupon rate only to determine the amount of the interest payments. After that, we used the current market interest rate—or, more correctly stated, an interest rate that is a derivative of the current market interest rate—for purposes of our present value calculation.

Only one cash flow is associated with the principal component of the bond: the $10,000 due to be paid on the maturity date of the bond. As a result, using the same n and i we utilized to calculate the present value of the interest payments, we use the present value of a lump sum formula (in conjunction with the present value of a lump sum table, if so desired) to calculate the present value of the bond principal amount:

$$PV = FV(PVF) = FV\left(\frac{1}{(1+i)^n}\right)$$

$$= \$10,000(0.6756)$$

$$= \$6,756$$

Adding together the present values of the interest and principal components of the bond, we arrive at the amount an investor would be willing to pay for a $10,000, five-year, 6 percent bond that pays interest semiannually when the current market interest rate is 8 percent:

$$\$2,433.27 + \$6,756 = \$9,189.27$$

You may be wondering why the issue price (i.e., the market value) of the $10,000, five-year, 6 percent bond in example 12.2 is only $9,189.27. The reason is that, because the current market interest rate is above the coupon rate of the bond, this bond is unattractive to potential investors. In order to make this bond more attractive to investors, the bond is, in effect, discounted by the market. Bonds that are sold for an amount below par value—usually because the current market interest rate is above the coupon rate of the bond—are sold at a discount. Bonds that are sold for an amount above par value—usually because the current market interest rate is below the coupon rate of the bond—are sold at a premium.

As alluded to earlier in this chapter, most significant bond issues are given a credit rating by a credit rating agency. The "Big Three" credit rating agencies—Moody's Investors Service, Standard & Poor's, and Fitch Ratings—control approximately 95 percent of the global credit rating industry. Investors should be aware that, until the early 1970s, credit rating agencies were paid for their efforts by investors who wanted professional opinions regarding the creditworthiness of securities issuers and their offerings, opinions that were backed by objective, in-depth research. Starting in the early 1970s, the Big Three began receiving payment for their work from the securities issuers whose securities they rate. This practice has led to charges by some that the rating agencies can no longer always be impartial when issuing ratings. Such charges have recently received more attention due to the role the Big Three appear to have played in contributing to the 2007–2008 U.S. financial crisis. Pre-crisis, the Big Three commonly issued favorable credit ratings for sub-prime mortgage-backed securities, the fast and precipitous decline in market value of which was triggered by the bursting of the U.S. housing bubble. After the crisis, information came to light that the agencies had given their highest ratings to securities that included more than $3 trillion of mortgages to home buyers with either bad credit or unsubstantiated incomes.[9]

Mutual funds and exchange traded funds (ETFs) are investment vehicles that can provide an investor with a professionally managed and diversified investment in bonds, similar debt instruments, or other types of securities. Mutual funds are investment vehicles set up by mutual fund companies (e.g., Blackrock and the Vanguard Group). Mutual fund companies collect funds from investors—who then become the mutual fund's shareholders—and then use the funds to purchase large blocks of bonds, stocks, and other types of investment securities. Every mutual fund is established with a specific risk level and financial return in mind. When you invest in a mutual fund, you're essentially hiring a professional manager to research and purchase those investment vehicles that match your specific investment goals—investment goals you've affirmed based on your choice of that particular mutual fund.

An ETF is an investment similar to a mutual fund, but ETFs are different from mutual funds in three major ways. First, like stocks, ETFs trade throughout the trading day. Mutual funds trade only after the end of the trading day at the net asset value calculated for the mutual fund for that day after the market closes. Second, most ETFs track a particular index, have no investment minimum, and charge no **sales load**, which is a fee charged when certain mutual fund shares are purchased or sold by an investor. EFTs therefore often have lower operating expenses and fees than many actively managed mutual funds. Third, most ETFs are more tax efficient than mutual funds due to the fact that they usually generate fewer taxable events. When an investor in a mutual fund (e.g., a large institutional investor) decides to redeem a significant amount of shares, the mutual fund manager is often forced to sell part of the mutual fund's holdings in order to have sufficient cash to pay for the shares being redeemed, thereby generating a capital gain or loss. In contrast, ETFs trade from investor to investor rather than being redeemed. In addition, most ETFs don't often sell their holdings. As a result, ETFs usually generate significantly fewer capital gain and capital loss events than mutual funds do.

> **sales load**
> a fee charged when certain mutual fund shares are purchased or sold by an investor

Mutual funds and ETFs are commonly categorized based on the types of securities in which they invest. One of the largest categories is **fixed income**. A fixed-income mutual fund or ETF purchases and manages investments that pay a fixed rate of return, such as government bonds, corporate bonds, and similar debt instruments. A mutual fund or ETF might be designed to focus on investing in municipal bonds, investment-grade corporate bonds, junk bonds, short-term bonds, long-term bonds, or a variety of other types of bond securities. Other mutual funds and ETFs are **index funds**, meaning they're constructed to track or follow a specific stock index (e.g., the Russell 1000) as a result of holding the same components that make up that specific index. Still other mutual funds and ETFs hold stocks and other securities associated with a specific industry (e.g., energy), geographic area (e.g., the Pacific Rim), or other investment criterion. Whatever their investment focus, the benefit of mutual funds and ETFs is that they both give investors the ability to diversify their investment in debt or equity securities via a single security purchase.

> **fixed income**
> a category of investments that pay a fixed rate of return, investments such as government bonds, corporate bonds, and similar debt instruments

> **index funds**
> exchange traded funds and mutual funds that are constructed to track or follow a specific stock index as a result of holding the same components that make up that specific index

Equities

Equities are stocks and other types of securities representing an ownership interest in a company. The stock of a C corporation is an equity often owned by the typical U.S. investor. Figure 12.1 illustrates the presentation of the stock of a C corporation on a corporation's balance sheet.

Common stock is an equity security representing the fundamental ownership of a company issued by a public or private corporation in order to raise financial capital. Common stockholders are the owners of a corporation. They exercise control over the corporation by electing the board of directors and voting on major corporate initiatives that, if approved, could change the fundamental nature of the goals or the operations of the company.

The very highly regulated and managed first sale of most or all of the stock of a previously private company—or mostly private company—to the general public is

West Corporation Equity Section of the Balance Sheet As of December 31, 2020	
Preferred stock, $100 par, 7% (10,000 shares)	$ 1,000,000
Common stock, $0.001 par (10,000,000 shares)	10,000
Paid-in capital in excess of par—common	12,490,000
Total paid-in capital	13,500,000
Retained earnings	19,452,886
Total stockholders' equity	$32,952,886

Figure 12.1. Example of the equity section of a C corporation's balance sheet.

called an initial public offering (IPO). Once a corporation has sold its stock via an IPO, all subsequent sales of the stock are usually carried out by the owners of the individual shares (not by the corporation), typically on a major exchange, such as the New York Stock Exchange (NYSE) or the Nasdaq Stock Market (commonly referred to as NASDAQ). Corporations do sometimes buy back and retire—cancel, according to SEC regulations—their own shares of stock in order to increase the stock's market price (as a result of reducing the supply of the shares available), thus benefiting its remaining shareholders. Shares of stock repurchased by the issuing corporation but not yet retired are called **treasury stock**.

The par value of a share of common stock is an arbitrary dollar amount indicated on a stock certificate, usually because a par value is required by state law. Common stock par values are typically small in dollar amount, such as $0.001, $0.01, or $0.10. The par value is multiplied by the number of issued and outstanding common shares to arrive at the "Common stock" amount included in the equity section of a corporation's balance sheet. The amount paid by shareholders for common stock that exceeds the par value of that stock is classified as "Paid-in capital in excess of par" or "Additional paid-in capital" on a corporation's balance sheet. For stocks that have no par value, the "common stock" amount represents the total amount paid per share for the common stock multiplied by the number of issued and outstanding shares. "Retained earnings" represents the cumulative earnings of the company not distributed to stockholders via dividends (C corporations) or distributions (S corporations) but instead retained in the corporation for future investment.

The **book value per share of common stock** is a number calculated from the information on a company's balance sheet and is typically viewed as the minimum value of a share of that company's common stock. The formula for book value per share of common stock is as follows:

$$\text{Book value per share of common stock} = \frac{\text{Total common stockholders' equity}}{\text{Number of shares of common stock outstanding}}$$

where

Common stockholders' equity = Total stockholders' equity – Book value of any preferred stock

Example 12.3 presents a calculation of book value per share of common stock.

Example 12.3

Calculate the book value per share of common stock for West Corporation. Figure 12.1 shows the equity section of the company's balance sheet.

$$\text{Book value per share of common stock} = \frac{\text{Total common stockholders' equity}}{\text{Number of shares of common stock outstanding}}$$

where

Common stockholders' equity = Total stockholders' equity – Book value of any preferred stock

$$\text{Book value per share of common stock} = \frac{\$32,952,886 - \$1,000,000}{10,000,000 \text{ shares}}$$

$$= \$3.20$$

---

treasury stock

shares of stock repurchased by the issuing corporation but not yet retired

book value per share of common stock

total common stockholders' equity divided by the number of shares of common stock outstanding, typically viewed as the minimum value of a share of a company's common stock

The **market value per share of common stock** is the price at which the current owners of a particular common stock are selling their shares, often via a regulated stock exchange, such as the NYSE or the NASDAQ. Several factors affect the market value of a share of common stock:

- the supply of and demand for the shares
- the recent earnings and anticipated future earnings of the corporation
- the book value per share of the stock
- the number of shares outstanding
- general economic conditions
- industry-specific conditions

The market value and book value of a share of common stock aren't consistently related, except that, unless a company is experiencing a crisis, the market value of a share of common stock typically doesn't go below its book value.

Similar to how discounting the expected cash flows of a bond to present day is a method used to determine the value of a bond, discounting the expected cash flows associated with a stock to present day (the discounted cash flow method) is a method often used to determine the value of a share of common stock. The discounted cash flow method is a theoretically strong valuation tool for stock because it focuses on the fact that a stock's value ultimately depends upon the associated company's ability to generate cash flows. As alluded to in chapter 11, however, a weakness of the discounted cash flow method derives from the fact that there's room for argument about how the future cash flows of the business, the long-term growth rate of the cash flows after the forecast period, and the discount rate used in the discounted cash flow calculation are determined. This said, a stock is generally considered a good investment if its value determined using the discounted cash flow method is higher than its current market value.

Due to time constraints and other factors, the typical investor doesn't usually perform sophisticated discounted cash flow or similar technical analysis in order to determine the value of a share of stock. Instead, most investors rely on paid professionals, purchased research, or simpler valuation methods. However, an instance where one would use the discounted cash flow method to determine the value of a share of stock would be in the event of an expected upcoming sale or transfer of the stock of a privately held company. The reason for this is because, unlike the stock of a publicly held company, no recent stock sale activity likely exists to suggest a market value for the privately held company's stock. Refer to chapter 11 for an illustration of how to use the discounted cash flow method to determine the value of a share of stock of a privately held company.

A corporation issues preferred stock—a class of ownership of a C corporation that has a higher claim on the assets and earnings of the corporation than the corporation's common stock—to raise financial capital. Preferred stock is a hybrid vehicle that includes the features of both common stock and bonds. Although they have a claim superior to the common shareholders (but subordinate to the firm's creditors) on the assets and income of a company, preferred shareholders are considered quasi-owners of a corporation because they usually have no voting rights but instead are guaranteed a specific return on their investment if the corporation pays a dividend.

There are different types of preferred stock. The most common are cumulative, convertible, and callable. When a corporation decides to pay a dividend, a stockholder holding **cumulative preferred stock** will receive both the current and any unpaid back dividends, called dividends in arrears, before any common shareholder receives any dividend.

Convertible preferred stock is preferred stock that may be exchanged for shares of common stock. This feature makes the preferred stock more attractive for two reasons. In the short run, dividend income is guaranteed. In the long run,

market value per share of common stock
the price at which the current owners of a particular common stock are selling their shares

cumulative preferred stock
preferred stock that will receive both the current and any unpaid back dividends, called dividends in arrears, before any common shareholder receives any dividend

convertible preferred stock
preferred stock that may be exchanged for shares of common stock

preferred stock can be converted into common stock in order to take advantage of any significant market price appreciation that may have occurred or is expected to occur.

Callable preferred stock is preferred stock that can be called back at a pre-specified price and then retired by a company. This type of preferred stock is usually not attractive to investors, so the company must usually include a **call premium**—an amount of money a company will pay above the current market price for a share of its preferred stock if it calls back the stock—as one of the terms associated with callable preferred stock. Companies generally call back callable preferred stock when interest rates are low, usually because they can pay less interest to a lender than they're paying in dividends to the preferred shareholder. Note that the features of cumulative, convertible, and callable can be mixed and matched and enhanced as desired by the issuing corporation.

As we learned in chapter 3, a dividend is a payment, usually in the form of cash, made by a C corporation to one or more of its shareholders, as authorized by the C corporation's board of directors. A corporation may or may not pay a dividend associated with its common stock. A company's board of directors determines if and when a dividend will be paid. Dividends are typically paid on a per-share basis. A dividend may be designated by a C corporation to be made to shareholders of more than one class of stock. Preferred stock dividends are generally paid first. Any remaining dividend authorized to be distributed is then paid to the common shareholders.

One would look at the statement of cash flows (or, for a very young company, the reconciliation of cash) to determine the total amount of dividends paid during any particular year. One would look at the balance sheet to determine the amount of any dividend declared but not yet paid to shareholders (a dividend payable). Note that dividends paid per share that involve fractional cents are not uncommon. Example 12.4 shows the dividend calculations for one company's common stock.

Example 12.4

West Corporation, which has 10 million shares of common stock outstanding and 10,000 shares of $100, 7 percent preferred stock outstanding, declares a $1 million dividend. Assuming there are no dividends in arrears related to the preferred stock, what is the amount of the dividend that will be paid related to each share of common stock?

$$\text{Total dividend} = \text{Total preferred dividend} + \text{Total common stock dividend}$$

$$\text{Total common stock dividend} = \text{Total dividend} - \text{Total preferred dividend}$$

$$= \$1,000,000 - [(0.07)(\$100)(10,000 \text{ preferred shares})]$$

$$= \$1,000,000 - \$70,000$$

$$= \$930,000$$

$$\text{Common stock dividend per share} = \frac{\text{Total common stock dividend}}{\text{Total number of shares of common stock outstanding}}$$

$$= \frac{\$930,000}{10,000,000 \text{ shares}} = \$0.093 \text{ per share of common stock}$$

Stock investment strategies include both long-term and short-term strategies. Long-term strategies include position trading and dollar cost averaging. **Position trading**, also known as buy and hold, involves buying stocks with the intent to hold them for a long period time. This investment strategy is based on the premise that, in the long run, the overall stock market generates a significant positive return (see figure 12.2), even when taking into consideration stock market downturns. The buy

---

callable preferred stock

preferred stock that can be called back at a pre-specified price and then retired by a company

call premium

an amount of money a company will pay above the current market price for a share of its preferred stock if the stock is called back by the company

position trading

an investment strategy that involves buying stocks with the intent to hold them for a long period of time; also known as buy and hold

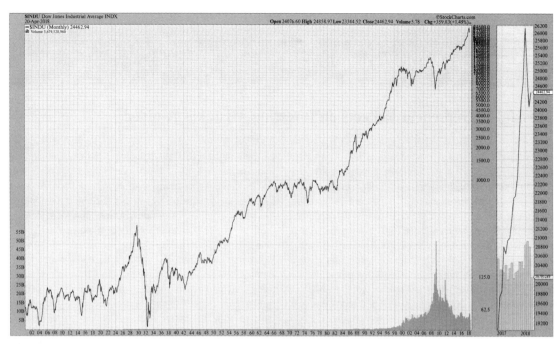

Figure 12.2. Dow Jones Industrial Average, 1900–present. Source: Chart courtesy of StockCharts.com.

and hold investment strategy is also based on the premise that attempting to "time the market"–attempting to buy a stock at or near its lowest price and sell it at or near its highest price–generally doesn't work, and that the investor who sells during a stock market downturn often irrevocably damages her portfolio's overall long-term return. Warren Buffett, arguably the most successful stock market investor of all time, suggests to the average investor that she buy quality stocks she knows and understands and hold them for the long run.

Entrepreneur in Action 12.1 (on page 358) illustrates the wisdom of buying quality stocks and holding them for the long run.

Dollar-cost averaging is the technique of accumulating a position in an investment by buying a fixed dollar amount of that investment on a regular basis, regardless of its price. As a result, more shares are purchased when market prices are low, and fewer shares are bought when market prices are high. Dollar-cost averaging is a prudent investment technique when an investor intends to buy and hold an investment long term because it lessens the risk of investing a large amount of money in a single security at the wrong time. Example 12.5 demonstrates an instance dollar-cost averaging.

> **dollar cost averaging**
> the technique of accumulating a position in an investment by buying a fixed dollar amount of that investment on a regular basis, regardless of its price

Example 12.5

You decide to purchase $450 of West Corporation's common stock each month for three months. In January, West's common stock is trading at $50, so you buy nine shares ($450 ÷ $50 per share = 9 shares). In February, the stock is trading at $75, so you buy six shares ($450 ÷ $75 per share = 6 shares). Finally, in March, the stock is trading at $45, so you buy 10 shares ($450 ÷ $45 per share = 10 shares).

At the end of the three months, in total, you've purchased 25 shares of West's common stock for $1,350. The average price is $54 per share, which is higher than the lowest price of $45 per share, but significantly lower than the highest price of $75 per share.

Entrepreneur *in Action* 12.1

A Successful Entrepreneur Reflects on Investing Mistakes Avoided

Omar Khan, a successful entrepreneur who had sold one of his companies in 2006 for $5M, a significant percentage of which he had soon after invested in the stock market, would never forget March 9, 2009. That day the Dow Jones Industrial Average closed at 6,547.05, having lost approximately 54 percent of its value since its October 9, 2007 record high close of 14,164.53.[10] That same day the S&P 500 Index closed at 676.53, having lost almost 57 percent of its value since its October 9, 2007 record high close of 1,565.15.[11] Most investors were in full panic mode and many were dumping their stocks, sometimes for pennies on the dollar. No one knew when—or at what level—the stock market would stabilize.

It was now March 28, 2013, and the S&P 500 Index had just closed at 1,569.19, surpassing its previous record high close on October 9, 2007.[12] Earlier in the month the Dow Jones Industrial Average had also closed above its October 9, 2007 record high close.[13] Omar felt it had been a long four years waiting for the stock market to recover. Omar knew some investors who, like him, congratulated themselves on keeping their wits about them and successfully weathering the steep stock market decline. He also knew others who were less enthusiastic about how they had handled the stock market crisis.

One investor Omar noted had weathered the storm well was Warren Buffett, arguably the most successful stock investor of all time. During the crisis, while many investors were selling their stocks—and other investors, like Omar, were struggling to find the confidence to hold onto their stocks—Warren Buffett was investing in and making deals with the likes of Goldman Sachs, Mars, Bank of America, and Dow Chemical.[14] For example, Omar had read that Mr. Buffett had pumped $5B into Goldman Sachs after the September 2008 collapse of Lehman Brothers and that this investment had ultimately profited Mr. Buffett to the tune of over

$3B.[15] Mr. Buffett had kept his cool and hadn't allowed himself to be rattled by the volatility of the stock market. He hadn't engaged in emotional selling.

As Omar knew from his reading, emotional investing often involves an investor buying stocks at or near the top of the market when a feeling of euphoria dupes the investor into believing that the stock market will keep going up "forever." That the investor must invest more money or he will "miss the boat." As Omar also knew from his reading, emotional investing's evil twin, emotional selling, leads many investors to sell at or near the bottom of the market in order to salvage at least some of their money from a stock market that seems like it will never stop going down. Unfortunately the losses resulting from emotional selling are permanent. Most of the stocks sold as a result of emotional selling in 2008 and 2009 did eventually rebound, but not to the benefit of the investors engaging in emotional selling, instead to the benefit of the stocks' new owners.

Omar had had to dig in deep to find the courage to hold on to his stocks—all of them stocks of quality companies (he had done his research)—when the stock market was crashing. There were many nights when he didn't sleep well, but while that was happening he had successfully kept in mind a quote from Warren Buffet: "[At Berkshire Hathaway, we] simply attempt to be fearful when other are greedy and to be greedy only when others are fearful."[16] On March 28, 2013, Omar was thinking that keeping in mind Warren Buffett's investing approach had served him well. Omar himself hadn't had the wherewithal to invest more money in the stock market when it was crashing, but he had had the courage to hold on to the quality stocks he already owned. Omar hadn't succumbed to emotional selling. And that—as they say—had made all the difference.

Stock investment strategies include multiple short-term strategies:

short-term trading
stock trading where entry and exit occurs within the range of a few days or a few weeks

- short-term trading
- margin trading
- selling short
- options trading

Short-term trading refers to stock trading where entry and exit occurs within the range of a few days or a few weeks. There are two general approaches to short-term trading: day trading and trend trading. **Day trading** involves buying and selling financial instruments within the same trading day. **Trend trading** involves buying a stock to hold short or medium term when its price is trending up and selling a stock "short" when its price is trending down. The expectation with trend trading is that a stock price will continue to move in the direction it's been moving.

day trading
a stock trading technique that involves buying and selling financial instruments within the same trading day

trend trading
a stock trading technique that involves buying a stock to hold short or medium term when its price is trending up and selling a stock "short" when its price is trending down

Margin trading, also called buying on margin, involves an investor borrowing money from the brokerage house where the investor has a brokerage account in order to buy stock. The percentage of a potential investment's total value that an investor must have on deposit with his broker before the broker will lend the investor money to purchase that investment is called a **margin requirement**. Margin requirements are typically 50 percent, except the margin requirement for certain ETFs can be up to 90 percent. Buying stock on margin has the advantage of allowing the investor to buy more stock than she could otherwise afford (bigger upside) and the disadvantage of allowing the investor to lose more money than she invests (bigger downside).

When an investor goes "long" on an investment, she has bought a stock believing its price will rise. Conversely, when an investor goes "short," she's anticipating a decrease in share price. **Selling short** (also called short selling) is a stock trading strategy that involves the sale and subsequent repurchase of stock that the seller has borrowed. Specifically, when you sell short, your broker will lend the stock to you from the brokerage's own inventory, another one of the firm's customers, or another brokerage firm. The shares are then sold, and the proceeds are credited to your account. The lender of the shares has the right to request that the shares be returned at any time; however, lender requests for the return of shares are not common. When a lender does request a return of shares, it's usually because the shares are trending up in price instead of down and there's a concern that the shares won't be returned at all.

Sooner or later, you must "close" the short, sometimes because the lender requests the return of the shares and there are no more shares available to borrow, but usually because of a margin call. A **margin call** is a demand by a brokerage house that an investor deposit additional cash or securities in order to cover potential losses. You close a short by buying back the same number of shares you borrowed and returning them to your broker (this is called "short covering"). If the price of the shares has dropped, you can buy back the stock at the lower price and make a profit on the transaction. If the price of the shares has risen, you have to buy back the stock at the higher price and lose money on the transaction. Unlike going long, where you can only lose the money you invest, when you go short, the amount you can lose is theoretically unlimited because the market price a stock can reach is theoretically unlimited.

Options (also called options contracts) are contracts that give the owner the right to buy or sell a security at a specified price for a specified period of time. A typical options contract in the United States relates to 100 shares of the underlying security. An option that gives the holder the right to buy a security is referred to as a **call option**. An option that gives the holder the right to require some other person or entity to buy a security from the holder is referred to as a **put option**. There are two basic approaches to the use of options: hedging and trading. The goals of hedging and trading are quite different. **Hedging** involves the use of options by an investor to limit her potential loss if the price of a security she buys heads in the direction opposite to that anticipated or desired. **Options trading** involves buying and selling options contracts with the hope of making a large profit from a small investment as a result of correctly anticipating the price movement of an option's underlying security. Example 12.6 illustrates using options to hedge an investment in a security.

Example 12.6

Suppose you want to buy 10,000 shares of West Corporation's common stock at the stock's current market price of $50 per share. This stock purchase will cost $500,000 (10,000 shares x $50 per share = $500,000). You expect the price of the stock to go up to $70, at which point, you plan to sell the stock and make a $200,000 profit (10,000 shares x $70 per share = $700,000; $700,000 – $500,000 = $200,000). However, you're a little worried that the stock price might go down instead of up.

To hedge your bet, you spend $7,500 to buy put options for 10,000 shares of West's common stock at $50 per share. As a result of buying the puts, because someone is now contractually obligated to purchase the 10,000 shares of West's common stock at $50 per share should you want to sell them, you just guaranteed that you can't lose money on this stock purchase (except for any commissions or fees you paid to purchase the $500,000 of stock and the $7,500 you paid for the put options).

---

margin trading
borrowing money from the brokerage house where the investor has a brokerage account in order to buy stock; also called buying on margin

margin requirement
the percentage of a potential investment's total value that an investor must have on deposit with his broker before the broker will lend the investor money to purchase that investment

selling short
a stock trading strategy that involves the sale and subsequent repurchase of stock that the seller has borrowed; also called short selling

margin call
a demand by a brokerage house that an investor deposit additional cash or securities in order to cover potential losses

options
contracts that give the owner the right to buy or sell a security at a specified price for a specified period of time; also called options contracts

call option
an option that gives the holder the right to buy a security at a specified price for a specified period of time

put option
an option that gives the holder the right to require some other person or entity to buy a security from the holder at a specified price for a specified period of time

hedging
the use of options by an investor to limit her potential loss if the price of a security she buys heads in the direction opposite to that anticipated or desired

options trading
buying and selling options contracts in the hope of making a large profit from a small investment as a result of correctly anticipating the price movement of an option's underlying security

Example 12.7 presents a scenario of using options to speculate a security.

Example 12.7

Suppose again that you think the price of West Corporation's common stock will go up from $50 to $70. But instead of spending $500,000 to buy 10,000 shares of the stock, you spend $10,000 to buy call options on 10,000 shares of the stock at its current market price of $50. That is, you spend $10,000, not $500,000.

When the market price of West's common stock increases from $50 to $51, the value of 10,000 shares of that stock has increased from $500,000 to $510,000, at which point, the gain in the stock equals the amount you paid for the call options. At this point, as a speculator, you're at breakeven because, theoretically at least, an investor would be willing to pay you $10,000 for the $10,000 of call options you own. When the market price of West's stock increases above $51, such as to $55, you're in a profit position that you can exploit in one of two ways:

1. You can sell the call options on the secondary market for more than your $10,000 investment.
2. If you have $500,000, you can exercise the call options, purchase the stock for $500,000, and then immediately sell the stock on the open market for $550,000, excluding commissions and fees.

A word of caution: Short-term trading, margin trading, selling short, and options trading are all generally considered speculative and high risk (i.e., riskier than buying and holding shares of stock long term) and are not advised for novice or unsophisticated investors.

The majority of large companies whose stock trades publicly choose to list their stocks on one of the major exchanges (i.e., NYSE or NASDAQ). However, many companies are either unable or unwilling to meet the financial and listing requirements of the major exchanges. Instead, these companies' securities often trade in the over-the-counter market. The **over-the-counter (OTC) market** is a market where investors trade directly with each other without the oversight of a formal securities exchange like the NYSE or NASDAQ. Investors typically participate in the OTC market by working with a broker involved in OTC trading. Orders for OTC securities are usually executed by such brokers through market makers. **Market makers** are companies or individuals who quote both a bid and an ask price for a security they hold in inventory. A **bid price** is the price that a prospective buyer is willing to pay for a security. An **ask price** is the price that a prospective seller is willing to accept for a security. The goal of a market maker is to make a profit on the difference between the bid and the ask price of a security.

Some brokers subscribe to the OTC Bulletin Board (OTCBB) and use it to look up prices or enter quotes for OTC securities. The OTCBB is an electronic quotation system operated by the Financial Industry Regulatory Authority (FINRA). Companies that wish to have their securities quoted on the OTCBB must file current financial reports either with the SEC or with the company's banking or insurance regulator, as applicable.[17]

The OTC Markets Group is a publicly held company that provides price and liquidity information for thousands of OTC securities through a variety of means, the most well-known of which is the pink sheets. The **pink sheets** list the bid and ask prices for the securities of companies that, unlike the companies included on the major exchanges and the OTCBB, do not have to meet any minimum disclosure requirements or file with the SEC. This creates the potential for fraudulent activity, which does indeed occur from time to time.

Many perfectly legitimate foreign companies, such as Nestle and Heineken, participate in OTC trading simply because they don't wish to file the reports required by

over-the-counter (OTC) market
a market where investors trade directly with each other without the oversight of a formal securities exchange like the NYSE or NASDAQ

market makers
companies or individuals who quote both a bid and an ask price for a security they hold in inventory

bid price
the price that a prospective buyer is willing to pay for a security

ask price
the price that a prospective seller is willing to accept for a security

pink sheets
a list of bid and ask prices for the securities of companies that, unlike the companies included on the major exchanges and the Over-the-Counter Bulletin Board, do not have to meet any minimum disclosure requirements or file with the SEC

the SEC in order to be included on a major exchange. Other companies trade in the OTC market after being delisted from a major exchange, either for a fairly innocuous reason (e.g., their stock price fell below a certain minimum prescribed level) or for a more alarming reason (e.g., failing to pay the listing fees owed to a major exchange).

A **penny stock** is a stock that trades at a relatively low price, often under $1, and usually in the OTC market via the pink sheets. The SEC's definition of penny stock includes all shares that trade below $5. Because they're often characterized by a small market capitalization, a limited following, and a general lack of disclosure, many penny stocks traded in the OTC market are considered highly speculative and high risk.

penny stock
a stock that trades at a relatively low price, often under $1, usually in the over-the-counter market via the pink sheets

Diversifying one's investment portfolio reduces portfolio risk. **Portfolio risk** is the risk that the combination of investment securities an investor owns will fail to meet the investor's desired financial objectives. Beyond choosing to diversify their portfolio by investing in a variety of individual stocks and bonds, investors may also diversify by investing in mutual funds and ETFs, both of which give investors the ability to diversify their investment in debt or equity securities via a single security purchase. Refer to the previous section of this chapter, "Bonds," for more information about mutual funds and ETFs.

portfolio risk
the risk that the combination of investment securities an investor owns will fail to meet the investor's desired financial objectives

Real Estate

Real estate investment is an investment in land or buildings. Real estate investments fall into three main categories that are treated differently for tax purposes:

1. owner-occupied residential
2. non-owner-occupied residential
3. commercial

Owner-occupied residential real estate is a house, condominium, housing cooperative, or apartment in which the owner lives. Owner-occupied residential real estate is limited by law to a person's primary residence and one additional vacation home. If taxpayers itemize their expenses, they can deduct on their tax return the interest paid on up to $750,000 of residential mortgage debt incurred on or after December 16, 2017 ($1 million of residential mortgage debt incurred before December 16, 2017).[18] If married and filing separately, the deduction is limited to the interest paid on $375,000 of residential mortgage debt incurred on or after December 16, 2017 ($500,000 of residential mortgage debt incurred before December 16, 2017).[19] Taxpayers can also deduct the property taxes paid related to owner-occupied properties.

owner-occupied residential real estate
a house, condominium, housing cooperative, or apartment in which the owner lives, limited by law to a person's primary residence and one additional vacation home

Non-owner-occupied residential real estate is property that the owner leases to a residential tenant for the purpose of generating income. This property may be in the form of houses, apartments, hotels, motels, or other types of property and becomes subject to depreciation because it's being used to generate income. The property owner may tax deduct the mortgage interest, depreciation, property taxes, repair and maintenance expense, and other business expenses typically incurred when owning and managing such property, including salaries.

non-owner-occupied residential real estate
property that the owner leases to a residential tenant for the purpose of generating income

Commercial real estate is land and buildings used by a property owner to generate rental income from businesses. Examples include commercial office buildings, shopping centers, factories, and warehouses.

commercial real estate
land and buildings used by a property owner to generate rental income from businesses

Most investments in real estate are made possible by the use of leverage. **Leverage** is the power the use of debt provides to an individual or business. Investing in real estate is an attractive option because it gives the investor the ability to use leverage to an extent not possible with many other investments. For example, if you want to buy stock, unless you're buying on margin, you have to pay the full value of the stock at the time of purchase. Even if you are buying on margin, the percentage

leverage
the power the use of debt provides to an individual or a business

of a stock's value that you can borrow is still much less than the percentage of a real estate property's value that you can borrow. A typical stock purchase on margin requires what amounts to a 50 percent down payment. Because a conventional real estate mortgage typically requires only a 20 percent down payment, sometimes less, an investor can control real estate property by paying only a relatively small portion of its value up front.

If you don't want to be a solo investor in real estate, or if you don't want the hassle of being a landlord, you might want to consider participating in a real estate investment group. A **real estate investment group** is typically founded by a lead investment company that builds or buys rental real estate units and then allows investors to buy the properties through the company, the investors thereby joining the investment group. The lead investment company usually manages all of the rental units in exchange for a percentage of the total monthly rents.

If you prefer to be an even more hands-off investor in real estate, a **real estate investment trust (REIT)**—an investment vehicle that pools investor funds to finance the investment in and operation of an array of income-producing real estate properties—might be the right alternative for you. Shares of private REITs are sold through brokers. Shares of publicly held REITs are traded on the major stock exchanges. REIT-specific mutual funds and ETFs also exist. REITs are attractive to investors because they usually pay healthy dividends owing to the fact that, in order to qualify as a REIT, a company must distribute at least 90 percent of its taxable income to its investors each year.

real estate investment group
an investment group typically founded by a lead investment company that builds or buys rental real estate units and then allows investors to buy the properties through the company, the investors thereby joining the investment group

real estate investment trust (REIT)
an investment vehicle that pools investor funds to finance the investment in and operation of an array of income-producing real estate properties

Commodities, Precious Metals, and Collectables

commodity
an article of commerce, such as a fuel, a metal, or an agricultural product, that can be traded, bought, or sold in bulk on a commodity exchange or other type of exchange

futures contract
an agreement to buy or sell a commodity at a specified future date at a specified price

A **commodity** is an article of commerce that can be traded, bought, or sold in bulk on a commodity exchange or other type of exchange. Fuels, metals, and agricultural products are examples of commodities. There are many ways to invest in commodities, including investing in agricultural, mining, and other commodity-related stocks, ETFs, and mutual funds. Investors can also invest in commodities via futures contracts. A **futures contract** is similar to a stock option in that a futures contract is an agreement to buy or sell an asset at a specified future date at a specified price. In the instance of a futures contract, however, the underlying asset is not a stock, it is a commodity. Each futures contract represents a specific amount of a given commodity. For example, the most widely traded commodity futures contract, crude oil, has a contract unit of 1,000 barrels.[20]

Commodity futures are generally highly leveraged. A commodity trader typically only has to post 5 to 15 percent of a contract's total value in order to control the contract. Therefore, as is the case when an investor buys stocks on margin, futures contracts allow the investor access to more of an asset than she could otherwise afford (bigger upside), with the disadvantage of allowing the investor to lose more money than she invests (bigger downside).

Commodities are a volatile investment class. It's not unusual for the price of a raw material to change 50 to 100 percent (or more) over a very short period of time. Making a short-term profit by speculating whether the price of an asset will go up or down is the main goal of many traders participating in the commodities markets. Considering the combination of price volatility, speculation, and leverage, commodities trading shapes up to be an extremely risky way to attempt to generate a profit.

The average investor, who typically doesn't have the time or inclination to participate in commodities trading, will sometimes elect to buy and hold certain commodities, especially precious metals (e.g., gold, silver, and platinum). Precious metals are in universal demand and hold their value when transported across international boundaries. Historically, however, precious metals have delivered a lower return than many other types of investments, especially stocks.[21, 22] This is because precious metals don't provide interest or dividend income, and their value depends on the whims of the market at the time of sale. An investment in precious metals is widely considered a hedge against inflation that should amount to no more than 5 percent of an individual's total asset holdings.

Collectables are items that become valuable over time because of their scarcity. Examples include baseball cards, coins, stamps, paintings, and antiques. The source of a collectable's value is usually that the demand for the item exceeds the supply of the item, typically because the item is no longer produced. Investing in collectables is considered highly speculative because the price the owner receives when she sells a collectable depends very much upon the whims of the market at the time of sale. Items that were once valuable collectables sometimes fall out of favor and lose their value as preferences change from one generation to the next.

collectables
items that become valuable over time because of their scarcity

Retirement Planning

If you're lucky, you'll live until you are old. Retirement planning involves creating a system of income for the time when you choose to retire or are forced to retire due to circumstances beyond your control. Retirement income in the United States comes from three main sources:

1. social security
2. employer-sponsored retirement plans
3. individual retirement accounts (IRAs)

Social security is a social safety net designed to keep people financially afloat during their old age. The U.S. social security program was signed into law in 1935 by Franklin D. Roosevelt in order to provide continuing income to retired U.S. workers age 65 and older.[23]

social security
a social safety net signed into law in 1935 by Franklin D. Roosevelt in order to provide continuing income to retired U.S. workers age 65 and older

Your eligibility for social security is based on the credits you earn during your working years. You acquire one credit for every $1,360 of income you earn (the amount of income required to earn a credit is adjusted each year; $1,360 is the amount for 2019), up to a limit of four credits per year.[24] People born after 1929 need 40 credits in order to receive social security retirement benefits. Your retirement benefit is based on the average of your highest 35 years of earnings (such earnings restated to today's dollars). When calculating the average of your highest 35 years of earnings, a year when you didn't work is considered a year of zero income, so not working a full 35 years prior to retirement is detrimental to the amount of the social security retirement benefit you'll receive.

An individual's spouse can also play a role in the amount of benefits a person receives. If you've worked long enough to qualify for full social security benefits, even if your spouse didn't work, didn't work enough to qualify for benefits, or has earned a benefit amounting to less than 50 percent of your benefit, your spouse will receive a benefit equal to 50 percent of your benefit.[25]

Employer-sponsored retirement plans may be defined benefit plans, defined contribution plans, or some combination or variation thereof. **Defined benefit plans**, often called pension plans, provide a pre-specified benefit to a company's retirees paid from a pool of funds contributed by the employer. The benefit to be received is usually determined based on an employee's earnings history, years of service, age, and other criteria. An example of a retirement benefit from a defined benefit retirement plan would be a $1,500 monthly pension payment made to a retired auto worker.

defined benefit plan
an employer-sponsored retirement plan that provides a pre-specified benefit to a company's retirees paid from a pool of funds contributed by the employer; also often called a pension plan

Defined contribution plans provide payments to a retiree from the retiree's individual account that has been accumulating funds and growing during the working life

defined contribution plan
an employer-sponsored retirement plan that provides payments to a retiree from the retiree's individual account that has been accumulating funds and growing during the working life of the retiree

of the retiree. In many instances, defined contribution plans include contributions from both the employee and the employer. Because of the cost savings involved, in recent decades, the popularity of defined contribution plans with employers has far outstripped that of defined benefit plans. In fact, only about 10 percent of U.S. workers are now covered by a defined benefit plan, compared to approximately 60 percent in the early 1980s.[26]

Except in the instance of a simplified employee pension (SEP) IRA or savings incentive match plan for employees (SIMPLE) IRA, both of which will be discussed later in this chapter, an **IRA** is a retirement account typically set up by an individual for her own benefit. Payments into an IRA are usually made by the individual the account will benefit.

Whether made by an employer or employee, the contributions made to a defined contribution plan account or IRA grow tax free. Because of this, it's in almost every individual's best interest to engage in active pension planning using a retirement vehicle that allows account earnings to accumulate tax free rather than saving money outside of a retirement vehicle in an alternative individual savings, brokerage, or other type of account.

Individuals may begin withdrawing funds from a defined contribution plan account or IRA at age 59-½ and, except in the instance of a **Roth IRA**—an individual retirement account that allows an individual to contribute after-tax dollars up to the same defined limit as for traditional IRAs but offers many advantages over traditional IRAs—must begin withdrawing funds by age 70-½. For defined contribution plan accounts and IRAs other than Roth IRAs, some or all of the amounts withdrawn after age 59-½ are taxed as ordinary income. If you withdraw money before you reach age 59-½, in most cases, you'll have to pay a 10 percent tax penalty for early withdrawal in addition to normal income tax on the withdrawal. Except in the instance of a Roth IRA, beginning the year you turn 70-½, you must start taking an annual required minimum distribution (RMD) from a defined contribution plan account or IRA. Generally, an RMD is calculated by dividing the prior year ending balance of a retirement account by the applicable life expectancy factor included in IRS Publication 590-B (available at irs.gov).[27] If you don't take enough withdrawals from your defined contribution plan account or IRA starting the year you turn 70-½, you'll have to pay a 50 percent tax penalty on the amount you should have withdrawn.

The most common defined contribution plans are 401(k) and 403(b) plans established by employers to accept employee contributions. A **401(k)** is typically offered by a for-profit company. Employees of nonprofits are often offered a **403(b)**. Employee contributions to both are often based on salary reduction. In other words, an employee contributes a certain percentage of her pretax salary to her retirement account via payroll deduction. Employers often match a portion of an employee's contributions on some predetermined basis. Note that wise financial planning suggests that such employer matching should be taken advantage of by an employee to the fullest extent possible if it's offered.

The rules can be complicated, but if you leave your job, you can usually roll a 401(k) or 403(b) account over into your new employer's 401(k) or 403(b) plan or, alternatively, into your IRA. There are limits regarding how much employees can contribute to a 401(k) or 403(b) account during any one year ($19,000 for 2019, more if age 50 or older).[28] Research "Retirement Topics—Contributions" at irs.gov to determine the current year contribution amount limitation related to any 401(k) or 403(b) account.

The owner of a business with no employees other than the business's owner and the owner's spouse can set up an individual 401(k), often called a **solo 401(k)**, and make contributions as both the employee and employer, up to a total of $56,000 for 2019 (more if age 50 or older).[29] Solo 401(k) plans have the same rules and requirements as any other type of 401(k).

individual retirement account (IRA)
a retirement account typically set up by an individual for her own benefit

Roth IRA
an individual retirement account that allows an individual to contribute after-tax dollars up to the same defined limit as for traditional IRAs but offers many advantages over traditional IRAs

401(k)
a type of defined contribution retirement plan typically offered by a for-profit company

403(b)
a type of defined contribution retirement plan often offered by a nonprofit entity

solo 401(k)
an individual 401(k) that can be set up by the owner of a business with no employees other than the business's owner and the owner's spouse

A **profit-sharing plan** is an employee benefit plan to which employees typically make no contribution. Rather, the plan is funded by a portion of a business's profit at the discretion of the employer. Annual contributions to these plans tend to vary as profits vary, and employers can choose to make no contribution. Profit-sharing plans are often incorporated into other types of employee benefit plans, such as 401(k) plans.

Returning to the topic of IRAs, there are five common types of IRAs:

1. (traditional) deductible
2. (traditional) nondeductible
3. Roth
4. SEP
5. SIMPLE

Deductible IRAs are those to which you can contribute pretax dollars up to an amount specified by current law ($6,000 for 2019, more if age 50 or older).[30] With a deductible IRA, when you withdraw the funds, you pay income tax on the dollars contributed and the earnings on the dollars contributed.

Nondeductible IRAs allow you to contribute the same amounts as are legally contributable to deductible IRAs, but the contribution is made with after-tax dollars. With a nondeductible IRA, when you withdraw the funds, you don't pay income tax on the dollars contributed, but you do pay income tax on all of the earnings on the dollars contributed.

Usually, a deductible IRA is a better deal (it depends upon your current and expected future tax rates and your ability to fund the IRA). Whether you qualify for a deductible IRA depends upon your income, your tax filing status, and whether you have access to an employee-sponsored retirement plan at work.[31] Check IRS Publication 590-A (available at irs.gov) to determine the tax deductibility of a contribution to your IRA account. Research "Retirement Topics—Contributions" at irs.gov to determine the current year contribution amount limitation related to any IRA account.

As mentioned earlier in this chapter, Roth IRAs allow you to contribute after-tax dollars up to the same defined limit as for traditional IRAs ($6,000 for 2019, more if age 50 or older) but offer many advantages over traditional IRAs:[32]

- Your contributions, but not the earnings on those contributions, can be withdrawn tax free at any time.
- There's no annual required minimum distribution beginning at age 70-½, and you can continue to contribute to a Roth IRA after age 70-½.
- If the funds are held in the Roth IRA for at least five years, after age 59-½, no income taxes are due on the earnings on the amounts contributed when those earnings are withdrawn.
- If the funds are held in the Roth IRA for at least five years, you can withdraw up to $10,000 before age 59-½ in order to purchase your first home. Note that you will have to pay ordinary income tax on any earnings withdrawn, but not the 10 percent tax penalty for early withdrawal.
- If the funds are held in the Roth IRA for at least five years, you may make withdrawals before age 59-½ for qualified education expenses, including tuition, fees, books, and room and board.[33] As is the case when you withdraw funds before age 59-½ for a first home purchase, you will have to pay ordinary income tax on any earnings withdrawn for qualified education expenses, but not the 10 percent tax penalty for early withdrawal.

You can roll a current non-Roth IRA into a Roth IRA provided you first pay any tax due related to the current IRA. In order to qualify to contribute to a Roth IRA in a particular year, you must make less than the IRS-established income limit for

profit-sharing plan
an employee benefit plan to which employees typically make no contribution; rather, the plan is funded by a portion of a business's profit at the discretion of the employer

deductible IRA
an individual retirement account to which an individual can contribute pretax dollars up to an amount specified by current law

nondeductible IRA
an individual retirement account that allows an individual to contribute the same amount as is legally contributable to a deductible IRA, but the contribution is made with after-tax dollars

simplified employee pension (SEP) IRA

a variation of an IRA designed for employers who wish to make contributions into an IRA for themselves and, if they have employees, into the individual IRAs they set up for the benefit of those employees

savings incentive match plan for employees (SIMPLE) IRA

a salary reduction plan to which the employer must contribute every year, established by an employer that does not offer any other qualified retirement plan and has fewer than 100 employees

that year (for 2019, the income limit was $137,000 if single and $203,000 if married filing jointly).[34]

Simplified employee pension (SEP) IRAs are a variation of an IRA designed for employers who wish to make contributions into an IRA for themselves and, if they have employees, into the individual IRAs they set up for the benefit of those employees. All contributions to a SEP IRA are funded by the employer, which has the flexibility to determine the annual contribution amount and the frequency of deposits, except the employer must contribute the same percentage of compensation to all participants when making a contribution.[35] In addition, the employer must include all employees who meet certain requirements. The employer can contribute up to 25 percent of each employee's income up to a defined annual limit ($56,000 for 2019).[36] SEP IRAs are easier to set up than solo 401(k) plans, so they're popular with the self-employed.

A **savings incentive match plan for employees (SIMPLE) IRA** is a salary reduction plan established by an employer that doesn't offer any other qualified retirement plan and has fewer than 100 employees. According to IRS requirements, the employer must contribute every year, and the plan must be offered to all employees who meet certain criteria.[37] Employees may elect to contribute up to a defined annual limit ($13,000 for 2019, more if age 50 or older).[38] SIMPLE plans are attractive to employers because they involve little administrative paperwork.

Other types of employer and combination plans exist beyond those discussed in this chapter, but they are more complicated and not as commonly used. Check IRS Publication 3998 (available at irs.gov) to learn more about the common retirement plan alternatives available to your business.

When embarking on retirement planning, you should establish the minimum lump sum or minimum annual distribution you desire when you retire, and you should consider the time value of money when determining either of these amounts. Most important, don't wait too long after you enter your working years to start a retirement account. If at all possible, start the account when you're young. The earlier dollars are contributed to a proper retirement vehicle and permitted to grow tax free, the more financially prepared you'll be for your retirement years. Note that, in Figure 12.3 (duplicated from chapter 9), $24,000 invested over a period of four years ($4,200 + $5,400 + $6,600 + $7,800 = $24,000)—an average of $500 per month

Carol Nightingale's SEP IRA Calculation of Expected Future Value							
Retirement age:	70						
Current age:	25						
Expected growth rate:	7%						
Compounding rate:	Monthly						
Year of Contribution	Years to Retirement at the Beginning of the Year	Monthly Contribution	FVOA Factor	End of Year Value	FVF	Future Value	Total Contributions
2020	45	$ 350.00	12.39258	$ 4,337.40	21.56419	$ 93,532.58	$ 4,200.00
2021	44	450.00	12.39258	5,576.66	20.11041	112,148.94	5,400.00
2022	43	550.00	12.39258	6,815.92	18.75465	127,830.18	6,600.00
2023	42	650.00	12.39258	8,055.18	17.49028	140,887.30	7,800.00
2024–2064	41	750.00	2826.92122			2,120,190.92	369,000.00
			Total retirement account value			$ 2,594,589.92	$ 393,000.00

Figure 12.3. Calculation of the expected future value of a SEP IRA.

invested from ages 25 to 28 ($24,000 ÷ 48 months = $500)—becomes worth $473,399 by age 70 ($93,532.58 + $112,148.94 + $127,830.18 + $140,887.30 = $473,399.00). Further, a total of $393,000 invested over a period of 45 years becomes worth almost $2,594,590 by age 70.

College Planning

In the United States, the most commonly used college savings vehicles are Section 529 plans and Coverdell Education Savings Accounts (ESAs). A **Section 529 plan** is a tax-advantaged college savings program operated by a state or state agency that allows for prepayment of qualified education expenses or contributions into an account whose earnings are tax free when used to pay qualified education expenses.

In a prepaid tuition plan, an account owner contributes cash for the beneficiary that purchases tuition credits for the beneficiary at current tuition rates. In a college savings plan, an account owner contributes cash that is invested according to the account owner's particular investment objectives until the funds are needed to pay the beneficiary's qualified education expenses. Contributions to a Section 529 plan aren't federally tax deductible, but they may be state tax deductible.

Section 529 plans feature tax-free distributions for qualified education expenses, such as tuition, fees, books, supplies, equipment, and room and board for both undergraduate and graduate education. Nonqualified distributions are subject to regular income tax plus an additional 10 percent tax penalty. There is no income phaseout for participation in a Section 529 plan, and transfers between beneficiaries belonging to the same family are permitted.

A **Coverdell Education Savings Account (Coverdell ESA)** is a tax-advantaged college savings vehicle set up by an account owner and usually administered by a private financial institution with the intention to pay some or all of the qualified education expenses of a designated beneficiary. Like Section 529 plans, the contributions to Coverdell ESAs are not federally tax deductible, but the earnings are tax free as long as they are used to pay qualified education expenses. Nonqualified distributions are subject to regular income tax plus an additional 10 percent tax penalty.

A Coverdell ESA has a number of disadvantages compared to a Section 529 plan:

- There's a $2,000 contribution limit per year per beneficiary, regardless of the number of accounts set up for a beneficiary.
- Continued contributions to a Coverdell ESA are generally not permitted once a beneficiary reaches age 18.
- Account assets must generally be fully distributed by the time the beneficiary reaches age 30.
- Income phaseouts exist for participation. The 2019 income phaseout for the ability to contribute to a Coverdell ESA starts for taxpayers with modified adjusted gross income above $95,000 for single filers and $190,000 for those married filing jointly.[39] Taxpayers with a 2019 modified adjusted gross income above $110,000 and $220,000 (single filers and those married filing jointly, respectively) won't be able to contribute to a Coverdell ESA at all.[40]

Less commonly used college savings vehicles—compared to Section 529 plans and Coverdell ESAs—include custodial accounts created under the Uniform Gifts to Minors Act (UGMA) and Uniform Trusts for Minors Act (UTMA), eligible Series EE and I savings bonds, and Roth IRAs. At one time, UGMA and UTMA custodial accounts were popular vehicles for college savings, but they have declined in popularity since the emergence of Section 529 plans. UGMA and UTMA custodial accounts are created at a bank, brokerage firm, or mutual fund company and managed by an

Section 529 plan
a tax-advantaged college savings program operated by a state or state agency

Coverdell Education Savings Account (Coverdell ESA)
a tax-advantaged college savings vehicle set up by an account owner and usually administered by a private financial institution with the intention to pay some or all of the qualified education expenses of a designated beneficiary

adult for someone who has not yet reached the age of majority (usually age 18 or 21, depending on the state).

Property transferred to a UGMA or UTMA account becomes the property of the child immediately and irrevocably. The child gains full control of the account at the age of majority, which means the funds can be used for whatever the child chooses, even if that choice isn't college. Additionally, the assets held in a UGMA or UTMA account can hurt a student's chances of qualifying for financial aid because a greater portion of a child's assets are expected to be allocated to pay for the child's education costs than a parent's assets.

The **savings bond education tax exclusion** permits qualified taxpayers to exclude from their gross income all or part of the interest received upon the redemption of eligible Series EE and I bonds issued after 1989 if, among other requirements, qualified higher education expenses are incurred during the same tax year in which the bonds are redeemed.[41] Other requirements to qualify for the exclusion follow:

- The taxpayer must be at least 24 years old on the first day of the month in which an applicable bond was purchased.
- The bonds must be registered in a parent's name, not the child's name, when using the bonds to pay for the child's education. The bonds must be registered in the applicable adult student's own name when using the bonds to pay for the adult student's own education.
- Married filers must file jointly in order to qualify for the exclusion.
- The applicable college, university, or vocational school must be a qualifying school, defined as meeting the standards for federal assistance.
- The bondholder's modified adjusted gross income cannot exceed a limit specified annually by the IRS. The limit for 2018 was $94,550 if a single taxpayer or $149,300 if a married taxpayer filing jointly.[42]

Parents often overlook a Roth IRA as a possible way to fund a child's college education. As noted earlier, assuming the funds are held in the account for at least five years, a Roth IRA allows early withdrawals for qualified education expenses, including tuition, fees, books, and room and board. The part of any withdrawal that represents a contribution to the Roth IRA is tax free, because the contributions to a Roth IRA can be withdrawn tax free at any time. The part of any withdrawal that represents earnings on the contributions to the Roth IRA will be taxed as ordinary income, but the 10 percent tax penalty that normally applies to early withdrawals will not apply.

The advantage of using a Roth IRA to save for college is that, should the child decide not to attend college, there need be no tax penalty. Any money saved in a 529 plan that isn't used for education expenses will ultimately become fully taxable as ordinary income and subject to a 10 percent tax penalty. Any money saved in a Roth IRA that isn't used for education expenses simply becomes money being saved for retirement or some other permitted purpose. But using a Roth IRA to save for college also has disadvantages:

- Contributions are limited to $6,000 per year per individual (for 2019, more if age 50 or older).[43]
- To qualify to contribute to a Roth IRA in a particular year, an individual must make less than the IRS-established income limit for that year (for 2019, $137,000 if single and $203,000 if married filing jointly).[44]

Because of the possibility of federal student financial aid, some parents believe it makes sense not to save for their child's college expenses. They think assets that don't exist can't be identified by the government to pay for college expenses. This strategy can backfire because even if parents haven't saved anything to pay for their child's college expenses, as part of the federal student financial aid determination

savings bond education tax exclusion

a tax exclusion that permits qualified taxpayers to exclude from their gross income all or part of the interest received upon the redemption of eligible Series EE and I bonds issued after 1989 if, among other requirements, qualified higher education expenses are incurred during the same tax year in which the bonds are redeemed process, the federal government still expects parents to contribute to their child's education based on the information included on their child's Free Application for Federal Student Aid (FAFSA) form. Another common error parents make is saving for their child's future before addressing their own long-term financial future. For this reason, college planning and retirement planning are often best done simultaneously.

Estate Planning

Despite the fact that you might want to, you will not live forever. Estate planning is the process of arranging for the tax-efficient, income-maximizing, and asset-protecting management and disposal of a person's assets and liabilities, both during life and after death. In other words, estate planning involves planning for the use, conservation, and transfer of your wealth as efficiently as possible both before and after your death. Note that if you don't have a plan for your estate, your state has one for you—one you may not like very much.

A **will** is a written document that provides direction regarding your final wishes and how you want your assets distributed after your death. **Probate** is a legal court process that addresses the will and the probate estate. The **probate estate** is property owned by a decedent that requires the appointment of a fiduciary, such fiduciary legally charged with managing and appropriately distributing the applicable property. The probate estate excludes the assets included in a **payable-on-death (POD) account**, which is an account for which the decedent has indicated to the financial institution holding the account prior to her death who should inherit the assets in the account. The probate estate also excludes assets placed in **trust**, which is a fiduciary relationship evidenced by a written trust agreement in which one party, the trustor, gives another party, the trustee, the right to hold assets for the benefit of a third party, the beneficiary. The probate process adds to the cost of estate distribution, increases the time to settle the estate, and exposes private family financial information to the public because probate is usually a matter of public record. Probate costs are typically a percentage of the probate estate, so good estate planning leaves as few assets as possible in the probate estate.

A person can remove assets from the probate estate via the following means:

- Joint ownership with right of survivorship with a spouse provides temporary removal from the probate estate. This type of removal from probate is only temporary because the possibility of probating the will come up again once the surviving spouse dies. Note that it is generally not wise for a child to be a part of joint ownership with right of survivorship with the child's parent because of the many complications this can create (e.g., it inextricably links the finances of a child with the finances of a parent until one of them dies, and it can create the need to pay significant gift taxes).

- Gifts reduce the value of the probate estate by giving it away. You can currently gift $15,000 per year, gift tax free, to each of your children, grandchildren, sons-in-law, and daughters-in-law. The even better news is that if you make a lump sum contribution of between $15,000 and $75,000 to a Section 529 account, you can elect to treat the contribution as being made over a five-year period for gift tax purposes, hence the gift is tax free.

- Trusts offer permanent removal from the probate estate. As mentioned previously, assets held in a trust are not part of the probate estate. In lieu of or in conjunction with a will, many individuals set up a **revocable living trust**, which is a trust whose provisions can be altered by the trustor during her lifetime and to whom the income of the trust is distributed during her lifetime. A properly set up revocable living trust can keep your assets out of probate after your death, maintain your family's privacy, prevent court control

will
a written document that provides direction regarding one's final wishes and how one wants one's assets distributed after death

probate
a legal court process that addresses the will and the probate estate

probate estate
property owned by a decedent that requires the appointment of a fiduciary, such fiduciary legally charged with managing and appropriately distributing the applicable property

payable-on-death (POD) account
an account for which the decedent has indicated to the financial institution holding the account prior to her death who should inherit the assets in the account

trust
a fiduciary relationship evidenced by a written trust agreement in which one party, the trustor, gives another party, the trustee, the right to hold assets for the benefit of a third party, the beneficiary

revocable living trust
a trust whose provisions can be altered by the trustor during her lifetime and to whom the income of the trust is distributed during her lifetime

of your assets at your incapacity, and bring your assets together under one easily managed umbrella. You can change your revocable living trust at any time until you die. After you die, your assets can stay in your trust, managed by the trustees you've selected, until your beneficiaries reach the age at which you wish them to inherit. Your trust can also be set up to provide long-term income and care for a loved one with special needs.

■ Payable-on-death (POD) accounts provide for removal of assets from the decedent's probate estate at the time of death. As mentioned previously, assets held in a POD account aren't part of the probate estate. POD accounts are a simple and efficient way to transfer assets on death while avoiding probate. The caution is that they should be utilized as part of an overall estate plan that carefully considers the desired distribution of all of an individual's assets upon death in order to not inadvertently favor one beneficiary over another. It's worth noting that the beneficiary of a POD account has no obligation to share the assets of that account with anyone else. For example, a daughter beneficiary of her father's POD account is under no obligation to share the assets of that account with any siblings. Note that, in order to overcome this limitation, multiple individuals can usually be indicated as equal beneficiaries on one POD account.

The Tax Cuts and Jobs Act of 2017 set the estate tax asset exclusion level at $11.18 million per taxpayer. The exclusion amount increased to $11.4 million in 2019. This means that your estate will pay federal estate tax only on the amount of assets that exceed $11.4 million. Federal estate tax rates range from 18 to 40 percent.[45]

State estate tax rates vary from 0 percent in many states to as high as 20 percent in Washington, D.C.[46, 47] State inheritance tax rates vary from 0 percent in many states to as high as 18 percent in Nebraska.[48, 49] Some states (e.g., Maryland and New Jersey) have both types of tax.[50] For those states that do have estate or inheritance taxes, asset exclusion amounts vary widely.[51]

An individual with an estate larger than $11.4 million or who lives in a state with estate or inheritance tax should contact an estate planning professional. In many instances, steps can be taken to reduce the overall amount of estate tax paid upon an individual's passing, thereby maximizing the amount of assets that can be passed on to that individual's chosen beneficiaries.

Summary

It is important to note that, as long as an entrepreneur owns a business, the personal finances of the entrepreneur and the finances of the business she has created continue to be linked. It is also important to note that whether an entrepreneur decides to dissolve her business, sell all or part of it, or keep the business long term, the personal wealth of the entrepreneur is often quite significantly enhanced by her business.

As an entrepreneur's personal wealth increases, the entrepreneur needs to increasingly focus on the following three tasks:

1. the protection of assets
2. the maintenance of adequate financial liquidity
3. the investment of excess cash in a manner that maximizes the probability of continued financial security

Protecting assets, maintaining adequate financial liquidity, and investing excess cash for continued financial security are all topics that were addressed in this chapter.

The protection of assets involves risk management. Approaches to risk management include risk avoidance, risk reduction, risk assumption, and risk transfer. The chapter discussed in great detail the topic of risk transfer achieved as a result of paying for various types of insurance policies.

Investment vehicles are the specific financial instruments used to maintain financial liquidity and furnish continued financial security as a result of generating income and providing for capital growth. Many different investment vehicles exist within each of the five main asset classes:

1. cash and cash equivalents
2. bonds and similar debt instruments, including fixed-income exchange traded funds and mutual funds
3. equities, including individual shares of stock and many exchange traded funds and mutual funds
4. real estate
5. commodities, precious metals, and collectables

Some investment vehicles are quite complex, represent exotic combinations of other investment vehicles, and are designed for only the most sophisticated investors. Chapter 12 familiarized the reader with the most common U.S. investment vehicles only.

Retirement planning involves creating a system of income for the time when an individual chooses to retire or is forced to retire due to circumstances beyond the individual's control. Retirement income in the United States comes from three main sources:

1. social security
2. employer-sponsored retirement plans
3. IRAs

When embarking on retirement planning, one should establish the minimum lump sum or minimum annual distribution desired upon retirement, and one should consider the time value of money when determining either of these amounts. Most important, one shouldn't wait too long after entering one's working years to start a retirement account. One should start a retirement account when one is young.

A common error parents make is saving for their child's future before addressing their own long-term financial future. For this reason, college planning and retirement planning are often best done simultaneously. The various tax-advantaged vehicles for saving for college were discussed in detail in this chapter.

Last, estate planning involves planning for the use, conservation, and transfer of one's wealth as efficiently as possible both before and after one's death. A will is a written document that provides direction regarding an individual's final wishes and how one wants one's assets distributed after death. Probate is a legal court process that addresses the will and the probate estate. Probate costs are typically a percentage of the probate estate, so good estate planning leaves as few assets as possible in the probate estate.

A person can remove assets from the probate estate via the following means:

- Joint ownership with right of survivorship with a spouse provides temporary removal from the probate estate.
- Gifts reduce the value of the probate estate by giving it away.
- Trusts offer permanent removal from the probate estate.
- POD accounts provide for removal from the probate estate at the time of death.

Key Terms

401(k)
403(b)
agency bonds
ask price
banker's acceptance
bid price
book value per share of
  common stock
business auto insurance
business interruption
  insurance
business liability
  insurance
call option
call premium
callable preferred stock
cash equivalents
collectables
commercial property
  insurance
commercial real estate
commodity
convertible preferred
  stock
coupon rate of a bond
Coverdell Education
  Savings Account
  (Coverdell ESA)
credit rating
cumulative preferred
  stock
day trading
deductible IRA
defined benefit plan
defined contribution plan
disability insurance
dollar cost averaging
financial liquidity

fixed income
foreign bonds
futures contract
hedging
high-yield bonds
index funds
individual retirement
  account (IRA)
insurance
investment-grade corpo-
  rate bonds
leverage
liability insurance
long-term care insurance
margin call
margin requirement
margin trading
market makers
market value per share of
  common stock
money market fund
mortgage-backed bonds
municipal bonds
mutual funds
nondeductible IRA
non-owner-occupied resi-
  dential real estate
options
options trading
over-the-counter (OTC)
  market
owner-occupied residen-
  tial real estate
par value of a bond
payable-on-death (POD)
  account
penny stock
pink sheets

portfolio risk
position trading
probate
probate estate
product liability
  insurance
professional liability
  insurance
profit-sharing plan
put option
real estate investment
  group
real estate investment
  trust (REIT)
revocable living trust
Roth IRA
sales load
savings bond education
  tax exclusion
savings incentive match
  plan for employees
  (SIMPLE) IRA
Section 529 plan
selling short
short-term trading
simplified employee
  pension (SEP) IRA
social security
solo 401(k)
term life insurance
treasury stock
trend trading
trust
umbrella insurance
whole life insurance
will
yield

Review and Discussion Questions

1. What are the five main asset classes in which investors most commonly invest?

2. Some investors charge that the "Big Three" credit rating agencies can no longer be relied upon to be impartial when issuing ratings. What are the Big Three credit rating agencies, and why do some investors make this charge?

3. What are mutual funds and ETFs, and what are the benefits associated with investing in them?

4. List and briefly describe the different stock investment strategies.

5. What are the advantages of investing in a Roth IRA compared to a traditional IRA?

6. What are the advantages associated with having a revocable living trust?

Exercises

1. Lakeville, Ohio, is issuing 6 percent interest rate, 15-year, tax-free municipal bonds. Cindy Baker, an Ohio resident who pays 35 percent of her income annually for federal, state, and local income taxes, is considering purchasing some of these bonds.

   a. When comparing this investment to taxable investment alternatives, what yield should Cindy use? Show your calculations.

   b. Assume the bond has an interest rate of 7 percent instead of 6 percent. When comparing this investment to taxable investment alternatives, what yield should she use? Show your calculations.

2. An investor is interested in purchasing a $100,000, five-year, 7 percent interest rate bond for which interest is payable quarterly.

   a. Assume the bond is to be issued today and the current market interest rate is 8 percent. What should the investor pay for this bond?

   b. Assume the bond is to be issued today and the current market interest rate is 6 percent. What should the investor pay for this bond?

3. Calculate the book value per share of common stock for East Corporation, whose equity section of the balance sheet looks as follows:

East Corporation Equity Section of the Balance Sheet As of December 31, 2020	
Preferred stock, $100 par, 6% (5,000 shares)	$ 500,000
Common stock, $0.01 par (10,000,000 shares)	100,000
Paid-in capital in excess of par–common	29,900,000
Total paid-in capital	30,500,000
Retained earnings	17,695,240
Total stockholders' equity	$48,195,240

4. East Corporation, which has outstanding 10 million shares of common stock and 5,000 shares of $100, 6 percent preferred stock, declares a $2.5 million dividend.

   a. Assuming there are no dividends in arrears related to the preferred stock, what is the amount of the dividend that will be paid related to each share of common stock?

   b. Assume that instead of 5,000 shares of $100, 6 percent preferred stock, East Corporation has 5,000 shares of $100, 8 percent preferred stock outstanding. Recalculate the dividend that will be paid related to each share of common stock.

5. You open a Roth IRA in January 2020 with the plan to contribute $250 to the account at the end of each month for the next 40 years. The Roth IRA will be invested in dividend-paying ETFs and mutual funds that average an 8 percent return, compounded monthly. You're currently 28 years old and plan to retire when you're 68. What's the value of this account expected to be when you're 68 and ready to retire?

Endnotes

1. "The National Flood Insurance Program," Federal Emergency Management Agency, https://www.fema.gov/national-flood-insurance-program, November 15, 2018.

2. "Yes, Renters Can Buy Flood Insurance," Federal Emergency Management Agency, https://www.fema.gov/news-release/2018/05/04/yes-renters-can-buy-flood-insurance, May 4, 2018.

3. "Business Interruption Insurance," Investopedia, https://www.investopedia.com/terms/b/business-interruption-insurance.asp, March 23, 2018.

4. Bradley Berman and Ze'-ev D. Eiger, "Considerations for Foreign Banks Financing in the United States, 2014 Update," *International Financial Law Review*, http://www.iflr.com/pdfs/IFLR-Considerations-for-Foreign-Banks-Financing-in-the-US-2014-Update.pdf, 2014.

5. "Commercial Paper Rates and Outstanding Summary," Board of Governors of the Federal Reserve System, https://www.federalreserve.gov/releases/cp/about.htm, May 5, 2017.

6. "Understanding Deposit Insurance," Federal Deposit Insurance Corporation, https://www.fdic.gov/deposit/deposits/, January 30, 2018.

7. Ibid.

8. Ibid.

9. Elliot Blair Smith, "Bringing Down Wall Street as Ratings Let Loose Subprime Scourge," Bloomberg, https://www.bloomberg.com/news/articles/2008-09-24/bringing-down-wall-street-as-ratings-let-loose-subprime-scourge, September 24, 2008.

10. Alexandra Twin, "Dow, S&P Break Records," CNN Money, https://money.cnn.com/2007/10/09/markets/markets_0500/index.htm, October 9, 2007.

11. Ibid.

12. Caroline Valetkevitch, "Key Dates and Milestones in the S&P 500's History," Reuters, https://www.reuters.com/article/us-usa-stocks-sp-timeline-idUSBRE9450WL20130506, May 6, 2013.

13. Peter Eavis, "As Fears Recede, Dow Industrials Hit a Milestone," The New York Times, https://www.nytimes.com/2013/03/06/business/daily-stock-market-activity.html, March 5, 2013.

14. Carmel Lobello, "How Warren Buffett Made $10 Billion during the Financial Crisis," The Week, https://theweek.com/articles/459166/how-warren-buffett-made-10-billion-during-financial-crisis, October 7, 2013.

15. Ibid.

16. Zack Friedman, "Here Are 10 Genius Quotes from Warren Buffett," Forbes, https://www.forbes.com/sites/zackfriedman/2018/10/04/warren-buffett-best-quotes/#798de55d4261, October 4, 2018.

17. "OTC Bulletin Board," Securities and Exchange Commission, https://www.sec.gov/fast-answers/answersotcbbhtm.html, October 25, 2012.

18. Bill Bischoff, "There Are Now Fewer Tax Breaks for Homeowners—Here Are the Ones That Remain," https://www.marketwatch.com/story/how-home-owners-win-and-lose-under-the-new-tax-law-2018-06-11, February 5, 2019.

19. Ibid.

20. "Crude Oil Futures Contract Specs," CME Group, https://www.cmegroup.com/trading/energy/crude-oil/light-sweet-crude_contract_specifications.html, 2019.

21. Brad Zigler, "The Real Story of Precious Metals' Returns," ETF.com, https://www.etf.com/sections/features-and-news/1035-the-real-story-of-precious-metals-returns-, August 25, 2008.

22. "Stocks vs. Gold Comparison," Longtermtrends.net, https://www.longtermtrends.net/stocks-vs-gold-comparison/, 2018.

23. "Pre-Social Security Period: Traditional Sources of Economic Security," Social Security Administration, https://www.ssa.gov/history/briefhistory3.html, February 1, 2018.

24. "Benefits Planner—Social Security Credits," Social Security Administration, https://www.ssa.gov/planners/credits.html, May 15, 2019.

25. "What Is the Eligibility for Social Security: Spouse's Benefits and My Own Retirement Benefits?," Social Security Administration, https://faq.ssa.gov/en-us/Topic/article/KA-02011?utm_source=twitter&utm_medium=social&utm_campaign=smt-cola-19&utm_content%20field=education, March 28, 2018.

26. Zina Kumok, "Why Defined Benefit Plans Are Being Phased Out," Investopedia, 2018.

27. "Publication 590-B," Internal Revenue Service, https://www.irs.gov/pub/irs-pdf/p590b.pdf, January 24, 2019.

28. "401(k) Contribution Limit Increases to $19,000 for 2019; IRA Limit Increases to $6,000," Internal Revenue Service, www.irs.gov/newsroom/401k-contribution-limit-increases-to-19000-for-2019-ira-limit-increases-to-6000, November 27, 2018.

29. "One Participant 401(k) Plans," Internal Revenue Service, www.irs.gov/retirement-plans/one-participant-401k-plans, November 6, 2018.

30. "401(k) Contribution Limit Increases to $19,000 for 2019; IRA Limit Increases to $6,000," Internal Revenue Service, www.irs.gov/newsroom/401k-contribution-limit-increases-to-19000-for-2019-ira-limit-increases-to-6000, November 27, 2018.

31. "IRA Deduction Limits," Internal Revenue Service, https://www.irs.gov/retirement-plans/ira-deduction-limits, October 20, 2017.

32. "401(k) Contribution Limit Increases to $19,000 for 2019; IRA Limit Increases to $6,000," Internal Revenue Service, www.irs.gov/newsroom/401k-contribution-limit-increases-to-19000-for-2019-ira-limit-increases-to-6000, November 27, 2018.

33. "What are Qualified Distributions?," Internal Revenue Service, https://www.irs.gov/publications/p590b#en_US_2017_publink1000231061, February 21, 2018.

34. "401(k) Contribution Limit Increases to $19,000 for 2019; IRA Limit Increases to $6,000," Internal Revenue Service, www.irs.gov/newsroom/401k-contribution-limit-increases-to-19000-for-2019-ira-limit-increases-to-6000, November 27, 2018.

35. "SEP Plan Fix-It Guide—Contributions to Each Participant's SEP-IRA Weren't a Uniform Percentage of the Participant's Compensation," Internal Revenue Service, https://www.irs.gov/retirement-plans/sep-fix-it-guide-contributions-to-each-participants-sep-ira-were-not-a-uniform-percentage-of-the-participants-compensation, January 14, 2019.

36. "How Much Can I Contribute to my Self-Employed SEP Plan if I Participate in my Employers SIMPLE IRA Plan?," Internal Revenue Service, https://www.irs.gov/retirement-plans/how-much-can-i-contribute-to-my-self-employed-sep-plan-if-i-participate-in-my-employers-simple-ira-plan, November 5, 2019.

37. US Department of Labor Employee Benefits Security Administration and the Internal Revenue Service, "Choosing a Retirement Solution for Your Small Business," Internal Revenue Service, https://www.irs.gov/pub/irs-pdf/p3998.pdf, February 1, 2019,

38. "How Much Can I Contribute to my Self-Employed SEP Plan if I Participate in my Employers SIMPLE IRA Plan?," Internal Revenue Service, https://www.irs.gov/retirement-plans/how-much-can-i-contribute-to-my-self-employed-sep-plan-if-i-participate-in-my-employers-simple-ira-plan, November 5, 2019.

39. "Intro to ESAs (Coverdell Educational Savings Accounts)," Saving for College, https://www.savingforcollege.com/intro_to_esas/?esa_faq_category_id=2, May 15, 2019.

40. Ibid.

41. U.S. Department of the Treasury, "Education Planning," Treasury Direct, https://www.treasurydirect.gov/indiv/planning/plan_education.htm, January 2, 2018.

42. "2018 Form 8815," Internal Revenue Service, https://www.irs.gov/pub/irs-pdf/f8815.pdf, May 15, 2019.

43. "401(k) Contribution Limit Increases to $19,000 for 2019; IRA Limit Increases to $6,000," Internal Revenue Service, www.irs.gov/newsroom/401k-contribution-limit-increases-to-19000-for-2019-ira-limit-increases-to-6000, November 27, 2018.

44. Ibid.

45. "What's New—Estate and Gift Tax," Internal Revenue Service, https://www.irs.gov/businesses/small-businesses-self-employed/whats-new-estate-and-gift-tax, February 8, 2019.

46. Scott Drenkard, "Does Your State Have an Estate or Inheritance Tax?" Tax Foundation, https://taxfoundation.org/does-your-state-have-estate-or-inheritance-tax/, May 5, 2015.

47. Julie Garber, "States Without an Estate or an Inheritance Tax," The Balance, https://www.thebalance.com/states-without-estate-tax-3505467, January 26, 2019.

48. Scott Drenkard, "Does Your State Have an Estate or Inheritance Tax?," Tax Foundation, https://taxfoundation.org/does-your-state-have-estate-or-inheritance-tax/, May 5, 2015.

49. Julie Garber, "States Without an Estate or an Inheritance Tax," The Balance, https://www.thebalance.com/states-without-estate-tax-3505467, January 26, 2019.

50. Scott Drenkard, "Does Your State Have an Estate or Inheritance Tax?," Tax Foundation, https://taxfoundation.org/does-your-state-have-estate-or-inheritance-tax/, May 5, 2015.

51. Ibid.

Glossary

401(k)   a type of defined contribution retirement plan typically offered by a for-profit company

403(b)   a type of defined contribution retirement plan often offered by a nonprofit entity

accounting information system   a usually software-based system that provides the data needed to effectively operate a business and prepare that business's period- or year-end financial statements, tax documents (i.e., W-2s and Form 1099s), and tax filings

accounts payable   a current liability that typically represents amounts owed to the vendors that provide essential products and services to a business so the business can, in turn, provide products and services to its customers

accounts receivable   the amounts customers owe a company related to their purchases from that company utilizing the credit or trade credit offered by that company

accounts receivable turnover ratio   a ratio that indicates how fast a company is turning its credit sales into cash

accredited investor   an individual who typically makes over $200,000 per year in income or has a net worth greater than $1 million, excluding her primary residence

accrued liabilities   obligations of a firm that accumulate over time during the normal course of operations and typically include items such as payroll, payroll taxes, certain employee-related benefits, property taxes, and sales taxes

accumulated depreciation   a contra-asset included on the balance sheet that represents the cumulative wearing out of certain of a business's fixed assets over time, valued in dollars

agency bonds   bonds issued by government-sponsored enterprises and U.S. federal agencies

aging of accounts receivable   a schedule that categorizes unpaid customer invoices based on the number of days they have been outstanding

amortization expense   a noncash expense that represents the systematic writing off of an intangible asset's cost over time

angel investor   an individual, usually a successful or retired entrepreneur or businessperson, who provides follow-up investment and free mentoring to start-up businesses; also referred to as an angel

annual exclusion for gifts   the amount of assets an individual can exclude when calculating the gift and estate taxes that may be due related to an individual tax year

annuity   a series of equal payments

annuity due   an annuity where the payments are made or received at the beginning of each time period

ask price   the price that a prospective seller is willing to accept for a security

asset   an item of value owned by a business

asset-based business valuation   a business valuation approach by which the value of a business is determined as a result of considering the total value of the company's tangible and intangible assets

audited financial statements   financial statements that have been successfully formally examined by an outside, independent auditor; examination includes an in-depth investigation of a business's accounting policies and practices, accounting records, and internal financial statements, with the goal of providing reasonable assurance that the final financial statements shared with those outside the company fairly present the financial position, performance, continued viability, and risks associated the company under audit

average collection period   the average number of days it takes a firm to collect its accounts receivable

banker's acceptance   a short-term debt instrument issued by a company that is guaranteed by that company's bank, widely used to provide some level of protection to a seller involved in a high-dollar-value international goods transaction with a purchaser the seller does not know

basic accounting equation   Total assets = Total liabilities + Total equity

bid price   the price that a prospective buyer is willing to pay for a security

book value per share of common stock   total common stockholders' equity divided by the number of shares of common stock outstanding, typically viewed as the minimum value of a share of a company's common stock

bootstrapping   borrowing noncash assets, bartering for noncash assets and services, and utilizing strategic negotiation tactics in order to avoid, delay, or minimize the outlay of cash

breakeven   the point at which the net income of a business, or a selected segment of a business (e.g., a product line), equals zero

breakeven price   the minimum price at which a product or service must be sold—under a given set of cost and sales unit conditions—in order to not lose money

breakeven revenue   the amount of revenue that must be brought in over an indicated period of time in order to not lose money

breakeven sales units   the number of units that must be sold over an indicated period of time in order to not lose money

business auto insurance   insurance that protects the cars, trucks, vans, or other vehicles used in a business and also protects the business from liability for most forms of damage or mayhem these vehicles might create

business broker   a professional who typically sells small companies to individuals

business interruption insurance insurance that compensates a business for the profits lost as a result of a catastrophic event

business liability insurance insurance that protects a business and its owners from most claims of bodily injury, personal injury, or property damage that arise as a result of the business's operations; also sometimes called general liability insurance

business model how a business concept will make a company—and ultimately the entrepreneur—money

business plan a comprehensive document that focuses on how to build a company, prepared by—and for the benefit of—the entrepreneurs involved, but written with an outside audience of potential investors, lenders, strategic partners, or major talent targets in mind

business succession planning a process that formally considers the question of who will take over the management of a business in the event the business owner is unwilling or unable to continue managing the business because of a planned retirement or an unplanned event, such as an accident, severe illness, or death

buy-sell agreement a contract between a business's owners that indicates the terms that will surround the purchase of an exiting owner's interest in the business

C corporation the formal corporate form of all corporations, by default, unless the corporation meets certain requirements and proactively requests Subchapter S tax status from the Internal Revenue Service, thereby becoming an S corporation

call option an option that gives the holder the right to buy a security at a specified price for a specified period of time

call premium an amount of money a company will pay above the current market price for a share of its preferred stock if the stock is called back by the company

callable preferred stock preferred stock that can be called back at a pre-specified price and then retired by a company

capital asset an asset that has an expected useful life in excess of one year

capital budgeting a process used to justify the acquisition of capital assets or the investment in projects that support the expansion of business operations

capital gain the profit made by an investor after selling an asset whose value has appreciated beyond the amount invested to acquire or build the asset

capitalization table a schedule that outlines the entire debt and equity structure of a business, including the order in which lenders and investors will be satisfied in the event of a company's liquidation

cash discount a discount offered to a credit customer to entice the customer to pay her bill early

cash equivalents investment securities designed for short-term investing, generally high-credit quality, low-risk, highly liquid investments that provide a lower yield than longer-term, higher-risk, less-liquid investments

cash flows from financing activities a section of the statement of cash flows that typically includes summary information regarding the sale or repurchase of stock, the receipt of debt proceeds or the repayment of debt, and the payment of dividends or distributions

cash flows from investing activities a section of the statement of cash flows that typically includes summary information regarding the purchase or sale of investments in the financial markets, the purchase or sale of fixed assets, the making or collection of loans, and any insurance settlement proceeds related to fixed assets

cash flows from operating activities a section of the statement of cash flows that considers a business's net income or net loss, adds back depreciation expense to net income or net loss because depreciation is a noncash expense, and identifies all the cash received and paid out by the business as a result of its day-to-day operations during a specified period by identifying the dollar change in balance sheet line items from the beginning of the period to the end of the period

certificate of deposit a promissory note whereby a bank promises to return to the depositor the principal amount deposited with the bank, plus interest, after a stipulated period of time

Certified Business Intermediary a broker certified by the International Business Brokers Association as being both educated and experienced in the art of business brokerage

charge-back when a customer uses a credit card to buy something and then cancels the transaction

collectables items that become valuable over time because of their scarcity

commercial paper an unsecured, short-term debt instrument, typically issued in a large denomination ($100,000 or more) by a large bank, a foreign government, or a large corporation with a strong balance sheet, the proceeds of which are typically used to finance accounts receivable or inventory or to meet short-term debt obligations

commercial property insurance insurance that protects a business's physical assets from theft, fire, vandalism, and the effects of many types of natural disasters

commercial real estate land and buildings used by a property owner to generate rental income from businesses

commodity an article of commerce, such as a fuel, a metal, or an agricultural product, that can be traded, bought, or sold in bulk on a commodity exchange or other type of exchange

common stock an equity security representing the fundamental ownership of a company issued by a public or private corporation in order to raise financial capital

comparative financial statements financial statements that present more than one period or date of financial statement information side by side in such a way that the reader can easily compare the different periods or dates

compiled financial statements financial statements that have been prepared by an accountant outside a company based on the data provided by that company; an accountant who prepares compiled financial statements does so without providing any of the assurances associated with an audit or a review

compound interest the amount of interest earned or charged on both the stated principal amount and the interest that has been previously earned or charged

convertible note a security that documents the terms of an investor's loan to a company, but also includes an option for the investor to convert the loan into an equity position in the company if desired by the investor at a future time; a commonly used tool of angel investors

convertible preferred stock   preferred stock that may be exchanged for shares of common stock

corporation   a legal entity authorized by state law to act as an artificial person in order to conduct business or engage in certain other activities

cost of goods sold   the amount it costs a company to create, build, or purchase the product it sells; the cost of inventory—once a company has sold that inventory—becomes cost of goods sold; often referred to as COGS

cost of sales   the direct costs associated with delivering services to the clients of service-based businesses; also called cost of revenue and cost of services

coupon rate of a bond   the rate of interest the bond issuer agrees to pay to the bondholder; also called the quoted rate or the stated rate

Coverdell Education Savings Account (Coverdell ESA)   a tax-advantaged college savings vehicle set up by an account owner and usually administered by a private financial institution with the intention to pay some or all of the qualified education expenses of a designated beneficiary

credit rating   an assessment of the creditworthiness of an entity or financial obligation, ideally provided by an objective third party

credit report   a detailed report of your credit history prepared by a credit bureau

credit score   a three-digit number, typically between 300 and 850, which is calculated from your credit report in order to gauge your reliability as a borrower

cumulative preferred stock   preferred stock that will receive both the current and any unpaid back dividends, called dividends in arrears, before any common shareholder receives any dividend

cumulative purchase discount   a discount or rebate—above and beyond any applicable trade, cash, or quantity discount—available after a designated purchase threshold has been met by a customer; also referred to as a cumulative purchase rebate

current asset   an item of value that's either cash or an asset that will likely be converted into cash within the next 12 months

current liability   an amount owed to others that will need to be paid within the next 12 months

current ratio   a ratio that indicates a company's ability to pay its obligations in the short run

day trading   a stock trading technique that involves buying and selling financial instruments within the same trading day

debt capital   capital acquired by a business with the understanding that the capital will have to be repaid by the business, within a defined time period, usually with interest

debt-to-equity ratio   a ratio that indicates what percentage of a business's assets are financed with debt compared to equity

debt-to-total assets ratio   a ratio that indicates what percentage of a business's assets are owned by its creditors

deductible IRA   an individual retirement account to which an individual can contribute pretax dollars up to an amount specified by current law

deferred taxes   a balance sheet line item unique to C corporations and entities taxed as a C corporation that usually arises due to differences in the treatment of an asset or expense for accounting versus tax purposes because of differences in accounting and tax rules

defined benefit plan   an employer-sponsored retirement plan that provides a pre-specified benefit to a company's retirees paid from a pool of funds contributed by the employer; also often called a pension plan

defined contribution plan   an employer-sponsored retirement plan that provides payments to a retiree from the retiree's individual account that has been accumulating funds and growing during the working life of the retiree

depreciation expense   an expense amount that represents the wearing out of certain of a business's fixed assets over time, valued in dollars; also called depreciation

disability insurance   insurance purchased to replace the income lost when an individual is temporarily unable to work due to an injury, illness, or pregnancy

discounted cash flow method of business valuation   a methodology that places a value on a business by determining, at a specified discount rate, the sum of the present values of all of the business's expected future cash flows

dissolution   legally terminating the existence of a business

distribution   a disbursement, usually in the form of cash, to an owner of a pass-through entity business

dividend   a payment, usually in the form of cash, made by a C corporation to one or more of its shareholders as authorized by the C corporation's board of directors

dollar cost averaging   the technique of accumulating a position in an investment by buying a fixed dollar amount of that investment on a regular basis, regardless of its price

due diligence   the process of a company willingly subjecting itself to a form of investigation by a potential buyer of the business or a potential new partner in the business

earnings per share of common stock   an element sometimes included on the income statement of a C corporation (but not on the income statement of an entity taxed as a C corporation) calculated by dividing net income by the number of the corporation's outstanding shares of common stock

earnings-based business valuation   a business valuation approach predicated on the idea that a business's true value lies in its ability to produce net income and positive cash flow in the future

economic order quantity   refers to the optimal quantity a business should purchase every time it places an order for an inventory item; often referred to as EOQ

effective annual interest rate   the actual interest rate paid by the borrower or earned by the investor after interest compounding is taken into consideration

employee stock ownership plan (ESOP)   an employee benefit plan designed to invest primarily in the stock of the sponsoring employer

enterprise value   an estimate of the value of a business, calculated as the estimated equity value of a company, plus any debt on the company's balance sheet, minus the cash on the company's balance sheet

entrepreneurial finance the study of resource acquisition, allocation, and management; financial planning and management; asset and business valuation; cash harvest strategy; and contingency planning in the context of a new business venture and the entrepreneur's personal financial goals

equity the amount by which the assets of a business exceed the liabilities of a business

equity capital capital acquired by a business as a result of selling some form of ownership of that business

equity crowdfunding the accumulation of small amounts of capital from a large number of individuals via a campaign on the internet, such individuals receiving an ownership interest in the company in which they invest

equity value the value of the equity of a company

exchange traded fund (ETF) a fund that invests in a basket of assets, such as stocks or bonds, and trades on a regulated exchange like the New York Stock Exchange, as many individual stocks do

factor a third party who, for a fee, provides a business owner with immediate cash for accounts receivable and then goes about collecting the accounts receivable themselves

feasibility analysis a document that concentrates on assessing the likelihood of economic success of a business, primarily for the benefit of the entrepreneurs contemplating starting that business

financial liquidity the preservation of a certain minimum level of cash coupled with the ability to quickly and easily get access to more cash

finished goods inventory inventory items that have been translated into a final product ready to be sold by the business

fixed assets a balance sheet subtotal made up of major assets that will likely not be converted into cash within the next 12 months; also called noncurrent assets, long-term assets, and property, plant, and equipment

fixed cost a cost that remains the same amount in total over a specified period of time

fixed income a category of investments that pay a fixed rate of return, investments such as government bonds, corporate bonds, and similar debt instruments

foreign bonds bonds issued or sold in the U.S. market by a non-U.S. entity, such bonds often denominated in U.S. dollars

franchise a business in which the buyer, who is the franchisee, purchases the right to sell goods or services using the systems, processes, or branding of the seller, who is the franchisor

free cash flow the cash flow generated by a business that's available for distribution to the providers of capital to the business

future value the value at some future point in time of an amount loaned, borrowed, saved, or invested today

futures contract an agreement to buy or sell a commodity at a specified future date at a specified price

Gordon growth model a model for determining the terminal value of a business that assumes a company exists forever and grows at a constant rate forever

grant an amount of money provided to an individual or an entity that does not have to be repaid to the provider of the money (the grantor) as long as the receiver of the money (the grantee) provides the goods or performs the services for which the grant was approved

gross margin the percentage of each dollar of net sales (or sales, if there is no net sales amount) that remains after cost of goods sold has been considered

gross profit net sales (or sales, if there is no net sales amount) minus cost of goods sold, cost of sales, cost of revenue, or cost of services

hedging the use of options by an investor to limit her potential loss if the price of a security she buys heads in the direction opposite to that anticipated or desired

high-growth start-up a business designed to be scalable

high-yield bonds bonds issued by less financially sound entities than those who issue investment-grade bonds and whose risk of default is distinctly higher than an investment-grade bond; also called junk bonds

horizontal analysis a determination of the percentage increase or decrease in each line item on a financial statement from a base time period to a successive time period

income statement a summary of the revenue and expenses of a business over a specified period of time

index funds exchange traded funds and mutual funds that are constructed to track or follow a specific stock index as a result of holding the same components that make up that specific index

individual retirement account (IRA) a retirement account typically set up by an individual for her own benefit

industry research research performed to provide insight regarding the size and complexity of an industry, the number and nature of its participants, and the economic, political, market, and other factors that affect it

initial public offering (IPO) a very highly regulated and managed first sale of most or all of the stock of a previously private company—or mostly private company—to the general public

insurance an arrangement evidenced in writing by which one party provides a guarantee of compensation for a specified loss incurred by another party in return for the payment of a premium

intellectual property intangible property created from human intellect, often evidenced by copyrights, trademarks, or patents

interest the price (i.e., rent) charged for money that's borrowed or loaned

interest expense the amount of interest incurred by a business related to its liabilities and debt; also called interest

internal rate of return (IRR) the actual rate of return of an investment

intrastate offering a security whose sale is limited to investors in one state

inventory turnover ratio a ratio that indicates how many times per year, on average, a company sells—and therefore must replace—all of its inventory

investment banking firm   a firm that usually assists in the sale of companies that are very large, very complex, or both

investment-grade corporate bonds   bonds issued by financially sound entities—typically large corporations—with a credit rating of at least Baa3 from Moody's Investor Service or BBB- from Standard & Poor's

lending-based crowdfunding   the accumulation of small amounts of capital from a large number of individuals via a campaign on the internet, such individuals expecting to be repaid by the company, with interest; also called crowd lending

leverage   the power the use of debt provides to an individual or a business

leveraged buyout (LBO)   a financial strategy whereby the debt used to purchase a company is collateralized fully or partially by the assets or cash flows of the company being purchased

leveraged recapitalization   a financial strategy whereby a company takes on substantial debt that is then used to make significant dividend or distribution payments to the company's owners

liability   an amount owed to others

liability insurance   insurance purchased to transfer to an insurance company the cost associated with damage to the property or person of others that might result from one's actions or the actions of one's business

lifetime basic exclusion for gifts   the amount of assets an individual can exclude when calculating the gift and estate taxes that may be due during the individual's lifetime or at the individual's death—over and above that allowed by an individual's annual exclusion for gifts

limited liability company (LLC)   a hybrid legal business entity authorized by state law featuring some of the characteristics of both partnerships and corporations

liquidation   concluding the affairs of a business by selling all of its assets, paying all of its liabilities, and distributing any remaining cash to the business's owners

liquidity (in relation to an asset on a balance sheet)   how quickly an asset can be turned into cash

liquidity (in relation to the general topic of finance)   the ease with which an asset can be converted into cash without significant loss of value

long-term care insurance   insurance that pays for the assistance one needs long term in order to perform daily living functions like eating, bathing, dressing, and walking, to the extent such assistance is not paid for by health insurance, Medicare, or Medicaid

long-term liability   an amount owed to others that doesn't need to be paid within the next 12 months; also called noncurrent liability

lowest total cost (LTC) method   a capital budgeting method similar to the net present value method commonly used by business owners who must replace fixed assets on a regular basis

maintenance, repair, and operating inventory   items that are kept on hand not to be sold, but instead to help the firm maintain consistent operations; often referred to as MRO inventory

management presentation   a flashy yet professional and sophisticated document designed to pique a potential buyer's interest in a large, complex business

manager-managed LLC   an LLC where only certain individuals, who may or may not be members of the LLC, are responsible for managing the business

margin call   a demand by a brokerage house that an investor deposit additional cash or securities in order to cover potential losses

margin requirement   the percentage of a potential investment's total value that an investor must have on deposit with his broker before the broker will lend the investor money to purchase that investment

margin trading   borrowing money from the brokerage house where the investor has a brokerage account in order to buy stock; also called buying on margin

market makers   companies or individuals who quote both a bid and an ask price for a security they hold in inventory

market research   research performed to identify one or more specific markets and determine their relative sizes and characteristics in order to identify and understand all the potential customers of the business under consideration

market value per share of common stock   the price at which the current owners of a particular common stock are selling their shares

market-based business valuation   a business valuation approach that attempts to establish the value of a business by comparing the business to be put on the market to similar businesses that have recently been sold

markup   the amount added to the cost of a good to determine its sales price

member-managed LLC   an LLC where all of the members participate in managing the business

merger and acquisition (M&A) advisor   a professional who usually assists in the sale of businesses larger than those represented by a business broker but smaller than those represented by an investment banking firm

mixed cost   a cost that includes elements of both variable and fixed costs

money market fund   a type of mutual fund that invests in short-term debt securities such as U.S Treasury bills, high-quality commercial paper, and banker's acceptances and generally aims to provide a higher return on excess cash than what is offered by a bank

mortgage-backed bonds   bonds backed by home mortgages, such bonds created when mortgages are pooled together by a sponsor who packages them for sale to the public in the form of a negotiable security that is sold in the financial markets; also called mortgage-backed securities

municipal bonds   bonds issued by a government or a government agency other than the federal government or one of its GSEs or agencies

mutual funds   investment vehicles set up by mutual fund companies, companies that collect funds from investors then use the funds to purchase large blocks of bonds, stocks, and other types of investment securities

net cost rate   the actual percentage of list price paid after taking advantage of a series of trade discounts

net fixed assets   for most businesses, fixed assets minus accumulated depreciation; also called net noncurrent assets, net long-term assets, and net property, plant, and equipment

net income   operating income minus interest expense for most sole proprietorships, partnerships, LLCs, and S corporations; for a C corporation or an entity taxed as a C corporation, net income equals operating income minus interest expense and minus the provision for income taxes; also called profit and net profit

net income before income taxes   a subtotal unique to the income statement of a C corporation or entity taxed as a C corporation that usually appears immediately before the line for the provision for income taxes

net present value (NPV) method   a capital budgeting method that considers the time value of money by discounting the future cash flows associated with a proposed project or asset purchase back to the present

net sales   sales minus returns and allowances; also called net revenue

non-compete agreement   an agreement that limits an individual's ability to compete with a business after the individual has been an employee of the business or sold the business

nondeductible IRA   an individual retirement account that allows an individual to contribute the same amount as is legally contributable to a deductible IRA, but the contribution is made with after-tax dollars

non-integer interest rates   interest rates that are not whole numbers

non-owner-occupied residential real estate   property that the owner leases to a residential tenant for the purpose of generating income

nonprofit organization   an entity that is run like a business, but whose main purpose is not to make a profit but instead to support some aspect of the public or private sector; also called a not-for-profit organization

note payable   for a start-up venture, typically a short-term loan to the company from a stakeholder—often a founder or an angel investor

operating expenses   all of an enterprise's expenses—except interest and income taxes—that are not included in cost of goods sold, cost of sales, cost of revenue, or cost of services

operating income   gross profit minus operating expenses; operating income represents the earnings from business operations—before interest and income taxes are considered—and is generally viewed as a key indicator of the relative success or failure of a business model

options   contracts that give the owner the right to buy or sell a security at a specified price for a specified period of time; also called options contracts

options trading   buying and selling options contracts in the hope of making a large profit from a small investment as a result of correctly anticipating the price movement of an option's underlying security

ordinary annuity   an annuity where the payments are made or received at the end of each time period

ordinary dividend   a dividend that is not a qualified dividend

over-the-counter (OTC) market   a market where investors trade directly with each other without the oversight of a formal securities exchange like the NYSE or NASDAQ

owner-occupied residential real estate   a house, condominium, housing cooperative, or apartment in which the owner lives, limited by law to a person's primary residence and one additional vacation home

paid-in capital in excess of par   the cumulative amount shareholders paid for the common stock of a company beyond its par value; also called additional paid-in capital

par value   an arbitrary dollar amount indicated on a stock certificate, usually because a par value is required by state law

par value of a bond   the amount paid to a bondholder at a bond's maturity, usually in the denomination of $1,000 or a multiple of $1,000; also called the face value or the principal value

partnership   an association of two or more persons who conduct business as co-owners for profit

pass-through entity   a business whose profits are not taxed at the company level, but instead pass through to the business owners' individual tax returns, where they are taxed

payable-on-death (POD) account   an account for which the decedent has indicated to the financial institution holding the account prior to her death who should inherit the assets in the account

payback method   a capital budgeting method that calculates the number of years it will take a business to get back the money it invests in a proposed project or asset purchase

penny stock   a stock that trades at a relatively low price, often under $1, usually in the over-the-counter market via the pink sheets

percentage of sales method   a technique used to develop a pro forma balance sheet based on the fact that the assets and liabilities of a company typically vary with its sales

personal guarantee   when a third party guarantees the financial obligations of another person or a business

pink sheets   a list of bid and ask prices for the securities of companies that, unlike the companies included on the major exchanges and the Over-the-Counter Bulletin Board, do not have to meet any minimum disclosure requirements or file with the SEC

portfolio risk   the risk that the combination of investment securities an investor owns will fail to meet the investor's desired financial objectives

position trading   an investment strategy that involves buying stocks with the intent to hold them for a long period of time; also known as buy and hold

preferred stock   a class of ownership of a C corporation that has a higher claim on the assets and earnings of the corporation than the corporation's common stock

prepaid asset   typically, an expense that's been paid for in advance of the period of its use

present value   the value in today's dollars of some amount to be received or paid in the future

primary market research   research conducted by communicating directly with current or potential customers

private equity firm   a type of firm that helps manage the mature companies of which it usually buys majority control or full control, often over time

private placement   the sale of securities directly to a private investor, rather than as part of a public offering

pro forma financial statements   financial statements that attempt to estimate the future financial situation of a company based upon certain identified assumptions

probate   a legal court process that addresses the will and the probate estate

probate estate   property owned by a decedent that requires the appointment of a fiduciary, such fiduciary legally charged with managing and appropriately distributing the applicable property

product liability insurance   insurance that provides coverage for bodily injury and property damage that result from the use of a product manufactured, assembled, or sold by a business

professional liability insurance   insurance that covers a business against negligence claims due to harm that results from professional mistakes or failure to perform; also known as errors and omissions (E&O) insurance

profit margin   the percentage of each dollar of net sales (or sales, if there is no net sales amount) that remains after all expenses, including interest and taxes, have been considered

profit-sharing plan   an employee benefit plan to which employees typically make no contribution; rather, the plan is funded by a portion of a business's profit at the discretion of the employer

proof of concept   evidence that a business concept is feasible

provision for income taxes   the amount of income taxes incurred by a C corporation or an entity taxed as a C corporation, related generally to the net income it generates; also called income tax expense

public offering   an issue of securities offered for sale to the public by a company or other entity

put option   an option that gives the holder the right to require some other person or entity to buy a security from the holder at a specified price for a specified period of time

qualified dividend   a dividend that meets the Internal Revenue Service requirements to—in most instances—be taxed at a lower rate than an ordinary dividend

quantity discount   a discount based on the number of units ordered by a customer

ratio analysis   a form of evaluation that uses a variety of ratios to determine the health of a business, especially as that business compares to other firms in the same industry

raw materials inventory   the fundamental materials or components a company uses to produce its final product

real estate investment group   an investment group typically founded by a lead investment company that builds or buys rental real estate units and then allows investors to buy the properties through the company, the investors thereby joining the investment group

real estate investment trust (REIT)   an investment vehicle that pools investor funds to finance the investment in and operation of an array of income-producing real estate properties

Regulation A   a regulation that allows an exemption from certain registration requirements of the SEC

Regulation A+   the name commonly applied to the 2015 updates to Regulation A

Regulation D   a regulation that allows companies to raise capital through the sale of securities without having to register those securities with the SEC

reorder point   the optimal quantity of an item that should be remaining in inventory when a business places an order for more of that item

reserve for bad debts   an estimate of the amount of the accounts receivable included on the balance sheet that won't be collected, typically included on a balance sheet as a contra-asset account to accounts receivable

retained earnings   the cumulative earnings of a company not distributed to stockholders via dividends (C corporations) or distributions (S corporations) but instead retained in the corporation for future investment

retainer   a usually nonrefundable deposit against which invoices for work performed and other fees and expenses may be charged

return-on-assets ratio   a ratio that indicates how much profit a firm is earning on its assets, calculated as a percentage of those assets; sometimes referred to as ROA ratio, also called return-on-investment (ROI) ratio

return-on-equity ratio   a ratio that indicates how much profit a firm is earning on the amounts invested in the company—and the profits retained in the company—by the company's owners, calculated as a percentage of the company's equity; sometimes referred to as ROE ratio

returns and allowances   refunded sales dollars; also called sales returns and allowances or simply sales allowances or returns

reviewed financial statements   financial statements that have been subjected to inquiry and analytical procedures by an outside accountant who expresses limited assurance that the financial statements fairly present the financial position, performance, continued viability, and risks associated with the company under review

revocable living trust   a trust whose provisions can be altered by the trustor during her lifetime and to whom the income of the trust is distributed during her lifetime

reward-based crowdfunding   the accumulation of small amounts of capital from a large number of individuals via a campaign on the internet, such individuals generally expecting nothing in return (other than a news update, a small token gift, or a promised product or service, usually of nominal value)

risk assumption   when one proactively assumes risk because one believes that the loss or cost one is likely to incur by assuming that risk is less than the loss or cost associated with risk avoidance, risk reduction, or risk transfer

risk avoidance   the avoidance of any hazard that exposes a business or an individual to risk

risk management   an individual planning for both his business's assets and his personal assets in such a manner as to reduce uncertainty and risk

risk reduction   engaging in behaviors and programs specifically designed to reduce risk

risk transfer   proactively transferring risk to another party

Roth IRA   an individual retirement account that allows an individual to contribute after-tax dollars up to the same defined limit as for traditional IRAs but offers many advantages over traditional IRAs

Rule 144 of the Securities Act of 1933   a rule that, under limited circumstances, provides an exemption from SEC registration requirements and permits for the resale of restricted or control securities, such as those issued in a private placement

S corporation   a private corporation with special tax status granted by Internal Revenue Service such that it is taxed similar to a partnership rather than as a corporation; more formally known as a Subchapter S corporation

safety stock   The number of units of an item of inventory a company expects will be remaining in inventory when a new order for that item arrives.

sales   the monies received as a result of a business selling its products and services; also called revenue and sales revenue

sales load   a fee charged when certain mutual fund shares are purchased or sold by an investor

salvage value   the amount for which an asset is expected to be sold after a business has fully depreciated the asset and ceased using it

savings bond education tax exclusion   a tax exclusion that permits qualified taxpayers to exclude from their gross income all or part of the interest received upon the redemption of eligible Series EE and I bonds issued after 1989 if, among other requirements, qualified higher education expenses are incurred during the same tax year in which the bonds are redeemed

savings incentive match plan for employees (SIMPLE) IRA   a salary reduction plan to which the employer must contribute every year, established by an employer that does not offer any other qualified retirement plan and has fewer than 100 employees

scalable   designed to perform well under continually increasing operational demands

Section 179 deduction   subject to a variety of limitations, Section 179 of the U.S. tax code allows businesses to immediately expense up to 100% of the cost of a fixed-asset purchase for tax purposes when that fixed-asset purchase meets certain criteria

Section 529 plan   a tax-advantaged college savings program operated by a state or state agency

secured credit card   a credit card whose application involves opening a certificate of deposit, the amount of which will be the card's credit limit

security   a negotiable financial instrument whereby an investor or lender expects to derive a profit or income

seed capital   the funding required to get a business started and actively pursuing full-scale operations

seed round   a startup's first significant seed capital received from a source other than the founders or their friends and families

selling memo   a comprehensive description of a business that business brokers, merger and acquisition advisors, and investment banking firms distribute to the individuals and companies they think will have an interest in buying the business

selling short   a stock trading strategy that involves the sale and subsequent repurchase of stock that the seller has borrowed; also called short selling

Series A   the first sophisticated round of investment capital to fund a young entity's growth after seed capital has already been provided

short-term loan   a loan that often fills the gap when a line of credit is temporarily unable to meet all of a company's short-term cash needs

short-term portion of long-term debt   a current liability that represents that portion of the principal of one or more major long-term borrowings that's due to be repaid within the next 12 months

short-term trading   stock trading where entry and exit occurs within the range of a few days or a few weeks

simple interest   the amount of interest earned or charged on a stated principal amount when there's no compounding of interest

simplified employee pension (SEP) IRA   a variation of an IRA designed for employers who wish to make contributions into an IRA for themselves and, if they have employees, into the individual IRAs they set up for the benefit of those employees

single equivalent discount   the total trade discount received, expressed in one percentage

small business investment companies (SBICs)   firms similar to venture capital firms that are licensed and regulated by the Small Business Administration

social security   a social safety net signed into law in 1935 by Franklin D. Roosevelt in order to provide continuing income to retired U.S. workers age 65 and older

sole proprietorship   a business owned and operated by an individual for profit

solo 401(k)   an individual 401(k) that can be set up by the owner of a business with no employees other than the business's owner and the owner's spouse

stated rate of interest   the rate of interest that's listed or quoted, normally on an annual basis, that disregards compounding

statement of cash flows   a summary of the cash receipts and cash expenditures of a business over a specified period of time

statement of financial position   a summary of the assets, liabilities, and equity of a business at a specific point in time; also called a balance sheet

stock option   a contract that gives its owner the right to buy or sell one or more shares of stock at a specified price for a specified period of time

stockout   running out of a particular item of inventory

strategic expense minimization   a process in which many entrepreneurs engage before starting a business with the goal of minimizing expected future outlays of cash

term life insurance   a life insurance policy for which one pays a yearly premium based primarily on the mortality rate of one's age group

term sheet   a usually bulleted list of the significant conditions and circumstances associated with a proposed business arrangement

terminal value   the value of all of a company's expected cash flows after a specified forecast period

time value of money   the loss of purchasing power that occurs as a result of the interest considerations associated with the passage of time

times-interest-earned ratio   a ratio that illustrates the relationship between the amount of interest a company must pay its creditors on an annual basis and a company's annual operating income

traction   evidence—such as sales or another form of positive customer response—that a product or service is being adopted at such a rate that the business model and the business's potential for sustainable growth appear to be validated

trade credit   a business-to-business arrangement by which the customer business can purchase items from the supplier business on account—paying no cash at the time of purchase, but instead paying for the items at a later date

trade customer   a recurring customer approved to purchase product on trade credit

trade discount   an amount deducted from the list price of an item when specific services are performed by a trade customer

treasury stock   shares of stock repurchased by the issuing corporation but not yet retired

trend trading   a stock trading technique that involves buying a stock to hold short or medium term when its price is trending up and selling a stock "short" when its price is trending down

trust   a fiduciary relationship evidenced by a written trust agreement in which one party, the trustor, gives another party, the trustee, the right to hold assets for the benefit of a third party, the beneficiary

umbrella insurance   liability insurance that's in excess of an individual's other specified policies and also potentially primary insurance for losses not covered by an individual's other insurance policies

variable cost   a cost that changes in total with a change in the volume of production or sales, but is generally fixed on a per-unit basis

venture capital firm   a firm typically set up as a limited partnership that gathers large sums of money from investors and deploys these monies by investing in the start-ups that survive the venture capital firm's vetting process

venture capital fund   monies accumulated by private venture capital firms, small business investment companies (SBICs), and certain large corporations that are typically used to invest in young, market-driven companies with a very large potential upside

vertical analysis   the process of using a single line item on a financial statement as a constant and determining how all the other line items relate as a percentage of that constant

whole life insurance   a life insurance policy that allocates part of the premium paid into building a cash value that can be used upon retirement or borrowed against in case of an emergency

will   a written document that provides direction regarding one's final wishes and how one wants one's assets distributed after death

working capital   the capital required to sustain operations and support business growth after a company's start-up phase

working capital management   the art of controlling current assets and current liabilities in such a way that a firm will maintain adequate cash and inventory levels, maximize the return on its assets, and minimize the size of the payments needed to settle its liabilities

work-in-process inventory   inventory items that are in the process of being assembled, modified, or otherwise translated into finished goods inventory

yield   the annual earnings—usually in the form of interest or dividends—produced by an investment, calculated as a percentage of the value of that investment

Index